BRIEF C

CONTENTS

THE MEDIA OF MASS COMMUNICATION

STUDY EDITION

TENTH EDITION

John Vivian
Winona State University

Allyn & Bacon

Boston Columbus Indianapolis New York San Francisco Upper Saddle River
Amsterdam Cape Town Dubai London Madrid Milan Munich Paris Montreal Toronto
Delhi Mexico City Sao Paulo Sydney Hong Kong Seoul Singapore Taipei Tokyo

Editor-in-Chief, Communication: Karon Bowers
Senior Acquisitions Editor: Jeanne Zalesky
Editorial Assistant: Stephanie Chaisson
Development Editor: Stephen Hull
Associate Development Editor: Angela Mallowes
Media Producer: Megan Higginbotham
Executive Marketing Manager: Wendy Gordon
Project Manager: Barbara Mack
Project Coordination, Text Design and Electronic Page Makeup: Integra Software Services Pvt. Ltd.
Operations Specialist: Mary Ann Gloriande
Art Director, Cover: Joel Gendron
Cover Designer: Wee Design Group
Cover Images: Hand holding phone and background: © DANNY MOLOSHOK/CORBIS All Rights Reserved; Globe: Shutterstock.com
Printer and Binder: Courier/Kendallville
Cover Printer: Lehigh-Phoenix/Hagerstown

1 2 3 4 5 6 7 8 9 10—CRK—14 13 12 11

Allyn & Bacon
is an imprint of

PEARSON

www.pearsonhighered.com

ISBN-13: 978-0-205-02936-5
ISBN-10: 0-205-02936-1

6 Motion Media 146

7 New Media Landscape 184

15 Mass Media Globalization 396

16 Media Law 424

PREFACE

Since the first edition of *The Media of Mass Communication* in 1991, more than a million students have found this book to be their first academic look at the media environment that so much shapes their daily routines, their lives, and their understanding of our whole culture. For a teacher this is gratifying.

Through *The Media of Mass Communication* and a growing network of colleagues who have adopted the book, my reach as a teacher has been extended far, far beyond the confines of my own classrooms. There are editions in several countries, including Canada, China and Indonesia. In all, *The Media of Mass Communication* has been published in 24 variations over the years, each updated specifically to keep students up to speed with ever changing media dynamics. I am indebted deeply to professors and their students, who pepper me almost daily with their reactions to the book and with news and tidbits to keep the next edition current.

Most gratifying to me is the community that has grown up around *The Media of Mass Communication*. These are people, many of whom have become valued friends, whose thoughts have made the book an evolving and interactive project. In countless messages, professors have shared what works in their classes and how it might work elsewhere. Students write me the most, sometimes puzzled over something that deserves more clarity, sometimes with examples to illustrate a point. All of the comments, questions and suggestions help add currency and effectiveness to every updated edition.

NEW TO THIS EDITION

Just as mass media are in major transition, so is the organization of *The Media of Mass Communication*. A new chapter on "Media Economics" places media within the economic context that helped trigger the revolution that is in progress today. Due to the shrinking role of print media, the printed book, newspaper and magazine industries no longer warrant distinct chapters and have been consolidated into a single chapter, "Ink on Paper," opening room for attention to new and growing components of media. Similarly, the closely related radio and sound recording industries now are covered in a single chapter, "Sound Media." The television and movie industries, once rivals, have been subsuming each other to the point that many old distinctions have vanished. Corporate mergers and acquisitions have led to common ownership. Distribution of products is spread over multiple media platforms. These formerly competing industries belong together in this single chapter, "Visual Media."

Nobody has come up with a satisfying umbrella term for the plethora of emerging media platforms, but clearly our media landscape is in major transition. The new chapter, "New Media Landscape," focuses on digitally delivered media, including the original military internet, the advent of the web, and the cavalcade of ensuing permutations as broad-ranging as Wikipedia, Google, Facebook and Twitter.

STAY IN TOUCH

Please feel free to contact me with questions and also ideas for improving the next edition. My e-mail: jvivian@winona.edu

May your experience with *The Media of Mass Communication* be a good one.

—John Vivian
Winona State University

Putting the Pieces Together

The Media of Mass Communication covers the important issues that confront students as consumers and purveyors of mass media. Issues such as culture, democracy, economy and audience fragmentation are addressed in each chapter. To provide a framework for the concepts and help bring these issues together for student understanding and retention, each chapter concludes with a highly visual "Thematic Summary." These summaries offer a unifying perspective—a kind of cross-referencing of material in every chapter to material in every other chapter.

Media Economics. Almost every aspect of media behavior is driven by economic considerations. This reality of capitalism is not only the focus of a new chapter in this edition, but is a recurrent theme throughout.

MEDIA ECONOMICS

Media Regulation. *The hold of government regulators over U.S. television and radio has been diminished by satellite program services that go directly to consumers. These signals bypass government-regulated local stations.*

The economic underpinnings of modern business and industry, including the economics of media industries, were set in place during the Industrial Revolution. Media companies in most countries need to make a profit to survive. As a result, these companies are highly sensitive to legal requirements established by governments for their operation, including restrictions of the content of messages. Scholars who have modeled the mass commu-

Media Technology. Mass communication is distinctive from other forms of human communication in being technologically based. This is a fundamental premise in understanding mass communication.

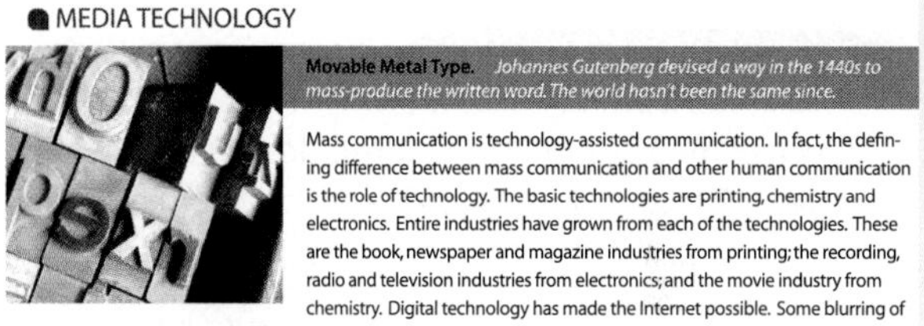
MEDIA TECHNOLOGY

Movable Metal Type. *Johannes Gutenberg devised a way in the 1440s to mass-produce the written word. The world hasn't been the same since.*

Mass communication is technology-assisted communication. In fact, the defining difference between mass communication and other human communication is the role of technology. The basic technologies are printing, chemistry and electronics. Entire industries have grown from each of the technologies. These are the book, newspaper and magazine industries from printing; the recording, radio and television industries from electronics; and the movie industry from chemistry. Digital technology has made the Internet possible. Some blurring of

Media and Democracy. Media and modern democratic governance have been in symbiosis since the dawn of libertarian political thought. This symbiosis is the thrust of an entire chapter on governance, and a significant focus in each chapter.

MEDIA AND DEMOCRACY

Garage Bands. *Technology that has reduced the cost of creating media products has also opened the way for low-power stations to make it big time. This has loosened the giant media companies' control on media content. Thunder Radio is a low-power station at North Dakota State University.*

The major mass media companies have humble origins, but now are so established and entrenched—and huge and powerful—that they are called "empires." With

Media and Culture. For better or worse, mass media shape values by which society defines itself. Simultaneously, media reflect values, including those that are fading and those that are rising. The complex relation of media and culture is an element of every chapter.

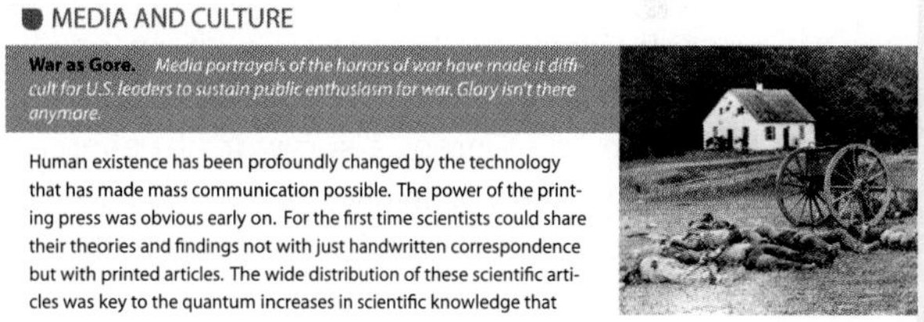
MEDIA AND CULTURE

War as Gore. *Media portrayals of the horrors of war have made it difficult for U.S. leaders to sustain public enthusiasm for war. Glory isn't there anymore.*

Human existence has been profoundly changed by the technology that has made mass communication possible. The power of the printing press was obvious early on. For the first time scientists could share their theories and findings not with just handwritten correspondence but with printed articles. The wide distribution of these scientific articles was key to the quantum increases in scientific knowledge that

Elitism and Populism. One of the most useful models for assessing the relationship of media and culture is the elitism-populism continuum. This is introduced early in the 10th edition and revisited frequently in subsequent chapters.

Media Effects. Through history, mass media have been scapegoats for fears about their potential to accelerate change. Often the fear manifests itself as paranoia about malicious agents manipulating media audiences to impose an unwanted agenda. Throughout the 10th edition, you will find discussions to dispel the most simplistic of these fears and to assess how media can and do have effects.

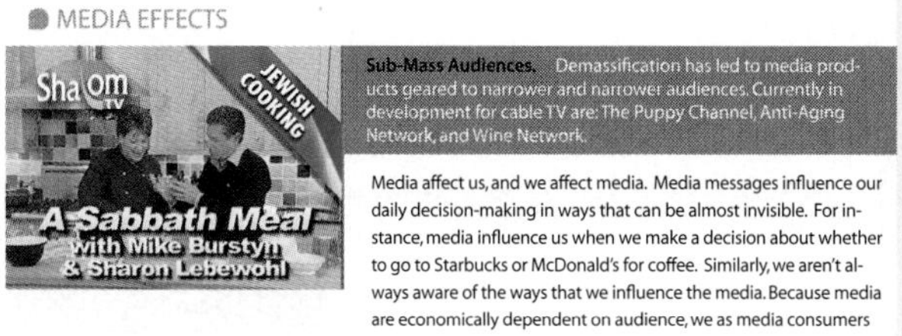

MEDIA EFFECTS

Sub-Mass Audiences. Demassification has led to media products geared to narrower and narrower audiences. Currently in development for cable TV are: The Puppy Channel, Anti-Aging Network, and Wine Network.

Media affect us, and we affect media. Media messages influence our daily decision-making in ways that can be almost invisible. For instance, media influence us when we make a decision about whether to go to Starbucks or McDonald's for coffee. Similarly, we aren't always aware of the ways that we influence the media. Because media are economically dependent on audience, we as media consumers

Audience Fragmentation. A permeating phenomenon of the transitions that media are undergoing is the diminished concern about mass audiences. The old measure of media success—the larger the audience the better—has given way to digital-based messages that target messages to audience segments.

Media Future. The point of honing your media literacy is to navigate mass media better in an uncharted future. This idea is to find ways to make better use of media and to understand the ways that media can be used to manipulate you. These include blatant spiels to buy goods and services, covert persuasion on values issues, and forthright attempts at persuasion on great social issues.

Mass Media on the Cutting Edge

You will find the most current treatment of the mass media available in this 10th edition.

▼ CUTTING EDGE TOPICS

- The lingering impact of the 2008 worldwide economic collapse, following the dotcom bust of 2000, which itself was a blow to some media industries. So profound is the 2008 economic implosion's effect that it constitutes a recurrent theme throughout the book.
- This edition draws on contemporary theories from other fields to explain what's happening in mass media, including the theory of business maturation cycles by scholar Andy Grove—the genius formerly behind Intel.
- Among print media, the book industry is in the best position to survive the transition to digital delivery. Why?
- The softening of network and affiliate audiences of old media—if television can be called old, then there must be fundamental changes in mass media.
- Everybody likes spectacles, especially the battle between Google and Yahoo to dominate the new media landscape.
- Gaming is a growing component of the new media landscape that is treated at several points in this edition.

Introductory Vignettes. Chapters open with evocative stories that illustrate important issues about the mass media and also colorful descriptions about people who contribute significantly to the mass media.

- Murdoch seems everywhere in the book, but a good starting point on his centrality in the emerging media landscape is a profile in Chapter 3.
- Tim Westergren, as you will discover in Chapter 5, is out-radioing web radio.
- How Environmentalism is a battleground for reformers and entrenched economic interests opens Chapter 8, which poignantly illustrates how media find themselves in the crosshairs.
- Paparazzi have a bad name, but don't cast your net too widely or be too broad in your criticism. See Chapter 9 for Keira Knightley on the red carpet with celeb shooters.
- Diane Van Deren, a survivor of epilepsy, may hardly seem a likely poster child for rugged outdoor gear. See why North Face likes her so much in Chapter 10.

LEARNING AHEAD

- More than most people realize, we are awash in a mass media environment.
- Media literacy begins with an awareness of our media environment.
- Communication through mass media has profoundly affected human existence.
- The mass media's role in binding people together is changing with more media choices.
- Profit potential drives mass media behavior in a capitalistic environment.

Michael J. Fox *Actor Michael J. Fox, who suffers from debilitating Parkinson's disease, chose to become a poster child for expanded stem cell research in 2006 political campaigns. His media presence was a powerful factor, perhaps a turning point, in the development of society-wide consensus on the morality of medical research using embryonic stem cells.*

GREAT MORAL ISSUES

Great moral issues define a society. Slavery, right or wrong? Abortion on demand? Stem cell research? Citizenship for illegal aliens? These are issues on which mass media comprise the primary forum for the debate as society struggles toward consensus.

On slavery, Quakers in the 1700s drew on their theology for an unequivocal position: evil. Later when the Constitution created the new American republic, slavery was debated as a constitutional issue. But not until the 1800s, with the proliferation of printing presses, did the

2

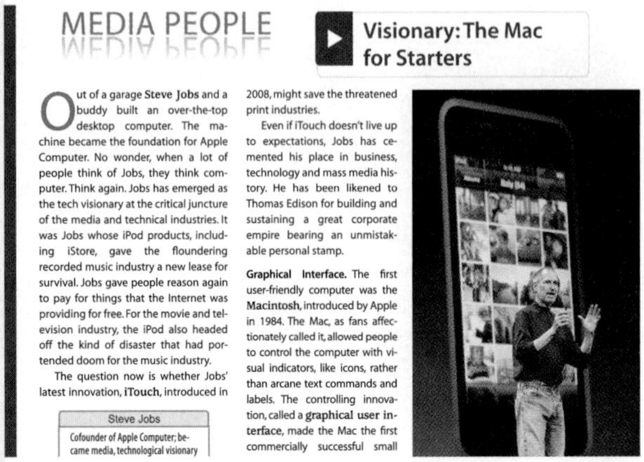

MEDIA PEOPLE

Visionary: The Mac for Starters

Out of a garage **Steve Jobs** and a buddy built an over-the-top desktop computer. The machine became the foundation for Apple Computer. No wonder, when a lot of people think of Jobs, they think computer. Think again. Jobs has emerged as the tech visionary at the critical juncture of the media and technical industries. It was Jobs whose iPod products, including iStore, gave the floundering recorded music industry a new lease for survival. Jobs gave people reason again to pay for things that the Internet was providing for free. For the movie and television industry, the iPod also headed off the kind of disaster that had portended doom for the music industry.

The question now is whether Jobs' latest innovation, **iTouch**, introduced in 2008, might save the threatened print industries.

Even if iTouch doesn't live up to expectations, Jobs has cemented his place in business, technology and mass media history. He has been likened to Thomas Edison for building and sustaining a great corporate empire bearing an unmistakable personal stamp.

Graphical Interface. The first user-friendly computer was the **Macintosh**, introduced by Apple in 1984. The Mac, as fans affectionately called it, allowed people to control the computer with visual indicators, like icons, rather than arcane text commands and labels. The controlling innovation, called a **graphical user interface**, made the Mac the first commercially successful small

Steve Jobs

Cofounder of Apple Computer; became media, technological visionary

Media People Boxes. This feature introduces personalities who have had a major impact on the media or whose story illustrates a major point of media history.

- Insidious forces are factors no less at home in media practices and performance than in other human endeavors—and just as hidden. One example on hidden financial influences is the documentary work of filmmakers Randy Baker and Beth Sanders, as detailed in Chapter 1 on media literacy.
- Cutting-edge personalities on the new media include Arianna Huffington and her *Huffington Post*.
- Rachel Maddow has been called the freshest commentator to hit television in cable's history. Cutting edge or not, controversial for sure. The edition is fresh with new media people, including the young speech-writer for President Obama, Jon Favreau.

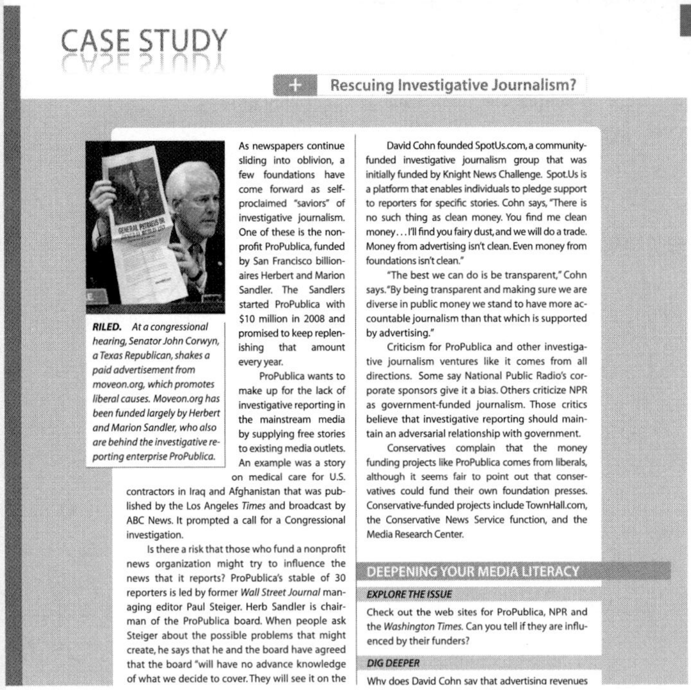

CASE STUDY

Rescuing Investigative Journalism?

As newspapers continue sliding into oblivion, a few foundations have come forward as self-proclaimed "saviors" of investigative journalism. One of these is the non-profit ProPublica, funded by San Francisco billionaires Herbert and Marion Sandler. The Sandlers started ProPublica with $10 million in 2008 and promised to keep replenishing that amount every year.

ProPublica wants to make up for the lack of investigative reporting in the mainstream media by supplying free stories to existing media outlets. An example was a story on medical care for U.S. contractors in Iraq and Afghanistan that was published by the Los Angeles *Times* and broadcast by ABC News. It prompted a call for a Congressional investigation.

Is there a risk that those who fund a nonprofit news organization might try to influence the news that it reports? ProPublica's stable of 30 reporters is led by former *Wall Street Journal* managing editor Paul Steiger. Herb Sandler is chairman of the ProPublica board. When people ask Steiger about the possible problems that might create, he says that he and the board have agreed that the board "will have no advance knowledge of what we decide to cover. They will see it on the

David Cohn founded SpotUs.com, a community-funded investigative journalism group that was initially funded by Knight News Challenge. Spot.Us is a platform that enables individuals to pledge support to reporters for specific stories. Cohn says, "There is no such thing as clean money. You find me clean money . . . I'll find you fairy dust, and we will do a trade. Money from advertising isn't clean. Even money from foundations isn't clean."

"The best we can do is be transparent," Cohn says. "By being transparent and making sure we are diverse in public money we stand to have more accountable journalism than that which is supported by advertising."

Criticism for ProPublica and other investigative journalism ventures like it comes from all directions. Some say National Public Radio's corporate sponsors give it a bias. Others criticize NPR as government-funded journalism. Those critics believe that investigative reporting should maintain an adversarial relationship with government.

Conservatives complain that the money funding projects like ProPublica comes from liberals, although it seems fair to point out that conservatives could fund their own foundation presses. Conservative-funded projects include TownHall.com, the Conservative News Service function, and the Media Research Center.

DEEPENING YOUR MEDIA LITERACY

EXPLORE THE ISSUE

Check out the web sites for ProPublica, NPR and the *Washington Times*. Can you tell if they are influenced by their funders?

DIG DEEPER

Why does David Cohn say that advertising revenues

RILED. *At a congressional hearing, Senator John Corwyn, a Texas Republican, shakes a paid advertisement from moveon.org, which promotes liberal causes. Moveon.org has been funded largely by Herbert and Marion Sandler, who also are behind the investigative reporting enterprise ProPublica.*

Case Studies. Case studies in every chapter encourage you to put together the knowledge, experience and values you brought to the course with new information and ideas from the book.

- The turmoil in media control is shown in the case study of real estate mogul Sam Zell, who acquired the Chicago *Tribune.* Within months not only was the *Tribune* in financial ruin, but Zell had been linked to Illinois Governor Rod Blagojevich, who found himself under indictment for bribery.
- A disregard for accuracy and truth are a growing problem with new media forms. The free-for-all is no better illustrated than in a case study on the abuses heaped on Al Gore for his documentary *An Inconvenient Truth.*
- How trustworthy are new sources of news information, like investigative reporting organization ProPublica? See Chapter 3 to learn how to assess the new media sources.

Media Timelines. These full-page features cast key developments in the mass media in a graphic chronology, and put these media developments in the context of what was happening intellectually, politically and socially in the larger society. You will find the timelines useful in connecting the dots between what you are learning about the mass media to what you already know.

- The demise of major daily newspapers and the desperate efforts of others to establish a viable web presence are explored in Chapter 4.
- See Chapter 11 for the shift of advertising subsidies of major media products to new and different products—and even some slippage in ad spending overall.

MEDIA TIMELINE

	TECHNOLOGY MILESTONES	PIVOTAL EVENTS
1400s/ 1500s	**Movable Type** Mass communication began with the Gutenberg printing process (1440 on).	Columbus discovered Americas (1492); Luther sparked Protestant Reformation (1517)
1600s	**Books** Cambridge Press issued first book in British North American colonies (1640). Cambridge Press also issued religious pamphlets, materials. **Newspapers** Ben Harris printed *Publick Occurrences*, first newspaper in the English colonies (1690).	Pilgrims established colony (1620); French and Indian wars (1689–1763)
1700s	**Magazines** Andrew Bradford and Benjamin Franklin introduced competing magazines in British colonies (1741). Meanwhile, weekly newspapers existed in larger colonial cities, reprinting items from Europe and each other.	Industrial Revolution began (1760s); Revolutionary War (1776–1781)
1800s	**Recording** Thomas Edison introduced Phonograph, which could record and play back sound (1877). Meanwhile, the book, newspaper and magazine industries flourished. **Movies** William Dickson devised motion picture camera (1888). Meanwhile, newspapers were in their heyday as dominant medium.	Size of United States doubled with Louisiana Purchase (1803); Morse invented telegraph (1844); U.S. Civil War (1861–1865); U.S. coasts linked by rail (1869)

Gutenberg

Publick Occurrences

Global Emphasis. The text highlights media diversity and cultural issues for students to help foster a deeper understanding of media literacy in today's global economy.

- In this era of growing globalization of media, how do companies in democratic-based societies, like Yahoo in the United States, function in countries with incredibly restrictive practices on human rights and free expression? Not consistently. And not always well. See Chapter 7 on the new media landscape.
- The Tweeter Revolution began as an easily dismissed fad. Then came the 2009 Iranian elections, with Tweeter and social networks functioning as the primary vehicle for the outside world to track the government's brutal attempts to keep itself in power. Chapter 7 on the new media landscape examines the new power of social media while Chapter 15 examines the dynamic role social media played in Iranian politics.
- The effect of media coverage in authoritarian governments including China are evaluated in Chapter 15 on Global Mass Media.

How to Use This Book

This edition retains many of the popular features that have helped your predecessors master the subject. These learning tools will help you understand central concepts and prepare for the course.

Learning Ahead Lists. Each chapter begins with learning goals to help you guide your thoughts as you read through the chapter.

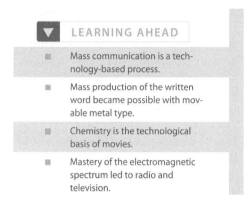

LEARNING AHEAD

- Mass communication is a technology-based process.
- Mass production of the written word became possible with movable metal type.
- Chemistry is the technological basis of movies.
- Mastery of the electromagnetic spectrum led to radio and television.

Study Previews. To help you prepare for the material ahead, each major section begins with a preview of the concepts to be covered there.

STUDY ***PREVIEW***

Historically, photography is rooted in chemistry. The distinct technology had come of ageby the time of the U.S. Civil War, creating a new kind of archival record. When techniqueswere devised to integrate photography into Gutenberg-legacy printing, the mass mediasuddenly were in a new visual era. Movies also drew on chemical technology but evolved along a separate path.

***CHECKING YOUR** MEDIA LITERACY*

- **Using a newspaper picture, show how halftones give the illusion of a photograph.**
- **Without halftones, what pre-Gutenberg methods could print media use forillustrations?**

Checking Your Media Literacy. Questions peppered throughout chapters help you be sure you've grasped the main points. These questions are intended also to help you relate what you've learned to your own experience that you have brought to the course.

Running Glossaries. You will also find glossary definitions in the margins, on the same page that the name of the concept is introduced in the text.

movable metal type
Innovative metal alphabet that made the printing press an agent for mass communication

Johannes Gutenberg
Metallurgist who invented movable metal type in mid-1440s

CHAPTER WRAP-UP

Financial Foundations (Pages 54–55)

- Mass media fit well into the profit-driven capitalistic system until two major revenue streams began drying up. Advertising revenue has fallen dramatically, dooming most daily newspapers and many magazines. The broadcast industry also faces new challenges with declines in advertising. A second significant U.S. media revenue source historically has been sales. This revenue too has declined for companies that have been losing audience. Might there be lessons from how other countries finance their media? Or from the experience-of-niche players in the U.S. media landscape?

Debate over Government Role (Pages 64–67)

- An ideal of government-press separation dates at least to democratic political philosopher John Locke in the late 1600s and still has many followers. Democracies have found ways, however, to channel public funding into the media to serve the common good—while avoiding government control. The British Broadcasting Corporation has functioned well since 1927. A U.S. variation on the British approach has a rocky record but generally has worked well. If government is to have a greater role in supporting the mass media financially, the challenge is to assure that the media retain the ability to be a watchdog on government for the people.

Ownership Structures (Pages 55–58)

- The structure of the mass media in the United States has followed a common business pattern. Most companies began with a hard-working entrepreneur, often a visionary whose media products bore a personal, sometimes

Historic Media-Government Links (Pages 67–70)

- Lessons about government involvement in media economics can be learned from a long record of government communication policies. The record began when the first Congress agreed to subsidize

Chapter Wrap-Ups. The end-of-chapter wrap-ups are expanded in this edition to include a summary paragraph on every section in the chapter. These are a handy review.

Review Questions. These questions are keyed to the major topics and themes in the chapter. Use them for a quick assessment of whether you have caught the major points.

Review Questions

1. How have mass media fit historically into the capitalist economic system?
2. How has media ownership changed in the United States through history?
3. Describe alternative business models for new revenue streams for mass media.
4. What different roles might government assume in the economics of the mass media?
5. What alternatives to historic mass media business models are being talked about? What are the upsides and downsides of each?
6. How is PPV an alternative concept to the newspaper as a bundled product?

Concepts, Terms and People. The most important concepts, terms and people introduced in the chapter are listed with their page numbers.

Concepts	Terms	People
channel (Page 43)	halftone (Page 28)	Arthur C. Clarke (Page 36)
gatekeeping (Page 45)	Industrial Revolution (Page 25)	Guglielmo Marconi (Page 34)
mass communication (Page 23)	movable metal type (Page 24)	Harold Lasswell (Page 43)
media convergence (Page 40)	noise and filters (Pages 45, 46)	Johannes Gutenberg (Page 24)
persistence of vision (Page 32)	regulators (Page 45)	Mathew Brady (Page 31)
		Philo Farnsworth (Page 35)

Media Sources. You also will find a brief list of suggested reading for further learning, some of it the latest thinking on the subject, some the classic works in the field.

Media Sources

- Linda Simon. *Dark Light: Electricity and Anxiety from the Telegraph to the X-Ray.* Harcourt, 2004. Simon, a literary scholar, finds both excitement and fear in 19th century novels and short stories about the transforming effect of electricity on life and values.
- Lev Manovich. *The Language of New Media.* MIT Press, 2001. Manovich, a media art theorist, offers a seminal and rigorous exploration of the concept of *new me-* this classic treatment, Littlejohn traces developments in communication theory and synthesizes the research. One chapter focuses on mass communication.
- Denis McQuail and Sven Windahl. *Communication Models for the Study of Mass Communication,* second edition. Longman, 1993. McQuail and Windahl include dozens of models from the first 30 years of

Resources in Print and Online

Name of Supplement	Available in Print	Available Online	Instructor or Student Supplement	Description
Instructor's Manual	√	√	Instructor Supplement	This comprehensive instructor resource contains chapter-by-chapter teaching material centering around seven major sections: the Chapter-at-a-Glance grids, Chapter Synopsis, Chapter Structure, Key Terms and Figures, Lecture Ideas, Activities, and Additional Resources. Available for download at www.pearsonhighered.com/irc; access code is required.
Test Bank	√	√	Instructor Supplement	The *Test Bank,* prepared by Keith Goldschmidt, University of West Florida, contains more than 2500 multiple-choice, true/false, completion, short answer, essay, and matching questions organized by chapter. Each question is referenced by page. Available for download at www.pearsonhighered.com/irc; access code is required.
MyTest		√	Instructor Supplement	This flexible, online test generating software includes all questions found in the *Test Bank.* This computerized software allows instructors to create their own personalized exams, to edit the existing test questions, and to add new questions. Other special features of this program include random generation of test questions, creation of alternate versions of the same test, scrambling of question sequence, and test preview before printing. Available at www.pearsonmytest.com (access code required).
PowerPoint™ Presentation Package		√	Instructor Supplement	This text-specific package, prepared by Andie Karras, The Art Institute - Hollywood, provides a basis for your lecture with PowerPoint™ slides for each chapter of the book. Available for download at www.pearsonhighered.com/irc (access code required),
Mass Communication Interactive Video	√		Instructor Supplement	Designed to help instructor's bring media issues to life in the classroom, the *Mass Communication Interactive Video* offers specially selected news segments dealing with a variety of media issues and problems. Videos focus on how mass media can be used in both ways that benefit society and in ways that can have harmful consequences for society. Each segment is accompanied by on-screen critical thinking questions to fully engage students in the issues. Please contact your Pearson representative for details.
Pearson Mass Communication Video Library	√		Instructor Supplement	This library of videos was produced by Insight Media and Films for the Humanities and Sciences and contains full-length videos such as *Functions of Mass Communication, Making of a Newspaper, Illusions of News,* and *The Truth About Lies.* Please contact your Pearson representative for details.
ClassPrep		√	Instructor Supplement	New from Pearson, ClassPrep makes lecture preparation simpler and less time-consuming. It collects the very best class presentation resources—art and figures from texts, videos, lecture activities, audio clips, classroom activities, demonstrations and much more—in one convenient online destination. You may search through ClassPrep's extensive database of tools by content topic (arranged by standard topics within the communication curriculum) or by content type (e.g., video, audio, activities). ClassPrep is found in the Instructor's section of MyCommunicationLab.
Answer Key for Study Edition Quizzes and Tests		√	Instructor Supplement	This instructor resource provides answer keys for all of the practice tests in the book as well as one additional quiz with answer key and Media Literacy Activity per chapter. Available for download at www.pearsonhighered.com/irc; access code is required.
Introduction to Mass Communication Study Site (open access)		√	Student Supplement	*Pearson's Introduction to Mass Communication Study Site* is an open access student resource featuring practice tests, weblinks, and flashcards of key terms for each major topic of your introduction to mass communication course. Each topic has been correlated to the table of contents for this book. http://www.abmasscommunication.com
Study Card for Introduction to Mass Communication	√		Student Supplement	Colorful, affordable, and packed with useful information, *Pearson Study Cards* make studying easier, more efficient, and more enjoyable. Course information is distilled down to the basics, helping you quickly master the fundamentals, review a subject for understanding, or prepare for an exam. Because they're laminated for durability, you can keep these Study Cards for years to come and pull them out whenever you need a quick review. Available for purchase and packaging with the text.
MyCommunicationLab		√	Instructor & Student Supplement	*MyCommunicationLab* is a state-of-the-art, interactive and instructive solution for communication courses. Designed to be used as a supplement to a traditional lecture course, or to completely administer an online course, *MyCommunicationLab* combines an eText, multimedia, video clips, activities, research support, tests and quizzes to completely engage students. See next page for more details.

Save time and improve results with

Designed to amplify a traditional course in numerous ways or to administer a course online, *MyCommunicationLab for Mass Communication* courses combines pedagogy and assessment with an array of multimedia activities—videos, assessments, research support, multiple newsfeeds—to make learning more effective for all types of students. Now featuring more resources including *MyMediaFeed* and *A Day In the Life* of video shorts, this new release of *MyCommunicationLab* is visually richer and even more interactive than the previous version—a leap forward in design with more tools and features to enrich learning and aid students in classroom success.

TEACHING AND LEARNING TOOLS

New *Mass Communication Instructor's Network* To help you stay current in the classroom, Vivian's *Mass Communication Instructor's Network* provides **current video clips and articles** accompanied by classroom discussion questions, sample assignments, and media literacy activities. Organized around each chapter of the book and **updated every week, this revolutionary online community helps you save time preparing current materials for class.** Participating instructors can communicate directly with each other to share best teaching practices, and upload and share files, including videos, as classroom presentations, exercises and case studies. Any file posted to the community, including links to video posted by another instructor, can be downloaded and shared. Users can add comments to network posts, ask questions, and participate in a discussion forum on a particular topic.

NEW VERSION! Pearson eText: Identical in content and design to the printed text, a Pearson eText provides students access to their text whenever and wherever they need it. In addition to contextually placed multimedia features in every chapter, our **new Pearson eText allows students to take notes and highlight, just like a traditional book.**

Videos and Video Quizzes: Interactive videos provide students with the opportunity to watch video clips that help highlight specific mass communication concepts including current events, news coverage, and interviews with scholars. Many videos are annotated with critical thinking questions or include short, assignable quizzes that report to the instructor's gradebook.

NEW! ABC News RSS feed: MyCommunicationLab provides an online feed from ABC news, updated hourly, to help students choose and research group assignments and speeches.

NEW! MySearchLab: Pearson's MySearchLab™ is the easiest way for students to start a research assignment or paper. Complete with extensive help on the research process and four databases of credible and reliable source material, MySearchLab™ helps students quickly and efficiently make the most of their research time.

ONLINE ADMINISTRATION

No matter what course management system you use—or if you do not use one at all, but still wish to easily capture your students' grades and track their performance—Pearson has a *MyCommunicationLab* option to suit your needs. Contact one of Pearson's Technology Specialists for more information and assistance.

A *MyCommunicationLab* access code is no additional cost when packaged with selected Pearson Communication texts. To get started, contact your local Pearson Publisher's Representative at www.pearsonhighered.com/replocator.

Acknowledgments

Infusing new energy and innovation at conceptual stages, experienced mass communication development editor Stephen Hull shepherded the project at critical early steps. This all has been done with the energetic support of Allyn & Bacon's mass communication editor, Jeanne Zalesky, to make this the most significant revision in the history of *The Media of Mass Communication*. It has been a team effort. Case studies, for example, came from Jenny Lupica, Brian Mickelson, Kay Turnbaugh, Emiley Zalesky and Jeanne Zalesky. Kudos go to production administrator Barbara Mack and project manager Eric Arima. Photo researcher Stephen Forsling's tireless pursuit of photographs and permissions to tell the story of the media of mass communication makes this edition dazzle.

Besides my students and colleagues at my academic home, Winona State University, who made contributions in ways beyond what they realize, I am indebted to many students elsewhere who have written thoughtful suggestions that have shaped this edition. They include Niele Anderson, Grambling State University; Krislynn Barnhart, Green River Community College; Michelle Blackstone, Eckerd College; Mamie Bush, Winthrop University; Lashaunda Carruth, Forest Park Community College; Mike Costache, Pepperdine University; Scott DeWitt, University of Montana; John Dvorak, Bethany Lutheran College; Denise Fredrickson, Mesabi Range Community and Technical College; Judy Gaines, Austin Community College; James Grades, Michigan State University; Dion Hillman, Grambling State University; Rebecca Iserman, Saint Olaf University; Scott Wayne Joyner, Michigan State University; David Keys, Citrus College; Chad Larimer, Winona State University; Amy Lipko, Green River Community College; Christina Mendez, Citrus College; Nicholas Nabokov, University of Montana; Andrew Madsen, University of Central Florida; Scott Phipps, Green River Community College; Colleen Pierce, Green River Community College; June Siple, University of Montana; and Candace Webb, Oxnard College.

I am grateful to the following reviewers who provided guidance for this new edition of *The Media of Mass Communication:*

Lisa Byerley Gary, University of Tennessee

Anita Howard, Austin Community College

Jennifer Lemanski, The University of Texas-Pan American

Bruce Mims, Southeast Missouri State University

John Reffue, Hillsborough Community College

Phillip A. Thompsen, West Chester University of Pennsylvania

I also appreciate the suggestions of other colleagues whose reviews over the years have contributed to *The Media of Mass Communication's* success:

Edward Adams, Brigham Young University

Ralph D. Barney, Brigham Young University

Thomas Beell, Iowa State University

Ralph Beliveau, University of Oklahoma

Robert Bellamy, Duquesne University

ElDean Bennett, Arizona State University

Lori Bergen, Wichita State University

Michelle Blackstone, Eckerd College

Bob Bode, Western Washington University

Timothy Boudreau, Central Michigan University

Bryan Brown, Missouri State University

Patricia Cambridge, Ohio University

Jane Campbell, Columbia State Community College

Dom Caristi, Ball State University

Michael L. Carlebach, University of Miami

Meta Carstarphen, University of North Texas

Michael Cavanagh, University of Louisiana at Lafayette

Danae Clark, University of Pittsburgh

Jeremy Cohen, Stanford University

Michael Colgan, University of South Carolina

Ross F. Collins, North Dakota State University

Stephen Corman, Grossmont College

James A. Danowski, University of Illinois, Chicago

David Donnelly, University of Houston

Thomas R. Donohue, Virginia Commonwealth University

John Dvorak, Bethany Lutheran College

Michele Rees Edwards, Robert Morris University
Kathleen A. Endres, University of Akron
Glen Feighery, University of Utah
Celestino Fernández, University of Arizona
Donald Fishman, Boston College
Carl Fletcher, Olivet Nazarene University
Laurie H. Fluker, Southwest Texas State University
Kathy Flynn, Essex County College in Newark, New Jersey
Robert Fordan, Central Washington University
Ralph Frasca, University of Toledo
Judy Gaines, Austin Community College
Mary Lou Galician, Arizona State University
Andy Gallagher, West Virginia State College
Ronald Garay, Louisiana State University
Donald Godfrey, Arizona State University
Tom Grier, Winona State University
Neil Gustafson, Eastern Oregon University
Donna Halper, Emerson College
Peggy Holecek, Northern Illinois University
Anita Howard, Austin Community College
Jason Hutchens, University of North Carolina at Pembroke
Elza Ibroscheva, Southern Illinois University, Edwardsville
Carl Isaacson, Sterling College
Nancy-Jo Johnson, Henderson State University
Carl Kell, Western Kentucky University
Mark A. Kelley, The University of Maine
Wayne F. Kelly, California State University, Long Beach
Donnell King, Pellissippi State Technical Community College
William L. Knowles, University of Montana
John Knowlton, Green River Community College
Sarah Kohnle, Lincoln Land Community College in Illinois
Charles Lewis, Minnesota State University, Mankato
Lila Lieberman, Rutgers University
Amy Lignitz, Johnson County Community College in Kansas
Amy Lipko, Green River Community College
Larry Lorenz, Loyola University
Sandra Lowen, Mildred Elley College
Linda Lumsden, Western Kentucky University
John N. Malala, Cookman College
Reed Markham, Salt Lake Community College
Maclyn McClary, Humbolt State University
Daniel G. McDonald, Ohio State University
Denis Mercier, Rowan College of New Jersey
Timothy P. Meyer, University of Wisconsin, Green Bay
Jonathan Millen, Rider University
Joy Morrison, University of Alaska at Fairbanks
Gene Murray, Grambling State University
Richard Alan Nelson, Kansas State University
Thomas Notton, University of Wisconsin–Superior
Judy Oskam, Texas State University
David J. Paterno, Delaware County Community College
Terri Toles Patkin, Eastern Connecticut State University
Sharri Ann Pentangelo, Purdue University
Deborah Petersen-Perlman, University of Minnesota–Duluth
Tina Pieraccini, State University of New York at Oswego
Leigh Pomeroy, Minnesota State University, Mankato
Mary-Jo Popovici, Monroe Community College
Thom Prentice, Southwest Texas State University
Hoyt Purvis, University of Arkansas
Jack Rang, University of Dayton
Benjamin H. Resnick, Glassboro State College
Rich Riski, Peninsula College
Ronald Roat, University of Southern Indiana
Patrick Ropple, Nearside Communications
Marshel Rossow, Minnesota State University, Mankato
Julia Ruengert, Pensacola Junior College
Cara L. Schollenberger, Bucks County Community College
Quentin Schultz, Calvin College
Jim Seguin, Robert Morris College
Todd Simon, Michigan State University
Ray Sinclair, University of Alaska at Fairbanks
J. Steven Smethers, Kansas State University
Karen A. Smith, College of Saint Rose
Mark Smith, Stephens College
Howard L. Snider, Ball State University
Brian Southwell, University of Minnesota
Alan G. Stavitsky, University of Oregon
Penelope Summers, Northern Kentucky University
Philip Thompsen, West Chester University
Larry Timbs, Winthrop University
John Tisdale, Baylor University
Edgar D. Trotter, California State University, Fullerton
Helen Varner, Hawaii Pacific University
Rafael Vela, Southwest Texas State University
Stephen Venneman, University of Oregon
Kimberly Vos, Southern Illinois University
Michael Warden, Southern Methodist University
Hazel G. Warlaumont, California State University, Fullerton
Ron Weekes, Ricks College
Bill Withers, Wartburg College
Donald K. Wright, University of South Alabama
Alan Zaremba, Northeastern University
Eugenia Zerbinos, University of Maryland

chapter 1

MASS MEDIA LITERACY

Michael J. Fox *Actor Michael J. Fox, who suffers from debilitating Parkinson's disease, chose to become a poster child for expanded stem cell research in 2006 political campaigns. His media presence was a powerful factor, perhaps a turning point, in the development of society-wide consensus on the morality of medical research using embryonic stem cells.*

LEARNING AHEAD

- More than most people realize, we are awash in a mass media environment.
- Media literacy begins with an awareness of our media environment.
- Communication through mass media has profoundly affected human existence.
- The mass media's role in binding people together is changing with more media choices.
- Profit potential drives mass media behavior in a capitalistic environment.

GREAT MORAL ISSUES

Great moral issues define a society. Slavery, right or wrong? Abortion on demand? Stem cell research? Citizenship for illegal aliens? These are issues on which mass media comprise the primary forum for the debate as society struggles toward consensus.

On slavery, Quakers in the 1700s drew on their theology for an unequivocal position: evil. Later when the Constitution created the new American republic, slavery was debated as a constitutional issue. But not until the 1800s, with the proliferation of printing presses, did the Quaker-inspired position for abolition bore into public consciousness as a defining moral issue for a new generation. Quaker-inspired newspapers, first published by white abolitionists, then also by blacks who had been freed from slavery, fanned the moral and intellectual struggle until it boiled over into politics. One by one the movement picked up followers. These included people who earlier hadn't had strong feelings on the issue. Also, there were converts.

The abolitionist movement spread from fringe publications to the mainstream. By the time of the Civil War in the 1860s, slavery was a leading subject in daily newspapers. Historians see a book, the novel *Uncle Tom's Cabin* by Harriet Beecher Stowe, as pivotal. The struggle was horribly painful and not entirely settled by the war. But over the next century, amid continuing media attention to social justice, consensus emerged. Nobody today would advocate slavery.

No less defining for society and its moral values is today's issue of stem cell research, with almost the entire debate going on in the mass media.

His body spasmodic because he'd chosen to forgo his medication that day, actor Michael J. Fox made a powerful case on television during the 2006 midterm elections for expanded stem cell research. Fox was hardly the first person to argue that the scientific tools are at hand to ease if not end the human misery wrought by chronic diseases like his own Parkinson's disease. Fox's involuntary convulsing gave potency to his argument. The television spots also provided the opposition with a springboard to argue the case that the medical use of embryonic stem cells is murder of human beings.

Someday the stem cell debate will be behind us, no matter its final outcome. A century from now historians will be pondering what the turning points were in the debate. The historians will focus on the role of the messages that the principals in the debate, all mass communicators, put into society-wide dialogue through the mass media. For now we'll leave it to commentators in the mass media to sort through whether Michael J. Fox's pleas will make a difference.

In the meantime, think about former cutting-edge issues that through debate in the mass media either have been resolved or are in the process of being resolved:

- Should women be allowed to vote?
- Are Darwin's provocative thoughts on the evolution of species the work of the devil?
- Are American Indians due restitution because of the U.S. government's history of genocidal policies?
- Is rap music the ruination of a generation?
- Do portrayals of violence in books beget real-life violence? How about portrayals on television? In the movies?
- Is the creation of jobs more important than the resulting environmental damage from industrial pollution?
- Do individuals have the right to choose to die?

That's a lot of weighty stuff to consider. As with all the profound issues with which educated people deal, mass communication's role is so key that it cannot be ignored.

This chapter is your start on a keener understanding of the media of mass communication and their significance in our lives, both individually and collectively. This understanding is called media literacy. The more sophisticated your media literacy, the better equipped you are to deal with the overwhelming deluge of messages from the mass media. You'll also be better able to participate intelligently in the dialogue.

Media Ubiquity

STUDY ***PREVIEW***

We swim in an ocean of mass communication, exposed 68.8 percent of our waking hours to media messages. So immersed are we in these messages that we often are unmindful of their existence, let alone their influences.

> **mass media**
> Strictly speaking, mass media are the vehicles through which messages are disseminated to mass audiences. The term also is used for industries built on mass media: *the television and book media.* Also, companies in the business of delivering mass messages with mass media: *Viacom is a media company.*

MEDIA EXPOSURE

So awash are we in **mass media** messages that most of the time we don't even think about them. Scholars at Ball State University found that people are intentionally involved in a media activity, like watching television or browsing the Internet, 30 percent of their waking hours—almost five hours a day. Additional media exposure is passive,

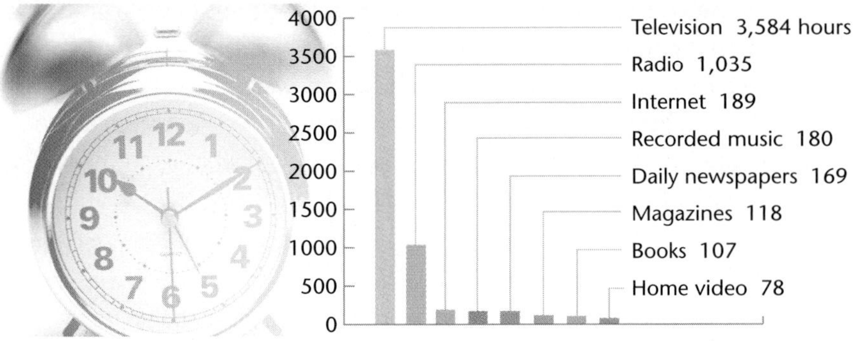

Media Usage. *The research firm Veronis Suhler Stevenson found that the reported amount of television viewing easily led other media in the average hours of consumer use per person in 2004. Veronis projected even more television viewing into the future.*

like audio wallpaper. In the 21st century, mass media are essential in most of our daily lives, sometimes in our faces, sometimes like air, ubiquitous but invisible. Or at least unnoticed, taken for granted.

CONCURRENT MEDIA USAGE

Incredible as it may seem, the Ball State study found that besides five hours of media involvement a day, people average more than an additional six hours with the media while doing something else. That's an additional 39 percent of our waking hours. This includes half-watching television while cooking dinner or catching a billboard while commuting. All tallied, the media are part of our lives about two-thirds of the time we're not sleeping—68.8 percent, to be precise. Perhaps we need the rest.

Mass media have become so integrated into people's lives that **media multitasking** is no chore. The Ball State researchers found that roughly one-third of the time people spend with mass media involves simultaneous contact with two or more other media. This includes reading a newspaper with one ear tuned to a television program, listening to the radio with the other ear, and simultaneously surfing the Net.

As startling as the Ball State study may seem, the findings are hard to dispute. Researchers tracked 294 Midwesterners for 12 hours a day, 5,000 hours in all, recording their media use every 15 seconds on a handheld device. That's a sample size and methodology that commands respect.

Strictly speaking, the media exposure tracked in the Ball State study was not all mass communication. By definition, **mass communication** is the technology-assisted transmission of messages to mass audiences. The Ball State study included technology-assisted one-on-one communication, such as instant messaging and e-mail, which primarily are forms of interpersonal communication. The fact, however, is that distinctions between mass communication and some interpersonal communication are blurring. Video gaming, for example, can be a solo activity. Video gaming can also be interpersonal, with two people together or apart. Also, video gaming can be a mass activity with dozens, theoretically thousands, clearly making it a form of mass communication. By lumping technology-assisted communication and mass media communication together, the Ball State data merely reflect the emerging reality that we are living a media-saturated existence.

CHECKING YOUR MEDIA LITERACY

- **Are you surprised at the Ball State University study on the amount of time people spend consciously and unconsciously with mass media?**
- **What are your own patterns and habits using mass media?**

media multitasking
Simultaneous exposure to messages from different media

mass communication
Technology-enabled process by which messages are sent to large, faraway audiences

INESCAPABLE SYMBIOSIS

As a demonstration of willpower, someone occasionally goes cold turkey and abstains from exposure to the mass media. The oddity makes it news, whether it's a grade-school class exercise or a scientific experiment with careful controls. Usually media-free demonstrations are short-lived. Except perhaps when we

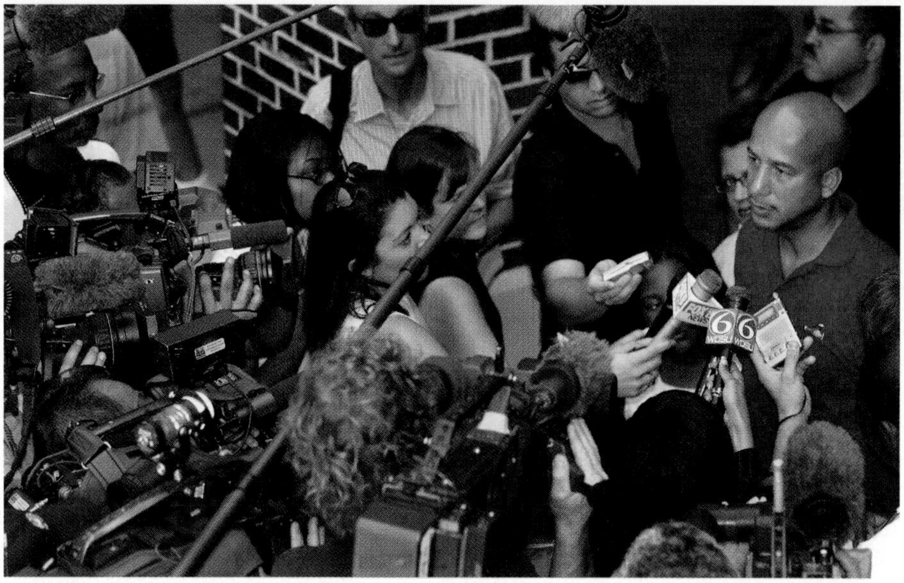

If Not from Reporters, from Whom? *It's through the mass media that people learn what's going on beyond the horizon. The media also are the vehicle through which leaders communicate with the public. Here, New Orleans Mayor Ray Nagin speaks with reporters about the Hurricane Katrina recovery. The reporters then packaged his account for their audiences.*

backpack into the remote wilds, most of us have a happily symbiotic dependence on mass media. We depend on media. And media industries, of course, are dependent on having an audience. What would be the purpose of a radio station, for example, if nobody listened?

>> **Personal Dependence.** Most days the most-listened-for item in morning newscasts is the weather forecast. People want to know how to prepare for the day. Not knowing that rain is expected can mean getting wet on the way home or not allowing extra time if the roads are slick. For most of us, modern life simply wouldn't be possible without media. We need media for news and information; for entertainment, amusement and diversion, and for the exchange of ideas.

>> **Information.** Mass-media-delivered information comes in many forms. Students heading for college, especially if they plan to live in a dorm, receive a brochure about the dread disease meningitis. It's a life-or-death message about reducing the contagion in cramped living quarters. The message "Inoculate now" is from a mass medium—a printed brochure or a mass-mailed letter from the campus health director.

Time Spent with Media. *Mass media are everywhere all the time. An extensive Ball State University study found that we spend 68.8 percent of our waking hours with the media, much of it while doing something else. Also, we sometimes expose ourselves to additional media messages at the same time.*

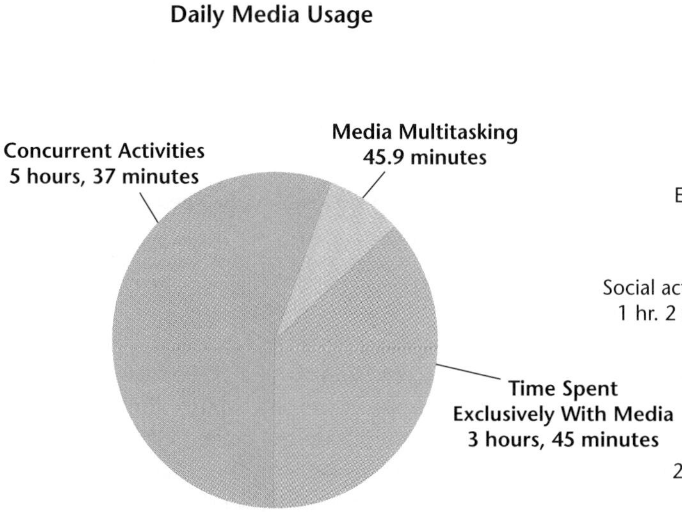

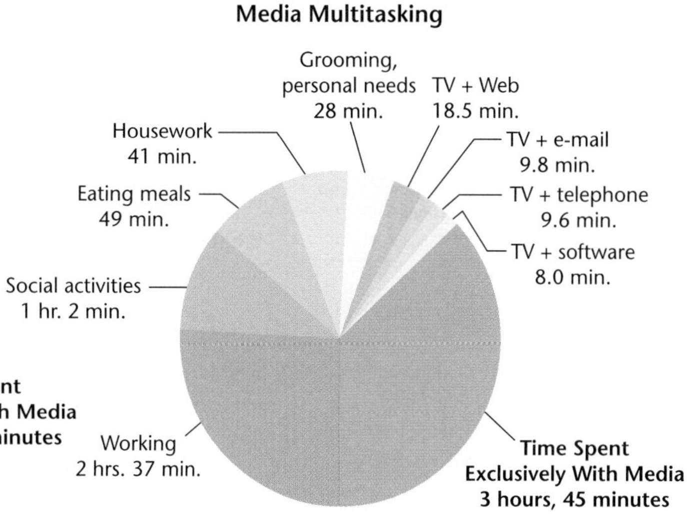

The most visible mass media-delivered information is news. People look to newscasts and news sites, even David Letterman and Argus Hamilton, to know what's going on beyond the horizon. If not for the mass media, people would have to rely on word of mouth from travelers to know what's happening in Iraq, Hollywood or the state Capitol.

Information takes many forms. For example, advertising offers information to help consumers make intelligent decisions.

>> **Entertainment.** Before mass media came into existence in the mid-1400s, people created their own diversion, entertainment and amusement. Villagers got together to sing and swap stories. Traveling jugglers, magicians and performers dropped by. What a difference mass media have made since then. In 2006 the Ron Howard movie *The Da Vinci Code*, in its first weekend, opened to 80 million people in the United States and 120 million abroad. Do you know anyone who hasn't had television or radio on for entertainment in the past week? The past 24 hours?

Marketplace of Ideas. *In his tract* Areopagitica *in the 1600s, English thinker John Milton made an eloquent case for free expression. Milton's idea was that individuals can use their power of reasoning to improve their situation and come to know great truths by exchanging ideas freely. The mass media are the primary vehicle for persuasive discourse.*

>> **Persuasion.** People come to conclusions on pressing issues by exposing themselves to competing ideas in what's called the **marketplace of ideas.** In 1644 the thinker-novelist John Milton eloquently stated the concept of the value of competing ideas: "Let truth and falsehood grapple; whoever knew truth put to the worse in a free and open encounter." Today more than ever, people look for truth by exposing their views and values to those of others in a mass media marketplace. Milton's mind would be boggled by the volume. Consider the diversity: talk radio, newspaper editorial pages, blogs, anti-war lyrics from iTunes.

The role of persuasion is especially important in a democratic society, where public policy bubbles up from the citizenry over time. Consider the debate for decades on limiting young people's access to alcohol. Should the legal drinking age be 18? 21? None at all? Or should booze be banned entirely? As the debate has worn on, with both sides making their cases, public policy representing a grassroots majority has evolved. The media have been essential in this process.

The most obvious persuasion that the mass media carry is advertising. People look to ads to decide among competing products and services. What would you know about Nikes or iPods if it weren't for advertising to which you exposed yourself or heard about from a friend who saw or heard an ad?

>> **Media Dependence.** Not only do people in their contemporary lifestyles need mass media, but the industries that have built up around the media need an audience. This is the interdependence—a **symbiosis**. To survive financially, a publishing house needs readers who will pay for a book. A Hollywood movie studio needs people at the box office or video store. Media companies with television, radio, newspaper and magazine products cannot survive financially unless they can deliver to an audience that advertisers want to reach. Advertisers will buy time and space from media companies only if potential customers can be delivered.

We live in an environment that interconnects with mass media. The interdependence is a generally satisfying although not problem-free fact of modern life.

CHECKING YOUR MEDIA LITERACY

- **Why do people need mass media today? And why do mass media need people?**
- **What is the role of persuasion in a democratic society?**

marketplace of ideas
The concept that a robust exchange of ideas, with none barred, yields better consensus

symbiosis
Mutually advantageous relationship

media literacy
Competence or knowledge about the mass media

HIERARCHY OF MEDIA LITERACY

By literacy, people usually mean the ability to read and write. Literacy also can mean command of a specific discipline such as history or physics. **Media literacy** is possessing the knowledge to be competent in assessing messages carried by mass media. Media literacy is essential in this Age of Mass Communication that envelops our lives dawn to dusk, cradle to grave. Think about not having modern media literacy.

Peter King

Bill Keller

Journalistic Treason? *Was it overblown political rhetoric for Peter King, a Republican member of Congress from New York, to accuse the New York* Times *of treason for revealing the breadth of Bush administration wiretapping? President Bush himself was irate at the revelations although he stopped short of using the T word. The executive editor of the* Times, *Bill Keller, admitted that the decision to publish did not come easily but that, in the end, the government's argument for secrecy was less compelling than the people's right to know. For citizens to sort through such issues requires that they have a competent level of media literacy.*

Thomas Jefferson, although brilliant and learned in his time, would be in absolute wonderment at hearing a radio for the first time. As foolish as he would seem to you and me today, a resurrected Jefferson might ask how so many little people could fit inside so tiny a box and make so much noise. Jefferson's lack of media literacy would be laughable.

MEDIA AWARENESS

Most of our media exposure is invisible or at least unnoticed at a conscious level—the background music at a mall store, the advertising blurb on a pen, the overblown entrée description on a menu with the stacked-higher-than-life photo of a burger. Many media messages blur into our landscape as part of the environment that we take for granted. One measure of media literacy is awareness of the presence of media messages.

Some awareness requires higher media literacy than others.

>> **Message Form.** Fundamental media literacy is the ability to see the difference between a one-on-one message and a mass message. This is not always easy. Consider a mass mailing with a personal salutation: "Hi, Karla." It's naïve—media illiteracy, we could call it—for Karla to infer from the salutation that she's getting a personal letter.

>> **Message vs. Messenger.** Once there was a monarch, as the story goes, who would behead the bearer of bad news. The modern-day media equivalent is faulting a news reporter for telling about a horrible event, or criticizing a movie director for rubbing your face in an unpleasant reality. Media literacy requires distinguishing between messages and the messenger. A writer who deals with the drug culture is not necessarily an advocate. Nor necessarily is a rapper who conjures up clever rhymes for meth.

>> **Motivation Awareness.** Intelligent use of the mass media requires assessing the motivation for a message. Is a message intended to convey information? To convince me to change brands? To sour me on a candidate? The answer usually requires thinking beyond the message and identifying the source. Is the message from a news reporter who is trying to be detached and neutral about the subject? Or is the message from the Democratic National Committee? It makes a difference.

>> **Media Limitations.** The different technologies on which media are shaped affect messages. CDs, for example, can deliver music superbly but books cannot. Both CDs and books are mass media, but they have vastly different potentials.

Someone who criticizes a movie for departing from the particulars of the book on which it's based may well lack sufficient media literacy to recognize that a 100-minute movie cannot possibly be literally true to a 90,000-word novel. Conversely, Ang Lee's 2005 movie *Brokeback Mountain* did things visually and audiologically that Annie Proulx could not do in her *New Yorker* short story on which the movie was based. It's as pointless to criticize a movie for not being a book as it is to criticize tuna for not tasting like spinach.

>> **Traditions.** The past informs our understanding of the present. A longstanding strain in U.S. journalism, for example, was born in the Constitution's implication that the news media should serve as a watchdog on behalf of the people against government folly and misdeeds. Another tradition is for artistic expression that is free from government restraint. Media literacy is impossible without an appreciation of the traditions that have profoundly shaped the parameters of media performance and reasonable expectations.

Too, media literacy requires an understanding of other traditions. The role of mass media in China, for example, flows from circumstances and traditions radically different from those in Western democracies. Even among democracies, media performance varies. News reporting about criminal prosecutions in Britain, as an example, is much more restrained than in the United States.

>> **Media Myth.** Video games are the latest whipping boys for violent crime. The fact is that the oft-heard conventional wisdom that media violence begets real-life violence has never been proved, despite hundreds of serious studies by social scientists. In fact, no matter how cleverly criminal defense attorneys have tried to scapegoat violent behavior on video gaming, television or movies, the courts always have rejected the argument. This is not to say that there is no link between violence in the media and violence in real life. Rather, it's to say that a simple, direct lineage has yet to be confirmed.

Media myths galore are afloat, polluting intelligent dialogue and understanding of important issues, including media violence. To separate real phenomena from conjecture and nonsense requires media literacy.

CHECKING YOUR MEDIA LITERACY

- **Give examples of media awareness as indicators of media literacy.**
- **How do media myths impede attaining a high level of media literacy?**

Saw Sequel. *Low-budget slasher flicks like the* Saw *flick franchise fuel criticism against media-depicted violence. Why do media companies keep pumping out such objectionable stuff? The first four* Saw *episodes, released annually just ahead of Halloween, earned $500 million worldwide, including more than 15 million DVDs.*

Human Communication

STUDY PREVIEW

Mass communication is a process that targets technologically amplified messages to massive audiences. Other forms of communication pale in comparison in their ability to reach great numbers of people.

ANCIENT COMMUNICATION

Human communication has many forms. Cave dwellers talked to each other. When Tor grunted at Oop, it was **interpersonal communication**—one on one. Around the campfire, when Tor recounted tales from the hunt for the rest of the tribe, he was engaging in **group communication.** Traditionally, both interpersonal and group communication are face-to-face. Technology has expanded the prehistoric roots of human communication. When lovers purr sweet nothings by telephone, it's still interpersonal communication. A rabble-rouser with a megaphone is engaging in group communication.

MASS COMMUNICATION

Fundamental to media literacy is recognizing the different forms of communication for what they are. Confusing interpersonal communication and mass communication, for example, only muddles an attempt to sort through important complex issues.

Mass communication is the sending of a message to a great number of people at widely separated points. Mass communication is possible only through technology, whether it be a printing press, a broadcast transmitter or an Internet server.

The massiveness of the audience is a defining characteristic of mass communication:

>> **Audience.** The mass audience is eclectic and heterogeneous. With sitcoms, for example, the television networks seek mega-audiences of disparate groups—male and female, young and old, liberal and right-wing, devout and nonreligious. Some media products narrow their focus, like a bridal magazine. But a bridal magazine's intended audience, although primarily young and female, is still diverse in terms of ethnicity, income, education and other kinds of measures. It still is a mass audience.

>> **Distance.** The mass audience is beyond the communicator's horizon, sometimes thousands of miles away. This is not the case with either interpersonal or group communication. Even technology-assisted group meetings via satellite or videoconferencing, although connecting faraway points, are not mass communication but a form of group communication.

>> **Feedback.** The mass audience generally lacks the opportunity for immediate **feedback.** In interpersonal communication, a chuckle or a punch in the nose right then and there is immediate feedback. With most mass communication, response is delayed—a letter to the editor, a canceled subscription. Even an 800-call to a television news quiz is delayed a bit and is certainly less potent than that punch in the nose. Also, the recipient of an e-mailed message doesn't necessarily read it right away.

interpersonal communication
Between two individuals, although sometimes a small group, usually face to face

group communication
An audience of more than one, all within earshot

feedback
Response to a message

CHECKING YOUR MEDIA LITERACY

- **Can you give examples of personal, group and mass communication besides those cited here?**
- **Is a football cheerleader with a megaphone a mass communicator? How about someone in a videoconference meeting?**

Media and Society

STUDY *PREVIEW*

With the advent of network radio, people across the geographically huge and diverse United States found themselves bound culturally as never before. Later television networks added to the cultural cohesion. That mass audience of yore, however, is fragmenting. Media companies cater increasingly to niches, not the whole.

UNIFICATION

Media literacy can provide an overview of mass media's effects on society and culture. The most sweeping effect of mass media has been as a cultural unifier.

>> **A Cultural Identity.** The mass media bind communities with messages that become a shared experience. History is peppered with examples. When Horace Greeley created a national weekly edition of his New York *Tribune* in the 1840s, readers throughout the country, even on the remote frontier, had something in common. Meanwhile, the first distinctly American novels, appearing in the early 1800s, helped give the young nation a cultural identity. The mass media of the time, mostly books and newspapers, created an awareness of something distinctly American. Shared knowledge, experience and the values flowing therefrom are, after all, what a culture is.

>> **Radio and Cultural Cohesion.** The national radio networks beginning in the 1920s, seeking the largest possible audiences, contributed intensely to cultural cohesion. Americans everywhere laughed together, simultaneously even, with the on-air antics of Eddie Cantor, Jack Benny, and Fibber McGee and Molly. Pop music became a coast-to-coast phenomenon. Even the networks' names suggested their role in making a national identity—the *National* Broadcasting Company and the *Columbia* Broadcasting System and later the *American* Broadcasting Company. It was radio that gave President Franklin Roosevelt a national audience in the Depression from which to rally massive majorities behind daring economic and social reforms. Hollywood shifted to patriotic war themes in feature movies, which, along with outright propaganda like Frank Capra's *Why We Fight* series, were a powerful part of the media mix that made it easy for Roosevelt to unify the nation for war in the 1940s, despite the country's ethnic, religious and social diversity.

A Nation Listening. *President Franklin Roosevelt calmed a desperate nation early in the Great Depression of the 1930s by talking in real time over the new national radio networks. Roosevelt's reassuring words are still quoted: "The only thing we have to fear is fear itself." It was a unifying message that built support for the President's daring economic reforms.*

>> **Television's Binding Influence.** Later the television networks became major factors in the national identity. Audiences of unprecedented magnitude converged on the networks, all promulgating the same cultural fare. Even network newscasts, when they were introduced, all had a redundancy.

Through most of the 20th century, the most successful mass media companies competed to amass the largest possible audiences. The companies sought to bring everybody into their tents. True, there were racist hate-mongers with radio programs. Also, political dissidents had their outlets. But the media, especially those dependent on advertising revenue, had a largely homogeneous thrust that simultaneously created, fed and sustained a dominant monoculture.

The role of mass media as a binding influence is most clear in news coverage of riveting events. Think 9/11. Think Hurricane Katrina. Even the Super Bowl. Onscreen news graphics are a regular binding influence: *America in Crisis, America's Most Wanted, Our Porous Borders*. Lou Dobbs on CNN has found broad appeal with his "War on the Middle Class" theme. Almost everybody's self-perception is as middle class or aspiring to be.

MORAL CONSENSUS

The mass media contribute to the evolution of what society regards as acceptable or as inexcusable. News coverage of the impeachment of President Clinton did this. On a lesser scale, so did revelations about the drug addiction of talk-show host Rush Limbaugh, after years of stridently calling for harsh crackdowns on sellers and users of illegal drugs. The lists of people convicted of underage alcohol consumption, a staple in many small-city newspapers, keep the question before the public about whether the legal age should be 21 or 18, or whether there should be any restriction at all or, at the other extreme, a return to prohibition. At many levels, the mass media are essential to the ongoing process of society identifying its values.

You might ask whether the media, in covering controversy, are divisive. The short answer: No. Seldom do the media create controversy. For the most part, media merely cover it. Thorough coverage, over time, helps to bring about societal consensus—sometimes for change, sometimes not. For example, most Americans once opposed legalizing abortion. Today, after exhaustive media attention, a majority belief has emerged that abortion should be available legally in a widening array of circumstances. Racial integration was settled upon as public policy in the latter 20th century. The debate, conducted almost entirely through mass media, is well along on many fundamental issues, such as gun control, universal health care, gay marriage and, never ending, government budget priorities.

demassification
Media's focus on narrower audience segments

sub-mass audience
A section of the largest mass audience, with niche interests

FRAGMENTATION

The giant Gannett newspaper chain launched a national daily, *USA Today*, in 1982, with editing techniques that pandered explicitly to an American identity. The paper had a first-person "our" tone throughout in referring to national issues. *USA Today* rose to become the largest daily in the nation, reflecting and also fueling a homogeneity in American culture. At the same time, however, a phenomenon was at work elsewhere in the mass media to turn the conventional wisdom about mass audiences on its head. In a process called **demassification,** media companies shifted many of their products from seeking the largest possible audience to focusing on audience segments.

Cable Niches. *Technology has enabled media companies to focus on sub-mass audiences. In planning are these cable channels: Puppy Channel, Anti-Aging Network, Wine Network.*

Demassification began on a large scale with radio. In the 1950s the major radio networks, NBC, CBS and ABC, pirated their most popular radio programming and put it on their new television networks. There was an exodus of audience and advertisers from radio. Suddenly, the radio industry was an endangered species. Stations recognized that they couldn't compete with network television for the mass audiences anymore and began seeking audience segments with specialized music. Radio became a demassified medium with a growing number of musical genres. Stations each sought only a local slice of the mass media—**sub-mass audiences,** they could be called. Or niche audiences. The new radio programming was designed not for universal appeal but for audience niches. These were audience segments that television networks didn't bother to seek in their quest to build mass audiences that left no one out.

Like radio, magazines geared for universal audiences lost national advertising to early network television. They survived only by reinventing themselves and focusing on audience segments.

ACCELERATING DEMASSIFICATON

Media demassification accelerated in the 1980s with technology that gave the cable television industry the ability to deliver dozens of channels. Most of these channels, while national, were taking the demassified course of magazines and gearing programs to audience niches—sports fans, food aficionados, speed freaks. The term **narrowcasting,** as opposed to broadcasting, entered the vocabulary for media literacy. Then a wholly new technology, the Internet, offered people more alternatives that were even narrower.

What has demassification done to the media's role as a contributor to social cohesion? Some observers are quick to link media fragmentation with the political polarization of the country, epitomized by Blue State and Red State divisions. Clearly there are cultural divides that have been nurtured if not created by media fragmentation. Music, as an example, is defined today by generational, racial, ethnic and socioeconomic categories, contrary to the homogenizing of tastes that radio fostered at the national level in its heyday in the 1930s and 1940s. At the same time, there remain media units that amass huge audiences in the traditional sense. Even in the slow summer months, CBS easily draws 9 million viewers to *CSI*. And *USA Today,* with a 2.3 million circulation, is by far the largest daily newspaper in the country.

A great drama of our times is the jockeying of the mass media for audience in an unpredictable and fast-changing media landscape. In pursuit of audience, whether mass or niche, media companies are experimenting with alternative platforms to deliver content that will find a following—or keep a following. Movies aren't only at the multiplex anymore and soon may be on iPods. ABC's *Lost* isn't only on prime time but is also downloadable. *USA Today* is online. CNN has multiple online platforms.

narrowcasting
Seeking niche audiences, as opposed to broadcasting's traditional audience-building concept

CHECKING YOUR MEDIA LITERACY

- **Historically, what was the effect of mass media's seeking the largest-possible audiences?**
- **What triggered media demassification? So what?**
- **Are mass media today a factor of unification or division in society?**

Media Finances

STUDY PREVIEW

An economic reality is that businesses, including media companies, need to turn a profit. One wag made the point this way in commenting on the struggling newspaper industry: "A newspaper is a business first, a newspaper second." The wag's point: A lot of media behavior and content is explained by economics.

REVENUE STREAMS

Media literacy requires an understanding of the dynamics that shape media content. In a capitalistic environment, economics is the primary driver of the behavior of media companies. With rare exceptions, media companies are businesses whose success is measured by their owners in profits. In short, **capitalism** rewards enterprises with **revenue streams** that generate profits.

How is this done? To succeed financially, media companies need to design products that will find an audience. This means slavish attention to audience interests. Sometimes the mass media work hard to appeal to unsophisticated mass tastes, when instead they could encourage a more elevated dialogue on important issues of the day. Example: celebrity magazines. But the reality is that without an audience, a media product cannot sustain itself. It's as simple as that.

Some media companies, like the book industry, rely almost exclusively on sales directly to their audience. Other media companies rely on revenue from advertisers, which means cultivating an audience that advertisers want to reach. Example: bridal magazines. For many media companies, turning a profit is a combination of direct sales to consumers and advertising.

ADVERTISING

The largest revenue stream for many media companies is advertising. Newspapers and magazines sell space to advertisers that seek to reach potential customers. Television and radio sell air time.

It's usually through advertising that corporations reach potential customers. Procter & Gamble, the largest U.S. advertiser, puts $5.4 billion a year into advertising in the United States alone. That's somewhere near $17 per capita. The purchase of media space and time is a major corporate activity. It's through advertising that corporations reach potential customers. In the process of buying access to potential customers, advertisers are also subsidizing consumer media habits.

If not for advertising, *Time* magazine wouldn't exist as we know it. Nor would CNN or the New York *Times.* Almost all newspaper, magazine, radio and television outlets have advertising as their main revenue stream and essential to maintain their cost structures.

The importance of advertising in the financial structure of mass media is hard to overstate. Some years ago it was estimated that a copy of *Time* would run $16 at the newsstand if it weren't for advertising. Today the cover price undoubtedly would be more. In effect, advertising subsidizes consumers who, for example, buy *Time* for only $5 off a news rack or subscribe for as little as 50 cents a copy.

What do advertisers get for their money? In their purchased time and space, advertisers generally are free to say whatever they want. It's their space. They paid for it.

Stories occasionally surface about advertisers that assume they also are buying control of what's called **editorial content**—the non-advertising part of a media product's content. In a classic case study, General Motors went into a tiff and yanked its advertising from the *Wall Street Journal* because it was unhappy with a news story. To its credit, the *Journal* stuck to the classic model of editorial independence for media-advertiser relations and refused to bend. GM eventually came back because it needed the *Journal* to reach potential customers. Not all media, however, have the financial wherewithal to stand up to advertiser pressure or bullying. In some communities, a major local advertiser, like car dealers and grocery chains, can wield tremendous power over editorial content.

A classic case of external pressure on media content occurred at the San Jose, California, *Mercury News* after reporter Mark Schwanhausser wrote about how car buyers could negotiate a better deal. The piece picked on some of the colorful stereotypes about slick and disingenuous sales pitches. Schwanhausser included examples of sales traps that car buyers should watch for. The article enraged car dealers. In knee-jerk unity, all 47 members of the Santa Clara County Motor Car Dealers Association stopped advertising in the *Mercury*—52 pages a week. The *Mercury*'s weekly car section shrank to 12 pages, some weeks less. The only ads were from parts houses.

capitalism
An economic system with profit as the incentive for producing goods and services

revenue stream
Source of income

editorial content
Mass media content other than advertising

MEDIA PEOPLE

Mass Media Fear and Favor

Nothing could be a more noble creed: To seek truth and to tell truth. Randy Baker and Beth Sanders bought into the creed early in their careers as documentary filmmakers. One of their films won a local Emmy Award after being aired on public station WTTW in Chicago. But Baker and Sanders' later documentary, *Fear and Favor in the Newsroom,* had no takers. WTTW took a pass. So did KQED in San Francisco, whose signal reaches Baker and Sanders' hometown. Was the new film a bad piece of work? Hardly. The Berkeley-based filmmakers got good reviews after, finally, their hometown KTEH put *Fear and Favor* on the air. But KTEH is a small-market station. What was going on at public television powerhouses like WTTW and KQED?

In *Fear and Favor,* Baker and Sanders offered case after case of media kowtowing to powerful corporate interests. Their theme was that media managers engage in self-censorship rather than face the fallout, usually subtle although unmistakable, for having crossed some invisible line. This media caution, which could be called cowardliness, has been characterized as a **Fortune 500** mentality.

So why was *Fear and Favor* such a hot potato that media companies didn't want it aired? Among revelations:

- The editor of the Atlanta *Journal and Constitution* stepped down under pressure from bankers for stories on racist lending practices and from Coca-Cola for stories on a bribery investigation.
- A reporter's story for the PBS *NewsHour* was edited so environmentalists objecting to a proposal by the company US Ecology to build a nuclear dump came across as shrill and mindless.
- The news president of NBC, owned by military contractor General Electric, fired a reporter who offered exclusive video of civilian casualties and damage from U.S. bombings in Iraq.
- The New York *Times* cancelled a column by a Pulitzer-winning journalist who had written about abuses of power by wealthy interests tied up with city government.

From the start Baker and Sanders had problems telling the truths they found. First, they couldn't get financing to produce the film. The usual funding sources for independent filmmakers—major corporations—wanted nothing to do with *Fear and Favor.* The Fortune 500 mentality also infects philanthropic foundations. The foundations themselves are dependent on Fortune 500 benefactors for the money they award for public-spirited projects including independent television documentaries.

Why were public television stations, and also the PBS network, skittish about *Fear and Favor*? Ironically, one of the reasons for the existence of the U.S. public broadcasting system is to be an alternative to the commercial system that had become part of the national corporate infrastructure. But as Baker and Sanders found, public broadcasting had become beholden to the corporations too.

At the time that Baker and Sanders were working on *Fear and Favor,* some members of Congress were mumbling about wiping out government subsidies that comprise a major part of the budgets for noncommercial television stations. It was common knowledge that members of Congress bow easily to corporate donors to their re-election campaigns. These were many of the same corporate donors that finance the noncommercial television system through a donation system called corporate underwriting. The whole U.S. noncommercial television system was treading on eggshells, unwilling to rock the boat for fear of jeopardizing its financial underpinnings.

Most one-hour independent documentaries take a few months to produce. *Fear and Favor* was in production seven years, mostly because Baker and Sanders couldn't find financing. Their funding requests were rejected by every major corporation and every major foundation, including those tied into the Public Broadcasting System. But in starts and spurts they kept working on the film with mini-grants from small foundations. As Sanders put it, "We'd get $3,000 here, another $3,000 there."

Randy Baker and Beth Sanders

Once *Fear and Favor* was ready to go, Baker and Sanders had another hurdle: getting the show on the air. PBS declined to accept it. Over a few weeks, 13 stations aired the documentary—a minuscule number in a country with 350 PBS-affiliated television stations. In some cities *Fear and Favor* aired only after local public-interest organizations mobilized viewers to deluge station managers with calls to air the film.

WHAT DO YOU THINK?

- What pattern do you see in the revelations in *Fear and Favor*?
- Do you see local parallels to a Fortune 500 mentality? Does hometown boosterism affect the news you read and hear? Consider sports: Is there a home team slant? Also look for local boosterism outside the sports section.
- Are any issues not being dealt with in media-delivered drama and entertainment? Does the home-improvement and reality promoting network HGTV get into any nitty-gritty on the dark underside of home financing that triggered the 2008 world economic meltdown? Can you cite other examples in which you as a media consumer get less than the whole picture?

The Federal Trade Commission investigated and rapped the car dealers for conspiring to restrain trade and deprive consumers of information to get a fair deal. The government ordered the dealers to stop the boycott. By then, the *Mercury* had lost more than $1 million in advertising. Worse, and embarrassing to media people, the *Mercury*'s publisher, Jay Harris, had obsequiously begged the car dealers to come back. At one point, Harris publicly criticized Schwanhausser's article as unfair. Harris also authorized a full-page apologetic in the *Mercury* headlined: "Ten Reasons Why You Should Buy Your Next Car from a Factory Authorized Dealer."

The Federal Trade Commission's investigator was not so compromising: "The boycott was designed to chill the publication from publishing similar stories in the future. And the *Mercury* hasn't."

The chilling effect of bullying the media is seldom open. It can be as quiet as a textbook company executive directing an author to explain a point with an example other than one unflattering about the company's chief executive. Or the decision of a Laramie, Wyoming, radio station to pass up national stories on contaminated soup in deference to a grocer who advertised with the station. It was neither a listener-oriented nor a consumer-oriented decision. It was a business decision, crass but largely unnoticed. In another example, a Chicago television station offered a feed to the NBC network on problems discovered on jet engines manufactured by General Electric for passenger planes. The story never made the air at the GE-owned network.

DIRECT SALES

Many media products are sold directly to consumers. Books are sold mostly one at a time. People buy music one song or album at a time. At the movies it's one ticket at a time.

>> **Direct Sales.** In one sense, direct sales are the purest relationship between a media product and audience. A book, for example, succeeds or fails on direct sales. Generally there is no advertiser as a third party in the relationship between a book and reader. It's the same for recorded music. Historically movies have relied on direct sales, although the growing number of paid product plugs in scripts is eroding the pristine movie-audience relationship.

>> **Subscriptions.** Another form of direct consumer sponsorship of media content is subscriptions. The role of subscription revenue varies. For most newspapers, newsrack coins and subscription orders are secondary revenue streams that at best cover delivery costs. The cost of producing the product is borne mostly by advertising. For most magazines also, subscriptions are a minor revenue stream.

Commercial radio and television in the United States have no mechanisms for subscriptions. For all practical purposes, selling time to advertisers is the sole source of revenue. There are notable exceptions, however. Cable networks charge local cable companies a monthly fee that is passed on to cable customers. Another example is the Sirius XM satellite radio service, which relies mostly on subscriptions.

A variation is the volunteer subscriptions that ad-free public television and radio stations encourage listeners to pay—a donation. Some web sites solicit donations. Corporations and charitable foundations are major donors for non-commercial television and radio.

OTHER REVENUE

A diverse range of other revenue supports various mass media to differing degrees. So-called public broadcasting, like PBS and National Public Radio, leans on government funding. Merchandise tie-ins, like Batman toys, are significant for Hollywood, not to mention DC Comics.

Fortune 500

Annual ranking by the business magazine *Fortune* of largest U.S. corporations

CHECKING YOUR MEDIA LITERACY

- **What are the mass media's most significant revenue streams?**
- **Which media are least vulnerable to advertiser pressure to shape content?**

CASE STUDY

Shaking Down a Newspaper

Out of His League. *With a fortune estimated at $5 billion, mostly from real estate, Sam Zell had earned a ranking as the 68th richest person in the United States. He could buy about anything: "Wouldn't a newspaper be fun?" Tragically, Zell knew nothing of the standard journalistic practices and customs that had made the Chicago* Tribune *a trusted and reputable newspaper.*

Were they to know Sam Zell, the founders of the Chicago *Tribune* would be rolling over in their graves. Spinning even. So would their heirs, who built the *Tribune* into a financial and journalistic powerhouse.

Zell, a rags-to-riches Chicago real estate mogul, bought the Tribune Com- pany in 2007. Disaster followed. Zell had no sense about great journalism or what had made the *Tribune* a great newspaper for more than 150 years. This included a firewall inside the *Tribune*'s organization that shielded editors and reporters from advertisers and other forces that might seek to compromise the journalistic integrity of the *Tribune*. For example, nobody from the *Tribune*'s advertising department sat on the newspaper's board of editorial writers. Nor did the mayor of Chicago, nor the governor of the state of Illinois.

In acquiring the *Tribune* Zell had overextended himself with debt. Soon finding himself in a financial bind, Zell began selling Tribune Company assets to make his loan payments. On the auction block went the Chicago Cubs baseball club, which the *Tribune* had owned since 1981. Zell sought help for the baseball sale from the Illinois Finance Authority, a state agency. The agency's participation could have boosted the value of Cubs' Wrigley Field by $150 million.

Therein was a wrinkle. The *Tribune*'s editorial board, which writes the newspaper's editorials, had been calling for the crooked governor of Illinois, Rod Blagojevich, to be investigated. With Zell asking for state help, the governor, who controlled the state Finance Authority, saw an opportunity to soften the *Tribune*'s editorial hostility. Blagojevich's top aide was quoted in devastating court documents as telling a Zell adviser: "There is a risk that all of this is going to get derailed by your editorial page." It was clear that Blagojevich wanted Zell to fire *Tribune* editorialists.

Behind closed doors the governor was attempting to shake down the *Tribune*. Worse from a journalistic perspective, Zell's people were returning signals that Zell was willing to comply. In a taped conversation, the governor's top aide told the governor that Zell "got the message and was very sensitive to the issue." Even more indicting, the aide told the governor that he understood that heads soon would be rolling on the *Tribune* editorial board. The governor responded: "Fantastic."

DEEPENING YOUR MEDIA LITERACY

Media literacy includes an ability to evaluate sources of information. This includes knowing the political and social agendas of filmmakers as diverse as Michael Moore, Oliver Stone and Ang Lee. And who calls the shots at your local newspaper? Your favorite radio station?

EXPLORE THE ISSUE

Most news organizations take positions on issues in separate sections labeled as opinion. These sections typically carry columnists, who write their own opinions, and editorials, which represent the views of the publisher or owner.

DIG DEEPER

Who owns the news organization on which you rely heaviest? What are some recent editorial positions that you find?

WHAT DO YOU THINK?

A privilege of ownership is being able do just about whatever you want with your property. But is it wise for a media owner to support politicians or special interests in exchange for financial favor?

Global Reach		
Movies	20th Century Fox Fox Searchlight 20th Century Fox Television	$5.9 billion
Television	Fox network 35 U.S. stations Latin American stations Asian stations	5.3 billion
Newspapers	New York *Post* London *Times* *News of the World* Australia newspapers	4.1 billion
Cable	Fox News Channel Fox Movie Channel Fox regional sports networks	2.7 billion
Satcast	StarTV Sky Italia Latin America services	2.3 billion
Books	HarperCollins	1.3 billion
Magazines	*TV Guide* *Weekly Standard* *InsideOut*	1.1 billion
Internet	MySpace.com Broadsystem Ventures	1.0 billion
Radio	Sky Radio	200 million

Rupert Murdoch. *Murdoch, heir to a Sydney daily newspaper in Australia, turned the silver spoon in his mouth at birth into platinum—and on a global scale. His News Corp. is one of the planet's largest media empires. His empire includes the Asian satellite television service StarTV, the 20th Century-Fox movie studio, the* Wall Street Journal, *HarperCollins books, and the Fox television networks.*

Murdoch is known to insert himself into content decisions when it's in his financial interest. Once he ordered his New York Post *to drop television listings of CNN, a rival to his Fox news channel. When he needed friends in Congress on a broadcast regulation issue, Murdoch offered the Speaker of the House $4.5 million for an autobiography. In courting the Chinese government leaders for permission for StarTV to transmit into China, Murdoch offered a book deal to the daughter of the head of state. Also, he cancelled another book that probably would have provoked the Chinese.*

What makes Murdoch tick? Making money. To a Congressional inquiry into the politically conservative thrust of his Fox News, Murdoch said he was apolitical. "Conservative talk is more popular," he explained. Period. End of explanation. In the 2008 U.S. presidential campaign, when many Democrats were spurning Fox because of its bias, Murdoch sensed a shift toward Democrats in public opinion and personally brokered an audience-building interview with Democratic nominee Barack Obama on Fox.

CHAPTER WRAP-UP

Media Ubiquity (Pages 3–6)

- Two-thirds of our waking hours is spent consciously or subconsciously with the mass media. The media is a major part of our environment. Mass media is so ubiquitous in our lives that we media multitask without even thinking about it. We can be oblivious to the media's effects unless we cultivate an understanding of how the media work and why. This understanding is called media literacy.

Media Literacy (Pages 6–9)

- Media literacy begins with a factual foundation and becomes keener with an understanding of the dynamics that influence media messages. There are degrees of awareness, including abilities to understand and explain media behavior and effects and to identify significant media issues.

Human Communication (Pages 9–10)

- Technology has expanded the original forms of face-to-face human communication. Today, we send amplified messages to great numbers of diverse people in mass communications. The audience for these mass communications generally has no opportunity to give immediate feedback.

Media and Society (Pages 10–12)

- The effect of mass media on society is changing. In the early days of radio and television, the same programs were beamed to everyone. Despite their cultural diversity, audiences across the country all watched and listened to the same comedy, drama and music shows. The result: a strong cultural cohesion. Today that audi- ence is fragmenting and the cultural cohesion is breaking apart. Today's media companies are constantly experimenting to find a following or a new niche audience, and the resulting audience fragmentation is some- times polarizing, at other times simply diverging.

Media Finances (Pages 12–16)

- Almost all media companies are businesses that need to make a profit, and this explains most media behavior. Most media companies deliver audiences to advertisers, not blanket audiences but sub-mass audiences. Should those advertisers be able to regulate the media's message? The problem is that the economic structure of many media companies creates a conflict between serving the interests of their advertisers and serving the interests of their audiences. Having two masters is problematic.

▼ Review Questions

1. How are interpersonal, group and mass communication different? Give examples of each.
2. What were your strengths in media literacy at the start of your current course? Any voids?
3. How are we dependent on media? Give examples.
4. Give an example of a shared experience that played a significant role in a recent event. What was the media's role in the shared experience?
5. How do revenue streams affect media products?

Concepts

demassification (Page 11)
marketplace of ideas (Page 6)
mass communication (Page 4)
media literacy (Page 6)
media multitasking (Page 4)

Terms

editorial content (Page 13)
feedback (Page 9)
narrowcasting (Page 12)
revenue stream (Page 13)
sub-mass audience (Page 11)

People

John Milton (Page 6)
Rupert Murdoch (Page 17)

Media Sources

- Newsmagazines, including *Time* and *Newsweek,* cover mass media issues more or less regularly. So do the New York *Times, Wall Street Journal* and other leading newspapers. Periodicals that track mass media as businesses include *BusinessWeek, Forbes* and *Fortune.*
- Art Silverblatt. *Media Literacy: Keys to Interpreting Media Messages,* 3rd edition. Praeger, 2007. Silverblatt, a leading scholar in media literacy, discusses numerous approaches for systematic analysis of media content.
- Mike Bloxham, Robert Papper, Mark Popovich, Michel Holmes. Center for Media Design, Ball State University, 2005.
- Robert Papper, Michael Holmes and Mark Popovich. "Middletown Media Studies: Media Multitasking and How Much People Really Use the Media." *The International Digital Media & Arts Association Journal* (2003).
- Ben Bagdikian. *The New Media Monopoly,* fifth edition. Beacon, 2004. Bagdikian, perhaps the best-known critic of media conglomeration, includes data, albeit dated, on the digital revolution in this update of his classic work.
- Benjamin M. Compaine and Douglas Gomery. *Who Owns the Media? Competition and Concentration in the Mass Media Industry,* third edition. Earlbaum, 2000. The authors update the 1979 and 1992 editions with details on further concentration, more attention to the cable and home video business, and the effect of technological convergence.
- Eric McLuhan and Frank Zingrone. *Essential McLuhan.* Basic Books, 1997. These scholars have edited the vast scholarship of Marshall McLuhan into this one-volume introduction to his theories and insights about the mass media. These include the global village, hot and cold media, the medium as the message, and media and culture.
- Judith Stamps. *Unthinking Modernity: Innis, McLuhan, and the Frankfurt School.* McGill-Queen's University Press, 1995. Stamps compares and contrasts the work of the Canadian theorists Innis and McLuhan and casts them within the larger Frankfurt School of philosophical thought.

MASS MEDIA LITERACY

In this chapter you have deepened your media literacy by visiting several themes. Here are thematic highlights from the chapter:

MEDIA ECONOMICS

Media Financial Problem. Plugs for products and services on blogs, through companies like PayPerPost, have become a revenue drain for mass media companies that relied historically on advertising for profits.

The mass media and the mass audience are interdependent. Without audience and the revenue that audiences generate, there would be no media system as we understand it. For the most part, media in a capitalistic environment derive revenue either from customers who buy media products or from advertising. Advertisers pay media for access to media customers. Media literacy requires a sense of how the economic base of the modern mass media, especially in capitalistic democracies, factors into media content and performance. (Page 6)

MEDIA TECHNOLOGY

Fireside Chats. President Franklin Roosevelt took to the radio networks in the 1930s, urging calm in the face of a global economic depression. Technology gave him a bigger audience than ever assembled before.

A distinction between mass communication and other forms of communication is technology. Without technology, like printing presses and broadcast transmitters, mass communication, would not exist. The advantage of mass communication over interpersonal and group communication is the size of the audience that can be reached. Think about how Simon Fuller could possibly parade *American Idol* performances before a national audience if it weren't for the amplifying technology of the mass media. (Page 9)

MEDIA AND DEMOCRACY

Consensus Builder. Media attention to divisive issues can help wring societal consensus. The Michael J. Fox pleas for stem-cell research funding in the 2006 political campaign stirred pro and con dialogues a step toward consensus.

Democracy cannot function without the mass media. Citizens need the information provided by mass media to participate in shaping their common course. This will be even more true in the future. People also need a forum for exchanging their reactions to information and their ideas. The mass media provide that forum. (Pages 6–8)

MEDIA AND CULTURE

Violence Progenitor? Slasher movies have reignited media criticism about negative effects on individuals and society. Research, however, is inconclusive as to whether media violence begets real-life violence. We need to know more about media effects.

We live in a culture that's increasingly media-saturated. So ubiquitous are mass media that their presence largely is invisible. Occasionally we're jarred by in-your-face content, but mostly the mass media are taken for granted—like air. Just as air affects us, and deserves scientific examination and monitoring, so do media. (Pages 3–4)

MEDIA EFFECTS

Sub-Mass Audiences. Demassification has led to media products geared to narrower and narrower audiences. Currently in development for cable TV are: The Puppy Channel, Anti-Aging Network, and Wine Network.

Media affect us, and we affect media. Media messages influence our daily decision-making in ways that can be almost invisible. For instance, media influence us when we make a decision about whether to go to Starbucks or McDonald's for coffee. Similarly, we aren't always aware of the ways that we influence the media. Because media are economically dependent on audience, we as media consumers influence the media when we decide which coffee to sip or which web sites to visit or magazines to read. (Pages 4–6)

AUDIENCE FRAGMENTATION

Hidden Influences. Documentary film makers Randy Baker and Beth Sanders themselves are a case study in how powerful forces affect media content, sometimes directly but almost always hidden from public scrutiny.

The American experience became a cohesive one with books in the early 1800s that fostered a sense of nationhood, and later with radio and television networks beaming the same comedies, dramas and newscasts to the country's diverse population. Today, media can still bond people, but increasingly messages are targeted to sub-mass audiences, a practice that is adding to the fragmentation of society. (Pages 10–12)

chapter 2

MEDIA TECHNOLOGY

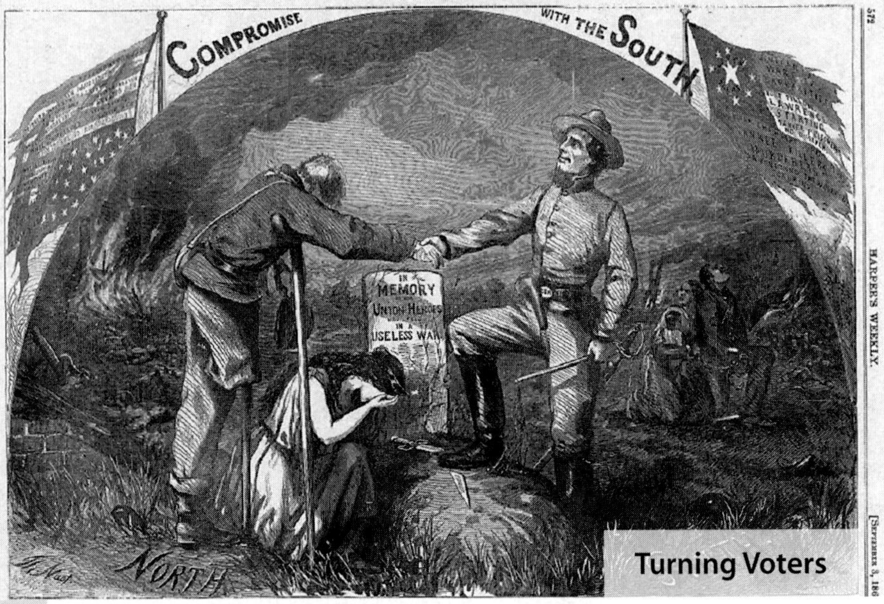

Turning Voters

After Democrats adopted an anti-war platform at their 1864 national convention, political cartoonist Thomas Nast held back nothing. His cartoon against a compromise to end the Civil War did no good for John Breckinridge. "John who?" you might ask. He was the Democratic candidate whom Abraham Lincoln, seeking re-election, defeated in November by a landslide. Today, with technology having transformed the mass media, the sway of political cartoonists has waned. Even so, the cartoonists' mighty pens remain a vital part of today's media mix and still draw blood and emotions.

LEARNING AHEAD

- Mass communication is a technology-based process.
- Mass production of the written word became possible with movable metal type.
- Chemistry is the technological basis of movies.
- Mastery of the electromagnetic spectrum led to radio and television.
- Orbiting satellites and fiber optics have improved media efficiency.
- Traditional media products and new products are emerging from digital technology.
- Models help explain the technology-driven process of mass communication.

PICTURE POWER

Despite the high regard in which Abraham Lincoln's presidency is remembered, his re-election in 1864 was hardly assured. With the nation asunder in civil war, it seemed that anti-war champion John Breckinridge had a shot at unseating Lincoln.

In September, with Election Day approaching, there appeared an emotion-rousing cartoon in the widely read magazine *Harper's Weekly*. Thomas Nast, the most powerful political cartoonist of his time, illustrated a compromise that had been proposed to end the war. A haughty Johnny Reb, representing the breakaway Confederate states, stands triumphantly beside a gravestone engraved

"Useless War." Shaking hands with Johnny Reb is a dejected peg-legged Union veteran on a cane. Nast added poignancy with a Northern widow sobbing graveside.

Lincoln supporters printed millions of copies of the Nast cartoon. They went up everywhere. Historians may quibble whether Thomas Nast swung the election. The fact is that Lincoln won with 180 electoral votes. Breckinridge had a mere 72. Lincoln called Nast the North's "best recruiting sergeant."

The influence of Nast's pencil, and that of other mid-1800s political cartoonists, was the child of new printing technology. In 1828 a revolutionary printing process, lithography, dramatically reduced the cost and time to reproduce line art. Suddenly, people had a window to see their political leadership other than in stuffy portraits. A generation of political cartoonists, wielding pens as mighty swords, became their generation's media heroes. Newspapers heralded their work atop front pages, magazines on their covers.

The rise of political cartooning is testimony to the dependence of mass media on technology. Lithographic technology was the underpinning for the new role for political cartoons in the late 1800s. Technology later would relegate cartooning to a lesser role. By the early 1900s most newspapers had begun regularly printing photographs, forcing cartoons to inside pages. Later on, color photography became a competitor for space. Television from the 1950s siphoned reader time to the screen, just as small screens and computer screens are doing now. The lesson: Mass media are technology-driven enterprises, and historically we have seen a parade of innovation that displaces old and familiar media platforms.

Even so, political cartooning has an ongoing niche. Few who saw it can forget Bill Mauldin's Lincoln Memorial after the assassination of President John Kennedy, with Lincoln's head bowed into his hands in tears. Then there was Kevin Kallaugher's 1992 depiction of a conflicted Democratic donkey blow-drying the hair of President Bill Clinton, who had suffered through after one sex scandal after another. The hair-dryer is whipping a woman's silky legs with a martini in hand out of the presidential coiffure. In a single frame a powerful political cartoonist can capture complex issues and make a point indelibly.

Through its history, political cartooning exemplifies the principle that technology is the fundamental underpinning of all mass communication. Cartooning also exemplifies how media content is in continuing flux as technology changes. Cartooning, as an example, was once the rage. Now less so. This chapter details the major technologies that have shaped and are shaping mass communication.

Media Technology

STUDY ***PREVIEW***

Technology is basic in mass communication. If not for the technology of printing presses, books as we know them wouldn't exist. If not for electronic technology, television and radio wouldn't be.

TECHNOLOGY DEPENDENCE

One defining characteristic of **mass communication** is its reliance on technology. People can communicate face-to-face, which is called **interpersonal communication,** without technological assistance. For centuries people communicated in large groups, as in town-hall meetings and concert halls, without microphones—just the human voice, albeit sometimes elevated to extraordinary volume. For mass communication, however, with audiences much more far-flung than those in the largest auditorium, machinery is necessary.

mass communication
Technology-enabled process by which messages are sent to large faraway audiences

interpersonal communication
Usually two people face-to-face

EVOLVING MEDIA LANDSCAPE

Media technology, the product of human invention, exists in several forms, each one distinctive. Around each of these technologies, industries have been built that are closely allied with each specific technology.

>> **Printing Technology.** The printing press, dating to the 1440s, spawned the book, newspaper and magazine industries. After centuries, each still exists in a largely cubbyholed niche in the media landscape.

>> **Chemical Technology.** Photography and movies have relied on chemical technology throughout most of their history.

>> **Electronic Technology.** The first of the electronic media, sound recording, actually preceded the widespread use of electricity but quickly became an electrically powered medium. Radio was electrical early on. Television was electronic from the get-go.

>> **Digital Technology.** Traditional mass media all adapted to digital technology to varying degrees beginning in the first decade of the 21st century, but the industries built on the original printing, chemicals and electronic forms remain largely distinctive. Book companies like HarperCollins still produce books. CBS is still primarily in the television business. The distinctive newest medium built on digital technology is the Internet. Even as companies built on older technologies have swirled in a frenzy to find ways to capitalize on the new medium, the Internet itself has created entirely new categories of media companies. Think Wikipedia. Think Facebook.com. Think Google.

Meanwhile, printed and bound books are still with us, as are Channel 2 on television, Paramount Pictures and commute-time radio.

CHECKING YOUR MEDIA LITERACY

- **What are the four primary technologies in which mass media are built?**
- **What industries have been built around the different media technologies?**

Printing Technology

STUDY PREVIEW

With the invention of movable metal type in the mid-1440s, suddenly the written word could be mass-produced. The effect on human existence was profound. Incorporating photographic technology with printing in the late 1800s added new impact to printed products.

MOVABLE METAL TYPE

Although printing can be traced back a couple thousand years to eastern Asia, an invention in the mid-1440s made mass production of the written word possible for the first time. The innovation: **movable metal type.** A tinkerer in what is now the German city of Mainz, **Johannes Gutenberg,** was obsessed with melting and mixing metals to create new alloys. He came up with the idea to cast the individual letters of the alphabet in metal, and then assemble them one at a time into a page for reproduction by pressing paper onto the raised, inked characters. The metal characters were sturdy enough to survive the repeated pressure of transferring the inked letters to paper—something not possible with the carved wood letters that had been used in earlier printing.

In time, industries grew up around the technology, each producing print media products that are still with us today—books, magazines and newspapers. But historically, the impact of Gutenberg's invention was apparent much earlier. Printing with Gutenberg's new technology took off quickly. By 1500 printing presses were in place throughout Europe. Suddenly civilization had the mass-produced written word.

movable metal type
Innovative metal alphabet that made the printing press an agent for mass communication

Johannes Gutenberg
Metallurgist who invented movable metal type in mid-1440s

GUTENBERG'S IMPACT

The impact was transformational. Scientists who earlier had carried on time consuming handwritten correspondence with colleagues now could print their theories and experiments for wide dissemination.

Modern science thus took form. Religious tracts could also be mass-produced, as could materials with serious challenges to religion. The growing quantity of printed materials fueled literacy and, slowly, a standardization in written languages. What Gutenberg begat can be called the Age of Mass Communication, but his innovation also spurred Western civilization into the ongoing Age of Science and Age of Reason. Civilization hasn't been the same since.

CHECKING YOUR MEDIA LITERACY

- **Would you rank Johannes Gutenberg among the 10 most influential persons in human history?**
- **What was the link between Gutenberg and the scientific revolution of the 1600s and 1700s?**

INDUSTRIAL REVOLUTION EFFECTS

The quality of Gutenberg's Bibles was incredible given the elements available. Consider the paper. Gutenberg printed some of his Bibles on **vellum,** a treated animal skin. Ink? From charcoal residue and linseed oil he stirred his own concoction. Gutenberg's ink still amazes museum curators for its blackness, even these centuries later.

>> Pulp Paper. Although taken for granted today, paper and ink were scarce for centuries. When the Reverend Joseph Glover set sail with the first press for the British colonies in North America in 1638, he packed his own stock of paper on board. When the supply ran low, the reverend's successors relied on shipments from England to replenish the stock.

When the **Industrial Revolution** approached its stride in the early 1800s, machines took over production of all kinds of products, including paper. Machine-made paper was introduced in 1803, manufactured from cotton and linen rags. The transition to wood pulp as the main ingredient occurred in 1840 with incredible cost efficiencies. Pulp-based paper helped fuel unprecedented production of printed materials. The term ***pulp fiction*** took hold for low-cost books for mass audiences. The first newspapers for mass audiences also were dependent on the new factory-produced pulp paper.

The simultaneous development of a petroleum industry made for cheaper inks.

>> High-Speed Presses. Products of the Industrial Revolution included presses that, like all the early machinery of the age, were powered by steam. The greatest innovation was the rotary press, which was perfected by **Richard Hoe,** whose name remains synonymous with high-speed printing production. An 1876 Hoe rotary press could produce 30,000 impressions an hour. In contrast, four centuries earlier with Gutenberg-style presses, printers could turn out 500 copies at most on a good day. Today, presses can print 160,000 copies an hour.

>> Paper Reels. Production was further accelerated when technology made it possible to manufacture paper in rolls. Paper could be pulled through the press continually and then cut and folded—all in a single operation in presses that were becoming more sophisticated all the time. Earlier, for four centuries going back to Gutenberg, paper was fed into the press one sheet at a time. It was a momentous event in the history of mass media technology when the Philadelphia *Inquirer* installed the first automatic reel-fed rotary press in 1865.

>> Typesetting. The Gutenberg process of hand-plucking metal-alloy characters and assembling them into words, paragraphs and pages was automated in 1884 by **Omar Mergenthaler.** With Mergenthaler's **Linotype** machine, a person at a 90-character

vellum
A treated animal skin used in early printing

Industrial Revolution
Use of machinery, notably steam-powered, that facilitated mass production beginning in late 1700s and through 1800s

pulp fiction
Derisive term for cheap novels

Richard Hoe
Perfected rotary press 1840

Omar Mergenthaler
Invented Linotype typesetting machine 1886

Linotype
Complex machine with typewriter-like keyboard to set type into line from molten lead

MEDIA PEOPLE

Johannes Gutenberg

Johannes Gutenberg was eccentric—a secretive tinkerer with a passion for beauty, detail and craftsmanship. By trade he was a metallurgist, but he never made much money at it. Like most of his fellow 15th-century Rhinelanders in present-day Germany, he pressed his own grapes for wine. As a businessman, he was not very successful, and he died penniless. Despite his unpromising combination of traits, quirks and habits—perhaps because of them—Johannes Gutenberg wrought the most significant change in history: the mass-produced written word. He invented movable metal type.

Despite the significance of his invention, there is much we do not know about Gutenberg. Even to friends he seldom mentioned his experiments, and when he did, he referred to them mysteriously as his "secret art." When he ran out of money, Gutenberg quietly sought investors, luring them partly with the mystique he attached to his work. What we know about Gutenberg's "secret art" was recorded only because Gutenberg's main backer didn't receive the quick financial return he'd expected on his investment and sued. The litigation left a record from which historians have pieced together the origins of modern printing.

The date when Johannes Gutenberg printed his first page with movable type is unknown, but historians usually settle on 1446. Gutenberg's printing process was widely copied—and quickly. By 1500, presses all over Western Europe had published almost 40,000 books.

Today, Gutenberg is remembered for the Bibles he printed with movable type. Two hundred **Gutenberg Bibles**, each a printing masterpiece, were produced over several years. Gutenberg used the best paper. He concocted an especially black ink. The quality amazed everybody, and the Bibles sold quickly. Gutenberg could have printed hundreds more, perhaps thousands. With a couple of husky helpers he and his modified wine press could have produced 50 to 60 pages an hour. However, Johannes Gutenberg, who never had much business savvy, concentrated instead on quality. Forty-seven Gutenberg Bibles remain today, all collector's items. One sold in 1978 for $2.4 million.

WHAT DO YOU THINK?

- Would you rank Johannes Gutenberg among the 10 most influential persons in history?

Movable Metal Type. *Johannes Gutenberg melted metals into alloys that he cast as individual letters, then arranged in a frame the size of a page to form words, sentences and whole passages. Once a page was full, the raised letters would be inked and a sheet of paper pressed onto them to transfer the impression. Dozens, even hundreds of impressions could be made, one page at a time. Then the type would be removed and reassembled for another page. Tedious? Yes, but it sure beat the tedium of scribists producing handwritten manuscripts letter by letter.*

Gutenberg Bible. *Although his technology for mass-producing the written word was primitive, Johannes Gutenberg's work was masterly. He mixed up excellent inks from scratch, his blacks the blackest blacks and his colors vibrant. Gutenberg was never rushed. He produced only 200 Bibles with his movable type. The survivors are now all museum pieces.*

Gutenberg Legacy

Among ways that Gutenberg changed history:

- **Scholarship.** Scholars were enabled to publish multiple copies of their discoveries and theories. Fueled by each other's progress, scholars made quantum advances that brought on the scientific revolution.
- **Oral Traditions.** With printed materials more widely available, people placed new value on reading. With the growing literacy, the tradition of listening to stories being told or read by others was displaced by reading as a silent and private act.
- **Languages.** Printing fostered a standardization of spelling and syntax in local languages that coalesced into national languages. One upshot was the modern nation-state in which citizens gradually replaced the local variations with a national language. The dominance of Latin as the only pan-European language began slipping.
- **Authorship.** The role of authors gained recognition. Hitherto, the names of authors often were lost as works were reproduced one copy at a time by scribes, often with idiosyncratic changes compounding one another with every new copy. Pre-Gutenberg translations added further confusion about authorship.
- **Commercialization.** Printed works became profitable, with some authors attracting what today would be called brand recognition. For the first time, authorship was profitable, publishing too. Copyright laws were created to protect the financial interests of the author or publisher by discouraging wanton copying.
- **Pagination.** With printing, page numbering became practical and useful. This was in contrast to handscribed works in which page breaks were a function of penmanship. Results included the first indexing and tables of content, both essential in optimizing the usefulness of printed material.
- **Religion.** Most written works in Europe before Gutenberg had been produced under church auspices to perpetuate religious beliefs. With secularization and commercialization of the printed word, the church leaders found they had to share their historic dominance in shaping Western civilization and values.

WHAT DO YOU THINK?

- How would your study habits be affected if your textbooks had no tables of content? Or indexes?
- Has standardization of languages damaged regional cultures that had distinctive language traditions before Gutenberg? What is the upside of post-Gutenberg standardization?
- Assuming that we are moving toward a universal language, how would it be like Latin? And how would it be different?

Chinese as a Problem

The first print culture, far preceding Gutenberg, was in Asia. Sometime before the year 600 the Chinese were using woodblocks, carved in reverse, to apply images with ink. The process is called negative relief printing. The Chinese also invented paper, which was an ideal medium.

With woodblock printing the Chinese produced hundreds of books on subjects as diverse as science, math and philosophy. It was printing that added to the influence of Confucius, whose teachings date to 500 years B.C.

But the Chinese printing technology was stalled. The Chinese written language comprised more than 5,000 basic characters. In contrast, Latin and derivative languages like Gutenberg's German had 26 characters. For the Chinese, their language had too many components for movable type to be a practical possibility.

WHAT DO YOU THINK?

- How did post-Gutenberg printing technology allow Europeans to leapfrog the Chinese in learning and understanding?

Gutenberg Bibles

Bibles printed by Gutenberg with movable type. Surviving Bibles all are collector items

keyboard could set in motion a process that created a mold for an entire line of type, poured melted lead into the mold and then, after a few seconds of cooling, dropped the lines of type into sequences for assembly into a page. After each line was created, the molds for the individual characters were automatically disassembled for use again.

Richard Hoe

Rotary Press. *Perfected by Richard Hoe, rotary presses had type molded onto a cylinder that rolled over sheets of paper that were fed into the press. This 1846 model was for the Philadelphia* Ledger. *Another major innovation was paper in rolls. Sheets then were not fed individually through the press.*

Post-Industrial Age improvements have included typesetting processes somewhat like a computer printer.

Even so, the printed media have direct lineage from Gutenberg, with enhancements from the Industrial Revolution and evolving technology. Books, newspapers and magazines remain mostly word-driven media. Production, however, now relies on chemical and electronic technology. Steam-powered presses? Electricity replaced steam a long time ago.

CHECKING YOUR MEDIA LITERACY

- **List printing innovations in the 1800s that accelerated mass production of the printed word.**
- **Contrast these innovations with Gutenberg-era technology.**
- **How do the new printing technologies of the Post-Industrial Age relate to the Industrial Revolution?**

PRINT-VISUAL INTEGRATION

Although visuals are not a mass medium, photography increased the communicative power of the printed word in the late 1800s. Experiments at Cornell University in the 1870s led to technology that could mass-produce images in books, newspapers and magazines. This new technology, pioneered by **Frederick Ives,** was the **halftone.** Ives divided a photograph into a microscopic grid, each tiny square having a raised dot that registered a separate tonal gray from a photograph—the bigger the dot, the more ink it would transfer to the paper and the darker the gray. At the typical reading distance of 14 inches, the human eye can't make out the grid, but the eye can see the image created by the varying grays. Although crude, this was the first halftone.

At the New York *Daily Graphic*, **Steve Horgan** adapted Ives' process to high-speed printing. In 1880, the *Graphic* published a halftone image of Shantytown—a break from the line drawings that were the *Graphic*'s original claim to distinction. Ives later improved on Horgan's process, and visual communication joined the Age of Mass Communication.

Frederick Ives
Invented halftone in 1876

halftone
Reproduction of an image in which the various tones of gray or color produced by variously sized dots of ink

Steve Horgan
Adapted halftone technology for high-speed newspaper presses

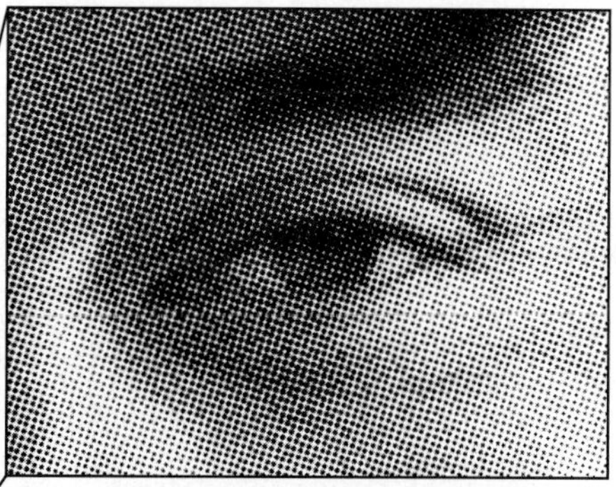

Frederick Ives

Halftone. *The halftone process, invented by Frederick Ives, uses variously sized dots to transfer ink to paper. The dots are invisible except under close examination. At a reading distance, however, the bigger dots leave darker impressions, the smaller dots a lighter impression. The effect looks like the varying tones in a photograph.*

Magazines, notably the early ***National Geographic,*** experimented with halftones too. When *Time* founder **Henry Luce** launched *Life* in 1934, photography moved the magazine industry into new visual ground. The oversize pages with slick, super-white paper gave *Life* photographs an intensity not possible with newsprint. *Life* captured the spirit of the times photographically and demonstrated that a wide range of human experiences could be recorded visually. Both real life and *Life* could be shocking. In 1938 a *Life* spread on human birth was so shocking for the time that censors succeeded in banning the issue in 33 cities.

National Geographic
Pioneer magazine in using visuals

Henry Luce
Magazine innovator whose *Life* exploited photographs for their visual impact

CHECKING YOUR MEDIA LITERACY

- **What breakthrough in technology made mass production of photographs possible in newspapers and other print media?**
- **Using a newspaper picture, show how halftones give the illusion of a photograph.**
- **Without halftones, what pre-Gutenberg methods could print media use for illustrations?**

Chemistry Technology

STUDY PREVIEW

Historically, photography is rooted in chemistry. The distinct technology had come of age by the time of the U.S. Civil War, creating a new kind of archival record. When techniques were devised to integrate photography into Gutenberg legacy printing, the mass media suddenly were in a new visual era. Movies also drew on chemical technology but evolved along a separate path.

MEDIA TIMELINE

TECHNOLOGY MILESTONES / PIVOTAL EVENTS

1400s/1500s

Movable Type
Mass communication began with the Gutenberg printing process (1440 on).

Gutenberg

>> Columbus discovered Americas (1492)

>> Luther sparked Protestant Reformation (1517)

1600s

Books
Cambridge Press issued first book in British North American colonies (1640). Cambridge Press also issued religious pamphlets, materials.

Newspapers
Ben Harris printed *Publick Occurrences,* first newspaper in the English colonies (1690).

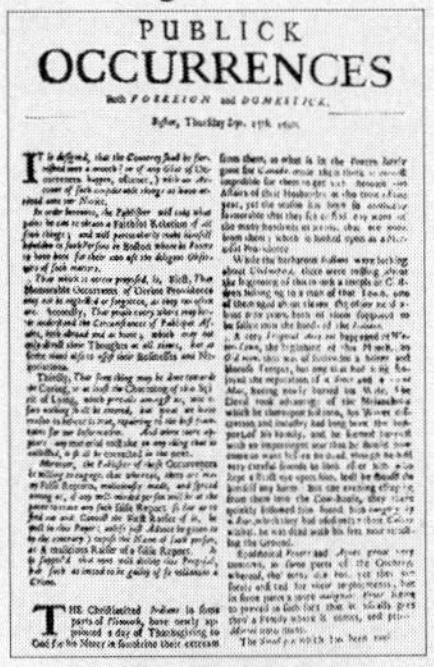

PUBLICK
OCCURRENCES

Publick Occurrences

>> Pilgrims established colony (1620)

>> French and Indian wars (1689–1763)

1700s

Magazines
Andrew Bradford and Benjamin Franklin introduced competing magazines in British colonies (1741). Meanwhile, weekly newspapers existed in larger colonial cities, reprinting items from Europe and each other.

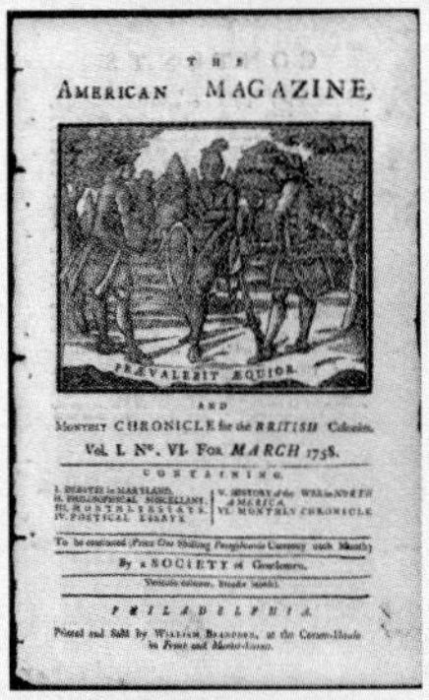

THE
AMERICAN MAGAZINE,
PRAEVALEBIT AEQUIOR
MONTHLY CHRONICLE for the BRITISH Colonies.
PHILADELPHIA

Bradford's Magazine

>> Industrial Revolution began (1760s)

>> Revolutionary War (1776–1781)

1800s

Recording
Thomas Edison introduced Phonograph, which could record and play back sound (1877). Meanwhile, the book, newspaper and magazine industries flourished.

Movies
William Dickson devised motion picture camera (1888). Meanwhile, newspapers were in their heyday as dominant medium.

Edison Invention

>> Size of United States doubled with Louisiana Purchase (1803)

>> Morse invented telegraph (1844)

>> U.S. Civil War (1861–1865)

>> U.S. coasts linked by rail (1869)

1900s

Radio
Guglielmo Marconi transmitted first message by radio waves (1895). Meanwhile, sensationalism and muckraking attracted growing newspaper and magazine audiences.

Television
Philo Farnsworth discovered how to pick up moving images electronically for live transmission (1927). Meanwhile, radio networks created national audiences unprecedented in their reach.

Internet
U.S. military established computer network that became the Internet (1969). Television firmly dominated as an entertainment medium and was maturing as a news medium.

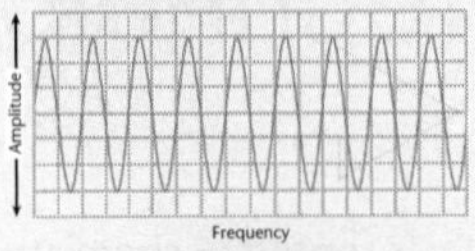

Mastering the Airwaves

>> Right to vote extended to women (1920)

>> Great Depression (1930s)

>> World War II (1941–1945)

>> Russian-Western rivalry triggered Cold War (1945)

>> Humans reached moon (1969)

>> Soviet empire imploded (1989)

2000s

Convergence
Delivery of mass messages fragmented into a growing number of digital mechanisms. By and large, the historic media industries remained in place producing content.

Digital Era

>> 9/11 terrorist attacks (2001)

>> Iraq War (2003–)

>> Hurricane Katrina (2005)

PHOTOGRAPHY

The 1727 discovery that light causes silver nitrate to darken was a breakthrough in mass communication. Scientists dabbled with the chemical for the next century. Then in 1826 **Joseph Níepce** found a way to capture and preserve an image on light-sensitive material. Photography was born—a chemical process for creating and recording a visual message. The technology was sufficiently established by the 1860s to create a new type of historical archive. Teams of photographers organized by **Mathew Brady** created an incredible visual record, much of it horrific, of the U.S. Civil War.

Over the next half-century, technology developed for reproducing photographs on printing presses. Brady's legacy was issued in book form. Emotional advertisements stirred sales, promising lifelike images of "soldiers dashing and flags flying and horses leaping all over." The time was right, and hundreds of thousands of copies were sold to a generation of Civil War veterans and their families. By the time World War I began, however, the market was saturated. Also, people had new gruesome photographs from the European front. New grisliness replaced the old.

Also, a new application of photographic chemistry—the motion picture—was maturing.

CHECKING YOUR MEDIA LITERACY

- **Explain this assertion: Photography and words are not mass media but are essential for the media to exploit their potential.**
- **How did Mathew Brady build public enthusiasm for photography in mass communication?**

Joseph Níepce
Preserved a visual image on light-sensitive material

Mathew Brady
Created photographic record of U.S. Civil War

MOVIES

The motion picture, a late-1800s development, was rooted in chemistry too. The new media linked the lessons of photography to the recognition of a phenomenon called

Mathew Brady

Visual Impact. *With new technology in the late 1800s that could produce photographs on printing presses, newspapers and magazines suddenly had new potency in telling stories. The potential of photography to send printed media in a new direction was illustrated with painfully gory battlefield scenes from the Civil War. This visual perspective on war was mostly the work of teams of photographers organized by entrepreneur Mathew Brady.*

persistence of vision. It had come to be recognized in the late 1800s that the human eye retains an image for a fraction of a second. If a series of photographs captures motion at split-second intervals, those images, if flipped quickly, will trick the eye into perceiving continuous motion. For most people the illusion of motion begins with 14 photos per second.

>> **Cameras.** At the research labs of prolific inventor and entrepreneur Thomas Edison, **William Dickson** developed a camera that captured 16 images per second. It was the first workable motion picture camera. Dickson used celluloid film perfected by **George Eastman,** who had popularized amateur photography with his Kodak camera. By 1891 Edison had begun producing movies.

persistence of vision
Fast-changing still photos create the illusion of movement

William Dickson
Developed first movie camera

George Eastman
Developed celluloid film

Lumière brothers
Opened first motion picture exhibition hall

>> **Projectors.** Edison's movies were viewed by looking into a box. In France the **Lumière brothers** Auguste and Louis brought projectors to motion pictures. By running the film in front of a specially aimed, powerful lightbulb, the Lumières projected movie images onto a wall. In 1895 they opened an exhibition hall in Paris—the first movie house. Edison recognized the commercial advantage in projection and himself patented a projector that he put on the market the next year.

CHECKING YOUR MEDIA LITERACY

- How are photography and motion pictures similar? Different?
- How does persistence of vision work?

Electrical Technology

STUDY PREVIEW

Electricity transformed people's lives beginning in the late 1800s with dazzling applications to all kinds of activities. The modern music industry sprang around these new systems for recording and playing back sound. Radio and television, both rooted in electricity, were among the technologies around which new industries were created.

ELECTRICITY AS TRANSFORMATIONAL

The harnessing of electricity had a profound impact on American life beginning in the late 1800s. The infrastructure for an electricity-based lifestyle was wholly in place half a century later when, in the 1930s, the government launched a massive project to extend electricity-distribution networks to every end-of-the-road farmhouse. During this period, inventors and tinkerers came up with entirely new media of mass communication.

For two centuries mass media had comprised only the print media, primarily books, newspapers and magazines. In the span of a generation, people found themselves marveling at a dizzying parade of inventions ranging from the lightbulb to streetcars. Among the new delights were phonographs, radio and then television.

Consider how much these new media transformed lifestyles. A person who as a child had read into the night by kerosene lantern could in adulthood be watching television.

CHECKING YOUR MEDIA LITERACY

- What new mass media were made possible by electricity?
- What lifestyle effects were generated by electricity?

RECORDINGS

Sound recording did not begin as an electronic medium. The first recording machine, the **phonograph** invented by **Thomas Edison** in 1877, was a cylinder wrapped in tinfoil that was rotated as a singer shouted into a large metal funnel. The funnel channeled the vibrations against a diaphragm, which fluttered and thus cut grooves into the rotating tin. When the cylinder was rotated in a playback machine, a stylus picked up sound from the varying depths of the groove. To hear the sound, a person placed his or her ear next to a megaphone-like horn and rotated the cylinder.

Inherent in Edison's system, however, was a major impediment for commercial success: A recording could not be duplicated, let alone mass-produced. In 1887 **Emile Berliner** introduced a sturdy metal disk to replace Edison's foil-wrapped cylinder. From the metal disk Berliner made a model and then poured thermoplastic material into the mold. When the material hardened, Berliner had a near perfect copy of the original disk—and he could make hundreds of them. The process was primitive by today's standards—entirely mechanical, nothing electronic about it. But it was a marvel at the time.

Those early machines eventually incorporated electrical microphones and electrical amplification for reproducing sound. These innovations, mostly by **Joseph Maxfield** of Bell Laboratories in the 1920s, had superior sensitivity. To listen, it was no longer a matter of putting an ear to a mechanical amplifying horn that had only narrow frequency responses. Instead, loudspeakers amplified the sound electromagnetically.

CHECKING YOUR MEDIA LITERACY

- **Why would be it be a mistake to call Thomas Edison's first sound recording and playback machine an instrument of mass communication?**
- **How would you rank the importance of these inventors in the history of sound recording: Thomas Edison, Emile Berliner and Joseph Maxfield? And why?**

phonograph
First sound recording and playback machine

Thomas Edison
Inventor of phonograph

Emile Berliner
Inventor of process for mass production of recorded music

Joseph Maxfield
Introduced electrical sound recording in 1920s

telegraph
Electricity-enabled long-distance communication, used mostly from Point A to Point B

Samuel Morse
Inventor of telegraph 1844

ELECTROMAGNETIC SPECTRUM

The introduction of electricity into mass communication occurred with the **telegraph.** After experimenting with sending electrical impulses by wire for more than a decade, **Samuel Morse** talked Congress into spending $30,000 to string electricity-conducting wires 41 miles from Washington to Baltimore. In 1844, using his code of dots and dashes, Morse sent the famous message "What hath God wrought." The demonstration's high visibility showed that real-time communication was possible over great distances. Morse's instantaneous-communication gizmo overcame an impediment of the printed word—the inherent delay of producing and delivering a physical product.

The possibilities of the Morse invention electrified people—and investors. Within only four years, by 1848, promoters had rounded up the money to construct a system that linked the most populous parts of the United States, up and down the eastern seaboard and inland as far as Chicago and Milwaukee. By 1866 a cable had been laid on the floor of the Atlantic Ocean to connect North America with Europe for telegraphic communication.

Although telegraph messages basically were Point A to Point B communication, the way was opened for applying electricity to explicitly mass communication—perhaps even without wires.

>> **Wireless.** The suggestion of wireless communication was inherent in a discovery by **Granville Woods** in 1887 of a way to send messages to and from moving trains. Railway telegraphy, as it was called, reduced collisions. Although the invention was

Granville Woods. *New possibilities for communication were suggested in his invention of railway telegraphy in 1887. The invention allowed train conductors to communicate with each other in transit and with dispatchers.*

intended for electric trains, which drew their power from overhead lines and on-ground rails, Woods' work also posed the question: Could communication be untethered?

For hundreds of years scientists had had a sense that lightning emitted invisible but powerful electrical waves. The word *radi,* from the Latin *radius,* was used because these waves rippled out from the electrical source. A German scientist, **Heinrich Hertz,** confirmed the existence of these waves in 1887 by constructing two separate coils of wire several feet apart. When electricity was applied to one coil, it electrified the other. Thus electricity indeed could be sent through the air on what soon were called Hertzian waves.

The scientific journals, full of theories about Hertzian waves, intrigued a young nobleman in Italy, **Guglielmo Marconi.** Whether he realized it or not, Marconi was educating himself as an engineer. Obsessed, refusing to take time even for food, he locked himself in an upstairs room at his father's estate near Bologna and contemplated and fiddled. By grounding Hertz's coils to the earth, Marconi discovered in 1895 that he could send messages farther and farther. Soon he was ringing a bell across the room by remote control, then downstairs, then 300 feet away—the first wireless messages.

Marconi suddenly was hopeful that he was disproving the notion among scientists at the time that Hertzian waves could not penetrate solid objects, let alone Earth. He devised an antenna, which further extended transmission range. Also, he hooked up a Morse telegraph key, which already was widely used to tap out dots and dashes for transmission on telegraph lines. Marconi had his brother go three miles away over a hill with instructions to fire a rifle if the Morse letter *s,* dot-dot-dot, came through a receiver. Metaphorically, it was a shot heard around the world.

Although Marconi didn't realize it at the time, the earth in fact impedes radio waves, but those waves that emanate upward then ricochet off the ionosphere back to Earth. Transmissions go far, far beyond the horizon. Marconi saw immediate business potential for establishing communication with ships at sea—something hitherto limited to semaphore flags and mirrors which, of course, meant that ships were incommunicado with anything over the horizon. Marconi made a fortune.

Heinrich Hertz

Demonstrated existence of radio waves 1887

Guglielmo Marconi

Transmitted first wireless message 1895

CHECKING YOUR MEDIA LITERACY

- **How was the telegraph a precursor of radio?**
- **Marconi's wireless was based on what scientific and technical breakthroughs?**
- **Marconi saw radio as a point-to-point medium rather than a mass medium. What's the difference?**

Guglielmo Marconi. *In 1895 he figured out how to hitch a ride on omnipresent but invisible electromagnetic waves to send messages. At first the imaginative young Italian-Irish tinkerer activated a bell by remote control. Seeing a future for telegraph-like communication without wires, Marconi made history and a fortune with ship-to-ship and ship-to-shore communication. Marconi failed, however, to see the potential of wireless telegraphy, as it was called, for anything more than point-to-point communication. Others would later make radio a mass medium, transmitting from a single point to a mass audience.*

>> **Television.** For most of its history, dating to experimental stations in the 1930s, television used the airwaves somewhat like radio does. But to capture movement visually for transmission, the technology of television involved drastically different concepts. Physicists at major universities and engineers at major research labs had been toying for years to create "radio with pictures," as early television was called.

But it was a south Idaho farmboy, **Philo Farnsworth,** who, at age 13 while out plowing the field, came up with a concept that led to his invention of television. Plowing the fields, back and forth in rows, the young Farnsworth had an epiphany. Applying what he knew about electricity from science magazines and tinkering, he envisioned a camera-like device that would pick up light reflected off a scene, with the image being sent radio-like to a receiver that would convert the varying degrees of light in the image and zap them one at a time across stacked horizontal lines on a screen, back and forth so rapidly that the image on the screen would appear to the human eye as real as a photograph. And then another electron would be zapped across the screen in, so to speak, "furrows," to replace the first image—with images coming so quickly that the eye would perceive them as motion. Farnsworth called his device an **image dissector,** which literally was what it did.

Like motion picture technology invented 40 years earlier, television froze movement at fraction-of-a-second intervals and played them in fast sequence to create an illusion that, like movies, capitalized on the persistence of vision phenomenon. Unlike movies, Farnsworth did not do this with photographic technology. Television uses electronics, not chemicals, and images recorded by the camera are transmitted instantly to a receiving device, called a *picture tube*, or to a recording device for later transmission.

Although Farnsworth had sent the first television picture from one room in his San Francisco apartment to another in 1927, the complexities of television technology delayed its immediate development. So did national survival while Americans focused on winning World War II. By the 1950s, however, a radio-like delivery infrastructure for television was in place.

Philo Farnsworth
Inventor of television

image dissector
First device in early television technology

CHECKING YOUR MEDIA LITERACY

- **Philo Farnsworth called his invention the image dissector. How were images dissected?**
- **What is the role of persistence of vision in television technology?**
- **How is persistence of vision employed differently in television and movies?**

New Technologies

STUDY PREVIEW

Satellite and fiber-optic technologies in the late 1900s improved the speed and reliability of delivering mass messages. These were backshop developments that were largely invisible to media consumers. Plainly visible, though, was the related advent of the Internet as a new mass medium.

ORBITING SATELLITES

More than 50 years ago the Russians orbited Sputnik, the first human-made satellite. The accomplishment ignited a rush to explore space near Earth. Technology surged. Weather forecasting became less intuitive, more scientific and many times more accurate. With geopositioning signals from satellites, maps had new, everyday applications that only Spock could have imagined. Communication was transformed too,

MEDIA PEOPLE

Philo Farnsworth

Philo Farnsworth was 11 when his family loaded three covered wagons and moved to a farm near Rigby in eastern Idaho. Cresting a ridge, young Farnsworth, at the reins of one wagon, surveyed the homestead below and saw wires linking the buildings. "This place has electricity!" he exclaimed. Philo obsessed about the electricity, and soon he was an expert at fixing anything electrical that went wrong.

The day when the Farnsworths settled near Rigby in 1919 was a pivotal moment in young Farnsworth's life that led to technology on which television is based.

The next pivotal moment came two years later when Philo Farnsworth was 13. He found an article saying that scientists were working on ways to add pictures to radio but they couldn't figure out how. He then went out to hitch the horses to a harvesting machine to bring in the potatoes. As he guided the horses back and forth across the field, up one row, down the next, he visualized how moving pictures could be captured live and transmitted to a faraway place. If the light that enables people to see could be converted to electrons and then transmitted one at a time, but very quickly as a beam, back and forth on a surface, then, perhaps, television could work.

The ideas simmered a few months and then, when he was 14, Farnsworth chalked a complicated diagram for "electronic television" on his chemistry teacher's blackboard. The teacher, Justin Tolman, was impressed. In fact, 15 years later Tolman would reconstruct those blackboard schematics so convincingly that Farnsworth would win a patent war with RCA and force RCA to abandon its claim that its Vladimir Zworykin invented television.

Farnsworth's native intelligence, earnestness and charm helped to win over the people around him. When he was 19, working in Salt Lake City, Farnsworth found a man with connections to San Francisco investors. With the investors' backing, the third pivotal moment in Farnsworth's work, he set up a lab in Los Angeles, and later in San Francisco, and put his drawings and theories to work. In 1927, with hand-blown tubes and hand-soldered connections, Farnsworth had a gizmo he called the image dissector. It picked up the image of a glass slide and transmitted it. The Idaho farmboy had invented television.

WHAT DO YOU THINK?

- Describe how Philo Farnsworth's image dissector worked.
- Farnsworth's horizontal electron zaps have been replaced by pixels, but the fundamental insight that led to his invention of television remains on video screens today. What is this enduring legacy?

Television Inventor. *Thirteen-year-old Philo Farnsworth came up with the concept of live transmission of moving images by zipping electrons back and forth on a screen—just as he was doing, back and forth, in harvesting a potato field. Barely in his 20s, Farnsworth moved from theory to practice with what he called an image dissector.*

geosynchronous orbit
A satellite's period of rotation that coincides perfectly with Earth's rotation

Arthur C. Clarke
Devised the concept of satellites in geosynchronous orbits for communication

with signals being bounced off satellites for a straight-line range that far exceeded anything possible with the existing network of ground-based relay towers located every 10 or so miles apart.

For communication, the key to utilizing satellites was the **geosynchronous orbit.** It was a concept of sci-fi author **Arthur C. Clarke,** who also was a serious scientist. Clarke figured out in 1945 that a satellite 22,300 miles above the equator would be orbiting at the same speed as Earth's rotation, thus always being

Arthur C. Clarke

Orbiting Relay Stations. *Dozens of satellites orbit Earth as communication relay stations. The concept dates to 1945 when Arthur C. Clarke, known mostly as a science fiction writer but also a serious scientist, conceived of satellites remaining stationary above a point on Earth if their speed matched the planet's rotation. Fifteen years later, in 1960, the first communication satellite Telstar proved Clarke right.*

above the same point below on Earth—an ideal platform for continuous service to pick up signals from Earth stations and retransmit them to other Earth stations. It was like a 22,300-mile-high relay tower. With only one relay, not hundreds, signals would move faster and with more reliability. The **Telstar** communication satellite, launched in 1960, took the first telephone signals from **uplink** stations on Earth, amplified them, and returned them to **downlink** stations. Television networks also used Telstar.

Satellite technology, however, did not change the fundamental structures of the industries that had built up around print, chemical and electronic technology. Rather, satellites were an efficient alternative for delivering traditional media products. Prime-time network programming still came from the networks. Although *USA Today* was sending pages by satellite to several dozen printing plants around the country, readers still picked up the paper every morning from newsracks. In short, satellite technology was important for enabling media companies to improve delivery of their products but was largely invisible to consumers.

Telstar
First communication satellite

uplink
A ground station that beams a signal to an orbiting communication satellite

downlink
A ground station that receives a relayed signal from a communication satellite

CHECKING YOUR MEDIA LITERACY

- **What was the genius of Arthur C. Clarke as a mass communication futurologist?**
- **How does a geosynchronous orbit work?**
- **Direct TV and Dish satellite television companies advertise they are available to homeowners anywhere in the United States as long as they have unrestricted access to the southern sky. Why south?**

BACK TO WIRES

Even as possibilities with satellites were dazzling scientists, the old reliable of mass communication—the wire, sometimes called a **landline**—was in revival. A radio repair-shop owner in Astoria, Oregon, wired the town in 1949 to receive television signals from Seattle, which was too far away for signals to be received unless they were intercepted by a high antenna. In mountainous West Virginia, entrepreneurs also were stringing up local cable systems to distribute television signals that were blocked by terrain. **Cable television,** as it was called, was a small-town success. On the television industry's radar, however, cable was merely a blip. Local cable operators only passed on signals from elsewhere. They didn't add any content.

The role of the cable industry changed in 1975 when the Time Inc. media empire put HBO on satellite as a programming service for local cable companies. With exclusive programming available to subscribers, cable suddenly was hot. More cable programming services, all delivered by satellite, came online. Wall Street investors poured billions of dollars into wiring major cities, where huge population masses were eager for HBO, CNN and other new programming available only through cable operators.

In the 1960s, meanwhile, Corning Glass had developed a cable that was capable of carrying light at incredible speeds—theoretically, 186,000 miles per second. The potential of these new **fiber-optic cables,** each strand carrying 60,000 messages simultaneously, was not lost on the telephone industry. So fast was the fiber-optic network that the entire *Oxford English Dictionary* could be sent in just seconds. Soon hundreds of crews with backhoes were replacing copper wires, which had constituted the backbone of telephone communication, with fiber-optic cables. Coupled with other new technologies, notably digitization of data, the new satellite-based and fiber-optic landline communication systems enabled the introduction of a new medium—the Internet.

landline

A conventional telecommunications connection by cable laid across land, typically buried or on poles

cable television

A television transmission system using cable rather than an over-air broadcast signal

fiber-optic

Thin, flexible fibers of glass capable of transmitting light signals

CHECKING YOUR MEDIA LITERACY

- **What has been the effect of geosynchronous-orbiting satellites on the television industry?**
- **What technologies transformed the sleepy small-town cable television industry beginning in the 1970s?**

Digital Integration

STUDY PREVIEW

Digital technology has brought efficiency to almost every aspect of human lifestyles, including products from traditional mass media companies. A wholly new medium, the Internet, is built entirely on binary digital signals. This newest media technology is melding the once-distinctive delivery systems of many products from old-line media companies.

SEMICONDUCTOR

Researchers at AT&T's Bell Labs knew they were on to something important for telephone communication in 1947. Engineers Jack Bardeen, Walter Brittain and William Shockley had devised glasslike silicon chips—pieces of sand, really—that could be used to respond to a negative or a positive electrical charge. The tiny chips, called **semiconductors,** functioned very rapidly as on/off switches. With chips, the human voice could be reduced to a stream of digits—1 for on, 0 for

Jack Bardeen, Walter Brittain and William Shockley Nobel Winners

Nobel Winners. *The 1956 Nobel Prize went to the inventors of the semiconductor. They had devised tiny, low-cost crystals that could be used as switches to transmit data that had been converted to binary codes of 0s and 1s. Digital communication followed, with innovations that led to today's global communication networks.*

off—and then transmitted as rapid-fire pulses and reconstructed so quickly at the other end of the line that the sound was like the real thing. Bardeen, Brittain and Shockley won a Nobel Prize.

Little did they realize that they had laid the groundwork for revolutionizing not just telephonic communication but all human communication.

Bell Labs then took digital on-off binary signals to a new level. By breaking messages into pieces and transmitting them in spurts, Bell suddenly, in 1965, could send multiple messages simultaneously. People marveled that 51 calls could be carried at the same time on a single line. The capacity of telephone systems was dramatically increased without a single new mile of wire being laid.

The potential of the evolving technology was no less than revolutionary. Not only could the human voice be reduced to binary digits for transmission but so could text and even images. Futurologists asked: "Who needs paper?" Might digitization even replace the still newfangled technology of television that had flowed from Philo Farnsworth's pioneering work?

Digitization, alas, did not replace Gutenberg-based print media, and the core media industries are still pigeonholed easily into their traditional categories—books, newspapers, magazines, movies, sound recordings, radio and television. The technology did, however, spawn new media industries built around the new technologies. America Online was in the first generation. Now Google, MySpace and YouTube are leaders. Tomorrow? Stay tuned.

CHECKING YOUR MEDIA LITERACY

- **What has proven to be the significance of binary digital signaling?**
- **How have traditional media industries been affected by binary digital signaling?**

INTERNET ORIGINS

Another building block for digitized communication was the **Internet.** The Net as it's called, originated with the military, which saw potential in digitized communication for a noncentralized network. Without a central hub, the military figured that the system could sustain itself in a nuclear attack. The system, called ARPAnet, short for Advanced Research Projects Agency Network, was up and running in 1969. At first, the network linked contractors and universities so that military researchers could exchange information. In 1983 the National Science Foundation, whose mandate is to promote science, took over and involved more universities, which tied their own internal computer-based communication systems into the larger network. As a backbone system that interconnected networks, the term *internet* fit.

MEDIA CONVERGENCE

The construction of a high-capacity network in the 1990s, which we call the Internet, is emerging as the delivery vehicle of choice for any and all media products. The technological basis, called **digital,** is distinctive. Messages, whether text, audio, image or a combination, are broken into millions of bits of data. The bits are transmitted one at a time over the Internet, which has incredibly high capacity and speed, then reassembled for reception at the other end. The process is almost instantaneous for text, whose digital bits of data are small and easily accommodated. Audio and visual messages can take longer because far more data bits are required to reconstruct a message at the reception point.

A digitization revolution, called **media convergence,** is in progress.

>> **Distribution.** The Internet has an unmatchable efficiency in delivering messages. In contrast, a newspaper company needs a fleet of trucks and drivers for predawn runs from the production point to intermediate distribution points. There, individual carriers pick up papers for delivery to individual customers. Magazine companies rely on the postal system, which takes at least a day and countless gallons of fuel for delivery. Book publishers have massive inventories, which require expensive warehousing, and then high shipping costs. Although books, newspapers and magazines have not vanished from the media landscape, these companies are shifting to delivering at least some of their content by the Internet.

>> **Devices.** With a single device, consumers can pick up media content whatever its origin. The device can be a desktop or laptop computer or something handheld. What the devices have in common is an Internet connection.

>> **Distinctions.** Digitization is breaking down old distinctions. Newspaper people increasingly talk about being in the news business, not the newspaper business. Radio people do likewise, talking about being in the music business, not the radio business. The new emphasis is on content. Consumers acknowledge this underlying shift. Instead of reading a newspaper, for example, more people talk about reading news. Instead of watching television, people watch a sitcom. This makes sense as digital devices supplant Gutenberg print technology and combine radio, television, movie and recording reception appliances into single devices.

>> **Production.** For almost a century, print media publishers have recognized their inherent disadvantage in production costs. Presses for a big-city daily require millions of dollars in investment. In contrast, as publishers have seen it, albeit simplistically, their broadcast counterparts merely flick a switch. But with digitized delivery, the broadcast equivalent of a printing press, even transmitter and tower maintenance seem hopelessly expensive. Production costs for newspaper content also can be cut drastically with Internet delivery.

>> **Democratization.** The relatively low cost of Internet production and delivery may have its greatest impact in broadening the sources of media content. Almost anybody can afford to create messages for Internet delivery and, theoretically anyway,

Internet
High-capacity global telephone network that links computers

digital
Technology through which media messages are coded into 1s and 0s for delivery transmission and then decoded into their original appearance

media convergence
Melding of print, electronic and photographic media into digitized form

Tim Berners-Lee — MEDIA PEOPLE

Single-handedly, Tim Berners-Lee invented the World Wide Web. Then, unlike many entrepreneurs who have used the Internet to amass quick fortunes, Berners-Lee devoted his life to refining the web as a medium of communication open to everyone for free. Berners-Lee, an Oxford engineer, came up with the web concept because he couldn't keep track of all his notes on various computers in various places. It was 1989. Working at CERN, a physics lab in Switzerland, he proposed a system to facilitate scientific research by letting scientists' computers tap into each other.

In a way, the software worked like the brain. In fact, Berners-Lee said that the idea was to keep "track of all the random associations one comes across in real life and brains are supposed to be so good at remembering, but sometimes mine wouldn't."

Working with three software engineers, Berners-Lee had a demonstration up and running within three months. As Berners-Lee traveled the globe to introduce the web at scientific conferences, the potential of what he had devised became clear. The web was a system that could connect all information with all other information.

The key was a relatively simple computer language known as HTML, short for "hypertext markup language," which, although it has evolved over the years, remains the core of the web. Berners-Lee also developed the addressing system that allows computers to find each other. Every web-connected computer has a unique address, a universal resource locator (URL). For it all to work, Berners-Lee also created a protocol that actually links computers: HTTP, short for "hypertext transfer protocol."

In 1992, leading research organizations in the Netherlands, Germany and the United States committed to the web. As enthusiasm grew in the scientific research community, word spread to other quarters. In one eight-month period in 1993, web use multiplied 414 times. Soon "the web" was a household word.

As you would expect, Berners-Lee had offers galore from investors and computer companies to build new ways to derive profits from the web. He said no. Instead, he chose the academic life. At the Massachusetts Institute of Technology he works out of spartan facilities as head of the W3 consortium, which sets the protocol and coding standards that are helping the World Wide Web realize its potential.

It's hard to overstate Berners-Lee's accomplishment. The Internet is the information infrastructure that likely will, given time, eclipse other media.

Some liken Berners-Lee to Johannes Gutenberg, who 400 years earlier had launched the age of mass communication with the movable type that made mass production of the written word possible.

WHAT DO YOU THINK?

- Would someone else have devised the World Wide Web if Tim Berners-Lee hadn't?
- Is Tim Berners-Lee in the same league as Gutenberg? Edison? Marconi? Farnsworth?

Original Webmaster. *Tim Berners-Lee and his associates at a Swiss research facility created new Internet coding in 1989, dubbing it the World Wide Web. Today the coding is the heart of global computer communication.*

reach everyone on the planet who has a reception device. In contrast to a generation ago, the price of entry into the mass media no longer requires millions of dollars for production facilities and millions more for startup costs, including costs for personnel. Ask any blogger or garage band. Media moguls are struggling to identify ways to maintain their dominance. We are in a turbulent environment of change that's still playing out but that has been described, perhaps with prescience, perhaps prematurely, as the democratization of mass communication.

CHECKING YOUR MEDIA LITERACY

- **What are the primary print media? And the primary electronic media?**
- **Did electronic media replace print media?**
- **What is the future for major mass media?**

CASE STUDY

Reuters' Mistaken Identity

No doubt about it, the news agency Reuters had egg on its face. After moving its U.S.-based photo editing operation to Singapore to cut costs, an editor in Singapore figured that a photo should be packaged with a news item on the iconic *Margaritaville* songster Jimmy Buffett. The photo-package was transmitted to clients worldwide.

Problem: The photo was the wrong Buffett. The Singapore editor, clueless to U.S culture, had pulled a photo of super-investor Warren Buffett from the archives. In business coat and tie, heavy eyeglasses on his nose, his receding gray hair cropped for a board meeting was a guy with a caption that read: "Buffett, known for such hits as *Margaritaville* and *Cheeseburger in Paradise,* promotes his upcoming tour."

Too Many Buffetts. *Can you figure out which guy is famous as a Wall Street investor? Which is famous for Margaritaville?*

Mistakes occur in the news business, like all human enterprises, and Reuters corrected the error.

The labor union representing U.S. employees of Reuters, however, glommed into the Buffett mix-up to take a slap at the decision by Reuters executives to outsource U.S. jobs. The union ran an advertisement in the New York *Times* with this message:

"This year Reuters has been covering important developments on Wall Street from Bangalore, India. A few months ago Reuters shifted its U.S.-based photo editing work to Singapore. This can't help but hurt the accuracy of news and photo services that we provide.

"We care about our company. We want Reuters to remain a timely and quality source of news and information. That means keeping skilled journalists on the job to report the news where it happens. Could we cover news in India from Indianapolis?"

A major U.S. political issue for decades has been the shifting of U.S. manufacturing jobs to countries with relatively cheap labor. Toyota and other Japanese cars were issues in the 1980s, then Hyundai from Korea. Now the outsourcing has shifted beyond manufacturing. U.S. banks and insurance companies, for example, have moved most backshop operations to India. U.S. advertising agencies contract for graphics and creative support services in China and south Asia.

In mass communication the issue is what changes, for better or worse, have been wrought by technology that enables economic globalization.

DEEPENING YOUR MEDIA LITERACY

EXPLORE THE ISSUE

For all its wonders, new technology can trigger major disruptions for many people. Consider the Luddites in the early 1800s. These English workers, angry at losing their livelihoods to the mechanization of the Industrial Revolution, took clubs and whatever else was handy and mobbed cotton and woolen mills and destroyed the infernal machines.

DIG DEEPER

What became of the Luddite movement?

WHAT DO YOU THINK?

The Newspaper Guild boils down its criticism of outsourcing: "Remote Control Journalism Is Bad News." How do you evaluate the Guild's position? Think about accuracy, thoroughness and competence in the news that's reported. How about the short term and the loss of U.S. jobs? How do you see historians evaluating the Guild position 200 years from now? Could this be Ludditism all over again?

Technology and Mass Communication

STUDY PREVIEW

Theorists have devised models to help understand and explain the complex and mysterious technology-dependent process of mass communication. But many models, now more than 50 years old, have been outdated by rapid changes in technology. These changes have added more complexity and mystery to how mass communication works.

LASSWELL MODEL

In the 20th century, scholars got serious about trying to understand how mass communication works. Theories came and went. One of the most useful explanations, elegant in its simplicity as an overview, was articulated in the 1950s by Yale professor **Harold Lasswell.** It is a narrative model that poses four questions: Who says what? In which **channel?** To whom? With what **effect?**

With his reference to *channel,* Lasswell clearly differentiated his model as not just another model for human communication. His channel component clearly made his model one of mass communication technology. Lasswell's channel was a technology-defined mass medium—a book, a movie, television.

The Lasswell model is easy to apply. Pick any media message, says former Vice President Al Gore's documentary *An Inconvenient Truth:*

- **Who says what?** Gore told a story based on expert testimony and recorded evidence about global warming. His message was that global warming is a human-accelerated phenomenon that threatens Earth as a habitat for life as we know it.
- **In which channel?** The documentary itself was a movie. Also, it was distributed widely in video form for home and group audiences. There also was a book bearing the same title.
- **To whom?** Although unfriendly critics tried to dismiss the work as intended for penguins, the movie's video and book quickly became best-sellers.
- **With what effect?** Public attention quickly embraced the notion that it was possible for human beings, acting quickly, to counter the deterioration of Earth as a habitable planet. Under Governor Arnold Schwarzenegger, California shifted into high gear with new public policies to reduce greenhouse emissions. The U.S. Supreme Court upheld tougher emission standards that big industries had resisted.

CHECKING YOUR MEDIA LITERACY

- **How does the Lasswell model of mass communication differ from models for interpersonal communication, like between friends conversing face-to-face?**
- **Clip a bylined newspaper article with a breakthrough on a recent controversial issue. Then apply the four steps in the Lasswell communication process to the article.**

VALUES AND LIMITATIONS OF MODELS

Harold Lasswell
Devised the narrative communication model

channel
The medium through which a message is sent to a mass audience

effect
The consequence of a message

For all their usefulness, models of mass communication fall short, way short, of capturing the complexities occurring in our media systems. The volume of messages is incalculable. The word *zillions* comes to mind. What we do know about the volume is that it's increasing rapidly. Nobody has come up with a model to portray the overlays and interplay of all the content moving through the mass media.

All models, whether of ships, planes, automobiles, have the same deficiency. By definition, a model is a facsimile that helps us see and understand the real thing. But no model shows everything. An aircraft engineer, for example, can create a model of an airplane's propulsion system. Although essential to illustrating how the plane will be powered, a model of its propulsion system doesn't illustrate the plane's aesthetic features, nor its ventilation system, nor its electrical system, nor any of hundreds of other important features. Engineers are able to overlay various models to show connections and interrelations—which itself is a major challenge—but far short of what it would take to illustrate all that is going on. It's the same with communication: Too much is occurring at any given nanosecond. So, like all models, mass communication models are useful illustrations but limited because there is far, far more to what's happening than can be reduced to a schematic.

Different models illustrate different aspects of the process. That the process is too complex for a single model to convey it all is clear from the Lasswell model. Sweeping as it is, the Lasswell model is far less than a detailed framework for understanding how mass communication works; but it is a starting point.

CHECKING YOUR MEDIA LITERACY

- **What are the advantages and disadvantages of any model?**
- **Can a complex phenomenon like mass communication be reduced to a model?**

CONCENTRIC CIRCLE MODEL

One of the most useful models from the late 20th century was conceived by scholars Ray Hiebert, Donald Ungurait and Thomas Bohn. It is a series of concentric rings with the source of the message at the center. The source encodes information or an idea, which then ripples outward to the outermost ring, which is the receiving audience. In between are several elements unique to the mass communication—including gatekeepers, a technologically based medium, regulators and amplification. The model creates a framework for tracking the difficult course of a message through the mass communication process. In effect, the model portrays mass communication as an obstacle course.

>> Medium. Hiebert, Ungurait and Bohn, aware that media affect messages, put the label *mass media* on one of their rings. Media make a difference. A message that lends

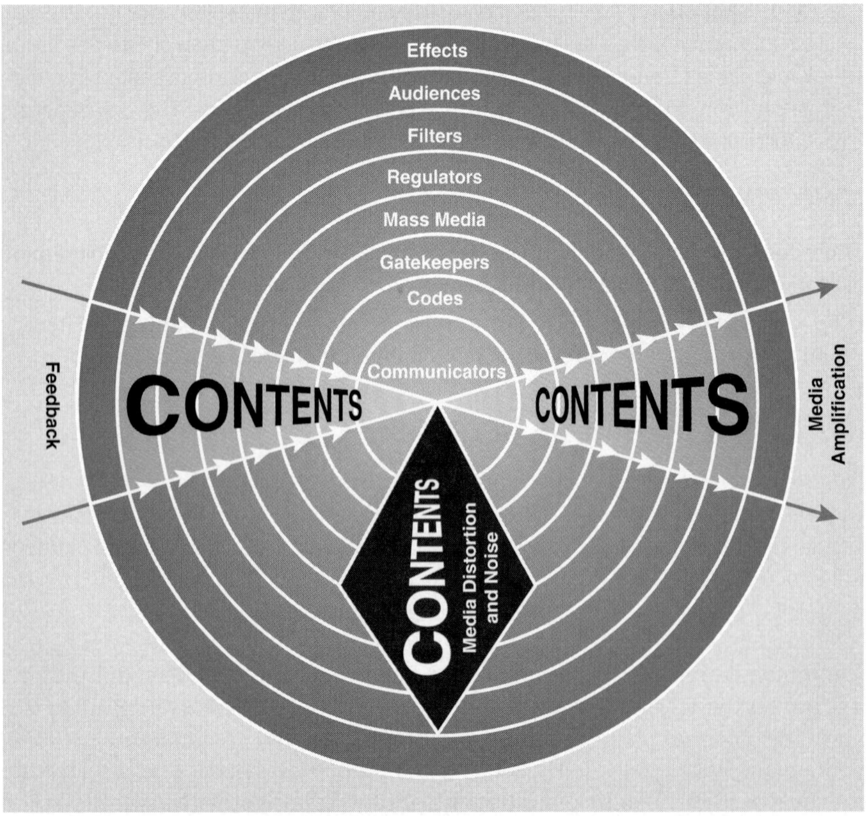

Concentric Circle Model. *The concentric circle model illustrates a great number of obstacles for a mass-communicated message to reach an audience. These include obstacles in the technology, including coding for transmission. It's a detailed model that acknowledges that the media amplify messages, which can compound their effects. Feedback is shown, too. In mass communication, feedback usually is muted and almost always is delayed.*

itself to visual portrayal, like a comedian's sight gag, will fall flat on radio. The medium is indeed critical in ensuring that an outward-rippling message makes its way to the goal—an effect, which Hiebert, Ungurait and Bohn place at the outermost ring.

>> **Amplification.** Important in understanding mass communication is knowing how a mass medium boosts a message's chance of reaching an audience and having an effect. Radio exponentially increases a commentator's audience. A printing press amplifies a message the same way. Indeed, it's the **amplification** made possible by media technology that sets *mass* communication apart from chatting with a neighbor or making a class presentation.

>> **Message Controls.** Most mass communication involves a team, usually dozens of people, sometimes hundreds. Consider video of a terrorist attack shot by an AP photographer in Iraq. The video passes through a complex gatekeeping process, with editors, packagers, producers and others making decisions on how much of the rough footage ends up in distribution to television stations—or whether the images will make the cut at all. **Gatekeepers** are media people who make judgments on what most merits inclusion in what is sent to networks, stations and web site operators.

Gatekeeping is an unavoidable function in mass communication because there is neither time nor space for all the messages that might be passed through the process. Gatekeepers are editors who decide what makes it through their gates and in what form.

Like gatekeepers, **regulators** can affect a communicator's messages substantially, but regulators are not media people. A military censor who stops a combat story is a regulator. Some regulators function more subtly than a censor but nonetheless powerfully affect messages. The Federal Communications Commission, which regulates U.S. broadcasting, is a mighty force in its authority to grant and deny licenses to over-air stations. In 2006 FCC fines for vaguely defined indecency prompted broadcasters to rein in scriptwriters and producers who had been pushing the envelope. The regulation process can be heavy-handed. China, for example, has insisted that U.S. and other countries' media companies comply with vaguely defined but stridently enforced bans on subjects the government sees as challenges to its authority. Censorship, yes, but Google, Yahoo!, StarTV and other transnational media companies eager to profit from access to potentially huge Chinese audiences have chosen to comply.

>> **In-Process Impediments.** If speakers slur their words, the effectiveness of their messages is jeopardized. Slurring and other impediments to the communication process before a message reaches the audience are called **noise.** In mass communication, based as it is on complex mechanical and electronic equipment, the opportunities for noise interference are countless because so many things can go wrong.

amplification
Giving a message a larger audience

gatekeepers
Media people who influence messages en route

regulators
Nonmedia people who influence messages

noise
Impediment to communication before a message reaches a receiver

Gatekeepers. *At the Baltimore, Maryland,* Afro American, *as at news organizations worldwide, editors sit down daily to decide what to include in their next edition or newscast. Not everything that could be reported will fit. This decision-making process is called gatekeeping. Some stories will make it, some will be trimmed, some will be spiked.*

Mass communicators themselves can interfere with the success of their own messages by being sloppy. This is called **semantic noise.** Sloppy wording is an example. So is slurring. **Channel noise** is something that interferes with message transmission, such as static on the radio. Or smudged ink on a magazine page. Or a faulty microphone on a television anchor's lapel. An intrusion that occurs at the reception site is **environmental noise.** This includes a doorbell interrupting someone reading an article, which distracts from decoding. So would shouting kids who distract a television viewer.

>> Deciphering Impediments. Unwittingly, people who tune in to mass messages may themselves interfere with the success of the mass communication process. Such interference is known as a **filter.**

If someone doesn't understand the language or symbols that a communicator uses, the communication process becomes flawed. It is a matter of an individual lacking enough information to decipher a message. This deficiency is called an **informational filter.** This filter can be partly the responsibility of the communicator, whose vocabulary may not be in tune with the audience. More often, though, filters are a deficiency in the audience.

There also are physical filters. When a receiver's mind is dimmed with fatigue, a **physical filter** may interfere with the communication process. A drunk whose focus fades in and out suffers from a physical filter. Mass communicators have little control over physical filters.

Psychological filters also interfere with communication. Conservative evangelist James Dobson and Parkinson's patient Michael J. Fox, for example, likely would decode a message on stem cell research far differently.

The Hiebert, Ungurait and Bohn model has been incredibly useful in diagramming the process of mass communication—until new technologies ushered in the Internet and transformed a lot of mass communication. Twentieth-century models quickly became, well, so old.

CHECKING YOUR MEDIA LITERACY

- **What are the similarities in the processes of interpersonal and mass communication? And the differences?**
- **What mechanisms does government use to influence media messages short of censorship?**

semantic noise
Sloppy message-crafting

channel noise
Interference during transmission

environmental noise
Interference at reception site

filter
Receiver factor that impedes communication

informational filter
Receiver's knowledge limits that impede deciphering symbols

physical filter
Receiver's alertness that impedes deciphering

psychological filter
Receiver's state of mind that impedes deciphering

21ST CENTURY MODELS

Scholars again are at work on devising models to help explain the new mass communication. Clearly, the coding of Internet messages has become largely automated. There are no typesetters or press operators. Nor are there broadcast control room engineers. Gatekeeping is minimal. Bloggers blog unfettered. The closest that Facebook comes to editing are anonymous monitors whose controls are so light-fingered as to be almost nonexistent. Regulators? Governments have scratched the surface on transnational copyright issues, but largely the governments of Western countries have dallied in trying to apply old regulation models to the Internet.

In part the problem is that the heart of the technology for the Internet is decentralized. There are no central sources that can be regulated—no newsroom, no production centers, no presses. In some ways it's a free-for-all. One useful way to envision the Internet is to think of old telegraph communication in the 1800s, in which messages went from Point A to Point B. In the 1900s, technology ushered in an explosion of mass communication. Radio, for example, picked up on the mass communication model of print media. Messages went from a single Point A to many, many recipients—magazine readers by the millions, radio listeners by the millions and television viewers by the millions. That was the process that Hiebert, Ungurait and Bohn's concentric circle model captured so well.

In the 21st century with the Internet, every Point A is theoretically reached by every Point B and C and also Points X, Y and Z. It's not a linear Point A to Point B. Nor

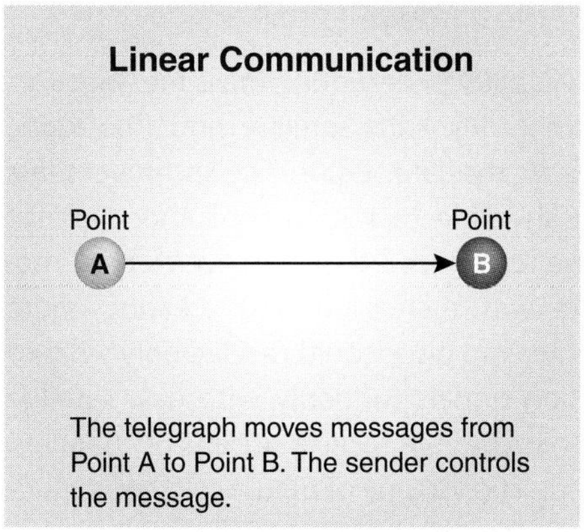

The telegraph moves messages from Point A to Point B. The sender controls the message.

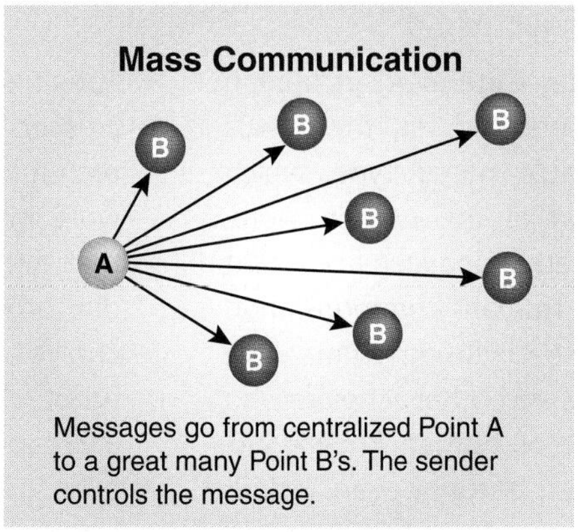

Messages go from centralized Point A to a great many Point B's. The sender controls the message.

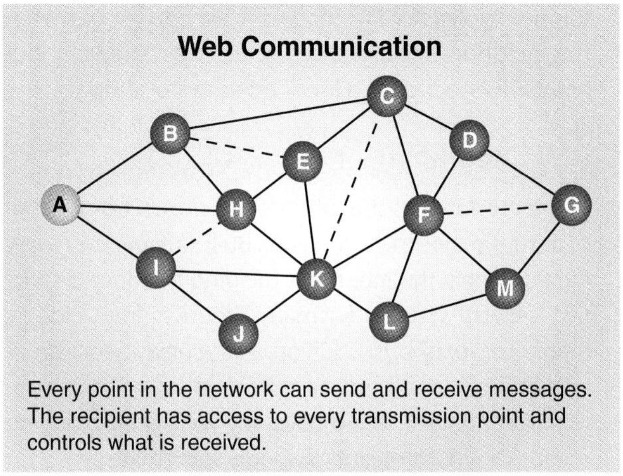

Every point in the network can send and receive messages. The recipient has access to every transmission point and controls what is received.

Points Model. *Web communication shifts much of the control of the communication through the mass media to the recipient, turning the traditional process of mass communication on its head. Receivers are no longer hobbled to sequential presentation of messages, as on a network television newscast. Receivers can switch almost instantly to dozens, hundreds even, of alternatives through a weblike network that, at least theoretically, can interconnect every recipient and sender on the planet.*

is it a message emanating from Point A to multiple points. It's a web of interactive messages reaching an incalculable number of points, which in part is why the term *World Wide Web* came to be.

CHECKING YOUR MEDIA LITERACY

- **How has the technology underlying the Internet rendered early mass communication models obsolete?**
- **Compare models for the new communication technology of the telegraph in the 1800s, radio and television in the 1900s, and the Internet in the 2000s.**

CHAPTER WRAP-UP

Media Technology (Pages 23–24)

- Mass communication is unique among various forms of human communication because it cannot occur without technology. These technologies include modern printing. Books, newspapers and magazines are rooted in printing technology. Motion pictures are rooted in chemical technology. Sound recording, radio and television are called electronic media for a reason. The latest media technology is binary digital signals.

Printing Technology (Pages 24–29)

- The importance of Johannes Gutenberg in human civilization cannot be overstated. In the 1440s Gutenberg invented movable metal type, which permitted mass production of the written word. Hitherto difficult communication between far-distant people became possible. Human communication multiplied exponentially. Especially important were exchanges among scientists and other scholars who were pressing the bounds of human knowledge. Pivotal movements in human history began, including the Age of Reason and the Age of Science and quantum leaps in literacy. These all could be called part of the Age of Mass Communication, now about 550 years old.

Chemical Technology (Pages 29–32)

- Photography was discovered through chemistry. With the invention of the halftone, photography became an important component of the printed media, notably newspapers and magazines. This dramatically increased the powerful effects of printed media messages. Movies also drew on chemical technology but evolved in a separate path.

Electrical Technology (Pages 32–35)

- Electricity and the mastery of electromagnetic waves brought us whole new delivery mechanisms for mass messages. Most notably these were radio, which established itself in the early 1900s, and later television. The electronic media transmitted messages invisibly through the air by shaping and warping electromagnetic waves that are omnipresent in the physical universe. Latter-day variations include cable delivery, but even the cable industry is dependent on over-air signals from program suppliers. Electronic media of a different sort include sound recording, which although not electronic to begin with has become so.

New Technologies (Pages 35–38)

- Speed and reliability in delivering mass messages increased dramatically with satellite and fiber-optic technologies in the late 1900s. The improvements were mostly invisible to media consumers, except that everyone recognized that the inventory of media products was increasing and creating more choices. People who once could receive only a handful of television signals suddenly, with new satellite and cable services, could receive dozens of channels, even hundreds. The volume of media content, including news coverage, grew exponentially. So did entertainment choices. For movies it was no longer what the neighborhood movie house was showing but what was stocked at a local video rental shop.

Digital Integration (Pages 38–42)

- In merely 40 years the Internet has grown from a concept to a major mass medium. Built entirely on binary digital signals, the Internet is melding the once-distinctive delivery systems for many products from old-line media companies. In addition, entire new media products and content forms have been invented. A generation ago nobody would have any idea what blogging meant. Or what it meant to Google something.

Technology and Mass Communication (Pages 43–47)

- The mass communication process is complex and mysterious. In attempts to understand the process, scholars have devised a broad range of models and schematics and invented terminology to explain some of the phenomena they observed when they dissected the process. Although useful in limited ways, modeling the mass communication process leaves many questions and issues open to further inquiry. If we had all the answers to how the process works, every advertising campaign would be a success, every book a best-seller, and every television pilot the next *American Idol*.

▼ Review Questions

1. What is the technology basis of books? Newspapers? Magazines? Sound recording? Movies? Radio? Television? The Internet?
2. What were early effects of Gutenberg's movable type on civilization? Can you speculate on what our culture would be like without Gutenberg's invention?
3. Photography and movies are both rooted in chemical technology, but one is a mass medium and one is not. Please explain this distinction with this paradigm: A photograph is to a book what a script is to a movie.

4. How were systems for delivering mass messages widened with electricity and electronic technology?
5. Describe components that led to the creation and refinement of our latest mass medium, the Internet.
6. The digital technology underlying the Internet changed industries that were built around older mass media. What are these changes? Will traditional media companies survive as we know them?
7. What are the strengths of the Lasswell mass communication model? The concentric circle model? What are their inadequacies?

Concepts

channel (Page 43)

gatekeeping (Page 45)

mass communication (Page 23)

media convergence (Page 40)

persistence of vision (Page 32)

Terms

halftone (Page 28)

Industrial Revolution (Page 25)

movable metal type (Page 24)

noise and filters (Pages 45, 46)

regulators (Page 45)

People

Arthur C. Clarke (Page 36)

Guglielmo Marconi (Page 34)

Harold Lasswell (Page 43)

Johannes Gutenberg (Page 24)

Mathew Brady (Page 31)

Philo Farnsworth (Page 35)

Media Sources

- Linda Simon. *Dark Light: Electricity and Anxiety from the Telegraph to the X-Ray*. Harcourt, 2004. Simon, a literary scholar, finds both excitement and fear in 19th century novels and short stories about the transforming effect of electricity on life and values.
- Lev Manovich. *The Language of New Media*. MIT Press, 2001. Manovich, a media art theorist, offers a seminal and rigorous exploration of the concept of *new media* in a cultural context.
- Stephen W. Littlejohn. *Theories of Human Communication*, eighth edition. Wadsworth, 2004. In this classic treatment, Littlejohn traces developments in communication theory and synthesizes the research. One chapter focuses on mass communication.
- Denis McQuail and Sven Windahl. *Communication Models for the Study of Mass Communication*, second edition. Longman, 1993. McQuail and Windahl include dozens of models from the first 30 years of mass communication research with explanatory comments. Included in the discussion are Shannon-Weaver and helix models.

EDIA TECHNOLOGY

In this chapter you have deepened your media literacy by revisiting several themes. Here are thematic highlights from the chapter:

MEDIA TECHNOLOGY

Movable Metal Type. *Johannes Gutenberg devised a way in the 1440s to mass-produce the written word. The world hasn't been the same since.*

Mass communication is technology-assisted communication. In fact, the defining difference between mass communication and other human communication is the role of technology. The basic technologies are printing, chemistry and electronics. Entire industries have grown from each of the technologies. These are the book, newspaper and magazine industries from printing; the recording, radio and television industries from electronics; and the movie industry from chemistry. Digital technology has made the Internet possible. Some blurring of distinctions among traditional media products is occurring. (Pages 22–51)

MEDIA ECONOMICS

Media Regulation. *The hold of government regulators over U.S. television and radio has been diminished by satellite program services that go directly to consumers. These signals bypass government-regulated local stations.*

The economic underpinnings of modern business and industry, including the economics of media industries, were set in place during the Industrial Revolution. Media companies in most countries need to make a profit to survive. As a result, these companies are highly sensitive to legal requirements established by governments for their operation, including restrictions of the content of messages. Scholars who have modeled the mass communication process call the forces responsible for these restrictions regulators. The role of regulators is most apparent in U.S. mass media in the over-air broadcast industry, whose operations are licensed by the Federal Communications Commission, a government agency. (Page 45)

MEDIA AND DEMOCRACY

Garage Bands. *Technology that has reduced the cost of creating media products has also opened the way for low-power stations to make it big time. This has loosened the giant media companies' control on media content. Thunder Radio is a low-power station at North Dakota State University.*

The major mass media companies have humble origins, but now are so established and entrenched—and huge and powerful—that they are called "empires." With control of the mass media concentrated in relatively few corporate hands, the voice of ordinary folks is squeezed out. This isn't how democracy is supposed to work. Newer technology, however, is reducing the price of entry for mass communication. Low-cost recording equipment and digital file-sharing have given garage bands the ability to produce and distribute music of a quality earlier possible only with costly studios controlled by major recording companies. Similarly, low-power radio and television has enabled mass communication with narrow niches within society. Blogging is another example of this democratization of mass communication. Just about anybody can blog. (Pages 40–41)

MEDIA AND CULTURE

War as Gore. *Media portrayals of the horrors of war have made it difficult for U.S. leaders to sustain public enthusiasm for war. Glory isn't there anymore.*

Human existence has been profoundly changed by the technology that has made mass communication possible. The power of the printing press was obvious early on. For the first time scientists could share their theories and findings not with just handwritten correspondence but with printed articles. The wide distribution of these scientific articles was key to the quantum increases in scientific knowledge that have been transforming our existence since Gutenberg. Structures that define society have been in transition too. Printing helped facilitate the Reformation that shook traditional religious structures beginning in the 1500s. Values have shifted over the decades with mass-produced and mass-distributed literature, in printed and other forms, including movies. The spread of values expressed in music and theater isn't limited any more to drama troupes and traveling balladeers. The argument can be made that the explosion of decentralized digital communication will have a cultural impact of the same magnitude as Gutenberg. Indeed, that impact is already occurring. (Pages 24-27 and 40-41)

chapter 3

MEDIA ECONOMICS

Rupert Murdoch

Global media mogul Rupert Murdoch is up front that he's driven not by politics but profits. Money explains the content of Murdoch's diverse media empire. In fact, economics explains most media behavior.

LEARNING AHEAD

- Economics explains most mass media companies' behavior.
- Most media companies, even conglomerates, began as an entrepreneur's vision.
- Financial alternatives are being pondered to sustain the mass media industries.
- A great issue: Are mass media a public good deserving government funding?
- Government policy has shaped U.S. media development and industry infrastructure.
- Hybrid revenue structures are likely for mass media in the future.
- Media follow traditional business patterns from innovative to mature stages.

MEDIA MOGUL OF OUR ERA

Journalists shuddered the day that Rupert Murdoch offered a phenomenal $5 billion to buy the *Wall Street Journal*. Media watchers were dumbfounded. Murdoch was the immensely rich Australia-born media baron whose empire included Fox television, HarperCollins books and an array mostly of lowbrow media ventures, indeed some sleaze. What would Murdoch want with the *Wall Street Journal,* one of the world's prestige newspapers? The question was all the more poignant because at that moment, in 2007, the newspaper industry, its heyday decades earlier, seemed on its deathbed.

Murdoch, some say, is hard to figure out and his success hard to explain.

Indeed, Murdoch, now approaching 80, is a complex human being, but two themes have marked his career. First, he latches onto goals, sometimes impetuously, and pursues them no-holds-barred. Second, in the end he acts in his economic self-interest. This means correcting, even reversing, impetuous decisions when it's clear the financial payoff is unlikely or too distant. Murdoch thus epitomizes a recurrent theme in media behavior—economic self-interest.

And Murdoch does OK for himself, thank you very much. His company, News Corp., pays him $30 million a year.

With the *Wall Street Journal,* as conventional wisdom has it, Murdoch, saw a way to vindicate his reputation as a media sleaze king. Yes while the low-budget tabloid New York *Post* is his, Murdoch was explicit that he wanted the *Journal* to compete directly against the gold standard in world journalism, the New York *Times.* Obsessed, he offered the Bancroft family more than every calculation as to what the parent company, Dow Jones, was worth.

After the deal was consummated, financial realities quickly caught up with Murdoch's dream for the *Journal.* To rein in costs, he ordered shorter stories and less-researched reporting. He trimmed page width, which cut postage expenses. Staff was reduced. Ad space was sold on the once-sacrosanct front page.

In earlier ventures Murdoch bailed when financial expectations turned bleak. He dumped his controlling interest in the DirecTV satellite delivery service in 2006 when, for example, he saw that the potential had peaked. He had controlled DirecTV only three years.

In the end the bottom line for Rupert Murdoch is the bottom line. He said as much at a Congressional hearing. To critics who contend that his Fox News is biased to the conservative right politically, Murdoch didn't deny the charge in his testimony but characterized himself as apolitical: "Conservative talk is more popular." His point: Money drives content. If liberalism would draw audience cost-effectively, then Fox, he was saying, would be liberal. In fact, in the 2008 presidential campaign, with the conservative-backed Republican candidate John McCain lagging badly, Murdoch endorsed Barack Obama, who was building a progressive, liberal coalition.

Murdoch's record shows a pattern of opportunism trumping values. In the 1980s, for example, Murdoch ran into an obstacle to building his network of Fox television stations because stations in the United States are licensed by the government only to U.S. citizens. So Murdoch applied for U.S. citizenship and took the exam. Problem solved. For Murdoch, citizenship was a means to an end.

When he needed friends in Congress on a broadcast regulation issue, Murdoch's book subsidiary, HarperCollins, offered House Speaker Newt Gingrich an extraordinarily sweet $4.5 million advance for an autobiography. Gingrich hadn't even started the book. When word about the deal leaked out, the book industry was aghast. There was no way a Gingrich book could ever earn back such an advance. In the glare of the negative publicity, the deal exposed, Murdoch denied he was trying to buy influence. His problems on the Hill and the book deal, he said, were an unfortunate coincidence.

Murdoch has no problem backpedaling. In one speech, waxing on the future of democracy, Murdoch predicted that advanced communication technology would spell the end of totalitarian regimes. He hadn't reckoned that the totalitarian leadership in China might hear the speech. They did. When the Chinese then threatened to deny permission for Murdoch's StarTV satellite to transmit into China, he moved quickly to placate the Chinese totalitarians. He signed a deal for HarperCollins to publish a book by the daughter of head of state Deng Xiaoping. Also, he canceled another book that probably would have provoked the Chinese. Knowing that the Chinese were wary of the BBC's independent news broadcasts, he discontinued BBC from his StarTV satcast service.

Murdoch has become synonymous with media power. Former CBS executive Howard Stringer once called him "the leader of a new Napoleonic era of communications." Critics claim that his emphasis on corporate profits has undermined the notion that the mass media have a primary responsibility to serve the public.

Financial Foundations

STUDY ***PREVIEW***

Most media behavior can be explained by economics. Who pays the bills? Advertising generates most of the revenue for newspapers, magazines, radio and television. Books and music rely largely on direct sales to consumers. The mix of revenue streams is in major upheaval, posing questions about the future shape of mass media industries.

CAPITALISM

The mass media function in the money-driven system of **capitalism.** As in all businesses, executives who don't deliver profits are replaced. If profits lag, investors pull out their money, reducing the capital available for operations and growth. Investors as a group couldn't care less whether their money is in the stock of a mass media company or a widget manufacturer. The investment with the greatest profit potential is a magnet.

Profit-generation is complex. Different media operations have a different mix of advertising and other revenue streams. A high-yield operation, as AOL once was for Time Warner, can fade and need either to be sold or somehow reinvented. Competition can change everything, whether a direct competitor or some new enterprise that sucks away audience—as the online news has for traditional news media. An enterprise that generates strong profits at the moment may not have strong prospects down the road. What to do? Cut expenses and ride the road to lesser revenue? Sell? Shut it down? And what effect do these questions have on you as a media consumer?

CHECKING YOUR MEDIA LITERACY

- **Why is profit a necessity for mass media in a capitalistic system?**
- **What happens when a media company fails to generate profits?**

PRIMARY REVENUE STREAMS

The primary mass media industries became economic behemoths through one of two ways—advertising or sales. Almost all the income of the book, recorded music and movie industries is from selling their products directly to consumers through the mail or downloads or through intermediaries like bookshops and box offices. Commercial television and radio, which dominate the U.S. broadcasting industry, depend solely on advertising. Major newspapers and magazines are a hybrid, dependent on subscriptions and so-called street or newsrack sales but even more so on advertising.

The dependence of media companies on a narrow range of revenue sources resulted in major changes in the media landscape early in the 21st century. Readership losses, largely to the Internet, eroded confidence among advertisers in whether their ad budgets were being spent wisely in newspapers and magazines. The broadcast media continued into a restructuring as advertisers moved budgets, generally gradually, from the long-established network-affiliate over-air delivery system to cable and satellite and, yes, to the Internet.

CHECKING YOUR MEDIA LITERACY

- **What have been the primary revenue streams of U.S. mass media historically?**
- **What dynamics have dwindled these primary revenue streams?**

Rupert Murdoch
a leading and stereotypical media mogul

capitalism
An economic system with private owners operating trade and industry for profit

ALTERNATIVE SYSTEMS

Alternatives to the U.S. commercial model for funding television, radio, newspapers and magazines have been developed in other nations. One alternative, used in some dictatorships, is for government to pay the bills and to control content. Less onerous from a U.S. perspective are Japanese and British systems to collect taxes explicitly for broadcasting.

>> **Japanese Broadcasting.** Anyone who owns a television set in Japan can expect a knock on the door every couple of months. It is the collector from NHK, the Japan Broadcasting Corporation, to pick up a $16 reception fee. The ritual occurs six times a year in 49 million doorways. The reception fee, required by law since 1950, generates $2.6 billion annually to support the NHK network. The fee does not support all Japanese television—only the two domestic NHK television networks and three NHK radio networks. The other networks—Fuji, NTV and the Tokyo Broadcasting System—must rely solely on their own advertising revenue streams. So do the few independent stations.

>> **British Broadcasting.** To support the venerable British Broadcasting Corporation, anyone buying a television set in Britain pays a fee of about $230. It's an annual fee, which prompts taxpayer grumbling when it's due but which figures out to about only 75 cents a day. The system has financed the growth of the "Beeb," as BBC is affectionately known, into a powerhouse in global broadcasting. Britain has additional networks and stations, all independent and separate from the BBC structure and advertising-dependent.

>> **Cuban Media.** Dictatorial regimes come in different stripes. All need, however, to control media content to minimize, if not to stifle, dissent. An effective form of control is to hold the pursestrings. Some dictatorships have made media entirely dependent on government funding and even appoint editors and managers. One model of government-financed and government-controlled media is the Cuban newspaper *Granma*. Rather than the freewheeling news coverage of newspapers in democracies, *Granma* is a government propaganda sheet, circulating only officially sanctioned "news."

A lesson from the global diversity in media economics, all successful in their own ways, for better or worse, is that they have been operating for decades.

CHECKING YOUR MEDIA LITERACY

What are Japanese, British and Cuban alternatives to advertising to finance mass media?

Ownership Structures

STUDY PREVIEW

One dynamic for media literacy is knowing the corporate structure within which media products exist. Knowing the entities comprising News Corporation, for example, explains a lot about the content issued by corporate stablemates Fox television and HarperCollins books.

ENTREPRENEURIAL ORIGINS

Media ownership patterns explain a lot about media performance. Through history most media operations began with an individual with a concept—dare we say vision—and a willingness to take on risk. Witness William Paley, who built the CBS radio network, then the CBS television networks. Or Henry Luce and his partner Briton Hadley, whose *Time* magazine grew into today's Time Life-CNN-AOL empire. Even the giant media operations that seem to burst full-blown in the marketplace have lesser origins. To many Americans, Rupert Murdoch's News Corporation suddenly was a major player with Fox television, movie studios, newspapers, books, magazines and home-delivery satellite television. But Murdoch began with a relatively small inheritance, a single newspaper in Adelaide, Australia.

CHECKING YOUR MEDIA LITERACY

- **How many brand-name media products can you trace to a visionary entrepreneur?**
- **Name them and their founder and their owner today.**

MEDIA CHAINS

The giant Gannett, like other media chains, started small. **Frank Gannett** and a few associates pooled enough money in 1906 to buy a half interest in the Elmira, New York, *Gazette*. They added a few nearby small-town papers. Eventually they created the Empire State group of dailies and moved the headquarters to Rochester. Gradually more papers were added. Today Gannett owns 99 daily newspapers coast to coast, including *USA Today*. The company also owns 17 dailies in Britain. The company's holdings include television stations. Along the way Gannett has been in and out of radio, billboard, magazine, polling and other related enterprises.

To gather capital for further expansion and to build its business, Gannett periodically sells ownership shares in the company to investors. These investors have a growing role in choosing managers of the company's properties and adopting policies to increase profits as a return on their investment.

CHECKING YOUR MEDIA LITERACY

- **How do you explain the phenomenon of media chain ownership?**
- **Who owns your daily newspaper? Your favorite local radio station? The dominant local television station?**

CONGLOMERATION

With media companies making stellar profits in the 1970s into the early 2000s, they became magnets for investors and for other companies looking to expand or to diversify. The result was media **conglomeration.** Acquired companies usually were left to continue their profit-making magic even though the new corporate policymakers could intervene at will if revenues faltered.

These conglomerates are giant enterprises. Time Warner generates revenue of $37 billion a year from movies, books, television, magazines, online sites and other media operations. The thing that the shareholders who control these conglomerates have in common is the goal of improving the return on their investment.

These are the largest U.S. media companies ranked by domestic revenue before the 2008 economic recession muddied data:

Time Warner	$ 37.0 billion
Google	21.8 billion
Viacom	21.5 billion
Comcast	20.1 billion
Disney	17.4 billion
NBC Universal	12.5 billion
News Corp.	11.4 billion
DirecTV	9.8 billion
Fox	8.6 billion
Yahoo!	7.2 billion
Echo Star	6.7 billion
Clear Channel	6.5 billion

Each company's board of directors chooses executives to achieve these goals. Those executives appoint subordinates to do the job. In a hierarchical business structure. Decisions by the board determine the shape of their subsidiary media

Frank Gannett
Founder of Gannett media corporation

conglomeration
Process of companies being brought into common ownership but remaining distinct entities

companies day-in and day-out—to buy or sell AOL, to reintroduce *Life,* to put more resources into *People* to strengthen its market dominance, to back off animated movies, or to further saturate the market with more animations. These are decisions, made in board rooms, that are off the radar of all but the most savvy and media-literate.

Most conglomerates leave day-to-day decision-making to the appointed managers of their subsidiary media products. Subsidiary managers, of course, can be replaced or, at minimum, overruled.

CHECKING YOUR MEDIA LITERACY

- **How do you explain the phenomenon of media conglomeration?**
- **Who makes the ultimate decisions on media products in conglomerate structures?**

MEGA-CONGLOMERATES

Some conglomerates stay with business enterprises they know best. Others reach into related enterprises. In fact, all of the largest media companies have tentacles all over the place. Comcast is an example. Originally a television cable-delivery company, Comcast now has telephone and Internet services and owns television production units for sports and game shows. In 2004, awash in cash and willing to take on debt, Comcast made an audacious bid to buy ABC-Disney. The offer failed, but, as it was later learned, Comcast wanted Disney not as much as Disney's ESPN television sports network. Had the deal gone through, industry observers expect that Comcast would have sold off the rest of Disney to keep the ESPN jewel.

The Comcast-Disney saga makes a case study in the realities of media conglomeration. The huge companies that own multiple, indeed sometimes dozens of media entities, have agendas that are invisible to most media consumers. If acquisition strategies go well, everything remains status-quo. When unanticipated consequences arise, disaster can result with grave consequences for media consumers. What if the risks of an acquisition were miscalculated? If too much loan burden was taken to make a purchase? If a revenue stream dries up? If the economy goes south?

The series of media bankruptcies that began in 2008, unthinkable only months earlier, had multiple causes, but financial overextension was a common thread. Media companies had borrowed too heavily to make acquisitions. The collateral for the loans for Sam Zell's leveraged 2007 buyout of the Tribune Company, as an example, included not only the flagship Chicago *Tribune* and other newspapers but also the company's radio and television stations and every company subsidiary. That included the Chicago Cubs baseball team. The effects can be far-flung. The Comcast-Disney deal, as another example, would have meant a sale of either Comcast's Philadelphia Flyers hockey club or Disney's Anaheim Mighty Ducks because of league regulations. Or think about the disruptions if the Chicago Cubs didn't attract fans to the stadium. In fact, Zell put the Cubs' stadium up for sale to raise cash for the Tribune Company after he realized he couldn't make payments on the debt he incurred to buy the company.

This gets all the more complicated when non-media companies venture into media properties. NBC and the Universal movie studio are owned by mega-conglomerate General Electric, whose credit subsidiary as well as other enterprises were hit hard by the recession that began in 2008. The MGM movie studio got tied up with casino hotels at one point. The Anaconda mining company once owned almost every daily newspaper in Montana.

With disparate entities, the top decision-makers at mega-corporations are focused on profitability of each entity and, truth be told, see a widget factory as just as precious as a media subsidiary. There is little conscience at the top corporate level other than to satisfy shareholder insistence on profitability. The pressure usually is to increase profits quarter after quarter, regardless of the impact on media companies and regardless of deleterious effects on media consumers. When times get rough, in fact, media subsidiaries are pressed to offset losses elsewhere in the conglomerate,. Inevitably these pressures affect the quality of the conglomerate's media products.

CHECKING YOUR MEDIA LITERACY

- **What is the downside of conglomerate ownership? Give examples.**
- **Can you name corporate stablemates of a chain or conglomerate that owns a media product on which you rely?**

DIVESTITURE

Media companies have a long history of jockeying their properties for new advantage. But in the recession that began in 2008, and leading up to it, divestiture became panic-driven. There were no buyers. The most obvious major crack in the conglomeration pattern of the previous 30 years, even going back longer by some measures, began in 2005. The landmark newspaper chain Knight Ridder exemplifies what happened. Knight Ridder, the second largest chain in the United States and a consistent Pulitzer Prize winner, wasn't making enough money in its shareholders' eyes. The decision was made to sell the company. Another chain, McClatchy, bought most of the Knight Ridder properties. Overextended, McClatchy's capitalized value plummeted. The company ended up with no choice but to sell assets and to put some of its newspapers into bankruptcy in an attempt to survive.

By 2010 it was clear that media ownership was no longer an avenue, so to speak, to print money. There were bright spots, to be sure, but few. The media landscape was fast changing.

CHECKING YOUR MEDIA LITERACY

- **What do media companies do when profitability flounders?**
- **What has happened to the old Knight Ridder newspaper chain?**
- **Are any former Knight Ridder newspapers still earning Pulitzer Prizes?**

Sponsored Media

STUDY PREVIEW

Many media products are sponsored by institutions as part of a larger mission. Among the most visible sponsored media since 1908 has been the newspaper the *Christian Science Monitor*, whose name is a giveaway to the sponsoring institution. Many media consumers, however, are unaware of institutional connections of sponsored media.

INSTITUTIONAL SPONSORSHIP

Sponsored media are not always visible. Many listeners of the historically powerful Chicago radio station WCFL had no idea that the call letters stood for the Chicago Federation of Labor. Yes, labor unions owned and operated the station. Going back to the 1920s, many churches have been in and out of station ownership.

By some measures, there are more sponsored media than financially stand-alone media. Of roughly12,000 magazines in the United States, most are issued by organizations to select audiences. These include corporate magazines for employees, shareholders, customers and other audiences. Every college has publications for alumni.

CHECKING YOUR MEDIA LITERACY

- **How aware do you believe media consumers are about institutions that sponsor some media products?**
- **How many sponsored media can you name?**

Mary Baker Eddy

'To injure no man, but to bless all mankind'

BOSTON · FRIDAY MARCH 27, 2009

THE CHRISTIAN SCIENCE MONITOR

Why are Germans buying so many cars? GOVERNMENT INCENTIVES AID BUYERS & DEALERS / 7

LATEST NEWS & EXTENDED COVERAGE: CSMonitor.com ONE DOLLAR

FAREWELL, DAILY PRINT

The New Monitor

This issue of The Christian Science Monitor represents a significant moment in our 100-year history. As of today, the daily Monitor makes its transition from print to online. Follow us 24/7 at CSMonitor.com and subscribe to our new print weekly. The Monitor move, which was announced last fall, is being watched by other news organizations, many of which are weighing changes of their own.

Editor's message John Yemma explains how our new formats – Web, weekly print, e-mail – will make Monitor journalism more relevant. Opinion, 9.

Past as prologue Former writers mark 'unique' moments – from crawling on the carpet with Reagan to being shot at with Arafat. Backstory, 20.

Beyond bailouts: reforms ahead

By MARK TRUMBULL, STAFF WRITER

The push to remake the financial industry's rules of the road in hopes of softening future boom-and-bust cycles gathered momentum this week with Treasury Secretary Timothy Geithner urging Congress Thursday to create new systems to monitor and control risks.

So far, Washington has acted mainly to contain the immediate damage to the economy. But any deeper fixes could also yield results quickly.

THE TREASURY SECRETARY is proposing new regulation for the financial industry.

By signaling a receptivity to increased regulation – a key European demand – the announcement might strengthen President Obama's ability to nudge Germany and other nations on a US priority at next week's meeting of the Group of 20 leaders: expanding government spending as an economic stimulus. Federal agencies would also have new authority to intervene at large, troubled financial institutions like AIG if parts of Mr. Geithner's plan are enacted into law.

Longer term, clarifying potential reforms could lift economic confidence.

See REFORM page 12

U.S. FORCES MAY NOT LEAVE KEY IRAQI CITIES

By JANE ARRAF, CORRESPONDENT

BAGHDAD – The US withdrawal from Iraq is under way. Some troops are preparing to go home and others have pulled back from outposts to bases. But the planned pullback of all American soldiers from Iraqi cities by the end of June will probably not be fully met.

In an exclusive interview, the top US ground commander in Iraq says Iraqi officials are likely to ask for US help in the key cities of Baquba and Mosul, meaning that American troops may stay there after the deadline for redeployment to major bases. Senior military commanders say US troops will also likely stay on in the southern city of Basra.

Did Al Qaeda in Iraq turn too violent? Dispute splits jihadis. Page 6.

"In Mosul and Diyala [Province], as we do a combined or joint assessment of the situation on the ground, I have every expectation that both sides will say we need to stay with this a little bit longer until this improves," says Lt. Gen. Lloyd Austin.

While US forces are to hand over combat missions to Iraqis

See IRAQ page 10

TROUBLE SPOT: US soldiers patrol Baquba, capital of Diyala Province, where fighting continues.

WHAT MAKES A TEACHER GOOD?

This series explores efforts to attract and cultivate more excellence at the head of the class. One central issue: How are future teachers best prepared for the work ahead? See page 13.

LAST OF THREE PARTS

IN TRAINING: Danielle Silverman (l) and Lakeyk Poston discuss a lesson at a K-8 school in Chicago.

PASSAGE TO INDIA?

US workers migrate overseas

By BEN ARNOLDY, STAFF WRITER

DELHI AND PUNE, INDIA – IBM announced a major round of US layoffs on Thursday, even as the company has been hiring workers in developing nations like India.

But over the past year, the company began offering US workers who are facing a job cut a novel carrot: If you apply for a new IBM position in a foreign country and are hired again at local wages, we will cover some of the transition costs like visa fees.

Few IBMers have taken the offer, and the firm has taken public relations lumps over it. But a handful of pioneering Americans at other firms have started to shop their skills on the Indian market, finding fulfillment and job security at a time of deep recession back home.

An IBM offer hints at a future where it's not just skilled Indians who travel the globe for work.

The IBM offer hints at a future where it's not just skilled Indians who might have to travel halfway around the globe for a job. It's likely that more American job seekers will have to think globally, say analysts, and the experiences of Americans who have taken jobs with companies here say it's not something to fear.

"I was making six figures when I left the States. I'm making six figures here – in *rupees*," laughs Jeanne Heydecker, a marketing

See JOBS page 11

Sponsored News. *Since its founding in 1908, the* Christian Science Monitor *has offered global news coverage from a solution-oriented perspective advocated by the Christian Science church. The goal of church founder Mary Baker Eddy was accurate and truthful reporting to help people address serious problems facing humankind. In 2009, short of funds to maintain the newspaper, the* Monitor *went completely to online delivery.*

THE *MONITOR* MODEL

Mary Baker Eddy, the influential founder of the Christian Science faith, was aghast at turn-of-the-century Boston newspapers. The Boston dailies, like papers in other major U.S. cities, were sensationalistic, overplaying crime and gore in hyperbolic battles to steal readers from each other. Entering the fray, Eddy introduced a newspaper with a different mission. Her ***Christian Science Monitor,*** founded in 1908, sought to deal with issues and problems on a higher plane and to help the world come up with solutions. The *Monitor* was a sponsored paper, produced by an institution as part of a larger purpose. Unlike many church-sponsored media, the *Monitor* has never been preachy either as a newspaper or in its new online format. As for all sponsored media, the church as the sponsor has underwritten expenses when subscriptions, newsstand sales and advertising revenue fell short.

Mary Baker Eddy
Founded the *Christian Science Monitor* in 1908

Christian Science Monitor
National daily newspaper sponsored by the Christian Science church

CHECKING YOUR MEDIA LITERACY

- **How does the *Christian Science Monitor* fit into the mission of the sponsoring church?**
- **Why would some sponsored media avoid bringing attention to their sponsorship?**

New Media Models

STUDY PREVIEW

Everyone has a stake in shaping new business models to take threatened mass media industries out of jeopardy. But nobody has come up with a blueprint. Brainstorming has examined the variety of current revenue sources to determine which hold promise into the future. And what about changing tax law, to encourage a return to yesteryear and family ownership of media companies?

BRAINSTORMING NEW MODELS

As advertising-dependent media went into a financial tailspin beginning in 2008, the quest for alternative business models became frenzied. The panic was worst for the hard-hit newspaper and magazine industries. Television and radio were cushioned somewhat by entertainment content, which suffered less audience slippage and maintained a sustainable although diminishing advertising base. Most of the concern focused on news-oriented media and the implications of their disappearance for the informed citizenry that is needed for democracy to function.

At an important conference of media thinkers at the Louisiana State University journalism school in 2008, brainstorming took many directions for future economic structures for mass media. Alternatives seemingly anathema to democratic traditions were broached, even government financing and operation of media. Other alternatives put on the table included overhauling the U.S. Tax Code to make it easier for media companies to stay in business.

CHECKING YOUR MEDIA LITERACY

- **Why is a fundamental rethinking of media business models occurring now?**
- **Who is best equipped to come up with sustainable plans for the mass media's future? Media industry leaders familiar with existing models? Non-media people? Business theorists? Scholars?**

COMMUNITY FOUNDATIONS

With the asset value of local newspapers plunging, some media analysts have suggested that owners donate them to charities that then could operate them tax-free. Ben Shute, director of the Rockefeller Brothers Fund for grants to encourage democratic practices, says community foundations, which are set up as charities, could identify voids that a newspaper's demise would leave and then take over the newspaper to meet those needs. **Community foundations,** common throughout the United States, are funded with donations. Their purpose is to support worthy community causes.

Skeptics are wary, however, whether all community foundations could provide the detached and neutral coverage that newspapers had offered under private ownership. Many foundations are community boosters, whose agenda would hardly countenance courageous investigative reporting. The concern is that many community foundations would wield a newspaper as a publicity machine and not a vehicle for public service through unbridled truth-seeking.

The jury remains out on how community foundations may fit into the future of economic support systems for mass media.

CHECKING YOUR MEDIA LITERACY

- **Should community foundations be encouraged to take over local media companies? What are the pros and cons?**

community foundation
Nonprofit entity to promote good in a community; generally supported by donations

NONPROFITS

cooperative
An organization owned and run jointly by members that share profits or benefits

Associated Press
World's largest news-gathering organization; a nonprofit and a cooperative owned by member newspapers

Another possibility is wider use of the **cooperative** model. In news, the largest model is the global news-gathering organization the **Associated Press.** The AP began in 1848 as a joint effort of several New York newspapers to pick up bundles of mail from Europe by sending boats out to transoceanic ships at anchor off Sandy Point and not yet docked. Rather than all the papers hiring their own newsboats to fetch the mail bundles, the papers agreed to share a single fleet and eliminated redundant costs. The Harbor News Association, as the co-op was known, evolved and grew into the AP. Then as now, in member newspapers control the AP and share the coverage as well as the costs of operation. The member newspapers also share the costs of operating

243 bureaus worldwide. To meet expenses, the AP also sells its coverage to broadcasters, investment firms, government agencies and other customers.

The cooperative model precludes profits as essential, which gives the AP an advantage over profit-driven enterprises. Over the years the AP's nonprofit status has given it a financial edge over competing for-profit news agencies, which have mostly disappeared. Does anybody hear any more about United Press? Or International News Service? The major players in international coverage are merely two—the AP and the British agency Reuters.

That nonprofits can work is clear from the AP model. An estimated 3 billion people a day see or hear news from the Associated Press. National Public Radio, another nonprofit although not a cooperative, reaches 21 million listeners a day in the United States.

In local news, a possible AP equivalent could be a consolidated newsroom serving newspaper, broadcast and web outlets. As with the Harbor News Association, duplicate costs could be eliminated. Alas, so would be the competition that historically has contributed to vibrant coverage.

>> **Sustaining Nonprofits.** Business economists are wary of switching a for-profit enterprise into a nonprofit because of the baggage that can come with the acquisition. Even if a nonprofit can generate sufficient revenue to underwrite operations, itself a challenge, the entity still accumulates expenses to maintain its own infrastructure. With a newspaper, for example, printing presses have a useful life of 30 years. And most newspapers have put off purchasing replacement presses. Eventually the presses will fall apart and need replacing. Other deferred capital expenses include maintaining facilities, replacing vehicles, upgrading software. A nonprofit may keep a media operation going for a period, but the longer-term issue is sustainability. Robert Picard, a media economist, casts the prospects bleakly in calling for a "sustainable model," rather than something that gets up and running for two or three years, maybe longer, and then fails because underlying financial problems don't go away.

>> **New Nonprofits.** New nonprofits, many organized by journalists from the shrinking newspaper industry, are filling voids left by for-profit news organizations. Worldwide, about 40 investigative reporting nonprofits are operating. These organizations are engaging in the most expensive and riskiest form of news reporting, the investigative story, which has been abandoned by many budget-strapped traditional media companies.

The new nonprofits take different forms. In Boston, the upstart Global News Enterprises operates as a newsroom. Philip Balboni, founder of New England Cable News, and Charles Senott, a Boston *Globe* reporter, who raised close to $8 million to get Global News going, have a network of 70 reporters, all freelancers. Another of the new nonprofits, the Center for Public Integrity, has a specific mission, to promote honesty in government and other powerful institutions. The center, in Washington, was founded by Charles Lewis, a frustrated producer of the CBS news program *60 Minutes*. With an annual budget of $5 million, the center's 40 reporters have issued 300 reports and 14 books. The center also has freelance contracts with hundreds of reporters around the world. Another nonprofit, ProPublica, also in Washington, is run by a former managing editor of the *Wall Street Journal*, Paul Steiger. He had a startup budget of $10 million a year. With a news staff of 30, ProPublica focuses on "important stories with moral force."

CHECKING YOUR MEDIA LITERACY

- **Why is investigative journalism the riskiest and most expensive form of news reporting?**
- **Can the Associated Press be called the granddaddy of nonprofit organizations in news?**
- **What problems confront moving for-profit media organizations into nonprofits?**
- **How do models for new nonprofit media organizations differ from the Associated Press?**

CASE STUDY

Rescuing Investigative Journalism?

RILED. *At a congressional hearing, Senator John Cornyn, a Texas Republican, shakes a paid advertisement from moveon.org, which promotes liberal causes. Moveon.org has been funded largely by Herbert and Marion Sandler, who also are behind the investigative reporting enterprise ProPublica.*

As newspapers continue sliding into oblivion, a few foundations have come forward as self-proclaimed "saviors" of investigative journalism. One of these is the nonprofit ProPublica, funded by San Francisco billionaires Herbert and Marion Sandler. The Sandlers started ProPublica with $10 million in 2008 and promised to keep replenishing that amount every year.

ProPublica wants to make up for the lack of investigative reporting in the mainstream media by supplying free stories to existing media outlets. An example was a story on medical care for U.S. contractors in Iraq and Afghanistan that was published by the Los Angeles *Times* and broadcast by ABC News. It prompted a call for a Congressional investigation.

Is there a risk that those who fund a nonprofit news organization might try to influence the news that it reports? ProPublica's stable of 30 reporters is led by former *Wall Street Journal* managing editor Paul Steiger. Herb Sandler is chairman of the ProPublica board. When people ask Steiger about the possible problems that might create, he says that he and the board have agreed that the board "will have no advance knowledge of what we decide to cover. They will see it on the day of publication."

But even if the people who fund foundation presses can refrain from influencing *which* news they cover, can their foundations be trusted to stay detached and neutral ideologically in their reporting? Critics say it's doubtful. They point to the Sandlers' involvement in liberal causes—and subsequent "liberal" reporting at ProPublica.

David Cohn founded SpotUs.com, a community-funded investigative journalism group that was initially funded by Knight News Challenge. Spot.Us is a platform that enables individuals to pledge support to reporters for specific stories. Cohn says, "There is no such thing as clean money. You find me clean money . . . I'll find you fairy dust, and we will do a trade. Money from advertising isn't clean. Even money from foundations isn't clean."

"The best we can do is be transparent," Cohn says. "By being transparent and making sure we are diverse in public money we stand to have more accountable journalism than that which is supported by advertising."

Criticism for ProPublica and other investigative journalism ventures like it comes from all directions. Some say National Public Radio's corporate sponsors give it a bias. Others criticize NPR as government-funded journalism. Those critics believe that investigative reporting should maintain an adversarial relationship with government.

Conservatives complain that the money funding projects like ProPublica comes from liberals, although it seems fair to point out that conservatives could fund their own foundation presses. Conservative-funded projects include TownHall.com, the Conservative News Service function, and the Media Research Center.

DEEPENING YOUR MEDIA LITERACY

EXPLORE THE ISSUE

Check out the web sites for ProPublica, NPR and the Washington *Times*. Can you tell if they are influenced by their funders?

DIG DEEPER

Why does David Cohn say that advertising revenues are only semi-transparent? Are there any differences between community-funded and privately funded investigative reporting? Is one better than the other?

WHAT DO YOU THINK?

Will foundation press save investigative journalism? Does it matter who provides the funding? Regardless of who does fund investigative journalism, is it crucial that they have no influence over it?

UNIVERSITY MEDIA GENERATORS

Charles Lewis of the Center for Public Integrity separately established a student investigative reporting unit at American University in Washington in 2009. Such university-based incubators of investigative reporting gained attention earlier when David Protess at Northwestern University created the Medill Innocence Project. Protess' students uncovered judicial lapses that sent 11 innocent men and women to prison, five to death row. At Brandeis University, former Washington *Post* reporter Florence Graves heads the Schuster Institute for Investigative Journalism. Lowell Bergman, formerly of the New York *Times* and PBS' *Frontline,* heads the Investigative Reporting Program at the University of California at Berkeley, which provides salaries, benefits and editorial guidance for journalists pursuing careers in in-depth public service reporting.

Campus-based generators of media content may be a long-term part of the emerging patchwork of new media organizations. The fact, however, is that not all universities, whatever their claims for academic freedom, have top-level administrators with the courage to support investigative journalism that tackles wrong-doing and abuses in powerful political and social institutions.

CHECKING YOUR MEDIA LITERACY

- **How do university-based news-gathering centers fit into a mosaic of the future of the mass media?**
- **How likely are most universities to accept a role as generators of investigative journalism?**

FAMILY OWNERSHIP

A nostalgia-driven alternative is a return to family ownership of media. Almost all media companies began as sole proprietorships. The usual pattern was for the founders to bequeath their companies to their heirs. Some families maintained ownership for subsequent generations, although federal inheritance tax laws in the latter 1900s forced most media families to sell outside the family, usually to chains that were eager to expand. Two factors figure into revised interest in family ownership, including a yearning for old ways:

>> **Personality-Driven Media.** Historically there were great contributions to media content during the era of individual and family ownership. Generally this family ownership has acquired an aura, perhaps rose-tinted, of a commitment to public service and commonweal. Certainly, media products bore the stamp of their founders and family owners more than in the successor phase of media ownership. The chains and conglomerates that acquired the family-run operations made policies that emphasized profits and, as the lore has it, a risk-averse blandness set in. Here are examples of the pattern:

	Media Unit	Early Proprietor	Later Ownership
Books	Scribner	Charles Scribner	Viacom
Newspapers	*Wall Street Journal*	Bancroft family	News Corp.
Magazines	*Time*	Henry Luce	Time Warner
Recordings	Motown	Berry Gordy	Universal Music
Movies	Paramount	Adolph Zukor	Viacom
Radio	CBS	William Paley	Viacom
Television	NBC	David Sarnoff	General Electric

This pattern toward chain ownership has been repeated throughout the United States in local newspaper, radio and television ownership. The often colorful characters associated with the earlier periods have been subsumed by a bland corporate mindset focused myopically on the bottom line.

>> **Pride of Ownership.** Whether the proverbial good ol' days were better can be debated. But there is a nostalgia that pride-of-ownership in the family media era made for better content. Indeed, a local family's reputation was inherent in the product. Jay Hamilton of the Louisiana State University journalism school has suggested that family owners may be willing to trade off maximum profits for doing the right thing for their community. Hamilton's point is that chain ownership put profits above community good, families less so.

Clearly, inheritance tax laws would need to be adjusted to encourage local family media ownership. The current tax code imposes unusually stiff levies on estates. Colloquially it is called the **death tax.** The rate is 55 percent, which means the heirs of a media property worth, say, $100 million would need to come up with $55 million for federal taxes. More would be due in states that have their own inheritance tax in addition. Raising the money to pay the tax usually means incurring significant if not impossible debt—or selling outside the family.

Doubters see a tax policy change to encourage family media ownership only as a Band-Aid solution. Media economist Robert Picard doesn't see it as a sustainable solution: "You can have all the tax breaks in the world to support family ownership, but the fact is about 80 percent of family firms never survive the second generation." Sometimes it's called the Rich Kids Syndrome. Often, too, it's just that the new generation develops other interests and priorities.

CHECKING YOUR MEDIA LITERACY

- **What is the history of family-owned media enterprises?**
- **Did mass media perform better in the era of family ownership?**
- **Should the U.S. inheritance tax be adjusted to encourage family media ownership?**

death tax
A tax on inheritances

Debate over Government Role

STUDY PREVIEW

Ideas for salvaging threatened mass media from extinction include such touchy possibilities as government ownership, which advocates say need not be as scary as it sounds. The nettlesome issue is whether he who pays the piper also calls the tune. Can government funding be separated from government influence on content or even control?

GOVERNMENT OWNERSHIP

The journalism dean at Louisiana State, Jack Hamilton, has raised the possibility of government owning the news media. Hamilton sees a parallel in parks and schools: "We know we ought to have public parks because the society needs parks. And we know that we need schools because schools are important things. Why can't we say the same for information?"

To those who worry about government controlling news and information, Hamilton advises against erecting obstacles against the idea of government ownership prematurely. First, he says, consider the reality that there is a need, whether for parks, schools or news. Then, he says, work to solutions that would allow government subsidies with buffers against government control of content.

Indeed, models exist for buffers against government intrusion into content. Government has subsidized the **British Broadcasting Corporation** since 1927. A royal charter defines BBC as a public service run by a quasi-autonomous corporation. The governing board, the BBC Trust, functions independently of private or government influence. Funding for domestic programming comes from a license fee on television sets, supplemented by advertising and selling programming to other broadcasters worldwide.

The United States, too, has buffers against government dabbling in content on subsidized noncommercial broadcasting. The U.S. record on government keeping its hands off, however, has been spotty. When Richard Nixon was president, the White House urged the U.S. equivalent of the BBC Trust, the **Corporation for Public Broadcasting,** to shift its financial support away from the national networks, like PBS and NPR, which the conservative Nixon considered liberal and unfriendly. Nixon wanted the funding to go instead to local stations that were less probing on political issues and, hence, said critics, to starve PBS and NPR. The Nixon initiative failed when the Watergate scandal subsumed the whole Nixon agenda and, finally, Nixon resigned the presidency.

Another conservative president, George W. Bush, took a different tack at trying to influence the content of noncommercial broadcasting. Bush appointed fellow conservative Kenneth Tomlinson to chair the Corporation for Public Broadcasting in 2005. Tomlinson, who was unabashed in his view that the PBS television network had "liberal bias," pushed for blatantly conservative programming until an internal investigation forced his resignation. Executives at PBS, of course, bristled at the accusation that the network's programming was anything less than detached and neutral truth-seeking. They were glad at Tomlinson's departure.

Although both the Nixon and Bush attempts to impose policy shifts on public broadcasting failed, the fact that the initiatives were launched suggests that the U.S. social and political culture is less sensitive to the public parks and schools model for mass media than the British.

CHECKING YOUR MEDIA LITERACY

- **Can parks and schools and mass media be lumped together easily in the same mold as a public good?**
- **Does government funding of mass media pose a risk of government control?**

GOVERNMENT-OPERATED MEDIA

British Broadcasting Corporation (BBC)
Government-funded radio and television system dating to 1927

Corporation for Public Broadcasting (CPB)
Quasi-government agency to channel funding into U.S. noncommercial television and radio

watchdog
Fanciful term for mass media as a monitor of government performance on behalf of citizens

Consensus seems solid in the United States that media content should be shielded from government control. It's a concept that was articulated powerfully by British philosopher John Locke in the late 1600s and by subsequent democratic political theorists. These thinkers saw government as a facilitator of people's needs and nothing more. They were fearful of government becoming too powerful and intrusive. Their concept was embodied in the U.S. Constitution when the new republic was created. The Constitution's First Amendment, ratified in 1791, acknowledged the role of the press as an independent check on government—a **watchdog** on behalf of the people against abuse of power.

Even so, the government has become a powerful generator and distributor of information. Government agencies produce reports, reviews and audits, almost all for public distribution. Every federal agency has a large public relations staff to tell the government's story the government's way. Mostly invisible are literally thousands of federal employees whose job is communications with the public. It was no accident

MEDIA TIMELINE

GOVERNMENT COMMUNICATION POLICY

1700s

Freedom of Press
First Amendment ratified, protecting media from government control (1791)

Postal Discounts
First federal communications policy with postage discounts for newspapers (1791)

John Locke: Democratic ideals

1800s

Cultural Wars
Congress gave weekly newspapers a postal break but not big-city dailies (1845)

Penny a Pound
Periodicals, books given new deep discounts on postage (1879)

Anti-Monopoly Law
Sherman Antitrust Act outlawed monopolies, price-fixing (1890)

Sara Josepha Hale's Ladies Book *benefited from subsidized postage*

1900s

Radio Law
Radio operators required to register with federal government (1912)

Broadcast Licensing
Congress tried to head off broadcast monopolies with limits on chain ownership (1927)

First Amendment
Courts decided that broad content-based licensing regulations for radio not a constitutional issue (1932)

Public Broadcasting
Congress created the agency CPB to support noncommercial broadcasting (1967)

Newspaper Preservation Act
Congress approved antitrust law exemptions for competing newspapers to merge (1970)

Internet
Congress turned Internet over to National Science Foundation for development (1983)

Broadcast Deregulation
Government eased limits on chain ownership of local over-air television, radio stations (1996)

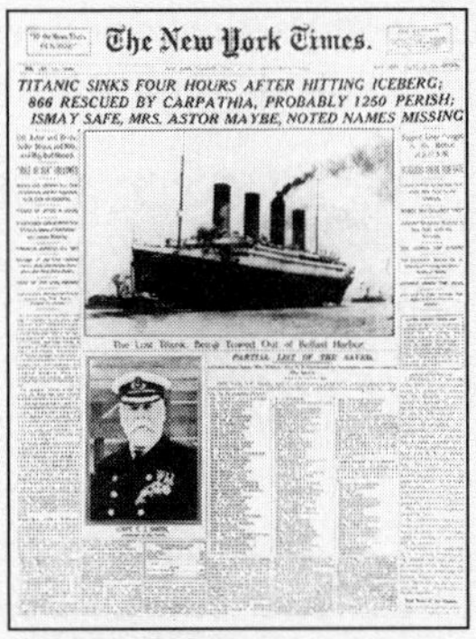
The New York Times.

TITANIC SINKS FOUR HOURS AFTER HITTING ICEBERG; 866 RESCUED BY CARPATHIA, PROBABLY 1250 PERISH; ISMAY SAFE, MRS. ASTOR MAYBE, NOTED NAMES MISSING

Sea disaster prompts government radio rules

Quack doctor denied federal radio station license

2000s

Newspaper Revitalization
Congress pondered tax breaks, other remedies to save newspaper industry (2009)

PIVOTAL EVENTS

1700s

- Revolutionary War (1776–1781)
- New U.S. republic constituted (1791)

1800s

- Books by native-born authors created an American culture (1820s on)
- Major cities in accelerating growth (1820s)
- Penny Press period (1833 on)
- Railroad linked East and West coasts (1869)
- Magazines became important national medium (1870s)
- Rapid corporate growth led to monopolies, abuses (1880s)

1900s

- Radio stations proliferated (1920s)
- Television emerged as commercial medium (early 1950s)
- Small-town depopulation (1950s on)
- Nixon presidency (1969–1974)
- Reagan presidency hastened deregulation (1981–1989)
- Internet emerged as commercial medium (1990s)

2000s

- iPod introduced, saps listeners from radio (2002)
- Newspapers, magazines in crisis with reader, advertising losses (2009)

that political scientist John Anthony Maltese chose the title *Spin Control* for his book on the White House Communications Office. Government publicists are everywhere. Even an Army company, the most basic of units, has a second lieutenant whose many hats include public information.

Until the advent of radio, most government-created mass communications were vetted through the news media. Radio, however, allowed government leaders to bypass the media as filter for the first time and talk directly to the people. This was epitomized in 1933 when the new president Franklin Roosevelt went live with the first of his "**fireside chats**" on network radio. The networks, of course, were nongovernment entities. It was the networks' choice to carry the Roosevelt addresses. Today, however, the government has full access to the Internet. Any and all government messages that are posted are unfiltered through any nongovernment intermediary. And with the demise of some traditional media filters, notably newspapers, the question is becoming whether the Constitutional assumptions of 1791 remain valid about the media as an intermediary on government-generated information. What is becoming of the traditional independent check on government? Is the watchdog asleep? Dying? And what are the implications for democracy? Who will keep the rascals honest?

A reality, like it or not, is that government itself gradually has become a major source of information in itself. Any new economic model for mass media companies, everyone agrees, needs to have built-in filters to guard against absolute government control of information about itself to the people.

fireside chats
Fanciful term for President Franklin Roosevelt's radio addresses

CHECKING YOUR MEDIA LITERACY

- **What is the watchdog function of mass media, especially news media?**
- **How has post-Gutenberg technology changed the role of the mass media as a filter of government-generated information?**

Historic Media-Government Links

STUDY PREVIEW

Critics of a government role in mass media need to acknowledge and address the fact that government policy has affected the structure and economics of U.S. mass media since the beginning of the republic. These policies have included favoring mass media over other businesses, by granting low postal rates. The structure of the U.S. broadcast industry has been shaped largely by government regulation. The U.S. newspaper industry also bears the imprint of government policy. The decline of the industry, for example, has been cushioned by government policy to preserve competitive newspapers.

POSTAL SUBSIDIES

Since the earliest days of the republic, government policy has shaped media economics.

>> Government Communication Policy. As one of its first acts, the First Congress gave periodicals a discount on postage in 1789. Newspapers could be mailed as far as 100 miles for a penny a copy and $1\frac{1}{2}$ cents beyond. It was a real deal. A newspaper could be sent 450 miles, for example, for $1\frac{1}{2}$ cents, compared to 45 cents for a three-page letter. The policy operationalized a point of Alexander Hamilton, one of the founders of the republic, about the value of newspapers. In the *Federalist Papers* essays Hamilton praised newspapers as "expeditious messengers of intelligence to the most remote inhabitants of the Union." In addition, the **1789 Postal Act** allowed editors to exchange their issues with each other postage-free. This facilitated the reprinting of news from the far reaches of the new nation and contributed to a sense of nationhood.

In a modest way, the 1789 law established a government role in the media business. The law gave an economic advantage to newspaper printers that other businesses did not have. The law's provision for free newspaper exchanges among editors was, in effect, a government subsidy for producing content, albeit only the re-publication of stories from afar.

>> **Postal Favoritism.** The 1789 law was the U.S. government's first communication policy but not the last. Congress went further in 1845 with free delivery for weeklies within 30 miles. In effect, Congress was taking sides in a growing wedge between rural areas and fast-growing cities. The goal, according to one member of Congress, was to protect small communities against "the poisoned sentiment of the cities, concentrated in their papers." By favoring small town weeklies over big-city dailies, the dominant rural faction in Congress at the time used the press as a pawn in the divisive agrarian-urban conflicts of the time. That issue from the mid-1800s remains a wedge today in the culture wars between perceived differences in rural and urban values.

The **1845 Postal Act** was controversial and was in ongoing revision and fine-tuning. One lesson, however, was clear. The government had assumed a further role in operations of the mass media, again with favorable postage rates, albeit only for outlying papers.

Under the next revision of the law, in the **1879 Postal Act,** the government subsidy of newspapers and magazines was standardized—a penny a pound for shipping. The word *subsidy* was not used, but in fact the government was using its resources to ease the cost of doing business for the press. At a token rate of a penny a pound, the nascent magazine industry boomed.

>> **Second-Class Rates.** Today postal subsidies for print media are institutionalized in **second-class postal rates.** Book and periodical publishing companies enjoy drastically reduced postal rates—but with conditions. To qualify for the subsidized delivery rate, newspapers and magazines must cap their percentage of paid advertising content at 70 percent.

Although media companies might be expected to object to almost any and all government policy affecting their content, none object to the government policy that gives them an economic advantage. Indeed, trade groups representing publishers aggressively lobby Congress for postage discounts. This is an example of media companies acting first and above all else in their economic self-interest.

1789 Postal Act
Provided government discounts for mailing newspapers

1845 Postal Act
Provided free postal delivery of weeklies

1879 Postal Act
Allowed periodicals and books to be mailed at a penny a pound

second-class postage
Discounted delivery rates for books and periodicals

CHECKING YOUR MEDIA LITERACY

- **How can government postal subsidies for the print media be justified?**
- **Has the government played favorites by giving the press advantageous postal rates?**

BROADCAST ECONOMICS

The government's biggest communication policy imprint has been on broadcasting. The government got into broadcast regulation even before there were stations.

>> **Safety and Necessity.** In 1909, 1,200 people were saved from a shipwreck because a shipboard wireless operator signaled distress messages. Impressed with the life-saving potential of the new radio technology, Congress acted quickly to require

large ships to have a radio operator. It was common-sense legislation. The wisdom of the law was underscored three years later by the *Titanic* disaster. Other common-sense legislation followed, including a requirement that stations register with the government. The idea was to enable the government to take control of the airwaves in event of a national emergency like war.

By the 1920s a commercial radio industry was taking root. Stations were seeking mass audiences so they could sell airtime to advertisers and make money. By 1927 there were 732 stations on the air in the United States but only 568 frequencies were available. In the quest to expand audiences, stations amped-up their signals to extend their range and power. The result: Stations drowned each other out with overlapping signals. The airwaves were becoming a useless cacophony. Stations formed an organization, the National Association of Broadcasters, to address the issue, but the NAB was unable to come up with a solution. Station owners then went to Congress, begging for government regulation to assign frequencies. Congress responded with the **1927 Federal Radio Act,** which created a new government agency to reduce the number of stations through licensing.

1927 Federal Radio Act
Created a government agency to license radio stations

scarcity model
Too few resources for demand

marketplace model
Supply and demand determines the enterprises that remain in business

By the time the new Federal Radio Commission set up licensing, technology had improved and there was room for 649 stations. Even so, the government had to shut down some stations to clear frequencies for others to broadcast. Also, stations were ordered to share frequencies, some broadcasting during the daytime, others only at night. Some stations were ordered to channel their signals directionally, like north-south, to avoid overlaps.

The New York Times.

TITANIC SINKS FOUR HOURS AFTER HITTING ICEBERG; 866 RESCUED BY CARPATHIA, PROBABLY 1250 PERISH; ISMAY SAFE, MRS. ASTOR MAYBE, NOTED NAMES MISSING

The Lost Titanic Being Towed Out of Belfast Harbor.

PARTIAL LIST OF THE SAVED.

CAPT. E. J. SMITH

Radio Regulation. *When* Titanic *struck an iceberg in the North Atlantic and sank in 1912, a radio operator on a nearby ship picked up the SOS. Although there already were some requirements for ships to have onboard radio operators, the* Titanic *tragedy led to more stringent regulation. This early regulation was designed for public safety but became part of the precedent for the 1927 Federal Radio Act that made broadcast a federally regulated industry through government licensing. Licensing created the economic infrastructure for the U.S. broadcasting industry.*

>> Broadcast Industry Structure. The station licensing system created in 1927 was based on a **scarcity model.** The shortage of available frequencies necessitated regulation if the young radio industry were to realize its potential for the common good of the American people. With the usual capitalistic marketplace dynamics displaced by regulation, the government became a protector of the radio industry's economic structure and, later, the structure also of the television industry. As a protector, government created a complex of policies to preserve the system it had created. In shielding the stations it licensed from marketplace dynamics, the regulatory agencies, first the FRC, then the Federal Communications Commission, became an obstacle against competition for its licensed stations. Examples:

- The FRC forbade the television cable-delivery systems from carrying lots of programming from local stations without the stations' permission. Acting out of their economic self-interest, stations rarely granted permission. The stations were fretting about losing viewers to cable systems, which offered many additional programming choices.
- For years, similarly, the FCC sided with its licensed over-air stations to prevent satellite-delivery systems from carrying local television stations.

The scarcity model became less useful for justifying tight protection of local over-air stations as technology gradually opened more frequencies for stations. Today 13,000 radio stations are on the air, many with sub-channels for additional signals. With scarcity no longer a significant issue, a traditional capitalistic **marketplace model** for broadcasting has emerged. Even so, the government still regulates frequency assignments through licensing. The government licensing system remains at the core of the shape of the U.S. broadcast industry.

CHECKING YOUR MEDIA LITERACY

- **How did the U.S. government get involved in the regulation of broadcasting?**
- **How did the 1927 Federal Radio Act shape the economics of the broadcast industry?**

Newspaper Preservation Act

1970 federal law for exception from antitrust laws for local newspapers that combine all but news-editorial operations

joint operating agreements (JOAs)

Combination under federal law of production, distribution, advertising and business operations of competing newspapers

Newspaper Revitalization Bill

Proposed law to allow newspapers to reorganize into a tax-exempt status for survival

FAVORED TAX TREATMENT

When a city loses a newspaper, loyal readers mourn the loss. Everybody bemoans that there is less journalistic competition. Always there is great hand-wringing about the implications for democracy with fewer news sources.

In 1970 after almost a decade of afternoon newspapers closing and others in imminent danger of collapse, Congress came to the rescue. The **Newspaper Preservation Act** encouraged competing local newspapers to combine their non-news operations by exempting the combinations from federal antitrust rules. Without the exemption, the joint operations could have been prosecuted as violations of anti-monopoly laws. In all, 56 newspapers created **joint operating agreements,** generally combining their advertising, production, distribution and business staffs but keeping independent news and editorial staffs. The result was to keep 26 cities as two-newspaper towns.

Alas, the law was artificial resuscitation. Gradually the weaker newspaper in the partnerships closed shop. Marketplace realities steered advertisers to the dominant paper. Eventually the artificial government-created safety net for the weaker paper was insufficient to maintain both publications. Few of the JOAs, as they are called, remain.

The same kind of concern prompted a 2009 proposal in Congress to allow newspaper companies to restructure as nonprofits, with advertising and subscription revenue being tax-exempt. The **Newspaper Revitalization Bill,** proposed by Senator Benjamin Cardin of Maryland, a Democrat, would classify newspapers as educational institutions, somewhat like public broadcasting stations. Cardin explained his proposal this way: "The business model for newspapers, based on circulation and advertising revenue, is broken, and that is a real tragedy for communities across the nation and for our democracy." Cardin said his plan would not bring any government influence in new coverage, but newspapers would be barred from their traditional role in endorsing political candidates.

Critics of the Newspaper Revitalization Act said it was time to let newspapers die a natural death.

CHECKING YOUR MEDIA LITERACY

- **Did the 1970 Newspaper Preservation Act indeed preserve newspaper competition?**
- **What are the pros and cons of the proposed Newspaper Revitalization Bill?**

New Media Funding

STUDY PREVIEW

Advertising and subscription revenue are weakening as a revenue source of mass media revenue but won't disappear entirely. What will pick up the slack? A patchwork, possibly of more government funding and charity support, seems likely. Also, media consumers themselves may pay for media access through new mechanisms.

ADVERTISING AND SUBSCRIPTIONS

New patchworks of revenue, some traditional, some not, are emerging to finance mass media. For some media, the role of advertising will diminish as advertisers find new ways on the Internet to connect directly with potential customers, rather than through traditional media. Also, subscription revenue will dry up for most periodicals. Already people are finding many of their information and other media needs can be met free on the Internet. Only a chump would pay for what can be had for nothing.

CHECKING YOUR MEDIA LITERACY

- **What is the future of advertising as a revenue stream for mass media companies?**
- **What is the future of subscription revenue for newspapers and magazines?**

NEW HYBRID MIX

In niches in the mass media, alternative funding mechanisms have been at work for decades. Every public broadcasting listener knows about on-air fund drives exhorting viewers and listeners to pony up. Until now, the legacy media ignored such alternatives. Not any more.

>> **Government Funding.** As the newspaper industry crumbled, Congress in 2009 launched hearings on what might be done. Senator John Kerry, who chaired subcommittee hearings, put the focus on newspapers even though the issue was broader: "The history of our republic is inextricably linked to the narrative of free and independent press," Kerry said. "Whatever the model for the future, we must do all we can to ensure a diverse and independent news media endures." Options included expanded government funding on the model of U.S. public television and radio.

A similar model is for state government funding. Several states already subsidize noncommercial radio. Among them are Minnesota and New Mexico, whose appropriations are essential to the budgets of state networks and stations.

Government support of media can be indirect for ostensibly unrelated reasons rather than a direct subsidy. At the behest of state newspaper associations, state legislators require counties and municipalities to designate an "official newspaper" to carry legal notices, usually called **legals.** These legals are detailed budget and other documents, usually from government agencies. The stated purpose is to provide the public with information on government policy and spending. The newspapers bill government agencies by the inch for the space these legals take, usually pages and pages annually. For some weeklies, legals are significant revenue sources. Competing papers engage in spirited bidding to win the "official" designation.

In some states, certain companies are required by law to publish periodic reports in the official local press. It's a condition of doing business, aimed mostly at out-of-state insurance companies. In effect, insurance policyholders are being taxed to subsidize local newspapers.

Similarly, the federal government requires some product manufacturers, including drug makers, to publish great detail about their product and its dangers in magazines. Too, federal and state governments buy lots of advertising time and space. Consider the Marines recruiting ads. Or, have you been exhorted recently to vacation in Arkansas?

>> **Philanthropy.** Significant gifts to support media organizations in recent years demonstrate untapped potential for philanthropy in the revenue mix for media into the future. The $200 million bequest to National Public Radio from Joan Kroc, from the McDonald's fast-food fortune, established a new mark for media **philanthropy.** Herbert Sandler, who built Golden Financial West into a mortgage giant and then sold it to the larger Wachovia banking empire, gave $10 million to create the ProPublica investigative reporting organization. Large charitable donations to media upstarts are becoming more common.

Loosely related to philanthropy is corporate .**underwriting.** Major oil companies, as an example, already underwrite costs of some programs, ostensibly from a civic-minded instinct. The supporters, however, are acknowledged on-air, which gives the companies a public association with the sponsored program. In reality, it's low-key advertising, although nobody wants to call it advertising because noncommercial stations licenses issued by the federal government forbid advertising. The term *underwriting* is used to sidestep the federal rules against advertising and yet allow on-air acknowledgments that include product descriptions.

legals

Paid advertising required by law, usually verbatim government documents

philanthropy

Generous donation for good causes

underwriting

On-air acknowledgments of non-commercial broadcast sponsors

>> **Fund Drives.** Nonprofit media organizations are not bashful about asking for gifts. Public broadcasting has made an art form of periodic fund drives. The 37-station Minnesota Public Radio Network, as an example, raises $12^1/_2$ percent of its $79 million budget from listener memberships and donations. Local public

television stations are no less successful in raising money from their viewers. WNET in New York has an annual fund-raising goal of $90 million. Many donations are less than $100 a year but an occasional $1 million or $2 million pledge comes in. Online sites have their palms out too. The Center for Public Integrity, which produces investigative journalism, asks readers for $5 a month with prestige donor recognitions for $500 or more.

>> **Micropayments.** Telephone companies mastered how to bill for tiny bits of long-distance time years ago. Its is a **micropayment** system that newspapers and magazines now are contemplating with the disintegration of their old model of a single charge for a bundle of content—like $1 a copy or a $150 a year subscription.

The unbundled model would charge per item, like 4 cents for a news story, and keep a running tab for periodic billing. The system would have efficiencies for many consumers. A sports fan with no other interests in life would not have to pay for unwanted political news or advice to lovelorns.

>> **Auxiliary Enterprises.** Rather than originating content, which is costly, many media organizations have taken to regurgitating more and more material from other sources. The diminishing quantity of original content has been widely decried, but the upside for media companies that continue to generate fresh content is that they can derive revenue from selling it for re-use. ProPublica, for example, peddles its investigative reporting to newspapers and other media companies. **Auxiliary enterprises** take many forms. PBS issues regular catalogs with DVDs of programs and spin-off products as wide-ranging as Barney dolls and program-keyed coffee mugs.

micropayment
A small sum generally billed with related charges, often on a credit card

auxiliary enterprise
A business sideline that generates revenue

CHECKING YOUR MEDIA LITERACY

- **What may emerge as important elements in funding mass media operations?**
- **What kind of revenue can be expected to dominate mass media business models in the future?**

Innovation-Triggering Patterns

STUDY PREVIEW

Media technology is the product of inventive genius, but the application of technology to create a medium that in fact reaches a mass audience is a trial-and-error process. Eventually some entrepreneur gets it right, which spawns imitators. It's an evolutionary process. Major media industries inevitably fall into a trap of their success and either fade in the face of new competition or radically reinvent themselves.

INVENTION

Invention is the first phase in a predictable pattern of mass media evolution through a cycle into maturity and, then, past prime. The origins of each mass media industry are easily identified. Everyone agrees that today's print media have roots in technology invented by Johannes Gutenberg in the 1440s. Gutenberg had no idea at the time that his movable metal type would enable the creation of massive industries in book, newspaper and magazine publishing. Newspapers? Magazines? Gutenberg could never have envisioned such things. Inventors focus mostly on their tinkering.

CHECKING YOUR MEDIA LITERACY

- **Do media innovators necessarily have a vision for their inventions?**

ENTREPRENEURSHIP

The transition from invention to commercial viability generally involves costly false starts. Consider the Internet, whose history as a business enterprise is littered with upstarts, some with big-buck financing and names that flashed into prominence and quickly dimmed. Remember General Electric's GEnie portal? Nobody else does much either. How about such other forgottens as Napster file sharing? Time Warner's Pathfinder magazine megasite?

The entrepreneurial phase of media evolution is a marriage of vision, capital and risk. Most initiatives flop. Finally, though, someone gets it right. An application of the technology finds an audience, and an industry is born.

Radio illustrates the point. Guglielmo Marconi's discovery in 1898 that messages could be carried through the air missed the potential of radio as a mass medium. His focus was on point-to-point communication modeled on the telegraph. In fact, he called his invention *radiotelegraphy*.

It was a Marconi employee, David Sarnoff, who had the vision for radio as a mass medium. In 1916 Sarnoff wrote a memo to his boss: "I have in mind a plan of development, which would make radio a 'household utility' in the same sense as the piano or phonograph. The idea is to bring music into the house by wireless. . . . The receiver can be designed in the form of a simple Radio Music Box." Sarnoff also proposed advertising to fund his vision for radio as a mass medium. The boss share didn't the young Sarnoff's enthusiasm for reinventing radio. On his other merits, however, Sarnoff rose quickly in a spinoff Marconi company, Radio Corporation of America. Then Sarnoff redefined radio as a new mass media industry under the banner of RCA subsidiary NBC.

A few inventors see commercial potential in their inventions. Thomas Edison, for example, forged his way into sound recording and movies as business enterprises. Generally, however, the entrepreneurial phase isn't dominated by inventors. It can be argued, for example, that Edison did less inventing as time went on. Instead, he left research and innovation to the people who ran his labs. George Eastman of Kodak camera was an Edison-like exception too. He also created labs where others did the later inventing under his name.

Failures in the entrepreneurial phase can be gigantic. In the 1990s, investors poured billions of dollars into Internet and other digital-medium enterprises. Most flopped. In the annals of business history, the collapse of hundreds of these companies, called the Dot-Com Bust of 2000, triggered a severe economic recession. In the ashes, though, were companies whose visions were economically viable. Steve Jobs of the resurgent Apple computer company typifies entrepreneurial success.

CHECKING YOUR MEDIA LITERACY

- **How do you respond to the maxim: "Let the inventors invent. Period"?**
- **What elements are necessary for the entrepreneurial phase to bring new media technology into a successful business enterprise?**
- **How does Guglielmo Marconi illustrate a failure at outside-the-box thinking about radio?**

AN INDUSTRY

Success breeds imitators. In radio, NBC was followed by CBS, then ABC. Television took the same course. As soon as one book publisher in the 1800s began a magazine to promote its books, others soon followed. There was *Harper's, Scribner's, Collier's.* Adolph Zukor created a new model for movie-making with his Paramount in 1912. So quickly did others follow that Hollywood became known for the studio system. Even within an industry, imitation is inevitable. *Time* was a significant innovation in 1923. Then came *Newsweek* and *U.S. News.*

MEDIA PEOPLE

Visionary: The Mac for Starters

Out of a garage **Steve Jobs** and a buddy built an over-the-top desktop computer. The machine became the foundation for Apple Computer. No wonder, when a lot of people think of Jobs, they think computer. Think again. Jobs has emerged as the tech visionary at the critical juncture of the media and technical industries. It was Jobs whose iPod products, including iStore, gave the floundering recorded music industry a new lease for survival. Jobs gave people reason again to pay for things that the Internet was providing for free. For the movie and television industry, the iPod also headed off the kind of disaster that had portended doom for the music industry.

The question now is whether Jobs' latest innovation, **iTouch**, introduced in 2008, might save the threatened print industries.

Even if iTouch doesn't live up to expectations, Jobs has cemented his place in business, technology and mass media history. He has been likened to Thomas Edison for building and sustaining a great corporate empire bearing an unmistakable personal stamp.

Graphical Interface. The first user-friendly computer was the **Macintosh**, introduced by Apple in 1984. The Mac, as fans affectionately called it, allowed people to control the computer with visual indicators, like icons, rather than arcane text commands and labels. The controlling innovation, called a **graphical user interface**, made the Mac the first commercially successful small computer.

Soon the Apple brand became personified in Jobs.

iPod. In 2002 Jobs introduced the **iPod** portable music device, which saved the music industry. The iPod was so nifty that people were willing to pay 99 cents a song at Apple's online **iStore** to download music. Almost overnight Apple became the world's largest music retailer. The numbers were staggering: In the first six years of the iPod, Apple sold 6 billion songs to 75 million people.

The device morphed into the video iPod in 2005. The first version could take 150 hours in video downloads from the Internet.

Meanwhile, Jobs had acquired Pixar Animation Studios, known for the blockbuster movies *Toy Story* and *Finding Nemo*. Jobs then sold Pixar to Disney for an incredible $7.4 billion. The deal made Jobs the largest Disney shareholder. That put Jobs on the Disney board of directors. With Disney and the ABC television network as corporate siblings, Jobs pushed for ABC content to be made available for Apple's video iPod. Negotiations took only three days, unbelievably fast by usual business standards. Mickey Mouse and Goofy features from Disney archives immediately were available on video iPods at $1.99. So were episodes from ABC's *Desperate Housewives* and *Lost*.

iPhone. With the **iPhone** in 2007, Apple entered the cellular telephone business—a johnny-come-lately, to be sure, but with a Jobs twist. The iPhone stood apart with a multi-purpose touchscreen face and iPod and Internet capabilities. Nobody had seen anything like it. Plus 10,000 free and cheap applications were available.

iTouch. The iPod, already the core for the iStore and iPhone enterprises, became the core for yet another Jobs creation in 2008. The iTouch device, with a nine-inch screen, was hailed as a savior for the traditional ink-on-paper industries because it was both portable and easy to read. Might Jobs do for books, newspapers and magazines what the iPod and its variations had done for the music, movie and television industries? In all of Apple's innovations was a theme that drew fans to the brand—easy-to-use elegance and stunning design.

Jobs returned in 2009, but the question became whether Apple was indeed a one-man show. Or did Jobs have a team in place not only to exploit the technological and market potential of iTouch but to keep Apple in the crucible of media and technology into the future?

WHAT DO YOU THINK?

- What common characteristics have there been in Apple products from the Mac through iTouch?
- Steve Jobs has been likened to Thomas Edison and Henry Ford as a technology innovator with a great sense not only of technology but also of business and marketing. How would you rank Edison, Ford and Jobs?

Tech Visionary. *Steve Jobs is a brilliant innovator who also built and sustained a great corporate empire. The question now, with Jobs' health in doubt, is whether Jobs' Apple media empire can survive without him. Will iTouch be an encore?*

Newspaper Row. *At their peak, sharing the media stage only with the book and magazine industries, newspapers built giant architectural monuments for their headquarters. In 1906 the* World, Tribune *and* Times *buildings dwarfed City Hall.*

Although competitors, successful upstarts and their imitators together come to comprise a rising industry. This has been the pattern in all of the enterprises rooted in media technology. The first attempts at radio stations in the 1910s hardly comprised an industry, but by the 1920s with a few hundred stations on the air, clearly an identifiable new business segment was functioning. This earlier was true with books, newspapers and magazines. At some point a critical mass of sound recording companies were a recognizable industry. The same with Hollywood. Later came television.

Within an industry, consolidation almost always occurs over time. Situations evolve that encourage competing companies to merge. Or blatant expansion can lead to buyouts. The result, played out in industries within the mass media and beyond, is an **oligopoly,** in which a few companies dominate an industry. Consider the monikers the *Big Four* in the recording industry, the *Big Six* in movies, *Big Four* in network television, the *Big Five* in trade book publishing.

Oligopolies fall short of **monopolies,** in which one company dominates production and distribution nationally or locally. In the United States, where there is a cultural preference for competition, monopolies have been illegal since 1890. Despite the cultural predilection, public policy has allowed consolidations into oligopolies. President Bill Clinton made the point that corporate bigness was essential for the United States to compete globally with international giants. Indeed, the largest media players are global, many based abroad.

Consider the recorded music industry, ranked by U.S. market share:

Universal (France)	MCA, Interscope, Geffen	27%
BMG-Sony (Germany-Japan)	Arista, BMG, Columbia, Epic, RCA	30%
Warner (United States)	Atlantic, Elektra	15%
EMI (Britain-Netherlands)	Capitol, Virgin	10%

Or trade book publishing:

Pearson (England)	Penguin	40%
Viacom (United States)	Simon & Schuster	21%
Bertelsmann (Germany)	Random House	21%
News Corp. (United States)	HarperCollins	12%

Today everyone recognizes that something is coming together with technological roots in digitization, but the outline of a new industry is still too blurry for a firm label. Attempts include the *software* industry, the *new media* industry, the *Internet* industry. Maybe what's happening will shake out into several distinctive industries. Or maybe we'll devise a new umbrella term drawn from what they all have in common. Stay tuned. These are exciting times to watch a new media industry, or perhaps industries, in formative stages.

The fact, though, is that consolidation is occurring, sometimes in bits and spurts, always unevenly. The proposed Yahoo!-Microsoft merger in 2008 fell apart but illustrates that an urge to merge is instinctive at the industry stage of the business maturation cycle. Consider all the consolidated corporate names—Time Life AOL, BMG-Sony, NBC-Universal. And also the myriad of contrived corporate

Steve Jobs
Cofounder of Apple Computer; became media, technological visionary

iTouch
Portable screen that displays book-like images

Macintosh
First commercially successful small computer to use graphical user interface; Apple product

graphical user interface
On-screen icons and visual indicators to instruct a computer

iPod
Portable player for downloaded music; Apple product

iStore
Apple retailer of music and other downloads

iPhone
Apple cellular phone with Internet capabilities, touch display

oligopoly
An industry in which a few companies dominate production, distribution

monopoly
Single company dominates production, distribution in an industry, either nationally or locally

names that camouflage a rich history of predecessor companies—Comcast, Cumulus, Entercom, Viacom.

CHECKING YOUR MEDIA LITERACY

- **At what point can it be stated for certain that a new media industry has come into existence?**
- **What is the difference between a company and an industry?**
- **Can you make a case that your local newspaper has a monopoly? How might the newspaper publisher respond that the newspaper is without competition?**

MATURATION

One mark in the evolution of media companies into something bigger than individual entities is the recognition of common issues that need to be addressed collectively. This point is when **trade groups** are formed. Some of the most powerful U.S. trade groups represent media industries, almost all with headquarters in Washington to influence government policies to their advantage.

trade groups
An organization created by related endeavors, sometimes competitors, to pursue mutual goals

Andy Grove
theorist on gentrification in industries

The Motion Picture Association of America, as an example, has entrenched itself in Washington policymaking. The association's long-time director, Jack Valenti, coupled his connections in the Lyndon Johnson White House in the 1960s with parading Hollywood stars in and out of Capitol offices to give MPAA the entree it needed in Washington policy circles. When Congress was grumbling about sex and violence in movies, Valenti headed off regulation by creating parental-advisory ratings. Although tweaked over time, Valenti's 1968 code remains an obstacle 40 years later against would-be censors. The MPAA was pleased to pay Valenti $1 million a year for his lobbying. At one point in Valenti's career, no other lobbyist earned more.

When Valenti retired in 2004 he was succeeded by Dan Glickman, a well-connected former member of Congress. Glickman, like Valenti, lines up Hollywood stars, which adds flash to Congressional hearings. He also brings stars to political events. Being on a first-name basis with Congressional leadership helps blunt political pressure on the movie industry. Also it gives Hollywood ears in important places on copyright and other issues affecting the industry's finances.

Trade groups, also, sponsor research, much of it on technology, to benefit their members. This includes developing industry-wide technical specifications. These include:

- A single standard for television transmission to avoid incompatible systems.
- Common newspaper column widths and page sizes so advertisers don't have confusing, multiple dimensions to sort through.
- Standard dimensions for magazines, which facilitates newsrack display.

Andy Grove. *Business leaders in aging industries fall into familiar patterns, including denial, according to former executive Andy Grove of giant computer-chip manufacturer Intel. By the time reality sets in, Grove says, it's too late. His advice to industries past their maturity, like newspapers: Heroic life-resuscitating efforts are futile. Accept the inevitable.*

CHECKING YOUR MEDIA LITERACY

- **Why do competing mass media companies join their rivals to form trade groups?**

DEFENDING INFRASTRUCTURES

Once solidly established, mass media industries risk complacency, gentrification and failure. **Andy Grove,** the fabled leader of computer-chip manufacturer Intel, later a scholar on business strategy at Stanford University, says that the final stages of an aging industry follow a predictable three-stage course.

>> **Ignore New Challenges.** Complacent in their companies' long-term rise and success, executives first minimize threats from cross-industry innovations. In short, they just don't get it. We see Grove's point over and over. The recording industry,

Media Trade Groups

The Motion Picture Association of America has a history of effectiveness in promoting the industry through lobbying, advertising, education, political donations and other public relations activities. Like other trade groups, MPAA works at collaboration by member companies for technical standards, sponsoring conferences on industry issues, and creating career-networking opportunities with other influential U.S. media trade groups and their major activities

- **Association of American Publishers.** Protects copyright owners against piracy, particularly bootleg foreign reproduction for black-market sales.
- **American Magazines Publishers Association.** Maintains discount mailing privileges for periodicals.
- **Recording Industry Association of America.** Curbs authorized downloads of music.
- **National Association of Broadcasters.** Protects over-air local station owners from competition from cable and direct-to-consumer satellite services.

Star Power. *Jack Valenti's long reign in effective lobbying for the Motion Picture Association of America on public policy included trotting out Hollywood stars and bigwigs. Members of Congress loved the photo opportunities with glamorous people, here actress Sophia Loren with Valenti.*

slavishly committed to its traditional distribution channels, turned a blind eye to Internet technology for music downloading. Similarly, the newspaper industry, after riding high for 140 years, deluded itself about slippages in readership until, wham, advertising as the industry's economic foundation began a free-fall plummet in 2001.

>> Resist Change. When crisis can no longer be dismissed, Grove says, industry executives move into a resistance mode. This can involve consolidations to find economies. Usually these mergers and acquisitions are heralded as steps toward a stronger future. That, says Grove, is delusional. The reality is that the disparate deal-making is merely staving off the inevitable.

Resistance can take other forms, like enlisting Congress and government agencies to adjust public policy to protect existing media infrastructures. The traditional television industry, based on locally licensed stations, has spent almost 30 years pressing the federal government to impede the natural growth of cable and satellite delivery alternatives. In the end, however, the customer appeal of cable and satellite reception eroded the lobbying effectiveness of local stations' trade groups and lobbyists.

>> **Radical Reforms.** Usually too late, an ailing industry launches heroic but doomed reforms for survival. How, for example, can local radio stations that have built themselves as music sources compete with iPods? Can daily newspapers ever again claim a monopoly as a news medium? Drastic overhauls and reinventions may work in some cases, but Grove is dubious: "Your doctor says you are going to die, but if you don't smoke you'll live a little longer."

CHECKING YOUR MEDIA LITERACY

- **What are the stages in an industry's decline, as Andy Grove sees them?**
- **Do you see Grove's three-stage pattern in your own experience? In what you are learning in this textbook and your mass media course?**

CHAPTER WRAP-UP

Financial Foundations (Pages 54–55)

- Mass media fit well into the profit-driven capitalistic system until two major revenue streams began drying up. Advertising revenue has fallen dramatically, dooming most daily newspapers and many magazines. The broadcast industry also faces new challenges with declines in advertising. A second significant U.S. media revenue source historically has been sales. This revenue too has declined for companies that have been losing audience. Might there be lessons from how other countries finance their media? Or from the experience-of-niche players in the U.S. media landscape?

Ownership Structures (Pages 55–58)

- The structure of the mass media in the United States has followed a common business pattern. Most companies began with a hard-working entrepreneur, often a visionary whose media products bore a personal, sometimes quirky imprint. Ownership then moved into chains or conglomerates. In general, the result was a blander product with the corporate imperative being to enhance profits and less on distinctive products to serve the commonweal. The chain and conglomerate structure hit rough sledding in some media industries, especially newspapers and magazines, when profits vaporized in the early 2000s. No longer financially viable, some chains broke up. Others were auctioned off, then broken up by new owners. It is unclear what new ownership structures will emerge from current uncertainties.

New Media Models (Pages 59–64)

- Tremendous energy is going into rethinking how the mass media need to be restructured to survive economically. The first to be hit hard in the Internet Age was the recorded music industry. After significant downsizing and painful adjustments, an equilibrium has been found for the radio industry to, it seems, sustain itself. More radical changes may be necessary for the dying newspaper industry and magazines. Brainstorming is as far-ranging as heavier government funding, as foundations taking on publications as charity cases, and as positing universities as newsgathering institutions. Nobody has come up with a panacea.

Debate over Government Role (Pages 64–67)

- An ideal of government-press separation dates at least to democratic political philosopher John Locke in the late 1600s and still has many followers. Democracies have found ways, however, to channel public funding into the media to serve the common good—while avoiding government control. The British Broadcasting Corporation has functioned well since 1927. A U.S. variation on the British approach has a rocky record but generally has worked well. If government is to have a greater role in supporting the mass media financially, the challenge is to assure that the media retain the ability to be a watchdog on government for the people.

Historic Media-Government Links (Pages 67–70)

- Lessons about government involvement in media economics can be learned from a long record of government communication policies. The record began when the first Congress agreed to subsidize newspapers with postal discounts. Although revised from time to time, the government break for media use of government services remains in effect. The structure of the U.S. broadcast industry has been shaped largely by government regulation since the 1920s. The decline of the U.S. newspaper industry has been cushioned for 40 years by government policy to preserve competitive newspapers.

New Media Funding (Pages 70–72)

- Losses in the twin traditional sources of U.S. mass media income—advertising and subscription revenue—have been substantial. One new model is for products like newspapers to give up their bundled content. The bundling concept, going back to the 1830s, was to create an affordable package with something for everyone. That model now is failing. One proposal is charging the audience by the item—a micropayment, perhaps just pennies for, as an example, a sports story. Customers pay a monthly bill for content they choose. Such a system already works in pay-per-view television and iPod downloads. More government funding and charity support is a possibility in a new patchwork of media revenue streams.

Innovation-Triggering Patterns (Pages 72–77)

- Some mass media are in a mature stage of their development. After a history dating to the 1830s, the daily newspaper industry probably is on its last legs, eclipsed by technology and unable to re-invent itself in time to save itself. These patterns of business are predictable, with industries moving through phases of innovation, entrepreneurship and maturation. The process is evolutionary. Major media industries are not exempt from the process and inevitably fall into a trap of their success and either fade in the face of new competition or radically reinvent themselves.

▼ Review Questions

1. How have mass media fit historically into the capitalist economic system?
2. How has media ownership changed in the United States through history?
3. Describe alternative business models for new revenue streams for mass media.
4. What different roles might government assume in the economics of the mass media?
5. What alternatives to historic mass media business models are being talked about? What are the upsides and downsides of each?
6. How is PPV an alternative concept to the newspaper as a bundled product?
7. Apply the maturation business model to newspapers, television and other media industries.

Concepts

conglomeration (Page 56)
cooperative (Page 60)
marketplace model (Page 70)
philanthropy (Page 72)
watchdog (Page 65)

Terms

Associated Press (Page 60)
micropayment (Page 72)
oliogopoly (Page 75)
Postal Acts of 1789, 1845, 1879 (Page 68)
underwriting (Page 71)

People

Andy Grove (Page 76)
Frank Gannett (Page 56)
Mary Baker Eddy (Page 59)
Rupert Murdoch (Page 54)
Steve Jobs (Page 74)

Media Sources

- Robert Burgelman, Andrew Grove and Philip Meza. *Strategic Dynamics: Concepts and Cases*. McGraw-Hill/Irwin, 2005.
- Kara Swisher. *There Must Be a Pony in Here Somewhere*. Crown, 2003. Swisher, a *Wall Street Journal* reporter, chronicles the giddy incorporation of AOL into Time Warner through the disenchantment that led to purging AOL from the corporate name in 2003.
- Benjamin M. Compaine and Douglas Gomery. *Who Owns the Media? Competition and Concentration in the Mass Media Industry*, third edition. Erlbaum, 2000. The authors update the 1979 and 1992 editions with details on further concentration, more attention to the cable and home video business and discussion of the effect of technological convergence.
- Ben Bagdikian. *The Media Monopoly*, fifth edition. Beacon, 1997. Bagdikian, perhaps the best-known critic of media conglomeration, includes data on the digital revolution in this update of his classic work.

MEDIA ECONOMICS

In this chapter you have deepened your media literacy by visiting several themes. Here are highlights from this chapter.

MEDIA ECONOMICS

THE CHRISTIAN SCIENCE MONITOR

Why are Germans buying so many cars?

Beyond bailouts: reforms ahead

The New Monitor

U.S. FORCES MAY NOT LEAVE KEY IRAQI CITIES

WHAT MAKES A TEACHER GOOD?

US workers migrate overseas

No More. Declining readership and advertising is sending dailies online Olympics?

The mass media are part of a capitalistic economic system in the United States, dependent almost entirely on finding consumers willing to buy media products. If no one wants to see a movie, the studio behind it will be in big trouble, maybe flop. It is the same for book publishers and music marketers that invest in new products. For some media, a more complex revenue steam is from advertising. Companies pay newspaper, magazines, radio, television and online companies for space and time for advertisements. In effect, advertisers are buying access through mass media to reach potential customers. (Pages 54–55)

MEDIA TECHNOLOGY

New York, 1906. Plants of huge media companies dominated sections in some cities.

Technology and advances, some incremental, some incredibly transforming, vastly increased the reach of mass media to larger audiences and created giant industries beginning in the 1800s. Since then, media companies, ranging from local newspapers to national magazines and broadcast networks, became major employers and significant components in the economy. Not unusual was for media companies in their heyday to hire leading architects to design production and other facilities as showcases. Some dwarfed other institutions, including schools, churches, banks and city halls. (Pages 73–75)

MEDIA AND DEMOCRACY

John Locke. Government hands off the press.

The concept that mass media must be independent from government for democracy to work is being rethought. Why? Because newspapers, magazines, radio and television today are vulnerable with advertising diminishing as their financial engine. The concept of media independence from government is mythical at least to some extent. Government policy from the earliest days of the nation has favored mass media in ways both small and significant. History has numerous models for using tax-generated government policy and revenue to maintain mass media as we know them. These models include the BBC broadcast empire in Britain and the public broadcasting infrastructure in the United States. (Pages 64–70)

AUDIENCE FRAGMENTATION

Steve Jobs. Audience demassification may be at its ultimate with wireless delivery of digitized messages.

The economic dislocations that are reshaping mass media are due largely to continuing shifts in audience habits and preferences. Every moment that someone spends on a web site is a minute less that could be spent with a book, for example, or a magazine. Modern life also has other alternatives for people. Do the math: Nobody has more than 24/7 available. People have unprecedented choices on how to spend their time. Consider television alone: Fifty years ago, three U.S. television networks dominated the nation's television programming. Today there are dozens and dozens of networks that gear programming to narrow audience segments. This kind of audience fragmentation is rewriting the economics of mass media industries. (Pages 55–58)

MEDIA TOMORROW

Special Interets. A bigger role for moveon.org and others?

Experts are looking deep into their crystal balls to see how mass media will emerge from current turbulent times. A core question: What, if anything, can replace advertising as the revenue stream that created the newspaper, magazine, radio and television industries? Might these industries soon be toast? Or might advertisers rediscover these media and fuel their revival. Other options? Being explored is media consumers somehow being weaned from their historically advertising-subsidized media into picking up the freight themselves. A possibility is the pay-per-view model in television, consumers making micro-payments, billed monthly, for each and every media item they choose. Consumers would pay not for a magazine but for access to an article, not for a newscast but for coverage of an event, not for an encyclopedia but for a reference item. Other revenue sources could be philanthropic grants, community foundations, universities, fund drives and government. (Pages 59–64)

MEDIA AND CULTURE

Jack Valenti. Media shape public policy through self-serving lobbying.

The shift from individual and family ownership of mass media has been consistent with the move to a corporate-created culture. A pattern for financially successful media companies has been to acquire other media companies. This trend is the result of inheritance taxes that make it almost impossible for heirs of media companies to keep them. The heirs have no choice but to sell the inheritance to pay the taxes. What happens goes by many terms, among them chain ownership and conglomeration. One result has been the rise of diverse shareholders controlling media companies. The primary focus of these shareholders is on improving profits. Often profitability has trumped community service, investigative journalism, cultural enrichment as values to which media can contribute. (Pages 55–58)

chapter 4

INK ON PAPER

Wikipedia Founder

Only a few employees led by Jimmy Wales keep Wikipedia humming. The entries, almost all from volunteers, are growing to many multiples of those in traditional encyclopedias.

LEARNING AHEAD

- Newspapers discovered a mass audience in 1830s and 1840s.
- The demise of the newspaper industry leaves a void in democratic function and changes culture.
- The magazine industry is also in difficult transition.
- Magazines have a history of innovations, including long-form journalism.
- Major segments of the book industry are likely to make the transition to a paperless media future.
- Reference book publishers are vulnerable to online competition.
- The future of the book industry hinges on young readers, the fate of blockbuster strategies, and retailing changes.

THE WIKIPEDIA BREAKTHROUGH

Sometime in the 1960s Jimmy Wales' folks bought a *World Book Encyclopedia* set from a door-to-door salesman. Jimmy became hooked on information. In college he became committed to the notion that people can best acquire wisdom by pooling what they know. He calls himself "an Enlightenment kind of guy."

Wales put his idea on the web in 2000 with an ambitious project for an online reference book. Nupedia, he called it. Like dozens of other encyclopedias before, all in printed form, Nupedia solicited experts to write articles, ran the articles by a review panel, and then posted them. Things went slowly. A year later, Nupedia had only 21 entries.

Then, secondhand from an assistant, **Jimmy Wales** heard about a simple software tool called *wiki*. The software enabled several people to collaborate on writing and editing. Why not thousands? Millions? By 2001 Wales had modified Nupedia to accept online contributions directly from, well, anyone—with anyone able to edit entries online and do so instantly. It was a process called open editing. An e-notice went out to 2,000 people on Nupedia's mailing list: "Wikipedia is up! Humor me. Go there and add a little article. It will take all of five or 10 minutes."

Five years later **Wikipedia,** as the project was renamed, carried 1 million articles, compared to 120,000 in *Encyclopaedia Britannica*, the printed encyclopedia against which all others are judged. Being on the web, Wikipedia has no physical limit on its size. The site has become the 17th-most visited on the Internet. There are 14,000 hits per second.

In many ways, Wikipedia represents much of the free-for-all that is the web. Among Wikipedia's few rules are these: First, articles must be from a neutral point of view. Second, content must be verifiable and previously published. Contributors must be anonymous.

Despite these rules, nonsense does get posted. Too, there are vandals who take perverse joy in messing up entries. Wales has robots that roam entries for disruptive submissions. When accuracy is an issue, administrators make judgment calls. When contributors differ on facts, Wales runs the facts by a mediation committee and an arbitration committee.

How accurate is Wikipedia? Stories are legion about members of Congress cleaning up entries posted about them. Voting records have been tampered with in self-serving ways. Some members of Congress modified entries about themselves in 2006 to distance themselves from President Bush when his popularity plummeted. Wikipedia, which tracks all changes, restored the distorted entries, although that took time. On several occasions every member of Congress has been barred from posting changes while Wikipedia administrators sorted out the facts and the truth.

A survey by the journal *Nature* in 2005 tested 43 entries in Wikipedia and in the *Encyclopaedia Britannica* and found both amazingly accurate. Wikipedia did, however, have four errors for every three in *Britannica*, but errors were rare both places.

Whatever the pros and cons of Wikipedia, it represents the techno-driven environment in which printed media, whether the book, the newspaper or the magazine industry, will survive or fail. For many companies solidly wedded to ink-on-paper technologies, the prospects are not good. A media revolution is in progress.

Newspaper Industry

STUDY ***PREVIEW***

The U.S. newspaper industry took form in the 1830s and dominated mass media for more than 160 years. The infrastructure of the industry, dependent on advertising, has entered a meltdown. Audiences have shifted elsewhere, largely to the Internet, for news and other content that newspapers historically had bundled successfully.

DISCOVERY OF MASS AUDIENCES

Jimmy Wales
Founder of Wikipedia

Wikipedia
User created and edited online encyclopedia

Benjamin Day
Published the New York *Sun*

Newspapers in the United States date to the first century of colonial times. These early papers were weeklies. Most were a sideline of printers struggling to make a living. The content largely was a hodge-podge of whatever a printer fancied or had handy to fill space. There were no reporting staffs. The concept of a newspaper as a comprehensive package of the day's events had yet to take form.

With new technology beginning in the 1840s, notably steam-power presses, the daily newspaper industry took form. A struggling New York printer, 22-year-old **Benjamin Day,** launched a penny-a-copy paper in 1833 that became an instant success. At a penny, the *Sun* was within reach of just about everybody. Other papers were expensive, an annual subscription costing as much as a full week's wages. Unlike other papers, which were distributed mostly by mail, the *Sun* was hawked every day on the streets. The *Sun*'s content was different too. It avoided the political and economic thrust of the traditional papers, concentrating instead on items of interest to common folk. The writing was simple, straightforward and easy to follow. For a motto for the *Sun*, Day came up with "It Shines for All," his pun fully intended. Day's *Sun* was an immediate success. Naturally, it was quickly imitated. The mainstream of American newspapers came to be in the mold of the *Sun*.

Merchants saw the unprecedented circulation of the **penny papers** as a way to reach great numbers of potential customers. Advertising revenue meant bigger papers, which attracted more readers, which attracted more advertisers. A snowballing momentum continued, with more and more advertising being carried by the mass media. A significant result was a shift in newspaper revenues from subscriptions to advertisers. As a matter of fact, Day did not meet expenses by selling the *Sun* for a penny a copy. He counted on advertisers to pick up a good part of his production cost. In effect, advertisers subsidized readers, just as they do today.

Several social and economic factors, all resulting from the Industrial Revolution, made the penny press possible:

- **Industrialization.** With new steam-powered presses, hundreds of copies an hour could be printed. Earlier presses had been hand operated.
- **Urbanization.** Workers flocked to the cities to work in new factories, creating a great pool of potential newspaper readers within delivery range. Until the urbanization of the 1820s and 1830s, the U.S. population had been almost wholly agricultural and scattered across the countryside.
- **Immigration.** Waves of immigrants arrived from impoverished parts of Europe. Most were eager to learn English and found that penny papers were good tutors with their simple style.
- **Literacy.** Also, literacy in general was increasing, which contributed to the rise of mass-circulation newspapers and magazines.

CHECKING YOUR MEDIA LITERACY

- **Can it be said that Ben Day discovered mass audiences?**
- **What cultural changes made the penny press possible?**
- **How did penny papers fuel cultural change?**

NEWSPAPER BUSINESS MODEL

The success of Day's New York *Sun* spawned imitators. Newspaper readership exploded exponentially within a few years. Newspapers became complex enterprises, following an emerging infrastructure model of industrialization with a division of labor. The era of the jack-of-all-trades printshop operator was over. In the new **business model,** newspapers had creative staffs that specialized in designing and creating the product. This creative core was mostly editors and writers in the newsroom and reporters in the field. Other staff specialized in production, including operation of complicated and sophisticated new presses. Another staff specialized in selling space to advertisers.

These were the typical divisions of labor at a newspaper:

- **News/editorial:** Headed by an editor, usually with a staff of assistants, news/editorial departments produced content. At its peak, the New York *Times* had one of the largest news/editorial staffs, about 1,200 reporters and editors.
- **Production:** Typesetters and other technicians performed the mechanical assembly of the product. The presses, gigantic machines whose complexities rivaled that of anything else in the Industrial Age, required separate staffs to operate and maintain.
- **Advertising:** The huge expenses of news/editorial and production functions were underwritten mostly by revenue from advertisers, which were willing to buy space to reach a newspaper's audience with their spiels.

penny papers
Affordable newspapers introduced in 1833 created Inprecedented mass audience

business model
A design operating a business, identifying revenue sources, customer base, products, financing

- **Circulation:** A separate department worked at building readership in order to attract advertising and also to distribute the product.
- **Business:** The immensity of a newspaper's operations required bookkeepers, accountants, lawyers and other standard business apparatus.

With modest refinements, the structure remained viable about 160 years.

MEDIA DOMINANCE

The long-running dominance of newspapers among mass media was built on a model of bundling news, information and entertainment in an accessible package. For a penny a copy, later a nickel, then a quarter, nothing provided the package of essentials like news and diversions like sports and comics, not to mention horoscopes, advice for the lovelorn and even serialized light fiction. The other print media, books and magazines, had niches but never approached the financial might of the newspaper industry.

>> **Newspaper Influence.** Newspapers were influential in the lives of generations of readers. What was reported was what people talked about. What wasn't reported generally didn't have alternate avenues into public dialogue.

Less clear is whether newspapers could dictate public opinion. Conventional wisdom was that support from a newspaper editorial was essential for political candidates. The conventional wisdom came into doubt in the 1930s and 1940s when a majority of newspapers wrote editorials supporting Republican candidates for the presidency, but the Democrat Franklin Roosevelt won four elections in a row by landslides. Of course, no candidate would spurn an editorial endorsement, but the maxim that newspapers could deliver elections was flawed. Still, a campaign ritual is for candidates to call on the editorial boards at newspapers to explain their positions, take questions and curry support.

>> **Newspaper Chains. Benjamin Franklin** was the first printer to get rich from owning a newspaper. By age 25, he was wealthy with his *Pennsylvania Gazette*. With his typical pragmatism, Franklin reasoned that if he could make money with one newspaper, he could make more money with more. Franklin financed former apprentices to start newspapers elsewhere in the colonies, which made him the first **chain newspaper** owner. He set up printers in Antigua, New York, Rhode Island and South Carolina. The former apprentices shared the profits with Franklin as their grubstake investor.

Franklin's chain was a piker compared to what came later. By the late 1800s, with newspapers in their heyday, publishers like William Randolph Hearst had multiple metropolitan dailies that created some of the largest personal fortunes in the nation. The phenomenon of chain ownership hit a new stride in the 1970s. Newspapers' profitability was skyrocketing, which prompted chains to buy up locally owned newspapers, sometimes in bidding frenzies. Chains bought up other chains. From 1983 to 1988 eight newspaper companies tracked by the business magazine *Forbes* earned the equivalent to 23.9 percent interest on a bank account. Only soft-drink companies did better.

The U.S. newspaper industry became concentrated in fewer and fewer companies in the late 1900s. At one point, four of five U.S. newspapers were in absentee ownership. The largest of the chains, Gannett, owned almost 100 dailies and corporate policies emanated from the company's skyscraper headquarters overlooking the Potomac. The Los Angeles *Times* may have looked local with *Los Angeles* prominent atop the front page, but business strategy and practices were dictated from chain bosses at the Tribune Company in Chicago.

The new industry mavens, in the corporate offices of the chains, rewrote the book on running newspapers. The new orientation was geared to the bottom line. Quality journalism became not a value for its own sake but merely a vehicle for sustaining and pushing profits. Despite a facade of language about an ongoing commitment to public service, the chains—indeed, most of the industry—were myopically focused on the bottom line and saw journalistic content as a burdensome cost center.

Benjamin Franklin
In U.S. colonial era, he created first newspaper chain

chain newspaper
Owned by a company that owns other newspapers elsewhere

New York *Times*

Although buffeted financially as part of the beleaguered U.S. newspaper industry, the New York *Times* remains the standard-bearer of journalistic excellence. Even critics of the *Times* are hard-pressed to name a better newspaper.

A Paper of Record. Since its founding in 1851, the *Times* has had a reputation for fair and thorough coverage of foreign news. It is a newspaper of record, for decades printing the president's annual State of the Union address and other important documents in their entirety. The *Times* is an important research source, in part because the *Times* puts out a monthly and an annual index that lists every story. More than 150 years of the *Times* pages are available online in many libraries. In an attempt to attract younger readers, the *Times* has followed the lead of other newspapers by adding some lighter fare to the serious coverage. In 2005 a Thursday style section was launched that includes more lifestyle-oriented advertising. The *Times* even added a 10-page "Funny Pages" section at the front of the glitzy Sunday *Magazine* that includes work by graphic artists, serialized genre fiction and a venue for humor writers called "True-Life Tales." The serious book review section and one of the world's most popular crossword puzzles remain.

***Times* Heritage.** The New York *Times'* journalistic reputation was cemented in the 1870s when courageous reporting brought down the city government.

- **Tweed Scandal.** City Council member **William Tweed** had built a fortune with fraudulent streetcar franchises, sales of nonexistent buildings to the city and double billing. In 1868 Tweed and like-minded crooks and scoundrels were swept into city offices in a landslide election, and the fraud grew like a spiderweb. The *Times* launched an exposé in 1870, which prompted Tweed to press the *Times'* largest advertisers to withdraw their advertising. Neither the management of the *Times* nor the main reporter on the story, **George Jones**, was deterred. With documents leaked from a disgruntled city employee, the *Times* reported that the Tweed Gang had robbed the city of as much as $200 million. Desperate, Tweed sent an underling to offer Jones $5 million in hush money—a bribe to back off. Jones refused and sent the underling packing.
- **Sullivan Libel Case.** In 1960, in the heat of the U.S. racial desegregation tensions, the Montgomery, Alabama, police commissioner, was incensed at criticism in an advertisement in the New York *Times* that promoted racial integration. He sued for libel and won in Alabama courts. The *Times* chose an expensive appeal to the U.S. Supreme Court to prove a First Amendment principle about free expression. The **Sullivan decision** came in 1964, establishing new rules on libel and untethering the U.S. news media in reporting public issues.
- **Pentagon Papers.** After being leaked a copy of a secret government study on U.S. policy in the Vietnam war, the *Times* conducted an exhaustive examination of the documents and decided to run a series of articles based on them. The government ordered the *Times* to halt the series, creating a showdown between the free press and the secretive Nixon administration. Not to be intimidated, the *Times* took the so-called **Pentagon Papers** case to the U.S. Supreme Court, arguing that the people in a democracy need information to make intelligent decisions on essential issues like war and peace. The Supreme Court sided with the *Times*, adding new legal obstacles to government censorship.
- **Wiretaps.** The *Times* broke the story in 2006 that the National Security Agency was tapping telephone conversations of U.S. citizens without constitutionally required court authorization. President Bush stopped just short of calling the stories treasonous, declaring the secret wiretap program essential to the government's war on terrorism. The *Times* responded that it had proceeded with its stories only after exhaustive consideration of security issues versus civil liberties issues. President Bush, although steamed, decided against pursuing the issue legally.

"All the News That's Fit to Print"
The New York Times
National Edition
SATURDAY, OCTOBER 10, 2009
Abortion Foes Tell of Journey To the Streets
Seeking Confrontation, and Fellowship
NEW WAY TO TAP GAS MAY EXPAND GLOBAL SUPPLIES
EXCITEMENT IN EUROPE
Extractions From Shale Could Create Huge Fuel Reserves
Surprise Nobel for Obama Stirs Praise and Doubts
Licensed to Sell Marijuana, but Still in Shadow
Greater Dialogue Cited — He's 'Humbled'
Watching a New Kind of Moon Shot
Another Landlord Worry: Is the Elevator Kosher?
Eat

WHAT DO YOU THINK?

- Why is a subscription to the New York *Times* a priority for librarians?
- What sets the content of the New York *Times* apart from other newspapers?
- What has contributed to the journalistic reputation of the New York *Times* over the years?

Old Gray Lady. *True to the graphic spirit of the 19th century, when it rose in eminence, the New York* Times *is sometimes called the Old Gray Lady of American journalism. Even after color photos were added in 1997, the* Times *had a staid, somber visual personality. The coverage, writing and commentary, however, are anything but dull, and it is those things that have made the* Times' *reputation as the world's best newspaper.*

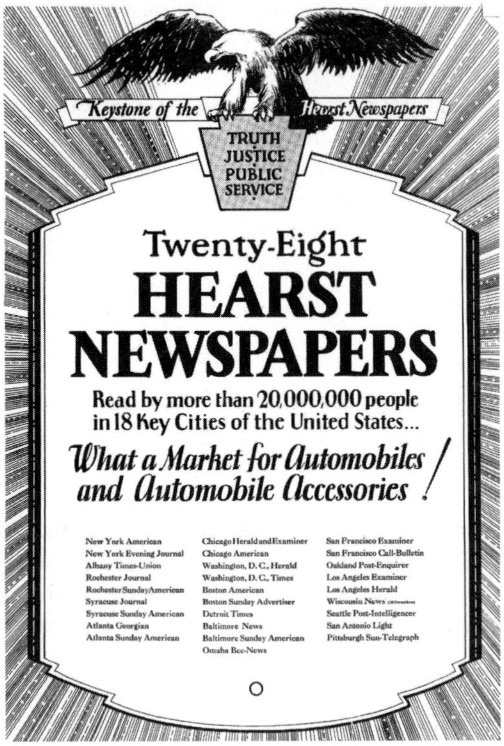

William Randolph Hearst

Chain Power. *The Hearst newspaper chain offered discounts for national advertisers that bought space in multiple newspapers. The chain, among the most profitable through the 20th century, included dailies in New York, Chicago, Los Angeles, Boston, San Francisco and Seattle. With his fortune, one of the largest in U.S. history, chain founder William Randolph Hearst lived well. His Beverly Hills, California, mansion had 29 bedrooms. His San Simeon, California, castle sits on a 240,000-acre site that today awes tourists. Twice Hearst was elected to Congress.*

William Tweed
Corrupt politician exposed by New York *Times*

George Jones
New York *Times* reporter who pursued Tammany Hall scandal

Sullivan decision
Landmark libel case in which New York *Times* argued for unfettered reporting of public officials

Pentagon Papers
Secret government-generated Vietnam war military documents revealed by New York *Times*

PMs
Afternoon newspapers

AMs
Morning newspapers

>> **Hidden Implosion.** The profits, however, masked an industry already in a slow implosion. Readership was largely stagnant or slipping. People had less time in their lives to spend with a newspaper. Television competed for eyeballs, then the Internet. More family members were spending more hours outside the home in full-time jobs. With more people in 9-to-5 jobs, in contrast to factory shifts that dominated earlier times, typically starting at 6 a.m. and ending in mid-afternoon, people had less time in the evenings for newspapers. **PMs,** as newspapers issued in the afternoon were called, had once outnumbered **AMs** but virtually disappeared in the 1980s. PMs either shut down or were absorbed into their morning competition. This goosed profits at the surviving morning papers because advertisers saw little alternative, but the upshot in revenue eventually dissipated. A traditional balance between producing a quality journalistic product as well as making money was lost.

For decades, historians will ponder when the U.S. newspaper industry began its decline. Circulation peaked at 62.8 million in 1988. By 2007 the number was 50.7 million. The drop, almost 20 percent, occurred even as the U.S. population continued to grow. As a financial analyst would put it, **market penetration** had slipped. The loss was undeniable. There was no way to gloss it over. In the first nine months of 2008, advertising revenue was down 19.3 percent from the year before, an accelerating free fall.

Chains slashed operating expenses to maintain profits. Pages were trimmed narrower to reduce newsprint costs. Trimmer products weighed less, which reduced fuel costs for distribution. Penny-pinching included cheaper grades of paper. Cost-cutting also damaged content. Staffing was cut at outlying bureaus, as in state capitals. The result was less coverage of policy issues and a disappearance of labor-intensive investigative reporting. The nation's leading dailies cut back on

Bye. *The contraction of the U.S. newspaper industry can be traced to the 1960s when cities with multiple dailies found themselves one-newspaper towns. The year 2008 ushered a whole new wave of shutdowns, including venerable papers like the* Rocky Mountain News *in Denver. The owner of the* News, *the Scripps-Howard chain of Cincinnati, Ohio, pulled the plug just short of the newspaper's 150th anniversary. Declining readership and advertising had rendered the* News *economically unviable.*

Washington bureaus and shut down foreign bureaus. These kinds of measures came about gradually to maintain profits. Generally the cuts went unnoticed outside the industry. By 2010, however, there was no way to mask continuing erosions in readership and the concomitant loss in advertising revenue. Owners took increasingly drastic steps to stay afloat, including further staff cutbacks that visibly diminished the product. The U.S. Labor Department estimated that 20,000 newspaper jobs were eliminated in 2008. In one swoop, not the first, the giant Los Angeles *Times* cut back 300 jobs.

market penetration
Sales per capita

In 2008, the *Rocky Mountain News,* a Denver fixture for 150 years, shut down. Up until then, the *Rocky Mountain News* was the largest newspaper to fail in the industry's implosion.

Post-Print Culture

STUDY ***PREVIEW***

For nearly 300 years the financial might of the newspaper industry enabled newspapers to contribute importantly to making democracy work. This included advancing free expression as a citizen right. Newspapers also have been at the forefront promoting openness in government. What will happen as newspapers vanish? What will replace the role of newspapers in society and culture?

DEMOCRACY WITHOUT NEWSPAPERS

One disparaging joke about newspapers is they make good wrappers for day-old fish. The loss of newspapers, however, is more worrisome than not having something for wrapping kitchen scraps.

HOLLYWOOD JUSTICE Weekend
THE WALL STREET JOURNAL.
WEEKEND EDITION
What's News—
Jobs Data Cloud Recovery
Rio Throws Chicago for a Loop
Rising Brazil's Win of 2016 Olympics Is Blow to Obama, Boon for Developing World
In China, the Forgotten Manchu Seek to Rekindle Their Glory
—Inside—
The Revolution at 60

49ers, Jets move on receivers
USA TODAY
Author turns to 'True-Life Novel'
Newsline
Home fields rule in Game 1 wins
For president, risks all around
Obama's 'defining moment' on Afghanistan
Goal of NASA moon shot: Finding water
COURTYARD Marriott
STAY THE WEEKEND AT COURTYARD AND GET A $25 ONLINE GIFT CARD

U.S. National Newspapers. The Gannett media chain introduced *USA Today* in 1982. With mostly single-copy sales, rather than individual subscriptions, *USA Today* gradually overtook the venerable *Wall Street Journal* in circulation. *USA Today* features flashy presentation and mostly short stories. The *Journal* shortened its stories after Rupert Murdoch bought the paper in 2008 but kept its focus on business and finance for a general audience. *USA Today* and the *Journal* are the only U.S. national dailies.

Newspaper Milestones

NEWSPAPER INDUSTRY | **PIVOTAL EVENTS**

1400s

>> Gutenberg invents movable metal type (1446)

1600s

Benjamin Day

>> Age of Science, Age of Reason begins (1600s)

>> Pilgrims found Plymouth colony (1620)

>> Isaac Newton discovers natural laws (1687)

1700s

Newspaper Chain
Ben Franklin expanded *Pennsylvania Gazette* into first chain (1734)

>> Industrial Revolution (1760s–)

>> Revolutionary War (1776–1781)

1800s

Penny Press
New York *Sun,* first penny newspaper (1833)

New York *Times*
Founded as serious alternative to penny papers (1851)

Mega-Chains
Hearst takes over San Francisco *Examiner*, which becomes flagship for major chain (1887)

William Randolph Hearst

>> Public education takes root as social value (1820s)

>> Machine-made paper widely available (1830s)

>> Civil War (1861–1865)

>> Public education spurs quantum growth in literacy (1880s)

1900s

Gannett
Upstate New York papers entered common ownership, grow into largest U.S. chain (1906)

USA Today
Founded by Gannett chains as a national daily (1982)

USA TODAY
Home fields rule in Game 1 wins
Obama's 'defining moment' on Afghanistan
Goal of NASA moon shot: Finding water

Largest U.S. daily

>> World War I (1914–1918)

>> Right to vote extended to women (1920)

>> Great Depression (1930s)

>> World War II (1941–1945)

>> Television emerges as commercial medium (early1950s)

>> Military founds predecessor to Internet (1969)

>> Internet emerges as commercial medium (late 1990s)

2000s

Newspaper Chains Falter
Historic chain Knight-Ridder fumbles financially, sold (2006)

Madison, Wisconsin, *Capital Times*
First U.S. daily to switch to online delivery (2008)

Readership Shift
More people get news online than from newspapers, magazines (2008)

Christian Science Monitor
Switches daily edition to online delivery (2009)

Failures
Rocky Mountain News, Denver,shuts down, largest newspaper to fold; others follow (2009)

THE CHRISTIAN SCIENCE MONITOR
California's age of megafires
Why Turkey is wary of Kurd rebel trap
WAR EXPENSE KEEPS RISING

Now online only

With their huge financial resources, newspapers built the largest news staffs in cities both large and small. Local radio and television news never matched the breadth and depth of local newspapers. No television network ever came close to staffing the world like the New York *Times*. These newspapers provided a core chronicle of events. They also dug for truths that would not otherwise have been uncovered.

>> **Democracy.** Investigative reporting has served democracy well. Intrepid digging by the New York *Times* in the 1870s sent brazenly crooked city leaders to prison. Municipal reforms followed. Similarly, a century later, the Watergate scandal was uncovered by dogged reporting by the Washington *Post*. President Nixon resigned amid *Post* revelations of an arrogance of power and contempt not only for democratic processes but also contempt for openness, honesty and decency and for the people. Regional and local newspapers too have carried the torch for tough, enterprising reporting. More than any other medium, newspapers have exercised the historic watchdog function of the press against wrongdoing in government, business and other institutions.

Newspapers have not had a monopoly as watchdogs, but until recently their wherewithal has enabled them to deliver more expensive, labor-intensive journalistic reporting than other media. No less important has been the ability of newspapers to dig into their deep corporate pockets to resist pressures from powerful corrupt forces to back off.

Without newspapers, a void will be left in investigative reporting. Who will "keep the rascals honest?" as a cynic once put it. An important check is being lost against dishonesty among those in positions of public trust.

>> **Free Expression.** Newspapers have been crusaders for free speech as a citizen right. In the pivotal 1964 legal case *New York Times* v. *Sullivan*, the *Times* fought for the right for people to comment on the performance of public figures. It was a case in which the *Times* had been accused of libeling a bullying Alabama police commissioner. The *Times* could have settled out of court for a fraction of the legal fees for an appeal to the U.S. Supreme Court. The *Times* went the costly route to do the right thing, not the easy thing—and prevail in a landmark ruling.

Not all newspapers historically have chosen to crusade for First Amendment rights, but newspapers and their trade associations have a far longer and stronger record on free expression than other media industries. Without newspapers, civil libertarians, indeed all citizens, have cause for concern.

>> **Government Openness.** Frequently newspapers have used laws requiring public access to government meetings and documents. These are laws designed to assure that government conducts the public's business with transparency: no closed-door deals for fat contracts to the mayor's brother-in-law, no short-circuiting of the civil rights of impoverished groups who don't have a voice, no pay-to-play political appointments. With less aggressive pursuit of news in general, a danger in a post-newspaper era is that more misfeasance, even criminal malfeasance, will go unnoticed.

CHECKING YOUR MEDIA LITERACY

- **What enabled newspapers to perform their historic role in a well-functioning democracy?**
- **What will happen to current levels of chronicling events without newspapers?**
- **What of investigative reporting?**

NEWSPAPERS AND CULTURE

Newspapers have contributed to culture in their content. By newspapers' very existence, these contributions have been in reporting, commentary and criticism on the arts. Also, newspapers have served as inspiration for countless books, movies and plays and constitute a whole category of drama, much as do cops, lawyers and doctors. But the contribution also has been deeper, probing into social values and questioning the

Kitchen Scraps. *The demise of newspapers has implications far beyond what* Time *magazine, tongue in cheek, suggested in this 2009 cover article. A void is being left in how democracy works.*

role of society's institutions. Important too has been the role of newspapers as incubators for great writers who have shaped the culture. In newsrooms and on news beats, the likes of Ernest Hemingway honed the skills and discipline essential for great writing. Their news experiences gave them insights into the human condition. Consider Stephen Crane, Edna Ferber, Jack London, Margaret Mitchell, Hunter S Thompson and Mark Twain. All were newspaper reporters at one time in their careers.

Besides great authors, the newspaper industry has been a starting point for significant careers. Newsroom skills have been springboards into pubic relations careers for thousands of people. Not uncommon among political leaders has been newspaper experience. Former Vice President Al Gore, a Nobel Prize winner for sounding the alarm on global warming, frequently refers to his start at the Memphis, Tennessee, *Commercial Appeal*.

Many of the concerns voiced about the disappearance of newspapers also can be raised about magazines. Can the magazine industry's social and cultural role survive in an online environment? Will there be sufficient revenues to maintain substantive content?

CHECKING YOUR MEDIA LITERACY

- **What traditional career avenues will be closed with the disappearance of newspapers?**

Magazine Industry Status

STUDY PREVIEW

Several high-visibility magazines have gone under, losing their audiences and advertising to Internet-based competition. Under pressure in the changing media environment, other magazines have survival strategies to shift to non-print delivery. Meanwhile, some shelter and celebrity magazines are among categories that are holding their own.

DECLINING MAGAZINE CIRCULATION

When Jon Meacham, the editor at *Newsweek*, was invited to drop in at Columbia University to discuss magazines with a group of 100 journalism grad students one day in 2008, he started by asking for a show of hands on how many read *Newsweek*. Nobody did. It was a telling moment. Two years later, *Newsweek's* long-time owner, the Washington Post Company, put the magazine up for sale. When he announced that *Newsweek* was on the block, Meacham said the magazine was caught in the same problems as historically print-centric publications—advertising declines, competition from digital media, and an increasingly fragmented audience for media products. Meacham cannot be faulted for innovation as *Newsweek's* fortunes wavered. He recognized that Internet-delivered news had pre-empted the magazine's forte, going back to 1933, of recapping the week's events. He shifted to commentary and analysis. The new thrust didn't stem reader and advertiser defections. The leading U.S. newsmagazine, *Time*, was in the same bind. A third newsmagazine, *U.S. News & World Report*, already had abandoned weekly issues and gone biweekly then monthly.

Magazines and Books Milestones

MAGAZINES AND BOOKS INDUSTRIES

1400s

1600s

First Press
Puritans establish Cambridge Press (1638)

1700s

Encyclopedia
French scholars began alphabetized reference book (1751)

Rise of Book Industry
J.B. Lippincott established as major publishing house (1792)

First Colonial Magazine
In Philadelphia, Andrew Bradford printed *American Magazine*, the first in the colonies; Ben Franklin followed with *General Magazine* (1741)

1800s

First Magazine Era
Saturday Evening Post ushered in era of general-interest magazines (1821)

Illustrated Magazine
Brother Jonathan first illustrated U.S. literary magazine (1840s)

Cheap Reading
Beadle Brothers introduced dime novels (1860)

Magazine Photography
Photography introduced in *National Geographic* (1899)

1900s

Muckraking
Ida Tarbell magazine exposé on Standard Oil (1904), Upton Sinclair's *The Jungle* (1906)

Magazine Innovation
The compendium *Reader's Digest* founded (1922), newsmagazine *Time* (1923), *New Yorker* (1924)

Photojournalism
Henry Luce founded *Life*, coined term *photo essay* (1936)

***Life* Dies**
Network television robbed general-interest magazines of advertisers (1960s)

Online Magazines
Time Warner creates Pathfinder web site (1994)

Digital Books
E-book introduced (1998)

2000s

Wikipedia
Wiki predecessor Nupedia launched (2000)

Google Print Library
Google began digitizing all books ever published (2005)

Daniel Defoe, 1209 magazine pioneer

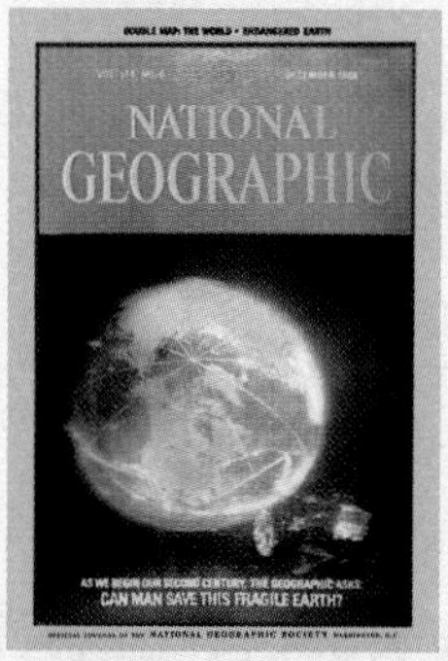

Photography pioneer

Muckraking Ida Tarbell

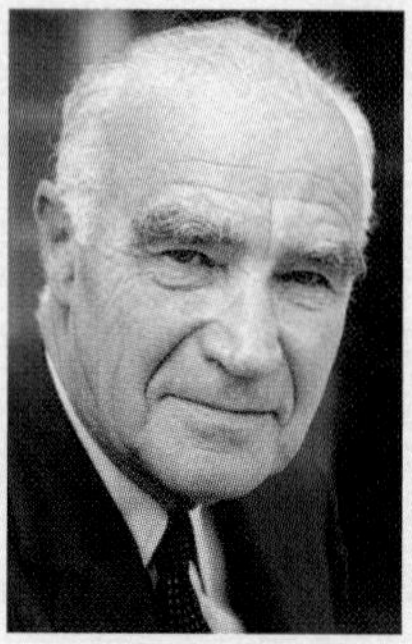

Henry Luce of Time Life

PIVOTAL EVENTS

- >> Gutenberg invents movable metal type (1446s)
- >> Age of Science, Age of Reason begins (1600s)
- >> Pilgrims found Plymouth colony (1620)
- >> Isaac Newton discovers natural laws (1687)
- >> Industrial Revolution (1760s–)
- >> Revolutionary War (1776–1781)
- >> Public education takes root as social value (1820s)
- >> Machine-made paper widely available (1830s)
- >> Civil War (1861–1865)
- >> Public education spurs quantum growth in literacy (1880s)
- >> World War I (1914–1918)
- >> Right to vote extended to women (1920)
- >> Great Depression (1930s)
- >> World War II (1941–1945)
- >> Television emerges as commercial medium (early1950s)
- >> Military founds predecessor to Internet (1969)
- >> Internet emerges as commercial medium (late 1990s)

The magazine industry was shaken. McGraw-Hill unloaded its venerable *BusinessWeek*, which re-emerged as an element of the multi-media Bloomberg financial reporting empire. Niche magazines that had thrived for years were hurting. The classy food and wine title *Gourmet* folded in 2009. Many shelter magazines hung on, but not all. When the slick women's magazine *Jane* folded, editor Jane Pratt explained it this way: "With so many women going online, it's possible that there isn't much need for it." Pratt spoke for an industry-wide problem: Readers aren't waiting for a monthly or even a weekend when the Internet is always available with convenient, readable content.

Like newspapers, magazines historically have enjoyed dual revenue streams. While cover and subscription prices make a dent in the business's fixed costs, it is advertising revenue that drives profits. Now, with circulation dropping, and also circulation revenue, advertisers are engaged in a mad search for alternate vehicles to carry their messages. Yes, magazines remain a major component of the mix of media, just less so at the moment as a shake-out occurs among the widening array of choices for readers and for advertisers. The bottom line for magazines is fewer ad dollars for magazine publishers.

CHECKING YOUR MEDIA LITERACY

- **Why are many major magazines losing readers? Where are they going?**
- **Why is advertising revenue declining at many magazines?**

MAGAZINE INDUSTRY SCOPE

Despite circulation and advertising slippage among historically high visibility categories of magazines, including women's titles and newsmagazines, some categories are holding their own and gaining. Shelter magazines, led by the monthly *Better Homes & Garden* and celebrity titles, like the weekly *People*, have growing circulations and advertising revenue. Also hot are magazines aimed at an Hispanic audience, in particular at Hispanic men: *Trucker News en Español*, *ESPN Desportes la Revista*, *Maxim en Español*, and *Si Latino*.

Although U.S. magazine industry revenue is slipping, titles number about 12,000. Most are focused on narrow audience segments with special interests, which offer advertisers targeted groups of readers on which to hone their messages. Less than 10 percent of the magazines produced in the United States, roughly 1,200, can be found at even the best newsstands. Most are distributed solely by mail. They exist, many thriving, under the radar of anybody outside the target audiences.

CHECKING YOUR MEDIA LITERACY

- **What kind of magazines have been least affected by the industry's general problems? Why?**

MAGAZINE TRANSITION PROSPECTS

Long-term prospects for magazines as ink-on-paper products are dimming, but the industry is in a better position than the newspaper industry to make a transition to online delivery.

>> Outsourcing. With *National Geographic* among the few rare exceptions, magazine companies long ago shed their presses and **outsourced** production to printing companies. Another print media function, **circulation,** also is mostly outsourced.

>> Staffing. Again unlike newspapers, many magazines even outsource substantial portions of their content to **freelancers.** These are unsalaried reporters and writers, many of whom work out of home offices and who are paid piecework. Common with magazines too are **contributing editors,** who receive a regular retainer for contributions. In general contributing editors don't edit but report and write in a kind of independent contractor arrangement. In some cases these "editors" are also additionally compensated for individual contributions.

outsource
Obtain services from an external supplier rather than internally

circulation
An activity to solicit and service subscribers and vendors

freelancer
A nonstaff writer or photographer who submits work on speculation or takes specific one-time assignments

contributing editor
A nonstaff magazine contributor, usually on continuing retainer

DeWitt and Lila Wallace

MEDIA PEOPLE

DeWitt and Lila Wallace had an idea but hardly any money. The idea was a pocket-size magazine that condensed informational, inspirational and entertaining nonfiction from other publications—a digest. With borrowed money, the Wallaces brought out their first issue of *Reader's Digest* in 1923.

The rest, as they say, is history. In 1947 *Reader's Digest* became the first magazine to exceed 9 million circulation. Eventually the total topped 15.1 million—not counting an additional 12.2 million in 18 languages. No other magazine, unless you count the Sunday newspaper supplements, had greater reach.

The Wallaces died in the 1980s, but the magazine continued with their formula. The Wallaces, both children of poor Presbyterian clergy, wanted "constructive articles," each with universal appeal. The thrust was upbeat but not Pollyannish. The Wallaces rejected advertising outside their moral bounds. At a time when cigarette manufacturers were major advertisers in U.S. magazines, for example, there was no tobacco stain in the pages of *Reader's Digest*. Even while spurning cigarette advertisers, the magazine thrived.

Condensed as they were, *Reader's Digest* articles could be quickly read. America loved it. At the magazine's peak, more than 90 percent of the circulation was by subscription, representing long-term reader commitment.

The *Digest* has slipped from its dominance. U.S. circulation is 8.2 million. That's substantial, true, but way down. Why?

As a digest, the magazine was an **aggregator**—a term now used, often derisively, for web sites that suck up content from elsewhere and produce little that is original. The *Digest* concept has been widely usurped: Quick reads are everywhere. The web is fresh 24/7 with digested and repackaged content. As with many magazines, newspapers too, many readers ask: "Why pay when I can go free to the Web?"

The *Digest* is not alone among magazines in circulation slippage, although some genres, including shelter and celebrity mags, are holding their own. At left are the leaders among consumer magazines available at large newsstands and also, in most cases, by subscription.

WEEKLIES	
Time	3.8 million
People	3.4 million
Sports Illustrated	3.2 million
Newsweek	2.7 million
BusinessWeek	2.7 million
BIWEEKLIES	
Forbes	3.4 million
Fortune	3.1 million
Rolling Stone	1.4 million
MONTHLIES	
Reader's Digest	8.2 million
Better Homes & Gardens	7.7 million
Good Housekeeping	4.7 million
TV Guide	3.3 million
Vogue	3.0 million
Cosmopolitan	2.9 million

Readers Digest *DeWitt and Lila Wallace founded Reader's Digest as a quick-read synopsis of articles from elsewhere. The concept has been so widely imitated that the magazine's attraction has been eclipsed.*

Most magazines have far less overhead than newspapers. For example, *Automobile*, a leading car magazine, has 23 staff people who work up the monthly content. The 23 include five people assigned to a web offshoot, an office receptionist and an intern. There are 21 contributing writers and artists. In contrast, the New York *Times* staff to generate content exceeds 1,000.

Like newspapers, magazines also have advertising and business infrastructures, but with most magazines these services are largely through corporate parents. With *Automobile*, as an example, the parent company, Source Interlink Media, publishes 75 magazines and provides management and back-office support.

With relatively lean staffs, magazines have adapted to online delivery without the massive infrastructure disruptions that have upended the newspaper industry. Even so, the low cost-of-entry to establish an online magazine has left traditional ink-on-paper magazine companies wallowing in a sea of new online competition. Readers can choose among hundreds of more diverse magazine-like sources online than were ever stocked the shelves at even the largest newsstands.

DeWitt and Lila Wallace
Founders of *Reader's Digest*

aggregator
An Internet site that collects and repackages content from other sources

CHECKING YOUR MEDIA LITERACY

- **How are magazine companies more nimble than newspaper companies in shifting to non-print delivery?**
- **What new competitive challenges face magazines in going online?**

Magazine Innovations

STUDY PREVIEW

What might be lost as the magazine industry navigates into a post-print era? Through their history magazines have been innovators in content. These include long-form journalism—thought-provoking commentary, essays and fiction. Some of the first investigative reporting was in magazines. Other innovations include personality profiles and photography.

LONG-FORM JOURNALISM

Although many flashy magazines have shifted toward fleeting treatments of issues and info-tainment tidbits, an enduring magazine tradition is articles of length and depth that cannot be boiled down to a few slick sentences.

>> Essays. Although remembered mostly for his adventure tale *Robinson Crusoe*, **Daniel Defoe** was also prominent in his era as a pamphleteer and journalist and also as a magazine pioneer. In 1704 Defoe established an influential journal in London, *Weekly Review*, which carried essays. Defoe's *Review* had a nine-year run, establishing a role for magazines as a bridge between society's intelligentsia and a broad audience.

Daniel Defoe
His 1704 *Weekly Review* established magazines as forum for ideas

This is a tradition remaining at its most obvious in what are called **highbrow slicks.** These magazines, of which *Atlantic* and *Harper's* are exemplars, work at being at the cutting edge of thinking on political, economic, social, artistic and cultural issues. The *New Yorker* prides itself on breaking ground on significant issues in articles that run as long as editors think necessary, some the length of a small book. Ideological magazines like the *New Republic, National Review* and the *Nation* frequently are both partisan and cerebral. Like other highbrow slicks, they are edited for **literati.**

highbrow slicks
Magazines whose content has intellectual appeal

literati
Well-educated people interested in literature and cerebral issues

The Defoe legacy is alive and well when *Time* and *Newsweek* excerpt books. Many niche magazines carry intellectually invigorating articles. On technology and its political, social and legal implications, for example, *Wired* is a must read.

CASE STUDY

Reformulating the Newsmagazines

Henry Luce

Richard Stengel

With breathless wonderment at the rise of U.S. culture after World War II, the genius magazine entrepreneur Henry Luce declared a new era: the American Century. Luce was as right about that as he was with his formula for one magazine success after another, beginning in 1923 with *Time*. Today, however, with hundreds of 24/7 news roundups on the Internet, the concept of a weekly news compendium is quaint. *Time*'s circulation has slipped. Many advertisers have gone elsewhere in search of sales. It's the same at rival newsmagazines.

Budget cuts unfathomable in the high-riding days of Henry Luce are taking place. *Time* eliminated many high-salary senior positions with voluntary retirement buyouts in 2007. *Newsweek* followed in 2008, with 111 employees leaving. Departures included film critic David Ansen and writer Cathleen McGulgan. Issues of both magazines are thinner, which reduces production and shipping expenses.

Meanwhile, editors are desperately trying to reinvent their magazines. At *Newsweek*, editor Jon Meacham has upped the space for text by 30 percent. He's done this in a smaller magazine by squeezing photographs. Images are smaller and fewer. Meacham has a model in the text-heavy British newsmagazine the *Economist*, whose circulation, counter to industry patterns, increased 8.5 percent in 2007. The open question is whether *Newsweek*'s readers, who still buy 2.7 million copies a week, will cotton to a grayer magazine. In 2007 circulation dropped 6.7 percent.

To reposition *Time*, editor Richard Stengel has a different tack. The magazine has added emphasis to health, science and technology with a consumer bent. There is less political thrust. Stengel also is hoping to stop the circulation decline, now at 3.4 million, by nurturing *Time*'s tradition as a home for big-name columnists.

Stengel knows why *Time* and also *Newsweek* are losing readers and, as a result, also advertisers: "There's more information out there than any time in human history. What people don't need is more information. They need a guide through the chaos." The question: Can a reformulation of content save the newsmagazines?

DEEPENING YOUR MEDIA LITERACY

EXPLORE THE ISSUE

Round up recent issues of *Time, and Newsweek*. A dozen would be good. If you could read only one article, which issue would you choose based solely on the cover? Why your choice? Again relying on what interests you, rank the other covers.

DIG DEEPER

Inside the magazines, identify the featured columnists and their subjects. Rank them in the order in which you would choose to read them. Explain your choices.

WHAT DO YOU THINK?

Based on your review of the newsmagazines, how can they fit into the lifestyle you are creating for yourself to stay abreast of important news and issues? What role do newsmagazines play in the mosaic of media sources available to you including the Internet, television and newspapers?

Daniel Defoe. *The British novelist and pamphleteer had his quill in many ink pots. Defoe's* Weekly Review, *in publication from 1704 to 1713, created a legacy for magazines as a vehicle for essays and thought-provoking commentary.*

Most of the worthy long-form journalism that is posted online today comes from magazines and newspapers as spin-offs of their core print editions. One troubling question: What will happen if the companies that produce the core ink-on-paper products are unable to survive financially? The fact is that online-only endeavors, some claiming to be in the magazine tradition, are pathetically paltry with essay explorations and muckraking. *Salon* is no *New Yorker*. *Slate* is no *Atlantic*. Unless the web develops an economic base to support high-quality infrastructures for content, authors and essayists and depth reporters may lose a home for their contributions to public dialogue.

CHECKING YOUR MEDIA LITERACY

- **Which magazines carry on the tradition of Daniel Defoe's *Weekly Review*?**
- **Why hasn't the magazine audience of literati and serious-minded readership shifted online?**
- **Will advertisers in highbrow slicks move online in sufficient numbers and at sufficient rates to underwrite the costs of highbrow content?**

>> Investigative Reporting. In the early 1900s magazines honed **muckraking**, usually called "investigative reporting" today. Magazines ran lengthy explorations of abusive institutions in society. It was **Theodore Roosevelt**, the reform president, who coined the term *muckraking*. Roosevelt generally enjoyed investigative journalism, but one day in 1906, when the digging got too close to home, he likened it to the work of a character in a 17th century novel who focused so much on raking muck that he missed the good news. The president meant the term derisively, but it came to be a badge of honor among journalists.

Muckraking established magazines as a powerful medium in shaping public policy. In 1902 **Ida Tarbell** wrote a 19-part series on the Standard Oil monopoly for ***McClure's***. **Lincoln Steffens** detailed municipal corruption, and reforms followed. Other magazines picked up investigative thrusts. *Collier's* took on patent medicine frauds. *Cosmopolitan*, a leading muckraking journal of the period, tackled dishonesty in the U.S. Senate. Muckraking expanded to books with **Upton Sinclair's** *The Jungle*. Sinclair shocked the nation by detailing filth in meat-packing plants. Federal inspection laws resulted.

muckraking
Early 1990s term for investigative reporting

Ida Tarbell
Exposed Standard Oil monopolistic practices in 1902 magazine series

Theodore Roosevelt
Coined term *muckraking*

McClure's
Pioneer muckraking magazine

Lincoln Steffens
Exposed municipal corruption

Upton Sinclair
Exposed bad meat-packing practices

CHECKING YOUR MEDIA LITERACY

- **Does the term *muckraking* capture what investigating reporting is about?**

>> Personality Profiles. The in-depth **personality profile** was a magazine invention. In the 1920s **Harold Ross** of the *New Yorker* began pushing writers to a thoroughness that was new in journalism. The conversational quality of Q-As, refined by **Hugh Hefner** at *Playboy* in the 1950s, added a cogent authenticity to long-form profiles. The obvious role of the interviewer in Q-As, often invisible in typical news stories, helps put what's said into context. Also, interviewees have opportunities to explain complex lines of reasoning with illuminating detail. The exhaustive nature of lengthy Q-As, such as *Playboy*'s, can draw out people in ways that other journalistic forms do not. Most *Playboy* interviews are drawn from weeks, sometimes months, of face time, all recorded and then spliced into a coherent article running 7,000 words or more. Many political and religious leaders, scientists and other thinkers, celebrities too, covet the opportunity that long Q-As give them to expand and elaborate on what they have to say.

The Q-A format has been widely imitated. It was in *Rolling Stone*, which uses Q-As regularly, that presidential candidate Wesley Clark, a retired general, said he knew from top-level Pentagon planners that the 2003 Iraq invasion was only the beginning of further U.S. military plans in the Middle East.

personality profile
In-depth, balanced biographical article

Harold Ross
New Yorker editor who pioneered the personality profile

Hugh Hefner
Playboy editor who created modern Q-A

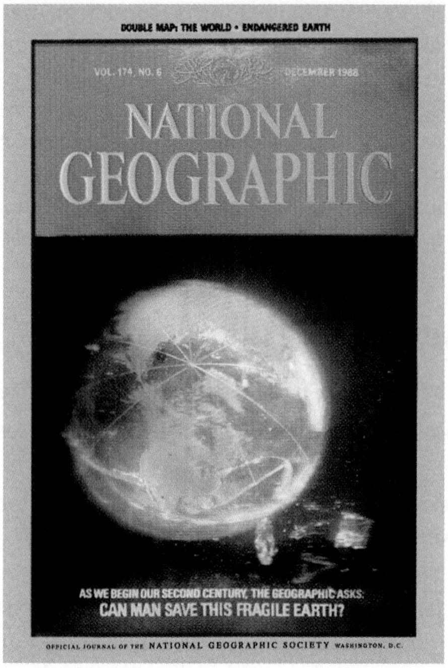

National Geographic. *The* Geographic *has remained in the vanguard of magazines photographically. In 1985 the magazine used a hologram, a three-dimensional photograph, of a prehistoric child's skull on its cover—the first ever in a mass-audience magazine. Three years later, for its 100th anniversary, the* Geographic *produced a three-dimensional view of Earth on the first fully holographic magazine cover. The* Geographic *is not only among the oldest U.S. magazines but also, with 6.7 million circulation, among the most read.*

Not all Q-A variations are breakthrough news. *Time* magazine, for example, has introduced a "10 Questions" feature that's tightly edited, with pointed questions and answers that fit on a single page. Readable and entertaining, yes, but usually also flighty and superficial and not what Hugh Hefner had in mind.

CHECKING YOUR MEDIA LITERACY

- **What were the contributions of Harold Ross and Hugh Hefner to long-form journalism in their very different magazines?**

PHOTOJOURNALISM

Perhaps the most enduring innovation from the rich legacy of the magazine industry will be media visuals. Before *Brother Jonathan*'s meager illustrations in the mid-1800s, magazines were entirely a word-driven medium. A breakthrough came in the Civil War when ***Harper's Weekly*** sent artists to draw battles, leading the way to journalism that went beyond words. Today visuals are a core element in all mass media except radio. For the digital age, visuals **pixelate** well.

Harper's Weekly
Pioneered magazine visuals

pixelate
To divide an image into tiny points, or pixels, for digital display with the points blurring to the human eye except when magnified

The young editor of the ***National Geographic,*** **Gilbert Grosvenor,** drew a map proposing a route to the South Pole for an 1899 issue, putting the *Geographic* on the road to being a visually oriented magazine. For subsequent issues, Grosvenor borrowed government plates to reproduce photos, and he encouraged travelers to submit their photographs to the magazine. This was at a time when most magazines scorned photographs. However, Grosvenor was undeterred as an advocate for documentary photography. Membership in the National Geographic Society, a prerequisite for receiving the magazine, swelled. Eventually, the magazine assembled its own staff of photographers and gradually became a model for other publications that discovered they needed to play catch-up.

National Geographic
Introduced photograph in magazines

Gilbert Grosvenor
Pioneer editor of *National Geographic*

Aided by technological advances involving smaller, more portable cameras and faster film capable of recording images under extreme conditions, photographers working for the *Geographic* opened a whole new world of documentary coverage to their readers.

Fearless Photojournalist. *Margaret Bourke-White not only would take her camera anywhere, but she had a sense of stories that were worth telling photographically. She is remembered mostly for her work in* Life *magazine over 20 years beginning in the mid-1920s. Her documentary work on the tragic lives of sharecroppers in the American South evokes emotions still today. So do her enduring images of Holocaust victims in Nazi concentration camps and of political leaders of the time in both triumph and defeat. She also created indelible images from South Africa by going underground with miners who were known only by numbers.*

Life magazine brought U.S. photojournalism to new importance in the 1930s. The oversize pages of the magazine gave new intensity to photographs, and the magazine, a weekly, demonstrated that newsworthy events could be covered consistently by camera. *Life* captured the spirit of the times photographically and demonstrated

Seeing the News. *Henry Luce's* Life *magazine pioneered photojournalism, beginning with Margaret Bourke-White's haunting shadows of the giant new Fort Peck Dam in Montana for the inaugural issue. When World War II came, "Life" dispatched Bourke-White and other photographers to capture the story, even the horrific details. With people eager for war news, circulation soared.*

that the whole range of human experience could be recorded visually. Both real life and *Life* could be shocking. A 1938 *Life* spread on human birth was so shocking for the time that censors succeeded in banning the issue in 33 cities.

CHECKING YOUR MEDIA LITERACY

- **Although different in mission, *National Geographic* and *Life* both established magazines firmly as a visual medium. How so?**
- **Might magazine-originated terms like *photojournalism* and *photo essay* outlive magazines?**

EARLIER MAGAZINE EPITAPHS

No matter how bleak the prospect for magazines as an ink-on-paper product, there remain observers, though few, who say don't count the magazine industry out. Their point is that magazines have survived crises in the past.

>> **Demassification.** In the 1950s the industry reinvented itself when, suddenly, the emerging national television networks offered advertisers larger audiences at less cost. The dynamic was **CPM,** short in advertising lingo for cost per thousand, the *M* for the Roman numeral meaning thousand. Television networks nibbled, then gobbled at the big magazines' CPM. In 1970 a full-page advertisement in *Life* ran $65,000, a $7.75 CPM. The networks' was $3.60. It's not hard to see why advertisers shifted to television. By then, 1970, once-leading magazines like *Saturday Evening Post, Look* and *Collier's* were out of business. *Life* held on a bit longer.

Doomsayers predicted the end of magazines as a mass medium. They were wrong. Rethinking the industry's traditional model that bigger was better, magazine companies focused on titles aimed at narrow audience segments that advertisers with products of limited interest needed to reach. For manufacturers of high-end audio systems, for example, *Stereo Review* made CPM sense. To go with network television, in contrast, would mean wasting advertising dollars on many viewers with no interest in buying big-buck sound systems.

By fragmenting the audience, a process called **demassification,** the magazine industry survived. The radio industry, under the same pressure from network television, did the same thing by focusing programming in niches that attracted advertisers whose products weren't a good fit for network television. These new niche business models, seeking **sub-mass audiences,** are widely applied today. In a comeuppance for the old

CPM
Cost per thousand

demassification
Process of media narrowing focus to audience niches

sub-mass audience
A segment within a mass audience that retains elements of a mass audience, usually with less heterogeneity

Magazine Demassification. *Advertisers favor magazines that are edited to specific audience interests that coincide with the advertisers' products. Fewer and fewer magazines geared to a general audience remain in business today.*

television networks, for example, the television industry is undergoing a latter-day demassification. There are hundreds of channels.

Demassification has roots in the women's magazines in the mid-1800s, but the phenomenon has mushroomed. The women's genre is now more appropriately characterized as **shelter magazines.**

>> **Newsmagazines** have fragmented as a genre too. There are business news magazines and sports news magazines. **Lifestyle magazines,** many hobby-oriented, are perhaps the most obvious result of demassification—car magazines, food magazines, travel magazines, celebrity magazines, you name it.

Demassification has critics. Look, for example, at a cat fancier magazine. The message is on what great people cat fanciers are, interspersed with advertising touting products and services in how to become an even greater cat fancier. This, as the late magazine traditionalist Norman Cousins said, is self-indulgent and superficial and contributes nothing to helping people understand what the world is about. Daniel Defoe would not be impressed either.

>> **The New Reality.** Most observers see the only chance this time for the magazine industry to survive is to abandon ink on paper and try to establish a primary presence online. The challenge is multifold. The online universe already is loaded with competition. Further, magazines have lost the advertising base that underwrote the costs of producing the best magazine content. Where have the advertisers gone? Advertisers are spreading their dollars among hundreds and thousands of these new Internet content outlets. Only crumbs are left of the loaf that magazines once claimed.

shelter magazines
Genre comprising traditional women's, home-improvement titles

newsmagazines
Focus on topical events, issues

lifestyle magazines
Genre comprising hobby, leisure titles

CHECKING YOUR MEDIA LITERACY

- **With demassification, have magazines forfeited an important role in society?**
- **How would you rate these magazines on a scale of demassification? *Sports Illustrated* and *Runner*? *MacAddict* and *Wired*? *Better Homes & Gardens* and *Wine Aficionado*? *Prevention* and *Diabetes Forecast*?**
- **How do you see the magazine industry making the transition into online products?**

Book Industry

STUDY PREVIEW

The book industry is well positioned to shift successfully to digital formats. Unlike newspapers and magazines, the book industry doesn't rely on advertising. Also, major book publishers have no expensive investment in printing presses.

PROSPECTS FOR PUBLISHING HOUSES

The U.S. book industry took a battering from the economic disaster that struck in 2008. High-visibility retailers began 2009 after horrible December holiday sales. Revenue at the largest chain retailer, Barnes & Noble, was off 7.7 percent from a year earlier, Borders off 14.4 percent, and Books a Million off 5.6 percent. Online retailer Amazon.com held its own, although it trimmed expenses by shuttering four warehouses. **Publishing houses** were affected too. HarperCollins was especially damaged, with revenue down 24.9 percent before the usual December sales surge. The new year began with layoffs and the consolidation of imprints.

publishing house
A company with a brand name identity that produces books

The setbacks triggered by the 2008 economy disaster exacerbated a few lean years, but the book industry seems more likely to recover over the long term than the other major ink-on-paper media of mass communication—newspapers and magazines. Consider these differences:

- **No Presses.** Unlike newspapers, book publishers have no huge capital investment in presses. The printing of almost all books is contracted out to companies that specialize in printing only. It is these printing companies, not the publishing houses, that will absorb the transition to paperless books that is ahead.
- **No Advertising,** The decimation of the newspaper and magazine industries followed the flight of advertising to online alternatives. The book industry, however, has no dependence on advertising. Almost all publishing house revenue comes from customer purchases. There is nothing akin to the advertising subsidy that underwrote the rise of the newspaper and magazines industries into media powerhouses. When the advertising base on which newspapers and magazines had relied for more than a century fell apart as a business model, newspapers and magazines went into a free-fall.

  With online delivery, the challenge for book publishers will remain, as it is today, to create well-edited, high-quality works that people will be willing to pay for. Likely to be lost in the transition to online delivery, which is already under way, will be the traditional bricks-and-mortar book retailer.
- **No Online Equivalent.** Most book publishers have no existing online competition. For newspapers and magazines, on the other hand, their type of content had been widely available from thousands of online sources before their business structures collapsed. But for novels, biographies, long-form journalism and textbooks, there is a dearth of serious online competition—except what's being created by the book industry itself.

SCOPE OF BOOK INDUSTRY

Uncertain is the shape and size of the book industry that will emerge from the setbacks that began in 2008. Some media conglomerates whose properties include books as well as newspapers and magazines will need to navigate the hazards of some of their operations to make it through the hard times. These include giants like Rupert Murdoch's News Corporation, Newhouse and Pearson. In recent years, before the recession, the U.S. book industry was issuing 195,000 titles a year. Sales revenue had been averaging 3.5 percent annual growth. Those numbers took major hits in 2009 but the industry can be expected to recover.

PUBLISHING HOUSES

Major publishing houses are widely recognized brand names: Simon & Schuster, Doubleday, HarperCollins, Penguin. To most people, though, a book is a book is a book, no matter the publisher—although there are exceptions, such as Harlequin, which is almost a household word for pulp romances. Scholars are exceptions. Their vocabularies are peppered with publishers' names, perhaps because of all the footnotes and bibliographies they have to wade through.

Major publishing houses once had distinctive personalities that flowed from the literary bent of the people in charge. Scribner's, for example, was the nurturing home of Tom Wolfe, Ernest Hemingway and F. Scott Fitzgerald from the 1920s into the 1950s and very much bore the stamp of Charles Scribner and his famous editor Maxwell Perkins. Typical of the era, it was a male-dominated business, everybody wearing tweed coats and smoking pipes. Today the distinctive cultures have blurred as corporate pride has shifted more to the bottom line.

BOOK INDUSTRY CONSOLIDATION

As with other mass media industries, book publishing has undergone consolidation, with companies merging with each other, acquiring one another, and buying lists from one another. Some imprints that you still see are no longer stand-alone companies but a part of international media conglomerates. Random House, a proud name in U.S. book publishing, is now part of the German company Bertelsmann. The company also owns the Bantam, Dell and Doubleday imprints, among other media subsidiaries, including numerous magazines. Harcourt was sold to Reed Elsevier of Europe and Thomson of Canada in 2001. Half of Simon & Schuster, once the world's largest book publisher, was sold to Pearson, a British conglomerate, in 1999. St. Martin's Press is now part of Holtzbrinck of Germany. HarperCollins is in the hands of Rupert Murdoch, whose flagship News Corp. has roots in Australia. Warner Books became part of French publishing giant Lagardere in 2006. In short, fewer and fewer companies are dominating more and more of the world's book output. And many once-U.S. companies now have their headquarters abroad.

CHECKING YOUR MEDIA LITERACY

- **Do you think the consolidation of the book industry into major publishing houses has reduced the diversity of new fiction in our society? Of nonfiction?**

Book Genres

STUDY PREVIEW

Reference works are vulnerable in this age of the Internet. Do you know anybody who's bought a set of encyclopedias lately? Wiki has taken a toll. Textbooks are less vulnerable. Textbooks each have a perspective that dovetails into how an adopting professor or school board sees how a course should be taught. Trade books can adapt easily to e-reading devices.

REFERENCE BOOKS

Publishing houses that produce **reference works** are vulnerable to Internet competition. A 2008 analysis by Comscore found that for every page viewed on Britannica.com, 184 pages were viewed on the user-authored and user-edited Wikipedia. The numbers are staggering: 3.8 billion page views per month for Wiki, 21 million for the online Britannica, which is drawn from the legendary ink-on-paper multi-volume encyclopedia. Sales of all traditional encyclopedias have plummeted. Why? In short, online reference works are free, easily accessible and frequently updated.

Although the user-authored Wikipedia and other online reference sites are redefining the reference publishing industry, the Wiki authoring concept is hardly new. Editors of reference works are no strangers to casting their nets widely for content. The Oxford English Dictionary, which dates to 1857 and is one of the greatest reference works in the English language, had its origins in a wiki model. Scholars put out the word to English speakers far and wide that they would welcome hard evidence of the earliest appearances of English words. So many submissions were received that the Britannica building began to sink under the weight of all the paper.

Even reference books that have been essential professional tools for generations, like the classic *Physician's Desk Reference* in medicine or the Associated Press stylebook in journalism, are at risk. The information in the compilations is readily available online, mostly free, with a quick search. The best hope for many reference publishers is to create subscription sites that aggregate the latest, reliable information that is scattered all around the globe on servers available at a click.

reference books
Compilations, including encyclopedias, dictionaries, atlases

CHECKING YOUR MEDIA LITERACY

- **How has the Internet affected publishing companies that produce reference works?**
- **What is the future of reference publishing in the Internet age?**

TEXTBOOKS

Wikipedia cofounder Larry Sanger proposed in 2006 that **textbooks** be written and edited anonymously online. Sanger's proposed **Citizendium** would invite anybody and everybody to contribute and update online, wiki-like, and to correct and adjust content from fellow contributors. Sanger's initial focus was **K-12** school books. College textbooks are also a possibility, he says: "This opportunity is low-hanging fruit."

The textbook industry is hardly quaking in its boots. Sanger's doubters point out that textbooks, unlike reference compilations, have the advantage of a perspective from a single author or a few coauthors. A creationist author, for example, has values that will permeate a biology textbook. Depending on the teacher, a creationism-leaning textbook will work well in some classes—although definitely not in others. Similarly, a Marxist historian will emphasize economic explanations in attempting to find meaning in the past. A cultural historian would have a very different treatment. Unlike reference works, textbook are more than mere compilations. A textbook has thematic coherence.

Also, textbook publishers are quick to note the convenience of their products. In one place, students have a well-organized presentation of what they need to know and understand. In other words, a textbook is a highly efficient learning tool—vastly more so than the Internet. Students don't need to wander hither and thither online in their learning quest and then end up with uneven jumbles of information, ideas and perspectives. Sanger's Citizendium? There are doubts.

textbooks
Curriculum-related titles for learning and understanding

Citizendium
Project for anonymously authored free-use textbooks

K-12
Kindergarten through 12th grade

CHECKING YOUR MEDIA LITERACY

- **What sets textbooks apart from reference works? What do these differences suggest for the future of textbooks?**
- **What is the inherent value of textbooks?**
- **A wag once commented that textbook sales are dependent on the coercion of the syllabus. What does this mean?**

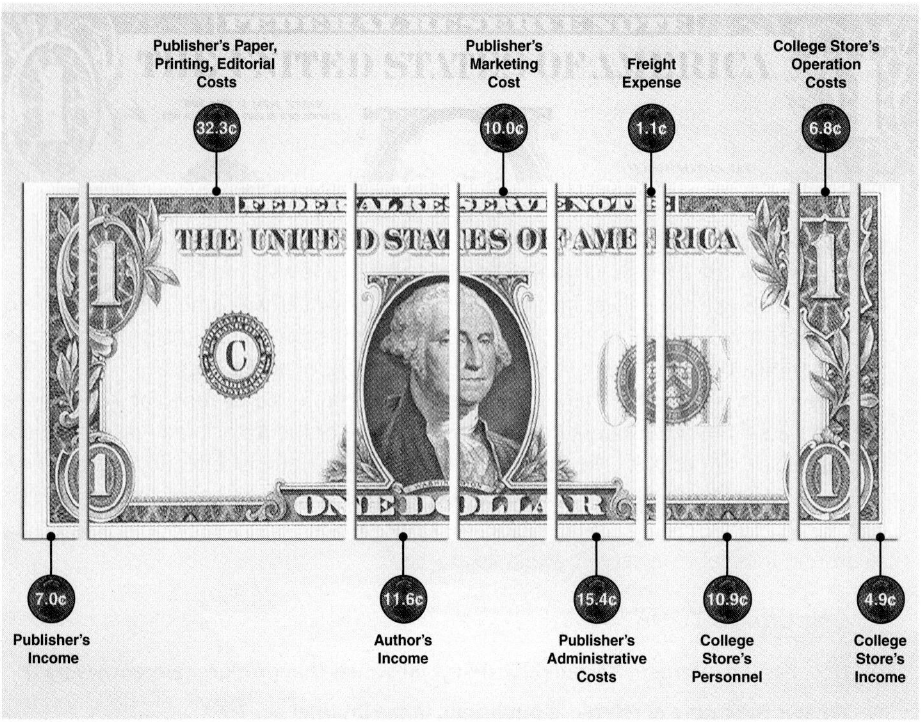

Textbook Dollar.
Students grumble about textbook costs, which fuel suspicions about profiteering. By most business and retail standards, however, profits are slim. The National Association of College Stores says pre-tax profits on new text books average 7.0 percent for publishers and 4.9 percent for retailers. Author royalties average 11.6 percent. For used books, however, the breakdown is drastically different. College stores often have twice the markup. On used books, there are no expenses for manufacturing, publishing house overhead, author royalties or marketing.

TRADE BOOKS

The most visible book industry product is the **trade book.** These are general-interest titles, including fiction and nonfiction, that people usually think of when they think about books. A 2008 Harris poll asked Americans to name their favorite books. The leaders:

The Bible
Gone With the Wind by Margaret Mitchell
The *Lord of the Rings* series by J. R. R. Tolkien
The *Harry Potter* series by J. K. Rowling
The Stand by Stephen King
The Da Vinci Code by Dan Brown
To Kill a Mockingbird by Harper Lee
Angels and Demons by Dan Brown
Atlas Shrugged by Ayn Rand
Catcher in the Rye by J. D. Salinger

All are trade books, except the Christian Bible. Most Bibles which are sold to churches or other groups or specialty retailers—not through the usual "book trade," as it's called.

Trade books can be incredible best-sellers. Since it was introduced in 1937, J.R.R. Tolkien's *The Hobbit* has sold almost 40 million copies. Margaret Mitchell's 1936 *Gone with the Wind* has passed 29 million. Most trade books, however, have shorter lives. To stay atop best-seller lists, Stephen King, J. K.Rowling, Danielle Steel and other authors have to keep writing. Steel, known for her discipline at the keyboard, produces a new novel about every six months.

Although publishing trade books can be extremely profitable when a book takes off, trade books have always been a high-risk proposition. One estimate is that 60 percent of them lose money, 36 percent break even, and 4 percent turn a good profit. Only a few become best-sellers and make spectacular money.

Trade book publishing is New York-centric, although the business also has deep historic roots in Boston and Philadelphia. The concentration in these cities is explained partly by career patterns. Upward mobility in the book industry is largely by jumping to a better job at a competitor that is, metaphorically, across the street. The result is a critical mass of experience and talent in a few places.

CHECKING YOUR MEDIA LITERACY

- **How many current or recent best-selling trade books can you name?**
- **How about long-term best-sellers?**
- **Why has book publishing in the United States become centered in New York and a few other publishing centers?**

trade books
General-interest titles, including fiction and nonfiction

copyright
An exclusive legal right to reproduce original works

public domain
Status of a creative work to which no one can claim ownership and thus belongs to the public as a whole

Michael Hart
Creator of Project Gutenberg

Project Gutenberg
First online digital library

PUBLIC DOMAIN LITERATURE

Among trade book publishers, the houses and imprints that specialize in issuing historic literature can be expected to retrench. These include imprints like Penguin Classics, which reproduce works whose authors never had **copyright** control, like Greek classics, or whose copyright has expired, like the works of Bunyan, Tolstoy and Voltaire. These publishers have thrived in a trade book niche with works that are in the **public domain.** The authors or the designated owners of their works have given up their claim to control the re-issuance or the ownership has expired under copyright law. Under current U.S. law, copyright claims typically expire 70 years after the author's death.

Public domain works are online. In 1971 an eccentric and colorful University of Illinois student, **Michael Hart,** began digitizing cultural works for online distribution. The endeavor, dubbed **Project Gutenberg,** attracted volunteers who scanned and keyboarded hundreds of public-domain works in the interest of making significant literature universally available.

Dozens of digital libraries followed. The most ambitious is the **Google Print Library,** a project of the Google search engine company. Google set out in 2005 to digitize the entire collection at the libraries of Harvard, Oxford, Stanford, the University of Michigan and the New York Public Library. The goal was massive: to put virtually all the books in the English language, 15 million titles, on a searchable database. The project will take years.

CHECKING YOUR MEDIA LITERACY

Google Print Library
Project to put all books in human history online

- **How did Project Gutenberg avoid legal issues in posting literature online without author permission?**
- **Why will the Google Print Library Project take so long?**

New Directions for Books

STUDY PREVIEW

Every publishing house covets having best-sellers, but the financial risks are steep. A larger role may be ahead for mid-list titles and other works that have longer, steadier sales potential than one-shot wonders that fade after a few weeks. The greatest change afoot in the book industry is in retailing. Bricks-and-mortar stores are in slow decline as Internet sales rise. The industry's greatest challenge is cultivating a new generation of young people as readers.

BLOCKBUSTER BOOKS

Since the huge success of *Uncle Tom's Cabin* in 1852, major publishing houses have been obsessed with finding the next blockbuster. How big can a best-seller be? No one knows. Every new top-seller sets a new goal to surpass. Two of the top-selling novels in history have appeared since 2000—J. K. Rowling's latest *Harry Potter* book, which averages 60 million copies worldwide, and Dan Brown's *Da Vinci Code*, at 60.5 million and still counting.

Critics fault publishing houses for their frenzied blockbuster emphasis. In an important book, *The Death of Literature*, Alvin Kernan makes the case that publishers look for what's marketable rather than what has literary quality. The blockbuster obsession, Kernan says, stunts good literature. A premium is put on works that are written, edited and marketed to a lesser literary level, which Kernan says

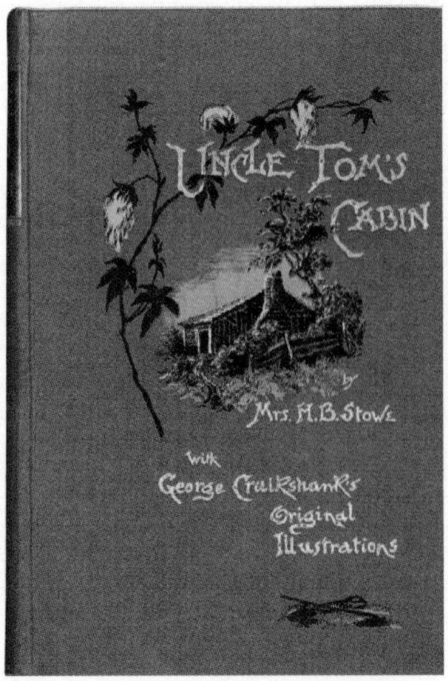

Harriet Beecher Stowe

First Blockbuster. *Publishers first tasted the immense potential of best-sellers before the Civil War, when* Uncle Tom's Cabin *by Harriet Beecher Stowe sold 200,000 copies within three weeks. The major focus at major publishing houses became finding potential mega-sellers and promoting them energetically. Sometimes, say critics, the promotion more than the literary quality creates the sales success. Put another way, the tail wags the dog.*

undermines cultural standards. Mediocre stuff, even bad stuff, displaces good stuff in the marketplace.

Critics say the fetish of major houses for best-sellers hurts talented mid-list authors, who write for modest advances and whose work languishes for want of a marketing budget. And, add the critics, society is culturally the poorer for the misguided emphasis on blockbusters.

The obsessive pursuit of mega-best-sellers is risky for book publishers because of large up-front investment. A flop or two can run corporate ledgers into red ink in a hurry. A shift is under way against concentrating corporate resources in a few major projects. Jane Friedman, long-time chief executive at HarperCollins, talks about long-term profits from what she calls "small books." She sees new life for books that now, after their introduction, languish in warehouses until they're shredded to make room for newer titles. With digital storage, these backlist books can remain available indefinitely. With **print-on-demand** technology, one copy at a time can be printed. Over the long term, Friedman says, many backlist books can generate continuing sales and profits.

Also, she says, small books could sell significantly better if marketed to people with specific interests and who otherwise have no idea the books are available. Friedman's ideas on targeted marketing are clearly contrarian in an industry where intuitive assessment of manuscripts has been the tradition. She's blunt: "Publishers have never looked at who the consumer is."

The book industry needs to reinvent itself, she says: "Chasing best-sellers is a fool's game."

The print-on-demand phenomenon already is making a dent. The output of on-demand, short-run and unclassified titles soared to 135,000 in 2007, six-fold from the year before. Combined with 277,000 new titles and editions, book production topped 411,000 in the United States, up 38 percent.

CHECKING YOUR MEDIA LITERACY

- **Why do major publishing houses obsess on best-sellers?**
- **What are downsides of the obsession for best-sellers?**
- **Do you see a stronger role for mid-list books in the future?**

print-on-demand (POD)
Printing and binding of books in low volumes, even a single copy

BOOK RETAILING

The book industry is undergoing major changes in delivering products to consumers. Retail booksellers have been under growing pressure for years. First, independent

Jeff Bezos. *As Jeff Bezos saw it back in 1994, the web had great potential for e-commerce. But what to sell? Figuring that products that lent themselves to direct mail would also work well on the web, Bezos settled on books. He founded Amazon.com in the garage of his Seattle home, pioneering book retailing on the web. By 2000 sales topped $1 billion.*

bookstores—traditionally a staple of every city neighborhood and every small town—gave way to chain superstores like Barnes & Noble and Borders. More recently, the surviving indies and the chains alike have been under siege from a new quarter—Internet booksellers led by the remarkable **Jeff Bezos** and his Amazon.com. Starting in 1994, Amazon's stunningly successful online retail model has changed the way that people browse and buy books and inaugurated a shift away from the bricks-and-mortar model that dates to the 1600s. Book retailing took a new turn in 2009 when the giant retailer Wal-Mart vowed to undercut Amazon pricing.

CHECKING YOUR MEDIA LITERACY

- **What kind of future do you see for bookstores as we know them?**

YOUNG READERS

A troubling aspect of the book industry's fundamentals is whether young people are reading as much as earlier generations. These are future book buyers. Studies come to contradictory conclusions. In the early 2000s, bookstores reported increases of 20 to 75 percent in young buyers. Some called it the **Harry Potter Effect,** which indeed prompted a swelling of new titles for 10- to 14-year-olds. Established authors including Isabel Allende, Clive Barker, Michael Crichton and Carl Hiaasen all wrote books for the juvenile market. Some observers noted that teenagers, spurred earlier than ever to do well on college admissions tests, worked harder at getting a sense of a larger world. Too, the book industry became increasingly clever with marketing lures, including Hollywood and celebrity tie-ins and book readings at teen clubs.

Even so, concern is growing that young people are drifting away from books. A landmark study by the National Endowment for the Arts, called *Reading at Risk,* found that fewer than half of American adults read literature, loosely defined as

Jeff Bezos (pronounced BAY-zos)
Founder of online book retailer Amazon.com

Harry Potter Effect
Impact of a single-best selling book

Stephenie Meyer

Fast-Seller. *Young people may not be as hungry for literature as earlier generations, but they will read. Stephenie Meyer's dark romance* Twilight *series, with Edward the hunky vampire and Bella the smitten rain forest maiden, sold 42 million copies starting in 2005. Edward and Bella displaced J. K. Rowling's* Harry Potter *series as the top-seller in 2008. Even so, Harry Potter's record remained a pinnacle in trade publishing—more than 400 million copies in a nine-year run.*

fiction or poetry. That was a 10 percent decline over 20 years. For young adults, the drop was 28 percentage points. It's not that people can't read, which would be illiteracy. Instead, people are increasingly **aliterate,** which means they can read but don't.

The findings of the National Endowment study, although alarming, may be overstated. The fact is that adult fiction titles grew 43.1 percent in 2004 to more than 25,000 titles, which perhaps means that fewer people are reading more books. Too, as book industry spokesperson Patricia Schroeder has noted, people in serious eras, like wartime and economic depression, spend less time with fiction and more time with biography, history, current events and other nonfiction. Clearly, more time now is being spent on alternatives to books, like on-screen news and blogs.

CHECKING YOUR MEDIA LITERACY

- **How would you respond to someone who sees books and other print media as past their heyday as major mass media?**
- **What can book publishers do to bring young people back to reading books, as did earlier generations?**
- **Do the findings of *Reading at Risk* coincide with your own observations and experiences?**

aliterate
A non-reader who can read but doesn't

New Book Technology

STUDY PREVIEW

In general, the book industry seems well poised to adapt to the Internet technology that has had devastating effects on other media industries. To be sure, ink-on-paper products will wither in coming years, but the book industry already has dabbled with alternate mechanisms to package and deliver its core product—long-form fiction and nonfiction and textbooks.

E-BOOKS

Like the other ink-on-paper media, the book publishing industry is migrating to digital ways of doing business, from scanning, archiving and searching on Google to print-on-demand technology to online bookselling. Two of the most talked about digital apps in publishing are e-books and e-readers. An **e-book** is usually a digital version of a print book formatted to be read on a computer, a dedicated e-reader or, increasingly, on a cell phone.

Sometimes e-books are created as original digital content, and never see the shelf as a printed book. The hottest sector of the Japanese publishing business recently has been the cell-phone novel: short novels, composed in short sentences on a cell-phone for distribution only to cell-phone networks. These novels are almost exclusively written by and for teens and young adults.

For over a decade e-books struggled to take hold in the marketplace, hampered chiefly by two drawbacks: first, by the lack of any standard **e-reader** platform; and second, by a distinct lack of urgency on the part of readers to migrate to these new devices. When the most advanced e-book software and e-reader hardware only mimics the look and feel of a printed book—a medium that has been in existence more than 500 years—what advantages do they confer that will compel people to give up their beloved books for them? It turns out, with the new generation of e-books and readers, such as the Kindle 2 from Amazon.com and Sony's EReader, there are several.

e-books
Digital files of book content that are stored, searched, sampled, downloaded and paid for online for use on computer, dedicated reader or cell phone

One is instantaneous access. With the Kindle, readers may browse tens of thousands of available books, and buy and download any of them instantaneously, a distinct advantage over previous generations of e-readers. Another is portability. You can store hundreds of books in a single device and carry them with you wherever you go.

e-reader
Portable electronic device for on-screen reading of books

These advantages, plus other improvements to the technology, are spurring growth in the e-book market up to 25 percent a year—enormous compared to the 2 percent growth of the book business as a whole.

Bezos Scores Again. *Amazon.com founder Jeff Bezos demonstrates his Kindle e-reader. Users buy entire books for $10 or so and download them. Periodical subscriptions also are available. Kindles can store more volumes than most people have physical library shelves. Kindle models are becoming lighter and thinner. What's next? Technology is at hand for flexible screens that can be scrolled up and jammed into a jeans pocket.*

But is any of this really new? Or are these innovations just mimes of a mass medium that's been around for centuries? Despite the glitz of e-books, the fact is that they are hardly transformational. As now, most books are still word-driven. They require literacy. A reader's progress through a book remains highly idiosyncratic and personal. Librarian Scott Condon, in assessing the core qualities of a book, puts it this way: "They are accessed and decoded through the sense of vision; the reading of books is self-paced; and they are evoked in the highly individualized circuitry of each reader's mind, heart and imagination." E-books will change none of that.

CHECKING YOUR MEDIA LITERACY

- **Are e-books a threat to the book publishing industry? How so?**

audio books
Recorded books, often abridged, for listening rather than reading

audio downloads
Digital audio files formatted for playback on a desktop or laptop computer, typically for a fee

podcasts
(contrivance of the words *iPod* and *broadcast*) A series of audio files for regular syndication. User's software automatically downloads later files associated with the podcast for use at listener's convenience

AUDIO BOOKS

Relatively low-tech **audio books** are more revolutionary than e-books. Audio books are non-literal. The language reaches us through the sense of hearing. The pace is not controlled by the user. The text is interpreted not by the reader but by a performer. It is perhaps telling that audio books, as a radical variant to the traditional book, comprise a minute fraction of the book industry. The lesson: Reading as an activity is what people enjoy. Listening? Not so much.

Conversely, the old audio book-on-tape is undergoing a digital renaissance of its own. **Audio downloads** of books for play on computers comprise a growing segment of the audio book business, and may make inroads into sales of print books. Authors have also been finding **podcasts** to be a robust new method of reaching an increasingly wired and far-flung audience.

CHECKING YOUR MEDIA LITERACY

- **How are low-tech audio books a radical departure from traditional ink-on-paper books?**

CHAPTER WRAP-UP

Newspaper Industry (Pages 83–88)

- The U.S. newspaper industry dominated mass media for more than 160 years. Even so, a contraction began in the 1970s as afternoon newspapers either shut down, were absorbed by morning competitors or switched to morning distribution. Why so? A major factor was the advent of the two-income household. Few people had free time in the evenings to read. Television attracted eyeballs too. The contraction was masked by an overheated economy with huge advertising spending and also by clever adjustments in the industry's business model, including economies of scale brought on with chain ownership. It all came apart in 2008 as major dailies were faced with advertiser losses brought on by the sinking economy and vaporizing ad revenue.

Post-Print Culture (Pages 88–91)

- The disappearance of major newspapers and magazines may profoundly change the way we live and our society operates. Through history the financial might of the newspaper industry enabled newspapers to contribute importantly to unearthing wrongs in government, business and other institutions and pushing for reforms. The term *muckraking* originated with magazines, which have contributed importantly to investigative reporting and social reform. These media gave voice to people who had no voice—the downtrodden, the impoverished and immigrants. In the future what will perform these functions that have been important in shaping our culture?

Magazine Industry (Pages 91–95)

- Several shelter and celebrity magazines are holding their own. But many high-visibility magazines have disappeared after losing their audiences and advertisers to Internet-based competition. Most magazines are well along into a transition to digital delivery on the Internet, but it's not easy. The advertising base that sustained magazines in their heydays is so scattered among countless web sites that magazines have far fewer resources to sustain the kinds of quality content of their past.

Magazine Innovations (Pages 95–101)

- When their advertising base was at peak levels, magazines pioneered innovations that have become standard in other media. These include visuals. The in-depth personality profile has remained the province of magazines. Some magazines remain committed to courageous investigative reporting in the muckraking tradition.

Book Industry (Pages 101–103)

- The book industry has components that produce books in different categories—trade books, which include best-sellers; textbooks; and reference books. Most publishing houses focus in one area, although some houses move in and out of categories. Also, there are dozens of subcategories.

Books and Technology (Pages 109–110)

- Components of the book industry are moving into digital delivery of products that largely are unavailable on the web. This includes well-selected, well-edited novels, biographies and long-form journalism. Textbooks are another genre for the web does not have an equal. Other genres, including reference works, are in rough times. With wiki, most traditional encyclopedias are having rough times. Does anybody buy a dictionary any more?

New Directions for the Book (Pages 106–109)

- Every publishing house covets having best-sellers, but the financial risks are steep. A larger role may be ahead for mid-list titles and works that have longer, steadier sales potential than one-shot wonders that fade after a few weeks. The greatest change afoot in the book industry is in retailing. Bricks-and-mortar stores are in slow decline as Internet sales rise. The digitization of every aspect of the business offers some hope of new markets, but the industry's greatest challenge is cultivating a new generation of young people as readers.

▼ Review Questions

1. What are the three major print industry components? What is the revenue source of each?
2. When did mass audiences come into existence? How so?
3. Describe some leading U.S. newspapers and what sets them apart.
4. Can democracy survive without newspapers and magazines? How about our culture?
5. How is the magazine industry coping with the transition to the Internet?
6. What have been magazine-pioneered innovations in media content?
7. What are the major components of the book industry?
8. How will the major components of the book industry fare in the Internet Age?
9. What other major challenges face the book industry?

Concepts

aliterate (Page 109)
business model (Page 84)
demassification (Page 100)
muckraking (Page 97)
public domain (Page 105)
sub-mass audience (Page 100)

Terms

audio books (Page 110)
audio downloads (Page 110)
e-book (Page 109)
e-reader (Page 109)
freelancer (Page 93)
penny papers (Page 84)
podcast (Page 110)
trade books (Page 105)

People

Benjamin Day (Page 83)
Henry Luce (Page 96)
Jeff Bezos (Page 108)
Jimmy Wales (Page 82)

Media Sources

- Sarah Ellison. *War at the Wall Street Journal: Inside the Struggle to Control an American Business Empire.* Houghton Mifflin Harcourt, 2010. Ellison, once a Journal reporter, portrays Rupert Murdoch variously as craft and resistant in adding Dow Jones to his global media empire. The Bancroft family us portrayed as hapless and mired in squabbles and dark secrets that doomed their rebuffs to Murdoch's persistence.
- Bertrand Lavédrine with Jean-Paul Gandolfo, John McElhone and Sibylle Monod; John McElhone, translator. *Photographs of the past: process and preservation,* Getty Conservation Institute, 2009. This is an encyclopedic illustrated review of photographic processes back to the early 1800s.
- Leading trade journals: *Editor & Publisher* for newspapers, *Folio* for magazines, *Publishers Weekly* for books.
- Numerous histories have been written on leading newspapers and magazines. So have biographies on leaders in the industries.
- Chris Anderson. *The Long Tail: Why the Future of Business Is Selling Less of More*. Hyperion, 2006. Anderson, editor of *Wired*, says blockbusters are becoming less important with the advent of technology that has expanded the marketplace into microniches.
- Jason Epstein. *Book Business: Publishing Past, Present, and Future*. Norton, 2001. Epstein, former editorial director at Random House, offers a history of book publishing.
- Gene Roberts and Thomas Kunkel, editors. *Breach of Faith: A Crisis of Coverage in the Age of Corporate Newspapering*. University of Arkansas, 2003. This collection of essays notes that newspapers have become more glitzy than ever but also formulaic and bland under new pressures from giant corporate owners.
- Michael Korda. *Making the List: A Cultural History of the American Bestseller 1900–1999*. Barnes and Noble, 2001. Korda, longtime editor at Simon & Schuster, argues that best-seller lists are telling indicators of changing social values. Korda is informed, witty and provocative.

A Thematic Chapter Summary

INK ON PAPER

In this chapter you have deepened your media literacy by revisiting several themes. Here are some thematic highlights from the chapter.

MEDIA TECHNOLOGY

Excess Press Capacity. Presses with less and less to print. Bye, bye, newspapers.

Printing technology begat the book, newspaper and magazine industries, which grew into giant influences in society. For newspapers, the machinery became an albatross early in the 21st century. The whole business model for the newspaper industry had been wedded to in-house presses, which constituted multi-million-dollar capital investments for even mid-size dailies. Then two essentials in the business model disappeared. Readership slipped, then advertising revenue. These presses had increasingly unused capacity. Magazine and book companies were less affected because they farmed out their printing.
(Pages 88–89 and 110–111)

MEDIA ECONOMICS

Without advertising revenue, newspapers and magazines scrambled to the Internet as a low-cost way to reach readers and win back advertising. By and large, it didn't work. Thousands of other companies were already entrenched online with the same kind of content as newspapers and magazines. Big-name publications, once the only place people could find news and sports, were suddenly just another player in a crowded, competitive field. The book industry, never dependent on advertising, was better situated. The Internet had little quality book-length competition for the book industry, which shifted adroitly into online delivery. (Pages 90–94 and 110–111)

MEDIA DEMOCRACY

Muckraking. Ida Tarbell dug up bad stuff on Standard Oil with the noble goal of reforms to prevent monopolistic abuses.

The mass media has played an essential role in democracy. Since the 1870s at least, newspapers, magazines and books exposed corruption and abuse in government and business that worked against the public's interest. Newspapers with daily frequency hammered away for prosecution and reform. What institutions of society will fill the void if newspapers and magazines aren't around? No online company has the advertising base to fund costly investigative reporting. In the 21st century, a new Tammany Hall gang might be running New York City without a press watchdog. Would a new Watergate coverup go unchecked?
(Pages 94–99 and 105–110)

ELITISM AND POPULISM

End of Blockbuster. Former publishing executive Jane Friedman sees high-risk blockbuster projects becoming passé.

Newspapers created in the penny press era built unprecedented circulation with stories that pandered to large audiences. These newspapers created the modern concept of mass audiences and mass communication. Although the audience has fragmented with a plethora of competition, there remains a strong populist strain in media content. The book industry, for example, has obsessed about best-sellers since *Uncle Tom's Cabin* in 1852. A book industry commentator, Alvin Kernan, makes a case that our culture has paid a heavy price for the obsession. Kernan believes that major publishing houses, in their quest for profits, are using resources for projects with mass appeal rather than for books that could contribute to moving the culture forward. He is making an elitist argument. By pandering to mass tastes, he said, the book industry is abdicating its responsibility to do good things. (Pages 115–117)

MEDIA FUTURE

E-Readers. Kindle and other devices may seal the fate of bricks-and-mortar retail booksellers. But will young people still be attracted to book-length reading?

Young people have glommed onto digital media that are less word-driven than ink-on-paper media. Does reading have a future? This generational shift has been a factor in the decline of newspapers. At the same time, studies go both directions on reading. Book publishers cite their survey that nonfiction is on the rebound. Indeed, until the recession beginning in 2008, book sales were growing 3 to 5 percent a year. And the incredible sales of the Harry Potter series demonstrates that the new generation is not averse to reading. (Pages 117–118)

MEDIA AND CULTURE

"It Shines for All." The New York *Sun* motto of 1833 wouldn't resonate as well in today's fragmented media environment.

At their strongest points in history, newspapers helped create communities by providing people with a common source of information and entertainment. Magazines and books did the same at national levels. Figuratively, everybody read *Uncle Tom's Cabin* and Ida Tarbell. Even if some content was contentious, everyone was on the same agenda on what constituted the pressing cultural, political and social values of the day. As ink-on-paper media lost their monopolies, first a little to broadcasting, then massively to the Internet, the mass media became less a binding force for local communities and the nation but a vehicle through which social fragmentation occurred. People had choices for media that catered to their individual interests rather than common interests. (Pages 90–91 and 99–100)

chapter 5

SOUND MEDIA

Tim Westergren

His Pandora Genome Project slices and dices the DNA of music, then with algorithms finds patterns in an individual music-lover's preferences. Subscribers, who pay nothing, are streamed a unique playlist. It could be called a "radio station for one"—you.

LEARNING AHEAD

- Four companies dominate the recording industry.
- File-swapping threatens to upend the industry's economics, but Apple's iPod and iTunes have eased swapping losses.
- Technology has given performers new control of pop music.
- The recording and radio industries are symbiotic.
- Radio is easily accessible, but audience for traditional stations is slipping.
- Music, news and talk are the primary radio content.
- Regulation relies on the idea of government and stations as trustees of the public airwaves.
- Chains have reshaped the radio industry.
- Public radio has filled a niche abandoned by commercial stations.
- Satellite radio has shaken the infrastructure of the radio industry.

TIM WESTERGREN'S PANDORA

It may not be easy at first to spot the core business that entrepreneur Tim Westergren is in.

At Stanford, Westergren studied computers, acoustics and recording technology. He is a piano player who later learned drums, bassoon and clarinet. He played in bands and produced music.

In 2000, like so many others in the early heyday of the Internet, Westergren saw potential for a new online business. It would combine his love and knowledge of music with a bold and clever new idea—create a product with an appeal to a core audience, and deliver it over the Internet. He cofounded the new company with a partner and pitched it successfully to venture capitalists.

The idea was simple: to develop a technology that would define and collect different attributes of music and organize them in such a way as to be maximally useful to people. The new company's first model, licensed to retailers such as Best Buy, helped music buyers find bands they liked. Westergren's classification and organization technology remains the heart of the business today.

So, what kind of business is Tim Westergren in? The music business? Online databases and catalogs? Internet and IT management? Web entrepreneurship?

Actually, Tim Westergren is in radio.

His company is called Pandora. With about 22 million users, it is one of the top three Internet radio sites in the world. Nearly 5 million users access Pandora on iPhones. By some measures, Pandora is the number one iPhone application.

Internet radio is not a new or unique idea. Radio stations have been streaming their signals online since the mid-1990s and many services, including Apple's iTunes, offer listeners a variety of free music channels by genre.

Pandora's innovation is to change the basic model of one-way communication common to all radio. Pandora transforms listeners from passive recipients into active partners in determining what they hear. It asks listeners to interact with its music classification algorithm by voting—thumbs up or down—on songs. This classification is called the Music Genome Project. It is a dizzyingly ambitious attempt to unpack and classify the hundreds of possible essential attributes of any song—to decode its musical DNA. All 600,000 songs in the growing Pandora database are analyzed by a professional musician. Each song is assigned a list of "genes" that mirror particular attributes of a song, for example, gender of lead vocalist, acoustic or electric bass, and distortion of rhythm guitar. Rock and pop songs have 150 genes, rap 350, jazz 400.

A Pandora user creates a radio station by naming a performer or individual song. Pandora plays a song that it calculates to share the genetic attributes of the song or artist named, not necessarily the song or performer itself. Pandora asks whether you like it. Based on your responses, Pandora continues to play new songs on your "station," getting continually smarter about what it plays as it learns more about what you want to hear. It is a simple idea, albeit difficult to execute, based on the original innovation of classifying music that Westergren started with.

With Pandora's booming popularity as an iPhone app, Internet radio is freed from the computer for the first time.

"People take their iPhone to the gym, and plug it into their car radio," Westergren says. "Rather than operate on the computer or office part of radio, we can actually play anywhere. Fifty percent of Pandora use on the iPhone is over wi-fi."

This means people are plugging it in to their docking bays at home, listening to Pandora away from their computer, the same way people have always listened to the radio.

"For folks like us in the radio world," says Westergren, "Our goal is to be as easy and ubiquitous as broadcast radio is."

The Recording Industry

STUDY ***PREVIEW***

The recording industry works mostly in the background of the mass media to which we are exposed daily. Ever heard of Bertelsmann? EMI? Most people haven't. Most music fans know artists and perhaps their labels, but the industry is in fact dominated by four global companies with corporate tentacles also in other media enterprises.

SCOPE OF THE RECORDING INDUSTRY

The recording industry that brings music to mass audiences, both the flashy stuff and everything else, is gigantic. Global sales in 2004 were estimated at $18.4 billion, with $4.9 billion in the United States alone. These totals don't include symbiotic industries like fan magazines, music television and radio that, all

David Geffen. *He parlayed drive and an ear for talent into a music fortune through Geffen Records, becoming Hollywood's first billionaire. Later Geffen joined Jeffrey Katzenberg and Steven Spielberg for a 12-year run with their own movie studio, Dreamworks. The studio produced one acclaimed movie after another, starting with* Saving Private Ryan.

together, claim revenues approaching $17 billion a year. Then there are concerts, performers' merchandise, sponsorships and a miscellany of related enterprises.

The stakes are big. The first billionaire in Hollywood history, **David Geffen,** became rich by building Geffen Records from scratch. He sold the enterprise for three-quarters of a billion dollars. Even in leaner times, with major losses to online music swapping, recordings from major acts sell well. Anglo-Dutch recording conglomerate EMI sold 5 million copies of pop singer Robbie Williams' greatest-hits collection. The Beastie Boys' *Hello Nasty* and Janet Jackson's *All for You* both topped 5 million. Two EMI albums by rapper Chingy have approached 4 million copies.

CHECKING YOUR MEDIA LITERACY

- **What are some measures of the size of the recording industry?**

RECORDING LABELS

The recording industry is concentrated in the major companies known as the Big Four, which have 84 percent of the U.S. market and 75 percent of the global market. Each of these companies, in turn, is part of a larger media conglomerate.

>> Majors. The Napster-induced online file-swapping crisis in the early 21st century shook up the industry's corporate landscape. Sony and Bertelsmann merged their music units. Bertelsmann, the German company that is the world's fifth-largest media company, runs the combined Sony BMG. Alarmed at declining sales in the new file-swapping era, Time Warner sold its Warner Music in 2004—just in time. The French media conglomerate Vivendi ended up with Warner Music and then, with recorded music sales plummeting, tried to unload the acquisition. Nobody wanted it.

The Big Four has twice nearly become the Big Three, with Warner Music, the fourth largest, and EMI, the third largest, twice going to the altar in merger talks, only to be derailed by regulators. The last time was in 2006. The European Union also has kept the Sony-Bertelsmann arrangement under scrutiny.

>> Indies. Besides the majors, independent recording companies called indies are a small but not unimportant segment. Typically indies claim about 15 percent of U.S. sales. An indie occasionally produces a big hit. When an indie amasses enough successes, it invariably is bought out by a major. The most famous of the indies, Motown, whose name became synonymous with a black Detroit style, maintained its independence for 30 years. In 1988, however, founder Berry Gordy received an offer he could not refuse—$61 million. Soon Motown was subsumed into the MCA empire, which later became Universal Music.

While struggling indies remain part of the record industry landscape, the latter-day indies are well-funded labels created by major artists who decide to go their own way, with themselves in charge, rather than dealing with cumbersome big-studio bureaucracies and machinery. The Beatles did it with Apple. Minnesota-based Prince did it. Today it's a common route.

These are the companies that dominate the recording industry, with their major acts by label and their percentage of the global market:

David Geffen
Recording, movie entrepreneur; first self-made billionaire in Hollywood

Universal Music (French) Guns N' Roses (Universal), Jay-Z (Def Jam), Brian McKnight (Motown), George Strait (MCA Nashville), Snoop Dogg (Geffen), Gwen Stefani (Interscope), The Killers (Island)	**25.5 percent**
Sony BMG (German) Bruce Springsteen (Columbia), Jennifer Lopez (Epic), Santa (Legacy), Travis Tritt (Sony Nashville), OperaBabes (Odyssey)	**21.5 percent**
EMI (Anglo-Dutch) Beastie Boys (Capitol), Janet Jackson (Virgin), Tina Turner (Capitol)	**13.1 percent**
Warner Music (U.S.) Doors (Elektra), Boyz N Da Hood (Bad Boy), Twisted Sister (Lava), Lil' Kim (Atlantic)	**11.3 percent**

CHECKING YOUR MEDIA LITERACY

- **What are the largest recording companies and the country in which each is based?**
- **Historically, what becomes of successful, independent record companies?**

A&R STRUCTURE

The heart of the recording industry once was the powerful **A&R** units, short for **artist and repertoire,** at major labels. In an arrogant tyranny over artists, A&R executives manufactured countless performers. They groomed artists for stardom, chose their music, ordered the arrangements, controlled recording sessions and even chose their wardrobes for public performances.

In his book *Solid Gold* Serge Denisoff quotes a Capitol executive from the 1950s explaining how the A&R system worked: "The company would pick out 12 songs for Peggy Lee and tell her to be at the studio Wednesday at 8, and she'd show up and sing what you told her. And she'd leave three hours later and Capitol'd take her songs and do anything it wanted with them. That was a time when the artist was supposed to shut up and put up with anything the almighty recording company wanted."

The muscle of the major record companies, aiming for mass market sales, contributed to a homogenizing of U.S. culture. Coast to coast, everybody was humming the same new tunes from Peggy Lee and other pop singers, who served a robotlike role for A&R managers. The A&R structure was a top-down system for creating pop culture. A relatively small number of powerful A&R executives decided what would be recorded and marketed. It was the opposite of grassroots artistry.

CHECKING YOUR MEDIA LITERACY

- **How would the Dixie Chicks respond if recording company A&R staffs tried to dictate their repertoire, even their style, as they did for Peggy Lee?**
- **Has the culture been enriched or damaged by the diminished A&R role today?**

A&R (artist and repertoire)
Units of a recording company responsible for talent

garage bands
A term coined for upstart performers without a studio contract

PERFORMER INFLUENCES

In the 1980s sophisticated low-cost recording and mixing equipment gave individual artists and **garage bands** a means to control their art. The million-dollar sound studio, controlled by major labels and their A&R people, became less important. As little as $15,000 could buy digital recorders and 24-channel mixing boards, plus remodeling the garage, to do what only a major studio could have done a few years earlier.

The upshot was liberation for creativity. Artists suddenly had an independence that big recording companies were forced to learn to accommodate. Linda Ronstadt, for example, shifted her recording to a home studio in her basement. Some artists, like LL Cool J, went so far as to create their own labels. The ability of artists to go out on their own gave them clout that was not possible in the A&R heyday. The Dixie Chicks, among others, used this new leverage in negotiating with their labels.

Another result has been greater diversity. A rap fan might never have heard the Dixie Chicks. The music of Barry Manilow is obscure to most Coldplay fans. In this sense, recorded music has become less of a unifying element in the whole society. The unification, rather, is in subsets of the mass audience.

Shawn Fanning

Pioneered music file-swapping through original Napster.

downloading

Installing a file on a computer from an Internet source

CHECKING YOUR MEDIA LITERACY

- **How has technology enabled artistic creativity?**
- **What is a cultural downside to the demassification that has come with greater artistic autonomy?**

New Digital Music Landscape

STUDY PREVIEW

Napster and other file-sharing technology that facilitates music swapping seriously eroded music sales until 2005, when the U.S. Supreme Court intervened. An older problem, pirate dubbing, continues to be a drain. The recorded music industry has moved to get on top of downloading technology with new retailing models. These include the iPod–iTunes distribution structure introduced by Apple. This shift in retailing has hurt bricks-and-mortar stores. Some chains have gone out of business.

Napster Guy. *Shawn Fanning introduced free-for-all online music-swapping technology that he dubbed Napster. The incredible popularity of swapping threatened the recording industry's traditional profit model. Why pay $15 for a CD? The industry went to court claiming that swap services were facilitating copyright infringements and won.*

FILE SWAPPING

Shawn Fanning's Napster technology ushered in a frenzy of free music swapping on the Internet in 2000. Suddenly, record stores found themselves unable to move inventory. Major music retailer Best Buy shut down its Sam Goody's, Musicland and other brand-name stores that had seemed sure moneymakers only a few months earlier. The free-fall continued. For the first time in its history, the record industry was not in control of new technology—unlike the earlier adjustments, when companies exploited developments to spur sales, like switches to high-fidelity and stereo and the introduction of eight-tracks, cassettes and CDs.

The Recording Industry Association of America, which represents recorded music companies, went to court against Napster. A federal judge bought the argument that Napster was participating in copyright infringement by facilitating illicit copying of protected intellectual property. Napster was toast.

In a surreal initiative in 2003, RIAA began legal action against individuals who **downloaded** music without paying. The association's goal was a few hundred highly publicized lawsuits, perhaps some showcase trials, to discourage download piracy. In one respect, the strategy backfired, only engendering hard feelings among people who were the industry's greatest consumers.

In 2005 the U.S. Supreme Court acted against file-swapping in what was quickly hailed as a landmark gain for the recording industry. The decision did not end music swapping immediately but so hobbled business as usual among swap services that RIAA was confident it had largely stopped the free-swapping drain on its revenues.

Download Solution. *Steve Jobs of Apple Computer gave the recording industry an online retailing outlet with his iTunes store, from which music could be downloaded into incredibly popular Apple iPod listening devices at 99 cents a song. Downloaders could feel good that they weren't violating the intellectual property rights of recording companies or performers, lyricists or composers. And recording companies, desperate to stem revenue losses from illegal but free downloading, could derive income from the sales.*

CHECKING YOUR MEDIA LITERACY

- **How did Shawn Fanning shake the recording industry out of its new-technology blind spot?**
- **How did the U.S. Supreme Court settle the recording industry's file-sharing disaster?**

ITUNES

The recording industry, comfortable and immensely profitable, was caught unawares by online music swapping. When the industry finally woke up to the threat, recording companies tried to tap into the new technology, but floundered. Numerous stabs at a new business model fell apart—until **Steve Jobs** of Apple Computer presented himself as a rescuing knight in shining armor with the online **iTunes** music store. From the iTunes site people can sample songs with a single click and then download with another click for 99 cents a song. In iTunes' first week, more than 1 million songs were downloaded, juicing a 27 percent spike in Apple stock.

Unlike download-swapping, iTunes wasn't free. But it had advantages. The sound quality was exceptional. Apple used a new format that compressed music efficiently, downloaded faster and consumed less disk space. It was a clean system, without the annoying viruses that affected swap systems. Apple benefited too from the guilt trip that RIAA was trying to lay on illegal downloaders.

Game Changers. *From its inception the Apple iPod changed the way we bought, stored, accessed, shared, and listened to music. Bands and record labels had no choice but to follow along with its pay-per-song paradigm. The iPhone combined a cell phone with music functionality and innumerable cool online applications for the decade's must-have device.*

Steve Jobs
The driving force behind the Apple Computer revival, iPod and iTunes

iTunes
Apple-owned online retail site for recorded music

CASE STUDY

Podcasting Evolution

Adam Curry. *He invented podcasting, which he sees as a revolutionary vehicle for just about anybody to assemble radio-like programs for indeed global listening. What's it cost? Not much more than a computer, a modem, and easy-to-use podcast software.*

Bands used to send their singles on a 45-rpm record to radio stations across the country, hoping for airplay. Today, musicians who want to reach a global audience send their music on a digital file to podcasters. These are the people who put together their own Internet audio shows, typically an MP3 file, that is delivered to a listener with an iPod, or other audio player, or a computer with an Internet connection and speakers. Listeners can access the podcast at their convenience, and it's free.

As of 2010 there were more than 72,000 podcasters in the music/radio category at Podcast Alley, a directory of podcasts for every type of music from jazz to metal. Chris McIntyre started Podcast Alley to index all the podcasts he could find. Music is only part of what his site indexes. "I truly believe that podcasting is a powerful communication tool and will have a profound effect on the way we communicate in the future," says the Purdue University graduate.

While musicians are hoping for exposure from the new medium, PodShow Inc. founder **Adam Curry** is poised to make big bucks from it. "Podfather" Curry and software pioneer Dave Winer developed the computer programs that make podcasting possible. Curry founded PodShow Inc. in 2005. The same venture capital companies that invested in Yahoo! and Google invested $9 million in PodShow.

The mainstream media "are so diluted, so packaged, so predictable. There's so very little that is new or interesting," Curry told the Los Angeles *Times*. "We've lost a lot of social connectedness that used to come from that. And what we're building here is a social media network for human beings." Curry's critics claim the former MTV VJ "promotes himself as a would-be revolutionary for the little guy, but he's actually as profit mad as the corporate giants."

Other companies are jumping on the podcast wagon. Nokia announced in 2006 that some of its new phones would include a podcasting client featuring the PodShow top 10, Podcast Alley Picks and podcasts from Digital Podcast.

"Thousands of bands are submitting their songs to the Podsafe Music Network. They're connecting with podcasters and listeners, and now they're figuring out that it makes sense to promote shows together and share their audience with each other," said Curry. "This is another way bands are benefiting from the DIY/digital revolution in music."

DEEPENING YOUR MEDIA LITERACY

EXPLORE THE ISSUE

Canvass 10 people around you on whether podcasts have become a part of their media habit. Ask what they seek from podcasts. Video stories? News? Music? And which podcasts seem most popular?

DIG DEEPER

Visit the most popular podcast sites. Rank them for ease of access. What are the access charges, if any?

WHAT DO YOU THINK?

Does music content available on podcasts comprise a significant shift in the retail delivery of recorded music? Or is it a blip in the music retailing landscape?

Jobs began iTunes with huge repertoires from some major labels. Other labels begged to sign on as soon as the iPod–iTunes success was clear. By 2005, 62 percent of all music downloads were from iTunes. To be sure, copycat services spawned quickly. Wal-Mart created WAM. The Napster name was resurrected as a subscription service with unlimited access to downloads, the whole collection playable as long as the subscription was kept current.

CHECKING YOUR MEDIA LITERACY

- **How does iTunes generate profits for both Apple and recording companies?**
- **Despite many products coming along to challenge iPod and iTunes, none have come close. Why?**

RETAILING

The iTunes concept drastically changed the retailing of recorded music. Record shops, once the core outlet for recording companies, already were under siege by retailers like Sam Goody and Musicland. With iTunes, even the chains were in trouble. Bankruptcies followed. The new retailing structure is largely iTunes-like download services, online retailers like Amazon.com, and giant retailers like Wal-Mart and Best Buy.

CHECKING YOUR MEDIA LITERACY

- **Who have been the losers in the retailing change introduced by iTunes?**
- **Who are the survivors?**

Adam Curry
Pioneer in podcasting technology

Regulatory Pressure

STUDY *PREVIEW*

The recording industry has been a scapegoat for social ills. To stay one step ahead of government censorship, the industry has taken a cue from other media groups and introduced self-regulation to head off First Amendment crises.

OBJECTIONABLE MUSIC

Campaigns to ban recorded music are nothing new. In the Roaring '20s some people saw jazz as morally loose. White racists of the 1950s called Bill Haley's rock "nigger music." War protest songs of the Vietnam period angered many Americans. Government attempts to censor records have been rare, yet the Federal Communications Commission indirectly keeps some records off the market. The FCC can take a dim view of stations that air objectionable music, which guides broadcasters toward caution. Stations do not want to risk their FCC-awarded licenses, which are subject to periodic renewal and can be yanked.

The FCC has been explicit about obnoxious lyrics. In 1971 the commission said that stations have a responsibility to know "the content of the lyrics." Not to do so, said the commission, would raise "serious questions as to whether continued operation of the station is in the public interest." The issue at the time was music that glorified drugs.

CHECKING YOUR MEDIA LITERACY

- **What form have objections to music lyrics taken?**
- **Has the government ever banned a song?**

LABELING

In the 1980s complaints about lyrics focused on drugs, sexual promiscuity and violence. **Parents Music Resource Center,** a group led by wives of influential members of Congress, claimed links between explicit rock music and teen suicide, teen pregnancy, parental abuse, broken homes and other social ills. The group objected to lyrics like those in Prince's *Sister,* which extol incest; Mötley Crüe's *Live Wire*, with its psychopathic enthusiasm for strangulation; Guns N' Roses' white racism; and rap artists' hate music.

The Parents Music Resource Center argued that consumer protection laws should be invoked to require that records with offensive lyrics be labeled as dangerous, like cigarette warning labels or the movie industry's rating system. After the group went to the FCC and the **National Association of Broadcasters,** record companies voluntarily began labeling potentially offensive records: "Explicit Lyrics—Parental Advisory." In some cases the companies printed lyrics on album covers as a warning. Online retailers, including iTunes, put a label of "explicit" on songs that might raise prudish eyebrows.

CHECKING YOUR MEDIA LITERACY

- **Why did recording companies embrace the idea of labeling music with objectionable lyrics? Was this a good thing?**
- **What is the purpose of labeling objectionable music? Does labeling accomplish its purpose?**

ARTISTIC FREEDOM

The usual defense against would-be censors is that artistic freedom merits protection, no matter how objectionable the art's content. When rapper Ice T seemed to push the envelope on acceptability with his song *Cop Killer* on a Warner Music label, police groups and others called for a ban. It was no wonder, with lyrics such as "I got my 12-gauge sawed-off/And I got my headlights turned off/I'm about to dust some cops off." Some defended the album as misunderstood. **Gerald Levin,** chief executive at Time Warner, catapulted the defense of Ice T to another level with an eloquent defense for artistic liberties as an essential value in a free society.

Free expressionists were enthusiastic that Levin had taken a pro-artist stance over a financially safer bottom-line position. A few months later, however, Levin waffled. He called on Warner artists to begin a dialogue on standards. Fervid support for Levin waned as his position shifted to safer ground for Time Warner's corporate well-being. In the end, Levin cut loose Ice T's label from the Warner collection—a more typical, albeit less heroic, action for a media executive. Ever-mindful of potential threats to their industry's autonomy, media executives almost always try to finesse their way out of confrontations that have the potential to precipitate serious calls for government censorship.

Parents Music Resource Center
Crusaded for labels on "objectionable" music

National Association of Broadcasters
Radio, television and trade organization

Gerald Levin
Time Warner chief executive who defended artists' free expression

CHECKING YOUR MEDIA LITERACY

- **How would you evaluate the Gerald Levin defense of Ice T's *Cop Killer* lyrics?**
- **Would you consider Gerald Levin a hero of free expression?**

Dependence on Radio

STUDY PREVIEW

The recording industry relies on radio for free advertising of its wares. Airplay has been essential for recordings to sell. This has led to legal issues, like under-the-table payments to decision makers at influential stations for airtime.

The Grammy Bounce. *In the two days after the 2005 Grammy Awards tribute to Ray Charles, sales of his* Genius Loves Company *album spiked 875 percent at the TowerRecords chain. The Grammy Bounce is a perennial phenomenon. In 2003 Norah Jones'* Come Away with Me *zoomed to number one within a week. Sales soon topped 9.2 million.*

RADIO PARTNERSHIP

The radio and record industries have been connected since the mid-1920s, when the bottom fell out of the record business. To stay afloat, record companies looked to advantageous partnerships with radio. The Victor Talking Machine Company began courting with the fledgling RCA radio network. In 1929 they merged. Columbia Phonograph Company acquired another network, which later became CBS.

Over time the value of radio to record makers became clearer in another context. In the 1940s, when records by performers like Bing Crosby and Frank Sinatra were promoted over the radio, sales soared. When radio shifted mostly to playing recorded music in the 1950s, **airplay** became essential for a new recording to succeed. Radio, in effect, became free advertising.

CHECKING YOUR MEDIA LITERACY

- **Radio needs music, and the music recording industry needs radio. Is this a mutual interdependence? Or is one party more dependent than the other?**

MARKETING THROUGH RADIO

Although radio has declined in importance for promoting records, with young people opting for iPods and similar devices, nothing beats free advertising. Record makers still supply stations with new music in hopes it finds its way on the air. In an imaginative step, country duo Montgomery Gentry recorded their single *Lucky Man* 81 times, each time with a different college or professional athletic team in the lyrics. The idea was to attract station music directors in key markets and encourage airplay. At the very least, figured Montgomery Gentry promoters, the local tie-in would prolong airplay more than normal.

CHECKING YOUR MEDIA LITERACY

- **Who at a radio station decides what music is aired?**

MEASURES OF SUCCESS

It would be wrong to suggest that successful recordings can result only from manipulation. Once new music crosses the threshold to exposure, its commercial success rests with public acceptance. Exposure, however, is key. The publicity that comes with a Grammy Award, for example, inevitably boosts sales, usually dramatically.

The most often-cited measure of success is sales. Once a single sells 1 million copies or an album sells 500,000 copies, the RIAA confers a **gold record** award. A **platinum record** is awarded for 2 million singles or 1 million albums. The measure of success for shareholders who own the conglomerates that own the record companies, however, is profit. A gold record for 1 million albums doesn't translate into profit if the artist has a lavish multimillion-dollar deal whose breakeven point is 2 million records.

airplay
Radio time devoted to a particular recording

gold record
The award for sales of 500,000 albums or 1 million singles

platinum record
The award for sales of 1 million albums or 2 million singles

CHECKING YOUR MEDIA LITERACY

- **What does it mean when a record goes gold? Platinum?**
- **What noneconomic measures can be used to score a recording's success?**

MEDIA TIMELINE

SOUND MEDIA MILESTONES / PIVOTAL EVENTS

1800s

Phonograph
Thomas Edison introduced a recording-playback device (1877)

Mass Production
Multiple copies of recordings possible with Emile Berliner's invention (1887)

Radio
Marconi transmitted first message (1895)

The New York Times.
TITANIC SINKS FOUR HOURS AFTER HITTING ICEBERG; 866 RESCUED BY CARPATHIA, PROBABLY 1250 PERISH; ISMAY SAFE, MRS. ASTOR MAYBE, NOTED NAMES MISSING

Making radio a household word

>> Emergence of a middle class in U.S., with new leisure time, discretionary income (1870s)

>> Congress created first regulatory agency, Interstate Commerce Commission (1887)

1900–1945

Titanic
News from the mid-Atlantic tragedy established radio in public mind (1912)

Commercial Radio
KDKA, Pittsburgh, became first licensed commercial station (1920)

Regulation
Congress created Federal Radio Commission (1927)

Shawn Fanning's Napster: A monster?

>> **Voice**
Audion tube for voice transmission (1906)

>> **Buzz**
Electricity added to recording, playback technology (1920s)

>> Recorded music added to movies (1927)

>> Great Depression (1930s)

1945–1950s

Television
TV networks drew audiences from radio (1950s)

Rockabilly
Hybrid musical form became rock 'n' roll (1950s)

Music Radio
Radio shifted to niche audience segments, mostly recorded music (1950s)

Transformational iPod

>> Rise of network television (1950s)

>> Supreme Court banned segregation in public schools, *Brown v. Board of Education* (1954)

>> Elvis Presley brings rock 'n roll to white audiences, transforms pop music (1956)

1960–1999

What A&R?
Record companies lost tight control of pop music (1960s)

Public Broadcasting
Congress established national noncommercial system (1967)

Digitization
Introduction of compact discs (1982)

Deregulation
Congress relaxed broadcast regulations, including caps on ownership (1996)

From orbit at 18,000 mph

>> Escalating war in Vietnam leads to protests, cultural upheaval (1965–1975)

>> Soviet Union collapses, end of Cold War (1989)

>> Rise of rap as major commercial force (1990s)

>> Rise of Internet as major commercial medium (late 1990s)

2000s

Internet Radio
Pandora streams customized medleys (2000)

MP3
Handheld iPod on market (2001)

Sirius and XM
Digital signal delivery to listeners via satellites (2001)

Podcasting
Adam Curry invented podcasting (2004)

Grokster
Online music-swap services outlawed (2005)

Adam Curry: Dooming radio as we know it?

>> 9/11 terrorist attacks (2001)

>> iPod introduced (2002)

>> Iraq war (2003–)

Influence of Radio

STUDY PREVIEW

Radio has become a ubiquitous mass medium, available everywhere, anytime. As an industry, however, there are troubling signs. Radio's primary programming, music, has become available through other devices, many with no advertising. A key radio audience, the segment aged 18 to 24, has fallen off dramatically.

UBIQUITY

Radio is everywhere. The signals are carried on the electromagnetic spectrum to almost every nook and cranny. Broadband is a new delivery means. So is direct-to-listener programming from satellite. Hardly a place in the world is beyond the reach of radio.

There are 6.6 radio receivers on average in U.S. households. Almost all automobiles come with radios. People wake up with clock radios, jog with headset radios, party with boomboxes, and commute with car radios. People listen to sports events on the radio even if they're in the stadium. Thousands of people build their day around commentators like Rush Limbaugh. Millions rely on hourly newscasts to keep up to date. People develop personal attachments to their favorite announcers and disc jockeys.

Statistics abound about radio's importance:

- **Arbitron,** a company that surveys radio listenership, says that teenagers and adults average 22 hours a week listening to radio.
- People in the United States own 520 million radio sets. Looked at another way, radios outnumber people 2:1.
- More people, many of them commuting in their cars, receive their morning news from radio than from any other medium.

Although radio is important, cracks are developing in the medium's reach. The audience is slipping from the traditional, federally licensed local stations to iPods, direct-to-listener satellite services, webcasts and cell phones. Yes, 200 million people, a sizable number, still tune in at least once a week, but the audience is shifting. The important 18- to 24-year-old listener block fell 22 percent from 1999 to 2004. The slippage continues.

CHECKING YOUR MEDIA LITERACY

- **What are some measures of radio's audience reach?**
- **Is the radio audience expanding or constricting?**

SCOPE OF THE INDUSTRY

More than 13,000 radio stations, each licensed by the federal government as a local business, are on the air in the United States. Communities as small as a few hundred people have stations.

Although radio is significant as a $16.1-billion-a-year industry, its growth seems to have peaked. Revenue, almost entirely from advertising, grew only 1.2 percent in one recent year—less than the other major mass media. Big radio chains, like Clear Channel with 1,200-plus stations, had remained hugely profitable until recently. The profits, however, were due less to audience and advertising growth, which are stagnant at best, than to the chains' economies of scale and radical cost-cutting.

Too, the big revenue growth of the chains had been fueled by their acquisitions. When federal caps on chains at 40 stations were dropped in 1996, there was massive consolidation. Chains bought up individually owned stations, and chains bought other chains. In effect, the chains now all have bigger shares of a pie that's not growing and may be diminishing. How much is the disparity between big operators and the others? The 20 largest chains, which together own

Arbitron
Radio listener survey company

2,700 stations, brought in $9 billion in advertising in 2008. The remaining 10,000-some stations split the other $7 billion.

CHECKING YOUR MEDIA LITERACY

- **How has chain ownership masked a softening in radio advertising?**

Radio Content

STUDY PREVIEW

Radio programming falls mostly into three categories: entertainment, mostly music; news; and talk. In addition, public radio has created a growing audience for its rich mixture of news and information programming, most originating with National Public Radio and free-lance producers.

RADIO ENTERTAINMENT

The comedies, dramas, variety shows and quiz shows that dominated network-provided radio programming in the 1930s and 1940s moved to television in the 1950s. So did the huge audience that radio had cultivated. The radio networks, losing advertisers to television, scaled back what they offered to affiliates. As the number of listeners dropped, local stations switched to more recorded music, which was far cheaper than producing concerts, dramas and comedies. Thus, radio reinvented itself, survived and prospered.

The industry found itself shaken again in the 1970s when the listeners flocked to new FM stations. Because FM technology offered superior sound fidelity, these became the stations of choice for music. AM listenership seemed destined to tank until, in another reinvention, most AM stations converted to nonmusic formats.

All-news radio hád its roots in 1961 with programming genius **Gordon McLendon,** who beamed the first 24/7 news into southern California from XTRA across the border in Tijuana. All-news then took off as a format in major cities. So did listener call-in shows with colorful, sometimes bombastic hosts.

Music, however, dominates radio, although the popularity of genres is always in flux as stations jockey among shifting public tastes.

CHECKING YOUR MEDIA LITERACY

- **How did radio content change dramatically in the 1950s? And why?**

RADIO NEWS

Radio news preceded radio stations. In November 1916, Lee De Forest arranged with a New York newspaper, the *American,* to broadcast election returns. With home-built receivers, hundreds of people tuned in to hear an experimental transmission and heard De Forest proclaim: "Charles Evans Hughes will be the next president of the United States." It was an inauspicious beginning. De Forest had it wrong. Actually, Woodrow Wilson was re-elected. In 1920 KDKA signed on as the nation's first licensed commercial station and began by reporting the Harding-Cox presidential race as returns were being counted at the Pittsburgh *Post.* This time, radio had the winner right.

>> **Radio News Forms.** Radio news today has diverse forms, some taken from the De Forest notion of drawing listeners to reports on breaking events as they happen, some more focused on depth and understanding. Mostly, though, radio news is known for being on top of events as they happen.

Gordon McLendon
Reinvented radio with narrow formats in the 1950s

Tom Joyner

MEDIA PEOPLE

Tom Joyner grew up during the Civil Rights movement. He remembers well the 1960s when Montgomery, Alabama, blacks boycotted merchants in an early display of collective economic power. In his native Tuskegee, 50 miles away, he remembers the weekly unity marches. Joyner got his first peek inside radio while protesting against a white-owned station that refused to play "black music." Joyner prevailed. The station manager left.

After college, majoring in sociology, Joyner landed a radio job in Montgomery. He moved from station to station in the 1960s in the burgeoning of black radio, by then 800-plus stations nationwide. Joyner honed his mix of music, guests and goofy comedy and appeals for donations to worthy causes. Even on incendiary issues with which he dealt, Joyner maintained his dulcet cool.

By 1985 Joyner was in demand. When KKDA in Dallas offered him a morning slot and WGCI in Chicago offered him an afternoon slot, he took both. The daily commute made Joyner the first frequent-flyer disc jockey and earned him the nickname "Fly Jock." In 1994 he went into syndication on the ABC network and was eventually piped through 95 stations and stayed home more.

Joyner knows the power of radio. When Christie's auction house in New York decided to auction off items from the slave trade, Joyner and buddy Tavis Smiley were quick to note that Christie's had a policy against trafficking in Holocaust items. Day after day, Joyner and Smiley called on listeners to jam Christie's phone lines in protest. Christie's canceled the auction.

Joyner has courage. For weeks he urged listeners to jam the lines at CompUSA, which didn't advertise on black radio. The company complained to ABC, which carried Joyner's show. In a decision that the network later regretted, ABC lawyers ordered Joyner to lay off. Joyner read the corporate ultimatum on the air, sparking a massive listener protest to the network. ABC backed off. So did CompUSA, which dispatched a representative for a guest appearance on the Joyner show to make nice.

When Hurricane Katrina devastated New Orleans, Joyner canvassed stations still on the air for the earliest comprehensive accounts of the damage. It was he who coined the catchy term *black folks' tsunami*. Joyner raised $1.5 million to provide housing for the displaced.

In the tradition of black radio generating money for social causes, Joyner has created a foundation to help students who have run out of money at historically black colleges. To his listeners, Joyner says, these students are our future.

WHAT DO YOU THINK?

- What are measures of Tom Joyner's success as a radio personality?
- How risky are the causes that Joyner takes up?

"Fly Jock." *A daily Dallas–Chicago commute for Tom Joyner.*

Edward R. Murrow
Pioneer broadcast journalist

breaking news
Reports, often live, on events as they are occurring

headline service
Brief news stories

>> **Breaking News.** Radio news came into its own in World War II, when the networks sent correspondents abroad. Americans, eager for news from Europe, developed the habit of listening to the likes of **Edward R. Murrow** and other giants of mid-20th-century journalism, including Walter Cronkite. As a medium of instantaneous reporting, radio offered news on breakthrough events even before newspapers could issue special extra editions. The term **breaking news** emerged to describe something to which radio was uniquely suited.

>> **Headline Service.** In the relatively tranquil period after World War II, with people less intent on news, the radio industry recognized that listeners tuned away from lengthy stories. News formats shifted to shorter stories, making radio a **headline service.** Details

RADIO STATION FORMATS

Country	2,041 stations
News/talk/sports	1,579 stations
Adult contemporary	1,213 stations
Religious	1,019 stations
Golden oldies	822 stations
Classic rock	639 stations
Top 40	444 stations
Alternative/modern rock	334 stations
Urban contemporary	312 stations

Country music dominates U.S. radio. Although numbers are in flux as stations jockey with format changes to attract audiences, this breakdown suggests the flavor of programming

and depth were left to newspapers. Gordon McLendon's influential rock 'n' roll format, which he introduced in the 1960s, epitomized the headline service, generally with three-minute newscasts dropped every 20 minutes amid three-minute songs, with no story seldom more than 20 seconds, most only two sentences.

>> **All-News.** As contradictory as it may seem, Gordon McLendon also invented **all-news radio,** also in the 1960s. For the Los Angeles market, McLendon set up a skeletal staff at XTRA across the border in Tijuana to read wire copy nonstop. When XTRA turned profitable, McLendon took over a Chicago station, renamed it WNUS, and converted it to all-news. This was a dramatic departure from the idea of radio as a mass medium with each station trying for the largest possible audience. McLendon's WNUS and later all-news stations sought niche listenerships, finding profitability in a narrow part of the larger mosaic of the whole radio market. Today all news stations prosper in many large cities, some going far beyond McLendon's low-cost rip-and-read XTRA with large reporting staffs that provide on-scene competitive coverage that goes beyond a headline service.

>> **News Packages.** When National Public Radio went on the air in 1970, its flagship *All Things Considered* set itself apart with long-form stories that ignored two premises that had become traditional in radio. These were stories that didn't necessarily fit the news peg of breaking news. Also, the stories ran as long as the reporter or producer felt necessary to tell the story, ignoring the premise that radio listeners had extremely short attention spans. The stories, called **news packages,** were slickly produced and reflected a commitment of time and energy in reporting that other news formats lacked. Many personified issues. News packages typically are full of sounds and recorded interviews and are often marked by poignant examples and anecdotes and powerful writing.

all-news radio
A niche format that delivers only news and related informational content and commentary

news packages
Carefully produced, long-form radio stories that offer depth; the hallmark of NPR

>> **Decline of Radio News.** Despite the ascendancy of all-news radio and National Public Radio, news is hardly a core element of radio programming anymore. By the 1990s, after the Federal Communications Commission dropped public service as a condition for license renewal, many stations, eliminated their expensive news departments. Instead, these stations emphasized low-cost programming based on playing recorded music. Many metropolitan stations, once major players in news, have cut to just one or two

Radio News Icon. *Edward R. Murrow's World War II coverage from Europe, with bombs in the background during his reports, gave CBS listeners the feeling of being there.*

people who anchor brief newscasts during commuting hours. Global and national headlines are piped in from a network, if at all. Some stations don't even commit one full-time person to local news.

CHECKING YOUR MEDIA LITERACY

- **What are the different formats for radio news?**
- **What stations and networks feature each of these formats?**

TALK RADIO

Talk formats that feature live listener telephone calls emerged as a major genre in U.S. radio in the 1980s. Many AM stations, unable to compete with FM's superior sound quality for music, realized that they were better suited to talk, which doesn't require high fidelity. Call-in formats were greeted enthusiastically at first because of their potential as forums for discussion of the great public issues. Some stations, including WCCO in Minneapolis and WHO in Des Moines, were models whose long-running talk shows raised standards. So did *Talk of the Nation* on NPR. However, many talk shows went in other directions, focusing less on issues than on wacky, often vitriolic personalities.

Much of the format degenerated into advice programs on hemorrhoids, psoriasis, face-lifts and psychoses. Sports trivia went over big. So did pet care. Talk shows gave an illusion of news but in reality were lowbrow entertainment.

Whatever the downside of **talkers,** as they're known in the trade, they have huge followings. **Rush Limbaugh** was syndicated to 660 stations at his peak, reaching an estimated 20 million people a week. Although slipping to 600 stations, Limbaugh remained a strong influence among his politically conservative audience until 2003. That year it was revealed, incredible as it seemed considering his on-air derision of drug addiction, that Limbaugh himself had a drug habit. Limbaugh's ratings also dropped partly because overwhelmingly conservative talk had become a crowded genre. Also, some ideological competition had developed.

Liberals are also talking. The alternatives to conservative talkers, however, have never attracted as many listeners. The most aggressive left-wing effort, the network Air America, has been floundering in financial difficulties since going on the air in 2004.

>> **Talk Listenership.** The influence of talkers can be overrated. A 1996 Media Studies Center survey of people who listen to political talk shows found that they are hardly representative of mainstream Americans. The political talk-show audience is largely white, male, Republican and financially well-off. It is much more politically engaged than the general population but on the right wing. Also, these people distrust the mainstream media, which they perceive as biased to the left.

talkers
Talk shows

Rush Limbaugh
The most listened-to talk-show host in the 1990s

>> **Effect on News.** Many stations with music-based formats used the advent of news and talk stations to reduce their news programming. In effect, many music stations were saying: "Let those guys do news and talk, and we'll do music." The rationale really was a profit-motivated guise to get out of news and public affairs, which are expensive. Playing recorded music is cheap. The result was fewer stations offering serious news and public affairs programming.

To many people, talk formats leave the perception that there is more news and public affairs on radio than ever. The fact is that fewer stations offer news. Outside of major markets with all-news stations, stations that promote themselves as newstalk are really more talk than news, with much of the talk no more than thinly veiled entertainment that trivializes the format's potential.

CHECKING YOUR MEDIA LITERACY

- **What technology was catalytic in creating talk radio as a major format?**
- **How is talk radio different from news radio?**

Commercial Terrestrial Radio

STUDY PREVIEW

The U.S. radio industry was shaped by federal regulation in the late 1920s. By regulation, stations were locally licensed with strictly limited range for their signals. The system assumed that stations would be financially self-sufficient from advertising. Networks soon bound major stations into a national system, however, blunting the localism envisioned in regulations.

> **First Amendment**
> Provision in U.S. Constitution against government interference with free citizen expression, including media content

TRUSTEESHIP CONCEPT

Unlike the print media, broadcasting is regulated by the federal government. This is something the government isn't supposed to do under terms of the **First Amendment** to the U.S. Constitution. The First Amendment's wording is unambiguous: "Congress shall make no law . . . abridging the freedom of speech or the press."

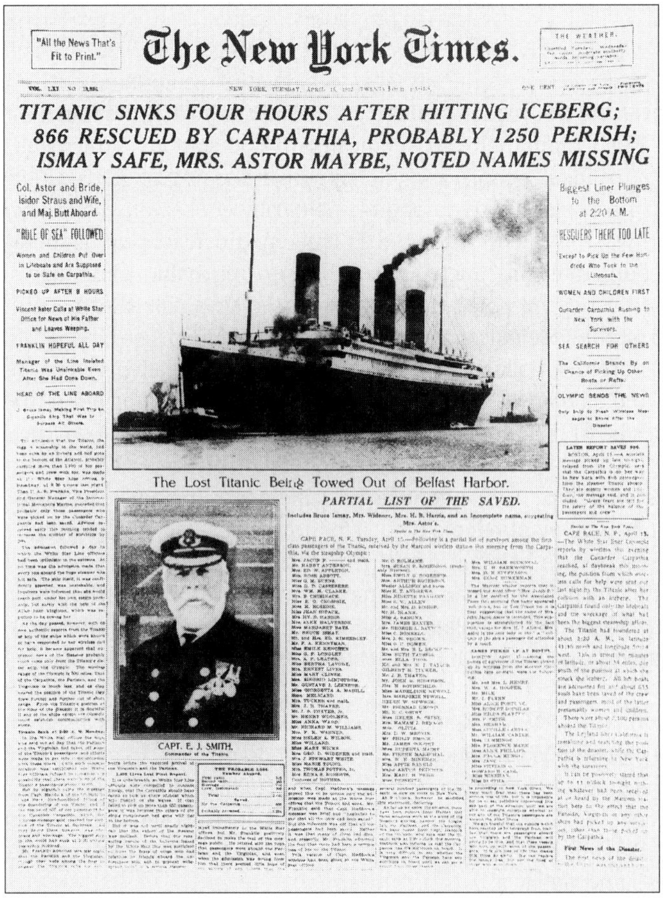

"All the News That's Fit to Print."

The New York Times.

TITANIC SINKS FOUR HOURS AFTER HITTING ICEBERG; 866 RESCUED BY CARPATHIA, PROBABLY 1250 PERISH; ISMAY SAFE, MRS. ASTOR MAYBE, NOTED NAMES MISSING

Col. Astor and Bride, Isidor Straus and Wife, and Maj. Butt Aboard.

"RULE OF SEA" FOLLOWED

Women and Children Put Over in Lifeboats and Are Supposed to be Safe on Carpathia.

PICKED UP AFTER 8 HOURS

Vincent Astor Calls at White Star Office for News of His Father and Leaves Weeping.

FRANKLIN HOPEFUL ALL DAY

Manager of the Line Insisted Titanic Was Unsinkable Even After She Had Gone Down.

HEAD OF THE LINE ABOARD

J. Bruce Ismay Making First Trip on Gigantic Ship That Was to Surpass All Others.

The Lost Titanic Being Towed Out of Belfast Harbor.

PARTIAL LIST OF THE SAVED.

CAPT. E. J. SMITH.

Biggest Liner Plunges to the Bottom at 2:20 A. M.

RESCUERS THERE TOO LATE

Except to Pick Up the Few Hundreds Who Took to the Lifeboats.

WOMEN AND CHILDREN FIRST

Cunarder Carpathia Rushing to New York with the Survivors.

SEA SEARCH FOR OTHERS

The California Stands By on Chance of Picking Up Other Boats or Rafts.

OLYMPIC SENDS THE NEWS

Only Ship to Flash Wireless Messages to Shore After the Disaster.

LATER REPORT SAVES 866.

CAPE RACE, N. F., April 15.

David Sarnoff

Radio a Household Word. *When* Titanic *sank in 1912, newspapers relied on young radio operator David Sarnoff for information on what was happening in the mid-Atlantic. For 72 hours Sarnoff sat at his primitive receiver, which happened to be on exhibit in a department store, to pick up details from rescue ships. The newspaper coverage of the disaster credited Sarnoff and radio, demonstrating the potential importance of this new medium for news.*

But an impossible situation, wrought by new radio technology, presented itself in the 1920s. More stations were on the air to fit on the available frequencies. The fledgling radio industry could not solve the problem and begged the government for regulation to sort out the problem.

public airwaves
Concept that broadcast should be subject to government regulation because the electromagnetic spectrum is a public asset

Federal Radio Commission
Agency to regulate U.S. radio; created in 1927; predecessor of Federal Communications Commission

public interest, convenience and necessity
Standard by which the U.S. government grants and renews local radio and television station licenses

trusteeship concept
States that government serves as a trustee for the public's interest in regulating broadcasting; so do the licensed station owners

>> **Public Airwaves.** To sidestep the First Amendment issue, Congress embraced the concept that the airwaves, which carried radio signals, were a public asset and therefore, somewhat like a public park, were subject to government regulation for the public good. The **public airwaves** concept was useful for justifying regulation of the 1927 chaos of overcrowded airwaves, but it also was problematic. What criteria would the government use in issuing and denying licenses? Congress came up with another concept: The **Federal Radio Commission** should award licenses to applicants who best demonstrated that they would broadcast in the **public interest, convenience and necessity.** Today, 80 years later, that standard remains in effect. Government regulates as a trustee for the public good. Station owners, as licensees, are also trustees.

Although the **trusteeship concept** phraseology was high-sounding, some already on-the-air stations that lost licenses cried foul and used the ugly word "censorship." A quack doctor in Kansas, who used his station to sell cure-all potions, went to court on First Amendment grounds. So did a hate-monger preacher who used his church-owned station in Los Angeles as a pulpit. The federal courts ruled glibly that the Federal Radio Commission was acting within its authority, leaving the First Amendment issue unaddressed for another day.

CHECKING YOUR MEDIA LITERACY

- **Why is radio, unlike print media, regulated by government?**
- **Why did early radio station operators embrace government regulation?**
- **Explain the trusteeship concept. Who is the trustee? Trustee of what? Trustee for whom?**

THE SHAPE OF RADIO

Federal regulation of radio made assumptions and established rules that gave the U.S. industry the following historic characteristics, some of which have been shaken in recent years:

Private Sector. Historically the industry has been privately owned in the U.S. capitalistic tradition. This was in contrast to most other countries, which used the concept of the airwaves being public to create government-sponsored national, broadcast structures.

Advertising Supported. The industry is financially self-supporting through advertising, also in the U.S. capitalistic tradition. There are, however, exceptions. In recognition of radio's potential as an educational tool that might not be commercially sustainable, several frequencies are reserved for noncommercial licenses.

Engineering Regulation. The government holds licensees strictly accountable to broadcasting precisely within their assigned space on the electromagnetic spectrum to avoid the pre-1927 chaos. This has allowed for as many stations as possible to be squeezed into the available spectrum.

Ownership. Stations are licensed for local communities to encourage diverse content, including news and ideas. Some group ownership was permitted, for years a maximum of seven stations, but until recent years it was strictly limited.

Content. The government never has had agents sitting at radio stations to keep things off the air, but the FCC is willing to consider listener complaints. The possibility of having their licenses yanked, although it rarely happens, is sufficient to keep stations from wandering too far from mainstream social acceptability and business practices.

Networks. Although not licensed, networks conform to government expectations for affiliates. The FCC clearly maintains that affiliates are responsible for whatever they retransmit from networks.

LOCALLY LICENSED STATIONS

The Federal Radio Commission used several mechanisms to guard against broadcasting becoming a one-voice government mouthpiece. There would be no powerful national stations. Stations were licensed to local service areas with local ownership. Further, there were strict limits on how many stations a single person or corporation could own. The goal of **localism** was a diversity of voices.

The law that established the Federal Radio Commission stated explicitly that stations would have First Amendment protection. The fact, however, was that the commission needed to assess station programming in deciding what was in the public interest, convenience and necessity. This inherent contradiction was glossed over during most of U.S. radio history because station license-holders were more than pleased to program whatever it took to satisfy the FRC and its successor, the Federal Communications Commission. That was the trade-off for stations to retain their licenses and stay in what, by and large, became one of the 20th century's most lucrative businesses. Also, the FCC, which was created in 1934, was gingerly about regulating content. Never, for example, did the FCC interfere with format issues, no matter how loud the protests from classical music fans when their favorite station shifted to rock.

Content regulation was mostly measuring the number of minutes per hour of news and public-service announcements, until even that was abandoned in the 1980s. Before shock jock Howard Stern, fines for on-air vulgarities were mere wrist slaps.

CHECKING YOUR MEDIA LITERACY

- **How did Congress try to avoid the growth of powerful radio chains, like those in the newspaper industry in the 1920s? Did it work?**

NETWORKS

Congress did not foresee the impact of radio networks, which were in their infancy when the Federal Radio Commission was created in 1927. By the 1930s NBC and CBS were piping programs to local stations, called **affiliates,** throughout the land.

Although the networks gave local exclusivity to affiliates, one per market, the high quality of the programming amassed unprecedented audiences. Then in 1924 came the Mutual Broadcasting System, which allowed any station to pick up any or all of its programming. Stations became less the forums of local issues and culture that Congress had intended with local licensing. For better or worse, local stations were becoming mere conduits for a powerful, emerging national culture.

Localism was further weakened in the 1950s when the networks shifted their emphasis to television and took much of radio's audience with them. Radio stations went almost entirely to recorded music, in effect displacing the original ideal of local talent with music geared for a national audience from the major music recording centers of New York, Los Angeles and Nashville.

CHECKING YOUR MEDIA LITERACY

- **How did radio networks weaken the idea of local stations geared to serving local audiences?**

MARKETPLACE CONCEPT

Ronald Reagan proclaimed that his presidency would "get government off the backs of business." In 1996, seven years after Reagan left office, it seemed that his **deregulation** dream had come true—at least in broadcasting. With the 1996 Telecommunications Act the age-old limits were relaxed on how many radio stations a single company could own. Right away, radio companies began gobbling one another up in mergers. Today the FCC has no limits on ownership except for a maximum of eight stations in a single market.

localism
Issuing broadcast licenses for service to a specified community and its environs

affiliates
Locally licensed stations that have an affiliation with a network to carry network programming

deregulation
A trend in the 1980s and later to reduce government regulation of business

The change in the corporate structure of U.S. radio represented a weakening of the trusteeship concept. No longer did the government see its role as an intermediary for the public as necessary to ensure that the industry performed in the public interest. The trusteeship concept had led to rules like the Fairness Doctrine, which required stations to air all sides of controversial issues and to air public-service announcements, and even micromanagement details like requiring the identification of a station by call letters and location on the hour and the half-hour. Those requirements were mostly gone by 1996 because one of the premises necessitating the trusteeship role for government, **channel scarcity,** had disappeared. Technology had found ways to squeeze 13,000 stations onto the available electromagnetic spectrum, which was plenty.

In place of the trusteeship concept had emerged a **marketplace concept,** in which the marketplace would have a far greater role in deciding the shape of radio broadcasting. If people were dissatisfied with a station, they had many other stations to go to—in effect, voting with a turn of the dial or the press of a preset button.

Stations that didn't meet public expectations would, given time, lose listeners and advertisers and cease to be viable businesses. Or so goes the rationale for the marketplace theory. The concept is simple: Let marketplace mechanics serve as a regulator, the people acting directly. Gradually the regulatory mechanisms that were a cocoon that protected the infrastructure of the radio industry from change are being shed. Even so, the National Association of Broadcasters, which represents radio station owners, as well as television owners, continues to lobby for government maintenance of the status quo to protect its interests. For example, the industry delayed for years the approval for XM and Sirius to use orbiting satellites as platforms for direct-to-listener broadcasting. On that issue, however, the FCC eventually applied the marketplace concept, allowed the satellites to go up, and let the people decide.

channel scarcity
An insufficiency of radio frequencies that necessitated government regulation in the 1920s

marketplace concept
Allowing people through marketplace mechanisms to determine the fate of a business; a successor in broadcasting to the trusteeship concept

CHECKING YOUR MEDIA LITERACY

- **How do the trusteeship and marketplace concepts differ?**
- **Can the trusteeship and marketplace concepts coexist?**

Corporate Radio

STUDY PREVIEW

A few corporations dominate the U.S. radio industry, using mostly centralized music and other programming geared to mass tastes. The approach, however, has earned the disapproving moniker "corporate radio" for its bland sameness. The chains have taken steps to win back listeners who had left for alternative sources of music, news and information.

CHAIN OWNERSHIP

Pressured by broadcasters to relax the limits on how many stations a single company could own, Congress in 1996 eliminated any cap. The only limit was that a chain could not own more than eight stations in a large market. Right away radio chains began buying up stations and also other chains. The 1999 merger of Clear Channel and AMFM created an 838-station group. The FCC then relaxed the limit further. By 2003, Clear Channel owned 1,200-plus stations. A new era of *corporate radio* had arrived.

To cut costs and thus maximize profits, these chains consolidated their new properties in the post-1996 era and centralized not only **playlists** but also disc jockeys. Most stations owned by Clear Channel, Viacom and other chains went to formulaic computerized scheduling, with stations each drawing from libraries of only 300 to 400 titles with the same 30 or 40 songs playing most of the time. Through a system called **voice tracking**, a handful of announcers at central sites played the songs over multiple stations in different markets. This robo-programming was efficient.

playlist
A list of songs that a radio station plays

voice tracking
A few announcers who prerecord music intros and outros for multiple stations to create a single personality for stations

Also to maximize profits, programming was larded with advertising. Some stations were running 22 minutes of ads an hour, some packages of ads going on for 10 minutes straight. A 2004 study by the investment banking firm J.P. Morgan found an average of 15 minutes an hour of advertising.

CHECKING YOUR MEDIA LITERACY

- What has happened to the goal of the 1927 Federal Radio Act to prevent radio chains?
- How has programming changed under the big radio chains?

NEW CORPORATE TUNE

Shifting a few gears, Clear Channel began striking deals with stations outside its ownership to pick up revenue from advertisers that were following listeners to alternative stations. An example is unorthodox Indie 103, a Los Angeles station whose music mix is personality-driven—pretty much whatever suits a disc jockey at the moment. It's quirky, but it also inspires about 700 listener calls a day. That's an intensity of listener loyalty that robo-radio can't match even with massively larger audiences. Hedging its course for the future, Clear Channel bought every minute of Indie 103's available advertising airtime. The deal allowed the station to meet expenses, and Clear Channel made money reselling the time at a premium with the advertising staff that served the chain's existing eight robo-programmed Los Angeles stations.

Clear Channel crafted another deal with the Bush-bashing liberal network Air America that kept the financially failing network in business. It's a strange deal indeed for a company whose Texas management strongly supported Bush financially in the 2004 election. Political ideology, it seemed, was less critical than stopping the leaks of listeners and ad revenue, even small ones, that were breaking out all over the Clear Channel landscape.

Some stations with robo-programming shifted gears in 2005 with **Jack,** a format developed by Rogers Media of Canada that has a decidedly more eclectic mix of music. Jack playlists typically include 1,200 songs. Unlike robo-formulas, few songs get played even once a day in Jack's unlikely patterns, with none of the segues that slide from one tune seamlessly into another. Eight U.S. stations licensed Jack from Rogers in 2005. Others are imitating it. At KSJK in Kansas City, which calls itself 105.1 Jack FM, program director Mike Reilly prides himself on "train wrecks," a collision of unlikely music in sequence: "If you hear MC Hammer go into the Steve Miller Band, I've done my job." It's the kind of programming excitement that people can create on an iPod. In fact, KSJK's print advertising shows an iPod with the line: "I guess you won't be needing this anymore, huh?"

Jack, say critics, is less than it seems. The playlists don't venture beyond what is familiar to listeners. A Jack consultant, Mike Henry, put it this way in a *Wall Street Journal* interview: "You're only challenging them on a stylistic level. You're not challenging them on a familiar/unfamiliar level." Nirvana grunge may butt up against Village People disco, but both are proven pop.

The big chains also have begun trimming commercials, a recognition that they had overdone it and driven listeners away. Radio companies don't like to talk about how much advertising they carry, but a brokerage firm, Harry Nesbitt, said Clear Channel was down to an average 9.4 minutes per hour at its 1,200 stations in 2004. Also, advertisers were encouraged to shorten their spots. It is believed that the decline has continued.

Jack
An eclectic, somewhat unpredictable musical radio format

CHECKING YOUR MEDIA LITERACY

- How have radio chains backed off their original goal of one-size-fits-all programming?
- What do you see as problems ahead for radio chains?

Public Radio

STUDY PREVIEW

For 40 years the noncommercial component of the U.S. radio industry, called *public radio*, has grown steadily with distinctive programming. A 1967 law provided federal funding—a response to a vision that radio could do better in serving the public good. A major gift from Joan Kroc, the widow of McDonald's founder, has secured the future for the backbone of the system, the network National Public Radio.

CORPORATION FOR PUBLIC BROADCASTING

From its beginnings in the 1920s, the U.S. radio industry was built around government licenses assigned to local communities and a financial advertising structure. In the backwaters were noncommercial stations, conceived originally as testbeds for experimentation. Many were licensed to universities, many to the physics departments.

There also were noncommercial licenses for educational purposes. These stations, barred from raising revenue through advertising, were merely a blip in the radio landscape until the privately funded blue-ribbon **Carnegie Commission for Educational Television** began rethinking noncommercial broadcasting. The influential commission concluded that noncommercial broadcasting was an undeveloped national resource.

Congress followed through on the Carnegie recommendations for a government funded television and radio system to meet "the full needs of the American public." The enabling legislation, the 1967 **Public Broadcasting Act,** was a slap at commercial broadcasting, whose content was mostly entertaining at a low and vapid level. The idea was for broadcasting to do better. Only a few years earlier, in 1961, FCC Chair Newton Minow had chastised broadcast executives at a convention as responsible for a "vast wasteland." The term stuck. So did the sting. But nothing changed in content.

The new law established the **Corporation for Public Broadcasting,** a quasi-government agency to channel federal funds into noncommercial radio and television. Right away, National Public Radio, which had been founded in 1970, created ***All Things Considered,*** a 90-minute newsmagazine for evening drive time. Many noncommercial stations offered *ATC,* as it's called in the trade, as an alternative to the headline services on commercial stations. The program picked up an enthusiastic

Terry Gross. *Her probing interviews on* Fresh Air, *marked by a disarming truth-seeking honesty, are among radio's longest-running programs. On 330 NPR affiliates, the daily show typically has 2.9 million listeners.*

Carnegie Commission for Educational Television
Proposed a government-funded educational system

Public Broadcasting Act
Established the Corporation for Public Broadcasting

Corporation for Public Broadcasting
Quasi-government agency that administers federal funds for noncommercial radio and television

All Things Considered
Pioneer NPR afternoon newsmagazine

albeit small following but grew steadily. In 1979 an early drive-time companion program, ***Morning Edition,*** was launched.

CHECKING YOUR MEDIA LITERACY

- **What motivated Congress to act on the Carnegie recommendations?**
- **How was the new *public radio* different from commercial radio? Have these distinctions survived?**

MCDONALD'S FORTUNE

Morning Edition
NPR's morning newsmagazine

Joan Kroc
Singlehandedly sextupled NPR's endowment

National Public Radio
Network for noncommercial stations

American Public Media
Program provider for noncommercial stations

Garrison Keillor
Long-running host of *A Prairie Home Companion*

satellite radio
Delivery method of programming from a single source beamed to an orbiting satellite for transmission directly to individual end users

Joan Kroc, widow of the founder of the McDonald's fast-food chain, was a faithful radio listener. She especially enjoyed programs from **National Public Radio.** When she died in 2003, Kroc bequeathed $200 million to NPR, sextupling the network's endowment.

The gift is transforming NPR into a powerhouse in radio in ways reminiscent of the commercial networks in their heyday. Today NPR claims more listeners than ratings-leader Rush Limbaugh does on commercial radio. Limbaugh's is the number one stand-alone program at 22 million listeners some weeks, but NPR does better overall. *Morning Edition* has 13.1 million listeners, and *ATC* has 11.5 million. In news, NPR has a lot to offer. With the Kroc gift and steeper charges to affiliates, the network has built a news staff of 300 in its Washington and Los Angeles bureaus and in 23 U.S. and 14 foreign bureaus. The programs are carried on 773 stations.

Although much of the Kroc endowment has underwritten NPR's growing news operations, the network also prides itself on cultural programming, much of it innovative and experimental, sometimes offbeat. The greatest audience that has evolved, however, has been news-related.

Although NPR is the most visible component of U.S. noncommercial radio, its programs constitute only about one-quarter of the content on its affiliate stations. These stations originate 49 percent of their own programming. Stations also buy about 19 percent of their programming from a competing program service, **American Public Media.** APM, a creation of the Minnesota Public Radio network, has the folksy **Garrison Keillor** live-audience variety show *A Prairie Home Companion,* which dates to 1974.

CHECKING YOUR MEDIA LITERACY

- **Trace the growth of public radio into a formidable second component of the U.S. radio industry.**

Satellite Radio

STUDY PREVIEW

Satellite radio, transmitting directly from national networks to individual listeners, is squeezing traditional locally licensed stations. Satellite networks Sirius and XM offer 100-plus channels, some commercial-free, some duplicating what's available on over-air stations.

SIRIUS AND XM

Two **satellite radio** operations, the first national U.S. radio stations, went on the air in 2001. Both Sirius and XM beamed multiple programs from multiple satellites, providing digital-quality sound, much of it commercial-free, for a monthly fee ranging between $10 and $13. The companies tried to build an immediate audience by lining up automobile manufacturers to install receivers into new vehicles—about 12 million a year. Both Sirius and XM offered at least a hundred channels—pop, country, news, sports and talk—but also specialized programming like chamber music, Broadway hits, NPR, audiobooks and gardening tips.

In 2004 Sirius and XM raised the stakes against each other and against traditional over-the-air radio. Sirius signed Howard Stern to a five-year deal worth $500 million, which began in 2006 when his previous contract expired with a traditional station. Stern's **shock jock** act on Sirius, laden with vulgarities and blue humor, is beyond the jurisdiction of the FCC, which licenses only the technical parameters of satellite radio. Signals downlinked from satellites are not considered use of the public's air.

Not to be outdone, XM signed a deal with Major League Baseball to broadcast every big-league game played through 2011, with an option for 2012 to 2014. That deal may be worth as much as $650 million to baseball. Raising their programming bar represents a huge gamble by both satellite firms, which, going into 2008, were hemorrhaging money. They merged in 2009.

CHECKING YOUR MEDIA LITERACY

- **How has satellite radio diversified the infrastructure of the U.S. radio industry?**
- **Why doesn't the concept for government regulation of public airwaves apply to XM and Sirius?**

shock jock
Announcer whose style includes vulgarities, taboos

terrestrial radio
The industry based on audio transmission from land-based towers, as opposed to transmission via satellite

ASSAULT ON TERRESTRIAL RADIO

While XM and Sirius were duking it out, a larger battle was shaping up between satellite radio and what's come to be called **terrestrial radio.** The term was devised to identify the traditional radio industry built around local stations that transmit from towers, in contrast to satellite transmission. Language purists object that *terrestrial radio* is a retronym like *print newspapers* and *broadcast television*. But boosted derisively by Howard Stern in hyping his 2006 move to Sirius, the term caught on.

Whatever the semantics tiff, the reality is that locally licensed commercial stations are under unprecedented competition for listeners. Among alternatives:

Snoop Dogg. *Satellite radio services have shared exclusive talent in their competition for listeners, including Snoop Dogg on XM and Howard Stern on Sirius. Satellite audiences are growing, but neither Sirius nor XM found profitability on its own and now have merged.*

>> Public Alternative. National Public Radio and its local affiliates have skimmed off the listenership whose demographics, including educational attainments and income, are coveted by advertisers. Although public stations cannot carry advertising, they are allowed to acknowledge supporters on the air, including purveyors of high-end products and services. These acknowledgments can sound like advertising as long as they don't exhort listeners to action.

>> Satellite Alternative. Every listener whom local commercial stations lose to Sirius-XM makes these stations less attractive to advertisers. The exodus has been major. Sirius-XM has 18 million subscribers.

Other technologies also are working against the traditional radio industry.

>> iPod. Handheld MP3 players, epitomized by the Apple iPod, are siphoning listeners from over-air local radio. With these devices and music downloaded from the Internet or ripped from their own CDs, people are able to create their own playlists—no inane disc jockey patter, no commercials, no waiting through less-than-favorite tunes for the good stuff.

>> Podcasting. Almost anybody who wants to create a show can prerecord a batch of favorite music, complete with narration, as an audio file on a personal computer. Then, by adding a hyperlink on a web server, they can let the world download the show for playback on a computer or MP3 player. Whenever the listener links to the server again, a new show from the same source will be downloaded automatically. Podcasting has the potential to make everybody a disc jockey. This too has cut into the audience of traditional radio.

>> On-Demand Radio. Like the earlier TiVo device for television, on-demand radio devices are available for recording programs for later playback. The leading service, RadioTime, offers a real-time database of 35,000 stations from 140 countries for a

$39 annual subscription. Some RadioTime models include an AM-FM tuner to grab local shows that aren't webcast.

CHECKING YOUR MEDIA LITERACY

Locally licensed terrestrial commercial radio is beleaguered. How has this happened?

Whither Radio?

STUDY PREVIEW

With deregulation, radio programming has become more populist, formulaic and bland. Many stations are devoid of local identity. Even so, some stations set themselves apart with local and distinctive content.

>> High-Definition. Happy with the heady profits in the 1990s, the radio industry missed an opportunity to upgrade with digital transmission technology. The technology, which would have improved clarity, was deemed too costly at $100,000 a station.

What a mistake. Joel Hollander, who came in as chief executive at the Infinity chain in 2005, is frank: "If we had invested three to five years ago, people would be thinking differently about satellite." By 2005, only 300 stations had gone digital.

The largest chains now have all committed to digital conversion. About 2,000 stations were be sending digital signals by 2008. The system requires two transmitters, one for the traditional analog signal and one for the new digital signal, but a new industry adopted standard, called **IBOC**, short for "in-band, on-channel," allows old-style analog and new-style digital receivers to pick up either signal at the same spot on the dial.

>> Bundled Transmission. Unlike analog radio, digital signals are encoded as binary 1s and 0s, which means that multiple programs can be **multiplexed** on the same channel. Segments of multiple programs are sent in packets, each coded to be picked out at the receiving end as a single unit and the others ignored. The company that holds the patents on high-definition radio, iBiquity Digital, has a system with which stations can spray six simultaneous messages to listeners, which opens opportunities for stations to regain listeners. Imagine a commuter setting a receiver to a music station with instructions to interrupt for traffic updates embedded in the same signal.

Receivers can be designed to store programs, TiVo-like. NPR's *All Things Considered* can be waiting on a commuter's car radio no matter what time the workday ends and the commute home begins.

CHECKING YOUR MEDIA LITERACY

What are possibilities for technological innovation for terrestrial radio?

REINVENTING RADIO

IBOC (in-band, on-channel)
A radio industry standard for digital transmission; allows multiple programming on the same channel

multiplexing
Sending multiple messages in bundles on the same channel

The structure of the U.S. radio industry that resulted from the 1927 Radio Act has had a long run. No one predicts a quick end to radio as we have come to know it—locally licensed, advertising-supported, over-air signals, and mostly lowbrow, middlebrow at best. But alternatives are coming on strong. Public radio, satellite services and iPod-enabled personal playlists are not friends of the old-line radio industry. They are taking away listeners, eroding bottom lines even for highly efficient chains like Clear Channel.

Radio has had doomsayers before, as when network television stole the audience and advertisers in the 1950s. Radio reinvented itself then. Gordon McLendon, the low-budget niche programming innovator, led radio into a survival mode. Will a new knight in shining armor come along to reinvent terrestrial commercial radio again?

Local radio stations have assets to reposition themselves. These include local news, which stations have largely abandoned but which could be revived. News is much costlier to program than recorded music, but it's a niche that is open in most markets—although public stations have established a small stake in local news and newspapers are moving into online delivery with audio.

Another unfilled niche is local culture. Stations spend little airtime on local concerts, drama, poetry and dialogue. Locally generated cultural programming is labor-intensive compared with piping in pop culture from Nashville, New York and Los Angeles in the form of recorded music. Piped-in network programming, by its nature, is hardly local.

When is the last time you heard a city council meeting live on radio? Or a poetry reading from a campus coffee shop? Or an intelligent interview with a local author? You're more likely to find a faraway Major League Baseball game than a local Legion game. Local content may not be riveting stuff for the large mass audiences that radio once garnered, but all signs point to those audiences continuing to dwindle. Radio's reinvention may be into niches even narrower than those to which McLendon was gearing programs in the 1950s. Even so, there indeed are things that radio can do that competitors don't or can't. Ironically, local programming would be nearer to what Congress envisioned in the **1927 Radio Act**—local stations recording and playing back their communities to themselves.

1927 Radio Act
Established the Federal Radio Commission

CHECKING YOUR MEDIA LITERACY

- **What threatens the future of commercial terrestrial radio?**
- **How can commercial terrestrial radio survive?**

CHAPTER WRAP-UP

The Recording Industry (Pages 117–120)

- The recording industry produces products that surround us. Recorded music is almost everywhere all the time. The industry is dominated by four major companies: Bertelsmann, EMI, Universal and Warner. All are international players, although invisible to people who buy recorded music, because their products are issued as labels—a kind of brand marketing. Despite the dominance of the Big Four, independent record companies have a strong history of innovation in music.

New Digital Music Landscape (Pages 120–123)

- The recording industry has been "technologically challenged." Focused on its traditional distribution channels, the industry missed the impact of the Internet for people to swap music until it was almost too late. In desperation, the recording industry attempted numerous online distribution mechanisms to combat unauthorized downloading. None worked. Then Apple introduced the iPod device and the iTunes music store, which gave recording companies a 21st century distribution system through which they could draw revenue.

Regulatory Pressure (Pages 123–124)

- With control by recording companies diminished, artists have gained artistic latitudes. These have included lyrics that are objectionable to some people but that also have resonated in segments of the marketplace. Record companies are in a bind between issuing products with strong profit potential and issuing products that draw condemnation, even boycott threats, from organized opposition. Boycotts are especially worrisome to companies like Time Warner, whose interests extend far beyond music. Also, government leaders rumble about censorship possibilities, especially during election years. But now technology has provided performers with independent access to audiences, and, for better or worse, the objectionable music has a following.

Dependence on Radio (Pages 124–126)

- The recording industry relies on radio to play new music. Airtime, basically free advertising, is essential for a song to become popular. With exposure comes the most often cited measure of success for music—sales.

Influence of Radio (Pages 127–128)

- With a growing multiplicity of portable listening devices, radio is everywhere. More people receive their morning news from radio than any other medium. Although large, the audience is fragmenting. Alternatives include webcasts, cell phones, and iPods with individually customized playlists that no station can match. Within the radio industry itself, fragmentation is occurring that especially threatens commercial terrestrial stations that the government has licensed for local service through the country since 1927.

Radio Content (Pages 128–132)

- Most radio programming is entertainment, primarily recorded music. Not much indigenous creative programming is offered. Although news once was a major component of radio programming, it's now been replaced with piped-in music. Talk programs are a significant programming mainstay at many stations but are mostly imported from faraway network sources and are not local.

Commercial Terrestrial Radio (Pages 132–136)

- The structure of U.S. radio was created by Congress in 1927—a system of stations almost all with strict limits on signal strength to serve local communities. It was a system based financially on advertising. For three-quarters of a century, the industry's core has been commercial terrestrial radio.

Corporate Radio (Pages 137–138)

- The 1927 regulatory legislation sought to avoid chain ownership in radio. Congress, indeed the American people, were leery about the possibility of a radio equivalent to the powerful newspaper chains of the time. Gradually limits on ownership were relaxed. In 1996 limitations were scrapped altogether, albeit for a provision against a single company buying up all the stations in large markets. The result has been exactly the chain ownership that Congress once sought to prevent.

Public Radio (Pages 138–140)

- A segment of the radio spectrum set aside in 1927 for educational broadcasting has evolved into a strong component of the industry—public radio. These noncommercial stations have long been resented and treated as outsiders by owners of advertising-based mainstream stations for taking even a sliver of the audience. Antagonism has grown since 1967 when Congress, tacitly criticizing commercial broadcasting for not living up to public service expectations, channeled major funding into the noncommercial system. Today noncommercial stations have a growing, loyal audience for news and public affairs that commercial stations had neglected. The public radio audience is growing even as the commercial audience is shrinking.

Satellite Radio (Pages 138–140)

- The technology for national stations to beam signals directly to listeners, bypassing local stations, was available long before the Sirius and XM satellite services went live in 2001. But the commercial terrestrial radio industry had fought successfully against the authorization of satellite services. The industry preferred the regulated infrastructure in which it found financial comfort. The industry's self-serving objections turned out to be well rooted. When authorization finally came, Sirius and XM lured a large part of the audience away from terrestrial stations.

Whither Radio? (Pages 140–141)

- The near-myopic focus on pop music may be the comeuppance of commercial terrestrial stations. Think iPod. How can a radio station compete with handheld devices that facilitate individual playlists? These devices put listeners in control. People no longer have to wait for songs they want to hear. Nor do they have to wait through commercial breaks. Where can commercial radio go from here? Narrower, local-oriented niches are a possibility, like miking civic events, concerts and other cultural events. Stronger local news and public affairs is another niche that commercial radio has largely forsaken.

Review Questions

1. What has transformed the retailing of recorded music?
2. How has the recording industry answered threats to censor objectionable lyrics?
3. How does the way indies do business differ from the practices of the Big Four?
4. Why did RIAA sue its fans?
5. How has the mix of entertainment and information changed through the course of radio's history in the United States?
6. How has the 1966 Telecommunications Act reshaped the U.S. radio industry?
7. What has contributed to the growth of public radio audiences?
8. How has satellite radio shaken the historic infrastructure of U.S. radio?

Concepts

deregulation (Page 146)
downloading (Page 120)
marketplace concept (Page 135)
public airwaves (Page 133)
public interest, convenience and necessity (Page 133)
terrestrial radio (Page 139)

Terms

1927 Radio Act (Page 141)
affiliate (Page 134)
garage bands (Page 119)
iTunes (Page 121)
Parents Music Resource Center (Page 124)
playlist (Page 135)
satellite radio (Page 138)

People

Adam Curry (Page 122)
David Geffen (Page 118)
Edward R. Murrow (Page 129)
Gerald Levin (Page 124)
Gordon McLendon (Page 128)
Joan Kroc (Page 138)
Rush Limbaugh (Page 131)
Shawn Fanning (Page 120)
Steve Jobs (Page 131)
Tom Joyner (Page 129)

Media Sources

- Steve Knopper. *Appetite for Self-Destruction: The Spectacular Crash of the Record Industry in the Digital Age.* Free Press, 2009. Knopper, a writer for *Rolling Stone*, blames lack of foresight and imagination, and, yes, also arrogance and stupidity, for the record industry's brush with death as the Internet came of age.
- Hugh Richard Slotten. *Radio's Hidden Voice: The Origins of Public Broadcasting in the United States* (Illinois, 2009). Slotten, a New Zealand scholar, offers a thoroughly researched, interpretive history back to the 1800s, yes, before radio, when government-sponsored agricultural extension services were looking for new ways to reach farmers.
- The biweekly *Rolling Stone* is the leading periodical for fans who want to track the music business.
- *Ethan* Brown. *Queens Reigns Supreme*. Anchor, 2005. Brown traces the roots of many big-name rappers to the 1988 shooting death of rookie cop Edward Byrne, which spurred a police crackdown on Queens drug barons. Many left the drug trade, turning to creating music about what they knew best. Although writing in a detached, neutral journalistic tone, Brown is unsympathetic.
- Barry Truax. *Acoustic Communication*, second edition. Greenwood, 2001. Truax, a Canadian scholar, draws on interdisciplinary studies to create a model for understanding acoustic and aural experiences.
- James Miller. *Flowers in the Dustbin: The Rise of Rock 'n' Roll, 1947–1977.* Simon & Schuster, 1999. Miller, an academic who also is a book and music critic, traces rock to earlier origins than most scholars.

A Thematic Chapter Summary

SOUND MEDIA

In this chapter you have deepened your media literacy by revisiting several themes. Here are thematic highlights from the chapter:

MEDIA TECHNOLOGY

Satellite Radio. Competition for a shrinking radio audience has been intensified by technology that allows direct-to-listener signals from satellite. Suddenly terrestrial radio is, well, so 20th century.

A pattern among established mass media companies is to miss transformational opportunities from new technology until it's almost too late. The recording industry, as an example, was caught unawares by Napster, which allowed fans to swap music free. Rather than embrace the fact that the new technology wouldn't go away, the industry resisted it and began filing lawsuits against fans. Now, a slightly different retailing model, Apple's iTunes, has been widely accepted. Radio too missed the opportunity to upgrade to digital transmission technology in the 1990s. As a result, satellite radio companies like Sirius and XM, which could deliver signals directly to listeners, have siphoned listeners away from terrestrial radio. The technology of terrestrial radio, beaming signals from towers on high points in the landscape, has been refined over the past century but fundamentally is unchanged. Terrestrial radio is attempting to regain its lost listeners. By 2008, about 2,000 radio stations were sending digital signals with improved clarity and IBOC, in-band, on-channel signals, which means that a single station can send simultaneous messages to listeners. (Pages 116–117, 120–122, 139–141)

MEDIA ECONOMICS

Filling the Gap. The radio industry's shift away from public affairs programming created somewhat of a vacuum that noncommercial stations have filled. Terry Gross of National Public Radio is a big draw.

Low-cost recording equipment, which gave rise to garage bands in the 1980s, has democratized music. Musicians no longer need support from a studio to produce marketable CDs. Marketing indeed remains a problem for upstart performers, but the stranglehold of record companies on the direction of music has been broken. When the bottom fell out of the record business in the mid-1920s, record companies looked to advantageous partnerships with radio. Radio stations found that music was their biggest draw and also their biggest source of advertising dollars after deregulation in the late 1900s. As the Federal Communications Commission eased license requirements on radio stations for public affairs and news, stations found that music was less costly to produce than staffs of news reporters and public affairs producers. The shift away from news to music was dramatic evidence of the fact that media companies are capitalistic enterprises that seek the least expensive routes to the greatest financial return. So secondary was promoting citizen participation in the life of the community and public affairs that it was all but forgotten, leaving the door open for public radio. (Pages 119–120, 124–125, 127–128, 134–136)

MEDIA AND DEMOCRACY

Live Audience Access. President Franklin Roosevelt tapped into radio's potential to reach larger audiences live than ever before. He rallied on national networks for support of his radical reforms to end the Great Depression of the 1930s.

The potential of radio as a medium for news has a long history. Returns in the 1916 presidential election were reported by radio. Television took over much of this role in the latter 20th century, but parts of the radio industry have continued the medium's role as a forum for discussion of public issues. Today this role is mostly played by talk stations, although much of the content is more showmanship and bluster than enlightenment. Noncommercial public stations, meanwhile, grew as a contributor to public affairs dialogue. (Pages 128–132, 137–138)

MEDIA AND CULTURE

Ray Charles Redux. The ways that mass media can shape public consumption of cultural output is demonstrated by spikes in music sales from factors apart from whether the music is good, bad or mediocre. The so-called Grammy Bounce, as with Ray Charles' Genius Loves Company album, is an example. The album won critical praise, but many Grammy winners are just secondary flashes in the pan and not long remembered.

Chain ownership of radio stations resulted in a centralization of their playlists in favor of pop music. Because radio permeates our society, complaints in the 1980s about objectionable lyrics that focused on drugs, sexual promiscuity and violence resonated with many parents. To stay one step ahead of government censorship, the recording industry followed the example of other media groups and introduced self-regulation to head off a First Amendment crisis. Government also has had a hand in the growing audience for news, public affairs and reporting on culture on noncommercial radio stations after Congress channeled major funding into the noncommercial system starting in 1967. (Pages 123–124, 135–136, 137–138)

chapter 6

MOTION MEDIA

Tyler Perry is the media's "new man." He sees seamless possibilities for developing content on multiple platforms. You may know his character Madea from the movies. It's also his stage play. He writes books. He produces television series. He acts. He directs. Print media? Sound media? Motion media? It doesn't matter. What matters to Perry is communicating content to mass audiences whatever the medium.

LEARNING AHEAD

- After early distrust between them, the television and movie industries have largely melded.
- Movies are most powerful viewed uninterrupted in a darkened auditorium.
- Besides feature films, there are subgenres including animated and documentary films.
- The movie industry is dominated by a handful of major studios.
- The exhibition component of the movie industry is in rapid transition.
- The television industry is under siege from new technology.
- U.S. television was built on the same dual infrastructure as radio.
- Cable and satellite delivery are challenging the affiliate network monopoly.
- Satellite delivery has further fragmented the television-delivery industry.
- New technology offers video on demand, which is reconfiguring the industry.
- Public television is an alternative to commercial television.
- Advertisers are eyeing alternatives created by time-shift devices and portable devices.

TYLER PERRY'S HOUSE OF MEDIA CONVERGENCE

Born to working-class parents in a poor neighborhood of New Orleans, a high-school dropout at 16, a self-taught playwright and actor who now lives in Atlanta, Tyler Perry seems an unlikely personification of the "new Hollywood." But he is all that and more: Tyler Perry just may be the thin end of the wedge—the next phase in the evolution of media content, platforms and channels. He is a new media *auteur* who creates, owns, brands, produces and distributes his creations across platforms completely without regard for the old lines that have traditionally divided movies, television, the stage, print and digital channels. He is media's "new man," and he's only 40.

In his early 20s Perry began writing and producing plays in his native Atlanta often for audiences of just 20 to 30 people. His actors were young, talented unknowns from the African often for audiences of just 20 to 30 people American community. Perry often played a part as well, sometimes appearing in wig and housedress as the formidable matriarch Madea, modeled on his grandmother. Perry did audience research after every performance, standing on stage, talking with the audience, finding out what they liked and what they wanted to see. Perry said recently of this experience, "African-American women were in the audience and what I found, as most men know, is if you are married, the women bring the men and the children and everybody to everything. So I know and I knew then that I needed to focus on them."

Perry's third play, *Diary of a Mad Black Woman,* centered on the character of Madea. It became his first movie, produced on a shoestring budget of $5.5 million. Distributed by indie LionsGate, it opened in 2005 and eventually grossed over $50 million. *Diary* was panned by critics, but it seemed to fill a gap with audiences who felt ignored by Hollywood, and it set a pattern for Perry's highly energetic output in the next several years, in which he wrote, produced and toured six more plays; a total of nine motion pictures; two television series; and a book.

All Perry's works regardless of medium are branded with the possessive, "Tyler Perry's . . ." His 2009 film *Tyler Perry's Madea Goes to Jail,* based on his play, had an opening weekend gross of $41 million, proving, as if further proof were needed, that a large and underserved market exists for middlebrow, middle-class comedies aimed at an African-American audience.

Perry to date has had two hit sitcoms running on the TBS network: *Tyler Perry's House of Payne* debuted in 2006, has logged over 100 episodes, and entered syndication. *Tyler Perry's Meet the Browns* debuted in 2009. It is, like many of his creations, a perfect example of content driving the convergence of media: *Meet the Browns* began life as a stage play; became a movie in 2008, opening at #2 with a $21 million weekend gross; and was quickly adapted to series television.

Perry recently told a gathering of network and advertising executives, "Audiences are starving for a show like *House of Payne* and *Meet the Browns.* To have someone paying attention to them, giving them what they want . . . images that look like themselves."

In addition to branding his own creative output, Perry has now turned to producing other artists' work, with the establishment in 2008 of Tyler Perry Studios, an enormous studio, soundstage and office complex in Atlanta from which he will guide the work of other filmmakers.

It may just also give him a base for his next dream: owning his own network.

"As I grow it from *House of Payne* to *Meet the Browns* and spread out with more and more shows, who knows?" he said. "I'm working on anchoring my own network, but this is a great place to sharpen the anchor."

The Television-Movies Meld

STUDY ***PREVIEW***

After early distrust between them, the television and movie industries have largely melded. Many major corporations are planted in both industries. Synergies have been found between both traditional television and Hollywood products.

COMMON AND DIVERGENT LEGACIES

Despite their current coziness, the Hollywood and the television industries once were rivals that saw each other as Darth Vaders. The rivalry dates to the 1950s when television grabbed eyeballs from the Big Screen by the millions. Until then, Hollywood had been entrenched as the sole media purveyor of screen sound-and-motion for half a century. Fueled by huge popularity and profitability, a distinctive Hollywood culture and lifestyle had evolved—celebrity-obsessed, gilded and flashy. Suddenly, there came the insurgent television with entirely different cultural roots in the buttoned-down New York-based radio industry. The insurgent was threatening to destroy the movie business.

The rivalry is hard to understand today. The television and film industries have subsumed each other as content-generators. In fact, the melding is evident in the new corporate titles: NBC Universal, Disney-ABC, Fox television and 20th Century Fox.

So what happened? And what distinctions remain in the blurring of these important media industries?

DISSECTING MOTION MEDIA INDUSTRIES

The traditional components of the movie industry—production, distribution and exhibition—have weathered rough times, albeit with some losses along the way.

>> **Production.** The original technologies underlying movies and television bore little in common. Movies were on film, a chemistry-based medium. Performances were filmed in bits and pieces over weeks or months, then painstakingly assembled, and audiences saw the product later. With early television, viewers saw events and performances live. In one sense, early television had the live tension and excitement of the stage. Movies, on the other hand, were edited, the final presentation slicker. For sure, television programs could be recorded on film, but for broadcast to an audience the transmission needed to be live in the early days.

The mindset for early television came from radio. The model was New York-centric network radio, and technicians and producers were from a technical tradition far afield. The continent away, from modes and traditions that had been evolving for more than half a century in Hollywood.

I Love Lucy. *The screwball sitcom transfixed millions of viewers on CBS from 1951 to 1957. More importantly and less visibly, the show pointed to the possibilities for a coexistence between disparate television and Hollywood cultures. Three-camera production of* I Love Lucy, *although new to television, was an innovation borrowed from movies. Also, producer-stars Desi Arnaz and Lucille Ball preferred a Hollywood to a New York lifestyle and insisted that production take place in California.*

The television-movie divide began to crumble with the television comedy series *I Love Lucy*. The show, launched in 1951, was filmed with three cameras, which brought television nearer to the conventions of Hollywood production. Editors chose from three sets of film, each from a different angle, for the greatest impact. Important too, actors Desi Arnaz and Lucille Ball, who had plenty of clout with the CBS network, insisted that they be allowed to produce the show in Hollywood. They liked West Coast sunshine and glamour.

Another breakthrough occurred in the mid-1960s when television networks began offering Hollywood blockbusters, like *Bridge on the River Kwai*, and then regularized them in prime-time Movie of the Week series. Financially these were a win-win for the networks and the movie studios, which suddenly discovered additional income in recycling their products. To be sure, local stations earlier had filled time with hand-me-down movies from Hollywood, but these mostly were from B lists and played at obscure times of the day.

>> **Distribution and Exhibition.** Television's greatest threat to Hollywood was in distributing and exhibiting its product. Since the early 1900s, the film industry had developed a complex system of shipping films, often in canisters weighing 85 pounds, to movie houses where people gathered, bought tickets, and watched a show. With television, distribution was by signals that moved freely through the air to in-home reception devices.

Families by the million made budget decisions over the kitchen table to buy a television set, often a hefty $500 at the time, and amortize the cost by staying home rather than going to the neighborhood Bijou for entertainment. Movie ticket sales plummeted. To Hollywood, with its survival in jeopardy, television was the enemy.

As Hollywood and television melded over the decades, it was companies in the exhibition business that took the greatest hit—movie houses. Attendance peaked in 1946 at 90 million tickets a week, at a time when the nation's population, 141 million, was less than half of today. Exhibitors have frantically tried to stem their box-office decline with multiple but smaller auditoriums, some spartan, some elegant. Movie-makers have tried to help with technical innovations from time to time—Cinemascope, 3D and THX. D-cinema now is coming on stream, promising to replace the distribution of film in those clunky 85-pound canisters. To offset box-office losses, exhibitors have put popcorn at ridiculous prices, buttered or not, and moved aggressively into selling on-screen advertising ahead of the main feature.

The fact is that 1946 won't come back. People have manifold more diversions, including television more than ever (the small screen) and online (the even smaller screen).

SYNERGIES

Overall, the barriers between Hollywood and television have come down. An early alliance between the ABC network and the Disney studio showed potential **synergies.** Popular movies begat television series, and popular television series begat movies. Digitization facilitated the shift of technicians from producing movies to television and back to movies. Distinctions blurred. And in corporate offices, executives were focused not on their old rival medium for eyeballs but on how to maximize profits by adapting products to any and all delivery vehicles.

Even actors dance among different media forms. Careers are built on exposure that is medium-neutral. This is in contrast to the time when some stage actors would consider appearing only on television, never in movies, because of the spontaneity of live performance. Then there were actors who took comfort in the control that filming and editing gave in exorcising slipups, and providing alternate takes for creating the perfect filmic moment.

synergy
An interaction that produces a combined effect greater than the sum of separate effects

CHECKING YOUR MEDIA LITERACY

- **What role did *I Love Lucy* play in easing tensions between the television and movie industries?**
- **How well has the rivalry between the movie and television industry been resolved?**

Movies: First of the Motion Media

STUDY ***PREVIEW***

Movies can have a powerful and immediate effect, in part because theaters insulate moviegoers in a cocoon without distractions. By some measures, the powerful effect is short-lived. Nonetheless, movies can sensitize people to issues and have a long-term effect in shifting public attitudes on enduring issues. To most people, the word *movie* conjures up the feature films that are the Hollywood specialty. Subspecies include animated films and documentaries.

MOVIE POWER

As Dan Brown's thriller *The Da Vinci Code* picked up steam en route to becoming a mega-selling book, the debate intensified on his account of Catholic church history. It was a big deal—but nothing compared to the fury that occurred when Sony moved Ron Howard's movie adaptation toward release. The full crescendo came when the movie premiered. The unprecedented fury in the dialogue demonstrates the impact of movies as a storytelling and myth-making medium, which for mass audiences can far exceed the impact of other media for at least short windows of time.

Movies with religious themes can strike loud chords, as did Mel Gibson's *Passion of the Christ* and Martin Scorsese's *Last Temptation of Christ*. But movies have an impact on other hot-button issues. Consider *Brokeback Mountain*, which catapulted homosexual affections into a new territory of public dialogue. The short story in the *New Yorker* magazine on which *Brokeback* was based had made merely a ripple in the mass consciousness. Al Gore's documentary *An Inconvenient Truth* gave new urgency in 2006 to finding solutions for global warming. Michael Moore and other docu-ganda producers have stirred significant issues far beyond what magazine and newspaper articles had been doing for years. *Guess Who's Coming to Dinner*, with a theme that was interracially edgy for the 1960s, moved the public toward broader acceptance.

CHECKING YOUR MEDIA LITERACY

- **What impact, perhaps indelible, have the movies mentioned here had on audiences?**
- **What recent movies would you add to the list? Why?**

COCOON EXPERIENCE

Why the powerful and immediate effect of movies? There may be a clue in one of Thomas Edison's first shorts, which included ocean waves rolling toward a camera on a beach. Audiences covered their heads. Instinctively they expected to be soaked. Such was their **suspension of disbelief.** Natural human skepticism gets lost in the darkened cocoon of a movie-house auditorium, compounding the impact of what's on-screen.

Although moviegoers are insulated in a dark auditorium, the experience is communal. You're not the only one sobbing or terrified or joyous. Among your fellow viewers is a reinforcement of emotions that other media can't match. A newspaper article, for example, may be read by thousands, but the experience is individual and apart. The emotional impact is less. Television, watched at home, often alone, is similarly disadvantaged, even though television has most of the accoutrements of movies—visuals, motion and sound.

suspension of disbelief
Occurs when you surrender doubts about the reality of a story and become caught up in the story

At their most potent, movies need to be seen in a theater. A movie may be good on a DVD at home, as computer downloads or as pay-per-view on television—but nothing compares to the theater phenomenon.

CHECKING YOUR MEDIA LITERACY

- **In what situation are movies most likely to encourage suspension of disbelief?**
- **What is the difference in the immediate and long-term effects of a movie theater experience?**
- **In fiction, what is the significance of suspension of disbelief?**

Suspension of Disbelief. *People are carrying their experiences and realities with them when they sit down for a movie. As a storyteller, a movie director needs quickly to suck the audience into the plot—to suspend disbelief, as novelists call it. Master directors, like James Cameron, best known for* Titanic, *strive to create this new reality in opening scenes to engross viewers in the story as it unfolds.*

GLOBAL ROLE

After Europe and its promising young film industry were devastated by World War I, Hollywood filled a void by exporting movies. Thus began Hollywood's move toward global pre-eminence in filmmaking. It happened again in World War II. The U.S. government declared movies an essential wartime industry for producing military training and propaganda films. After the war, Europe again in ruins, Hollywood was intact and expanded its exports.

Today, movies are among the few products that contribute positively to the balance of trade for the United States. More movies are exported than imported. Indeed, the potential for foreign box office

MEDIA TIMELINE

MOTION MEDIA MILESTONES / PIVOTAL EVENTS

1700s

Pivotal Events

- Photographic technology discovered, essential for early movies (1727)

1800s

Pivotal Events

- U.S. middle class with discretionary time for amusement emerged (1870s–)
- Edison lab invented movie cameras, projectors (1888)

1900–1949

Motion Media Milestones

Strand
First of the opulent movie palaces (1912)

Paramount
Hollywood studio system took form (1912–)

Popularity
U.S. movie box office peaked at 90 million a week (1946)

Breakup
U.S. Supreme Court broke up Hollywood's vertical integration 1948)

Networks
First television network feeds (1948)

Major studios concentrate in Hollywood

Philo Farnsworth, image dissector inventor

Pivotal Events

- Fox introduced sound in newsreels (1922)
- *Black Pirate,* first color movie (1927)
- Warner distributed first talkie, *The Jazz Singer* (1927)
- Philo Farnsworth invented a tube to capture and transmit moving images (1927)
- FCC adopted standards for U.S. television (1941)
- Cable television introduced (1949)

1950–1999

Motion Media Milestones

Television
Network television hurt movie attendance (1950s)

Public Television
Congress established Corporation for Public Broadcasting (1967)

Disney
Disney produced weekly television show (1954)

Multiplex
Multiscreen theaters attempted to recover movie audience (1970s)

VHS
Home movie rentals hurt home theater attendance (1990s)

HBO
First satellite-delivered programming to cable systems (1975)

Dishes
Satellite-direct programming began (1994)

Digital
FCC adopted digital standards for gradual phase-in (1996)

Flying way high

Computer-assisted special effects

Pivotal Events

- FCC chair Newton Minow characterized television as "vast wasteland" (1961)
- Telstar in orbit (1961)
- Internet emerged as commercial medium (late 1990s)

2000s

Motion Media Milestones

Movie-House Make-Over
10-year conversion to digital projection began (2006)

Television anywhere, any time

Pivotal Events

- Apple introduced video iPod (2005)

presence is essential for Hollywood in working out the financial details for film projects. Movie proposals with good prospects for a foreign box office revenue are more likely to get a green light.

Consider this mid-2006 snapshot of leading Hollywood films:

	U.S. Box Office	Foreign Box Office
X-Men: Last Stand	$231.2 million	$205.5 million
The Da Vinci Code	213.2 million	515.1 million
Cars	205.9 million	64.6 million
Ice Age: The Meltdown	194.3 million	446.9 million
Superman Returns	141.6 million	35.8 million
Pirates of the Caribbean: Dead Man's Chest	135.6 million	48.6 million
Mission: Impossible III	133.0 million	219.4 million

About 60 percent of U.S. film exports go to Europe, 30 percent to Asia. It is action films that do best abroad. There usually is minimal dialogue to impede the transcultural experience. Media scholar George Gerbner once explained it this way: "Violence travels well."

CHECKING YOUR MEDIA LITERACY

- **How did Hollywood establish itself as a global moviemaking center?**
- **About Hollywood movie exports, scholar George Gerbner once said, "Violence travels well." What did he mean?**

Movie Products

STUDY PREVIEW

To most people, the word *movie* conjures up the feature films that are the Hollywood specialty. Subspecies include animated films and documentaries. Also, the historic distinction between Hollywood and television as rivals is melding.

FEATURE FILMS

Movies that tell stories, much in the tradition of stage plays, are **narrative films.** These are what most people think of as movies. They're promoted heavily, their titles and actors on marquees. Most are in the 100-minute range. A French magician and inventor, Georges Méliès, pioneered narrative films with fairy tales and science-fiction stories to show in his movie house in 1896. Méliès' *Little Red Riding Hood* and *Cinderella* ran less than 10 minutes—short stories, if you will. In 1902 Edwin Porter directed *Life of a Fireman*, the first coherent narrative film in the United States. Audiences, accustomed to stage plays and being a distance away from the actors, were distressed, some shocked, at his close-ups, a new technique. They felt cheated at not seeing "the whole stage."

narrative films
Movies that tell a story

Gradually, audiences learned what is called **film literacy,** the ability to appreciate moviemaking as an art form with unique-to-the-medium techniques that add impact or facilitate the telling of a story. Porter's next significant film, *The Great Train Robbery,* was shocking, too, for cutting back and forth between robbers and a posse that was chasing them—something, like close-ups, that film can do and the stage cannot. Slowly movies emerged as a distinctive art form.

>> **Talkies.** At Thomas Edison's lab, the tinkerer William Dickson came up with a sound system for movies in 1889, but it didn't go anywhere. The first successful commercial application of sound was in Movietone newsreels in 1922. But it was four upstart moviemakers, the **Warner brothers,** Albert, Harry, Jack and Sam Warner, who revolutionized **talkies,** movies with sound. In 1927 the Warners released ***The Jazz Singer*** starring Al Jolson. There was sound for only two segments, 354 words total, but audiences in movie houses the Warners had equipped with loudspeakers were enthralled. The next year, 1928, the Warners issued ***The Singing Fool,*** also with Jolson, this time with a full-length sound track. The Warners earned 25 times their investment. For 10 years no other movie attracted more people to the box office.

film literacy
Ability to appreciate artistic techniques used for telling a story through film

Warner Brothers
Introduced sound

talkies
Movies with sound

The Jazz Singer
The first feature sound movie

The Singing Fool
The first full-length sound movie

The Black Pirate
The first feature movie in color

computer-generated imagery (CGI)
The application of three-dimensional computer graphics for special effects, particularly in movies and television

>> **Color.** Overtaking *The Singing Fool* in 1939 was a narrative movie with another technological breakthrough, *Gone with the Wind* with color. Although *Gone with the Wind* is often referred to as the first color movie, the technology had been devised in the 1920s, and ***The Black Pirate*** with Douglas Fairbanks was far earlier, in 1925. But *GWTW*, as it's called by buffs, was a far more significant film. *GWTW* marked the start of Hollywood's quest for ever-more-spectacular stories and effects to attract audiences—the blockbuster.

>> **Computer-Generated Imagery.** You can imagine why early moviemaker Alfred Clark used a special effect for his 1895 movie *The Execution of Mary Queen of Scots*. "Illusion" was what special effects were called then. Although audiences were amazed, the effects were nothing like today's *CGI*, the shoptalk abbreviation that movie people use for three-dimensional **computer-generated imagery.**

The first use of three-dimensional CGI in movies was *Futureworld* in 1976. University of Utah grad students Edwin Catmull and Fred Parke created a computer-generated hand and face. There were CGI scenes in *Star Wars* in 1977, but the technology remained mostly an experimental novelty until 1989 when the pseudopod sea creature created by Industrial Light & Magic for *The Abyss* won an Academy Award. Photorealistic CGI was firmly in place with the villain's liquid metal morphing effects in *Terminator 2*, also by Industrial Light & Magic and also recognized by a 1991 Oscar for special effects.

Computer-generated imagery soon became the dominant form of special effects with technology opening up new possibilities. For stunts, CGI characters began replacing doubles that were nearly indistinguishable from the actors. Crowd scenes were easily created without hiring hundreds of extras. This raised the question of whether movie actors themselves might be replaced by pixels.

Movie commentator Neil Petkus worries that some filmmakers may overuse their toy. "CGI effects can be abused and mishandled," Petkus says. "Directors sometimes allow the visual feasts that

What's Old Is New Again.

CASE STUDY

In-Your-Face Documentaries

Al Gore. *His documentary* An Inconvenient Truth *turned former Vice President Al Gore into a movie star of sorts. Suddenly he had riveted public attention on climatic issues that environmentalists as far back as Rachel Carson in the 1950s have been arguing threaten the habitat of the planet for humans and other species.*

Not so long ago, moviegoers deemed documentaries dreary, dull and dry. Today some documentaries are the hottest money-makers in Hollywood. Michael Moore's in-your-face *Fahrenheit 9/11* grossed $100 million its first month.

As with all his documentaries, including *Sicko* in 2007, Moore has critics who say he's neither fair nor balanced. Moore stands by his accuracy but explains that his documentaries are his take on issues. He sees them as "balancing" to dominant interpretations offered in the mainstream media.

That contrarian thrust, says television writer Debi Enker, is addressing a void in general media coverage of issues: "The current interest suggests people are seeking not just immediacy but also context and the kind of perspective that time, research, thoughtful analysis, and intelligent storytelling can bring." Dawn Dreyer of the Center for Documentary Studies at Duke University puts it this way: "It's narrative. It's storytelling. It's becoming engaged with people's lives."

Dreyer's characterization of documentaries explains, also, the success of former Vice President Al Gore's *An Inconvenient Truth*. The movie grossed more than $41 million worldwide. A documentary typically has a far lower budget than other movies, which can mean higher profits even if there is only a limited theatrical release. *An Inconvenient Truth*, the first carbon-neutral documentary, started as a low-tech slide show. Filming took six months and a little more than $1 million—pocket change by Hollywood standards.

One of *An Inconvenient Truth*'s producers, Lawrence Bender, said: "Everything about this movie was a miracle." Not only did the film rake in cash, it earned two Oscars. Also, it made Al Gore a movie star. "When we took Gore to Sundance and Cannes, people just went crazy around him," said Bender. "It was really amazing. He doesn't sing or act, but he actually is kind of a rock star. He has this message that's drawing people to him, making him larger than life."

The British government purchased 3,385 DVDs to distribute to every secondary school. In the United States, 50,000 copies were given to teachers. The Documentary Organization of Canada launched a new green code of ethics for documentary filmmakers. Paramount Classics donated 5 percent of all box office receipts to The Alliance for Climate Protection. The Alliance also received 100 percent of Gore's proceeds from the film.

DEEPENING YOUR MEDIA LITERACY

EXPLORE THE ISSUE

Pick a new muckraking documentary and a television news report on the same subject.

DIG DEEPER

What makes the documentary different from the way a television news report might treat the same subject? Would the documentary resonate as well with the audience if the filmmaker did not feel passionately about the subject and it was completely fair and balanced?

WHAT DO YOU THINK?

Do you think these new documentaries fill a need? How have they contributed to the movie industry? To society?

computers offer to undermine any real content a movie may have had." Petkus faults director George Lucas for going too far in later *Star Wars* movies: "Any interesting character developments that could have occurred in these movies were overwhelmed by constant CGI action sequences."

Faster computers and massive data storage capacities have added efficiencies to computer-generated movie imagery, but offsetting the efficiencies has been pressure for greater detail and quality. CGI is labor-intensive. A single frame typically takes two to three hours to render. For a complex frame, count on 20 hours or more. The Warner Bros. budget for the 2006 *Superman Returns*, a record $204 million, was eaten up largely with CGI effects.

CHECKING YOUR MEDIA LITERACY

- **How would you define feature films?**
- **How has technology shaped feature films?**

ANIMATED FILMS

Walt Disney
Pioneer in animated films

animated film
Narrative films with drawn scenes and characters

Steamboat Willie
Animated cartoon character that became Mickey Mouse

Snow White and the Seven Dwarfs
First full-length animated film

Robert Flaherty
First documentary filmmaker

documentary
A video examination of a historical or current event or a natural or social phenomenon

Frank Capra
Hollywood movie director who produced powerful propaganda movies for the U.S. war effort in World War II

Why We Fight
Frank Capra's war mobilization documentary series

Fairness Doctrine
A U.S. government requirement from 1949 to 1987 that broadcast presentations had to include both sides on competing public issues

The 1920s were pivotal in defining genres of narrative films. In his early 20s, **Walt Disney** arrived in Los Angeles from Missouri in 1923 with $40 in his pocket. Walt moved in with his brother Roy, and they rounded up $500 and went into the **animated film** business. In 1928 ***Steamboat Willie*** debuted in a short film to accompany feature films. The character Willie eventually morphed into Mickey Mouse. Disney took animation to full length with ***Snow White and the Seven Dwarfs*** in 1937, cementing animation as a subspecies of narrative films.

Animated films were labor-intensive, requiring an illustrator to create 1,000-plus sequential drawings for a minute of screen time. Computers changed all that in the 1990s, first with digital effects for movies that otherwise had scenes and actors, notably the *Star Wars* series by George Lucas, then animated features. Disney's *Toy Story* in 1995 was the first movie produced entirely by computers. The new technology, brought to a high level by Lucas' Industrial Light & Magic and Steve Jobs' Pixar, has led to a resurgence in the issuance of animated films after a relatively dormant period. Recent years have seen huge audiences for *Shrek, Finding Nemo* and *Monsters vs Aliens*, among others.

CHECKING YOUR MEDIA LITERACY

- **What were pioneer successes in animated films?**
- **How can you explain the resurgence of animated films?**

DOCUMENTARIES

Nonfiction film explorations of historical or current events and natural and social phenomena go back to 1922 and **Robert Flaherty**'s look into Eskimo life. With their informational thrust, early **documentaries** had great credibility. Soon, though, propagandists were exploiting the credibility of documentaries with point-of-view nonfiction. Propagandist films found large audiences in World War II, including **Frank Capra**'s seven 50-minute films in the ***Why We Fight*** series.

>> Television Network Documentaries. Television journalists sought to bring balance and fairness to documentaries in the 1950s. In part it was that journalists of the just-the-facts mold were doing the documentaries. Also, it was the television networks that underwrote the budgets of these documentaries. Their purpose was to build corporate prestige, not propagandize. A factor in the neutral thrust of most of these documentaries also was the Federal Communications Commission's licensing dictate to stations for fairness in whatever was broadcast.

>> Docu-Ganda. The FCC's **Fairness Doctrine** was withdrawn in 1987, setting in motion a new rationale for documentaries that, in many cases, seeks not so much to

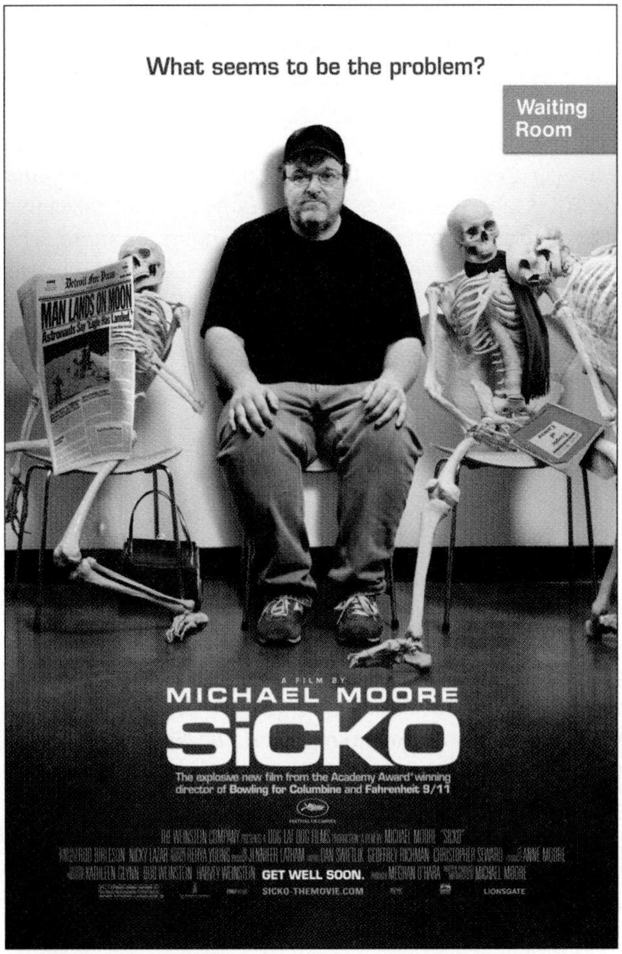

Sicko. *Michael Moore taunted the pharmaceuticals industry with his 2007 documentary* Sicko. *In one sense, Moore's documentaries, although fact-based, carry slants and use rhetorical techniques that short-circuit what could be honest persuasion. The techniques leave Moore an easy target for responses from those whom his films attack.*

inform as to influence the audience. What emerged was a new-form genre critics call **docu-ganda,** which plays not on the major television networks but in movie houses and niche outlets. Independent filmmaker **Michael Moore** has epitomized the new generation of documentary-makers, first with *Roger and Me*, a brutal attack on General Motors. Moore was no less savage in *Bowling for Columbine*, this time aiming at gun access advocates, and *Fahrenheit 9/11*, aimed during the 2004 elections at President Bush and his Iraq war motivations. *Fahrenheit* was the largest-grossing documentary in history—a demonstration of the economic viability of documentaries.

Relatively inexpensive digital filmmaking equipment has also driven the new documentaries. For his *Super Size Me*, linking fast food and obesity, Morgan Sperlock could never have persuaded a major studio to cover the budget, several million dollars upfront, for a documentary attacking an American icon like McDonald's. But with a $3,000 digital camera, $5,000 in software and an Apple computer, Sperlock created his personal statement on fast food. So compelling was *Super Size Me* that 200 theaters showed it and grossed $7.5 million in a month. In all, Sperlock had spent only $65,000 to create the movie.

>> Single Point of View. Critics fault many recent documentaries for usurping the detached, neutral tone of earlier documentaries while delivering only a single point of view. Guilty as charged, respond the new documentary-makers. David Zieger, who raised eyebrows with his *Sir! No Sir!* on the anti-war movement within the military during the Vietnam war, says: "If you make a film with both sides, you're going to make a boring film." Film is not journalism, Zieger says.

In other words, a docu-ganda requires viewers to have a higher level of media literacy than in the heyday of television's network documentaries, which laid out competing viewpoints within a single package. Some critics say that the contemporary documentaries that make the biggest splash are, in fact, dangerous because they can dupe viewers into accepting them as the whole truth.

docu-ganda
Documentaries that seek to influence their viewers

Michael Moore
Producer–director of point-of-view documentaries

CHECKING YOUR MEDIA LITERACY

- **What are historically important documentaries?**
- **Who are significant current documentary producers? What are their signature works?**
- **Some documentaries are journalistic explorations. Others are highly opinionated. How can moviegoers recognize the difference?**

Hollywood Studios

STUDY PREVIEW

Hollywood is dominated by six movie studios, all engaged in both producing and distributing movies. These studios, each part of a conglomerate, are enmeshed with the television industry through corporate connections.

STUDIO SYSTEM

The structure of the U.S. movie industry is rooted historically in a few major companies that tightly controlled everything beginning in the 1920s. In this studio system, a handful of companies produced, distributed and exhibited movies. The companies had oligarchic control, successfully excluding outsiders and using their power to coerce the marketplace. No studio better illustrates the system than Paramount under Adolph Zukor.

PARAMOUNT

Hungarian immigrant **Adolph Zukor** started poor in Hollywood, but in a series of innovations, none of them artistic, he invented the movie business as we know it. Before Zukor there were no movie stars, nothing approaching mass production and only a loose distribution and exhibition structure. Zukor changed all that, becoming the stereotypical Hollywood mogul.

>> **Star System.** When Zukor started his studio, Famous Players, in 1912, moviemakers kept the names of their actors secret. The idea was to dead-end a nascent fan base that might give actors a star complex and calls for better pay. Fifteen dollars a day was tops then. Zukor saw things differently. He tracked fan letters for mentions of actors. Those most mentioned he signed to exclusive contracts. So to speak, Zukor put their names in lights. It cost him. Mary Pickford was soon at $15,000 a week. The payoff for Zukor was that Mary Pickford's name attracted repeat customers just to see her, even in lackluster movies.

The **star system,** as it was called, was imitated by competing studios, which had no choice. Meanwhile, Zukor had a head start. Soon his enterprise took on the name Paramount.

Adolph Zukor
Innovative creator of Paramount as a major movie studio

star system
Making actors into celebrities to increase the size of movie audiences

studio system
When major studios controlled all aspects of the movie industry

>> **Production Efficiencies.** Zukor brought mass production to moviemaking, in part because he needed to have projects to keep his stars productive, as well as other contract employees, including hundreds of directors, writers, editors and technicians. Paramount movies became factory-like products. On tight mass-production schedules with programmed progress, Paramount eventually was issuing a movie a week. So were competitors in what came to be called the **studio system.**

Adolph Zukor

Hollywood Survivor. *Most studios sold their huge sound lots to real estate developers for cash to see them through revenue slumps after big-budget flops. Today only Paramount has retained its facilities in Hollywood.*

By the mid-1930s, the big movie companies—Columbia, MGM, Paramount, RKO, 20th Century Fox, Universal and Warner—owned acre upon acre of studios and sets. These were money machines but only as long as production kept moving. So whether scripts were strong or weak, the movie factories needed to keep churning out products on predictable schedules to meet what at the time seemed an insatiable public demand for films at movie houses. The movie houses were part of the studio system, many owned by the big studios.

>> **Vertical Integration.** Studios like Paramount, which controlled the production, distribution and exhibition of movies, squeezed out independent operators. **Block booking** was an example. Zukor booked his Paramount movies into his Paramount-owned theaters. Paramount indeed also provided movies to independent movie houses but only in packages that included overpriced clunkers. To book a movie they wanted, theaters were forced to take many movies that they didn't. Profits for the studios were immense, funding the lifestyle and other excesses that gave Hollywood its gilded reputation.

The major studios, controlling the whole process from conception of a movie to the box office, had put the industry into what businesspeople call **vertical integration.** Their control, including coercive practices like block booking, in time attracted the antitrust division of the U.S. Justice Department. In a case decided by the U.S. Supreme Court in 1948, the studios were told to divest. As a result of the so-called **Paramount decision,** studios gave up their ownership of movie houses. It was a setback for the studio system. Suddenly the studios had to compete for screen time in movie houses. Without a guaranteed outlet for movies, including proverbial B movies, the studios had no choice but to scale back on payrolls and facilities. The lavish excesses of Hollywood's gilded age were over.

Studios, including Paramount, turned more to outside directors. Ongoing contracts for big-name stars disappeared. Instead, actors, directors and others were hired project by project. Those acres of sound studios, as movie sets were called, were sold in lucrative real estate deals in the booming Los Angeles area. Also, some studios found new business in producing television programs in the 1950s.

CHECKING YOUR MEDIA LITERACY

- **What were Adolph Zukor's enduring contributions to the U.S. movie business?**
- **Distinguish the so-called studio system from the star system.**
- **How did the U.S. Supreme Court reshape Hollywood?**

DISNEY

Disney isn't just Mickey Mouse anymore. It was Disney's unmatched animated cartoons, however, that launched the company and propelled it into a distinctive role among major Hollywood studios. Although ranking studios is tricky because one megahit or one clunker can upset a listing, Walt Disney Studio Entertainment is consistently among the leaders of the major studios.

>> **Classic Disney.** Although not realizing it, illustrator Walt Disney created the Disney franchise with Mickey Mouse in a synch-sound cartoon in 1928. In 1937 Disney risked it all with a full-feature animated film, *Snow White and the Seven Dwarfs*. Audiences wanted more. Disney responded with *Pinocchio, Dumbo* and *Bambi*.

While other studios were fighting a losing battle with network television in the 1950s, Disney embraced the enemy. He struck a deal with the ABC network in 1954 to produce an original television series. In effect, he recycled his film content for television. The program *Disneyland*, a Sunday night ritual for millions of television viewers, accounted for almost half of ABC's billing in its first year.

Disney also launched the *Mickey Mouse Club* on ABC in the afternoons, with kids singing and dancing and acting in episodic serials.

block booking
A rental agreement through which a movie house accepts a batch of movies

vertical integration
One company owning multiple stages of production, to the detriment of competition

Paramount decision
U.S. Supreme Court breakup of movie industry oligarchy in 1948

Not only did Disney cross-fertilize his corporate growth with television. In 1955 he opened the Disneyland amusement park in Los Angeles. The term *theme park* was coined. The Disney park theme? All the movie characters. Talk about cross-promotion. When Disney died in 1966 he was still on the rise. What next?

>> **Disney Brand.** Disney had become a brand name for family-oriented entertainment and for the next 20 years the mandate at Disney was to cultivate the brand.

Corporate managers worked to exploit the synergies, reissuing the earlier films in cycles, creating new ones in the Disney spirit, and building more theme parks, first in Orlando and then laying the groundwork for parks in Paris, Tokyo and elsewhere around the globe. Disney was indeed an international franchise, but without Walt the luster was fading, and revenue projections were uninspiring.

>> **Eisner Era.** To jump-start the company, Disney shareholders in 1984 brought in an energetic executive from Paramount, **Michael Eisner.** In a 20-year run Eisner indeed rejuvenated the company. Eisner engineered a merger with ABC to create in-house outlets for Disney products. He moved Disney beyond family fare with cutting-edge and niche movies, like *Powder* and *Dangerous Minds*, but buffered the projects under subsidiary units and partnerships to shield the wholesome Disney aura. Films were produced through Touchstone, Caravan, Hollywood Pictures and Miramax. Meanwhile, Disney's distribution unit, Buena Vista, the largest in the world, moved into producing Broadway plays.

>> **Post-Eisner.** Not all was perfect under Eisner. After *The Lion King*'s success in 1995, Disney had a run of animated feature flops. Profits slumped occasionally, which, although typical of the vagaries of the movie business, raised shareholder concerns.

In a messy shareholder battle, Eisner was thrown out. The post-Eisner leadership, concerned that Disney had lost its edge in animation, offered $7.4 billion to Steve Jobs, the genius behind Apple's resurgence, for his Pixar animation studio. It was Pixar that had stolen Disney's animation pre-eminence with blockbusters like *Toy Story, Finding Nemo* and *The Incredibles*. The deal, in 2006, made Jobs the largest Disney shareholder and put him on the Disney board of directors.

OTHER MAJOR STUDIOS

The remaining Big Six studios, besides Paramount and Disney, are Columbia, 20th Century Fox, Universal and Warner.

>> **Columbia.** Founded in 1919, Columbia has moved through high-visibility ownership, including Coca-Cola and the Japanese electronics company Sony. Movies are produced and distributed under brand names Columbia and TriStar, and through frequent partnerships with independent producers Phoenix and Mandalay. The company is also in television production and distribution, including the venerable game show *Jeopardy*.

>> **20th Century Fox.** With roots dating to 1915, this studio is now part of the global media empire of Rupert Murdoch's News Corp., whose roots are in Australia. Corporate siblings include Rupert's Fox television network.

>> **Universal.** The U.S. conglomerate General Electric bought Universal from the financially overextended French media giant Vivendi in 2002. The deal made sense as synergy. Universal came under the same corporate roof as NBC, also owned by General Electric. Entering 2010, GE was in the process of selling its NBC Universal unit to the U.S. cable system giant Comcast. Synergy was the name of the game again, Comcast's chief executive Brian Roberts said the deal would make Comcast "a leader in the development and distribution of multiplatform anytime-anywhere media that American consumers are demanding.

Michael Eisner

Post-Walt Disney executive who expanded Disney while protecting its wholesome cachet; engineered a merger with ABC

Michael Eisner. *He's the second-most-important person in Disney corporate history. Before being ousted, Eisner's accomplishments included the 1995 merger with ABC that gave Disney a new outlet for its creative output.*

>> **Warner.** Founded in 1918, Warner Bros. became part of the Time Inc. media empire in a 1989 acquisition, prompting the parent company to rename itself Time Warner. The company produces and distributes movies and television programs mostly through units carrying the Warner name but also the names Castle Rock, New Line and Lorimar. The CW television network is a joint Warner and Paramount venture.

CHECKING YOUR MEDIA LITERACY

- **The movie industry once saw television as a rival but no more. What happened?**
- **What is the extent of foreign ownership in the U.S. movie industry?**

INDEPENDENTS

Besides the major studios that dominate Hollywood, independent studios and producers come and go—often with a single breakthrough film, then not much that attracts attention. The term *independent* is misleading in a sense because these indies frequently lean on majors for financing. Also, there are no suitable options for distribution other than through the corporate siblings and subsidiaries of the major studios. The history of independents is that those that establish a track record end up being acquired by a major studio. A notable exception is United Artists.

>> **United Artists.** Unhappy with profit-obsessed studios limiting their creativity, friends Charlie Chaplin, Douglas Fairbanks, D. W. Griffith and Mary Pickford broke away in 1919. They created United Artists. With full creative control, they produced movies that scored well among critics and attracted huge audiences. United Artists has been among only a few insurgent movie companies to make a long-term mark on Hollywood after the giants established themselves early on.

Despite box office successes, United Artists has had its share of movies in red ink. After Michael Cimino's costly *Heaven's Gate* in 1980, United needed a white knight. The Transamerica insurance company bought the studio, then unloaded it on MGM. The new company, MGM/UA, produced one disaster after another.

>> **Dreamworks.** In the United Artists spirit, three Hollywood legends—David Geffen, Jeff Katzenberg and Steven Spielberg—founded a new studio, Dreamworks SKG, in 1994. The three founders were well-connected and seasoned Hollywood people, each with a fortune from successful entertainment industry careers. They were called the Hollywood dream team. Spielberg's *Saving Private Ryan* in 1998 established an early Dreamworks benchmark for filmic excellence. Then came *Gladiator*, named 2000's best picture at the Academy Awards. Like most upstarts, even the most successful ones, Dreamworks has disappeared. Geffen, Katzenberg and Spielberg sold the enterprise in 2005 to Paramount for $1.6 billion.

>> **Miramax.** Brothers Bob and Harvey Weinstein blew into Hollywood in 1979, introducing themselves as concert promoters from Buffalo, New York. They set up a movie distribution company, Miramax, with a simple premise: Find low-budget, independently produced movies and buy them cheap, then promote them lavishly.

After 10 years of struggling, the Weinsteins hit gold with the biopic *My Left Foot*, on Irish writer-painter Christy Brown. An Academy Award nomination for best picture

MEDIA PEOPLE

Steven Spielberg

Although born in 1946, Steven Spielberg couldn't have made films like *Jaws, E.T.* and *Indiana Jones* if he weren't still a kid himself. At the dinner table when his seven kids were growing up, Spielberg used to start with a few lines from a story that popped into his head, then each of the kids would add a few lines. Where it would go, nobody knew, but everybody kept the story moving.

Spielberg loves stories, especially with ordinary characters meeting extraordinary beings or finding themselves in extraordinary circumstances. Another theme is that of lost innocence and coming-of-age. A persistent theme is parent-child tensions, which has been attributed to Spielberg's own distress as a child at his parents divorcing.

Critics, however, see unrealistic optimism and sentimentalism in Spielberg films although they admit exceptions. Certainly *Indiana Jones* is not all that has earned Spielberg his reputation as one of history's great moviemakers. One ranking has him number one. Twice he has won Academy Awards as best director, for *Schindler's List* and *Saving Private Ryan*, both gritty films set in wartime misery. *Schindler* took an Oscar for best picture.

As a kid, Spielberg was infected with a love for making movies. At 12 he put two Lionel toy trains on a collision course, turned up the juice to both engines and made a home movie of the crash. By that time he already had shot dozens of short films. For one of them, he coaxed his mother into donning a pith helmet and an Army surplus uniform, and then rolled the film as she bounced the family Jeep through backhill potholes near Phoenix. That was his first war movie.

Later, on a family trip to Los Angeles he lined up an unpaid summer job on the Universal Studios lot. He enrolled at California State University in Long Beach in 1965 but interrupted his studies to take a television director job at Universal before finishing his degree. Ironically, Spielberg tried three times for admission to the prestigious film program at the University of Southern California and failed—although in 1994 he was awarded an honorary USC degree.

Most Spielberg films, although wide-ranging in subject matter, have family-friendly themes with a childlike wonderment. There also are strong emotions, as in the *Schindler* depiction of the horrors of the Holocaust, social and sexual injustice in *The Color Purple*, slavery in *Amistad* and terrorism in *Munich*. But amid the heavy-duty treatments he mixes in rollicking adventures, like yet another in the *Indiana Jones* series or a *Jurassic Park* sequel.

Spielberg's financial success, $250 million alone for the first *Jurassic Park*, has given him the wherewithal to make whatever movie he wants. In 1994 he teamed with Hollywood legendaries David Geffen and Jeffrey Katzenberg to create Dreamworks, a stand-alone movie studio outside of Hollywood's Big Six. *Amistad* and *Saving Private Ryan* set a benchmark for achievement for the enterprise, which produced acclaimed movies although not in huge numbers. Twelve years later, Geffen, Katzenberg and Spielberg sold Dreamworks to Paramount for $1.6 billion. Before then Spielberg had made the *Forbes* magazine ranking of the richest people in the United States with a net worth at $2.7 billion, second among Hollywood figures only to his buddy George Lucas at $3.5 billion.

The sale of Dreamworks, however, didn't mean an end to Spielberg's moviemaking. A fourth in the *Indiana Jones* series was finished in 2007. An Abraham Lincoln bio-pic is coming along. Might we meet the thoroughly ugly but oh-so-lovable E.T., the extraterrestrial, at least one more time?

WHAT DO YOU THINK?

- What do Steven Spielberg movies have in common?
- What did Dreamworks have in common with earlier independent Hollywood studios?

Compelling Storyteller. *Spielberg makes a point with cinematographer Janusz Kaminski and actor Diego Luna for* The Terminal. *Since* Jaws *in 1975, he has directed movies involving history and science, including many on issues that kids deal with.*

stirred the box office. So did Daniel Day-Lewis' winning the Oscar for best actor. In the same year they released the indie favorite, *Sex, Lies and Videotape*. Other hits followed, prompting Disney to buy into Miramax in 1993. The deal left creative control with the hands-on Weinsteins, who seemed to have a deft touch for cultural edginess that Disney lacked. The arrangement produced Quentin Tarantino's *Pulp Fiction* in 1994, an $8 million film that grossed $200 million worldwide and earned an Oscar.

More financial and critical successes followed, including *The English Patient*, *Good Will Hunting*, *Shakespeare in Love*, *Kill Bill*, and the *Scary Movie* franchise. Like any studio the Weinsteins had their failures, including *Cold Mountain* and *Gangs of New York*, which never earned back their $100 million production budgets.

>> **Lions Gate.** Founded in 1997 by a Canadian investor, Lions Gate found early financial success in acquiring and producing tight-budget movies and then promoting them aggressively and imaginatively. Typical was *Crash*. Production cost $3.3 million, and marketing sextupled that—to $21 million. The U.S. and global box office generated $254 million. To create buzz for the Academy Awards, Lions Gate sent 110,000 DVDs to members of the Screen Actors Guild. The movie subsequently won the 2005 Academy Award for best picture. That generated the predictable bump for *Crash* in movie attendance and rentals. Alongside critical favorites like *Crash*, Lions Gate has made big money with the slasher franchise of *Saw* films—six, to date.

Lions Gate releases fewer than 20 pictures in a typical year. In 2005 there were 18, of which 15 were profitable, an unusually high ratio in Hollywood. To see itself through slumps, Lions Gate invested in film libraries and gradually amassed an archive of 5,500 titles that generate continuing revenue through domestic and overseas licensing. The catalog includes *Basic Instinct*, *Total Recall*, *Dirty Dancing* and the lucrative *Leprechaun* horror series.

D. W. Griffith
Early director known for innovations in *Birth of a Nation* and loose spending in *Intolerance*

blockbuster
A movie that is a great commercial success; also used to describe books

CHECKING YOUR MEDIA LITERACY

◇ **What is the role of independent studios in the U.S. movie industry?**

RISE OF THE BLOCKBUSTER

Early directors, including **D. W. Griffith,** tested the storytelling potential of the new film medium. Growing public enthusiasm was the proof of what worked. Griffith's 1915 Civil War epic *Birth of a Nation* was cinematically innovative and a commercial success. By the standards of the time, it was a **blockbuster.** The movie fueled Griffith's imagination to push the envelope further in a more complex project, *Intolerance*. In the new movie Griffith wanted to examine social justice through all of human history. He built huge sets and hired hundreds of actors. In all, he spent an unprecedented $2 million. In 1916, when *Intolerance* debuted, the critics were ecstatic at Griffith's audacity and artistry as a director. With audiences, however, the movie bombed. People were baffled by the movie's disparate settings, including ancient Babylon, Renaissance France and the Holy Land at the time of Christ.

Broke, Griffith had to obtain outside financing to make further movies. This meant that bankers and financiers sent agents to look over Griffith's shoulders, always with a pencil and balance sheet in hand, to control expenses. Not infrequently the money men overruled Griffith's creative impulses. The second-guessing involved not only cost issues. Sometimes the on-site agents of the bankrollers imposed their assessment of what would work with audiences. In effect, accountants gained a pivotal role in storytelling.

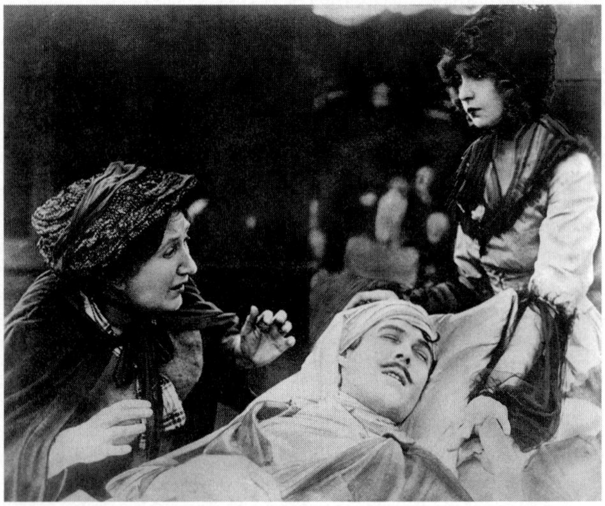

Birth of a Nation. *In a dramatic moment in D. W. Griffith's 1915 Civil War epic, Josephine Crowell and Lillian Gish are distressed over Henry Walthall. The powerful and cinematically innovative movie was the blockbuster of its time.*

D. W. Griffith. *On set with Billy Bitzer for* Way Down East *in 1920.*

The *Intolerance* experience demonstrated a dynamic that continues to play out in Hollywood—the tension that erupts not infrequently between financiers and directors. A second lesson from *Intolerance* was another Hollywood reality—boom or bust. The quest for super-earning blockbusters has escalated, often with risky big budgets. There are spectacular payoffs, like *Titanic* of 1997, the reigning box office triumph, and *Gone with the Wind* in 1939, which in inflation-adjusted dollars has done even better. On the other hand, blockbuster disasters can haunt a studio or production company for years. MGM, once a reigning studio, slipped with miscalculations. United Artists almost went under with the costs of Michael Cimino's obsession with historical details in *Heaven's Gate* in 1980.

Even so, with the conglomerate structure of the movie industry, involving all major U.S. studios as part of larger corporate structures, there is growing pressure to produce spectacular moneymakers. A blockbuster will satisfy the bosses at corporate headquarters—and thus the quest to outdo *Titanic* spirals upward with bigger and bigger production and promotion budgets. With great expectations can come great risk.

RISK REDUCTION

To balance the risk of blockbusters, studios look for safe bets. There can be profits if production costs can be contained. The result is a preponderance of formulaic movies that offer little in creative storytelling and don't advance the art of moviemaking but that turn a profit. Called **B movies,** these include sequels, remakes and franchises that, although hardly great movies, are almost sure to outearn their expenses.

Fast action, which doesn't require fine acting and which is cheap to produce, has figured heavily into low-budget and mid-budget movies. So too have violence and sex. Dialogue is minimal in many of these movies, which makes them easily adaptable for distribution to non-English-speaking audiences abroad.

Studios, also, have hedged their bets by building product names into scripts for a fee. This is called **product placement.** Some New York and Los Angeles advertising agencies specialize in product placement, as do talent agencies such as Creative Artists. No, it was no accident that Tom Hanks' character in *Cast Away* worked for FedEx. Or that hulky Chrysler 300s appeared in so many 2005 movies or Cadillacs appeared in MGM's *Be Cool*. In 2006 product placement worked its way into movie titles—*How Starbucks Saved My Life* and *The Devil Wears Prada*. Universal changed *Flight 93* to *United 93*.

Studios have found revenue too in **merchandise tie-ins,** including trinkets at Burger King and entire lines of toys.

B movie
Low-budget movie; usually with little artistic aspiration

product placement
Including a product into a script for a fee

merchandise tie-in
Products spun off from a movie, usually trinkets and toys

RISE OF LITTLE MOVIES

New structures have evolved for moviemaking newcomers to interest the distribution units of major studios in their work.

>> Film Festivals. Every January in Park City, Utah, Hollywood dispatches teams to audition films by independent filmmakers at the Sundance Film Festival. These are low-budget projects that sometimes bring substantial returns on investment. *The Blair Witch Project*, by a team of University of Central Florida grads, is classic. The movie cost $35,000 to produce. The young colleagues on the project made a killing when scouts from Artisan Entertainment watched a Sundance screening of it in 1998 and paid $1.1 million for distribution rights. For Artisan, the movie generated $141 million at the box office.

>> **Exhibition Niches.** For half a century, major cities and college towns have had **arthouses,** small movie houses that show mostly foreign films. In recent years the theater chains have booked niche films onto a few multiplex screens. Since 1999 Regal has played only specialty titles on 70 of its 546 screens. In 2006 AMC designated 72 of its 3,232 screens for its AMC Select program.

The fare isn't just foreign art films anymore. The AMC Select program included *Little Miss Sunshine* from the Sundance Film Festival, Robert Altman's *A Prairie Home Companion* and Al Gore's environmental documentary *An Inconvenient Truth*. For specialty screens, the chains are nurturing potentially major films to build up word-of-mouth promotion. These included *March of the Penguins* and *Brokeback Mountain* in 2005. Neither would have survived long in the usual make-it-or-break-it frenzy of opening-weekend competition.

>> **Demographic Niches.** Hollywood has an uneven history of gearing movies to demographic niches, except for teen flicks, whose low budgets consistently yield solid returns. Many niches are tricky and fickle. The optimistic civil rights films of Sidney Poitier had strong crossover appeal in the 1960s, then faded. So called blaxploitation films had a brief run with black audiences in the 1970s, only to be succeeded by urban action films like *New Jack City*. The main lesson has been that racial pandering has less box office appeal than good movies that have broader appeal regardless of racial theme.

>> **Foreign Movies.** Abroad, local-language movies are taking a large slice of their home markets. The result: more homegrown competition for Hollywood-produced films in foreign countries. Hit hardest have been mid-range U.S. pictures that once had a sure market abroad. Part of the plight for Hollywood pictures is that the growing number of homemade foreign movies has squeezed the availability of opening weekends and screens.

Beyond the foreign box office, the competition also is for financing. Commercial investors that once financed only Hollywood productions now are recognizing the investment potential in other countries. The result: More producers in more countries are vying for funding to do movies.

arthouses

Movie houses specializing in artistic films, often from abroad, for highbrow niche audiences

CHECKING YOUR MEDIA LITERACY

Why have little movies become a growing segment in Hollywood?

The Box Office

STUDY PREVIEW

The 90 million-tickets-a-week heyday of U.S. movie houses in 1946 is ancient history. It's been a bumpy road since. The exhibition business has problems with the continuing erosion of box office revenue. Attempts to address the declines include spiffier theaters, enforced audience conduct codes and new technology—d-cinema.

THEATERS: RISE AND DECLINE

The movie **exhibition** business has been boom and bust. The beginnings, early in the 1900s, were modest. Images were projected onto a white sheet spread across a wall in low-rent storefronts and onto white-washed plywood hoisted upright in circus tents. By 1912, there was a new standard—the Strand in New York, an opulent 3,300-seat theater

exhibition

What local movie houses do

Movie Palaces. *The 3,300-seat Strand, which opened in 1912, became the model for opulent downtown movie theaters. Many featured elaborate Roman, Oriental and other themes, with lavish lobbies and furnishings and doormen groomed to fit the fantasy of a night at the movies.*

that rivaled the world's best opera houses. Nattily groomed and uniformed doormen and ushers made moviegoing an experience. So did expansive lobbies, lavish promenades, columns and colonnades and plush velvet wall upholstery. The first air-conditioning was in theaters, using technology invented at Chicago meatpacking plants. Downtown movie palaces were built throughout the land.

>> **Attendance Peak.** To capitalize on the popularity of movies, and to keep access affordable, less ostentatious movie houses were built in neighborhoods and small towns. These were the core of the exhibition part of the movie industry at its peak. Although neither as large nor as lavish as the downtown palaces, the neighborhood movie houses were the heart of movie going when U.S. attendance peaked in 1946 at 90 million tickets a week. People even watched movies from automobiles parked row upon row in front of huge outdoor screens with clunky loudspeakers hooked into car windows. Movies were handy and affordable. For many people they were a habit two or three times a week.

The advent of network television in the 1950s cut into movie attendance. A lot of marquees went dark, some permanently, some at least a few nights a week.

>> **Multiplexes.** The exhibition business adapted. Beginning in the 1970s, moviehouse chains followed their customers to the suburbs and built a new form of movie house—the multiscreen **multiplex.** Attendance revived, although far short of the 1946 peak and also dependent on what was showing. People, newly discriminating, turned out mostly for movies that had received good reviews—unlike in the heyday of the Strands and the neighborhood theaters, when even weak movies drew crowds. Also, by the 1970s, people had many alternatives for entertainment.

The multiplexes addressed the unevenness in attendance. With multiple auditoriums, each with different seating capacity, movies could be switched among auditoriums to coincide with demand. Boffo films could be shown simultaneously in several auditoriums. With multiplexes the new measure of a movie's success was not in how many theaters it was booked but onto how many screens it was projected.

CHECKING YOUR MEDIA LITERACY

Trace the history of movie exhibition from the earliest days to the multiplex.

EXHIBITION CONSTRICTION

In the 1990s, sensing better days ahead, major movie-house chains went on a spending spree to expand and spiff up theaters. Attendance was strong at multiplexes, some with as many as 30 screens. State-of-the-art sound systems were installed. Some auditoriums were outfitted with plush stadium seating.

>> **Overexpansion.** The expansion and upgrades, however, overextended some chains financially. Bankruptcies followed. Then came a wave of consolidations that eliminated some chains and left Regal dominant with 5,800 screens, followed by Carmike at 3,700 and AMC at 3,300. The situation worsened with continued box office slippage, down 7 percent in 2005, further reflecting competition from DVD sales and rentals for home viewing on television sets. Pay-per-view home satellite and cable options also hurt. So did video games, which particularly attracted young men who had been core moviehouse patrons.

multiplex
Movie theater with multiple screens

The movie-house crisis is no better illustrated than in these 2005 figures:

Box office revenue: $9.5 billion
DVD revenue: $24.5 billion

>> **Release Windows.** What the exhibition business craves and relies on most is the period of exclusivity when a film may only be seen in theaters. Ever since Hollywood had begun releasing movies to television in the 1950s, there had been a guaranteed window of exclusivity for movie houses. Studio-owned distribution also protected the exhibition business by not releasing films to video and DVD right away but distributors kept shrinking the window. What had been a window of six months in 1994 shrank to 4 months, 13 days in 2008, with studios talking about possibly going to simultaneous release. Clearly, Hollywood was coming to see that its best profit potential was not in staggering the release of new movies in different channel, but in maximizing a single promotional burst with simultaneous theatrical and DVD/Blu-Ray releases.

Despite the social and psychological impact of the communal moviegoing experience, the future doesn't bode well for movie theaters, with the expansion of home broadband access, making an era of home downloading and pay-per-view purchasing of feature-length movies increasingly common.

CHECKING YOUR MEDIA LITERACY

- **Discuss how the interests of Hollywood and movie exhibition companies once coincided but now do so less.**
- **What is the effect of broadband on movie attendance at theaters?**

D-CINEMA

Mark Cuban
Early advocate of converting to digital exhibition

d-cinema
Movies that are filmed, edited, distributed and exhibited digitally

The exhibition business, with a financial boost from Hollywood, is planning to outfit theaters with digital projectors. Owners had resisted because of the cost, at least $100,000 minimum per screen, but finally decided there was no choice.

Mark Cuban of the 270-screen Landmark chain was first. Cuban began converting his theaters in 2005, saying that once people saw their first digital movie on a big screen, they would settle for nothing less. Digital projection is not the same as HDTV technology, but its clarity and impact are similar. With **d-cinema,** as it is called, colors are more vivid, graininess is gone and projection-room goofs,

Mark Cuban. *Although known mostly as the excitable owner of the Dallas Mavericks, Mark Cuban, who made his fortune in software, is an advocate of digital video. He owns the pioneering HDNet television movies network. His Landmark movie-house chain has been a leader in switching to digital projection. Cuban also is an advocate of plush furnishings to make a night at the movies a memorable experience.*

like reels out of sequence, are no more. Nor will there be any more distracting focus adjustments or scratchy reels that have been pulled over the sprockets too many times.

In 2006, taking a cue from Cuban, the entire movie industry recognized the obvious—that people are becoming more enamored of digital images on computer screens, a trend that is sure to accelerate with television's shift to digital transmission. With Hollywood advancing the money, movie-house chains began a 10-year project to convert to digital projection equipment at all of the 36,700 screens in the United States and thousands of screens around the world. In March 2009 AMC Entertainment announced that it closed on a $315 million deal with Sony to replace all of its movie projectors with digital projectors.

D-cinema also has economic benefits. Digital movies can be distributed on hard drives, optical discs or via satellite, and don't require transportation in bulky film canisters. One estimate was that $568 million a year could be saved in transportation and handling. Meanwhile, Hollywood studios have begun issuing movies in double versions, on film and digitally, through a transition period.

CHECKING YOUR MEDIA LITERACY

- **What is d-cinema?**
- **How likely is the conversion of movie houses to digital projection to draw audiences back?**

THE NEXT PLATFORM

Hollywood distributors have been keen on DVD sales and rentals, which had buoyed their revenues as box office revenue declined. But by 2007 the DVD market had plateaued. Concerned that the industry may have maxed-out the potential of both theatrical and DVD releases, studios earnestly pondered what their next delivery platform might be. Computer downloads remained broadband hogs with little appeal. Downloads to handheld and other devices were mostly short features, not movies, and they were competing with all kinds of other Internet content for attention.

Confronted with the possibility that Hollywood may have reached the end of its cycle as a growth industry, major studios turned cautious. Disney reduced its output in 2006 and laid off 650 employees. Studios cut back on deals with independent producers. The situation was put in startling financial terms by a Kagan Research study that found studios recouped only 84 percent of production and domestic marketing costs from domestic theatrical releases and home video sales in 2005. The shareholder-sensitive corporations that own the studios ordered more scrutiny on spending until bottom lines improve. The trade journal *Variety* put it this way: "In the eyes of Wall Street, studios are now seen as bloated entities."

Still, Hollywood has faced challenges before, always adapting to a changing environment and emerging stronger than ever. In the current technological, cultural and financial flux, many look to the accelerating convergence of the movie and television industries, as natural allies of the motion media.

Television in Transition

STUDY PREVIEW

Once, television was so influential that its cultural influence was described as "a molder of the soul's geography." The question now is whether television as a medium can retain its social role amid a changing technological environment.

TELEVISION INDUSTRY IN CRISIS

Television transformed the mass media. In the 1950s, television, the new kid on the block, forced its media elders, notably movies, radio and magazines, to reinvent themselves or perish. Year by year television entrenched itself in the latter 20th century, first as a hot new medium, then as the dominant medium. Now the industries that developed around television technology are themselves in crisis. They have been overtaken by innovations in delivering video through other channels.

Can the television industry reinvent itself? Can the industry get on top of the new technology? Or will television as an industry find itself subsumed, perhaps even replaced, by new competition? High drama is being played out even as you read this chapter.

CULTURAL ROLE OF TELEVISION

Despite questions about how the U.S. television industry will adapt to an era of iPods, blogs and online gaming, the medium itself is hardly on its deathbed. Almost every U.S. household has at least one television set. On average, television is playing about seven hours a day in those households. Many people, sometimes millions, still shape their leisure time around the television, like when CBS runs *CSI*. Somewhere around 134 million people assemble ritual-like for the Super Bowl.

As a medium, television can create cultural icons. Just ask *American Idol*'s Simon Cowell, or the Geico gecko. Even though many advertisers are shifting their spending to alternative media, Procter & Gamble spends $5.2 billion touting its wares on television, AT&T $3.2 billion. For important messages to U.S. citizens, President Obama, who seems quite at home in the medium, has no more effective pulpit. It is rare for a candidate for public office not to use television to solicit support. For information, millions of people look to network news—and also Jon Stewart, Oprah Winfrey, David Letterman and Conan O'Brien.

Fictional television characters can capture the imagination of the public. Perry Mason did wonders for the reputation of the legal profession in the 1960s. Mary Tyler Moore's role as a television news producer showed that women could succeed in a male-dominated business. Roles played by Alan Alda were the counter-macho model for the bright, gentle man of the 1970s. Today, Kiefer Sutherland's Jack Bauer is the model for principled cool under pressure. The sassy belligerence of Bart Simpson still makes parents shudder.

CHECKING YOUR MEDIA LITERACY

- **What are some measures of television's role in our culture?**
- **What are examples of this role? Include some from your own experience.**

ENDURING TELEVISION EFFECTS

Although television can be effective in creating short-term impressions, there are also long-term effects. Social critic Michael Novak, commenting on television in its heyday, called television "a molder of the soul's geography." Said Novak: "It builds up incrementally a psychic structure of expectations. It does so in much the same way that school lessons slowly, over the years, tutor the unformed mind and teach it how to think." Media scholar George Comstock made the point this way: "Television has become an unavoidable and unremitting factor in shaping what we are and what we will become."

Whether the influence ascribed to television by Novak and Comstock will survive the fast-changing media landscape of the 21st century remains to be seen. Nobody, however, is predicting the imminent disappearance of television. The question is whether the television industry will lose its legacy as a mass medium to technological innovations from new media of mass communication.

CHECKING YOUR MEDIA LITERACY

- **What did Michael Novak mean by calling television "a molder of the soul's geography"?**

Terrestrial Television

STUDY ***PREVIEW***

The regulatory mechanism created by Congress for television in the 1930s resulted in a two-tier U.S. television system. Corporate entities that entered television comported with the regulatory infrastructure. The original television industry comprised local stations, generally with the most successful carrying programs from the Big Three national networks of the time.

DUAL INFRASTRUCTURE

With television on the horizon in the 1930s, Congress looked at how its regulation of radio had worked. Congress was pleased with the **Federal Radio Act** of 1927. If the regulatory system worked for radio, why wouldn't it work for television? The **Federal Communications Act** of 1934 tidied up the 1927 law and expanded the scope to television.

The powerhouse in making television technology viable commercially was **David Sarnoff.** He had parlayed his fame as the kid picking up signals from the *Titanic* rescue drama in 1912 into leadership at the Radio Corporation of America. With a patent from **Philo Farnsworth,** the inventor of television, Sarnoff demonstrated television—"radio with pictures," some called it—at the 1939 World's Fair in New York. People marveled. The FCC licensed the first station in 1941, but World War II interrupted Sarnoff's plan to replicate the successful NBC radio network as a television system.

After the war more stations were licensed. By 1948 heavy-duty **coaxial cables** that were necessary to carry television signals from the head end, or point of origin, to local transmission towers, had been laid out to the Midwest, and NBC began feeding programs to local stations. The coaxial linkup, with some stretches covered by microwave relays, connected the East and West coasts in 1951.

The backbone of the national television system was local stations. The first stations, all in larger cities, took affiliations with the fledgling NBC, CBS, ABC and short-lived Dumont networks. Larger cities also had unaffiliated, independent stations. Noncommercial stations were licensed for educational programming, mostly operated by school districts.

Federal Radio Act
Original law in 1927 for government regulation of U.S. broadcasting

Federal Communications Act
Revision of Federal Radio Act in 1934 to include television

David Sarnoff
Broadcast visionary who built RCA, NBC

Philo Farnsworth
Invented the electronic technology for television

coaxial cable
A high-capacity wire with dual electric current conductors

Big Three
ABC, CBS, NBC

two-tier system
Original U.S. broadcast infrastructure had two tiers, one of locally licensed stations, the other of national networks

Pat Weaver
NBC program innovator, 1950s

CHECKING YOUR MEDIA LITERACY

- **How did David Sarnoff create the structure of the early U.S. television industry?**

NETWORKS

For most of television's history, three networks, ABC, CBS and NBC, provided programming to local stations in prime time at night and parts of daytime. NBC dominated early on, but the **Big Three,** as they were called, came to be evenly matched with about 200 affiliates each. Their programs reached the whole country, with the exception of remote and mountainous areas unreachable by signals.

As with radio earlier, the infrastructure of television became a **two-tier system.** Stations, licensed for local communities by the government, were one tier. The networks provided a national tier of infrastructure. The largest television chains.

>> NBC Television. The genius who had built the NBC radio network within the RCA empire, David Sarnoff, moved into television as soon as the government resumed licensing local stations after World War II. For early programming NBC raided its radio repertoire of shows and stars. Then came innovations. **Pat Weaver,** an ad executive recruited by NBC as a vice president in 1951, created a late night comedy-variety talk show, precursor to the venerable *Tonight Show*. Weaver also created a wake-up show, the still-viable *Today*. With those shows NBC owned the early morning and late-night audience for years.

CASE STUDY

Television as Babysitter

Spongebob and Friends. *At what price does a child's screen time displace physical exercise? Has Barney been a factor in the new obesity epidemic?*

The scene is typical. Dad plunks the kids in front of the television so he can do laundry. Mom does the same while cooking dinner. In school, kids also find themselves being babysat by television. Teachers use it to give students a break from real learning or just to settle them down.

A 2005 study by the Kaiser Family Foundation found that 83 percent of children under age 6 use what's called screen media (television, video or computers) about two hours a day. And media use increases with age. Sixty-one percent of babies watch screen media in a typical day. For 4-year-olds to 6-year-olds it's 90 percent. Other studies have found that kids in lower-income homes kids watch more television and are more likely to have a television set in their bedrooms, a practice discouraged by pediatricians.

Strong cases can be made that too much television isn't good for kids. Why aren't they out exercising? And nobody would prescribe watching violence. At the same time, shows like *Sesame Street, Blue's Clues* and *Dora* can teach spelling, arithmetic, problem-solving and social skills. These shows employ experts with doctoral degrees to work with writers to set goals and review scripts. *Sesame Street* tests its shows in day-care centers.

In the early 1970s, researcher and psychologist Daniel Anderson watched kids watching *Sesame Street* and found that "television viewing is a much more intellectual activity for kids than anybody had previously supposed."

Demand for quality children's shows increased after Congress passed the Children's Television Act in 1990. The PBS network, creator of *Sesame Street*, launched *Barney & Friends*. *Sesame*-derived merchandise flew off the shelves. According to Joseph Blatt, of the Harvard Graduate School of Education, *Dora*, created by Nickelodeon's Brown Johnson, proved that it is possible to do quality programming for kids in a commercial environment. Now marketers spend a lot of money trying to convince parents that their shows will help children's brains develop. It has worked. The Kaiser study found that many parents are enthusiastic about the use of television. Two-thirds say their child imitates positive behavior, such as helping or sharing, as seen on television.

The phenomenon of using television as a babysitter has been debated since the first picture flickered on the small screen. "Like alcohol or guns, TV will be used sensibly in some homes and wreak havoc in others," writes Daniel McGinn in *Newsweek*. "Debating its net societal value will remain a never-ending pursuit."

DEEPENING YOUR MEDIA LITERACY

EXPLORE THE ISSUE

Check out the PBS Kids: Sesame Street—Caregivers web page and the Playhouse Disney Guide for Grownups web page.

DIG DEEPER

What do you notice about these pages? What do you think their message is to parents?

WHAT DO YOU THINK?

Does the quality of children's shows matter in the debate about television as a babysitter? Are shows without commercials or merchandise marketing inherently better than commercialized shows?

Making Fox. The Simpsons *was among a handful of programs that helped Fox, a Johnny-come-lately television network, establish itself with a young audience. Some early Fox programs floundered, like* Married . . . with Children, *which faded after a few seasons. The Simpson brood, however, maintained its following, spawning a profitable movie version in 2007.*

>> CBS Television. Sarnoff's longtime rival in radio, **William Paley** of CBS, was not far behind in moving soap operas and other programs from radio to television. Soon CBS was fully competitive with its own innovations, which included the *Twilight Zone* science-fiction anthology. By 1953 the *I Love Lucy* sitcom, which eventually included 140 episodes, was a major draw. Paley worked at creating a cachet for CBS, which he relished calling the "Tiffany network" after the ritzy New York jewelry store.

CBS established a legacy in public affairs when **Edward R. Murrow,** famous for his World War II radio reporting from Europe, started *See It Now*. Three years later, in 1954, when Senator Joseph McCarthy was using the prestige of his office to smear people as communists even though they weren't, it was Murrow on *See It Now* who exposed the senator's dubious tactics. Many scholars credit Murrow not only for courage but also for undoing McCarthy and easing Red Scare phobias.

>> ABC Television. ABC established its television network in 1948 but ran a poor third. Two programs, though, gave ABC some distinction—*Disneyland* in 1954 and the *Mickey Mouse Club* in 1955. ABC picked up steam in 1961 with *Wide World of Sports*, a weekend anthology that appealed to more than sports fans. **Roone Arledge,** the network's sports chief, created *Monday Night Football* in 1969. Network television was a three-way race once again. By 1976 ABC was leading by a hair.

William Paley
CBS radio, television founder

Edward R. Murrow
Pioneer broadcast journalist

Roone Arledge
ABC sports programming innovator, 1960s, 1970s

Rupert Murdoch
His media empire includes Fox television and 20th Century Fox movies

Barry Diller
Creator of early, profitable Fox network programming

>> Fox. Rupert Murdoch, the Australian-born media magnate, made a strategic decision in 1986 to become a major media player in the United States. He bought seven nonnetwork stations in major markets and also the 20th Century Fox movie studio. The stations gave Murdoch a nucleus for a fourth network. With 20th Century Fox, Murdoch had production facilities and a huge movie library to fill airtime. Murdoch also recruited **Barry Diller,** whose track record included a series of ABC hits, to head the new network; Murdoch called it Fox.

There were doubts that Fox would make it, but Diller kept costs low with low-budget shows like *Married . . . with Children*, which featured the crude, dysfunctional Bundy family. *The Simpsons* attracted young viewers, whom advertisers especially sought to reach. Fox outbid CBS to televise half of the Sunday National Football League games in 1994. Soon some CBS affiliates defected to Fox.

The Murdoch strategy worked. With almost 200 affiliates, Fox made network television into the Big Four.

CHECKING YOUR MEDIA LITERACY

- **List the programming innovators who shaped each of the major networks. What were their contributions?**

Cable and Satellite Television

STUDY PREVIEW

Early cable companies were small-town enterprises that merely relayed signals from over-air stations to townspeople, but in the 1970s networks were formed to provide exclusive programming to these local cable companies. Explosive growth followed. Television delivery fragmented further with satellite signals delivered directly to viewers via their own reception dishes. This so-called satcom system bypassed the federally licensed system of over-air local stations as well as cable distributors.

CABLE SYSTEMS

Entrepreneurs in mountainous sections of Oregon, West Virginia and western Pennsylvania figured out how to bring television to their communities in the late 1940s even though mountains blocked the signals. The only stations at the time were in big cities. By hoisting a reception tower on a nearby mountain top, these entrepreneurs caught the faraway signals and strung a cable down to town, and from there to every house. Voila, places like Astoria, Oregon, had television. Gradually every small town beyond the reach of over-air television signals had a local cable system—all low-cost distribution systems. Few offered local-origination programming, however.

Urban television stations and the networks too were pleased with the upstart **CATV** enterprises, short for *community antenna television*. With no investment, the big city stations picked up additional viewers, which permitted the stations to charge more to advertisers. Small-town people were enthusiastic to be able to watch Jack Benny. Although not a technological leap, the locally owned small-town cable systems were a new wrinkle in television delivery. The systems were a minor, relatively passive component in the U.S. television industry. Even into the 1970s nobody sensed what a sleeping giant they had become.

CHECKING YOUR MEDIA LITERACY

- **Why was cable television only a small-town phenomenon for a quarter century?**

CABLE NETWORKS

A young executive at Time Inc. in New York, **Gerald Levin,** put two and two together and came up with a new direction for television in the early 1970s. His idea was to create a network exclusively for local cable systems to augment what they were picking up from over-air stations. The network, built on a floundering Time entity called Home Box Office, HBO for short, would send programming via orbiting satellites.

With only 265,000 households at its 1975 launch, the first cable network, HBO, barely dented the viewership of over-air stations. But HBO grew. A year later Atlanta station owner Ted Turner put his WTBS on satellite as mostly a movie channel for local cable systems. Turner called WTBS a "superstation," and it quickly became a money machine. Leveraging the revenue, Turner then created CNN, then bought a fledgling competitor and started Headline News, a second 24/7 news service. Then Turner created TNT, a second movie channel.

These networks avoided most government regulation because their programming was delivered to viewers by cable, bypassing FCC-regulated airwaves. It was an alternative that shook up the over-air television industry, siphoning viewers.

CATV

Early local cable television systems; short for *community antenna television*

Gerald Levin

Used orbiting satellite to relay exclusive programs to local cable systems in 1975

Sopranos Attraction. *Since its inception, HBO has hastened the fragmentation of television programming. Beginning in 1975 with post-release movies, HBO was an exclusive network for cable systems, then became a power to be reckoned with in original programming. Series like* The Sopranos *built HBO as a brand and attracted more subscribers. The torments of Carmela Soprano, a tough, independent, religious yet rationalizing mob wife, played by Edie Falco, made irresistible viewing for millions of HBO subscribers until the 2007 finale.*

Seeing the potential, other cable channels soon were competing for space on local cable systems—ESPN for sports, a weather network, music video networks, home shopping networks. By 2008 there were more than 330 national cable networks.

CHECKING YOUR MEDIA LITERACY

- What transformed cable into a major player in the television industry?
- How did Gerald Levin transform cable? How did Ted Turner do likewise?

MULTISYSTEM OPERATORS

The potential of the cable television industry that Gerald Levin had recognized did not go unnoticed on Wall Street. For investors, cable suddenly was hot. CATV systems were gobbled up in hundreds of acquisitions. What emerged were **multisystem operators,** called MSOs in the industry. These companies, many of them subsidiaries of larger media companies, simultaneously were raising money from investors to wire big cities so that cable programming could be offered for a monthly subscription. Today, more than 90 percent of U.S. households have access to cable, although only about two-thirds of them subscribe.

The company Comcast catapulted into becoming the largest multisystem operator in 2002 by buying AT&T Broadband and claiming, with earlier acquisitions, more than 21 million subscribers. Time Warner is second at 11 million. The consolidation of cable systems into large ownerships has reduced the number of MSOs nationwide to 25—a far cry from the individual local systems that began in the late 1940s.

CHECKING YOUR MEDIA LITERACY

- What has happened to all those CATV systems?

OWNERSHIP MELD

For years, over-air networks resented the intrusion of cable networks as a competitor for national advertising, but the tension cooled as media conglomerates added cable networks to their bevy of holdings. It was an **ownership meld.** Advertising revenue that the over-air networks lose to cable may still end up in the parent company's coffers. In recent years, for example, NBC's advance revenue guarantees from advertisers were about the same as the year before, but stablemate Bravo's **upfront** advertising commitments doubled. Senior sales executives cut deals with advertisers to buy time on both the networks serving over-air affiliates and on the network-owned cable services. Consider that the five major network companies have cable siblings:

	Over-Air Networks	Among Cable Networks
Disney	ABC	ABC Family Channel, Disney Channel, ESPN, SoapNet
NBC Universal	NBC, Telemundo	Bravo, CNBC, MSNBC, Mun2TV, SciFi Channel, Trio, USA Networks
News Corp.	Fox	Fox Movie, Fox News, Fox Sports, Fuel, National Geographic Channel
Time Warner	CW	Cartoon Network, CNN, TBS, Turner Classic Movies, TNT
Viacom	CBS, CW	BET, MTV, MTV2, The N, Nickelodeon, Nick at Nite, Noggin, Spike, VH1

CHECKING YOUR MEDIA LITERACY

- How have major television networks hedged their bets against cable as a competitor?

multisystem operator (MSO)
A company that owns several local cable television delivery units in different, usually far-flung, communities

ownership meld
When a company is subsumed into the ownership of a competing company

upfront
Advance advertiser commitments to buy network advertising time

SATELLITE-DIRECT DELIVERY

The cost of entry for satellite-direct transmission has limited the number of U.S. satcom operators to two. **DirecTV,** the larger, has 15.5 million subscribers. For several years media mogul Murdoch controlled DirecTV with 34 percent ownership. He sold his interest in 2006 but continues with similar satellite services on other continents—Star TV in Asia, B-Sky-B in Britain, Sky Italia in Italy and Foxtel in Australia. The **Dish Network,** the trade name for EchoStar, has 11 million subscribers. EchoStar has a fleet of nine satellites in orbit, DirecTV eight.

Both DirecTV and EchoStar are growing, taking subscribers away from cable. In 2003 Dallas became the first major city with more satellite than cable customers. The growth accelerated when the Federal Communications Commission cleared the way for the satellite-delivery companies to include local over-air stations and their network programs among their array of cable channels. Both services also carry pay-per-view movies, pornography and sports packages.

DirecTV
Larger of two U.S. satellite-direct companies

Dish Network
Satellite-direct company

CHECKING YOUR MEDIA LITERACY

- **What is a satcom?**
- **How many satcoms serve the United States? Name them.**
- **How big a factor are satcoms in the U.S. television industry? Globally?**

Video on Demand

STUDY PREVIEW

Time-shifting devices enable viewers to decide when they watch television. Portable devices let them decide where. These video-on-demand devices, as well as content designed for watching on the go, are undermining some long-term attractions of networks, stations, cable systems and satcoms as advertising vehicles.

TIME SHIFTING

Devices that allow people to watch what they want when they want, **video on demand,** date to Betamax videotape players introduced by Sony in 1976. Later devices, like **TiVo** digital recorders, provide other options for what's called **time shifting.** People don't have to schedule their activities around a channel's schedule. It's possible to program a TiVo to record the news at 6 p.m. and then watch it whenever. The same is true with *Survivor* or the *Daily Show*. Time shifting has dramatically reduced the tyranny that network and station programmers once had over people's lives. Direct Video Recording, on-demand movies, sports, television shows and special events available through cable and satellite providers allow viewers to watch whatever they want, in whole or in part, on their own schedule. Also, with the increasing migration of television content online, it is possible to watch a lot of television without actually even owning a television. Many shows are archived online and deliverable free through a variety of official and unofficial portals. Many are partially uploaded before they actually air, and fully uploaded immediately upon airing.

Video on demand
Viewer controlled access to content at anytime

TiVo
Digital recording and playback device for television

time shifting
Ability of viewer to change when they access programming

A troubling upshot of the technology for networks and stations is that they are losing their power to amass great numbers of people in front of the screen at the same time. That had been a selling point to advertisers. An advertiser for time-of-day products like Subway sandwiches wants to reach viewers at mealtime—not whenever viewers decide to watch a show. What good is an advertisement designed to stir excitement for the weekend introduction of the new Chevy Volt if viewers don't see the spot until a week later? Also, those DVR devices allow viewers to skip commercials entirely.

CHECKING YOUR MEDIA LITERACY

- How was Betamax revolutionary?
- How did TiVo further empower viewers?

PORTABLE DEVICES

In 2005 a video-playing Internet device introduced by Apple fully liberated viewers from planting themselves before large and stationary television sets. The Apple **video iPod** suddenly splintered television as an industry. By 2008 handheld iPods could store as many as 150 hours of video and display the images on a $2\frac{1}{2}$-inch color screen. People could watch television shows on the road or wherever—and whenever. It was true video on demand, with people downloading programs from the Internet to catch any time they wanted. Next Apple came up with iPhone, which had video-on-demand capabilities, followed by upgrades with greater capabilities. Not to be left out, the major television networks, ABC, CBS, Fox and NBC, scrambled to sell archived programming for iPods. The one-time monopoly of the big networks providing programming through over-air local affiliates was further fractured. Meanwhile, cell phone providers led by Verizon added VOD capabilities to their phones. Verizon's subscription service, rolled out in 2006, offered snippets, then longer video features, some truncated from programs to which rights had been purchased from the big networks and other television program creators.

Mobile Television. *Comic-strip detective Dick Tracy of the 1950s would love cell phone television. All Tracy had was a two-way wrist radio. Today for $15 a month, the telephone company Verizon's V Cast offers newscast snippets and clips from the previous night's Jon Stewart show. Longer programs are available from the iTunes store and other sources for downloading.*

CHECKING YOUR MEDIA LITERACY

- How has television viewing become untethered?

VOD CHALLENGES

VOD is the great unknown in the future of television as we know it. Apple has positioned itself with the handheld video iPod and its Disney ABC connection. In 2006 Warner made a deal to put 14,000 free episodes of vintage shows, including *Welcome Back, Kotter, Wonder Woman* and *Kung Fu*, on the America Online subscription service owned by its parent company, Time Warner. AOL started with a drama channel, a comedy channel and four others. By 2006 about half of U.S. households had fast broadband connections to accommodate larger-than-ever-before downloads from the Internet, including ever-longer videos.

The VOD revolution has only begun. The cost of entry is so low that almost anyone with a few hundred dollars in software can create videos for VOD distribution. Just about everyone has easy access to post on YouTube.

CHECKING YOUR MEDIA LITERACY

- How do affiliate stations view network forays into VOD?
- Who owns massive inventory assets of programming for VOD?
- How can a case be argued that VOD is democratizing television?

Public Television

STUDY PREVIEW

Government financial support of a national noncommercial television system grew out of concern in the 1960s that television was a "vast wasteland" of lowbrow content. Programming at the time came mostly from the three networks. Then PBS came into being as an alternative. Today, with a great array of programming available, a question is whether public funding is necessary anymore.

NONCOMMERCIAL STATIONS

Many universities and school districts set up stations as noncommercial operations in the 1950s and 1960s as part of their mission to broaden their reach. These stations, as a condition of their licenses from the Federal Communications Commission, could not sell time to advertisers. As educational experiments, the **ETV** stations, as they were called, had mixed results. Most programs were dull lectures. The following was small. In some cities, meanwhile, citizen groups obtained licenses for noncommercial stations. By the late 1960s there were 300 of these stations, but viewership was sparse.

educational television (ETV)
Stations that supplement classroom lessons, also extend learning beyond school

Meanwhile, commercial television was drawing unprecedented audiences nightly. Lifestyles changed dramatically, as barkeeps and movie-house operators nationwide could attest. Many lodges surrendered their charters because of membership declines. Heard much about Freemasons lately? The big alternative draws were local news and network entertainment. While popular, the entertainment fare was criticized by elitists as downscale and a horrible default on television's potential to make positive and enduring contributions. In a notable 1961 speech, the chair of the Federal Communications Commission, **Newton Minow,** accused the industry of presiding over a "vast wasteland."

Newton Minow
FCC chair who called television a "vast wasteland"

CHECKING YOUR MEDIA LITERACY

- Put Newton Minow's 1961 "vast wasteland" indictment of television in a modern context. Is it still true?
- Where would you put Minow on an elitist-populist scale?
- What was the original purpose of noncommercial television stations?

Carnegie Commission on Educational Television
Recommended ETV be converted to the public television concept

public television
Noncommercial television with an emphasis on quality programs to meet public needs

Corporation for Public Broadcasting (CPB)
Quasi-government agency that channels tax-generated funds into the U.S. noncommercial television and radio system

PUBLIC BROADCASTING SERVICE

In 1967 a blue-ribbon group, the **Carnegie Commission on Educational Television,** examined the situation and saw a grossly underdeveloped national resource. The commission recommended an alternate concept and used the term **public television** to "serve the needs of the American public." Within months, Congress responded by creating the **Corporation for Public Broadcasting** to develop a national noncommercial broadcasting system for both television and radio. The goal was

The War. *Documentary producer Ken Burns drew more viewers to PBS with his 1990 Civil War series than any other program in the network's history. His 10-part series* Jazz, *which tracked the history of the distinctive U.S. musical genre, was in the same spirit in 2001, as is his recent documentary that explores World War II from the perspectives of the soldiers on the ground and the loved ones they left behind.*

high-quality programming distinct from that of the commercial networks, which, by their nature, pandered to mass audiences. Thus was born the **Public Broadcasting Service** as a network serving the former ETV stations, most of which shifted to the new public television model.

To pay the bills, public television has cobbled together motley sources of revenue. Until recent years, congressional appropriations, buffered from political control through a quasi-government agency, the Corporation for Public Broadcasting, were a mainstay. As federal funding has declined, the public television system has stepped up its drive for donations from public-spirited corporations and viewers themselves. Although prohibited from selling advertising time, stations can acknowledge their benefactors. These acknowledgments, once bare-bones announcements, have become more elaborate over the years and sometimes seem close to advertising.

Public television has never been much liked by the commercial television industry. Public stations take viewers away, even though relatively few. Also, that public television receives what amounts to government subsidies seems unfair to the commercial stations. The upside of the arrangement for commercial television is that the presence of high-quality programming on public television eases public and government pressure on them to absorb the cost of producing more high-culture fare as a public service that would attract only niche audiences and few advertisers. Public television, like its commercial counterpart, has not been immune from encroachments on its turf. The explosion of cable and satellite original programming has created channels and whole networks—Discovery, National Geographic, The History Channel, to name just a few—devoted to the kinds of programming once exclusively on PBS.

Public Broadcasting Service (PBS)
Television network for noncommercial over-air stations

CHECKING YOUR MEDIA LITERACY

- **What did the founding of PBS say about the quality of television programming at the time?**
- **What happened to educational television?**
- **Somebody has to pay the bills to keep public television on the air. Who?**

CHAPTER WRAP-UP

The Television-Movies Meld (Pages 147–149)

- Beginning in the 1950s, television transformed lifestyles in the United Staes. Until recently, movies and television were enemies, fighting for the same audience. Today, the two industries have largely melded and created new synergies. They share corporate owners, content and stars.

Hollywood Studios (Pages 156–164)

- Six studios, all parts of conglomerates, dominate Hollywood movie production and distribution. These studios are enmeshed with the television industry through corporate connections. A growing component in movie distribution channels is independent films, which originate outside the Hollywood structure but which the directors sell to studio-owned distribution companies to market them. Massive profits from a runaway movie success lure studio executives into big-budget epics and spectaculars, but some bomb. Historically, studios have issued a mix of big-budget, mid-budget and low-budget movies, but in tight times the emphasis has shifted to caution.

Movies: First of the Motion Media (Pages 149–152)

- For more than a century, movies have been an important element of U.S. culture. Movies can be great entertainers that also sensitize people to issues and have a long-term effect in shifting public attitudes on enduring issues. Measuring the cultural impact is difficult, but conventional wisdom, almost certainly overstated, is that Hollywood can change fundamental values. This notion has made Hollywood a target in the culture wars that have divided American society in recent years. Comedian Bill Maher has challenged the idea that movies threaten traditional values with a quip that Hollywood is not geared to Red States or Blue States but to green—whether a movie will attract audiences. Producers, he says, don't sit around and work at conceiving movie projects that people in Iowa will really hate.

The Box Office (Pages 164–167)

- The exhibition component of the industry, presenting movies to audiences, is in transition. Movie-house attendance and box office revenue have slipped dramatically. Video rentals and sales have offset the revenue decline from Hollywood's perspective, although there are signs that video revenue has peaked. Movie houses have responded with a wide range of tactics, but they seem mostly to be floundering. D-cinema is one new initiative to improve the visual experience in a movie house and also to reduce exhibition costs. Still to be felt is the coming technology that will allow home downloading of feature-length movies.

Movie Products (Pages 152–156)

- Although most people associate movies with heavily promoted Hollywood feature films, the medium lends itself to a wide range of content besides escapist fiction. Documentaries, a nonfiction genre, have a long tradition. The popularity of documentaries has peaks and ebbs. Propagandist films were a growth industry for Hollywood in World War II. Rock concert documentaries peaked in the 1980s. Today documentaries range from journalistic explorations to opinionated docu-ganda. Another genre that comes and goes in popularity is the animated film. Animation production has changed in recent years with digital technology, which makes production less labor-intensive than in the Disney heyday.

Television in Transition (Pages 167–168)

- Television transformed lifestyles in the United States beginning in the 1950s. It's hard to imagine the Super Bowl without television. Lodge meetings, Wednesday night vespers and evening socializing at neighborhood taverns suddenly were relegated to something from the not-so-much-regretted good ol' days. Today, however, that huge audience is fragmenting. The fragmentation began with the arrival of cable networks in the 1970s and accelerated with satellite-direct delivery systems. Video on demand via the Internet is the latest technology to beleaguer the traditional structure of television. For clarity, perhaps the term today should be *screen media* instead of *television*. Even so, the medium has had a powerful influence. Social critic Michael Novak calls television "a molder of the soul's geography."

Terrestrial Television (Pages 169–171)

- The original U.S. television system was modeled on radio—local stations licensed by the national government. As with radio, national networks soon were providing local stations with their most popular programming, particularly in the evening. The evening hours came to be called prime time because that's when networks could charge advertisers premium rates for the biggest audiences. The first television network was created by radio pioneer David Sarnoff, who applied lessons from radio to organize NBC. Not far behind was rival William Paley at CBS. ABC was a late arrival, but by the mid-1950s the industry was dominated by the Big Three. The truly late arrival was Fox in 1986.

Video on Demand (Pages 174–176)

- The Internet's impact on television has been just as great as its impact on other media. With portable devices, including advanced cell phones, people can pick up video programming on the go. Because of technical download issues, live programs tend to be short—like five-minute webisodes. But long-form programs can be downloaded in advance for viewing any time, anywhere. This is another challenge for older over-air and cable delivery and even newer satellite-direct delivery to deal with. Other technology also is giving traditional television fits. Devices that allow time shifting, like TiVo recording and playback machines, are cutting into the massive audiences that networks and their over-air affiliates once could rely on to sit down and watch *I Love Lucy* simultaneously, along with the interspersed ads. With TiVo, viewers can even skip the ads.

Cable and Satellite Television (Pages 171–174)

- Cable television sat in the backwaters of the television industry for its first quarter-century. Originally, cable systems were merely mechanisms for relaying big-city and Big Three over-air television programming to faraway communities beyond the reach of over-air signals. That changed dramatically in 1975 when HBO began offering exclusive programming to cable systems, followed by Ted Turner's WTBS superstation, then CNN. Today, 330 cable networks compete for viewers. Those small-town CATV systems, short for "community antenna television," now have been absorbed by giant multisystem cable companies that have wires in big cities. Cable is no longer a small-town business. The television industry opposed satellite-direct delivery because it would bypass local stations and cable too. But in 1984 DirecTV won authorization to establish the satcom business, followed by EchoStar's Dish Network. This further fragmented the television industry.

Public Television (Pages 176–177)

- Responding to the television industry's focus on programming that appealed to the widest possible audience, necessarily a lowbrow strategy, Congress in 1967 established a structure for federal funding to develop noncommercial stations as an alternative. The result was a financial base for programming that otherwise would not be aired for want of sufficient advertising revenue. Noncommercial stations that had been licensed for educational purposes redubbed themselves *public television* and built their programming around a new network, the Public Broadcasting Service. Public funding always has been controversial. One severe critic, radio talk-show host Rush Limbaugh, epitomized the opposition this way: "Why should tax dollars fund broadcasting that people don't want to watch?" The fact is that with the proliferation of cable and satcom channels, PBS and its affiliates' programming is less distinctive than it was originally.

Review Questions

1. What are the signs that old feuds between the movie and television industries have been resolved ?
2. What is required for movies to have their great impact on viewers?
3. What are Hollywood's primary products? Give examples of each.
4. What has happened to Hollywood's studio system?
5. Would you invest your money in a movie exhibition chain? Explain.
6. What technological innovations are beleaguering the original television industry?
7. What ended the happy relationship between CATV operators and over-air stations? And how are satcoms affecting the television industry?
8. What are examples of video on demand?
9. Has public television addressed the 1961 observation of FCC chair Newton Minow that television is a "vast wasteland"?
10. Will advertisers abandon over-air, cable and satcom television channels because of time-shift and portable devices? Explain.

Concepts

exhibition (Page 164)
ownership meld (Page 173)
public television (Page 176)
star system (Page 157)
studio system (Page 157)
suspension of disbelief (Page 150)
time shifting (Page 174)
two-tier system (Page 169)

Terms

B movie (Page 163)
blockbuster (Page 162)
CATV (Page 172)
computer-generated imagery (CGI) (Page 153)
Corporation for Public Broadcasting (CPB) (Page 176)
d-cinema (Page 166)
multisystem operator (MSO) (Page 173)
upfront (Page 173)
vertical integration (Page 158)
video on demand (Page 174)

People

Adolph Zukor (Page 157)
D. W. Griffith (Page 162)
Gerald Levin (Page 172)
Mark Cuban (Page 166)
Newton Minow (Page 176)
Robert Flaherty (Page 155)
Walt Disney (Page 155)

Media Sources

- Colin McGinn. *The Power of Movies*. Pantheon, 2006. McGinn, a philosopher, builds an easy-to-follow case for the long-analyzed Dream Theory of Cinema to explain the compelling nature of the medium.
- David L. Robb. *Operation Hollywood: How the Pentagon Shapes and Censors Movies*. Prometheus, 2004. Robb, a veteran Hollywood reporter, chronicles the coerciveness of the government in providing and denying technical support for war movies.
- Dade Hayes and Jonathan Bing. *Open Wide: How Hollywood Box Office Became a National Obsession*. Miramax, 2004. Hayes and Bing, both editors at the movie trade journal *Variety*, examine the role of marketing with *T3, LB2* and *Sinbad*, each from a different studio, as case studies. They provide a historical context of movie marketing back to the 1950s.
- Bill Carter. *Desperate Networks*. Doubleday, 2006. Carter, a television reporter for the New York *Times*, tracks network television programming for a season.
- J. D. Lasica. *Darknet: Hollywood's War Against the Digital Generation*. Wiley, 2005. Lasica draws on a wide range of interviews in making a case that the framework for U.S. broadcasting is outdated for the digital age.
- Roger P. Smith. *The Other Face of Public Television: Censoring the American Dream*. Algora, 2002. Smith, a widely recognized television producer, argues that U.S. public television is substantively the same as commercial television, only in a cosmetically different wrapping. He rhetorically asks whether public television can be truly independent as long as it is dependent on government funding. He concludes with a call for an alternative television production organization endowed with a nongovernment trust fund.

MOTION MEDIA

In this chapter you have deepened your media literacy by revisiting several themes. Here are thematic highlights from the chapter:

MEDIA TECHNOLOGY

Satcom. Is satellite programming delivered directly to viewers the future of television? Ask Rupert Murdoch. Ask John Malone. You'll find different takes on the question. Both media barons have been out of the satellite-direct television business.

Movies were the first medium with visual motion. It was a technology that marveled people. Then came television, a fast-growth industry built on a new technology that also marveled people. "Radio with pictures," it was called. Networks supplied programming to local affiliates for relay to anyone within a signal's reach. Now that's all old technology. The new technology, digital and Internet-based, delivers video any time, anywhere. One result is a challenge to the traditional U.S. television infrastructure and the program forms built around it—30-second spots and 30-minute and 60-minute scheduled programs. (Pages 166–167, 171–174, 174–175)

MEDIA EFFECTS

Too Much TV? Ongoing issue for researchers is its effects on kids.

While some researchers focus on whether movies, television and other media affect public attitude and opinion, cultural sociologists focus on lifestyle effects that lend themselves to firmer conclusions. The effect of early television was obvious. Wednesday-night boxing, an early program fixture, kept people home and dented the attendance at older venues for out-of-home activities. And who in America in the 1950s would have missed the *$64,000 Question*? Today, devices that enable time shifting and on-the-go video pickups are putting the audience in charge. (Pages 170, 174–176)

MEDIA ECONOMICS

Webisodes. How far is our fast-paced 21st century lifestyle taking us? No more sitting down for 60-minute television shows? Thirty minutes too long, too? How about Susan Zirinsky's five-minute webisode news items taken from *Jericho* scripts?

The economics of the movie industry became bumpy with the rise of television. In the early years of television, the networks and their affiliates were in money-making bliss. Advertisers lined up to buy every spot available, particularly in prime time. The whole industry was built on charging advertisers what the market would bear, which was on a roll with double-digit annual growth. Today the economic structure is fracturing. Advertisers have options galore in which to make visual appeals to consumers, not only on cable and satcom channels but also via Internet venues and a dizzying array of digital-based alternative media. Where the unraveling of the traditional economic infrastructure will end is for clairvoyants to predict. In the meantime, the major over-air networks are testing other venues, like selling programs for Internet viewing. Parts of the movie industry, notably exhibition, also are being upended by technology-triggered economic change. (Pages 148–149, 150–152, 156–158, 162–164, 164–166, 173–174)

ELITISM AND POPULISM

PBS. A little good history, anyone? Documentary producer Ken Burns has drawn big audiences on public television. His 2007 series on World War II drew a large audience in terms of numbers. However, most PBS offerings draw a mass audience yawn. Is there a place for serious-minded works on television?

The new medium of television, quickly engaging millions of viewers in the 1950s, seemed to have great potential as a force for cultural enlightenment and for encouraging public participation in the great issues. A decade later FCC chair Newton Minow had, in effect, given up on this potential. He called television a "vast wasteland," a label that has stuck ever since. The networks pandered to low tastes with programming that neither excited the mind nor motivated political engagement. In the main, television was narcoticizing, lowbrow stuff—comedy geared to momentary chuckles, drama with predictable outcomes, and superficial takes on news. Whether television overall is less a wasteland today can be debated, but at least public stations are in existence as an alternative. (Pages 176–177)

AUDIENCE FRAGMENTATION

"Tracy, Here." The miniaturization of electronics envisioned for comic-strip detective Dick Tracy more than half a century ago has arrived—with unanticipated consequences. The way that television content is delivered, for example, is being transformed even as you read this. Seen Jon Stewart on an iPod? How about on a Tracy-like wristwatch screen? Oh, that's next week.

The explosion of television as a new medium ruined the magazine, radio and movie industries, at least for a while, and took away time that people had spent with books. The consolidation of audiences around the new medium was phenomenal. Magazines and radio demassified to survive, seeking segments of their former audiences. No question about it, the magazine and radio industries surrendered large segments of their audiences to television. In a comeuppance, the television audience itself now is fragmenting. The core network-affiliate over-air system has lost audience to hundreds of channels available on cable systems and by satcom delivery. (Pages 164–167, 171–175)

MEDIA AND DEMOCRACY

Liberation Tool. Portable video viewing is freeing people from half a century of lifestyle tyranny by television network executives, who schedule when programs will air.

Video-on-demand technology has liberated people from being tied down to a television set. The control that networks once had over lifestyles with their tantalizing prime-time and other fare is breaking down. People can watch television at their convenience with recording and playback devices. Portable devices enable people to choose not only when to watch but where. This has been called the democratization of television, the power shifting from national network program schedulers at corporate offices in New York to individual viewers. (Pages 174–178)

chapter 7

NEW MEDIA LANDSCAPE

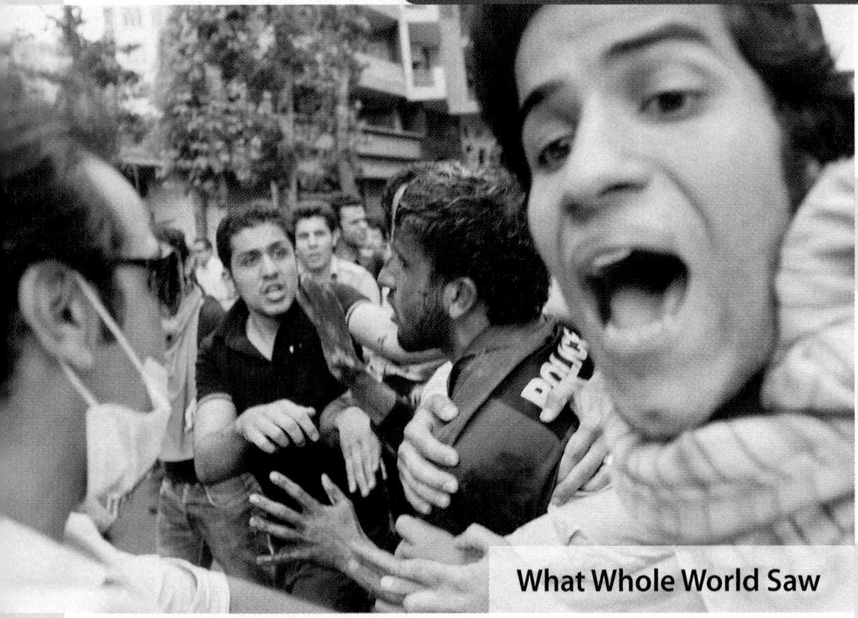

What Whole World Saw

Despite efforts of the Iran government to squelch news about massive citizen protests after a disputed election, thousands of images and videos made their way worldwide through video-sharing sites. New tools are shifting the power of mass communication to the people.

LEARNING AHEAD

- Browsers transformed the original walled-garden business model for web sites.
- Search engines are essential in the new media landscape.
- E-mail is a core Internet activity.
- Sites built on user-based content have profound possibilities for shaping the future.
- The shape of the Internet industry is still taking form.
- The Internet is democratizing mass communication, albeit with side effects.
- Internet technology is blurring distinctions among traditional media.

THE TWITTER REVOLUTION

It was an online showdown.

It started when the Iranian government tried to block media coverage of events following the disputed 2009 presidential election. Supporters of an opposition candidate, Hossein Mousavi, claimed the election was rigged. Mousavi supporters took to the streets. Demonstrations became violent when the government of President Mahmoud Ahmadinejad cracked down. There was blood in the streets.

The Ahmadinejad government banned both foreign and local media from reporting on what it called unauthorized opposition protests and rallies. Foreign reporters, most with short-term visas, were pressed to leave the country.

When news of the opposition continued to leak out of the country, the government confined foreign journalists to their bureaus. The reporters couldn't get to the demonstrations.

At that point in what is now being called the "Twitter Revolution," everyone became a reporter. Ordinary Iranians sent real-time updates to Twitter about the protest marches. They took video from their windows of government agents beating

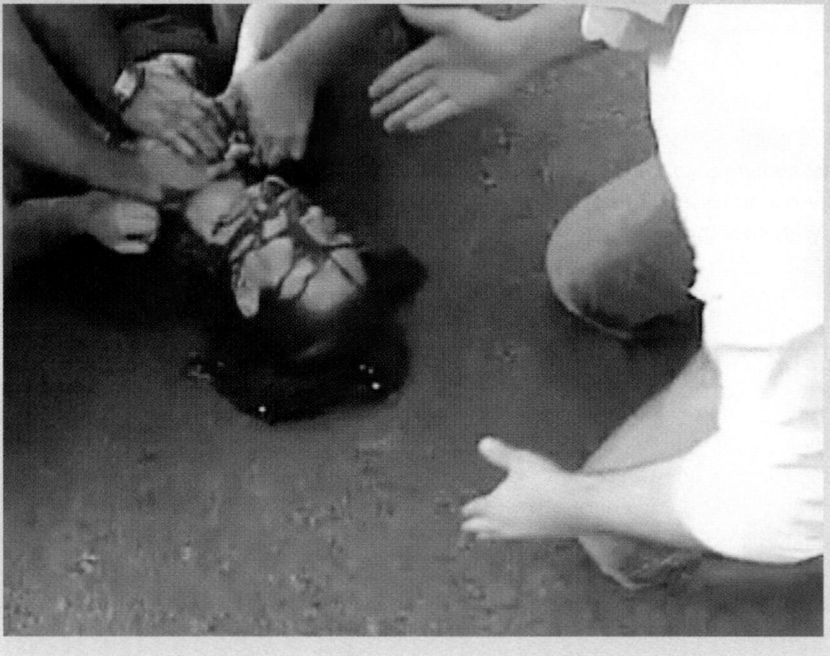

Martyred Through Twitter. *Exactly what happened before Neda Agha Sultan was shot by Iranian militia during citizen protests isn't clear. One account has it that she was riding with her music teacher in a car. Trapped in a street blocked by the protest, she opened the car door because of the heat and got out—and took a bullet in the chest. Almost immediately, dramatic video of her dying moments on the pavement was on Twitter worldwide, then archived on YouTube and other video-sharing services. Neda was a new martyr against government brutality.*

Neda Agha Sultan

protesting citizens. As people walked the streets, they used their cell phones to shoot images of people shouting from the rooftops.

Twitterers also picked up powerful, sometimes shocking photos and video from YouTube, Flickr and other sites and passed them on. One video on YouTube showed a young woman named Neda as she died after being shot. The video sent shock waves around the world.

Without any alternatives, mainstream media used the reports on Twitter and other social media for their stories.

The government's actions were swift, brutal—and stupid. Somehow they forgot that Iranians had been learning and practicing social networking skills for years. Sixty percent of Iranians are under age 30. Most own cell phones. This is a population accustomed to blogging and text-messaging to organize everything from poetry readings to underground rock concerts. Indeed, Iran ranks near the top of the worldwide list of bloggers per capita. It should have been no surprise to the government that citizens would put their new media tools to political use.

The Iranian government fought back. Agents posed online as opposition activists or foreign journalists to catch dissidents. The government tried to shut down Internet access but then found it needed the Internet as much as the dissidents did. The government also was accused of slowing down Internet access, and in return Mousavi supporters around the world treated the web sites of Ahmadinejad and Iran's supreme cleric, Ayatollah Khamenei, to a Twitter-wide effort to overload their servers.

All this was online warfare—and also a challenge for the mainstream media. How to verify these reports from untrained and sometimes partisan observers? Various blogs claimed that anywhere from 30 to 3,000 people were killed. Some photos posted by the Iranian government appeared doctored. Most reports in the mainstream media were couched in the words "unable to verify." But the mainstream media had to keep up. And they used these citizen reports because there was no other way to provide up-to-date coverage.

Is the Twitter Revolution truly a revolution? Are we at last embracing new media and using them to their fullest potential? This chapter examines the new and emerging landscape of mass communication.

Portals

STUDY PREVIEW

Early attempts to draw mass audiences to the Internet with "walled gardens" of services, such as America Online offered, were successful but short-lived. The AOL concept was doomed by the invention of browsers. With browsers, even first-time computer owners at home found access to the whole Internet. There is a lot beyond the garden wall.

WALLED GARDENS

Visionaries recognized in the 1990s that the Internet had potential to transform the mass media, but the visions were blurred. The first concept to take root was the **walled garden.** A one-time online games company redubbed itself **America Online** and set out to offer an encyclopedic array of features by subscription. For $20 a month, people could buy access to news, games, e-mail and whatever AOL posted inside the "garden."

AOL executive Steve Case became legendary with an audacious marketing scheme. He mailed millions of CDs that gave nontechnical people quick and easy access to AOL from their new home computers. The AOL "software suite," as it was called, had advantages over other walled gardens, like the techno-oriented CompuServ. Case's savvy marketing ploy gave AOL 30 million subscribers, outpacing not only CompuServ but also Prodigy and GEnie.

The success of America Online attracted executives at media giant Time Warner. In their quest to get on top of the future, Time Warner had floundered with Internet versions of their magazines. AOL seemed the right path. The companies merged in 2001. Such was the exuberance that the new company was named Time Warner AOL.

With the walled-garden business model, AOL provided limited interfaces with the Internet as a whole. But things were already changing, and fast. People already were using new technology, through software called **browsers,** for direct access to the Internet without a subscription. Gradually AOL lowered or dismantled the "wall." AOL mounted frenzied attempts to reinvent itself but never recovered. Recognizing the flaws in its original hopes for AOL as the model for the future of the mass media, Time Warner dropped AOL from the company name in 2007. In 2009, with subscriptions slipping below 10 million, Time Warner spun off AOL to become a separate entity.

walled garden
Early business model for online portals with access limited mostly to proprietary content

America Online (AOL)
Once-dominant Internet service provider

CHECKING YOUR MEDIA LITERACY

- **Why did the walled-garden online business model peak and then flounder?**
- **How could Time Warner have so misjudged the potential for America Online?**

BROWSERS

While America Online was in its formative ascendency, **Marc Andreessen** and some grad-school buddies at the University of Illinois were designing software to connect disparate operating systems with the Internet and each other. Their invention was the browser.

When Andreessen was graduated in 1993, he and some friends created a company called **Netscape.** With Netscape, computer newbies could uncrate their first home computer and point-and-click their way to just about anything on the Internet. Well, maybe not quite that easily, but almost. No matter how untechnical, anyone with a computer could unlock more content than ever before possible in human history. At first Netscape charged for the software, but with no

browser
Software to navigate the Internet, specifically World Wide Web sites

Marc Andreessen
Software wunderkind who designed pioneer browser Netscape

Netscape
First Internet browser

sub-scription fees. No AOL. The Netscape advertising line said it all: "The web is for everyone."

In 1996 Andreessen was on the cover of *Time* magazine, age 25, barefoot and a multimillionaire.

Netscape revenues zoomed to $100 million in 1996. Meanwhile, Microsoft introduced its own browser, Explorer. Other companies also entered the field. Clearly, the sun was setting on the walled-garden online business model.

Sensing the changing playing field, America Online bought Netscape in 1998 for $4.2 billion. Andreessen was given an executive title at AOL but his job was mostly chief resident thinker. He quickly grew bored and left for other ventures. Meanwhile, AOL tinkered with its business model and took down more garden walls, but a new era had arrived. AOL missed the boat.

The question then became: What to do once you got to the vast, seemingly infinite territory of unsorted content? With hundreds of thousands of sites, updated daily if not more often, how could anyone figure out where to go? True, browsers had bookmarking capability that allowed users to create a list of personally useful sites, but what about all those hundreds and thousands of sites that could be useful but that nobody in a lifetime could conceivably run across by random trips through the aptly named web?

Marc Andreessen. *His browser Netscape sealed the fate of subscription-only walled-garden access to the Internet. Netscape and copycat products offered free access to just about anything posted by anyone anywhere.*

CHECKING YOUR MEDIA LITERACY

- **How was Netscape the beginning of the end for walled gardens?**
- **Browsers were a quantum leap in online technology but still fell short. How so?**

Search Engines

STUDY PREVIEW

Search engines are essential in the new media landscape as a tool for access to the billions of sites on the Internet. Google and Yahoo are the major search engines. Each is a multimillion-dollar player. Both seek to grow into other Internet-related activities.

GOOGLE

Just as important as browsers for making the Internet useful to most people are **search engines.** Using elaborate software, search engines dispatch animated crawlers through the Internet to take snapshots of web pages and key words. The search engines amass huge reference files, update them continuously and organize them by the frequency that certain words appear in the text. For example, if someone searches the term *FM radio,* the search engine produces a list of sites, probably hundreds, ranked by the frequency of the word on each site.

search engine
Tool to identify and rank web sites by key terms

Sergey Brin, Larry Page
Creators of Google search engine

At Stanford University two doctoral students, **Sergey Brin** and **Larry Page,** developed an idea in 1996 to refine the search process with algorithms that ranked web pages by the number of links to them from other relevant web pages. Brin and Page tested their idea on the Stanford web site with the domain google.stanford.edu.

Google Guys. *With the fortune they amassed from Google, Sergey Brin and Larry Page have cast their net widely for new projects. The in-process Google Print Library aims to digitize the entire inventory of books ever published into a giant reference source. Google would sell on-screen advertising, as it does for its other search engine products.*

The term *google* actually was a common misspelling among mathematicians of the word *googol,* which means 1 to the power of 1 followed by 100 zeroes. In one sense, the word overstates what **Google** delivers. Only 1,000 results are provided max for any specific search query. But who's complaining? Or counting? The word *google* nonetheless captured the literal and ever-changing infinity that Brin and Page were trying to index—and it stuck. Dictionaries have canonized the word into a verb—*to google* is to use the Google search engine to obtain information on the Internet.

Search engines were free to users, placing another nail in the coffin of subscription sites whose walled gardens were hardly as extensive. How was it, then, that Brin and Page became multimillionaires within a couple of years? Most of Google's revenue, 99 percent at one point, was from advertising. Text-based ads—nothing gaudy, not even flashy—appeared with lists of searchable sites based in the term entered by a user. The ads, quietly appearing to one side of the screen, didn't interfere with the search or delay downloads. Advertisers liked the targeting of likely customers. Google's advertising revenue approached $20 billion in 2010.

Google has expanded into other services, including its e-mail brand, gmail. Its core business, though, remains its search engine. Among search engines Google clearly is the leader by market share:

Google	54 percent
Yahoo	20 percent
Live Search	13 percent

A culture has arisen around Google and created an aura. Corporate quips and truisms abound. Some are serious and brilliant in the message they capture in a few words, like the company mission: "To organize the world's information and make it universally accessible and useful." Perhaps the most enduring line came from a Google engineer, Paul Buchheit, which has numerous variations on the idea: "You can make money without doing evil." However, Googlisms can be problematic. How, for example, can a company succeed without doing what's evil in at least someone's eyes somewhere? Even for Google, doing business has required decisions about censorship, copyright and privacy that have not met with universal approval.

CHECKING YOUR MEDIA LITERACY

- **What is a search engine?**
- **What set Google apart from other search engines?**

Google
Dominant search engine

Yahoo
A major search engine and Internet services company

David Filo, Jerry Lang
Founders of Yahoo

YAHOO

Before Google there was **Yahoo,** also created by two Stanford grad students. **David Filo** and **Jerry Yang** created their search engine in 1994 and chose the name *Yahoo,* to which they attached an exclamation mark affectation—Yahoo. An odd name, true, but catchy. In a playful, sophomoric spirit, Filo and Yang said Yahoo was an acronym for "Yet Another Hierarchical Officious Oracle." The inspiration actually came from Jonathan Swift's name for a bumpkin in his 1726 novel, *Gulliver's Travels.* Whatever its name, Yahoo was something new and incredibly useful—a web directory. Within a year, Yahoo had 1 million hits.

Yahoo became an instant magnet for venture capital in the heady overinvestment period in computer-related companies in the 1990s. The value of Yahoo plummeted in

Complicity with Chinese Censorship

When Chinese authorities asked the U.S.-based Internet service provider Yahoo for information on Wang Xiaoning's Chinese e-mail account, Yahoo gave it to them. Promptly Wang Xiaoning, an engineer, was arrested. Why? In anonymous posts to an Internet mailing list, he had called for democratic reforms in China.

Such is life in authoritarian China, which presents a dilemma for companies like Yahoo with roots in democratic ideals that value free expression as a human right.

The case of Wang Xiaoning is not isolated. In at least four cases Yahoo has handed over user information from its China-based e-mail service to Chinese authorities, according to Rebecca MacKinnon, a consultant to Human Rights Watch. As a result, four Chinese dissidents were locked up.

Yahoo is not alone among U.S.-based international Internet companies in facilitating censorship in China. Others include Cisco, AOL, Skype and Nortel.

So why would Chinese citizens risk their freedom to swap information and thoughts on the Internet? The major U.S.-based Internet companies, Yahoo, Microsoft and Google, say that people are better off having Internet access even if they are censored and spied on. Google cofounder Sergey Brin notes that political searches are not that big a portion of the searches coming out of China: "You want to look at the total value picture that a search engine like Google brings and think of all that it's used for."

The issue, in part, for profit-oriented companies like Yahoo is that China represents a huge market. By 2008 the number of Internet users in China reached 253 million, making it the world's biggest Internet market. And at 19 percent of the population, the China market showed enormous potential for growth. By contrast, at the same time, about 220 million Americans were online—about 70 percent of the U.S. population.

Huddle Before Congress. *Yahoo chief executive Jerry Yang whispers to a company attorney during testimony at a Congressional inquiry into disclosing the identities of Yahoo users in China. The Chinese government has used Yahoo-provided information to jail its citizens.*

DEEPENING YOUR MEDIA LITERACY

EXPLORE THE ISSUE

To comply with laws in Germany, France and Switzerland, Google has blocked access to sites with material likely to be judged racist or inflammatory. Can you find other evidence of Internet intervention?

DIG DEEPER

Human Rights Watch has compiled a list of principles on corporate responsibility to uphold human rights. What would be on your list for Internet companies?

WHAT DO YOU THINK?

What role should ethics play when Internet companies do business in other cultures? Should the companies consider the bottom line when making ethical decisions?

the burst of the bubble—the so-called **dot-com bust** of 2000, but by then, already well diversified, the company was substantial enough to survive. Today Yahoo is worldwide, with web businesses in 20 languages on a wide range of subjects, together averaging more than 3.5 billion visits a day.

The scope of Yahoo is a dream-come-true for marketing. A 2007 study concluded that Yahoo could collect far more information on individual consumers for advertisers than any other data-aggregation agency. On average Yahoo could build a profile of 2,500 records per month about each of its visitors.

Indeed, Yahoo has become an advertising powerhouse by delivering the relatively precise segments of potential customers that advertisers covet. Eighty-eight percent of Yahoo revenue comes from selling screen space to advertisers. Advertisers pay 2.5 to 3 cents for every click-through from a notice on Yahoo. The company also sells advertising space on Yahoo News, Yahoo Movies, Yahoo Finance, Yahoo Sports and other sites.

The company has many branches, including the largest e-mail service in the world, and the social and user-generated sites Flickr, My Web, Yahoo Buzz, Yahoo Personals, and Yahoo 360°. Most of the company's units are acquisitions that have been given the same prefix—Yahoo Mail, Yahoo Games, Yahoo Pager. Indeed, Yahoo is a brand.

Besides acquiring companies, Yahoo has been an acquisition target. The software giant Microsoft has tried several times to finesse and even force a merger. There have been talks of combinations with Google, News Corp. and AOL.

One measure of the significance of search engines has been the wealth created for their founders. The business magazine *Forbes* lists Google's Larry Page as the 33rd richest American at $18.6 billion and Sergey Brin as the 72nd at $14.1 billion. They have established a foundation endowed with $90 million to tackle global poverty and energy and environmental problems. Yahoo's David Filo, 117th on the *Forbes* list at $2.5 billion, and Jerry Yang, 140th at $2.2 billion, remember their alma maters. Filo has donated $30 million to Tulane and Yang $75 million to Stanford.

dot-com bust
Economic collapse of most investments in Internet commerce in 2000

CHECKING YOUR MEDIA LITERACY

- **What was the dot-com bust?**
- **How does Yahoo make money with no-charge access to many of its sites?**

Messaging

STUDY ***PREVIEW***

A core element of the new media landscape is e-mail and related text-based messaging. E-mail is a computer-based system whose history dates to a military communication network launched in 1969. A similar but more limited variation for mobile phones is texting, generally with a maximum of 140 characters per message.

E-MAIL

One of the first mass uses of the Internet was **e-mail,** a shortened form of the term *electronic mail.* The history of e-mail goes back to 1969 when the U.S. military created a computer network, called **ARPAnet,** which stood for Advanced Research Projects Agency Network. The Pentagon built the network for military contractors and universities doing military research to exchange information. In 1983 the National Science Foundation, whose mandate is to promote science, took over. New software coding evolved that enabled disparate computer systems to talk with each other.

e-mail
A system for computer users to exchange messages through a network

Advanced Research Projects Agency Network (ARPAnet)
Military network that preceded Internet

Today, anyone with a computer and a modem can exchange e-mail messages with anyone on the planet who is similarly equipped. E-mail has become a nearly universal communication tool. Most users prefer e-mail to letters, now derisively called *snail mail,* and also to the telephone.

The unadorned text of e-mail messages is quick to compose and straightforward, and can be left in the in-boxes of busy and away-from-the-desk recipients. Endless telephone tag became less an irritant to everyday business and social transactions.

Despite all its roots in new and dazzling technology, e-mail generally is not mass communication. People use e-messages mostly one to one. True, multiple parties can be coded into a message. Also true, hucksters have devised **spams** that blanket thousands, even millions of people with pitches and pleas. In one sense, spams meet the definition of mass communication because of the size, heterogeneity and distance of the audience. But even e-mail spams are mostly unpolished and amateurish. Few bear the marks of carefully and professionally crafted mass-communication messages.

E-mail did take on more earmarks of mass communication when new software integrated plain-vanilla text with hypertext, which is the underlying coding for the web, and with graphics. Even then, however, organizations seeking slick presentations for mass audiences generally use web sites.

CHECKING YOUR MEDIA LITERACY

- **Is e-mail mass communication?**

TEXTING

A variation on e-mail is texting, which is using a mobile telephone keypad to tap messages that a recipient with a mobile phone can read on a tiny phone screen live or later. Text messages usually are brief and text-only. In fact, the cellular networks that carry texting have a 140-character limit per message, about 20 words.

Texting originally was an idea for telephone-like point-to-point communication, not mass communication. But businesses and organizations have come to use newer software to send notices to select groups, like a reminder for a club meeting or an upcoming real deal. Some news services sell premium services and flash blurbs on breaking news, sports scores and market ups and downs. After several campus massacres, including Virginia Tech in 2007 and Northern Illinois University in 2008, many colleges set up systems to alert students by texting their cell phones.

The proliferation of cell phones and enthusiasm for texting, especially among young people, has had wide-ranging impact. It's not all idle chitchat. Police know, for example, that raiding a college kegger is more difficult because one person who spots congregating officers can get the word down the street by texting silently and undetected. Imagine this late-night party scene: The only illumination is from handheld telephone screens. Texting also can work for police. In the Netherlands, police routinely issue text alerts for citizens to be vigilant if something is awry—like a kidnapping or a robbery in progress.

Political organizers—yes, including rabble-rousers—have found texting a superior 21st-century substitute for bullhorns. It is thought, too, that texting campaigns have turned elections in several countries. Backers of Philippines President Joseph Estrada blamed his ouster in 2001 on what was called a "smart mob."

The United States is hardly the leader among nations in the rise of texting, but the U.S. data nonetheless are staggering. Four of five mobile-phone users in the United States use texting. Among teenagers and young adults, it's 87 percent. The U.S. average is six texts per user a day. U.S. usage got a boost when AT&T opened its texting network to viewers to vote for their favorite talent in the runaway TV success, *American Idol.* In 2009, fans sent 178 million text messages to the show, more than double the year before. Do the math: U.S. population, 306 million; *American Idol* texts, 178 million. True, many viewers sent multiple messages over the season.

CHECKING YOUR MEDIA LITERACY

- **How are texting and e-mailing similar? Different?**
- **How has texting affected how people live their lives?**
- **What are political implications of texting?**

spam

E-mail message sent indiscriminately to large numbers of recipients

MEDIA TIMELINE

NEW MEDIA LANDSCAPE MILESTONES

PIVOTAL EVENTS

1960–1969

ARPAnet
U.S. military linked computers of contractors, researchers (1969)

Breakthrough game

- >> Telstar in orbit (1961)
- >> Vietnam war (1964–1975)
- >> Nixon presidency (1969–1974)
- >> Humans on moon (1969)

1970–1979

1980–1989

SimCity
Will Wright created simulation game (1984)

"Walled Garden"
AOL founded (1989)

Andreessen: widening Internet access

- >> Reagan presidency (1981–1989)
- >> Soviet empire imploded (1989)

1990–1999

Browser
Netscape introduced (1994)

Social Networking
Facebook predecessor Facemash (1993)

Search Engine
Yahoo created (1994); Google created (1996)

Video Game Advertising
Chex Quest (1996)

First Blog
Rob Marta created slazhdot.org (1997)

Metaverse
Philip Rosedale created *Second Life* (1999)

- >> George H. W. Bush presidency (1989–1993)
- >> Persian Gulf war (1990–1991)
- >> Investor exuberance in dot-coms (1990s)
- >> Clinton presidency (1993–2001)
- >> Legislation fuels rapid fiber-optic network growth (1996)

Jimmy Wales: Wikipedia creator

2000–2009

Wikipedia
Collaboratively edited online encyclopedia (2001)

Google Print Project
To digitize all books ever published (2005)

Game Growth
Video game sales twice the music industry's (2008)

Bye, AOL
Time Warner severs AOL (2009)

Nanotube
U.S., Chinese research perfected mass production (2009)

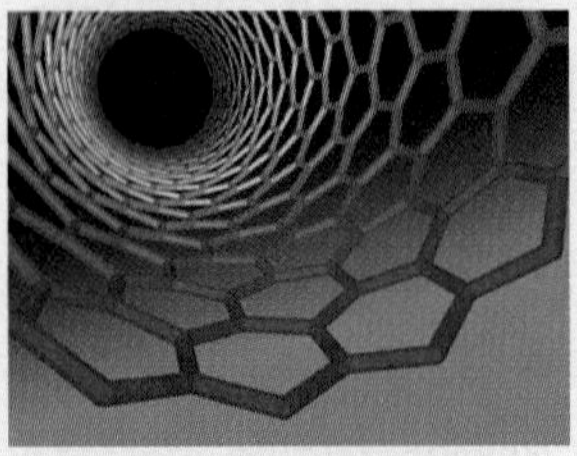
From Duke, Beijing universities

- >> Dot-com bust (2000)
- >> George W. Bush presidency (2001–2009)
- >> 9/11 terrorist attacks (2001)
- >> iPod introduced (2002)
- >> Iraq war and occupation (2003–2009)
- >> Major recession (2008–)
- >> Obama presidency (2009–)

2010–

User-Generated Sites

STUDY PREVIEW

Bloggers have made a potent presence in the mass media landscape. Blogs may be uneven in quality, but they have demonstrated that they can be watchdogs for the public. Important, too, is that blogging demonstrated potential for additional new and important mass communication vehicles, including social networking sites.

BLOGS

The ease with which individuals can create a personal media presence has been made possible by software from Internet service providers to create simple web pages. Because these pages were like personal journals or logs, they were called *web logs*, or **blogs** for short. Some bloggers developed followings and added software features that allowed visitors to chime in. A running narrative became a running dialogue.

Blogs have become a distinct and influential mass medium. Blogger Joshua Marshall, for example, reported on his talkingpointsmemo.com in 2002 that the most powerful member of the U.S. Senate, Trent Lott, had made comments in a speech that were, depending on your point of view, either racist or racially insensitive. Lott had uttered his comments at the 100th birthday party of Senator Strom Thurmond, once a strong segregationist. Mainstream media missed the implications of Lott's comments. Not Joshua Marshall. On his blog, Marshall hammered away at Lott day after day. Other bloggers, also outraged at Lott's comment, joined in. Three days later the story hit NBC. Four days later Lott apologized. Two weeks later, his Senate colleagues voted him out as majority leader.

As a blogger who made a difference, Joshua Marshall is hardly alone. Best known is Matt Drudge, whose revelations propelled the Bill Clinton-Monica Lewinsky dalliances in the Oval Office into a national scandal. Another blogger, college student Russ Kirk, at his computer in Arizona, looked for information on government refusals to release photographs of caskets of fallen U.S. soldiers in Iraq and Afghanistan, which he regarded as documents to which the public, himself included, had legal access. Kirk filed a request for the documents under the Freedom of Information Act. Then on his web site thememoryhole.org, he posted the photographs of the flag-draped coffins and also of the astronauts who had died in the *Columbia* disaster. The photos became front-page news. At one point, Kirk's blog was receiving 4 million hits a day—almost twice the circulation of *USA Today*.

Blogging not only is important in the new media landscape but for spawning a wide range of **user-generated** Internet content. The effect has been transformational on the mass media. Just about anybody can create and distribute content—in contrast to the traditional model with monumentally high costs of entry, like starting a newspaper or putting a television station on the air. With user-generated content, the Internet has democratized the mass media by enabling anyone with a computer and a modem to become a mass communicator.

blogs
A journal-like web site with continuing narrative, generally personal in nature, on a narrow subject. Short for *web log*.

user-generated content
Internet messages that originate with an individual to communicate directly with a mass audience

CHECKING YOUR MEDIA LITERACY

- **What is a blog, and who are bloggers?**
- **Does blogging matter?**
- **How can it be said that bloggers have democratized mass communication?**
- **What mass media innovations have flowed from blog technology and the blogging experience?**

King Tweeter. *Actor Ashton Kutcher's Twitter followers include actress-wife Demi Moore. Kutcher is the first user of Twitter to have 1 million followers. Why? Ask them.*

SOCIAL NETWORKING

The giant social networking site **Facebook** had dubious beginnings. In 2003 when Mark Zuckerberg was a sophomore at Harvard, he raided sorority house membership rosters for photos of members. He paired the pictures on his blog, then invited his visitors to vote for the "hotter" of the paired women. Zuckerberg's Facemash didn't last long. The university shut it down for a host of issues, including privacy.

However, the reception for Facemash among students—some anyway—was enthusiastic, and Zuckerberg figured he was onto something. He re-mounted the site on a non-university server as Facebook, named for those photo pamphlets that small colleges once issued for freshman orientation to help new students get to know each other. First it was Harvard mugs, then Stanford, Columbia and Yale. Zuckerberg kept tweaking the concept.

Today Facebook is not only the granddaddy of social networking sites but the largest. People post their own photos, choose friends with whom they want to keep in touch and exchange messages easily. On their pages, people can update their personal profiles to notify friends about themselves. Facebook allows an individual 60 photos.

The success of Facebook has been phenomenal. One tracking service says Facebook is the fifth most-visited site worldwide. Fourteen million photos were being uploaded a day. Facebook's reputation has been especially strong among college students. One study concluded that only beer outranked Facebook among collegians' favorite things. A competing site in the Fox media family, **MySpace,** is stronger among high-schoolers, but that demographic distinction seems to be fading as Facebook moves into more broader-based use, including business communication.

Facebook and MySpace are among user-generated sites, so called because the content originates with users—again a contrast with the early AOL concept of a walled garden. Other major players include **Flickr,** for posting photos, and **YouTube,** for videos. The usual revenue model is on-screen advertising that directs ads to users based on lifestyle profiles.

The impact of social networking sites on traditional media has been twofold. The sites are one more competitor for advertising revenue, which has been slipping away from traditional media. Also, the sites are an additional competitor for audience time: every minute on Facebook is one less minute for something else—like reading a magazine or watching a sitcom.

CHECKING YOUR MEDIA LITERACY

- **What is the immense attraction of Facebook?**
- **How do social networking sites make money to stay in business?**

Twitter
Platform for 140-or-fewer-character communications among computer and cell phone users

TWITTER

Who knows what whimsy captured actor Ashton Kutcher in April 2009. What we do know is that Kutcher set a goal of becoming the first user of **Twitter,** then a four-year-old social networking site, to have 1 million followers. It may seem a dubious distinction to have 1 million people tracking your daily commentary, like whether you chose sandals or flipflops for the beach, but such statistics are why the *Guinness Book of World Records* sells in the millions.

Although Twitter was a distant third among social networking platforms at the time of Kutcher's record, its growth was phenomenal, up 14-fold globally in a year:

	Users	Growth
Twitter	17 million	1,298%
Facebook	132 million	217%
MySpace	50 million	7%

tweets
Messages on the Twitter platform

passed links
References to web sources shared among computer users

Jack Dorsey. *At 14 Dorsey was intrigued with designing software to improve the dispatching of taxis. By 23 he was making a living with his inventions for dispatching couriers, taxis and emergency services from the web. Then he became interested in instant messaging and came up with the concept for Twitter. It was a blend of IMing and blogging that gave new dimension to social networking–and opened significant new potential for human communication.*

What made Twitter different? Like texting, **tweets,** as they are called, are limited to 140 characters. Unlike texting, Twitter integrates communication among cell phones and computers. It's all seamless. And it's not limited to one-to-one communication. If you decide to become an Ashton Kutcher follower, for example, you sign on and then receive all the latest postings from Kutcher and fellow followers, each posted sequentially with the latest at the top.

Twitter took a lot of early ribbing: How much depth is there in a message limited to 140 characters? Who cares whether Ashton Kutcher chose Wheaties or Lucky Charms for breakfast? Or to tool the L.A. freeways in a Ferrari or Hummer? Indeed, is Twitter a messaging form for an attention-deficit-disordered society?

To that question, technology author Steven Johnson, who assessed the Twitter phenomenon for *Time* magazine, has answered resoundingly: No. Johnson cited a conference for 40 invited educators, entrepreneurs, philanthropists and venture capitalists on the future of education. Everyone was encouraged to post tweets of live commentary during the presentations and discussions for display on a screen everyone could see. Distracting? Johnson recapped the six-hour experience by describing a "shadow conversation." There were summaries of discussion, occasional jokes, suggested links for further reading. "At one point a brief argument flared up between two participants in the room—a tense back-and-forth that transpired silent as the rest of us conversed in friendly tones." Yes, Johnson's lesson is that people indeed can multitask. Those 140-character twits can be enriching.

Then, to Johnson's surprise, outsiders got wind of the interesting dialogue inside the conference and joined in. The interloping followers of the Twitter thread were adding their observations and ideas, which the participants inside the conference room integrated into their thinking and face-to-face conversation. Said Johnson: "Integrating Twitter into that conversation fundamentally changed the rules of engagement. It added a second layer of discussion and brought a wider audience into what would have been a private exchange."

Important too, Johnson said, was that a public record of hundreds of Tweets, none more than 140 characters, had been created. The whole was far more than the sum of the parts. And then, the record continued for weeks with follow-up twitters. The conference has "an afterlife" on the web.

These points can be made to counter frequent claims that tweets constitute an alarming dumbing-down of the culture:

- Brevity is not necessarily without profundity.
- Individual tweets are part of a thread of dialogue and thought that should be considered in its entirety.
- Twitter discussions include links to additional materials, like supporting data elsewhere on the Internet or a fresh perspective in *Atlantic Monthly*. These are called **passed links.**

Watch This Book. *Book publishers have been assigning part of their promotional budgets to videos with authors pitching their books. Novelist Chuck Palahniuk has staged interviews with his fictional porn star Cassie Wright, in a series produced by publisher Doubleday.*

The possibilities for passed links could be a next step in the new media landscape. Johnson sees shared links as "a fantastic solution for finding high-quality needles in the immense spam-plagued haystack that is the contemporary web."

CHECKING YOUR MEDIA LITERACY

- **How is Twittering different from texting?**
- **What is the basis for Twitter being characterized as a tool for people with short attention spans?**
- **Can an argument be made that tweets are a sign of a declining culture? What is the counter-argument?**

VIDEO SHARING

Measures of the social impact of user-generated sites are as elusive as measuring media effects in general. Since its creation in 2005, however, the video sharing site YouTube has shown the significant effect of user-generated media. Users can upload videos and do so 65,000 times a day. Put another way, people post 20 hours of new video a minute. Most are amateur videos, but other media, including television networks, post snippets to draw attention to their programming. The site is a major media stopping point in the lives of many people. There are 100 million video views a day.

YouTube is ingrained in the new Internet culture. The impact goes further: Two of the presidential debates for the 2008 U.S. elections, carried on the CNN television network, were built around questions on video from YouTube users. The debates extended YouTube's visibility beyond its core younger viewers. One of the debates had an unusually high viewership of 2.6 million.

Authoritarian governments have found YouTube vexatious in tense times. During the 2009 Iranian election crisis, the government tried to block access to YouTube and other sites to prevent the upload of video footage of mass demonstrations and police violence against citizens. Iran and other regimes, including the democratic government of Turkey, have cut off access to YouTube on grounds of morality and decency.

In 2006 YouTube was acquired by Google. The selling price: $1.7 billion.

CHECKING YOUR MEDIA LITERACY

- **What has been the social and political impact of video sharing?**

Online Commerce

STUDY PREVIEW

The Internet was conceived as a commercial-free communication network. The concept evaporated as the Internet's potential for commerce became evident. Commercial sites are mostly catalog-like, offering products that can be shipped to customers or downloaded.

SALES SITES

As the Internet was coming together under National Science Foundation auspices in the 1980s, the creators were of one mind about keeping the system commercial-free. The goal was a serious medium of mass communication uncontaminated by a free-for-all in quest of filthy lucre. Early users policed the system to keep it pristine, sending sharp rebukes to offenders. The "police" gave up as the commercial potential of the medium burst into everyone's consciousness. When it came time to organize the Internet into useful segments with **domain names,** the suffixes approved by the **Corporation for Assigned Names and Numbers,** the chief Internet oversight agency, included the telling .com and later .biz. Now even some sites with the suffix .edu, reserved for educational institutions, carry commercial messages.

CHECKING YOUR MEDIA LITERACY

- **Why the early disdain for commercial content on the Internet?**

AUCTION SITES

No story better illustrates the transformation of the Internet into a commercial medium than the rise of the auction site **eBay.** It was only in 1995 that computer programmer **Pierre Omidyar** of San Jose, California, added an auction function on his personal site. Somebody posted a broken laser pointer, which sold, to Omidyar's amazement, for $14.83. Omidyar figured he was onto something, and found investors, and the company grew exponentially. When ownership shares were offered to the public in 1998, three years after the launch, Omidyar was an instant billionaire.

Today eBay operates globally with 84 million active users. In 2007, the total value of goods sold through eBay was almost $60 billion. Put another way, eBay users trade more than $1,900 worth of goods on the site every second. As an auction site, eBay is not alone. Some are narrowly focused, like diecast.com, which specializes in scale automobile models.

CHECKING YOUR MEDIA LITERACY

- **Can a case be made that eBay forced the commercialization of the Internet?**

domain name
An identification label for a web site, each with a suffix like .com, .org, .gov.

Corporation for Assigned Names and Numbers
Internet's chief oversight agency

eBay
Pioneer online auction site

Pierre Omidyar
Creator of eBay online auction site

Amazon.com
Electronic commerce company that upended traditional book retailing

Jeff Bezos
Created Amazon online site, originally for selling books

iTunes Store
Online digital media for consumer downloads, originally music

MAIL ORDER

The Internet has transformed retailing, with many brick-and-mortar stores losing sales. In response, retailers across the spectrum from giant Wal-mart to mom-and-pop shops have created an online presence to, at minimum, steer customers to their physical stores or to make online sales for shipping to customers.

The pioneer in rewriting the rules of retailing on a large scale was **Amazon.com.** It was the concept of **Jeff Bezos,** who saw great potential in the Internet for e-commerce but didn't know what to sell. Figuring that products that lent themselves to mail delivery would work well on the Internet, Bezos settled on books. He founded Amazon.com in the garage of his Seattle home and went live in 1995, pioneering online book retailing. Amazon sales topped $1 billion by 2000. Today Amazon is a department store with a wide range of products, like the Sears Roebuck catalogs of earlier times, with everything delivered directly to buyers through the Postal Service or other carriers.

The book retailer Barnes & Noble responded with its own Internet sales site, but Amazon had a head start. Many local independent book retailers failed to get with the new retailing model. Their market share shrank. Many closed down.

CHECKING YOUR MEDIA LITERACY

- **Why did Jeff Bezos choose books for online commerce?**
- **How has Amazon.com affected traditional book retailing?**

PRODUCT DOWNLOADS

The computer manufacturer Apple took e-commerce in a new direction with their **iTunes Store,** which, unlike Amazon, delivered an intangible product—music. Digitized music was downloaded to customers' computers. The delivery was non-physical. Like Amazon, the Apple iStore quickly won customers and hurt traditional music retailing through stores and mail order. As download technology improved to allow video downloading in reasonable times, the iStore inventory grew to include television episodes and movies.

At Amazon, Bezos picked up on the Apple iTunes model. In 2008 Amazon introduced an e-book, **Kindle,** and offered books by download for reading on the device. Clearly, the Internet had certainly become a major medium for commerce.

Kindle
Amazon e-book to which books and periodicals can be downloaded

CHECKING YOUR MEDIA LITERACY

- **List similarities between the original Amazon.com and iTunes Store concepts.**
- **List differences.**
- **How does Kindle move Amazon nearer the iTunes model?**

Online Domination

STUDY PREVIEW

The search engine Google dominates the Internet with intuitive and focused search algorithms. Advertising revenue has grown because commercial messages can be targeted to likely customers. The social networking site Facebook is in a position to offer even more precisely targeted information to advertisers because so much personal information is stored on its servers.

AMASSING TARGET AUDIENCES

The new media landscape is being shaped by traditional media economics. The company that dominates will be the company that can attract the largest audiences, or, in today's parlance, the most eyeballs. Advertisers want eyeballs and are willing to pay for the access. The potential of the Internet for commerce remains largely untapped. Of an estimated $500 billion a year spent on brand advertising globally, only about 10 percent goes to the Internet.

With 54 percent of the search engine market, Google has so many visits every day, every hour, every second, that advertisers pay handsomely for on-screen advertising space on pages with search results. It's **targeted marketing.** Someone searching for information on, say, mosquitoes, is a more likely customer for an anti-itch spray than someone searching for spaghetti sauce recipes or Nordic winter vacations. Google's search algorithms offer an unrivaled linkage of products and potential customers—a marketing dream. Although Google has created revenue streams besides advertising, much of its near $20 billion income a year is from advertising.

In effect, Google slices and dices the mass audience in ways that give advertisers unusual efficiency in reaching the people they seek. In advertising lingo, there is less *wastage.* Why, for example, should a marinara company buy space in a food magazine whose readers include people with tomato allergies when Google offers a targeted audience of people looking for spaghetti sauce recipes with nary a one among them who's allergic to tomatoes?

CHECKING YOUR MEDIA LITERACY

- **How can search engines target potential customers for advertisers?**

targeted marketing
Matching advertisers with potential customers with relative precision

BEHAVIORAL TARGETING

The social networking site Facebook has positioned itself to outdo Google for delivering audience segments to advertisers. Unlike Google, whose algorithms build an atlas of the online universe, Facebook amasses personal information on its users—the people who make purchases. The users' personal data, when organized and sorted, can be a gold mine for marketing goods and services with new precision. Consider these facts: Every month the 200 million individuals with Facebook accounts post 4 billion bits of information, 850 million photos and 8 million videos. All this is held exclusively on Facebook's 40,000 servers.

Facebook has incredible potential to deliver customers to advertisers based on information that members submit themselves, albeit unwittingly, when they communicate with friends. In the technology magazine *Wired,* business writer Fred Vogelstein noted that people behave differently on Facebook than anywhere else online: They use their real names, connect with real friends, link to their real e-mail addresses and share their real thoughts, tastes and news. In contrast, Vogelstein notes, Google knows little about its users except their search histories and some browsing activity.

That Facebook is positioned to become the central component in the new media landscape has not been lost on investors. Microsoft bought a chunk of Facebook stock in 2007 at a price that suggested the company was worth $15 billion. It's thought that Google, although bigger at $23 billion, may have peaked in the potential reach of its once cutting-edge technology to target customers for advertisers.

Vogelstein explains the Facebook-Google contrast colorfully with the example of a friend whose Facebook profile has the usual stuff—birthday, address, resume and pictures of his wife and kids. Plus, Vogelstein notes, his friend explained that he likes to make beer, ate at one of Vogelstein's favorite restaurants the week before and likes to watch cartoons. The friend pondered in a Facebook message to a friend whether his son's Little League game might be rained out. Also, he asked friends for help figuring out how the impeller in his central heating unit works. In contrast, a search of the name of Vogelstein's friend on Google yielded that he holds a doctorate in computer science on a dated personal web site with links, most of them expired, and a list of scholarly papers he had written over the years.

The future of the Internet may well be the **behavioral targeting** that Facebook and other social networking sources can offer advertisers. There are hurdles. Users objected loudly in 2007 when Facebook began injecting advertising into news feeds. Users were concerned about privacy. Accused of betraying users' privacy expectations through data mining for commercial purposes, Facebook backed off. Then in 2009 Facebook quietly modified its terms of service, to which users must agree or leave, so anything posted on the site gives ownership of the material to Facebook in perpetuity. The small print read: "We may share your information with third parties, including responsible companies with which we have a relationship." To a new batch of criticism, the company denied an intention to provide information to third parties. Even so, the language remained in the terms of service.

behavioral targeting
Using personal information and patterns in activities to match advertisements with potential customers

CHECKING YOUR MEDIA LITERACY

- **What is the advantage of using social networking sites to target customers for advertisers?**
- **What obstacles does Facebook have as a behavioral targeting service?**

Games

STUDY PREVIEW

Online video games have emerged slowly from checkers, tic-tac-toe and Scrabble-style games. With growing sophistication in software, new broadband capacity and interactivity, games have acquired qualities akin to mass communication. This includes expanding acceptability as an advertising medium.

ONLINE GAME AUDIENCE

Firmly established in the Internet universe is online video gaming. Gaming has grown from the simple games added to software packages with the first generation of home computers even before people had heard of the Internet. These games were hardly mass communication, any more than a Monopoly board is. Gradually, though, games went online. Today, the top online role-playing games such as *World of Warcraft* and *Halo 3* boast tens of thousands of players worldwide at any given time.

With their huge and growing following, video games have become a natural target for advertising. It's an attractive audience. The Entertainment Software Association says that players average 6.5 hours a week at their games. Players include a broad range of people, and 39 percent earn $50,000 a year or more—an attractive demographic that advertisers have a hard time tapping with other media.

Among entertainment industries, video games vaulted ahead of music in revenue rankings in 2008 in the United States and also globally. A comparison of U.S. sales:

Books	$35.7 billion
Movies	$32.5 billion including DVD sales, rentals
Video games	$21.3 billion
Music	$10.0 billion

Some projections are 9.1 percent annual growth for the video and online game industry. Globally that would be to $48.8 billion in 2012, making the industry the fastest growing among media sectors.

CHECKING YOUR MEDIA LITERACY

- **Why have video games surpassed music sales?**
- **Do you see online video games surpassing movies as an entertainment medium?**

GAME ADVERTISING

One question has been whether video and online games are actually a medium of mass communication. The earliest computer games were solitary time-passers, like shooting an on-screen missile at a moving target. An iota of *mass* was added when scores were registered online. It was an incremental step toward mass communication—a primitive tally allowing players to compare their prowess with others'.

New ground was broken in 1961 when Steve Russell and fellow students at the Massachusetts Institute of Technology designed *Spacewar.* With new computer technology, two players, each with a spacecraft, lobbed missiles at a black hole. Innovations led to video arcade games in the 1980s, but these resembled high-tech pinball machines more than anything close to mass communication.

Arcade games moved to home computers with early IBM and Apple machines in the mid-1980s. The genre moved closer to mass communication with so-called **multi-user dungeons,** MUDs for short, with online multi-player capability. Even so, these were structured games. In one sense, game designers were communicating to players but only with a structure, certainly no message. Even platforms like handheld devices and mobile phones didn't make video games mass communication.

multi-user dungeons (MUDs)
Video games with multi-player capabilities

Will Wright. *He created the SimCity series, the first big-seller video games that allowed players to interact with one another creatively. The series offered scenarios for designing and building urban environments and solving problems as they arose, often unexpectedly.*

>> Advertising. A shift occurred when advertisers began recognizing games as a platform to reach a significant and growing audience comprising mostly younger men—an elusive audience for advertisers. Early games ads were simple, like a billboard or poster in the background.

Brand names, including Chef Boyardee and Coca-Cola, dabbled with **advergames** in the 1990s. The games were issued on disks for home computers. In 1996 Ralston Purina created an on-disk game, *Chex Quest,* and boxed it with its breakfast cereals. It featured the battles of the humanoid Chex Warriors against an invasion of slimy Flemoids on a distant planet. *Chex Quest* morphed in sophistication as technology improved. In 2008 a multi-player online variation with chatrooms was introduced. Hosted games had 9 million registered fans. There were daily matches.

The lessons of the *Chex Quest* campaign were not lost on other advertisers. The Chex advertising agency WatersMolitor was credited with almost quadrupling the volume of Chex sales. Market share grew 48 percent in the crowded breakfast cereal field.

Online and with advertising, video games suddenly had not only a foothold in mass communication but also a future. Projections have games eroding advertising revenue from network television.

advergames
Video games sponsored by an advertiser to promote sales

artificial life
Games that put players in control of a character in make-believe situations

simulation games
Video games in which players interact with one another in situations that they create

Will Wright
Game designer known mostly for *SimCity* and spin-offs

metabrain
Computers that collect human intelligence to assess and disseminate

Philip Rosedale
Creator of *Second Life* game; a.k.a Philip Linden

Second Life
Video game in which players create roles and interact in a virtual world they create

avatar
Any *Second Life* character created by a player. The word is adapted from the Hindu concept of a soul being released from earthly limitations.

>> Simulation Games. A genre called **artificial life** puts players in control of a character in make-believe situations. These **simulation games** are built around the social interaction of the individual characters controlled by the players. The player lives the life of someone else. Best known are the best-selling Sim series by U.S. game designer **Will Wright.** In Wright's first major game, *SimCity,* players build a city, including power grids and transit systems, amid obstacles that include changing tax rates, floods and even a meteor strike.

Wright is exuberant about the potential of simulation games and talks about players collectively creating what he calls a **metabrain.** In a 2008 interview, Wright put it this way: "People are making this stuff, and computers collect it, then decide who to send it to. The computer is the broker. They are aggregating human intelligence into a system that is more powerful than we thought artificial intelligence was going to be." Wright has called simulation games "the world's most important pizza party."

>> Role Playing. Role-playing games began simply enough. Players assumed a role—say, of an adventurer—and progressed through a predetermined story line programmed with lots of unexpected twists. In the mid-1990s, multi-player online games were developed. Players, sometimes hundreds, would interact in real time and amass points by completing quests.

CHECKING YOUR MEDIA LITERACY

- **How did advertising move video games more into a medium of mass communication?**
- **Explain Will Wright's concept of computers and interactivity through mass media as a "metabrain."**

SECOND LIFE

Philip Rosedale, a self-taught software master, took lessons from his physics studies at the University of California at San Diego, and moved role playing into new territory with the platform ***Second Life.*** In the game, players choose another identity, called an **avatar,** and interact with other avatars in a constantly

Philip Rosedale

His Avatar. *Of course, the inventor of Second Life plays a role in his online never-never land. Rosedale's avatar is Philip Linden. Not uncoincidentally, the make-believe currency in this make-believe place are Linden dollars. Players use them to buy whatever anyone else wants to sell.*

changing reality that they create. Avatars can travel, create property and sell, buy and rent using *Second Life* currency, known as Linden dollars. Rosedale's avatar is Philip Linden.

As many as 88,000 avatars have been engaged in second lives simultaneously in this never-never land. The average is 38,000. In one month, avatars spent 28.3 million hours "in world," as it's called.

Scenarios can be topical and full of intrigue. During the 2008 U.S. presidential primaries, avatars representing Republicans who supported the Bush re-election campaign raided the headquarters of Democrat John Edwards. They defaced the office with obscenities and slogans and Marxist posters. Only a month later the headquarters of French presidential candidate Jean-Marie Le Pen was attacked. Bloodshed ensued between the invading marauders and security police. As scenarios unfold with whatever twists that avatars concoct, they chat through an instant-messaging function.

Where *Second Life* may grow is open to conjecture and also, importantly, a function of imagination. In 2007 the Maldives became the first country to open an embassy on *Second Life's* Diplomacy Island. Sweden soon established an embassy to promote a national image for culture. For a while, the global news agency Reuters created a bureau on *Second Life* with two reporters keeping avatars abreast of news from the place. Not finding enough general interest in *Second Life* news, Reuters closed the bureau after two years. The CNET web site and network and *Wired* magazine also dabbled with *Second Life* bureaus. The news network CNN has taken a route requiring less investment. Avatars can be citizen journalists and post news themselves through a CNN outpost.

CHECKING YOUR MEDIA LITERACY

- **Thirty thousand *Second Life* avatars were insufficient to warrant a Reuters bureau. What do you see as a critical mass for Reuters to reopen the bureau? Consider a one-reporter bureau costs $100,000 a year to operate. Consider possibilities for advertising revenue.**

Online Archives

STUDY PREVIEW

The capacity to store digitized data seems infinite. The impact is at its most obvious with library collections. Who needs miles of shelf space? The online encyclopedia Wiki and specialized banks of data and information have revolutionized the reference book industry. On-call digitized data has profound social and political effects.

DIGITAL STORAGE

The seemingly endless capacity for digital storage has eliminated the scarcity of space for moving and storing text, images, sound and video. Theoretically, librarians no longer will need to shred the least-used parts of their collections for want of shelf space. Encyclopedia editors no longer have arbitrary limits, whether 10 volumes or 20, to encapsulate all human knowledge. Archivists, rejoice! There's plenty of room for anything that can be digitized.

CHECKING YOUR MEDIA LITERACY

- **What is digital storage replacing?**

GOOGLE PRINT PROJECT

In terms of previous human experience, a proposal by the search engine company Google to digitize every book ever produced is boggling. Google's collection will far surpass the holdings of any library. That includes Harvard University, whose collection of 15 million volumes is the largest academic library in the world. The **Google Print Library** will also exceed the Library of Congress (42.3 million volumes), and the British Library (25 million). When the project expands to additional languages, the collection will dwarf French Bibliothéque's 13 million volumes in French.

Google Print Library
Project to put all books in human history online

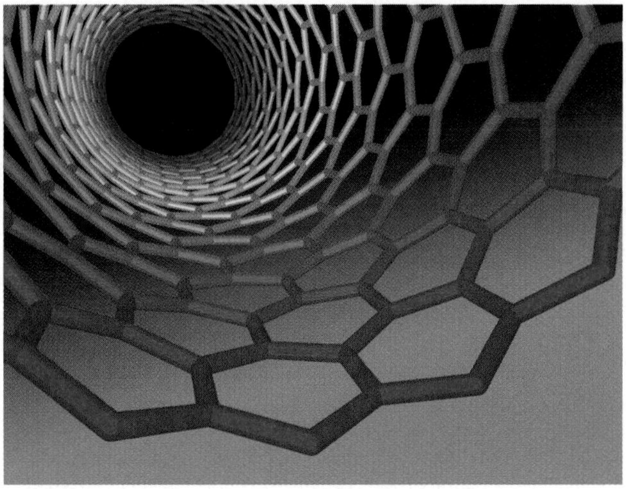

Carbon Nanotube. *The capacity to move data is entering another phase with thin-wall carbon nanotubes to conduct data bits. Nanotubes are one molecule thick—about 1/1,000th of the finest human hair. Technology is proving that Gordon Moore, the so-called godfather of microprocessing, was right in 1965 when he predicted the capacity of computers to move data would double every 18 months. Incredibly, we also are growing the capacity to store it all.*

Gordon Moore

The new challenge is organizing the digitized material to facilitate access. Good-bye to the Dewey decimal and other indexing systems. Digitized materials can be searched in infinite ways—not just titles and authors and subjects but even passages. Book retailer Amazon.com has dabbled with searches for passages and phrases in books in its inventory.

The Google project has raised issues about who owns published works. With Shakespeare and Aristotle, the core works have long been in the public domain and, in effect, belong to everyone. Old-line media companies have resisted Google's digitizing more recent works on grounds that publishers and authors have exclusive rights to control their dissemination—and to charge for it. The issue is a core one involving copyright protection, which involves almost all media products. A fundamental question is whether the concept of encouraging creative production by offering creators the incentive of profiting from their work has been rendered obsolete.

CHECKING YOUR MEDIA LITERACY

- **Why are many book publishers and authors concerned over the Google Print Library project?**
- **How can the Google Print Library possibly have room for every book ever printed?**

WIKIPEDIA

The archival potential of digitization has been demonstrated by Wikipedia, an online encyclopedia whose users volunteer the articles, which then go through a free-wheeling editing process by fellow users. In its first eight years the collaborative process generated 2.9 million articles in English and almost five times that many in additional languages. The scope of the endeavor, and also the process, could not have been fathomed as practicable even a few years before.

The impact: Bound encyclopedias like the Britannica, currently at 32 volumes, have become the digital era's horse and buggy. Traditional encyclopedia companies are in crisis. How can Britannica, with overhead that includes 100 full-time and 4,000 expert contributors, compete against Wiki? Even a DVD edition drawn from various Britannica versions has but 120,000 entries—impressive by earlier standards but a pale one-25th of Wiki's total in English alone.

The collaborative model is not without its critics. While many—perhaps the majority—of Wikipedia entries are generally accurate, mistakes, inaccuracies and even deliberate falsehoods can flourish unchecked in the online environment. For that reason, Wikipedia is not yet considered an acceptable source of information for most school or college papers, much less professional research.

The effect of a 2009 decision at Wiki to add professional staff editors is unclear. The goal is to improve entries in general.

CHECKING YOUR MEDIA LITERACY

- **Contrast the Wikipedia collaborative process with how the Britannica is edited.**

NEWS RECORD

School teachers once lectured students that a knowledgeable citizen read several newspapers a day to be well-informed. While once good advice, every student today has easy access online to dozens of news sources—and to digitized archives of earlier news. Yesterday's newspaper no longer is used to wrap up leftover fish from dinner for the garbage. The new digital version is archived for reference in perpetuity. It's the same with magazines.

Internet-only news services may tout their latest coverage, but posterity will value the archives. A paperless age for news is upon us.

CHECKING YOUR MEDIA LITERACY

- **What advantage do digital archives of news have over traditional news archives?**

New-Style, Old-Style News

MEDIA PEOPLE

Could it be that old-style personality-driven journalism can make it in the digital age? Take a look at the liberal-leaning *Huffington Post,* an Internet news site begun in 2005. Flashy headlines, with sharp witticisms and exclamation points, hark back to the days of muckraking. *HuffPo* is a rich, unpredictable brew of breaking news and pop culture. Coverage of Sarah Palin's hair ranks next to a piece on a new Supreme Court justice. For founder and editor-in-chief Arianna Huffington, it's been a winning combination.

The site was conceived in 2005 as a foil to the politically right-wing *Drudge Report.* By Election Day 2008 it was the ninth-most-visited news site online (Drudge was fourth; Washington post.com, 11th).

Its worth has been estimated at $90 million.

HuffPo's success is partly anchored in its understanding of the unique nature of the Internet. Importantly, there also is Huffington's personality and her connections.

Arianna Huffington didn't start out as a liberal. Born Arianna Stassinopoulos, she moved from Greece to London with her mother to attend Cambridge University. She became enamored with the debating society and eventually rose to its presidency. She told *New Yorker* magazine: "I went to every debate. I must literally have sat there with my mouth open. I was so spellbound by the spectacle of great speakers and people being moved or angered by their words."

Huffington has written 12 books, including a biography of opera soprano Maria Callas. That book was Huffington's admission ticket to New York high society. Soon she knew almost everyone who was anybody, and married Michael Huffington, an oil multimillionaire. Barbara Walters was a bridesmaid. The Huffingtons moved to Washington, where Michael worked for the Reagan administration as deputy assistant secretary of defense. Arianna stumped for her Republican husband in an unsuccessful bid for the U.S. Senate in 1994. After the campaign, Michael wanted to fade into obscurity, but Arianna was ready to hit the big-time. They agreed to divorce.

After the break-up of her marriage, Huffington did an about-face and took on liberal causes. She ran for governor of California but withdrew before the election. Then she found her calling with *HuffPo.* A year later, in 2006, she was named to *Time*'s list of the 100 most influential people in the world.

She runs *HuffPo* from her home in the wealthy neighborhood of Brentwood near Los Angeles. The operation has 55 paid staffers. Twenty-eight are in editorial, including Huffington. Compare that to the 1,000-plus at the New York *Times.* In addition, *HuffPo* has six paid and 11,000 unpaid "citizen journalists." *HuffPo* also has 3,000 bloggers, many of them her former political foes.

Basically an aggregator site, *HuffPo* rehashes a couple of paragraphs from other sources and then links to the original story. The home page often features stories from the Associated Press and blogs from the opinionated and famous. Although *HuffPo* has been credited with an occasional scoop, most stories are ripped from other sources.

Predictably, traditional media take umbrage with the practice, likening it to "stealing." Huffington is quick to note that the original sources pick up "millions of page views" from *HuffPo* links, implying that the originating sites should be grateful. She says, "The question for newspapers is how they monetize those links." Huffington likes to say that *HuffPo* "curates" the news, finding good stuff and "artfully" exhibiting it.

Time magazine says Huffington's success is based in her ability to reinvent herself when needed, this time from Bush-bashing pundit into a media mogul and digital pioneer. Huffington sees *HuffPo* as the future of journalism. She may be onto something: The no less famous Tina Brown launched her news and culture aggregator site *The Daily Beast* in 2008.

WHAT DO YOU THINK?

- Are aggregator sites the future of journalism? Why?
- Would sites like *Huffington Post* be as prominent with less visible, less well-connected founders?

Arianna Huffington. *A master at self-reinvention, she is reigning now as editor-in-chief of the liberal* Huffington Post *news site. Starting from scratch in 2005,* HuffPo *has become a major destination for news served up in ways that the once-Republican and conservative Huffington could not have anticipated in earlier days.*

CHAPTER WRAP-UP

Portals (Pages 186–187)

- Desktop computers became a standard household appliance in the 1980s. A gateway to the Internet opened for millions of people. Everybody sensed a new media landscape was being formed. One popular idea, epitomized by America Online, was modeled loosely on subscribing to a newspaper or magazine. With a subscription, people would buy access to a rich array of online material from AOL or a competing "walled garden" of content. That concept disintegrated with the introduction of browsers like Netscape, which gave everybody—geeky and otherwise—access beyond walled gardens.

Search Engines (Pages 187–190)

- The Internet was so vast—and also growing—that it was easy to get lost. Search engines were the answer. Software tracked the Internet and clumped sites by subjects. Computer users could type in a search term and their search engine would rank hundreds of relevant sites. Google became dominant, listing as many as 1,000 possible sites every search and making the new media landscape navigable.

Messaging (Pages 190–192)

- The Internet became a major artery for interpersonal communication. E-mail ranks with the Postal Service and the telephone for communicating from Point A to Point B and also for mass communication. A variant, texting with portable telephones, added mobility to communication.

User-Generated Sites (Pages 193–196)

- Software that allowed anyone with a computer and a modem to upload content was the last nail in the coffin of the "walled-garden" concept. No longer did media companies have a monopoly on content. Blogging became a national, indeed global, pastime. Facebook and Myspace facilitated an online presence for millions of people. YouTube made everybody a movie producer or, gee whiz, a star. Twittering stands to transform participatory communication profoundly.

Online Commerce (Pages 196–198)

- The founders of the Internet had a typically American disdain for filthy lucre. They didn't want commerce to taint their wonderful new medium for communication. Another American value, capitalism, emerged as dominant. Today the Internet is a primary vehicle for commerce with online catalogues and ordering, auctions and product downloads. Rare is a company without an online presence to, at minimum, promote itself.

Online Domination (Pages 198–199)

- The search engine Google mapped the Internet and made it functional for everyday use. By selling on-screen advertising space, Google became a media juggernaut financially. But the social networking site Facebook has a potential and huge advantage in attracting advertisers. Facebook maps not the Internet but Internet users and has amassed incredible quantities of data to help advertisers target potential customers with unprecedented precision. Facebook users keep pumping personal data in Facebook servers and updating it regularly.

Games (Pages 199–202)

- The video game industry has surpassed the music industry in sales and is gaining on movies and books. Interactivity among players has created huge audience. In one month, players of the real-life simulation game *Second Life* spent 28.3 million hours "in world."

Online Archives (Pages 203–205)

- Digitization enables the storage of incredible quantities of data. Would you believe every word published in human history? Who needs bricks-and-mortar libraries with miles of shelf space? Every breaking news story, including text, image, audio and video, can be archived for posterity and almost instant retrieval. The effect of digital archiving on traditional media is enriching new content with readily available background. One example: Consider how illuminating an interview can be when a journalist plays back a politician's words from last week, last month, last year or the last campaign: "Yes, senator, how do square what you said today with what you said last January? Take a listen."

Review Questions

1. How did browsers doom the walled-garden business model for the Internet?
2. Why are search engines essential for making full use of the Internet?
3. How are e-mailing and texting different? Similar?
4. What new dimension has user-based content added to the new media landscape?
5. How has commerce become the economic driver of Internet growth?
6. Contrast the potential of Google and Facebook in attracting advertising into the future.
7. When do video games become mass communication rather than a solitary activity?
8. How is digitized data storage enriching mass communication and society and culture?

Concepts

behavioral targeting (Page 199)
passed links (Page 195)
user-generated content (Page 193)
walled garden (Page 186)

Terms

advergames (Page 201)
browser (Page 186)
dot-com bust (Page 190)
search engine (Page 187)
Twitter (Page 194)

People

David Filo, Jerry Yang (Page 188)
Marc Andreessen (Page 186)
Pierre Omidyar (Page 197)
Sergey Brin, Larry Page (Page 187)

Media Sources

- Jean Burgess and Joshua Green with Henry Jenkins and John Hartley. *YouTube: Online Video and Participatory Culture*. Polity, 2009. The authors, all scholars, argue that YouTube is an important vehicle for social critique in the new participatory culture.
- Jack Goldsmith and Tim Wu. *Who Controls the Internet?: Illusions of a Borderless World.* Oxford University Press, 2006. Goldsmith and Wu see cracks in the widespread notion that governments are powerless at controlling Internet content.
- J. Storrs Hall. *Nanofuture.* Prometheus, 2005. Certain that technology challenges can be overcome, Hall, a futurist with a software background, waxes enthusiastic about the ability of individual constructs of atoms to be manufactured to create any and everything.
- David Bondanis. *Electric Universe.* Crown, 2005. Bondanis, who teaches mathematical physics at Oxford, offers a parallel to the Internet's quick remaking of the world by chronicling the 19th century inventions of Michael Faraday, Samuel Morse and Alan Turning.

NEW MEDIA LANDSCAPE

In this chapter you have deepened your media literacy by revisiting several themes. Here are thematic highlights from the chapter:

MEDIA TECHNOLOGY

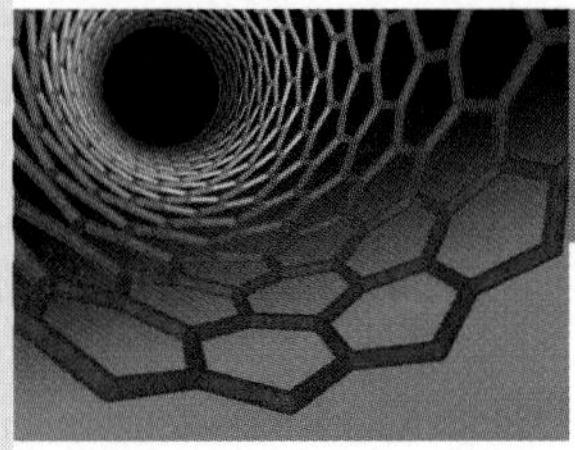

Age of Refinement. The technologies transforming the mass media landscape are in place. Next will be cascades of refinements and improvements. Expect more speed, more capacity, more applications.

Change arrives rapidly with each new development in the underlying technologies of computers and the Internet. Portals grew few walled gardens. They became public parks where everyone was invited to play on new laptops with wi-fi access. Starting with the World Wide Web protocols of Tim Berners-Lee and Marc Andreessen's revolutionary Netscape browser, the Internet began its domination of new media. E-mail, search engines, social networking, texting, blogging, printing books on-demand, on-call digital storage in online archives, gaming and real-life simulations—each new advancement has been revolutionary. Who knows what will be next? (Pages 186–192)

MEDIA ECONOMICS

Google Guys. Great business wars have been fought already for control of new media businesses. These range from patent battles, marketing deals, copyright court fights. Google founders Larry Page and Sergey Brin are kings of the mountain. Wait 'til next week.

The walled garden business model was innovative for its time, but it was quickly replaced with browser software that allowed anyone access to Internet content. Soon, entrepreneurs saw the potential for making money through the Internet. Google, a powerful search engine, added text-based ads to its search results, and made its founders multimillionaires. Larry Page is worth $18.6 billion, and Sergey Brin is worth $14.1 billion. Yahoo, another powerful search engine, also has made billions for its founders David Filo and Jerry Yang by delivering ads to precise segments of potential customers. Both Yahoo and Google have branched out into e-mail services, social networking and gaming. Social networking sites, like Flikr, Twitter and Facebook, and video sharing sites like YouTube have successfully used ads to generate revenue, usually by directing those ads to users based on lifestyle profiles. Almost every business these days has a web site either to disseminate information or for online commerce. Commercial web sites offer products that can be shipped to customers or downloaded. Auction sites like eBay are another way people are using the Internet to make money. The potential of the Internet for commerce remains largely untapped. It's estimated that only about 10 percent of the annual $500 billion spent on brand advertising globally goes to the Internet, but the Internet's potential for targeted marketing is making inroads in the traditional model for advertising. (Pages 185, 193–195)

MEDIA AND DEMOCRACY

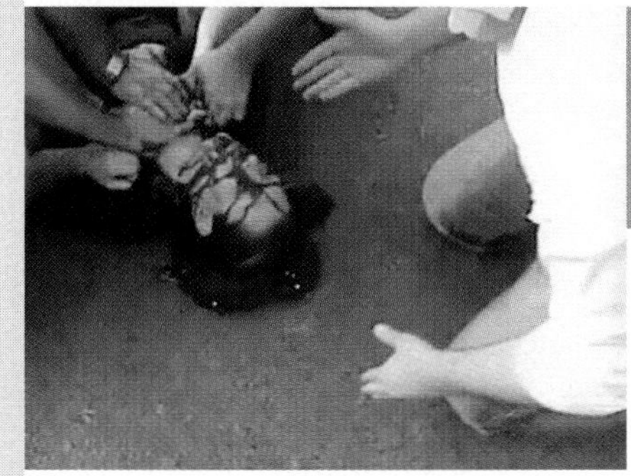

Empowerment. Repressive political regimes remain as brutal as ever in history. But resistance and uprisings have new tools in social network sites. These tools are so fast and visual and ubiquitous, as shown in Iraq, that governments cannot conceal their brutality.

In the 2008 elections, YouTube users could pose questions during presidential debates. Candidates put their messages out to voters through e-mail, YouTube, Facebook and Twitter. Just about anyone can create and distribute content on the Internet. Individuals can open their own blogging sites, or they can send content to social networking sites like Facebook, Twitter, YouTube or Flickr. Unlike traditional media, which relied on trained reporters, anyone with a cell phone or a computer can become a citizen journalist. This has become problematic for authoritarian governments around the world, which regularly try to block access to YouTube and other sites. The advent of user-generated content has had the effect of democratizing the mass media. (Pages 184–185, 191)

MEDIA AND CULTURE

New media have had profound effects on our culture. Hardly anyone still writes letters and sends them through the U.S. mail. E-mail has become the dominant form of communication. We do business, send party invitations, birthday cards and pictures via e-mail. Facebook and other social networking sites keep us in touch with our friends and colleagues. Even when someone lives across the globe, we know what they're having for lunch, who they're dating, and how they're doing in school—and we know almost instantly. We no longer need to look at bulky catalogs for mail-order shopping—we can shop and order online. Researching school papers and finding obscure information is only a few key taps away thanks to powerful search engines and faster connections to the Internet. We can even have a *Second Life* in a parallel Internet world. All of these innovations are not without controversy. Since almost everything we do on the Internet is trackable, advertisers and marketers are anxious to tap that information in spite of the inherent privacy issues. (Pages 190–195)

chapter 8

NEWS

Counter Science *Scholars Jules and Maxwell Boykoff see journalists getting trapped in a desire for balance. For too long, journalists gave equal play to sources lined up by big energy companies to downplay the seriousness of global warming despite overwhelming evidence that it was occurring at a pace accelerated by environmentally reckless human activity. The Boykoffs make the point that truth doesn't necessarily come from tit-for-tat balance of opposing views.*

LEARNING AHEAD

- Many news media practices originated during periods of major change in U.S. history.
- The notion of objectivity in news is vexing.
- Journalists bring personal, social and political values to their work.
- Variables affect what ends up being reported.
- The free-for-all in the new multiplicity of news sources makes for a cacophony.
- Journalistic trends include exploratory reporting, soft news and 24/7 coverage.

WHEN BALANCED REPORTING ISN'T

In a massive study of news coverage on global warming, brothers Jules Boykoff, a political scientist, and Maxwell Boykoff, a geographer, reviewed four leading U.S. newspapers—the New York *Times, Wall Street Journal,* Washington *Post* and Los Angeles *Times*. Over 14 years they identified 3,542 news items, editorials and other articles on global warming. Randomly they chose 636 articles for analysis. Fifty-three percent, more than half, gave equal weight to the opposing views. The easily inferred impression, they said, was that the scientific community was "embroiled in a rip-roaring debate on whether or not humans were contributing to global warming." The fact is, there was no such debate.

How could the news media in their reporting of science be so out of synch with scientists? It's a question at the heart of this chapter on news, which examines definitions of news and, importantly, how media-literate consumers can decide which reporting to trust.

The Boykoffs have a theory about what was wrong: In a sense, as counterintuitive as it seems, journalists try too hard to be fair. "The professional canon of journalistic fairness requires reporters who write about a controversy to present competing points of view," the Boykoffs explained. "Presenting the most compelling arguments of both sides with equal weight is a fundamental check on biased reporting. But this canon causes problems when it is applied to issues of science. It seems to demand that journalists present competing points of view on a scientific question as if they had equal scientific weight, when actually they do not."

The fairness chink in journalistic armor has given special interests an opportunity to manipulate news by making misleading and even false information easily available to reporters who, dutifully if not mindlessly, apply the principle of fairness. A legion of spokespersons, many funded by special interests, end up with roles in journalists' stories. The Boykoffs cite many examples, one being the New York *Times* quoting a global warming skeptic that carbon dioxide emissions aren't a threat to the climate but "a wonderful and unexpected gift from the Industrial Revolution."

Who are these special interests? Former Vice President Al Gore, himself a journalist early in his career, has been blunt: "A relatively small cadre of special interests including Exxon Mobil and a few other oil, coal and utilities companies." Why? "These companies want to prevent any new policies that would interfere with their current business plans that rely on the massive, unrestrained dumping of global-warming pollution of the Earth's atmosphere every hour of every day."

The Boykoffs put it this way: "Balanced reporting has allowed a small group of global-warming skeptics to have their views amplified." Balanced coverage, according to the Boykoffs, has not translated into accurate coverage.

Are journalists dishonest? Jules Boykoff doesn't blame the journalists. Boykoff notes that giant media companies, intent on improving profits, have cut back on newsroom staffs and labor intensive investigative reporting. The result: More and more reporters are called upon to be generalists and are being denied time to build expertise on a complex subject such as climate change.

Journalism Traditions

STUDY PREVIEW

U.S. journalism has evolved through four distinctive eras: the colonial, partisan, penny and yellow periods. Each of these periods made distinctive contributions to contemporary news media practices.

colonial period
From the founding of the colonies to the American Revolution

Benjamin Harris
Published *Publick Occurrences*

Publick Occurrences
First colonial newspaper, Boston, 1690

John Peter Zenger
Defied authorities with his New York *Journal*

COLONIAL PRESS

In the American **colonial period, Benjamin Harris** published the first newspaper, ***Publick Occurrences,*** in Boston in 1690. He was in hot water right away. Harris scandalized Puritan sensitivities by alleging that the king of France had dallied with his son's wife. In the colonies, just as in England, a newspaper needed royal consent. The governor had not consented, and Harris was put out of business after one issue.

Even so, Harris' daring was a precursor for emerging press defiance against authority. In 1733 **John Peter Zenger** started a paper in New York in competition with the existing Crown-supported newspaper. Zenger's New York *Journal* was backed by merchants and lawyers who disliked the royal governor. From the beginning, the newspaper antagonized the governor with items challenging his competence. Finally, the governor arrested Zenger. The trial made history. The jury found for Zenger, who had become a hero for standing up to the Crown. He was freed. To the government's chagrin, there was great public celebration in the streets of New York that night.

Zenger Trial. *Printer John Peter Zenger, in the dock, won his 1735 trial for criticizing New York's royal governor. The victory fed a colonial exuberance that culminated 46 years later in winning the revolution against British rule.*

Zenger's success against the Crown foreshadowed the explosive colonial reaction after Parliament passed a stamp tax in 1765. The colonies did not have elected representatives in Parliament, so the cry was a defiant "No taxation without representation." The campaign, however, was less ideological than economic. It was led by colonial printers, who stood to lose from the new tax, which was levied on printed materials.

These traditions from the colonial period remain today:

- The news media, both print and broadcast, relish their independence from government censorship and control.
- The news media, especially newspapers and magazines, actively try to mold government policy and mobilize public sentiment. Today this is done primarily on the editorial page.
- Journalists are committed to seeking truth no matter who is offended.
- The public comes down in favor of independent news media when government becomes too heavy-handed, as demonstrated by Zenger's popularity.
- In a capitalistic system the news media are economic entities that sometimes react in their own self-interest when their profit-making ability is threatened. Newspaper opposition to the stamp tax illustrates this point.

CHECKING YOUR MEDIA LITERACY

- **The colonial campaign against the 1765 stamp tax has been called the newspaper war against Britain. What does the campaign tell us about the news media?**
- **Both Harris and Zenger were slapped down by colonial governors for their early newspapers, but the cases were dramatically different. Which of these early printers would you regard as more heroic? More important?**

PARTISAN PRESS

After the Revolution, newspapers divided along partisan lines. What is called the Federalist period in U.S. history is also referred to as the partisan period among newspaper historians. Intense partisanship characterized newspapers of the period, which spanned roughly 50 years to the 1830s.

Initially, the issue was over a constitution. Should the nation have a strong central government or remain a loose coalition of states? James Madison, Alexander Hamilton, Thomas Jefferson, John Jay and other leading thinkers exchanged ideas with articles and essays in newspapers. The ***Federalist Papers,*** a series of essays printed and reprinted in newspapers throughout the nation, were part of the debate. Typical of the extreme partisanship of the era were journalists who reveled in nasty barbs and rhetorical excesses. It was not unusual for an ideological opponent to be called a "dog," "traitor," "liar" or "cheat."

Federalist Papers
Essays with diverse views on the form the new nation should take

John Adams
Federalist president

Alien and Sedition acts
Discouraged criticism of government

David Bowen
Punished for criticizing the majority party

After the Constitution was drafted, partisanship intensified, finally culminating lopsidedly when the Federalist party both controlled the Congress and had the party leader, **John Adams,** in the presidency. In firm control and bent on silencing their detractors, the Federalists ramrodded a series of laws through Congress in 1798. One of the things the **Alien and Sedition acts** prohibited was "false, scandalous, malicious" statements about government. Using these laws, the Federalists issued 25 indictments, which culminated in 10 convictions. Among those indicted was **David Bowen,** a Revolutionary War veteran who felt strongly about free expression. He put up a sign in Dedham, Massachusetts: "No stamp tax. No sedition. No alien bills. No land tax. Downfall to tyrants of America. Peace and retirement to the president [the Federalist John Adams]. Long live the vice president [the Anti-Federalist

Thomas Jefferson] and the minority [the Anti-Federalists]. May moral virtues be the basis of civil government." If only criticisms of recent presidents were so mild! But the Federalists were not of a tolerant mind. Bowen was fined $400 and sentenced to 18 months in prison.

Public outrage showed itself in the election of 1800. Jefferson was elected president, and the Federalists were thumped out of office, never to rise again. The people had spoken.

Here are traditions from the partisan period that continue today:

- Government should keep its hands off the press. The First Amendment to the Constitution, which set a tone for this period, declared that "Congress shall make no law . . . abridging freedom . . . of the press."
- The news media are a forum for discussion and debate, as newspapers were in the *Federalist Papers* dialogue on what form the Constitution should take.
- The news media should comment vigorously on public issues.

CHECKING YOUR MEDIA LITERACY

What lesson can political leaders of today draw from public reaction to the Alien and Sedition acts?

PENNY PRESS

Benjamin Day started the penny press period in 1833 with the creation of the *Sun,* which he sold for a penny a copy.

Another leading penny press editor was **James Gordon Bennett,** who, in the 1830s, organized the first newsroom and reporting staff. Earlier newspapers had been either sidelines of printers, who put whatever was handy into their papers, or projects of ideologues, whose writing was in an essay vein. Bennett hired reporters and sent them out on rounds to gather information for readers of his New York *Herald.*

Another penny press editor, **Horace Greeley,** used his newspaper to fight social ills that accompanied industrialization. Greeley's New York *Tribune,* especially in its editorial section, was a voice against poverty and slums, an advocate of labor unions, and an opponent of slavery. It was a lively forum for discussions of ideas. Karl Marx, the communist philosopher, was a *Tribune* columnist for a while. So was Albert Brisbane, who advocated collective living. Firm in Greeley's concept of a newspaper was that it should be used for social good. He saw the *Tribune* as a voice for those who did not have a voice; a defender for those unable to articulate a defense; and a champion for the underdog, the deprived and the underprivileged.

In 1844, late in the penny press period, **Samuel Morse** invented the telegraph. Within months the nation was being wired. When the Civil War came in 1861, correspondents used the telegraph to get battle news to eager readers. It was called **lightning news,** delivered electrically and quickly.

The Civil War also gave rise to a new convention in writing news, the **inverted pyramid.** Editors instructed their war correspondents to tell the most important information first in case telegraph lines failed—or were snipped by the enemy—as a story was being transmitted. That way, when a story was interrupted, editors would have at least a few usable sentences.

The inverted pyramid, it turned out, was popular with readers because it allowed them to learn what was most important at a glance. They did not have to wade through a whole story if they were in a hurry. Also, the inverted pyramid helped editors to fit stories into the limited confines of a page—a story could be cut off at any

Thomas Jefferson
Anti-Federalist president

James Gordon Bennett
Organized the first methodical news coverage

Horace Greeley
Pioneered editorials

Samuel Morse
Invented the telegraph

lightning news
Delivered by telegraph

inverted pyramid
Most important information first

MEDIA PEOPLE

James Gordon Bennett

James Gordon Bennett, a young man seeing the success of Ben Day's penny paper, the New York *Sun*, rounded up $500 and rented a basement. There, in 1835, with a plank across two flour barrels for a desk, a dilapidated press and barely enough type, Bennett produced his own humble penny paper—the New York *Herald*, with pages slightly larger than sheets of a legal pad.

Bennett quickly recognized that being first with news gave him an advantage over competitors. His obsession with getting news to readers quickly brought an emphasis on timeliness as an important element in the concept of news. It also contributed to the fact-oriented telling of news because reporters rushing to get a dispatch together are too pressed to be analytical.

Bennett made a fetish of timeliness. He used small, fast boats to sail out to Sandy Point, on the coast beyond New York, to pick up parcels of newspapers and letters from arriving oceanic ships and then sail back to the city before the ships themselves could arrive and dock. He beat other papers by hours with fresh news.

In one case Bennett himself went to Halifax, Nova Scotia, where many European vessels landed before continuing down the coast. With a news packet in hand he hired a locomotive to take him to Boston, Worcester and New London, where he took a ferry to Long Island, and then another locomotive to New York. That news was days ahead.

The *Herald* was a quick success, surpassing the circulation of Ben Day's *Sun*. Bennett never relented in his quest for quick news. After Samuel Morse invented the telegraph in 1844, Bennett instructed reporters to use the infant network that was being built around the country to send back their dispatches without delay.

Bennett organized the modern newsroom, applying the division of labor principle. Reporters were assigned subjects to cover and were responsible for being first with news on their subjects. These news beats, as they were called, included the police, the courts and other fertile subjects for news. New York, then 150,000 people, was large and complex enough that nothing short of a beat system could come close to comprehensive coverage. It was a recognition that finding a broad audience meant covering a wide range of subjects and issues.

Today's journalism eschews euphemisms and obscurities. So did Bennett. Call a leg a leg, not a limb, he told his reporters. Don't call a shirt a linen. A pantaloon is a pantaloon, not an "unmentionable," which the Victorian morality preferred. Bennett's direct language sparked condemnation from the pulpits, which brought him readers. Bennett was not without eccentricities. When Harriet Agnes Crean agreed to his marriage proposal in 1840, Bennett put it on Page One. The stacked headline:

> To the Readers of the Herald
> Declaration of Love.
> Caught at last.
> Going to Be Married.
> New Movement in Civilization.

Bennett wrote daily dispatches from the honeymoon in Niagara Falls. To say the least, his was a highly personal style of journalism.

WHAT DO YOU THINK?

- It's been said that James Gordon Bennett invented news as we think of it today. How so?
- How did Bennett capitalize on the invention of the telegraph?

Inventor of News. *Bennett organized the first newsroom with reporters assigned to beats. His* Herald *was known for comprehensive, timely coverage.*

paragraph and the most important parts remained intact. The inverted pyramid remains a standard expository form for telling event-based stories in newspapers, radio and television.

CHECKING YOUR MEDIA LITERACY

- **News as we think of it today has roots in the penny press period. What are these roots?**
- **What was the connection between the telegraph and the inverted pyramid?**

Yellow Press

yellow period
Late 1800s; marked by sensationalism

Joseph Pulitzer
Emphasized human interest in newspapers; later sensationalized

Nellie Bly
Stunt reporter

The quest to sell more copies led to excesses that are illustrated by the Pulitzer–Hearst circulation war in New York in the 1890s, in what came to be known as the **yellow period.**

Joseph Pulitzer, a poor immigrant, made the St. Louis *Post-Dispatch* into a financial success. In 1883 Pulitzer decided to try a bigger city. He bought the New York *World* and applied his St. Louis formula. He emphasized human interest, crusaded for worthy causes and ran lots of promotional hoopla. Pulitzer's *World* also featured solid journalism. His star reporter, **Nellie Bly,** epitomized the two faces of the Pulitzer formula for journalistic success. For one story Bly feigned mental illness, entered an insane asylum and emerged with scandalous tales about how patients were treated. It was enterprising journalism of great significance. Reforms resulted. Later, showing the less serious, show-biz side of Pulitzer's formula, Nellie Bly was sent out to circle the globe in 80 days, like Jules Verne's fictitious Phileas Fogg. Her journalism stunt took 72 days.

Yellow Journalism's Namesake. *The* Yellow Kid, *a popular cartoon character in New York newspapers, was the namesake for the sensationalist "yellow journalism" of the 1880s and 1890s. Many newspapers of the period, especially in New York, hyperbolized and fabricated the news to attract readers. The tradition remains in isolated areas of modern journalism, like the supermarket tabloids and trash documentary programs on television.*

Stunt Journalism. *When newspaper owner Joseph Pulitzer sent reporter Nellie Bly on an around-the-world trip in 1890 to try to outdo the fictional Phileas Fogg's 80-day trip, stunt journalism was approaching its peak. Her feat took 72 days.*

In San Francisco, Pulitzer had a young admirer, **William Randolph Hearst.** With his father's Nevada mining fortune and mimicking Pulitzer's New York formula, Hearst made the San Francisco *Examiner* a great success. In 1895 Hearst decided to go to New York and take on the master. He bought the New York *Journal* and vowed to "out-Pulitzer" Pulitzer. The inevitable resulted. To outdo each other, Pulitzer and Hearst launched crazier and crazier stunts. Not even the comic pages escaped the competitive frenzy. Pulitzer ran the *Yellow Kid,* and then Hearst hired the cartoonist away. Pulitzer hired a new one, and both papers ran the yellow character and plastered the city with yellow promotional posters. The circulation war was nicknamed "yellow journalism," and the term came to be a derisive reference to sensational excesses in news coverage.

The yellow excesses reached a feverish peak as Hearst and Pulitzer covered the growing tensions between Spain and the United States. Fueled by hyped atrocity stories, the tension eventually exploded in war. One story, perhaps apocryphal, epitomizes the no-holds-barred competition between Pulitzer and Hearst. Although Spain had consented to all demands by the United States, Hearst sent the

Joseph Pulitzer

William Randolph Hearst

Journalistic Sensationalism. *Rival New York newspaper publishers Joseph Pulitzer and William Randolph Hearst tried to outdo each other daily with anti-Spanish atrocity stories from Cuba, many of them trumped up. Some historians say the public hysteria fueled by Pulitzer and Hearst helped to precipitate the Spanish-American War, especially after the U.S. battleship* Maine *exploded in Havana harbor. Both Pulitzer and Hearst claimed that it was a Spanish attack on an American vessel, although a case can be made that the explosion was accidental.*

artist **Frederic Remington** to Cuba to cover the situation. Remington cabled back: "Everything is quiet. There is no trouble here. There will be no war. Wish to return." Hearst replied: "Please remain. You furnish the pictures. I'll furnish the war."

William Randolph Hearst
Built circulation with sensationalism

Frederic Remington
News illustrator whose work included Spanish-American War

jazz journalism
Updated yellow journalism, often in tabloid format and featuring photography

The yellow tradition still lives. The New York *Daily News,* founded in 1919 and almost an immediate hit, ushered in a period that some historians characterize as **jazz journalism.** It was just Hearst and Pulitzer updated in tabloid form with an emphasis on photography. Today, newspapers like the commercially successful *National Enquirer* are in the yellow tradition.

CHECKING YOUR MEDIA LITERACY

- **What stunt journalism have you seen in recent months that would make Nellie Bly proud?**
- **News that's sensationalized beyond what the facts warrant can be dangerous. Give an example from the yellow press period. Can you cite recent examples from your experience?**

Concept of News

STUDY PREVIEW

News is a report on change that survives the competition for reporting other change that is occurring. What ends up being reported is the result of news judgments by reporters and editors who package their regular updates on what they believe their audiences need and want to know.

DEFINITION OF NEWS

Ask anybody: "What's news?" Everybody thinks they know, but press them and you'll hear a lot of fumbling. So why is consensus elusive about something as much a part of everyday life as news? In part it's because the U.S. Constitution forbids government from interfering with almost anything that the media report. This freedom has led to diverse presentations under the label of news. Compare the outrageous tabloid *News of the World*, which for many years reported on alien creatures visiting earthly celebrities weekly, and the New York *Times*, the pillar of U.S. daily journalism. Not even mainstream media report events and issues in lockstep.

A useful definition of news involves two concepts—news and newsworthiness.

In short, **news** is a report on change. This is no more apparent than in traditional newspaper headlines, which contain a verb—the vehicle in a language to denote change:

Obama wins Democratic Iowa caucus
Roadside Iraq bombs kill four soldiers
Paris Hilton *leaves* jail a "new person"

Not all change can fit into the limited time in a newscast or the limited space in a newspaper. Nor does all change warrant audience time online. So what change makes the news? Journalists apply the concept of **newsworthiness** to rank change. When Barack Obama sniffles, it's change—and the whole world cares. A lot is at stake. For most of us, when we sniffle, only Mom cares. Applying a newsworthiness test to a series of events that might be reported requires judgment. No two people will assign all priorities the same. See for yourself: Rank these hypothetical events by newsworthiness and ask a friend to do the same:

Yankees win World Series
Congress votes to remove Mexico fence
Navy launches new aircraft carrier
Bin Laden found dead in Afghan mountains
Scientology founder returns from dead
Airline crash kills 220 in Kenya

A lot of factors go into determining newsworthiness—proximity to audience, prominence of people involved, timeliness, impact on society, even the so-called gee-whiz factor. But there is no clinical formula for newsworthiness. A subjective element flowing from journalists' values and sense of the world and sense of audience is at the heart of what is reported and how it's reported.

CHECKING YOUR MEDIA LITERACY

- **News is a report on change, but clearly more change is occurring than is possible to report. What principles do journalists apply to identify change that most merits reporting?**
- **Why is it unavoidable that journalists disagree among themselves on what merits being reported on a given day?**

news
A report on change

newsworthiness
A ranking of news that helps decide what makes it into news packages

objectivity
A concept in journalism that news should be gathered and told value-free

OBJECTIVITY

Despite the high quotient of judgment in deciding what changes to report, a lot of people use the term ***objectivity*** to describe news. By this they mean a value-free process in making choices about what to tell and how to tell it. It's a self-contradictory concept: Choice, by definition, is never value-free. So how did we end up with this idea that news should be objective when it cannot be? History has the answer.

- **Penny Press.** Part of the answer goes back to the era of Ben Day and his New York *Sun,* the first of the penny papers with a mass audience. Day looked for stories with mass appeal. Suddenly, what made the paper was not the opinionated ramblings of the preceding partisan press but stories chosen to appeal to the largest possible audience. Opinion was out, storytelling in. The writer became subordinate to the tale, even to the point of near-invisibility. No more first person. Facts carried the story.
- **Associated Press.** Several cost-conscious New York newspaper publishers agreed in 1848 to a joint venture to cover distant news. The Associated Press, as they called the venture, saved a lot of money. It also transformed U.S. journalism in a way that was never anticipated. Inherent in the AP concept was that its stories needed to be nonpartisan to be usable by all of its member newspapers, whose political persuasions spanned the spectrum. The result was an emphasis, some say fetish, on fact-driven journalism devoid of even a hint of partisanship.
- **Newspaper Economics.** Another fundamental shift cemented the detached, neutral AP tone, often characterized as objective. News became profitable—highly so. The fortune that Benjamin Day made with the New York *Sun* in the mid-1830s was puny compared with the Pulitzer, Hearst and other news empires that came within 50 years. These super-publishers saw their newspapers as money machines as much as political tools. The bottom line gradually and inevitably gained more weight. The safest route to continue building their mass audiences and enhancing revenue was to avoid antagonizing readers and advertisers. There was money to be made in presenting news in as neutral a tone as possible. Picking up a lesson from the AP, but with a different motivation—to make money rather than save money—profit-driven publishers came to favor information-driven news.

By the early 20th century, when news practices became institutionalized in the first journalism textbooks and in the formation of professional organizations, the notion of a detached, neutral presentation was firmly ensconced. Ethics codes, new at the time, dismissed other approaches as unacceptable and unethical, even though they had been dominant only three generations earlier. The word *objectivity* became a newsroom mantra.

To be sure, there are exceptions to the detached, neutral presentation, but traditionalists are quick to criticize the departures. The goal is to keep the reporter, even the reporter's inherently necessary judgment, as invisible in the presentation as possible.

CHECKING YOUR MEDIA LITERACY

◇ **How did so many people come to the vexatious opinion that news should be objective?**

Personal Values in News

STUDY PREVIEW

Journalists make important decisions on which events, phenomena and issues are reported and which are not. The personal values journalists bring to their work and that therefore determine which stories are told, and also how they are told, generally coincide with mainstream American values.

ROLE OF THE JOURNALIST

Even with the values-free pretext under which most U.S. journalism functions, values cannot be wished out of existence. The fact is that journalists make choices. NBC newscaster Chet Huntley, after years of trying to come up with a definition of

MEDIA TIMELINE

NEWS MILESTONES / PIVOTAL EVENTS

1700s

Zenger Trial
Colonial jury freed John Peter Zenger (1735)

Stamp Tax
Colonial newspapers campaigned against stamp tax (1760s)

Challenged the Crown

- Puritans established Cambridge Press (1638)
- French and Indian wars (1689–1763)
- *Publick Occurrences,* first colonial newspaper (1690)
- First colonial magazines (1741)
- Revolutionary War (1776–1781)

1800s

Penny Press
Ben Day founded New York *Sun,* first penny paper (1833)

Modern News
James Gordon Bennett pioneered systematic news coverage (1840s)

Editorials
Horace Greeley established editorial page (1841)

Telegraph
Samuel Morse invented the telegraph (1844)

Yellow Press
Sensationalistic excesses (1880s)

Penny press, unprecedented mass audiences

Yellow Kid, the cartoon namesake for an era

- Public education took root as a social value (1820s)
- Factory jobs fueled urban growth (1830s–)
- Waves of immigration added to urbanization (1830s–)
- U.S. Civil War (1861–1865)
- Populism widened effective political participation (1880s–)
- Spanish-American War (1898)

1900s

Muckraking
Ida Tarbell and journalism aimed at reform (1902–)

Radio
Presidential returns were broadcast (1916)

Watergate
Confidential sources became issue in reporting the Watergate scandal (1972)

Television
CNN introduced 24-hour television news (1980)

Television Construction
Local stations trim staffs, budgets with collapsing advertising base (2008)

Newspaper Industry Collapse
Denver daily *Rocky Mountain News* prints last edition (2009)

New York Daily News, *reporting Watergate*

- Radio emerged as commercial medium (late 1920s)
- Great Depression (1930s)
- World War II (1941–1945)
- Russian-Western Cold War (1945–1989)
- Television emerged as commercial medium (early 1950s)
- Vietnam war (1964–1973)
- Internet emerged as commercial medium (late 1990s)

2000s

Iraq War
Government manipulation intensified as people took issue with the information used to justify war (2005)

- 9/11 terrorist attacks (2001)
- Iraq war (2003–)
- Hurricane Katrina (2005)

news, threw up his hands and declared: "News is what I decide is news." Huntley wasn't being arrogant. Rather, he was pointing out that there are no clinical criteria for news that sidestep human judgment on what to put in the paper or on the air. Even if an event has intrinsic qualities as news, such as the prominence of the people involved and the event's consequence and drama, it becomes news only when it's reported. Huntley's point was that the journalist's judgment is indispensable in deciding what is news.

Huntley's conclusion underscores the high degree of autonomy that individual journalists have in shaping what is reported. Even a reporter hired fresh out of college by a small daily newspaper and assigned to city hall has a great deal of independence in deciding what to report and how to report it. Such trust is unheard of in most other fields, which dole out responsibility to newcomers in small bits over a lengthy period. Of course, rookie journalists are monitored by their newsroom supervisors, and editors give them assignments and review their stories, but it is the city hall reporter, no matter how green, who is the news organization's expert on city government.

The First Amendment guarantee of a free press also contributes to the independence and autonomy that characterize news work. Journalists know that they have a high level of constitutional protection in deciding what to report as news. While most reporters will agree on the newsworthiness of some events and issues, such as a catastrophic storm or a tax proposal, their judgments will result in stories that take different slants and angles. On events and issues whose newsworthiness is less obvious, reporters will differ even on whether to do a story.

CHECKING YOUR MEDIA LITERACY

- **What personal values would shape your judgment as a journalist?**
- **In what kinds of situations would you expect your values to influence your reporting?**

JOURNALISTS' PERSONAL VALUES

The journalistic ideal, an unbiased seeking of truth and an unvarnished telling of it, dictates that the work be done without partisanship. Yet as human beings, journalists have personal values that influence all that they do, including their work. Because the news judgment decisions that journalists make are so important to an informed citizenry, we need to know what makes these people tick. Are they left-wingers? Are they ideological zealots? Are they quirky and unpredictable? Are they conscientious?

As a sociologist who studied stories in the American news media for 20 years, **Herbert Gans** concluded that journalists have a typical American values system. Gans identified primary values, all in the American mainstream, that journalists use in making their news judgments:

>> Ethnocentrism. American journalists see things through American eyes, which colors news coverage. In the 1960s and 1970s, Gans noted, North Vietnam was consistently characterized as "the enemy." U.S. reporters took the view of the U.S. government and military, which was hardly detached or neutral. This **ethnocentrism** was clear at the end of the war, which U.S. media headlined as "the *fall* of South Vietnam." By other values, Gans said, the communist takeover of Saigon could be considered a *liberation*. In neutral terms, it was a *change in government*.

This ethnocentrism creates problems as the news media become more global. In the 2003 Iraq war, news reporters embedded with U.S. units advancing toward Iraq used the term "the enemy" for Iraqi resistance, which was hardly neutral considering that many Iraqis regarded the invading army as the enemy. It is hard for all people, including journalists, to transcend their own skins.

Herbert Gans
Concluded that journalists have mainstream values

ethnocentrism
Seeing things on the basis of personal experience, values

>> Democracy and Capitalism. Gans found that U.S. journalists favor U.S.-style democracy. Coverage of other governmental forms dwells on corruption, conflict, protest and bureaucratic malfunction. The unstated idea of most U.S. journalists, said Gans, is that other societies do best when they follow the American ideal of serving the public interest.

Gans also found that U.S. journalists are committed to the capitalist economic system. When they report corruption and misbehavior in U.S. business, journalists treat them as aberrations. The underlying posture of the news coverage of the U.S. economy, Gans said, is "an optimistic faith" that businesspeople refrain from unreasonable profits and gross exploitation of workers or customers while competing to create increased prosperity for all. In covering controlled foreign economies, U.S. journalists emphasize the downside.

It may seem only natural to most Americans that democracy and capitalism should be core values of any reasonable human being. This sense itself is an ethnocentric value, which many people do not even think about but which nonetheless shapes how they conduct their lives. Knowing that U.S. journalists by and large share this value explains a lot about the news coverage they create.

>> **Small-Town Pastoralism.** Like most of their fellow citizens, U.S. journalists romanticize rural life. Given similar stories from metropolitan Portland and tiny Sweet Home, Oregon, editors usually opt for the small town.

Cities are covered as places with problems; rural life is celebrated. Suburbs are largely ignored. Gans' understanding of small-town pastoralism helped explain the success of the late Charles Kuralt's *On the Road* series on CBS television.

>> **Individualism Tempered by Moderation.** Gans found that U.S. journalists love stories about rugged individuals who overcome adversity and defeat powerful forces. This is a value that contributes to a negative coverage of technology as something to be feared because it can stifle individuality. Gans again cited the long-running CBS series *On the Road,* in which Charles Kuralt presented pastoral features on rugged individuals. Today the *Everybody Has a Story* series by Steve Hartman serves the same role at CBS.

Journalists like to turn ordinary individuals into heroes, but there are limits. Rebels and deviates are portrayed as extremists who go beyond another value: moderation. To illustrate this bias toward moderation. Gans noted that "the news treats atheists as extremists and uses the same approach, if more gingerly, with religious fanatics. People who consume conspicuously are criticized, but so are people such as hippies who turn their backs on consumer goods. The news is scornful both of the overly academic scholar and the oversimplifying popularizer. It is kind neither to highbrows nor to lowbrows, to users of jargon or users of slang. College students who play when they should study receive disapproval, but so do 'grinds.' Lack of moderation is wrong, whether it involves excesses or abstention."

In politics, Gans said, both ideologues and politicians who lack ideology are treated with suspicion: "Political candidates who talk openly about issues may be described as dull; those who avoid issues entirely evoke doubts about their fitness for office."

>> **Social Order.** Journalists cover disorder—earthquakes, hurricanes, industrial catastrophes, protest marches, the disintegrating nuclear family and transgressions of laws and mores. This coverage, noted Gans, is concerned not with glamorizing disorder but with finding ways to restore order. Coverage of a hurricane, for example, lasts not much longer than the storm, but coverage of the recovery goes on for days. The media focus is far more on restoring order than on covering death and destruction.

The journalistic commitment to social order also is evident in how heavily reporters rely on people in leadership roles as primary sources of information. These leaders, largely representing the Establishment and the status quo, are the people in the best position to maintain social order and to restore it if there's disruption. This means government representatives often shape news media reports and thus their audiences' understanding of what is important, "true" or meaningful. No one

MEDIA PEOPLE

Seymour Hersh

Seymour Hersh broke a story about U.S. soldiers wiping out a remote village of civilians during the Vietnam war. Finding official denials everywhere he turned, Hersh tracked veterans to their homes after their tours of duty to piece together an account of the horrible incident. Becoming known as the My Lai Massacre, it led, as it should have, to court-martials. But the story so embarrassed the Pentagon that Hersh became a pariah in top Pentagon circles. Even so, he was so respected for his dogged truth-seeking that knowledgeable sources within the Pentagon and the Central Intelligence Agency continued to feed him leads on other stories.

Hersh was no one-shot wonder with his 1969 My Lai stories. En route to becoming one of the pre-eminent investigative reporters of our time, he focused on clandestine operations of the U.S. government. These included the CIA's covert role in the overthrow of Salvador Allende in Chile. Hersh exposed secret bombing in Cambodia that had been authorized by presidential aide Henry Kissinger.

In 2004 in the *New Yorker* magazine Hersh exposed prisoner abuses at the Abu Ghraib prison in Iraq. Even though the Pentagon's initial response was to label Hersh's Abu Ghraib account "outlandish and conspiratorial," the photos that Hersh showed could not be ignored.

In 1975, when Donald Rumsfeld was President Ford's chief of staff, he and Dick Cheney, then a high administration official, exchanged memos on how to contain damaging reporting by Hersh. At the time Hersh was with the New York *Times*. In new positions in the second Bush administration—Rumsfeld as secretary of defense, Cheney as vice president—they were no less angry at Hersh. But despite the denials and pooh-poohing of Hersh's revelations, the accuracy of Hersh's reporting still was proving unshakable. No matter how hard the Pentagon tried at the highest levels to make Hersh an outsider, he has become, in fact, an insider. Sources came to him, especially, it seems, midlevel and some senior civilian and military leaders in the defense establishment with grudges against President Bush for ignoring their experience and advice in setting new policy courses, including the Iraq war.

Hersh has won five George Polk awards for journalistic integrity and investigative reporting in magazine reporting. It's no wonder that when Hersh speaks, people listen. Sometimes, he admits he is too loose-lipped when speaking, as happened in an address at the University of Minnesota in 2009. For a future book he said he was working on an "executive assassinating ring" that reported directly to Vice President Dick Cheney. It was a bombshell assertion.

Later Hersh backed off the claim but hardly retracted. He said his comment arose from reporting he is doing for a book that might be a year or two away and that he wants to dig deeper so the point is "effective, that is, empirical, for even the most skeptical."

Caught in a similar lapse in an earlier speech, Hersh conceded that he allows himself leeway in speaking, especially if in unscripted question-answer sessions, that he would never take in his writing: "I can't fudge what I write. But I can certainly fudge what I say." He explained too that he will blur information to protect his sources. "Sometimes I change events, dates and places in a certain way to protect people."

WHAT DO YOU THINK?

- For 40 years White House news secretaries have found themselves denying information dug up by Seymour Hersh. In the end, Hersh has always been right. If you were the White House news secretary, how would you respond to a new and embarrassing revelation from Hersh about secret military operations?
- What sets Hersh's reporting apart from that of most other reporters?

Military Beat. *Hersh's scoops began with the My Lai Massacre in the Vietnam war and have continued through the Abu Ghraib prison torture during the war in Iraq.*

Because all reporting is investigative in the sense that it seeks truth through inquiry, the term *investigative reporting* is tricky. Here is a useful definition:

- A story that would not have been revealed without the enterprise of a reporter.
- A story that is pieced together from diverse and often obscure sources.
- A story that may be contrary to the version from officials, who might have tried to conceal the truth.

Examples:

St. Louis *Post-Dispatch*	Police routinely write up sex crimes not as official reports but as informal memos, which aren't included in crime statistics.
Seattle *Post-Intelligencer*	Oil companies have sidestepped environment-sensitive regulations imposed after the *Exxon Valdez* shipwreck disaster that spoiled an Alaska bay.
South Florida Sun-Sentinel	Inspectors hired by the government to enter Hurricane Katrina-damaged homes to verify damage claims included criminals convicted of robbery, embezzlement and drug dealing.

Investigative Journalism. *Dogged pursuit of meticulous factual detail became a new wrinkle in 20th-century journalism after* Washington Post *reporters Carl Bernstein and Bob Woodward unearthed the Watergate scandal. For months they pursued tips that a break-in at the Democratic Party national headquarters in the Watergate hotel, office and apartment complex in Washington, D.C., had been authorized high in the Republican White House and that the White House then had tried to cover it up. In the end, for the first time in U.S. history, a president, Richard Nixon, resigned.*

receives more media attention than the president of the United States, who is seen, said Gans, "as the ultimate protector of order."

CHECKING YOUR MEDIA LITERACY

- **Which of the values that Herbert Gans attributed to American journalists do you share?**
- **What additional values do you hold?**

JOURNALISTIC BIAS

Critics of the news media come in many flavors. Conservatives are the most vocal, charging that the media slant news to favor Democrats and liberal causes. Numerous studies, some shoddily partisan, others not, fuel the conservatives' accusations. Although his work is dated, Ken Walsh of *U.S. News & World Report* is often quoted for a survey that found 50 White House correspondents had voted Democratic and only seven Republican in 1996. To be sure, some news organizations offer partisan spin, for years most notably the Washington *Times*. More recently Fox News took a lesson from the most successful talk-radio shows and intentionally positioned itself to appeal to right-wing viewers.

In general, though, most U.S. newsrooms pride themselves on neutral presentation and go to extraordinary lengths to prove it. To avoid confusion between straight news and commentary, newspaper opinion pieces are set apart in clearly labeled editorial sections. Broadcast commentaries are also flagged.

>> **Professional Standards.** Most news reporters, even those with left or right leanings, profess a zealous regard for detached, neutral reporting. In the United States this is the journalistic creed, embodied in every professional code of ethics. Almost all reporters see their truth-seeking as unfettered by partisanship. In self-flagellating postmortems, they are the first to criticize lapses.

Editors and news directors say they have no political litmus test in hiring reporters. They recruit reporters for their skills and intelligence, not their politics. Joe

Strupp, who interviewed dozens of editors for the trade journal *Editor & Publisher,* found that editors rely on peer dynamics in the newsroom to keep the focus on complete and thorough reporting, which trumps any ideological bent. At the San Diego *Union-Tribune,* editor Karin Winter said: "We know how to turn off our affiliation when we walk through the door. It does not come up."

The editing process, an elaborate kind of peer review to which virtually all stories are subjected, also works against bias in coverage. Reporters know that the final word on their copy rests with editors, who recognize that the main product a newsroom has to offer the audience is accurate, truthful and believable reporting. The media have an economic incentive to tell news straight. Bruce Bartlett of the National Center for Policy Analysis noted that people will cancel their subscriptions if they perceive "liberal claptrap."

>> **News as Change.** If the news media indeed are obsessed with avoiding partisan reporting, how do the charges of bias retain currency? A historical reality in the bipolar U.S. political tradition is that the extremes have been conservatives, who by and large prefer things as they are, and liberals, who seek reform and change. Critics who paint the news media as liberal usually are forgetting that news, by its nature, is concerned with change. Everybody, journalists and news media consumers alike, is more interested in a volcano that is blowing its top than in a dormant peak. People are interested congenitally in what is happening, as opposed to what is not happening. Friends don't greet each other: "Hey, what's not new?" News stories on Krakatoa in 1883 hardly meant that journalists favor volcanic eruptions. The fact is that change is more interesting than the status quo, although usually less comforting and sometimes threatening. News is about change—proposed, pending and occurring. And change is not what political conservatism is about.

When journalists write about a presidential candidate's ideas to, for example, eliminate farm subsidies, it's not that journalists favor the proposed change. Rather, it's that the topic is more interesting than stories about government programs that are in place, functioning routinely and unchallenged. In short, to conclude that journalists' concern with change is necessarily born of political bias is to overlook the nature of journalism—and also the natural human interest in what's new.

>> **Watchdog Function.** Some accusations of journalistic bias originate in confusion between message and messenger. Incumbent officeholders often are quick to blame the media when news is less than hunky-dory. The classic case was in 1968 when the White House was beset with unfavorable news. Vice President Spiro Agnew, addicted as he was to fanciful alliteration, called the press "nagging nabobs of negativism." Successive presidential administrations, Democratic and Republican alike, have been no less gentle in charging the media with bias when news is less than flattering.

The news media frequently are whipping boys for performing their constitutionally implied **watchdog function.** Since the founding of the Republic, journalists have been expected to keep government honest and responsive to the electorate by reporting on its activities, especially shortcomings. Unless the people have full reports, they cannot intelligently discuss public issues, let alone vote knowledgeably on whether to keep or replace their representatives.

This is not to suggest that journalists are perfect or always accurate, especially in reporting confusing situations against deadline. Nor is it to suggest that there are no partisans peppered among reporters in the press corps. But critics, usually themselves partisans, too often are reflexive with a cheap charge of bias when reporters are, as one wag put it, doing their job to keep the rascals in power honest. In the process of doing their work, journalists sometimes indeed become facilitators of change—but as reporters, not advocates.

CHECKING YOUR MEDIA LITERACY

- **Most mainstream media in the United States package or label opinion as separate from news. How does this work? Does it work well?**
- **How well do your local news media perform their watchdog function? Give recent examples.**

watchdog function

The news media role to monitor the performance of government and other institutions of society

Variables Affecting News

STUDY ***PREVIEW***

The variables that determine what is reported include things beyond a journalist's control, such as how much space or time is available to tell stories. Also, a story that might receive top billing on a slow news day might not even appear on a day when an overwhelming number of major stories are breaking.

NEWS HOLE

A variable affecting what ends up being reported as news is called the **news hole**. In newspapers the news hole is the space left after the advertising department has placed all the ads it has sold in the paper. The volume of advertising determines the number of total pages, and generally, the bigger the issue, the more room for news. Newspaper editors can squeeze fewer stories into a thin Monday issue than a fat Wednesday issue.

In broadcasting, the news hole tends to be more consistent. A 30-minute television newscast may have room for only 23 minutes of news, but the format doesn't vary. When the advertising department doesn't sell all seven minutes available for advertising, it usually is public-service announcements, promotional messages and program notes—not news—that pick up the slack. Even so, the news hole can vary in broadcasting. A 10-minute newscast can accommodate more stories than a five-minute newscast, and, as with newspapers, it is the judgment of journalists that determines which events make it.

CHECKING YOUR MEDIA LITERACY

- **Why does the news hole frustrate journalists?**

NEWS FLOW AND NEWS STAFFING

Besides the news hole, the **news flow** varies from day to day. A story that might be displayed prominently on a slow news day can be passed over entirely in the competition for space on a heavy news day.

On one of the heaviest news days of all time—June 4, 1989—death claimed Iran's Ayatollah Khomeini, a central figure in U.S. foreign policy; Chinese young people and the government were locked in a showdown in Tiananmen Square; the Polish people were voting to reject their one-party communist political system; and a revolt was under way in the Soviet republic of Uzbekistan. That was a heavy news day, and the flow of major nation-rattling events pre-empted many stories that otherwise would have been considered news.

Heavy news days cannot be predicted. One would have occurred if there had been a confluence on a single day of these 2005 events: Hurricane Katrina, the Samuel Alito nomination to the U.S. Supreme Court, the 2,000th U.S. combat death in Iraq, the Michael Jackson acquittal and the Afghanistan-Pakistan earthquake.

Staffing affects news coverage, for example, whether reporters are in the right place at the right time. A newsworthy event in Nigeria will receive short shrift on U.S. television if the network correspondents for Africa are occupied with a natural disaster in next-door Cameroon. A radio station's city government coverage will slip when the city hall reporter is on vacation or if the station can't afford a regular reporter at city hall.

CHECKING YOUR MEDIA LITERACY

- **Look at your local newspaper over the past week. Which was the heaviest news day? The slowest news day? Explain.**
- **Which is cheaper for a newspaper or television station to report? A session of the city council or a session of the British Parliament? Explain.**

news hole
Space for news in a newspaper after ads are inserted; time in a newscast for news after ads

news flow
Significance of events worth covering varies from day to day

staffing
Available staff resources to cover news

PERCEPTIONS ABOUT AUDIENCE

How a news organization perceives its audience affects news coverage. The *National Enquirer* lavishes attention on unproven cancer cures that the New York *Times* treats briefly if at all. The *Wall Street Journal* sees its purpose as news for readers who have special interests in finance, the economy and business. The Bloomberg cable network was established to serve an audience more interested in quick market updates, brief analysis and trendy consumer news than the kind of depth offered by the *Journal.*

The perception that a news organization has of its audience is evident in a comparison of stories on different networks' newscasts. CNN may lead newscasts with a coup d'état in another country, while Bloomberg leads with a new government economic forecast and MTV with the announcement of a rock group's tour.

CHECKING YOUR MEDIA LITERACY

- **How do your expectations differ regarding the news coverage on the *Daily Show* and CNN?**

COMPETITION

Two triggers of adrenaline for journalists are landing a scoop and, conversely, being scooped. Journalism is a competitive business, and the drive to outdo other news organizations keeps news publications and newscasts fresh with new material. Competition has an unglamorous side. Journalists constantly monitor each other to identify events that they missed and need to catch up on to be competitive. This catch-up aspect of the news business contributes to similarities in coverage, which scholar Leon Sigal calls the **consensible nature of news.** It also is called "pack" and "herd" journalism.

In the final analysis, news is the result of journalists scanning their environment and making decisions, first on whether to cover certain events and then on how to cover them. The decisions are made against a backdrop of countless variables, many of them changing during the reporting, writing and editing processes.

consensible nature of news
News organization second-guessing competition in deciding coverage

CHECKING YOUR MEDIA LITERACY

- **How can similar content in competing news media be explained?**

New Realities in News

STUDY PREVIEW

The Internet has given rise to a multitude of sources of news and information. But are more voices good for democracy and the common good? While diversity is valued in a democracy, fewer hurdles for flawed and petty and self-serving voices make for a confusing cacophony. Traditional newsroom values and ethics, honed for more than a century, have a lesser role in the universe of news today.

CYBER NEWS

Upstart web sites wield influence that could never have been imagined a quarter century ago. Some of the sites are in the tradition of detached, neutral reporting, like Politico.com. Others are not.

The site *Little Green Footballs* was focal of conservative bloggers who hounded CBS into forcing anchor Dan Rather into retirement. For years Rather's solid reporting had survived the antipathy of right-wingers who never forgave his persistent reporting on moral turpitude in the Nixon White House. Rather's detractors picked up new ammunition after producers at the CBS news program *60 Minutes* prepared a story that President George W. Bush had received preferential treatment while in the Texas Air National Guard. Rather provided the on-air narrative. It turned out that the producers had been duped by a forged document. The story about whether Bush was an inveterate slacker in the Texas Guard was never disproven, but the *60 Minutes* report was circumstantial, not smoking gun evidence. After months of bombardment, seeded by *Little Green Footballs,* Rather relinquished the CBS Evening News anchor seat and left the network.

One of the first of the political web sites, the *Drudge Report,* began humbly in 1994. A low-level employee at a CBS gift shop in Hollywood, Matt Drudge, shared celebrity gossip online with friends. Within months Drudge developed a following, and the *Drudge Report* was born. The power of a news source, outside the mainstream media, became clear when Drudge picked up that President Clinton and White House intern Monica Lewinsky had engaged in sex in the Oval Office. Quickly a magnet for information from confidential sources, Drudge pounded away at the scandal. Finally the House impeached Clinton, although the president was spared a trial before the Senate.

Liberal freelancer Joshua Michal Marshall drew on a legion of readers of his site *Talking Points Memo* during the George W. Bush administration. Marshall pursued a story that Attorney General Alberto Gonzales, a Bush crony, had fired U.S. attorneys around the country for not pursuing the administration's political agenda. A crescendo of criticisms for political meddling in the U.S. judicial system eventually forced Gonzales to resign. Marshall was awarded a George Polk award, the first blogger to receive the vaunted journalism award.

CHECKING YOUR MEDIA LITERACY

- **How influential are web upstarts on governance and politics?**
- **How can media literacy affect choices in news in the web?**

AGGREGATION NEWS

The incredibly low cost of entry into web news has spawned thousands of news sites. Drudge had merely a primitive 286 computer and a modem. Today, with his site generating advertising revenue, Drudge is a millionaire. Like many news sites, the *Drudge Report* offers less original reporting than aggregated news from elsewhere, including core Associated Press coverage and links to many sources, plus a bevy of opinion writers. These **aggregation sites** serve largely as portals to comprehensive coverage.

A miniscule staff, sometimes one person, can operate an aggregation site—just as Drudge did at the outset.

Some aggregation sites have had a jump start. The well-connected Arianna Huffington, wealthy almost beyond imagination from a flashy divorce settlement, launched her *Huffington Post* in 2005 as a liberal alternative to the *Drudge Report.* Huffington put up $11 million. Huffington started by aggregating news and gossip mostly from print and television sources or somebody's cell phone or video camera. By the 2008 presidential campaign season, the *Huffington Post* had 46 full-time employees. There were 11 million clicks a day from different computers. Only eight newspaper sites had more. Advertising revenue approached $7 million, enough to break even.

CHECKING YOUR MEDIA LITERACY

- **What is the difference between originating news and aggregating news?**
- **Which is better? Which is more convenient? Which is more reliable?**

DISTRIBUTIVE JOURNALISM

For all of the online excitement created by the exploding multiplicity of news sites, there is a downside. Ask Jeffrey Davidson, a San Francisco allergist. Davidson Googled his own name online one day and found patients had posted negative comments about him on the site RateMDs.com. To be sure, there were positive comments too, but Davidson grimaced at the bad ones: "False and unbelievable." Such is a fact of life with blog sites and rating sites, some tied in with news sites. The phenomenon, to which traditional news organizations had built-in safeguards, is a result of what has

aggregation sites
News sites that regurgitate news compiled from elsewhere or that offer pass-through links to other sources

come to be called **distributive journalism.** With information from widely distributed or diverse sources, anybody can say almost anything, often with anonymity. No heed need be given for the traditional journalistic standard of detached and neutral presentations and a penchant for accuracy in pursuit of truth.

By and large it's a free-for-all. Federal law shields web site owners from liability for comments posted on their sites. There is no recourse at all as long as comments are opinions of hyperbole. In reporting the issue with RateMDs.com, *Forbes* writer Claire Cain Miller noted it's legally safe, for example, to say "This doctor has the bedside manner of an orangutan." Not so for "This doctor killed two patients last week," unless, of course, it's true.

Then too, how easily can an anonymous posting be traced to its origin? Even the FBI, with all its investigative tools, has a hard time, even with high-priority criminal cases.

Some web sites do self-policing. Activist Randall Robinson once asserted on *Huffington Post* that Hurricane Katrina survivors were eating corpses to survive. Arianna Huffington doubted the claim and herself contacted Robinson and he backed off and immediately retracted the post.

Not all false, misleading or scurrilous posts are intercepted—and some whoppers occasionally make it to the mainstream media if not for any other reason than that, spreading like wildfire, they themselves cannot be ignored as news.

CHECKING YOUR MEDIA LITERACY

- **How are nasty disparaging comments allowable legally online but factual incorrect statements are not?**
- **What is meant by the term *distributive journalism?***

distributive journalism

Information included in news from widely diverse sources of unchecked veracity

QUALITY OF NEWS

The advent of web news has eroded some of the standard operating practices in newsrooms that historically had given readers a high level of expectation for accuracy and judgment.

Great Moon Hoax. *As a lark, Richard Locke penned a brief news item for the New York* Sun *in 1835 that a South Africa telescope had spotted winged humanlike creatures flitting from crater to crater on the moon. Locke offered further embellishment for several days and goosed* Sun *readership. But then Locke was found out and resigned. The upshot was a firm focus on accuracy in news reporting, albeit with notable lapses and, of course, human error.*

810.13 RICHARD ADAMS LOCKE (1800-1871).
Credit: The Granger Collection, New York

Richard Locke

Reporter's Choice: Tell or Go to Jail?

Forty-nine states have shield laws or other protections in place that recognize reporters' privilege to protect their confidential sources. But there is no national shield law, which leaves journalists vulnerable to court orders to break promises that they won't identify their sources. When subpoenaed, journalists must reveal their sources or go to jail for refusing a judge's order.

A 2007 attempt in Congress at a federal shield law, the Free Flow of Information Act, was supported by dozens of media companies and journalistic organizations. Supporters included the Free the Media organization, established by Josh Wolf. The 24-year-old blogger had spent almost eight months in prison for not giving the FBI video he shot in San Francisco during a protest facilitated by a group called Anarchist Action against the G-8 Summit in Scotland.

Wolf posted some of his video on his blog. Also, he sold some of the video to television news outlets. A few days later the FBI turned up at his door.

Wolf was subpoenaed by a federal grand jury, which had been called to determine if arson charges should be brought against protestors for damaging a police car, even though it had only a damaged taillight. The federal court circumvented the state's shield law and got involved because the purchase of the police car was funded in part by federal anti-terror money.

"What I caught on videotape was a cop choking a guy," Wolf said, not the car incident, but FBI agents still wanted his video, and they wanted him to identify protestors, who were wearing masks. They wanted all documents, writings and recordings related to the protest, as well as all his cameras and recording devices and his computer. Wolf refused to comply. "There was a trust established between people in the organization that I was covering," he said in one interview. "I wasn't an investigator for the state turning over piles of tape for fishing expeditions."

After Wolf spent 226 days in jail, longer than any other journalist in U.S. history, an agreement was reached. Wolf gave federal prosecutors his tape, and at the same time he published it on his web site. He answered no to two questions about what he had seen at the demonstration. A statement on his site declared victory for "a free press." U.S. Attorney Kevin Ryan said in a court filing that it was "only in Wolf's imagination that he is a journalist."

The Society for Professional Journalists and the National Newspaper Guild disagreed. The SPJ Northern California chapter honored Wolf as Journalist of the Year and gave him the James Madison Freedom of Information Award. He also received the Herb Block Freedom Award from the National Newspaper Guild.

Josh Wolf. *A prosecutor argued that Josh Wolf, as a blogger, had no right to refuse to divulge information about an anti-G-8 demonstration. The prosecutor said it was "only in Wolf's imagination that he is a journalist." Wolf spent 226 days in jail for refusing to divulge information that he said was acquired only because sources trusted him not to rat on them.*

DEEPENING YOUR MEDIA LITERACY

EXPLORE THE ISSUE

Do you think blogger Josh Wolf is a journalist who deserves the protection of a shield law?

DIG DEEPER

Tom Rosenstiel of the Project for Excellence in Journalism says the proper question should be not whether you call yourself a journalist but whether your work constitutes journalism. With this definition in mind, analyze the Josh Wolf case.

WHAT DO YOU THINK?

Do you think a federal shield law is necessary? Why? Do you think it should include bloggers and independent journalists? Why?

>> Accuracy. A penchant for accuracy can be traced to the first criticisms of falsity and distortions in news. This became explicit in the outrage over the Great Moon Hoax, a series of items in Benjamin Day's New York *Sun* in 1835. Writer Richard Locke described bird-like creatures spotted on the moon through a new powerful telescope. Readers gobbled up the story. Whether competing newspaper publishers were outraged more at the fantasy-as-news or at losing readers can be debated. The fact, however, is that a chorus erupted for accuracy and truthfulness in news.

A penchant for accuracy became institutionalized in codes of ethics, first with a code from the American Society of Newspaper Editors in 1923.

As 'tis often said, to err is human. And mistakes creep into news, which is regrettable but usually forgiven. Serial sloppiness with facts, however, has become a near-cardinal sin in traditional newsrooms and fabrication a cause of immediate dismissal. Sad but true, with everybody and their cousins able to create one-person news operations online, the widely held standard for accuracy has become less, well, less a standard. Many of these new self-styled and self-proclaimed journalists have never been to j-school. They are untrained in post-Moon Hoax news ethics and practices and unsteeped in traditional newsroom traditions.

>> Gatekeeping. More complex than accuracy is the newsroom function of gatekeeping, which also is less at work in small-staff upstart newsrooms. So what is gatekeeping? Not everything can be reported because of practicalities—not enough room in the paper, not enough time in a newscast, not enough staff to pursue all stories. Decisions need to be made on what to tell. These decisions are made by **gatekeepers.** Their job is to exercise news judgment, deciding what most deserves to be told and how.

Gatekeeping can be a creative force. Trimming a news story can add potency. A news producer can enhance a reporter's field report with file footage. An editor can call a public relations person for additional detail to illuminate a point in a reporter's story. A newsmagazine's editor can consolidate related stories and add context that makes an important interpretive point. Most gatekeepers are invisible to the news audience, working behind the scenes and making crucial decisions in near anonymity on how the world will be portrayed in the evening newscast and the next web site update.

With the smaller staffs of many web newsrooms, some of them one-person shops, fewer hands and eyes and minds process and sort incoming information and material. Among these people, the commitments are uneven compared to traditional newsroom values—like truth and accuracy, democratic ideals, an honestly informed citizenry, the common good.

Also, so many voices are out there that it becomes more difficult for civic-minded citizens to find the kind of journalistic leadership that marked an earlier era. Jill Edy, a communication scholar at the University of Oklahoma, says that the "collective memory" created for the public by professional news people is at risk: "It's likely instead that 'the media' will continue to multiply and morph into a thousand different voices and versions and visions. Under such conditions: How will a collective memory be formed? Will it be observed? Where, in the future, will we find collective memory?"

Columnist Frank Rich of the New York *Times* also decries the multitude of voices the public hears today and suggests that even today's leading commentators have less influence than the Walter Lippmann or James Reston of earlier eras: "Now, there are so many sources of news and opinion in so many competing media, from the Internet and radio and television to print, that no single voice can have that kind of impact."

CHECKING YOUR MEDIA LITERACY

- **Why is gatekeeping unavoidable in the process of reporting news?**
- **What are the good purposes served by gatekeeping? What are the dangers?**
- **Evaluate the argument of Frank Rich that more is not better for democracy.**

gatekeepers
Media people influencing messages en route

Journalism Trends

STUDY **PREVIEW**

The explosion of 24/7 news on television and the Internet is transforming news gathering and redefining news practices and audience expectations. Traditional avenues for news, sometimes called mainstream media, were shaken in the 2004 political campaign by individuals, mostly without journalistic training, generally operating alone, who created hundreds of blog sites. Bloggers offer an interconnected web of fascinating reading. Sometimes they score scoops.

NEWSROOMS IN TRANSITION

Two dynamics are reshaping newsrooms. One is the transition into Internet delivery of news, which is pushing editors to find ways to stretch their staffs to produce their traditional products—plus offer competitive web sites. The other dynamic is financial, primarily at newspapers where recent years have seen drastic staff reductions. Newspaper industry reporter Joe Strupp, writing in the trade journal *Editor & Publisher,* put it this way: "So with newsrooms shrinking and corporate demands growing, the question inevitably may be asked: 'What gives?'" Most television newsrooms face the same issue. How can the extra duty of a 24/7 web site or perhaps multiple sites, some interactive, be absorbed by existing staff?

Among the new realities:

>> **Less Comprehensive Coverage.** Newsrooms once put lots of energy into catching up on their competitors' scoops and taking the coverage further. Less so now. Ken Paulson, editor of *USA Today,* said he now applauds the New York *Times* and Washington *Post* when they break an exclusive story. Applauds—and forgets it. Said Paulson: "We have to make judgment calls on what our priorities are."

The new *USA Today* practice, common in all financially strapped newsrooms, doesn't speak well for the kind of excellence that competition has generated historically in U.S. journalism. The coverage of historically significant stories, like the Pentagon Papers and Watergate in the 1970s, was marked by intense competition. Independent coverage by competing newsrooms led to revelations that no one news organization could have managed single-handedly. Every breakthrough from competing newsrooms in Watergate, for example, further peeled away at the truth and became a stepping stone for new rounds of pursuit.

>> **Less Enterprise.** With smaller, stretched staffs, newsrooms are opting for easier stories. This has meant a greater quotient of stories that chronicle events and fewer stories that require labor-intensive digging. This further means fewer reporters being freed for what David Boardman, executive editor at the Seattle *Times,* calls "two- and three-day stories." There was a time in the lore of the *Wall Street Journal* that editors would work up a promising story possibility with a veteran reporter, give the reporter an American Express card, and say "Come back with a story in six months." Although the *Journal* still features exhaustive journalistic examinations, they are becoming less common in American journalism and even in the *Journal* too.

>> **Less Outlying News.** Many newsrooms have trimmed or shuttered bureaus in outlying areas. Typical is the Memphis, Tennessee, *Commercial Appeal.* The bureaus in Jackson, Mississippi, and Little Rock, Arkansas, have been shut down. The state capital bureau in Nashville, once with three reporters, has been trimmed to one.

>> **Fewer Beats.** Reporters assigned to cover specialized areas are being given broader beats. Some police beat reporters, for example, now also cover the courts. To cover some beats, editors in some newsrooms have shuffled reporters from general assignment duties to beats, which means there are fewer resources for day-to-day coverage of breaking news that doesn't fall in the bailiwick of one of the surviving beats.

>> Less Independent Reporting. Newsrooms are sharing stories among corporate siblings, which fills space cheaply but reduces the traditional value of competitive reporting yielding better coverage overall. Many newspapers and newscasts fill up with a growing percentage of faraway content from the Associated Press, which is far less costly per story than staff-generated local coverage. One upshot is less diversity in content when AP stories, appearing word for word in news packages statewide, even nationwide, displace local coverage.

The trend toward shared stories is most obvious with so-called multimedia newsrooms. One of the first was the integrated newsroom of the Tampa, Florida, *Tribune*, television station WFLA and TBO.com. Some local television stations are sparing themselves the cost of operating a newsroom and contracting with crosstown stations to provide the newscasts. Efficient? Yes. That repackaging is better than fresh content, however, is hard to argue.

CHECKING YOUR MEDIA LITERACY

- **The Watergate coverage by Carl Bernstein and Bob Woodward of the Washington *Post* began with a brief, routine account of a break-in at the Democratic Party's national headquarters. Discuss whether Bernstein and Woodward in a newsroom like today's would have had the time to pursue the story. What if their coverage had stopped with the burglary item?**
- **How much duplicate reporting—competing reporters all doing the same stories—do you see in your local news media?**

NONSTOP COVERAGE

Reporters for the Associated Press and other news agencies were a breed apart through most of the 20th century. In contrast to most newspaper reporters, who had one deadline a day, agency reporters sent dispatches to hundreds of news organizations, each with its own deadlines. Agency reporters literally had a deadline every minute.

The advent of all-news radio and then CNN expanded **nonstop coverage** beyond the news agencies. Network reporters at the White House, for example, once concentrated on a piece for the evening newscast. They had time to think through issues, line up sources, and frame questions. Today correspondents seem always in a frantic race, over and over and often breathless, to Pebble Beach, as they call a camera area with a White House backdrop.

Consider a day in the life of NBC reporter Chuck Todd:

> First, Todd scans newspapers and other competitors to orient himself for the day. Then he writes an item for the NBC blog "First Read." Next is an appearance live on NBC "Today" or MSNBC "Morning Joe." On a heavy news day he makes more than a dozen stand-up reports from Pebble Beach, never fewer than six. In addition, he adds three to five blog entries during the day and posts as many as a dozen tweets or Facebook updates. Too, Todd has the one-hour newscast "The Daily Run-Down."

The work is important, the adrenaline rush exciting. But Todd, like reporters everywhere, acknowledges that the pressure to produce quantity diminishes the opportunity for fresh reporting, for turning up news angles, for developing good stories that end up untold. He uses his Blackberry to scour sources for tidbits, knowing, as all reporters do, that texting is hardly a substitute for a substantive sit-down interview.

Not only are reporters pressed to produce more stories for 24/7 news cycles, tighter news budgets in recent years mean that fewer news reporters are doing the work.

Quality erosion shows up in small ways. Reporters shudder at their typos making it online because fewer editors are assigned to check copy. At the Baltimore *Sun*, Bill Salganik, the president of the Newspaper Guild, which represents reporters as a collective-bargaining agent, says the new pressures make more mistakes inevitable: "How do we maintain ethical and journalistic standards?"

In short, nonstop coverage, whatever the advantage of keeping people on top of breaking events, has shortcomings. The pressure for new angles tends to elevate the trivial. Also, context and understanding are sacrificed.

nonstop coverage
News reporting geared to ever-present deadlines, as 24/7 formats

Rachel Maddow

MEDIA PEOPLE

Rachel Maddow was no ordinary kid. At 4, her mother remembers, little Rachel would perch on a kitchen stool as her mom fixed breakfast and, still in pajamas, read the newspaper. At 7, during the 1980 presidential campaign, Maddow remembers an intense repulsion at Ronald Reagan on television.

Maddow, now a leading political commentator on the political left, can't explain her Reagan-loathing as a gradeschooler. Noting Reagan's political conservatism, Maddow quips that some kind of "reverse engineering" must have set in. It's a self-deprecating line typical of Maddow's quick humor that draws audience chuckles and then double takes as the irony settles in.

The fact is that Maddow is hardly a slouch intellectually. She roots what she says on premises, not on whatever instinctive gut reactions may have been playing on her when she was 7. Maddow holds a degree from Stanford University in public policy. Then she won a Rhodes scholarship for an Oxford doctorate in political science.

Maddow has a common touch that goes beyond her trademark 501 baggy jeans and sneakers. Yes, that's how Maddow shows up for work at the radio network Air America, where she started a talk show in 2004. Maddow didn't change her style when, at age 35, the MSNBC television network gave her a show during the 2008 heated presidential campaign. The button-down MSNBC culture in Manhattan hasn't affected Maddow. She says she's still comfortable dressing like a 13-year-old boy. Before going on the air nightly at MSNBC, however, she pulls a pantsuit from a closet of identical suits. She calls her style "butch dyke."

The common touch is more than wardrobe. Maddow earned money in college heavy-lifting. For a while she unloaded trucks. She also did yard-clearing for a landscaper. Then there was a job putting stamps on coffee packets. For reading she's as at home with Malthus and Machiavelli as with graphic novels.

At MSNBC in the intensive 2008 presidential campaign Maddow quickly doubled the 9 p.m. Eastern audience to 1.9 million. Among viewers 25 to 54, she outdrew the CNN icon Larry King 27 of 44 nights in her first two months.

Her work ethic from college has carried into her career. Her days run 16 hours. She admits to getting only a couple hours of "drunk sleep" some nights.

Maddow's drive is contagious. Her crew at MSNBC, political junkies in their 20s and 30s, uses the same term "drunk sleep" and concedes to crankiness as they show up at mid-afternoon to brainstorm themes with Maddow for the night's show. The sessions harken to those all-night free-form college dorm jams on imponderables.

Maddow, lanky and 6 foot, flops on the floor however she's comfortable at the moment. Bubbling through the give-and-take is a rich mixture of optimism for the future and skepticism about politicians—and bedrock patriotism. The session is heavy on the day's events and questions that need to be asked and on guests to line up to address the issues. Maddow twirls and lobs a foam basketball. Shifting her body on the floor, she scribbles ideas in a notebook.

The loosely structured planning is all rehearsal for Maddow—a kind of free-form cerebral internalizing. On air there is focus, although an informal feel that has attracted the young audience that the major television networks covet. There's a practiced sneering, her sarcasm punctuated with a trademark "Duh." Cliches, none. There is no doubt of Maddow being bright, authentic and original.

To be sure, Maddow has detractors. Her innuendos and nudge-nudge, wink-wink comments have been called theatrical and biased. Others see Maddow as finding a flavorful balance that is substantive and distinctly refreshing. For sure, Maddow resonates with a mass audience that finds the old boys' club that has dominated cable television suddenly stuffy.

WHAT DO YOU THINK?

- How do you explain the ratings success for Maddow for MSNBC?
- Is Maddow too smart, too witty, too political for most prime-time network viewers?

Clever. Smart. Dorky? *Rachel Maddow broke into the old boys' club of cable television, dominated by Bill O'Reilly at Fox, Larry King at CNN and Keith Olbermann at MSNBC, with a distinctive take on political news.*

CHECKING YOUR MEDIA LITERACY

- How has 24/7 news changed journalism?
- Do these changes have a downside?

LIVE NEWS

Over the past 150 years the news media in the United States, elsewhere too, have evolved standard and accepted practices. These practices, taught in journalism schools and institutionalized in codes of ethics, guide reporters and editors in preparing their summaries and wrap-ups. In general the traditional practices worked well when newspapers were the dominant news medium, and they worked well in broadcasting too—until the advent of highly portable, lightweight equipment that enabled broadcasters to report news events live, bypassing the traditional editing process.

With television cameras focused on the towers of the World Trade Center as they turned into infernos in the 2001 terrorist attack, trapped people began jumping from windows hundreds of feet above ground. The plunges were desperate and fatal, and audiences viewing the scene live were shocked and horrified. Neither the video nor still photographs were included in most later newscasts.

Whatever the virtues of live coverage, a significant downside is that the coverage is raw. Nobody is exercising judgment in deciding what to organize and how to present the material. There is no gatekeeper. Live coverage, of course, obviates the criticism of those who, rightly or wrongly, distrust journalism.

Following live coverage is time-consuming for the audience. Compare, for example, the efficiency of reading or listening to a 60-second report on a congressional hearing or watching the whole four-hour session live.

CHECKING YOUR MEDIA LITERACY

- How has the role of gatekeeping been changed by live broadcast coverage?

UNEDITED BLOGS

When *Columbia Journalism Review* created a web site for commentary on reporting of the 2004 presidential campaign, the magazine went out of its way to distance the new site from the thousands of web log sites, called **blogs,** on which amateurs post whatever is on their minds. No, said *CJR,* its campaigndesk.org would be held to the highest journalistic standards. The point was that a lot of irresponsible content gets posted on the web by people without any journalistic training or sense of journalistic standards. The web has made it possible for anyone to create a blog that is as easily accessible as are sites from news organizations that consciously seek to go about journalism right.

No gnashing of teeth, however, will make blogs go away—and their impact is substantial. Blog rumors, gossip and speculation, even when untrue, sometimes gain such currency that the mainstream media cannot ignore them. It's become a bromide, drawn from the tail-wags-dog metaphor, that blogs can wag the media.

blog
An amateur web site, generally personal in nature, often focused on a narrow subject, such as politics; short for "web log"

CHECKING YOUR MEDIA LITERACY

- What do you think of *Columbia Journalism Review*'s distinction between good blogs and bad blogs?

EXPLORATORY REPORTING

Bob Woodward
Bernstein's colleague in the Watergate revelations

Carl Bernstein
Washington *Post* reporter who dug up Watergate

Although in-depth reporting has deep roots, the thrust of U.S. journalism until the 1960s was a chronicling of events: meetings, speeches, crimes, deaths and catastrophes. That changed dramatically in 1972. Two persistent Washington *Post* reporters, **Bob Woodward** and **Carl Bernstein,** not only covered a break-in at the Democratic national headquarters, at a building called the Watergate, but also linked the crime to the White House of

Republican President Richard Nixon. The morality questions inherent in the reporting forced Nixon to resign. Twenty-five aides went to jail. The **Watergate** scandal created an enthusiasm for **investigative reporting** and in-depth approaches to news that went far beyond mere chronicling, which is relatively easy to do and, alas, relatively superficial.

The roots of investigatory reporting extend back to the **muckraking** period in U.S. history. **Ida Tarbell,** a leading muckraker, uncovered abusive corporate practices at Standard Oil in 1902, triggering government reforms that broke up the Rockefeller oil monopoly and paved the way for antitrust legislation. Today's newspapers continue this tradition. But is anybody listening? The New Orleans, Louisiana, *Times-Picayune* won a fistful of awards for John McQuaid and Mark Schleifstein's 2002 series "Washing Away," a chilling prediction of the Hurricane Katrina disaster that came true three years later. Government didn't do anything at the federal, state or local level.

Watergate
Nixon administration scandal

investigative reporting
Enterprise reporting that reveals new information, often startling; most often these are stories that official sources would rather not have told

muckraking
Fanciful term for digging up dirt but that usually is used in a laudatory way for investigative journalism; aimed at public policy reform

Ida Tarbell
Muckraker remembered for her series on monopolistic corruption at Standard Oil

soft news
Geared to satisfying audience's information wants, not needs

CHECKING YOUR MEDIA LITERACY

- **All reporting results from inquiry. What sets investigative reporting apart?**
- **List five examples of investigative reporting that have affected history.**

SOFT NEWS

In contrast to hard investigative reporting came a simultaneous trend toward **soft news**. This includes consumer-help stories, lifestyle tips, entertainment news and offbeat gee-whiz items often of a sensational sort. The celebrity-oriented *National Enquirer*, whose circulation skyrocketed in the 1960s, was the progenitor of the trend. Time-Life launched *People* magazine. The staid New York *Times* created *Us*. Newspaper research found that readers like soft stuff. Soon many dailies added "People" columns. The television show *Entertainment Tonight* focuses on glamour and glitz, usually as a lead-in to the evening news on many local stations. Traditionalists decry the space that soft news takes in many newspapers today, but hard news remains part of the product mix.

CHECKING YOUR MEDIA LITERACY

- **In what divergent directions is news moving today?**
- **How has live reporting changed journalism, in contrast to eras when newspapers were dominant?**
- **How has 24/7 coverage changed news?**

CHAPTER WRAP-UP

Journalism Traditions (Pages 211–216)

- In the colonial period, people made a hero of John Peter Zenger, whose newspaper represented an anti-Establishment voice. The tradition continues of U.S. news media as an independent voice apart from government. In 1833, a century after Zenger, fast-growing cities created the first mass audiences. In the new penny papers, facts trumped opinion in vying for space and spawned the idea that news reporting should be values-free. Later came the sensationalism of the so-called yellow press, which continues as part of American journalism.

Concept of News (Pages 216–218)

- News is a report on change that journalists deem most worth their audience's attention. In the United States there is a high premium on a detached, neutral presentation in which reporters keep their presence as much in the background as they can. The emphasis generally is on the story, not the storyteller, even though the reporter's role in seeking and organizing stories requires judgments that are subjective and flow from personal values.

Personal Values in News (Pages 218–224)

- Since news cannot be values-free, the question is what values do journalists bring to their work? Values include those that prevail in society. In the United States these include broad values often taken for granted, like family, education and health. Studies have found other values that flavor American journalism. These include a national ethnocentrism, a commitment to democracy and capitalism, a romanticism about rural and small-town lifestyles, a favoring of individualism tempered by moderation, and a commitment to social order.

Variables Affecting News (Pages 225–226)

- Practical matters shape much of what appears in the news. How much space is there in an edition? Never enough to tell all that journalists would like to tell. Time on a newscast? Never enough either. Nor does the audience have the time to be engaged in everything that gets reported. Also, more stories are worth telling than any news organization has the staff and resources to pursue.

Journalism Trends (Pages 231–235)

- Journalism is going in many directions. Lengthy treatments, typified television network documentaries, are long-form journalism—labor-intensive to produce but often with breakthrough revelations. At another extreme are snippets sometimes only a couple lines long that are packaged in radio newscasts. The advent of 24/7 news on television and the web has stretched the resources of many newsrooms. With a limited number of reporters being asked to repackage stories for multiple outlets, there has been a shift to stories that are quicker to report. The result: a decline in significant enterprise reporting that takes major commitments of newsroom time and resources.

▼ Review Questions

1. What contemporary news practices are rooted in the major periods in U.S. journalism history?
2. How are all journalists captives of the personal values they bring to their work?
3. What variables about news gathering and news packaging are beyond the control of reporters and even editors but nonetheless affect what people read, hear and see?
4. What pressures from outside the media affect news reporting?
5. What are the pros and cons of the new multiplicity of news sources through the Internet?
6. Trends in news reporting are going in divergent directions. Why? Evaluate these trends and their long-term prospects.

Concepts

gatekeepers (Page 230)
news (Page 217)
objectivity (Page 217)
soft news (Page 235)
yellow period (Page 215)

Terms

aggregation sites (Page 227)
Alien and Sedition acts (Page 212)
distributive journalism (Page 228)
investigative reporting (Page 235)
Watergate (Page 235)

People

Bob Woodward (Page 234)
Carl Bernstein (Page 234)
Herbert Gans (Page 220)
James Gordon Bennett (Page 213)
John Peter Zenger (Page 211)
Rachel Maddow (Page 233)

Media Sources

- Evan Thomas. *The War Lovers: Roosevelt, Lodge, Hearst, and the Rush to Empire, 1898*. Little, Brown, 2010. Thomas, a *Newsweek* editor, enters into psychohistory in analyzing powerful U.S. war-mongers, including newspaper mogul William Randolph Hearst, as well as voices against the U.S. war on Spain.
- Tammy Boyce and Justin Lewis, editors. *Climate Change and the Media.* Lang, 2009. Boyce and Lewis, British scholars, include work of 24 contributors, some with strong content analysis on media coverage of climate change in a range of locations.
- Barbie Zelizer, editor. *The Changing Faces of Journalism: Tabloidization, Technology and Truthiness* (Routledge, 2009). Zelizer has compiled essays that encourage new, positive paradigms about the move toward visualization, personalization, sensationalism, narratives and convergence. Several essays see the shift from objectivity as yielding new broader, diverse understandings.
- Kate Kaye. *Campaign '08: A Turning Point for Digital Media*. Kate Kaye, 2009. Kaye, a journalist on marketing news, offers a breezy account of the McCain and Obama media strategies.
- Costas Panagopoulos, editor. *Politicking Online: The Transformation of Election Campaign Communications.* Rutgers University Press, 2009. Panagopoulos has collected observations from fellow political scientists on new media applications in election campaigns and the effect on democracy.
- Loren Ghiglione. *CBS's Don Hollenbeck: An Honest Reporter in the Age of McCarthyism.* Columbia, 2008. Ghiglione, a newspaper publisher-turned-professor, tells the career story of Hollenbeck, a radio reporter and commentator, in a larger media context, including newspapers and then early television, in the 1940s and 1950s.
- Myra MacPherson. *"All Governments Lie:" The Life and Times of Rebel Journalist I.F. Stone*. Scribner, 2006. MacPherson, a biographer, offers a well-researched account of Stone as an eclectic pursuer of truth in high places.
- Mike Conway. *The Origins of Television News in America: The Visualizers of CBS in the 1940s.* Peter Lang, 2009. Conway, a media scholar, examines the precursor years to television network news with illuminating anecdote and detail.
- Joe Strupp. "What Gives?" *Editor & Publisher* (May 2007), pages 36–44.
- William David Sloan, editor. *The Media in America,* seventh edition. Vision Press, 2009. This textbook is the standard for U.S. media history.
- David Wallis, editor. *Killed: Great Journalism Too Hot to Print.* Nation, 2004. Wallis has compiled great magazine articles that never made it to print, mostly to avoid litigation or not to offend advertisers or the editors' sensitivities. Among the stricken are works by Betty Friedan, George Orwell and Terry Southern.
- Bob Woodward and Carl Bernstein. *All the President's Men.* Simon & Schuster, 1974. The reporters' own chronicle of the obstacles they overcame in the classic unfolding series of investigative reports in the Nixon Watergate scandal.

NEWS

In this chapter you have deepened your media literacy by revisiting several themes. Here are thematic highlights from the chapter:

MEDIA TECHNOLOGY

Mass Audience. Ben Day, publisher of the *Sun*, the best known of the penny papers, chose stories for their broad appeal.

News as we know it today did not exist before the 1830s and 1840s, when presses were invented that could produce thousands of copies an hour. The question became: What content will sell all this product? Stories on current events displaced the opinion thrust that had marked earlier papers. In the 1920s when broadcasting was introduced, stories became briefer. Internet technology is now changing the rules again, with many mainstream news media conventions being ignored in the shaping and exchanging of information. Whether these changes are merely amateur-hour bloggers breaking rules they never knew is unclear. Some changes may have long futures. (Pages 213–215, 226–235)

MEDIA ECONOMICS

Celebrity News. The Associated Press experimented with a blackout on partygoing celebrity Paris Hilton. The blackout lasted one week. Not a single AP subscribing media outlet complained. But other news organizations continued pouring out Paris copy. The AP rejoined the mania but promises a case-by-case assessment of newsworthiness.

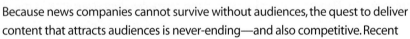

Because news companies cannot survive without audiences, the quest to deliver content that attracts audiences is never-ending—and also competitive. Recent years have seen a rise in celebrity news, mostly inconsequential but followed avidly. This is an example of news following the dollar. Economics also shapes news in other ways. To varying degrees, news companies are cautious about reporting events and issues that might offend their advertisers. The issue is whether serving the audience or serving advertisers comes first. In some newsrooms, it's an easy call. In others, advertisers usually win out. (Pages213–216, 235)

MEDIA AND DEMOCRACY

Global Warming. Al Gore got everyone's attention with *An Inconvenient Truth*. Now global warming and the environment are hot-button issues in the news.

An independent streak has been present in American news media going back to Ben Harris. Government banned Harris' *Publick Occurrences* in 1690 after one issue. Although Ben Harris' paper hardly contributed to the making of public policy, the independence of the news media became an enduring and important element in U.S. democracy. News media convey information, ideas and opinions that enable the people to participate in the creation of public policy. The mechanisms of participation are uneven, but without them the people would be woefully lacking in what they need to know to participate in governance. Democracy needs an independent media. (Pages 211–212, 220, 224)

MEDIA EFFECTS

Watergate. Richard Nixon did it to himself, but the news media were catalysts that led to his resignation.

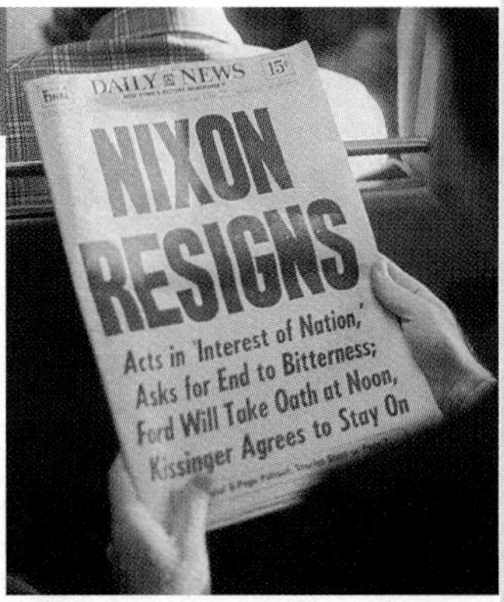

The news media can have powerful effects. The resignation of Alberto Gonzales as attorney general in 2007 was fueled by the news coverage in which he demonstrated continuing ineptness. The 1971 Watergate scandal that sent Richard Nixon packing midterm was the result of news coverage of dirty tricks and deceits that he and his lieutenants committed. Today, news coverage of the pending global-warming disaster is mobilizing public alarm, which is translating into public policy reform. (Pages 210–211, 224, 231–235)

ELITISM AND POPULISM

"It Shines for All." Ben Day's motto for his New York *Sun* in 1833 captured his innovation—a newspaper for everyone, a true mass audience.

Publications in the early days of the Republic were too expensive for most people. Articles were narrowly focused. These publications were forums where the thinkers and ideologues of the time shared their views. The political, economic and not uncommonly philosophical thrust was elitist. The commercialization of newspapers, with the mass audience beginning in the 1830s, sparked a shift to news of interest to all strata of society. Ben Day's motto for his New York *Sun* in 1833 said it all: "It Shines for All." The beginning of marketing that relied on advertising, which changed the financial base of newspapers from subscriptions to advertisers, made it essential economically that news be found to attract and keep as many readers as possible. Advertisers went with papers with the largest circulations. (Pages 212–216, 230, 235)

MEDIA FUTURE

Divergent Paths. Long-form journalism survives armid the emergence of softer, briefer, less consequential news. The *Wall Street Journal,* for example, has a huge audience for seriousness and depth.

Turkey's PM On Armenia And Genocide
Jessica Seinfeld Has a Recipe For Book Sales
Inside College Sports' Biggest Cash Machine
THE WALL STREET JOURNAL.
What's News—
Google Under Fire Over a Controversial Site
Insulin Flop Costs Pfizer $2.8 Billion
New Trend in Germany: Food Handouts for the Poor

No media maven has all the answers on where the news media are headed. Trends point in no single direction. Faster-pace lifestyles and spare-time diversions are robbing people of time once spent tracking news. The upshot is briefer coverage that's often superficial. At the same time, news junkies abound. Long-form journalism thrives on national and specialized subjects, albeit not so much in local daily coverage. A major change involves the around-the-clock news cycle, particularly with CNN and other cable channels and the Internet. The competition to be first is changing reporting conventions. Not long ago reporters had time, albeit not much, to think and assess their reportage before telling their stories. Today more and more reporting is going live—now. (Pages 231–232)

chapter 9

ENTERTAINMENT

Through the lenses of celebrity photographers, actress Keira Knightley is in the eyes of the world at a red-carpet photo opportunity. The enthusiasm and eagerness of such celeb shoots epitomize a confounding question about what is the best role that mass media can serve—sustaining and fueling cultural superficiality or just giving people what they want.

LEARNING AHEAD

- Mass media technology has magnified the audience for storytelling and entertainment.
- Pure performance and mediated performance are different.
- Mass media powerfully extend the reach of literature.
- Technology has accelerated music as a social unifier.
- Mass media feed an insatiable demand for sports.
- Gaming has become a mass medium with advertisers pursuing gamers.
- Mass media have championed the right of adult access to sexual content.
- Mass media entertainment quality is compromised by factory-style production.
- Mass media often fall short in elevating cultural sensitivity.

CELEBRITY SHOOT

The English actress Keira Knightley could not have looked grander. Her gown glimmering in spotlights, Knightley paraded gracefully, all smiles, along the cordoned-off red carpet. Celebrity photographers vied for exclusive shots. From behind the rope Steve Granitz, a celeb shooter since 1980, shouted a proven line: "It's me!" Like every fellow shooter in the horde, Granitz wants a new expression—a searching expression, a carefree toss of the locks, a really, really toothy smile. Says Granitz: "We're just trying to get a nice shot so we can publish it."

Because red-carpet shoots have become news events, celeb shooters are among the most visible of media content-creators. Although not obnoxious paparazzi, these photographers are magnets for criticism that the mass media have become crazed about entertainment and celebrities. Usually the criticism is that superficiality, glamour and glitz displace substance when the media obsess on amusement and diversion.

The criticism is not without merit, but celeb shooters are quick to excuse themselves as not being the cause of society's growing star obsession. The media are meeting a demand. Granitz explains it this way: "We want colorful outfits, nice hats and nice jewelry that will get published." Those images, he says, are what the audience wants.

Critics respond that media people like celeb shooters are to blame for debauching the mass media's potential to encourage and elevate widespread dialogue on significant issues. The bottom line: Does the public's appetite for vapid sleaze force the media to aim low? Or is the media so at home in the gutter that it gives the public no other choices? Either way, it's a race to the bottom, and in the end, a chicken-or-egg kind of question.

What's undeniable is that the economic imperatives of modern life are the dynamics that drive the obsession. Many interests have a financial stake. These include a powerful triad of media content shapers. These include profit-driven media companies, like movie-maker Disney that seeks as much lavish attention as possible for Keira Knightley in order to plug its *Pirates of the Caribbean* series.

A second major factor are media content-creators like the celeb shooters along Keira Knightley's red carpet. These media people practice their craft, often excellently, and earn a livelihood.

The most powerful leg of the triad is, get ready for this: you. OK, OK, you may bristle at being lumped with star-crazed groupies and other fawning fans who, if Granitz is right, drive the whole thing. But, no question about it, the audience for this stuff is huge and seemingly insatiable. Directly and indirectly, the audience finances media content.

Meanwhile, along the red carpet, the celeb shooters try every trick they can muster for an exclusive star reaction. English-born Frazer Harrison, a news photographer since 1985, has done his homework and his plotting. Resurrecting his best Blighty accent in the strobe-studded Keira Knightley shoot, Harrison shouts out: "Over to the English guy!" She can't resist a searching stare for a fellow Brit. Snap. Harrison has his shot.

Entertainment in History

STUDY ***PREVIEW***

The mass media, during their 550-year existence, have magnified the audience for entertainment. Technology has wrought many refinements, but the core categories of media entertainment remain storytelling and music.

PRE-MASS-MEDIA ROOTS

Entertainment predates the written history of the human species. Around the prehistoric campfire there was music. We know this from Neolithic animal hide drums that archaeologists have unearthed. Certainly, the cave dwellers must have told stories. Who knows when the visual arts began? The record goes back to paintings on cave walls. Through the eons, entertainment became higher and higher art. Archaeologists know that the elites of ancient civilizations enjoyed lavish banquets that included performing entertainers—acrobats, musicians and dancers. Sports and athletics became institutionalized entertainment by the time of ancient Greece with the Olympic games and huge stadiums. Then came ancient Rome with athletics and competition on an even larger scale. Circus Maximus in Rome could hold 170,000 spectators for chariot races and gladiator games.

Entertainment that has survived the ages includes music, literature, sports and sex. Other breakdowns can be made, like performing arts and visual arts. Some people distinguish entertainment from art, relegating entertainment to a somehow less worthy category. On close examination, however, these distinctions blur. Art is in the eye of the beholder, a highly personal and subjective issue.

CHECKING YOUR *MEDIA LITERACY*

- **What are categories into which entertainment can be sorted for analysis?**

TECHNOLOGY-DRIVEN ENTERTAINMENT

What distinguished the Age of Mass Communication, which began with Gutenberg's movable type in the 1440s, was that messages, including entertainment, could be mass-produced to reach audiences of unprecedented size. The post-Gutenberg press gave literature wider and wider audiences. But even 200 years after Gutenberg the audience for John Milton's *Paradise Lost,* to take one example, was remarkable for the time but minuscule compared to the audience for every book now on the New York *Times* weekly list of leading titles. Too, literature has taken on diverse forms today, from academic tomes in the Milton tradition to pulp romances and Westerns—and it's not all in printed form.

As media technology leapfrogged into photographic and electronic forms, literature adapted to the new media. Movies extended the reach and the artistic form of books. So did radio and then television. Music, a rare treat in people's lives before audio recording was invented, is everywhere today. Indeed, the impact of the entertainment content of today's mass media is hard to measure. With television turned on seven hours a day in U.S. homes on average, most of it tuned to entertainment content, it's obvious that people are being entertained more than ever before in history.

CHECKING YOUR MEDIA LITERACY

- **What is the role of media technology in entertainment?**

ENTERTAINMENT GENRES

genres
Broad thematic categories of media content

To make sense of the gigantic and growing landscape of entertainment in the mass media, people have devised **genres** that are, in effect, subdivisions of the major categories of storytelling and music.

Perennial Cop Shows. *The police story, almost always a whodunit, is an enduring story genre that spikes periodically in popularity. The latest generation is led by the prime-time CBS series* CSI *and its spin-offs. Here, true to the series' title, characters played by William Petersen and Jorja Fox are at a crime scene investigation.*

MEDIA PEOPLE

Cecile Frot-Coutaz
Producing Lowbrow

Cecile Frot-Coutaz is the queen of schlock television. She has a golden feel for high-performance reality television. She played a key role in selling *American Idol* to Fox, and she's the force behind *America's Got Talent.*

As a child in Lyon, France, Frot-Coutaz didn't watch television. Her biochemist father allowed her to watch only the low-brow English classic, *The Benny Hill Show.* Television held the allure of the forbidden for the young Cecile.

She earned a graduate business degree at the prestigious Insead in Paris in 1994. She said no to the first two offers she received from Goldman Sachs and Morgan Stanley and took a job as a corporate strategist at Pearson's television division in London. Her boss, Greg Dykes, who later became the head of the BBC, taught her fearlessness. He told her, "We're all going to get fired. It just happens, so you might as well take risks."

Among Frot-Coutaz's fearless acts was overseeing Pearson's acquisition of the company that would become Fremantle, which brought with it the game shows *The Price Is Right* and *Password* and the rights to *Baywatch.*

In 2000 Pearson Television, a unit of Bertelsmann, was renamed Fremantle-Media. As Fremantle, the company's focus began to shift from syndication to producing new shows like *Pop Idol.* In 2002, Fremantle sent Frot-Coutaz to the United States to sell an American version of the show. Three networks said no, but Frot-Coutaz helped make the pitch to Fox, which who said yes. *American Idol* became Fox's highest rated show and propelled the network to first place among the coveted 18-to-49 demographic. The show is now in 42 countries. Frot-Coutaz says that *American Idol* has become more than just a television show—she calls it a "pop-cultural phenomenon." Her team works with Fox to make tweaks in the show every year so it remains fresh and engaging.

She convinced Fox not to run the *Idol* competition twice a year, arguing that it would shorten *Idol's* life span. It seems she was right. CBS decided to run *Survivor* twice a year, and its viewers dropped to less than half that for *Idol.*

After *Idol*, Frot-Coutaz created *The Swan,* a show about ordinary women who undergo plastic surgery. It bombed. But then she found the hugely successful *America's Got Talent.*

Next up was Frot-Coutaz's version of a weird Japanese game show called *Hole in the Wall,* in which contestants must squeeze themselves through openings in a moving wall or get knocked into a swimming pool. Although it and a new variety show with Ozzy and Sharon Osbourne for Fox were disappointing compared to the success of *Idol,* Frot-Coutaz hardly blinked in her quest for the next hit show.

In early 2009, she was working on *The Phone* for MTV with co-producer Justin Timberlake. The show is based on a Dutch format that places contestants in the middle of an action movie. "It's a new way to do reality," said Frot-Coutaz, who seems to be prescient about new reality show trends. "We script scenarios and put real people in the script." The *Bourne Identity*-like show also has great opportunities for integration with phone and car partners.

Frot-Coutaz was promoted to chief executive of FremantleMedia North America in 2005. She makes a lot of money for Fremantle. The public filings of the Bertelsmann subsidiary that is Fremantle's parent showed its U.S. revenues—the bulk of which are generated by her group—were $310 million in 2007, up from $280 million the year before and $177 million in 2005.

Cecile Frot-Coutaz. *FremantleMedia's Cecile Frot-Coutaz has a knack for sniffing out the next lucrative trend in reality shows. She is a key player on the international programming scene and the creative force behind* American Idol, America's Got Talent, *and* The Phone.

WHAT DO YOU THINK?

- As more women break the glass ceiling and enter the executive suites in the entertainment industry, what kind of role model is Cecile Frot-Coutaz?
- What in her professional background helped prepare Frot-Coutaz for her role in developing hit shows for Fremantle?

>> **Storytelling.** Whether novels, short stories, television drama or movies, literature can be divided into genres. Popular genres include suspense, romance, horror, Westerns, fantasy, history and biography. Further slicing and dicing are possible. There are subgenres, such as detective stories. Also, some subgenres cut across two or more genres, such as sci-fi Westerns: Remember the 1999 movie *Wild Wild West?* Some genres are short-lived. In the 1960s a movie genre dubbed *blaxploitation* emerged, for better or worse, with a black racist appeal to black audiences. The genre culminated in the *Shaft* series, which, although updated in 2003, had been eclipsed by the ongoing racial integration of society.

>> **Music.** A lot of crossover makes for genre confusion in music. Wanting to define their tastes, aficionados keep reinventing thematic trends. The array of subgenres is dizzying. How is acid rock different from hard rock, from solid rock, from progressive rock, from alternative rock, from power rock, from metal rock? Don't ask. Categorizing is not a neat, clinical task.

>> **Sports.** Genres are clearest in sports because the rules, although not set in granite, have been agreed on, as have the procedures for revising the rules. Nobody confuses baseball with soccer or the shot put with Formula One auto racing. Attempts at crossover genres, like the wrestling-inspired XFL football experiment, don't do well.

CHECKING YOUR MEDIA LITERACY

What are major genres of media-delivered entertainment?

Performance as Media Entertainment

STUDY PREVIEW

The mass media's entertainment content is performance, but it's not pure performer-to-audience. The media change the performance. Authentic performance is live and eyeball-to-eyeball with the audience. Mediated performance is adapted for an unseen and distant audience.

AUTHENTIC PERFORMANCE

When liberal commentator Al Franken used to do a routine before a live audience, before entering politics as a candidate himself, it was uproariously funny unless his bite hit a raw ideological nerve. That's why conservatives avoided his shows. But in 2004, when Franken took his humor to radio in a talk show on the new Air America network, his humor and bite didn't translate well. On radio he was flat. The fact is that the media change performance. There are many reasons for this.

>> **Audience.** At a play, whether on Broadway or in a high school auditorium, the audience is assembled for one purpose. It's **authentic performance,** live with the audience on-site. Everyone is attentive to the performance. Nuances are hard to miss.

>> **Feedback.** Performers on stage are in tune with their audience's reactions. There can be reaction and interplay. For the same performance through a mass medium, performers guess—some better than others—at how they are coming across. The fact is, taking television as an example, what resonates in one living room does not necessarily resonate in another. Some performers are more gifted at maximizing their impact, but to reach the massive, scattered, heterogeneous mass audience requires pandering to some extent to common denominators. There is less edge.

authentic performance
A live performance with an on-site audience

>> Technology. The equipment that makes mass communication possible is what sets it apart from interpersonal and group communication. Technology imposes its own requirements on performance. The aural beauty of operatic trills in an acoustically optimal concert hall cannot be duplicated by a home stereo, no matter how many woofers it has. Andrew Lloyd Webber's stage musical *Starlight Express,* with roller-skating singers on ramps in front of, behind and above the audience, would be a different audience experience in a movie or on television. Media transform a performance. In ways large and small, it becomes a **mediated performance.**

By definition purists prefer pure, unmediated performance. There will always be a following for Broadway, live concerts and ghost stories around the campfire.

CHECKING YOUR MEDIA LITERACY

What are advantages of live performances over mediated performances?

MEDIATED PERFORMANCE

In ways we don't always realize, media technology affects and sometimes shapes the messages the media disseminate. The changes necessary to make a **mediated message** work are a function of the technology that makes it possible to reach a mass audience.

mediated performance
A performance modified and adjusted for delivery to an audience by mass media

mediated message
Adjusted to be effective when carried by the mass media

>> Music. Edison's mechanical recording technology, which captured acoustic waves in a huge horn, picked up no subtleties. Brass bands and loud voices recorded best. Scratchy background noise drowned out soft sounds. It's no wonder that the late 1800s and early 1900s were marked by the popularity of martial music and marching bands. High-pitched voices came through best, which also shaped the popular music of the period.

When Joseph Maxwell's electrical technology was refined in the 1920s, subtle sounds that now could survive the recording and playback processes came into vogue. Rudy Vallee and Bing Crosby were in. John Philip Sousa was out. Improvements in fidelity beginning in the 1950s meant that music could be played

A Gore-Bon Jovi Moment. *Live performance has become rooted in mediated performance. This is no better illustrated than by former Vice President Al Gore's 2007 Live Earth concert to exploit the power of music to elevate global warming as a public policy agenda item worldwide. Top-tier performers, including Jon Bon Jovi, took to stages on every continent. Their repertoire was almost wholly music from their recordings. Although performed live, the performances were mediated to maximize audience. Nineteen million watched worldwide on television, 10 million on the Internet.*

louder and louder without unsettling dissonance—and many rockers took to louder renditions.

>> **Movies.** Media technology profoundly affects art. When audio and film technology were merged to create talkies, moviemakers suddenly had all kinds of new creative options for their storytelling. Directors had more new possibilities when wide screens replaced squarish screens in movie houses. When technology changes the experience for the moviemaker, it also changes the experience for moviegoers.

>> **Sports.** Technology has dazzled sports fans. Instant replays on television, tried first during an Army-Navy football game in the early 1960s, added a dimension that in-stadium fans could not see. Then came miniature cameras that allow viewers to see what referees see on the field. Putting microphones on referees, coaches and players lets the mass audience eavesdrop on the sounds of the playing field that no one in the stands or sidelines can pick up.

Some digital cable channels allow viewers to select various static camera angles during a game. Viewers, in effect, can participate in creating the media coverage they see. This is a profound development. Watching television, once a largely passive activity, now can involve the viewer at least to some degree.

CHECKING YOUR MEDIA LITERACY

What are advantages of mediated performances over live performances?

Storytelling

STUDY PREVIEW

The media are powerful vehicles for exponentially extending the reach of literature. The most enduring genres include romances and mysteries, but variations and hybrids come and go in popularity.

GENRES OF LITERATURE

Some of literature's storytelling genres have lasted through the centuries. Shakespeare was neither the first to do romances and mysteries, nor the last. Genres help us make sense of literature, giving us a basis for comparison and contrast. Literature can be categorized in many ways, one as basic as fiction and nonfiction, another being prose and poetry. There are periods: medieval, antebellum, postmodern. There are breakdowns into geographic, ethnic and cultural traditions: Russian, Hispanic and Catholic. Ideologies comprise genres: Marxist, fascist and libertarian. Bookstores use thematic genres to sort their inventory, including mysteries, romances, sports, biographies and hobbies.

CHECKING YOUR MEDIA LITERACY

What genres of media content can you identify besides those mentioned here?

MEDIA-DEFINED TRENDS

Genres rise and fall in popularity. Early television was awash with variety shows, which featured a range of comedy, song and dance, and other acts. Then came the wave of 1950s quiz shows, then Westerns, then police shows. Going into the 21st century, the television programming fads were talk shows in the style pioneered by Phil Donahue

Genre du Jour. *Television series built around complex female characters—antiheroines, they could be called—have been a recent genre rage. Kyra Sedgwick's character on* The Closer *was squarely in the genre. Minnie Driver played an ex-con drug addict in FX's* The Riches. *Other edgy lead portrayals of flawed and non-stereotypical women included Mary-Louise Parker, a drug-dealing widow on Showtime's* Weeds, *Courteney Cox on FX's* Dirt, *Glenn Close on FX's* Damages, *and Holly Hunter on TNT's* Saving Grace. *As with all genres, no one knows when this one will run its course.*

and sustained by Oprah Winfrey, reality shows epitomized by the unending CBS *Survivor* series, and yet another rush of whodunit police shows.

Some categories are short-lived. A wave of buddy movies was ushered in by *Butch Cassidy and the Sundance Kid* in 1969. Later *Thelma and Louise* spawned girlfriend movies.

Genre trends are audience-driven. People flock to a particular book, song, film or television show and then to the thematic sequels until they tire of it all. Although a lot of genre content is derivative rather than original art, new twists and refinements can reflect artistic fine-tuning by authors, scriptwriters and other creators. People may quibble about whether Francis Ford Coppola's *The Godfather* or *The Godfather Part II*, was the better, but almost everyone, including the critics, concurs that both were filmic masterpieces. At the same time, nobody serious about creative media content is looking forward to Sylvester Stallone in *Rocky XXXIII*. At some point the possibilities for fresh treatments within a theme are exhausted.

CHECKING YOUR MEDIA LITERACY

- **What genres of media content have you seen come and go?**

Music

STUDY PREVIEW

Audio technology accelerated the effect of music as a social unifier. This is no better illustrated than by the integration of traditional black music and white hillbilly music into rock 'n' roll, a precursor to the furthering of racial integration of U.S. society. The potency of music has been enhanced by its growing role in other media forms, including movies and television.

ROCKABILLY REVOLUTION

Most music historians trace contemporary popular music to roots in two distinctive types of American folk music. There was the black music emanating from the enslaved black culture. Another form was hillbilly music, also from the South but with roots in rural Appalachia.

>> Black Music. Africans who were brought to the colonies as slaves used music to soothe their difficult lives. Much of the music reflected their oppression and hopeless poverty. Known as **black music,** it was distinctive in that it carried strains of slaves' African roots and at the same time reflected the black American experience. This music also included strong religious themes, expressing the slaves' indefatigable faith in a glorious afterlife. Flowing from the heart and the soul, this was folk music of the most authentic sort.

black music
Folk genre from American black slave experience

After the Civil War, black musicians found a white audience on riverboats and in saloons and pleasure palaces of various sorts. That introduced a commercial component into black music and fueled numerous variations, including jazz. Even with the growing white following, the creation of these latter-day forms of black music remained almost entirely with African-American musicians. White musicians who picked up on the growing popularity of black music drew heavily on black songwriters. Much of Benny Goodman's swing music, for example, came from black arranger Fletcher Henderson.

In the 1930s and 1940s a distinctive new form of black music, **rhythm and blues,** emerged. The people who enjoyed R&B were all over the country, and these fans included both blacks and whites. Mainstream American music had come to include a firm African-American presence.

>> Hillbilly Music. Another authentic American folk music form, **hillbilly music,** flowed from the lives of Appalachian and Southern whites. Early hillbilly music had a strong colonial heritage in English ballads and ditties, but over time hillbilly music evolved into a genre in its own right. Fiddle playing and twangy lyrics reflected the poverty and hopelessness of rural folk, "hillbillies" as they called themselves. Also like black music, hillbilly music reflected the joys, frustrations and sorrows of love and family. However, hillbilly music failed to develop more than a regional following—that is, until the 1950s, when a great confluence of the black and hillbilly traditions occurred. This distinctive new form of American music, called **rockabilly** early on, became rock 'n' roll.

CHECKING YOUR MEDIA LITERACY

What distinctive American musical genres melded in rockabilly?

ROCK 'N' ROLL

If **rock 'n' roll** as a musical genre has a single progenitor, it may be Memphis disc jockey and promoter **Sam Phillips.** In 1951 Phillips recorded a cars and girls song, *Rocket 88,* an ode to a new Oldsmobile. The recording itself was technically flawed. Willie Kizart's guitar had a cracked amp, but, folded into a boogie-woogie piano, a blues sax and Jackie Brenston's rhythm and blues vocals, the fuzzy guitar sounds seemed to fit. Right away, *Rocket 88* was atop the R&B charts.

Rock 'n' roll was hardly calculated. *Rocket 88* had come from four buddies, Ike Turner and His Kings of Rhythm. Infatuated with the new Oldsmobile and driving to a recording session in Memphis, they scribbled rhymes about the Oldsmobile. A blown tire, a rainstorm and a night in jail later, they were in Sam Phillips' recording studio and jamming impromptu—Turner boogie-woogieing his piano, Raymond Hill blowing his blues sax, Willie Kizart hitting fuzzy chords on his failing guitar, and Jackie Brentson intoning those on-the-fly lyrics from the trip.

Sam Phillips was pleased that *Rocket 88,* from a black group, caught on with white as well as black teenagers. But Phillips realized that this emerging hybrid musical genre needed a white face in order to find an enduring place in mainstream pop. In 1954 a white crooner, Elvis Presley, was in the studio recording ballads. During a break Presley belted out a variation of black composer Arthur Crudup's *That's All Right*. Phillips knew he had found what he called, at least apocryphally, his "white boy who sang colored."

Elvis wasn't the first, but he put a white face on rock 'n' roll. A cultural race barrier was transcended on an unprecedented scale. It can be argued that the racial integration of music paved the way for the accelerated civil rights movement in the 1960s that profoundly changed U.S. society.

CHECKING YOUR MEDIA LITERACY

How did Elvis Presley personify the music traditions that fused into rock 'n' roll?

rhythm and blues
Distinctive style of black music that took form in 1930s

hillbilly music
Folk genre from rural Appalachia, Southern white experience

rockabilly
A splicing of rock 'n' roll and hillbilly, used for early rock music

rock 'n' roll
A popular dance music characterized by a heavy beat, simple melodies, and guitar, bass and drum instrumentation, usually on a 12-bar structure

Sam Phillips
A Memphis music producer who recorded and promoted early rock music

Birth of Rock 'n' Roll. *A strong claim can be made that a two-minute ode to a powerful new Oldsmobile, the* Rocket 88 *model, with a firm backbeat, launched rock 'n' roll as a musical genre in 1951. Other claimants: Louis Jordan's* Caledonia, *Fats Domino's* Fat Man, *and Lloyd Price's* Lawdy Miss Clawdy.

MUSIC OF DISSENT

Entertainment can be political, potently so. A folk revival was a centerpiece of the anti-Vietnam war movement of the late 1960s into the 1970s. There were countersingers too, who sold lots of vinyl. *The Ballad of the Green Berets* cast soldiers in a heroic vein. *An Okie from Muskogee* glorified blind patriotism.

This was nothing new. Stephen Foster's *Nothing but a Plain Old Soldier* kept the legend of George Washington going. *The Battle Hymn of the Republic* still moves people. The Civil War generated a spate of patriotic music. The catchy *Over There* did the same in World War I.

It was an offhand remark, not their music, that made the sassy Dixie Chicks the bad girls among George W. Bush loyalists. In 2003 at the height of public enthusiasm for the Iraq war, lead singer Natalie Maines, a Texas native, told a London audience that she was "ashamed" that the president, who had launched the war, was from Texas. Despite the popularity of their music, the Chicks were banned by many radio stations whose managements were cowed by the volume of listener outrage. The Chicks had the last word, however. In 2006, with public sentiment shifted against the war, the group rebuffed the angry reaction with *Not Ready to Make Nice* on a CD that opened at Number 28 on *Billboard*'s Hot 100.

Classic rockers Pearl Jam added to the anti-war revival with an album that included *World Wide Suicide,* which opened with a newspaper casualty report. Then came the dark lyrics: "Now you know both sides / Claiming killing in God's name / But God is nowhere to be found, conveniently." The new anti-Iraq war repertoire was perhaps most strident with Neil Young's track *Let's Impeach the President,* in which he sings "flip" and "flop" amid Bush quotes. Paul Simon, whose popularity, like Young's, dated to the Vietnam period, entered the anti-war revival in 2006 with the politically tinged album *Surprise*.

Political leaders know the power of incorporating popular music into their campaign personas. Can you imagine a documentary on Franklin Roosevelt without Jack Yellen and Milton Ager's *Happy Days Are Here Again*? The first President Bush paraphrased the Nitty Gritty Dirt Band on the campaign trail, then borrowed from Paul Simon's *Boy in the Bubble* to make a point about the economy: "If this age of miracles has taught us anything, it's that if we can change the world, we can change America."

The mobilizing power of recorded music was demonstrated with Michael Jackson and Lionel Richie's *We Are the World,* the fastest-selling record of the 1980s. Four million copies were sold in six weeks. Profits from the recording, produced by big-name entertainers who volunteered, went to the USA for Africa project. In six months $50 million was raised for medical and financial support for drought-stricken people. *We Are the World,* a single song, had directly saved lives. Willie Nelson has done the same with recordings from his Farm Aid concerts.

The worldwide Live Aid and Live Earth concerts were in the same spirit. In short, music has tremendous effects on human beings, and the technology of sound recording amplifies these effects. The bugle boy was essential to World War II's Company B, but today reveille is digitized to wake the troops. Mothers still sing Brahms' *Lullaby,* but more babies are lulled to sleep by Brahms on disc. For romance, lovers today rely more on recorded music than on their own vocal cords. The technology of sound recording gives composers, lyricists and performers far larger audiences than would ever be possible through live performances.

CHECKING YOUR MEDIA LITERACY

- **What has historically been the role of protest music?**

Mixing Music and Politics. *The Dixie Chicks were no friend of the Iraq war even before Bush-bashing became a national pastime in the waning months of his presidency. After Natalie Maines lashed out at the president in an aside at a London performance, Bush supporters pressured radio stations to stop playing their music. Sales of their music fell, but the group, unapologetic, didn't back off. Within months, record sales rebounded. The saga demonstrated how the role of music and performers is perceived in public policy.*

RAP

As transforming as rock was, so too 40 years later was **rap.** Born in the impoverished Bronx section of New York, this new style of music had an intense bass for dancing and rhyming riffs, often a strong and rapid-fire attitude, overlaid on the music. Slowly rap spread to other black urban areas. Indie-produced *Run-DMC* and *King of Rock* were the first black rap albums to break into the U.S. music mainstream. Major record companies soon were signing up rap acts. Controversial groups Public Enemy and N.W.A., with violence and racism as themes of their songs, made rap a public issue in the 1990s, which only fanned diehard enthusiasm.

Like rock 'n' roll, major labels missed the significance of early rap, scrambling to catch up only after the catchy lyrics were siphoning sales from older pop genres. A maxim in media studies is that large enterprises become mired in tradition with an aversion for risk taking.

CHECKING YOUR MEDIA LITERACY

- **What was the role of independent labels in the rise of rap?**
- **Why was significant innovation, such as rock 'n' roll and rap, a business challenge for major media companies?**

rap
Dance music with intense bass, rhyming riffs, the lyrics often with anti-establishment defiance

MUSIC AS MULTIMEDIA CONTENT

Although music often is studied as the content issued by the recording industry, music is hardly a one-dimensional form of media message. Even in pre-mass media eras, going back to prehistoric times, music was integrated with dance and theater. When

"I Love College." *White rappers are rare, but performer Asher Roth has given the genre a white suburban spin. His rhymes and riffs make no apology for his non-dysfunctional upbringing in the Philadelphia suburb of Morrisville. His style has been called by critics, amateurish and uneven, but his music reflects a coming-of-age experience laced with Nintendo, Ford Tauruses and getting high on marijuana. Roth calls it "yoga and yogurt covered in fruit." And he's built a college following.*

movies were establishing themselves, music was an important component. Even before movie sound tracks were introduced with the "talkies," many movie houses hired a piano player who kept one eye on the screen and hammered out supportive music. D. W. Griffith's *The Birth of a Nation* of 1915 had an accompanying score for a 70-piece orchestra.

Some movies are little more than musical vehicles for popular performers, going back to Bing Crosby and continuing through Elvis Presley and the Beatles. Rare is the modern movie without a significant musical bed. Just count the number of songs in the copyright credits at the end of today's movies.

Early radio recognized the value of music. Jingles and ditties proved key to establishing many brand names. Today many composers and lyricists derive significant income from their work being built into advertisements for television, radio and online. Think about the Intel and NBC tones or the grating "Hey, Culligan Man."

CHECKING YOUR MEDIA LITERACY

- **What is the difficulty of separating music from other forms of entertainment?**

Sports as Media Entertainment

STUDY PREVIEW

Early on, mass media people sensed the potential of sports to build their audiences, first through newspapers, then through magazines, radio and television. The media feed what seems an insatiable demand for more sports. Why the huge public intrigue with sports? One expert suggests it's the mix of suspense, heroes, villains, pageantry and ritual.

MASS AUDIENCE FOR SPORTS

The brilliant newspaper publisher **James Gordon Bennett** sensed how a public interest in sports could build circulation for his New York *Herald* in the 1830s. Bennett assigned reporters to cover sports regularly. Fifty years later, with growing interest in horse racing, prizefighting, yacht racing and baseball, **Joseph Pulitzer** organized the first separate sports department at his New York *World*. Sportswriters began specializing in different sports.

> **James Gordon Bennett**
> New York newspaper publisher in 1830s; first to assign reporters to sports regularly

> **Joseph Pulitzer**
> New York newspaper publisher in 1880s; organized the first newspaper sports department

> **KDKA**
> Pittsburgh radio station that pioneered sports broadcasting in 1920s

Audience appetite for sports was insatiable. For the 1897 Corbett-Fitzsimmons heavyweight title fight in remote Nevada, dozens of writers showed up. The New York *Times* introduced celebrity coverage in 1910 when it hired retired prizefighter John L. Sullivan to cover the Jeffries-Johnson title bout in Reno.

Sports historians call the 1920s the Golden Era of Sports, with newspapers glorifying athletes. Heroes, some with enduring fame, included Jack Dempsey in boxing, Knute Rockne and Jim Thorpe in football, and Babe Ruth in baseball. The 1920s also marked radio as a medium for sports. In 1921 **KDKA** of Pittsburgh carried the first play-by-play baseball game, the Davis Cup tennis matches and the blow-by-blow Johnny Ray versus John Dundee fight. Sportswriter Grantland Rice, the pre-eminent sportswriter of the time, covered the entire World Series live from New York for KDKA, also in 1921.

Sports magazines have their roots in *American Turf Register*, which began a 15-year run in Baltimore in 1829. The *American Bicycling Journal* rode a bicycling craze from

1877 to 1879. Nothing matched the breadth and scope of *Sports Illustrated,* founded in 1954 by magazine magnate **Henry Luce.** The magazine, launched with 350,000 charter subscribers, now boasts a circulation of 3.3 million a week.

Although television dabbled in sports from its early days, the introduction of *Wide World of Sports* in 1961 established that television was made for sports and, conversely, that sports was made for television. The show, the brainchild of ABC programming wizard **Roone Arledge,** covered an unpredictable diversity of sports, from Ping-Pong to skiing. In this period, professional athletic leagues agreed to modify their rules to accommodate television for commercial breaks and, eventually, to make the games more exciting for television audiences.

Television commentator Les Brown explains sports as the perfect program form for television: "At once topical and entertaining, performed live and suspensefully without a script, peopled with heroes and villains, full of action and human interest and laced with pageantry and ritual."

The launching of ESPN as an all-sports network for cable television systems prompted millions of households to subscribe to cable. The success of ESPN spawned sibling networks. Regional sports networks have also emerged, including many created by Fox as major revenue centers.

CHECKING YOUR MEDIA LITERACY

- **What have been landmarks in the growth of media sports for amusement?**

AUDIENCE AND ADVERTISER CONFLUENCE

The television networks and national advertisers found a happy confluence of interest in the huge audience for televised sports. This goes back at least to *Friday Night Fights,* sponsored by Gillette, and *Wednesday Night Fights,* sponsored by Pabst beer, in the 1950s. Today, sports and television are almost synonymous. Not only does the Super Bowl pack a stadium, but 90 million U.S. households tune in. The World Cup soccer tournament draws the largest worldwide television audiences.

In part to keep their names on screen, some firms have bought the rights to put their name on sports stadiums. The value of brand-name exposure at places like the Target Center in Minneapolis, the Bank One Ballpark in Phoenix and Coors Field in Denver is impossible to measure.

Advertiser interest flows and ebbs, as do audiences. The 1950s audience for Wednesday night fights, for example, grew fickle. The phenomenal success of the World Wrestling Federation lost steam after the September 11 terrorist attacks in 2001. Too, there seems to be a saturation point. The WWF's colorful promoter, Vince McMahon, bombed with his new XFL professional football league in 2001. Even with its own rules, designed to add excitement for television audiences, and even with tireless promotion by NBC, it seemed that football fans already had their plates full.

CHECKING YOUR MEDIA LITERACY

- **Why are advertisers attracted to sports?**

COST OF SPORTS BROADCASTING

Sports attract huge audiences to television. Roughly 71 percent of U.S. households tuned in to the 2004 Olympics from Athens. For the Super Bowl 70 percent's typical. Advertisers pay millions of dollars for commercial time to reach these audiences. Anheuser-Busch spent $222.8 million on sports advertising in one recent year, Chevrolet $182 million, and Coca-Cola $131.2 million. With the exception of the 2008 Beijing Olympics, for which NBC budgeted $1 billion, the networks seldom generate enough revenue to offset fees negotiated by sports leagues. Broadcast rights exceeded $6.9 billion in 2004 for the Big Four professional leagues and NASCAR.

Henry Luce
Magazine publisher known for *Time, Life, Sports Illustrated* and others

Roone Arledge
ABC television executive responsible for *Wide World of Sports* in 1961

Data are hard to come by, but these are estimates from industry insiders of recent bottom lines for U.S. television networks:

2003	Major League baseball	$370 million
2003	National Football League	$270 million
2004	National Basketball Association	$246 million
2003–2004	NASCAR	$106 million
2003–2004	National Hockey League	$77 million
2004	Athens Olympics	$65 million
2003–2004	College basketball	$55 million
2003	College football	$10 million

Considering the economics, the networks occasionally retreat from the bidding frenzy for broadcast rights. NBC opted out of bidding to renew its four-year $1.6 billion National Basketball Association contract after losing $100 million in 2003. What happened? ESPN won the rights for $2.4 billion.

Madness, you say? Maybe not. Consider the experience of CBS, which was the leading sports network in 1994. CBS executives, trying to make the numbers work to continue its National Football League coverage, was outbid by Fox. Six local affiliates switched to Fox. CBS fell to fourth among the networks with male viewers, an important demographic group for advertisers. Smarting at the setbacks, CBS was not to be outdone. When CBS regained the NFL rights in 1998, the network resumed leadership in terms both of total viewers and of men 18 and older. Now CBS and Fox have bid $8 billion for NFL games from 2007 to 2010, 25 percent more than the previous deal.

The networks have adjusted their business model from seeing sports as a profit center. Instead, sports has become recognized as a **loss leader.** The goal now is to use sports programs to promote other network programming, to enhance the network as a brand, and to deny coverage to competing networks—and at the same time generate enough in advertising and in some cases subscription revenue to minimize the loss. Les Moonves, president of CBS, explained the new thinking this way: "Broadcast networks must look at sports as a piece of a much larger puzzle and not focus on the specific profits and losses of sports divisions."

Culturally the Moonves mindset has negative effects. The sports drain has forced CBS and other networks to emphasize more low-cost programming, like reality shows, for the rest of their schedules. The question: After sports, what's worth watching? Also, critics note that the huge licensing fees paid in broadcast rights make possible the mega-salaries of top athletes.

loss leader
A product sold at a loss to attract customers

CHECKING YOUR MEDIA LITERACY

- **Why do broadcast companies compete to air sports even though the programming generally is a money loser?**

Sex as Media Content

STUDY PREVIEW

Despite the risk of offending some people's sensitivities, the media have long trafficked in sexual content. Undeniably, there is a market. The media have fought in the U.S. courts for their right to carry sexually explicit content and for the right of adults to have access to it.

ADULT ENTERTAINMENT

Sexually oriented content has bedeviled the mass media in the United States for longer than anyone can remember. Clearly, there is a demand for it. Sales of banned books soared as soon as the courts overruled government restrictions, no better illustrated than by the Irish classic ***Ulysses*** by James Joyce in 1930. Firm data on the profitability of sexual content are hard to come by, partly because definitions are elusive. *Ulysses*, as an example, is hardly a sex book to most people, yet its sexual content is what once prompted a federal import ban. The difficulty of a definition gives partisans the opportunity to issue exaggerated estimates of the scope of the sexual media content.

Even so, there is no denying that sex sells. Although revenues are difficult to peg precisely, most estimates are in the range of $8 billion to $10 billion annually for the entire U.S. sex industry, a major part of which is media content. About 8,000 adult movie titles a year are released. Pay-per-view adult movies on satellite and cable television generate almost $600 million in revenue a year.

It was no sleazy outfit that first imported *Ulysses* but the venerable publisher Random House. Today the major purveyors of adult content include Time Warner's HBO and Cinemax, which pipe late-night adult content to multiple-system cable operators including Time Warner. Satellite providers DirecTV and Dish Network offer porn to their subscribers. Big-name hotel chains pipe adult movies into rooms. In addition, moralists periodically picket Barnes & Noble and other mainstream bookstores to protest the books and magazines they stock.

CHECKING YOUR MEDIA LITERACY

- **What has been government's role in curbing sexual content in entertainment?**
- **Why is government regulation of sexual media content difficult?**

DECENCY REQUIREMENTS

Most media companies have found comfort in the definition of sexually acceptable content that has evolved in free expression cases in the U.S. courts. Today the courts make a distinction between **obscenity,** which is not allowed, and **pornography,** which the courts find to be protected by the First Amendment guarantee not only of free expression but also of adult access to other people's expressions.

How are obscenity and pornography different? Since 1973, when the U.S. Supreme Court decided the case *Miller* v. *California*, the courts have followed the **Miller Standard.** In effect, sexual content is protected from government bans unless the material fails all of these tests:

- Would a typical person applying local standards see the material as appealing mainly for its sexually arousing effect?
- Is the material devoid of serious literary, artistic, political or scientific value?
- Is the sexual activity depicted offensively, in a way that violates a state law that explicitly defines offensiveness?

The Miller Standard protects a vast range of sexual content. Only material for which the answer is "yes" to all three Miller questions can be censored by government agencies.

The Miller Standard notwithstanding, the Federal Communications Commission fined CBS $550,000 for the Janet Jackson breast flash during the 2004 Super Bowl halftime show. The producer, CBS's Viacom cousin MTV, called the incident a "wardrobe malfunction." About 89 million people were tuned in. Some complained.

CHECKING YOUR MEDIA LITERACY

- **How are obscenity and pornography different?**
- **What is the Miller Standard?**
- **How useful do you find the Miller Standard?**

Ulysses
James Joyce novel banned in the United States until 1930 court decision

obscenity
Sexually explicit media depictions that the government can ban

pornography
Sexually explicit depictions that are protected from government bans

Miller Standard
Current U.S. Supreme Court definition of sexually explicit depictions that are protected by the First Amendment from government bans

Filthy Words. *After Pacifica radio station WBAI in New York aired a 12-minute recorded George Carlin monologue, the U.S. Supreme Court authorized government restrictions on indecency at times of the day when children might be listening.*

SEXUAL CONTENT AND CHILDREN

Although government limits on sexual content gradually eased in the late 20th century, there remained restrictions on media content for children. State laws that forbid the sale of sexually explicit materials to children are exempted from regular First Amendment rules. The U.S. Supreme Court established the childhood exception in 1968 in a case involving a Bellmore, New York, sandwich shop owner, **Sam Ginsberg,** who had sold girlie magazines to a 16-year-old. The local prosecutor went after Ginsberg using a state law that prohibited selling depictions of nudity to anyone under age 17. The U.S. Supreme Court upheld the constitutionality of the state law.

In broadcasting, the U.S. Supreme Court has upheld restrictions aimed at shielding children. After New York radio station WBAI aired a comedy routine by **George Carlin** with four-letter anatomical words and vulgarities, the Federal Communications Commission, which can yank a station's license to broadcast, took action against the station's owner, the Pacifica Foundation. In the **Pacifica case,** as it came to be known, the U.S. Supreme Court upheld the FCC's limits on indecency during times of the day when children are likely to be listening. Carlin's monologue, *Filthy Words,* had aired at 2 p.m. In response, stations now are careful to keep the raunchiest stuff off the air until late night.

The courts also have upheld laws against sexual depictions of juveniles as exploitative. Many prosecutors come down hard even for the possession of such materials. Child pornography is one of society's last taboos.

CHECKING YOUR MEDIA LITERACY

- **Describe attempts by the government to create a double standard, one for adults and one for children, on sexual media content.**

Gaming as Media Content

STUDY PREVIEW

Gaming has grown as a form of mass entertainment. Some games outdraw television. As typical with new media content, gaming has become a whipping boy for society's ills with calls for restriction. The courts have not found compelling reasons to go along with restrictions.

Sam Ginsberg
Figure in U.S. Supreme Court decision to bar sales of pornography to children

George Carlin
Comedian whose satires on vulgarities prompted rules on radio programming to shield children

Pacifica case
U.S. Supreme Court ruling to keep indecency off over-air broadcast stations at times when children are likely to be listening or watching

GROWING ENTERTAINMENT FORM

Nobody could doubt the significance of video games as a media form after 2001. Sales in the United States outpaced movies. In 2004 when Microsoft introduced its *Halo2,* it was a news event. At 6,800 retailers nationwide, the doors opened at midnight on the release date to thousands of fans waiting in line, some for as long as 14 hours. Within 24 hours, sales surpassed $125 million—way ahead of the $70 million opening-weekend box office for the year's leading film, *The Incredibles*.

The time enthusiasts spend with video games is catching up with television. Players of *Madden NFL 2004* spend an estimated average of 100 hours a year on the game. With 4 million players, that is 400 million hours. The full season of *The Sopranos,* then at its heyday, was claiming 143 million viewing hours. Do the math: *The Sopranos* averaged 11 million viewers for 13 episodes that year.

To catch consumers who spend less time with television and more time with video games, advertisers have shifted chunks of their budgets to gaming.

Madden NFL. *The sudden potency of gaming as a media content form was no better illustrated than with Electronic Arts'* Madden NFL 2004, *which earned $200 million within four months. The Oscar-winning movie at the time,* Chicago, *took nine months to earn $171 million.*

The potential is incredible. Half of Americans 6 and older play games, and that elusive target for advertisers, men 18 and older, makes up 26 percent of the gamers.

CHECKING YOUR MEDIA LITERACY

Why is gaming attractive as an advertising vehicle?

IMPACT OF GAMING

Although gaming is distinctive as a form of media content, market-savvy executives have extended their franchise to other forms. The 2001 movie *Lara Croft Tomb Raider,* adopted from a 1996 game and six sequels, generated $131 million in U.S. box offices. *Resident Evil* grossed $90 million, *Mortal Kombat,* $135 million. There is inverse cross-fertilization too. Games have been based on movies, including *James Bond, Matrix, Shrek, Spider-Man* and *Star Wars*. Gaming shows on television and gaming magazines have proliferated.

Music ranging from orchestral to hip-hop has replaced the blips and bleeps of early generation games. For recorded music companies and artists, landing a spot in a game can provide wider exposure than MTV. For one annual edition of *Madden NFL,* game manufacturer Electronic Arts auditioned 2,500 songs submitted by recording companies. Twenty-one ended up in the game. The Phoenix band Minibosses plays nothing but Nintendo music, note for note.

Not surprisingly, the integration of gaming into larger media conglomerates is under way. The Warner Brothers movie studio now has a gaming division. So does Disney's Buena Vista. Sumner Redstone, whose media empire includes CBS and MTV, has bought into the Midway gaming company. Hollywood and New York talent agencies have divisions that look for game roles for their client actors.

CHECKING YOUR MEDIA LITERACY

Why is gaming shedding its status as a niche media?

CENSORSHIP AND GAMING

Like other entertainment forms, gaming is a lightning rod of concern about the effects of explicit violence and sex on children. The industry devised a voluntary rating system with EC for "early childhood" to AO for "adults only," but critics have called the system a joke among retailers. Three high-visibility U.S. senators, Evan Bayh of Indiana, Hillary Clinton of New York and Joe Lieberman of Connecticut, once went so far as to propose $5,000 fines for every time a retailer violates the code for kids under 17.

Similar attempts to codify ratings through law at the state level have not been viewed kindly in the courts. Since 2001 federal judges have found a lack of compelling evidence from opponents who claim that games like *Grand Theft Auto: San Andreas* cause harm. If anyone ever demonstrates that a game begets violent behavior, the courts may change their stance. Meanwhile, the First Amendment gives constitutional protection to game makers as freedom of expression and to game players as freedom to inquire and explore.

CHECKING YOUR MEDIA LITERACY

How have gaming companies responded to calls to censor violence and sex?

Artistic Values

STUDY PREVIEW

The mass media are inextricably linked with culture because it is through the media that creative people have their strongest sway. Although the media have the potential to disseminate the best creative work of the human mind and soul, some critics say the media are obsessive about trendy, often silly subjects. These critics find serious fault with the media's concern for pop culture, claiming it squeezes out things of significance.

MEDIA CONTENT AS HIGH ART

Mass media messages can be art of a high order, as was perhaps no better illustrated than by early filmmaker D. W. Griffith. In the 1910s Griffith proved himself a filmmaking author whose contribution to the culture, for better or worse, was original in scale, content and style. Griffith had something to say, and the new mass medium of film was the vehicle for his message.

In the 1950s, when French New Wave directors were offering distinctive stories and messages, film critic **Andre Bazin** devised the term ***auteur*** to denote significant and original cinematic contributions. European auteurs included Jean Luc Godard, who made *Breathless,* and François Truffaut, who made *The 400 Blows*. Their work was marked by distinctive cinematic techniques—freeze-frames, handheld cameras and novel angles, many of them common in movies now. Perhaps the most famous of these highbrow filmmakers who developed a global following was the Swedish director Ingmar Bergman, with his *The Seventh Seal* and other dark, moody and autobiographical works.

American filmmakers have also contributed to the auteur movement. The original auteurs were those Hollywood directors working within the constraints of the studio system who nevertheless imparted their unique artistic vision across their body of work. John Ford, John Huston, Howard Hawks and Elia Kazan all left their distinctive mark on otherwise homogenous Hollywood products. More recent auteurs include Stanley Kubrick, who directed *2001: A Space Odyssey;* Martin Scorsese, whose films include *Taxi Driver* and *Goodfellas;* David Lynch, who made *Blue Velvet;* and Spike Lee, who focuses on African-American life.

Culturally significant media content is hardly limited to movies. Older media forms, including novels and short stories, have long been home for creative people whose work adds insight to our lives and deepens our understandings and appreciations.

The impact of great composers from eras before the mass media has been exponentially extended through recording, film and television. The printing press greatly expanded the audience for religious scriptures, whose messages go back to prehistoric times.

CHECKING YOUR MEDIA LITERACY

- **Which media content easily ranks as worthy art?**

LESSER ART

To be sure, not all media content is high art.

Andre Bazin
French film critic who devised the term *auteur* for significant cutting-edge filmmakers

auteur
A filmmaker recognized for significant and original treatments

>> Production-Line Entertainment. A television soap opera, whatever its entertainment value, lacks the creative genius of Shakespeare's enduring *Romeo and Juliet*. Why can't all media content rank high on an artistic scale? Besides the obvious explanation that not everyone is born a Shakespeare, the modern mass media are commercial enterprises that must produce vast quantities of material. In the 1920s, for example, an insatiable public demand for movies led to the creation of the

Hollywood **studio system,** in effect turning moviemaking into a factory process. Production quotas drove movie production. The studios, awash in money, hired leading authors of the day, including F. Scott Fitzgerald and William Faulkner, for creative story lines and scripts, but inexorable demands for material drained them. It has been said that Hollywood had some of the most gifted writers of the time doing their weakest work.

The factory model, a product of the Industrial Age, extends throughout the media. The Canadian book publisher **Harlequin** grinds out romance novels with their bodice-busting covers. Nobody confuses them with high art. Imagine, also, filling a television network's prime-time obligation, 42 half-hour slots a week. It can't all be great stuff, despite the promotional claims in preseason ramp-ups. Also, many in the mass audience don't want great art anyway.

>> **Copycat Content.** Significant amounts of media content are imitative. Copycat sounds abound in material from the recording industry. In network television a sudden success, like ABC's *Who Wants to Be a Millionaire* in 2001, spawned other, albeit less successful, quiz shows. Alas, even *Millionaire* was hardly original. The concept was licensed from an already-running show in Britain.

>> **Cross-Media Adaptations.** The demand for content creates a vacuum that sucks up material from other media. Movie studios draw heavily on written literature, from best-selling novels to comic books like *Spider-Man* and *The X-Men*. Conversely, fresh movies sometimes are adapted into book form.

Cross-media adaptations don't always work well. Movie versions of books often disappoint readers. Scenes change. So do characters. Inevitably, a lot is left out. Some of the criticism is unfair because it fails to recognize that movies are a distinct medium. How, for example, could a screenwriter pack everything in a 100,000-word novel into a 100-minute script? These are different media. Passages that work brilliantly in a word-driven medium, like a magazine or short story, can fall flat in a medium with visual enhancements. Conversely, the nuances compactly portrayed by a master actor, like Meryl Streep or Jack Nicholson, could take pages and pages in a book and not work as well. Also, movie studio producers, almost always needing to appeal to the widest possible audience, will alter plots, scenes and characters and sometimes even reverse a story line's climactic events.

Some cross-media adaptations are commercial disasters. With limited success, movie studios have tried to cash in on the popularity of video games. Despite high expectations, *Super Mario Bros*. flopped in 1993. The explanation? Some critics cite the same difficulties that occur in transferring messages from books to movies. With video games the audience member plays an active role by exercising some control over the story line. Watching a movie, however, is relatively passive.

studio system
A production-line movie system devised by Hollywood in the 1920s

CHECKING YOUR MEDIA LITERACY

- **What mass media dynamics work against consistent delivery of quality content?**

Harlequin
Canadian publisher known for romances with clichéd characters, settings and themes; the term is applied generically to pulp romances

UNPRETENTIOUS MEDIA CONTENT

Although critics pan a lot of media content as unworthy, the fact is that lowbrow art and middlebrow art find audiences, sometimes large audiences, and have a firm place in the mix that the mass media offer. There is nothing artistically pretentious in **pulp fiction,** including the Harlequin romances, nor their soap-opera equivalents on television. The lack of pretension, however, can have its own campy charm.

pulp fiction
Quickly and inexpensively produced easy-to-read short novels

ELITIST VERSUS POPULIST VALUES

The mass media can enrich society by disseminating the best of human creativity, including great literature, music and art. The media also carry a lot of lesser things that reflect the culture and, for better or worse, contribute to it. Over time, a continuum has been devised that covers this vast range of artistic production. At one extreme is artistic material that requires sophisticated and cultivated tastes to appreciate. This is called **high art.** At the other extreme is **low art,** which requires little sophistication to enjoy.

One strain of traditional media criticism has been that the media underplay great works and concentrate on low art. This **elitist** view argues that the mass media do society a disservice by pandering to low tastes. To describe low art, elitists sometimes use the German word ***kitsch,*** which translates roughly as "garish" or "trashy." The word captures their disdain. In contrast, the **populist** view is that there is nothing unbecoming in the mass media's catering to mass tastes in a democratic, capitalistic society.

In a 1960 essay still widely cited, "Masscult and Midcult," social commentator **Dwight Macdonald** made a virulent case that all popular art is kitsch. The mass media, which depend on finding large audiences for their economic base, can hardly ever come out at the higher reaches of Macdonald's spectrum.

This kind of elitist analysis was given a larger framework in 1976 when sociologist **Herbert Gans** categorized cultural work along socioeconomic and intellectual lines. Gans said that classical music, as an example, appealed by and large to people of academic and professional accomplishments and higher incomes. These were **high-culture audiences,** which enjoyed complexities and subtleties in their art and entertainment. Next came **middle-culture audiences,** which were less abstract in their interests and liked Norman Rockwell and prime-time television. **Low-culture audiences** were factory and service workers whose interests were more basic; whose educational accomplishments, incomes and social status were lower; and whose media tastes leaned toward kung fu movies, comic books and supermarket tabloids.

Gans was applying his contemporary observations to flesh out the distinctions that had been taking form in art criticism for centuries—the distinctions between high art and low art.

high art
Requires sophisticated taste to be appreciated

low art
Can be appreciated by almost everybody

elitist
Mass media should gear to sophisticated audiences

kitsch
Pejorative word for trendy, trashy, low art

populist
Mass media should seek largest possible audiences

Dwight Macdonald
Said all pop art is kitsch

Herbert Gans
Said social, economic and intellectual levels of audience coincide

high-, middle- and low-culture audiences
Continuum identified by Herbert Gans

highbrow, middlebrow and lowbrow
Levels of media content sophistication that coincide with audience tastes

>> **Highbrow.** The high art favored by elitists generally can be identified by its technical and thematic complexity and originality. High art is often highly individualistic because the creator, whether a novelist or a television producer, has explored issues in fresh ways, often with new and different methods. Even when it's a collaborative effort, a piece of high art is distinctive. High art requires a sophisticated audience to appreciate it fully. Often it has enduring value, surviving time's test as to its significance and worth.

The sophistication that permits an opera aficionado to appreciate the intricacies of a composer's score, the poetry of the lyricist and the excellence of the performance sometimes is called **highbrow.** The label has grim origins in the idea that a person must have great intelligence to have refined tastes, and a high brow is necessary to accommodate such a big brain. Generally, the term is used by people who disdain those who have not developed the sophistication to enjoy, for example, the abstractions of a Fellini film, a Matisse sculpture or a Picasso painting. Highbrows generally are people who, as Gans noted, are interested in issues by which society is defining itself and look to literature and drama for stories on conflicts inherent in the human condition and between the individual and society.

>> **Middlebrow. Middlebrow** tastes recognize some artistic merit but don't have a high level of sophistication. There is more interest in action than abstractions—as in Captain Kirk aboard the starship *Enterprise,* for example, than in the childhood struggles of Ingmar Bergman that shaped his films. In socioeconomic terms,

CASE STUDY

When Extremism Trumps Entertainment

Surviving Movie House. *Pashto movies were hardly great film-making, but they built an audience over the years in the remote Khyber Pass region of Pakistan and Afghanistan. Today, after vigilante fire-bombings and intimidation by religious extremists, the Pashto movie industry has largely vanished. The Shabistan Cinema in Peshawar is among the few remaining movie houses. Go at your own risk.*

Perhaps nowhere on earth is entertainment as suspect, even loathed, as in regions with a strong presence of Taliban religious fundamentalism. Through intimidation, the fundamentalists have shut down the movie industry in northwest Pakistan. *Time* magazine reporter Aryn Bakers tells the story of Aziz ul-Haq, a shopkeeper in the frontier city of Peshawar. One day a Taliban devotee visited the shop and accused Haq of selling pornography. The Taliban jabbed a finger at a DVD cover depicting a man and woman about to kiss. "These movies are destroying the character of our children," the Talib declared. Haq defended the movie: "This is a family drama, a romance, nothing more."

Next: Haq's shop was destroyed in a pre-dawn firebombing. Over several months, vigilantes also left messages with their bombs at other shops. Afraid not only for their livelihoods but also for their lives, shopkeepers one by one stopped stocking videos. Some, like Haq, went out of business.

Peshawar once had a small, thriving movie industry. Although never known for great films, the studios issued movies that depicted values of Pashto-speaking people in northwest Pakistan and southeast Afghanistan. Today, what's left of the Pashto movie business is underground. Movies are produced secretly. DVDs are distributed through anonymous channels. Most Pashtun movie-makers have moved to safer cities to avoid the wrath of zealous Tailiban mullahs and their adherents.

The Peshawar music industry has been decimated too. Without distribution channels, there is no market. A Peshawar professor explained: "These entertainers are stealing an audience away from the mullahs, so the musicians have become their enemies."

DEEPENING YOUR MEDIA LITERACY

EXPLORE THE ISSUE

The U.S. entertainment industry faces occasional threats of boycotts by people objecting to the content of movies and other media. Consider campaigns against movie houses for *The Last Temptation of Christ* in 1988, rapper Ice-T for *Cop Killer* in 1992, and against CBS for shock-jock Don Imus in 2007.

DIG DEEPER

What form have these campaigns taken? What was objectionable? With each boycott, identify the target. Retailers? Distributors? Advertisers? Others? Add to the list of boycotts in recent years.

WHAT DO YOU THINK?

Civil libertarians object to shutting down expression, and call boycotts coercive. They favor responding with reason and dialogue. Their mantra: "The answer to bad speech is more speech." What would you say to Taliban mullahs in Peshawar? How would you say to the boycott organizers in this country? Or are the issues different?

middlebrow appeals to people who take comfort in media portrayals that support their status-quo orientation and values.

>> **Lowbrow.** Someone once made this often-repeated distinction: Highbrows talk about ideas, middlebrows talk about things, and **lowbrows** talk about people. Judging from the circulation success of the *National Enquirer* and other celebrity tabloids, there must be a lot of lowbrows in contemporary life. Hardly any sophistication is needed to recognize the machismo of Rambo, the villainy of Darth Vader, the heroism of Superman or the sexiness of Lara Croft.

CHECKING YOUR MEDIA LITERACY

- **What kinds of scales can be used to rank creative activity?**

CASE AGAINST POP ART

Pop art is of the moment, including things like body piercings and hip-hop garb—and trendy media fare. Even elitists may have fun with pop, but they traditionally have drawn the line at anyone who mistakes it as having serious artistic merit. Pop art is low art that has immense although generally short-lived popularity.

Elitists see pop art as contrived and artificial. In their view, the people who create **popular art** are masters at identifying what will succeed in the marketplace and then providing it. Pop art, according to this view, succeeds by conning people into liking it. When capri pants were the fashion rage, it was not because they were superior in comfort, utility or aesthetics but because promoters sensed that profits could be made by touting them through the mass media as new and cashing in on easily manipulated mass tastes. It was the same with pet rocks, Tickle Me Elmo and countless other faddish products.

The mass media, according to the critics, are obsessed with pop art. This is partly because the media are the carriers of the promotional campaigns that create popular followings but also because competition within the media creates pressure to be first, to be ahead, to be on top of things. The result, say elitists, is that junk takes precedence over quality.

Much is to be said for this criticism of pop art. The promotion by CBS of the screwball 1960s sitcom *Beverly Hillbillies,* as an example, created an eager audience that otherwise might have been reading Steinbeck's critically respected *Grapes of Wrath*. An elitist might chortle, even laugh, at the unbelievable antics and travails of the Beverly Hillbillies, who had their own charm, but an elitist would be concerned all the while that low art was displacing high art in the marketplace and that society was the poorer for it.

CHECKING YOUR MEDIA LITERACY

- **Why do elitists frown on pop art?**

popular art
Art that tries to succeed in the marketplace

pop art revisionism
The view that pop art has inherent value

Susan Sontag
Saw cultural, social value in pop art

POP ART REVISIONISM

Pop art has always had a few champions among intellectuals, although the voices of **pop art revisionism** often have been drowned out in the din of elitist pooh-poohing. In 1965, however, essayist **Susan Sontag** wrote an influential piece, "On Culture and the New Sensibility," that prompted many elitists to take a fresh look at pop art.

>> **Pop Art as Evocative.** Sontag made the case that pop art could raise serious issues, just as high art could. She wrote: "The feeling given off by a Rauschenberg painting might be like that of a song by the Supremes." Sontag soon was being called the High Priestess of Pop Intellectualism. More significantly, the Supremes were

Susan Sontag. *Her defense of less-than-highbrow art earned Susan Sontag the title of High Priestess of Pop Art. Sontag, a thinker on cultural issues, said paintings, music and other art with wide, popular appeal can evoke significant insights and sensitivities for some people.*

being taken more seriously, as were a great number of Sontag's avant-garde and obscure pop artist friends.

>> Pop Art as a Societal Unifier. In effect, Sontag encouraged people not to look at art on the traditional divisive, class-conscious, elitist-populist continuum. Artistic value, she said, could be found almost anywhere. The word *camp* gained circulation among 1960s elitists who were influenced by Sontag. These highbrows began finding a perversely sophisticated appeal in pop art as diverse as Andy Warhol's banal soup cans and ABC's outrageous *Batman*.

>> High Art as Popular. While kitsch may be prominent in media programming, it hardly elbows out all substantive content. In 1991, for example, Ken Burns' public television documentary *The Civil War* outdrew low-art prime-time programs on ABC, CBS and NBC five nights in a row. It was a glaring example that high art can appeal to people across almost the whole range of socioeconomic levels and is not necessarily driven out by low art. Burns' documentary was hardly a lone example. Another, also from 1991, was Franco Zeffirelli's movie *Hamlet*, starring pop movie star Mel Gibson, which was marketed to a mass audience yet could hardly be dismissed by elitists as kitsch. In radio, public broadcasting stations, marked by highbrow programming, have become major players for ratings.

CHECKING YOUR MEDIA LITERACY

- **How do pop art revisionists defend pop art?**

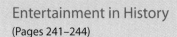

CHAPTER WRAP-UP

Entertainment in History
(Pages 241–244)

- Entertainment far predates its modern eminence as a mass media enterprise. People always have loved stories and music. Media technology, beginning with printing, dramatically changed entertainment. Master storytellers and musicians, for example, could have audiences whose size could never have been anticipated in earlier times. Entertainment of a high caliber became available widely. People gradually took less responsibility for creating their own entertainment, becoming consumers of entertainment.

Performance as Media Entertainment
(Pages 244–246)

- Mass media affect performance. A stage product transferred to television, for example, needs to be adapted to camera possibilities such as close-ups. The relationship to the audience is far different. So are cutaway possibilities to multiple additional scenes. Audio technology has brought dramatic changes to music. Early acoustic technology was crude, which put a premium on loud if not blaring martial music. Amplification technology brought the crooners. Changes are not entirely wrought by technology, however. Economics can affect performance. The NFL, for example, has changed football rules to accommodate television's requirement for commercial breaks.

Storytelling (Pages 246–247)

- Mass media companies have made storytelling in its various forms a commodity. Always looking for a competitive edge, companies shift in their promoting of different genres of literature programming. A book or program that catches the public's fancy becomes hot and spawns imitators. The public inevitably grows weary of a genre. Having run their course, genres are displaced by what's newly hot.

Music (Pages 247–251)

- The impact of music is impossible to measure. Think about Scottish pipes at a funeral, a love ballad in a romantic tragedy, a patriotic march in a Fourth of July parade. Then there's *Here Comes the Bride.* In a broader sense, music can help society adjust its attitudes, especially when performance is broadened to audiences of millions of people by the mass media. The genius of independent record-maker Sam Phillips in the 1950s was apparent when, so goes the story, he recognized Elvis Presley as a "white boy who sang colored." The result was a breakdown in racial divisions in U.S. music. The impact reverberated in the civil rights movement of the 1960s and new laws to end racial segregation.

Sports as Media Entertainment (Pages 251–253)

- Mass media have taken sports beyond the amphitheater, exponentially compounding the audience. The huge fan base created by the mass media is an attractive target for advertisers, especially because male consumers are hard to reach as a demographic cluster. But guys come together for sports, by the millions in front of television receivers for some events. Sports has shaped the media in ways not always recognized. What percentage of the pages of your daily newspaper is devoted to sports? It's easy to argue that sports coverage panders disproportionately to an audience mania. The media also shape sports. Time-outs and period lengths have been adjusted in the rules to accommodate broadcast and advertiser priorities.

Sex as Media Content (Pages 253–255)

- The presence of sexual content in mass media products has been largely settled by the U.S. Supreme Court. Adults, according to the Court, have constitutional rights to sexual depictions. 'Twasn't always so. The federal government once banned James Joyce's *Ulysses* through import regulations. Postal regulations were also used to stop distribution of other literary works, as well as some works of dubious literary merit. The issue has mostly been settled with the Court saying, in effect, that government should not be allowed to determine the material to which people can and cannot have access. Among major purveyors of sexually explicit material in recent years have been General Motors, when it controlled DirecTV, and Rupert Murdoch, when he controlled the company. Among the last bastions of restrictions is over-air broadcasting. The Federal Communications Commission has statutory controls to maintain decency on the public airwaves, although defining *decency* remains contentious.

Gaming as Media Content (Pages 255–256)

- Advertisers have not missed the growing audience, largely male, for Internet games. Advertising takes the form of billboards in game landscapes, scripted plugs and game sponsorship. The popularity of gaming has found critics who focus on violent and sexual elements. To blunt criticism, game makers have followed the lead of the recorded music and movie industries and incorporated product labeling.

Artistic Values (Pages 257–262)

- Significant creative content can be found in the mass media. In movies there are auteurs. In literature there are Ernest Hemingways, Pearl Bucks and Toni Morrisons. Masterpieces, however, are exceptions in the huge ocean of media content. The economics of modern mass media pressures companies to produce quantities to meet huge demands. It's like zookeepers needing to keep the lions fed. Production lines for television series, romance novels and the latest hot genres are designed to produce quantities to meet low thresholds of audience acceptability.

Review Questions

1. What categories of entertainment from prehistoric times to now reach people through mass media?
2. Do you prefer live or mediated performance? Why? In which do you participate more?
3. How do genres both clarify and cloud serious discussion of the quality of mass media content?
4. How has recorded music radically changed the social complexion of U.S. society?
5. How do you explain the exponential growth of sports as a form of entertainment?
6. What is driving gaming into its new status as a mass media vehicle?
7. What are the legal obstacles facing people who oppose sexual content in mass media?
8. What works against the presence of significant art and creativity in mass media content?
9. How well do mass media elevate cultural sensitivity? Explain.

Concepts	Terms	People
auteur (Page 257)	genre (Page 242)	Dwight Macdonald (Page 259)
highbrow (Page 259)	*kitsch* (Page 259)	George Carlin (Page 255)
mediated performance (Page 245)	rhythm and blues (Page 248)	Roone Arledge (Page 252)
popular art (Page 261)	rockabilly (Page 248)	Sam Phillips (Page 248)
pornography (Page 254)	studio system (Page 258)	Susan Sontag (Page 261)

Media Sources

- Gail Dines. *Pornland: How Porn Has Hjacked Our Sexuality.* Beacon, 2010. Dines, an anti-porn activist, has reviewed narratives and visuals in concluding that pornography is humanizing results, but she draws only lightly on social-science research to support her thesis and relies on loose addiction terminology to make a case that critics say is simplistic and overdrawn.
- Barbara Ching and Jennifer A. Wagner-Lawlor, editors. *The Scandal of Susan Sontag.* Columbia University, 2009. Scholars assess Sontag's contributions on a range of subjects, including the bridges she created between haute culture and middle-brow and low-brow culture.
- Jonathan Pieslak. *Sound Targets: American Soldiers and Music in the Iraq War.* Indiana University Press, 2009. Pieslak, a scholar and himself a composer, examines the psychological impact of music, particularly in motivating soldiers into combat.
- Elijah Wald. *How the Beatles Destroyed Rock 'n' Roll: An Alternative History of American Popular Music.* Oxford University Press, 2009. Music historian Wald sees a demarcation in pop music with the Beatles. It was the Beatles' artier instincts as they matured, he says, that moved beyond the rhythmic, danceable qualities that set earlier rock apart.
- Steven Johnson. *Everything Bad Is Good for You.* Riverhead, 2005. Johnson, a thinker and essayist, draws on neuroscience, economics and media theory to present the contrarian perspective that media content that's often maligned as lowbrow, middlebrow at best, actually is intellectually enriching.
- Glenn C. Altschuler. *All Shook Up: How Rock 'n' Roll Changed America.* Oxford University Press, 2004.

Altschuler, a writer specializing in the media, explores the social effects, including racial integration, of rock from the 1950s on.

- Guthrie P. Ramsey Jr. *Race Music: Black Culture from Bebop to Hip-Hop.* University of California Press, 2003. Ramsey, a scholar, sees popular music in the United States from the 1940s to the 1990s as a window into the diverse black American culture, society and politics.

- Steven L. Kent. *The Ultimate History of Video Games: From Pong to Pokemon—The Story Behind the Craze That Touched Our Lives and Changed the World.* Random House, 2001. Kent, drawing on hundreds of interviews, offers a comprehensive history of video games, starting from the first pinball machines.

- Dolf Zillmann and Peter Voderer. *Media Entertainment: The Psychology of Its Appeal*. Erlbaum, 2000.

ENTERTAINMENT

In this chapter you have deepened your media literacy by revisiting several themes. Here are thematic highlights from the chapter:

MEDIA TECHNOLOGY

Fan Base. The global sports industry is built on media coverage and attention. It's hard to imagine the World Cup or the NFL without the mass media. The Olympics? Sure, the Athenians had the Olympics, but how dull the ancient games must have been compared to today's sequenced quadrennial winter and summer games. On radio and television, sports is a big draw. Sports is the second-largest section in most daily newspapers. The Internet game *Madden NFL* earns more for Electronic Arts, its corporate parent, than Hollywood studios take in from most leading movies.

Entertainment's role has been amplified in human existence by media technology. Amusement and diversion are available any time, anywhere. Consider background music. How about 24/7 sports channels? Then there's handheld access to news and YouTube. Technology also shapes entertainment. Actors once needed strong voices that could carry to the back of the theater. Now audiences hear even hushed whispers from the lips of miked actors. With movies, screen tests are part of the audition process. Book publishers, too, want to know whether the author of a prospective book will look good during talk-show interviews. (Pages 242, 244–246)

ELITISM AND POPULISM

Peaking Genre? Quick, can you name the spin-offs of the successful *CSI* series plus copycat variations that have created a major primetime genre? As with all entertainment genres, the high-rolling crest of these dramas surely will peak and fade—only to be replaced by another genre that catches the ever-shifting fancy of mass audiences and advertisers.

The interplay between mass media content and public tastes may never be understood fully. Do media reflect public tastes and values? Or are media reshaping tastes and values? No one denies that mass media have the potential to put values to rigorous tests. Great authors have done this for centuries, posing and examining issues through fictional situations. Nonfiction can be just as influential. But lots of media content is not driven to help audiences seek understandings and appreciations. The goal instead is to attract audiences of sufficient size and variety to be platforms for advertisers to reach potential customers. This is true of books, magazines, radio, television and more and more the Internet. Book and movie companies work to satisfy shareholders with direct sales, the more the better. Elitists fault media as failing in their responsibility to leave the world a better place by focusing too much on audience building, in contrast to promoting human knowledge and understanding. (Pages 240–241, 243, 257–262)

MEDIA AND CULTURE

The elitist-populist tension is apparent in merit ratings of art. High art requires sophisticated and cultivated tastes to appreciate. Sergey Rachmaninoff was no rockabilly composer. This doesn't mean rockabilly is

(continued)

Not So Quick. Although lots of mass media content is easy to dismiss as second-rate, essayist Susan Sontag cautioned against being too quick to judge. An often-quoted line from a Sontag essay is: "The feeling given off by a Rauschenberg painting might be like that of a song by the Supremes." Also, Sontag made the point that pop art has social value in broadening the common experience of a society.

without value, but it falls into a category like pop art and folk art. Whether middlebrow or lowbrow on a merit rating, rockabilly is easy to appreciate. Anyone can get the message. A school of thought defends media on the lower rungs of rating scales if they bridge the gaps among the abilities of audience segments. Disney's *Fantasia* may be as close as some people get to a symphony hall. It's the same with Richard Strauss' or Wagner's prominence in space movie sound tracks. (Pages 257–262)

MEDIA ECONOMICS

Factory-like production lines are among the techniques that mass media companies use to keep costs down. The factory model works well to increase profits for products that are imitative and attract audiences, which explains in part the rise of genres of media content. Imitative stuff lends itself to expanding a genre until it runs its course. In television, horse operas had their day in the 1960s *(Wagon Train)*. So have police dramas *(Cagney and Lacey)*, prime-time soaps *(Dallas)*, talk shows *(Donahue)* and reality shows *(Survivor)*. But audiences, ever fickle, tire of old stuff. Even the long-running sitcom genre seems in a fall from grace. If nobody's buying, further production is pointless, no matter the efficiency. Media companies then need to create a hot new genre or glom onto somebody else's next hot genre. (Pages 257–258)

AUDIENCE FRAGMENTATION

Entertainment is easily dissected into genres, but the mass media have created such a massive audience that subgenres and sub-subgenres also are economically viable. Consider music formats in radio a half century ago. What once was country now is splintered into country rock, bluegrass, urban country, and a half-dozen others. Rock 'n' roll, once dominant in radio, is no less fragmented. (Page 246)

MEDIA AND DEMOCRACY

Natalie Maines. Her offhand slap at President Bush during a 2003 Dixie Chicks concert was in the vein of a long-running history of protest music. Politics and music can mix potently.

Mediated entertainment can give voice and feeling to ideas and build pressure for political and social change. Powerful sympathy for the mentally ill, as an example, has been generated in novels, movies and television in recent years, manifesting itself in growing pressure for public policy reforms. One all-time classic was Upton Sinclair's novel *The Jungle* in 1906, which led to government setting health standards for the meat-processing industry. Organized crime has been done no favors by Mario Puzo or Francis Ford Coppola. The debate over public policies is acted out through entertainment, no better illustrated than by Merle Haggard's *An Okie from Muskogee,* extolling blind patriotism, and the rising tide of anti-war music in the Vietnam war period. (Pages 247–249)

chapter 10

PUBLIC RELATIONS

Diane Van Deren *Prepping in the San Juan Mountains near her Colorado home, Diane Van Deren gives North Face outdoor gear a trial. She is a champion athlete after radical brain surgery for seizures—and a public face for North Face products.*

LEARNING AHEAD

- Public relations is a persuasive communication tool that uses mass media.
- Public relations grew out of public disfavor with big business.
- Public relations is an important management tool.
- Public relations includes promotion, publicity, lobbying, fund-raising and crisis management.
- Advertising and public relations are distinctive undertakings.
- Public relations usually involves a candid, proactive relationship with mass media.
- Public relations organizations are working to improve the image of their craft.

BROADENING THE ENDURANCE AURA

Thirty miles from finishing the grueling 430-mile Yukon Arctic Ultra race, Diane Van Deren stopped for a photograph. The ice cracked underneath her, and she fell into a tributary of the freezing Takhini River. A competitor pulled Van Deren out with a trekking pole—back into the minus-40 February air. Drenched and freezing, Van Deren pushed on. Survival meant generating as much body heat as possible. She dragged her own 45-pound sled of supplies to finish her 13-day endurance trek. She came in fifth. Among women she was first.

Van Deren's accomplishment was especially notable. Years earlier, pregnant with her third child, Van Deren had been diagnosed with epilepsy. That was a blow to the former professional tennis player. Ten years of seizures followed. Although sporadic, the seizures were nonetheless frightening. The seizures ended after radical brain surgery to remove part of her right temporal lobe. That began Van Deren's passion as an endurance athlete, like 100-mile snowshoe races and, ultimately, the Yukon Arctic Ultra.

It was only natural that Van Deren became a spokesperson for children with spinal cord and traumatic brain injuries. She also became an endorsement athlete for North Face, which markets a wide range of sports gear and garb.

For North Face, whose cachet is authentic ruggedness, Van Deren was a real find. The company was looking to extend its market beyond hard-core adventurers. Who better than Van Deren to inspire more people into the outdoors? Van Deren has no hesitation in touting North Face gear for her success in the Arctic Ultra.

An easy hero in the media, Van Deren is glad to share her story. "I enjoy talking about how we all have obstacles in our lives," she says. "Mine is epilepsy."

A North Face vice president, Letitia Webster, is responsible for sustaining the North Face brand and promoting Van Deren as a magnet for media attention, to their mutual benefit. North Face profiles Van Deren in videos and on the company web site. Webster has encouraged a stream of articles in publications that cater to endurance sports, like *Outsider, Backpacker* and *Powder.* But Webster sees the Van Deren story in broader terms than sustaining the interest of North Face's traditional clientele. Her job, in marketing parlance, is to "grow the brand."

Webster is a public relations professional, focusing on promotional projects that contribute to North Face corporate goals. It's not advertising. Webster is not involved in pushing sales, at least not directly. Her mission, as she puts it, is to make people step away from sedentary at-home television and computer habits and go outside.

One Webster tactic has been the North Face endurance team and Van Deren. The team allows North Face, says Webster, "to weave in more about the athletes and their phenomenal personal stories" into the company aura.

Letitia Webster. *Public relations for North Face outdoor garb and equipment is her game. Her title is vice president for corporate sustainability and communication.*

North Face has been consistent with advancing its image of authentic ruggedness since the brand was introduced in the 1960s. That's a long run for a brand. Webster's job as vice president for corporate sustainability and communication is not only to keep the ball rolling but to, as she puts it, "broaden the message and touch more people."

This is no easy task in a world increasingly crowded with brand names. North Face even has competitors inside its corporate owner, the $7.2 billion a year VF Corp. VF brands include Jansport, Lee, Nautica and Wrangler.

Webster is not alone. She has a staff at North Face. Also, beginning in 2004 she has been drawing counsel from Ruder Finn, one of the largest U.S. public relations firms.

Meanwhile, for her own sake, as well as that of North Face, Diane Van Deren keeps on trekking.

Importance of Public Relations

STUDY ***PREVIEW***

Public relations is a persuasive communication tool that people can use to motivate other people and institutions to help them achieve their goals.

DEFINING PUBLIC RELATIONS

The public relations pioneer **Edward Bernays** lamented how loosely the term ***public relations*** is used. To illustrate his concern, Bernays told about a young woman who approached him for career advice. He asked her what she did for a living. "I'm in public relations," she said. He pressed her for details, and she explained that she handed out circulars in Harvard Square. Bernays was dismayed at how casually people regard the work of public relations. There are receptionists and secretaries who list public relations on their résumés. To some people, public relations is glad-handing, backslapping and smiling prettily to make people feel good. Public relations, however, goes far beyond good interpersonal skills. A useful definition is that public relations is a management tool for leaders in business, government and other institutions to establish beneficial *relationships* with other institutions and groups. Four steps are necessary for public relations to accomplish its goals:

>> **Identify Existing Relationships.** In modern society, institutions have many relationships. A college, for example, has relationships with its students, faculty, staff, alumni, benefactors, the neighborhood, the community, the legislature, other colleges, accreditors of its programs and, perhaps, unions. The list could go on and on. Each of these constituencies is called a *public*—hence the term *public relations.*

>> **Evaluate the Relationships.** Through research, the public relations practitioner studies these relationships to determine how well they are working. This evaluation is an ongoing process. A college may have excellent relations with the legislature one year and win major appropriations, but after a scandal related to the president's budget the next year, legislators may be downright unfriendly.

>> **Design Policies to Improve the Relationships.** The job of public relations people is to recommend policies to top management to make these relationships work better, not only for the organization but also for the partners in each relationship. **Paul Garrett,** a pioneer in corporate relations, found that General Motors was seen in unfriendly terms during the Great Depression, which put the giant automaker at risk with many publics, including its own employees. GM, he advised, needed new policies to seem neighborly—rather than as a far-removed, impersonal, monolithic industrial giant.

>> **Implement the Policies.** Garrett used the term ***enlightened self-interest*** for his series of policies intended to personalize GM in the eyes of many of the company's publics. Garrett set up municipal programs in towns with GM plants and grants for schools and scholarships for employees' children. General Motors benefited from a revised image, and in the spirit of enlightened self-interest, so did GM employees, their children and their communities.

Public relations is not a mass medium itself, but PR often uses the media as tools to accomplish its goals. To announce GM's initiatives to change its image in the 1930s, Paul Garrett issued news releases that he hoped newspapers, magazines and radio stations would pick up. The number of people in most of the publics with which public relations practitioners need to communicate is so large that it can be reached only through the mass media. The influence of public relations on the news media is extensive. Half of the news in many newspapers, some studies say much more, originates with formal statements or news releases from organizations that want something in the paper. It is the same with radio and television.

Edward Bernays
Early public relations practitioner whose practice and scholarship helped define the field

public relations
A management tool to establish beneficial relationships

Paul Garrett
Devised the notion of enlightened self-interest

enlightened self-interest
Mutually beneficial public relations

CHECKING YOUR MEDIA LITERACY

- **What does it mean to describe public relations as a management function?**
- **What did Paul Garrett mean by the term *enlightened self-interest*?**

Paul Garrett

MEDIA PEOPLE

At one of the most precarious times in U.S. history, the Great Depression, Paul Garrett led public relations in new directions to win public support. Amid worries that people—many hungry, all distressed—would see huge corporations as scapegoats and perhaps upend capitalism, Garrett had an unprecedented challenge as General Motors' public relations chief. How precarious was the situation? Sit-down strikes were occurring at GM plants. Discontent was bubbling throughout the country.

Garrett, in the first generation of public relations people who had learned their craft from the government's Creel Committee in World War I, immediately sought to minimize the image of General Motors as some sort of monolithic giant that, being big and distant, was an especially easy target for hate. To head off problems, Garrett introduced a public strategy: *enlightened self-interest.* It was in GM's self-interest, he argued, to touch the lives of people in personal ways, such as with grants for local schools and scholarships for employees' children. General Motors, of course, nurtured publicity about these corporate good deeds.

Garrett summed it up this way: "The challenge that faces us is to shake off our lethargy and through public relations make the American plan of industry stick. For unless the contributions of the system are explained to consumers in terms of their own interest, the system itself will not stand against the storm of fallacies that rides the air." Garrett also worked on GM's image at a macro level, aiming for consumers in general to think well of the company.

A GM caravan, called the Parade of Progress, traveled from coast to coast in 1936 with a message that new technologies would facilitate progress and social change. In the same spirit, prominent radio announcer Lowell Thomas narrated a feature film, *Previews of Science,* that cast business, big business in particular, in heroic terms. In short, the genius of corporate science and initiative was creating a better tomorrow.

The National Association of Manufacturers caught Garrett's spirit. Garrett worked with the association to tie the public impression of big corporations into warm, albeit fuzzy, notions about Americanism. At a 1939 meeting, the association's public relations division, with Garrett on board, said that its job was to "link free enterprise in the public consciousness with free speech, free press and free religion as integral parts of democracy."

Public relations had become widely embraced as a way to channel the thinking of the country.

WHAT DO YOU THINK?

- Paul Garrett's term *enlightened self-interest* has been preserved in the PR lexicon. Why?
- Why are behavior and actions as essential to public relations as words?

Enlightened Self-Interest. *Paul Garrett, a pioneer in corporate public relations, encouraged General Motors to act both in its corporate interest and in the interest of employees and other constituencies. It is possible to serve multiple masters, Garrett said. He called his approach to public relations enlightened self-interest.*

PUBLIC RELATIONS IN DEMOCRACY

Misconceptions about public relations include the idea that it is a one-way street for institutions and individuals to communicate to the public. Actually, the good practice of public relations seeks two-way communication between and among all the people and institutions concerned with an issue.

A task force established by the **Public Relations Society of America** to explore the stature and role of the profession concluded that public relations has the potential to improve the functioning of democracy by encouraging the exchange of information and ideas on public issues. The task force said public relations practitioners:

Public Relations Society of America
Professional association for public relations practitioners

- Communicate the interests of an institution to the public, which broadens and enriches public dialogue.
- Seek mutual adjustments through dialogue between institutions in the society, which benefits the public.

- Create a safety valve for society by helping work out accommodations between competing interests, reducing the likelihood of coercion or arbitrary action.
- Activate the social conscience of organizations with which they work.

CHECKING YOUR MEDIA LITERACY

- **Draw on your knowledge and experience for examples of public relations serving the democratic ideal of the fullest dialogue on important issues.**

Origins of Public Relations

STUDY PREVIEW

Many big companies found themselves in disfavor in the late 1800s for ignoring the public good to make profits. Feeling misunderstood, some moguls of industry turned to Ivy Lee, the founder of modern public relations, for counsel on gaining public support.

MOGULS IN TROUBLE

Nobody would be tempted to think of **William Henry Vanderbilt** as having been good at public relations. In 1882 it was Vanderbilt, president of the New York Central Railroad, who, when asked about the effect of changing train schedules, said: "The public be damned." Vanderbilt's utterance so infuriated people that it became a banner in the populist crusade against robber barons and tycoons in the late 1800s. Under populist pressure, state governments set up agencies to regulate railroads. Then the federal government established the Interstate Commerce Commission to control freight and passenger rates. Government began insisting on safety standards. Labor unions formed in the industries with the worst working conditions, safety records and pay. Journalists added pressure with muckraking exposés on excesses in the railroad, coal and oil trusts; on meat-packing industry frauds; and on patent medicines.

The leaders of industry were slow to recognize the effect of populist objections on their practices. They were comfortable with **social Darwinism,** an adaptation of **Charles Darwin**'s survival-of-the-fittest theory. In fact, they thought themselves forward-thinking in applying Darwin's theory to business and social issues. It had been only a few decades earlier, in 1859, that Darwin had laid out his biological theory in *On the Origin of Species by Means of Natural Selection*. To cushion the harshness of social Darwinism, many tycoons espoused paternalism toward those whose "fitness" had not brought them fortune and power. No matter how carefully put, paternalism seemed arrogant to the "less fit."

George Baer, a railroad president, epitomized both social Darwinism and paternalism in commenting on a labor strike: "The rights and interests of the laboring man will be protected and cared for not by labor agitators but by the Christian men to whom God in His infinite wisdom has given the control of the property interests of the country." Baer was quoted widely, further fueling sentiment against big business. Baer may have been sincere, but his position was read as a cover for excessive business practices by barons who assumed superiority to everyone else.

Meanwhile, social Darwinism came under attack as circuitous reasoning: Economic success accomplished by abusive practices could be used to justify further abusive practices, which would lead to further success. Social Darwinism was a dog-eat-dog outlook that hardly jibed with democratic ideals, especially not as described in the preamble to the U.S. Constitution, which sought to "promote the general welfare, and secure the blessings of liberty" for everyone—not for only the chosen "fittest." Into these tensions at the turn of the century came public relations pioneer Ivy Lee.

William Henry Vanderbilt
Embodied the bad corporate images of the 1880s, 1890s with "The public be damned"

social Darwinism
Application to society of Darwin's survival-of-the-fittest theory

Charles Darwin
Devised survival-of-the-fittest theory

CHECKING YOUR MEDIA LITERACY

- **How was social Darwinism appealing to religious people who found themselves with massive wealth while others suffered at their expense?**

MEDIA TIMELINE

PUBLIC RELATIONS MILESTONES

1800s

Promotional Excesses
P. T. Barnum made huckster promotion a high art (1870s)

"The Public Be Damned"
Yes, incredibly, railroad titan William Henry Vanderbilt said it (1882)

1900–1949

Ivy Lee
Founder of first public relations agency (1906)

George Creel
Head of first government public relations agency (1917)

Edward Bernays
Wrote *Crystallizing Public Opinion* (1923)

Arthur Page
First corporate public relations vice president (1927)

Paul Garrett
Created term *enlightened self-interest* (1930s)

Office of War Information
Elmer Davis headed federal agency to generate war support (1942)

1950–1999

Ethics
Public Relations Society of America ethics code (1951)

Accreditation
PRSA accreditation system (1965)

Strike-Back PR
Herb Schmertz pioneered adversarial practices (1970s)

Tylenol Crisis
Classic campaign aided recovery from product-tampering crisis (1982)

Integrated Marketing
Attempt to subsume public relations into marketing (1990s–)

2000s

Consolidation
Advertising agencies bought up many public relations agencies to broaden client services (2002)

Dialogics
Scholars applied dialogic theory to public relations (2002)

Lobbying Scandal
Washington master lobbyist Jack Abramoff went to jail (2006)

Large-scale public relations *Government rallies public enthusiasm for World War I*

Ivy Lee *Father of PR*

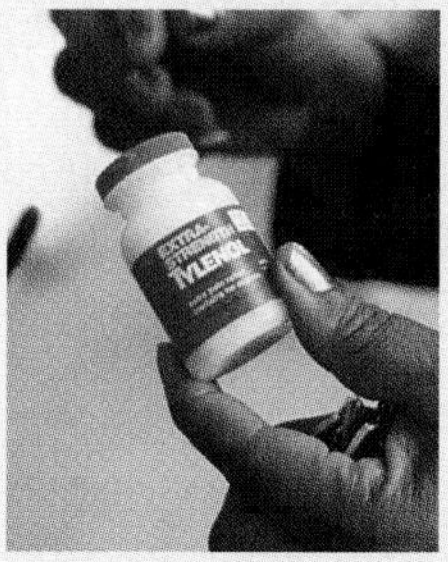

Tylenol scare *Model case study in public relations*

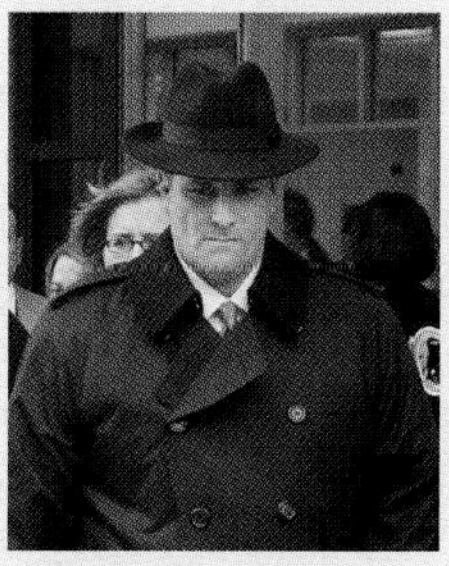

Jack Abramoff *Lobbyist bad boy gets prison time*

PIVOTAL EVENTS

1800s

- >> Public education took root as a social value (1820s)
- >> Charles Darwin wrote *Origin of Species* (1859)
- >> U.S. Civil War (1861–1865)
- >> Rise of banks, major corporations (1870s–)
- >> Populist political movement aimed against monopolies (1880s–)
- >> Samuel Gompers formed predecessor of American Federation of Labor (1881)
- >> Social Darwinism used to justify corporate excesses (1890s)

1900–1949

- >> Labor crisis in coal industry (1902)
- >> Ludlow Massacre (1914)
- >> Right to vote extended to women (1920)
- >> Great Depression (1930s)
- >> World War II (1941–1945)

1950–1999

- >> Korean War (1950–1953)
- >> Vietnam War (1964–1973)
- >> Humans reached moon (1969)

2000s

- >> 9/11 terrorist attacks (2001)
- >> Iraq War (2003–)
- >> Hurricane Katrina (2005)

THE IDEAS OF IVY LEE

Coal mine operators, like railroad magnates, were held in the public's contempt at the start of the 1900s. Obsessed with profits, caring little about public sentiment or even the well-being of their employees, mine operators were vulnerable to critics in the growing populist political movement. Mine workers organized, and 150,000 in Pennsylvania went on strike in 1902, shutting down the anthracite industry and disrupting coal-dependent industries, including the railroads. The mine owners snubbed reporters, which probably contributed to a pro-union slant in many news stories and worsened the owners' public image. Six months into the strike, President Theodore Roosevelt threatened to take over the mines with Army troops. The mine owners settled.

Shaken finally by Roosevelt's threat and recognizing Roosevelt's responsiveness to public opinion, the mine operators began reconsidering how they went about their business. In 1906, with another strike looming, one operator heard about **Ivy Lee,** a young publicist in New York who had new ideas about winning public support. He was hired. In a turnabout in press relations, Lee issued a news release that announced: "The anthracite coal operators, realizing the general public interest in conditions in the mining regions, have arranged to supply the press with all possible information." Then followed a series of releases with information attributed to the mine operators by name—the same people who earlier had preferred anonymity and refused all interview requests. There were no more secret strike strategy meetings. When operators planned a meeting, reporters covering the impending strike were informed. Although reporters were not admitted into the meetings, summaries of the proceedings were given to them immediately afterward. This relative openness eased long-standing hostility toward the operators, and a strike was averted.

Lee's success with the mine operators began a career that rewrote the rules on how corporations deal with their various publics. Among his accomplishments:

>> **Institutional Openness.** Railroads had notoriously secretive policies not only about their business practices but even about accidents. When the Pennsylvania Railroad sought Ivy Lee's counsel, he advised against suppressing news—especially on things that inevitably would leak out anyway. When a train jumped the rails near Gap, Pennsylvania, Lee arranged for a special car to take reporters to the scene and even take pictures. The Pennsylvania line was applauded in the press for the openness, and coverage of the railroad, which had been negative for years, began changing. A "bad press" continued plaguing other railroads that persisted in their secretive habits.

>> **Finding Upbeat Angles.** When the U.S. Senate proposed investigating International Harvester for monopolistic practices, Lee advised the giant farm implement manufacturer against reflexive obstructionism and silence. A statement went out announcing that the company, confident in its business practices, not only welcomed but also would facilitate an investigation. Then began a campaign that pointed out International Harvester's beneficence toward its employees. The campaign also emphasized other upbeat information about the company.

Ivy Lee
Laid out fundamentals of public relations

Ludlow Massacre
Colorado tragedy that Ivy Lee converted into a public relations victory

John D. Rockefeller Jr.
Ivy Lee client who had been the target of public hatred

>> **Giving Organizations a Face.** In 1914, when workers at a Colorado mine went on strike, company guards fired machine guns and killed several men. More battling followed, during which two women and 11 children were killed. It was called the **Ludlow Massacre,** and **John D. Rockefeller Jr.,** the chief mine owner, was pilloried for what had happened. Rockefeller was an easy target. Like his father, widely despised for the earlier Standard Oil monopolistic practices, John Jr. tried to keep himself out of the spotlight, but suddenly mobs were protesting at his mansion in New York and calling out, "Shoot him down like a dog." Rockefeller asked Ivy Lee what he should do. Lee began whipping up articles about

Ivy Lee

Ludlow Massacre. *Colorado militiamen, called in to augment company guards, opened fire during a 1914 mine labor dispute and killed women and children. Overnight, John D. Rockefeller Jr. became the object of public hatred. It was a Rockefeller company that owned the mine. Even in New York, where Rockefeller lived, there were rallies demanding his head. Public relations pioneer Ivy Lee advised Rockefeller to tour the Ludlow area as soon as tempers cooled to show his sincere concern and to begin work on a labor contract to meet the concerns of miners.*

Rockefeller's human side, his family and his generosity. Then, on Lee's advice, Rockefeller announced that he would visit Colorado to see conditions himself. He spent two weeks talking with miners at work and in their homes and meeting their families. It was a news story that reporters could not resist, and it unveiled Rockefeller as a human being, not a far-removed, callous captain of industry. A myth-shattering episode occurred one evening when Rockefeller, after a brief address to miners and their wives, suggested that the floor be cleared for a dance. Before it was all over, John D. Rockefeller Jr. had danced with almost every miner's wife, and the news stories about the evening did a great deal to mitigate antagonism and distrust toward Rockefeller. Back in New York, with Lee's help, Rockefeller put together a proposal for a grievance procedure, which he asked the Colorado miners to approve. It was ratified overwhelmingly.

>> **Straight Talk.** Ivy Lee came on the scene at a time when many organizations were making extravagant claims about themselves and their products. Circus promoter **P. T. Barnum** made this kind of **puffery** a fine art in the late 1800s, and he had many imitators. It was an age of *puffed-up* advertising claims and fluffy rhetoric. Lee noted, however, that people soon saw through hyperbolic boasts and lost faith in those who made them. In launching his public relations agency in 1906, Lee vowed to be accurate in everything he said and to provide whatever verification anyone requested. This became part of the creed of good practice in public relations, and it remains so today.

P. T. Barnum
Known for exaggerated promotion

puffery
Inflated claims

CHECKING YOUR MEDIA LITERACY

- **How did public relations pioneer Ivy Lee help revolutionize the way business conducted itself in the early 1900s?**
- **What are enduring pillars of Ivy Lee's concept of good business practice?**

War Popularizer. *World War I did not begin as a popular cause with Americans. There were anti-draft riots in many cities. This prompted President Woodrow Wilson to ask journalist George Creel to launch a major campaign to persuade Americans that the war was important to make the world safe for democracy. Within months Americans were financing much of the war voluntarily by buying government bonds. This poster was only one aspect of Creel's work, which demonstrated that public relations principles could be applied on a massive scale.*

George Creel

PUBLIC RELATIONS ON A NEW SCALE

The potential of public relations to rally support for a cause was demonstrated on a gigantic scale during World War I and again during World War II.

>> **World War I.** In 1917 President Woodrow Wilson, concerned about widespread anti-war sentiment, asked **George Creel** to head a new government agency whose job was to make the war popular. The Committee on Public Information, better known as the Creel Committee, cranked out news releases, magazine pieces, posters, even movies. A list of 75,000 local speakers was put together to talk nationwide at school programs, church groups and civic organizations about making the world safe for democracy. More than 15,000 committee articles were printed. Never before had public relations been attempted on such a scale—and it worked. World War I became a popular cause even to the point of inspiring people to buy Liberty Bonds, putting up their own money to finance the war outside the usual taxation apparatus.

>> **World War II.** When World War II began, an agency akin to the Creel Committee was formed. Veteran journalist **Elmer Davis** was put in charge. The new Office of War Information was public relations on a bigger scale than ever before. The Creel and Davis committees employed hundreds of people. Davis had 250 employees handling news releases alone. These staff members, mostly young, carried new lessons about public relations into the private sector after the war. These were the people who shaped corporate public relations as we know it today.

George Creel
Demonstrated that public relations works on a mammoth scale in World War I

Elmer Davis
Led Office of War Information in World War II

CHECKING YOUR MEDIA LITERACY

- **How did George Creel contribute to the expansion of public relations?**
- **What happened to the thousands of people on George Creel's payroll after World War I?**

Structure of Public Relations

STUDY PREVIEW

In developing sound policies, corporations and other institutions depend on public relations experts who are sensitive to the implications of policy on the public consciousness. This makes public relations a vital management function. Besides a role in policymaking, public relations people play key roles in carrying out institutional policy.

POLICY ROLE OF PUBLIC RELATIONS

When giant AT&T needed somebody to take over public relations in 1927, the president of the company went to magazine editor **Arthur Page** and offered him a vice presidency. Before accepting, Page laid out several conditions. One was that he have a voice in AT&T policy. Page was hardly on an ego trip. Rather, he had seen too many corporations that regarded their public relations arm merely as an executor of policy. Page considered public relations itself as a management function. To be effective, Page knew that he must contribute to the making of high-level corporate decisions as well as executing them. Today, experts on public relations agree with Arthur Page's concept: When institutions are making policy, they need to consider the effects on their many publics. That can be done best when the person in charge of public relations, ideally at the vice presidential level, is intimately involved in decision-making. The public relations executive advises the rest of the institution's leaders on public perceptions and the effects that policy options might have on perceptions. Also, the public relations vice president is in a better position to implement the institution's policy for having been a part of developing it.

CHECKING YOUR MEDIA LITERACY

What is the role of public relations at the policymaking level of an institution?

HOW PUBLIC RELATIONS IS ORGANIZED

No two institutions are organized in precisely the same way. At General Motors 200 people work in public relations. In smaller organizations PR may be one of several hats worn by a single person. Except in the smallest operations, the public relations department usually has three functional areas of responsibility:

External Public Relations. Public relations helps organizations engage with groups and people outside the organization. These include customers, dealers, suppliers, community leaders and policymakers.

Internal Public Relations. Organizations need internal communication for optimal relations among employees, managers, unions, shareholders and other internal constituencies. In-house newsletters, magazines and brochures are common elements in internal public relations.

Media Relations. For communication with large groups, organizations rely largely on mass media. It is media relations people who respond to news reporters' queries, arrange news conferences, issue statements to the news media and often serve as an organization's spokespersons.

Arthur Page
Established the role of public relations as a top management tool

CHECKING YOUR MEDIA LITERACY

Would you classify media relations more as an external or an internal public relations function?

PUBLIC RELATIONS AGENCIES

Even though many organizations have their own public relations staff, they may go to **public relations agencies** for help on specific projects or problems. In the United States today, hundreds of companies specialize in public relations counsel and related services. It is a big business. Income at global PR agencies like Edelman runs about $260 million a year.

The biggest agencies offer a full range of services on a global scale. These agencies will take on projects anywhere in the world, either on their own or by working with local agencies.

These are the largest agencies with significant U.S. accounts:

	Global Income	Employees Worldwide
Edelman	$262.9 million	1,711
Waggener Edstrom	96.6 million	667
Ruder Finn	83.2 million	350
MWW	48.3 million	243
Chandler Chicco	31.5 million	148

Some agencies bill clients only for services rendered. Others charge clients just to be on call. Hill & Knowlton, for example, has a minimum $5,000-a-month retainer fee. Agency expenses for specific projects are billed in addition. Staff time usually is charged at an hourly rate that covers the agency's overhead and allows a profit margin. Other expenses are usually billed with a 15 to 17 percent markup.

public relations agencies
Companies that provide public relations services

CHECKING YOUR MEDIA LITERACY

- **When does an organization with its own public relations operation need also to hire an outside public relations agency?**

Public Relations Services

STUDY PREVIEW

Public relations deals with publicity and promotion, but it also involves less visible activities. These include lobbying, fund-raising and crisis management. Public relations is distinct from advertising.

publicity
Brings public attention to something

promotion
Promoting a cause, idea

lobbying
Influencing public policy, usually legislation or regulations

PUBLICITY AND PROMOTION

Full-service public relations agencies provide a wide range of services built on two of the cornerstones of the business: **publicity** and **promotion.** These agencies are ready to conduct media campaigns to rally support for a cause, create an image or turn a problem into an asset. Publicity and promotion, however, are only the most visible services offered by public relations agencies.

LOBBYING

No doubt about it, **lobbying** is a growth industry. Every state capital has hundreds of public relations practitioners whose specialty is representing their clients to legislative bodies and government agencies. In North Dakota, hardly a populous state, more than

300 people are registered as lobbyists in the capital city of Bismarck. The number of registered lobbyists in Washington, D.C., exceeds 10,000 today. In addition, there are an estimated 20,000 other people in the nation's capital who have slipped through registration requirements but who nonetheless ply the halls of government to plead their clients' interests.

In one sense, lobbyists are expediters. They know local traditions and customs, and they know who is in a position to affect policy. Lobbyists advise their clients, which include trade associations, corporations, public interest groups and regulated utilities and industries, on how to achieve their goals by working with legislators and government regulators. Many lobbyists call themselves "government relations specialists."

CHECKING YOUR MEDIA LITERACY

- **Why does lobbying have a bad name? Is it deserved? Undeserved?**

POLITICAL COMMUNICATION

Every capital has political consultants whose work is mostly advising candidates for public office in **political communication.** Services include campaign management, survey research, publicity, media relations and image consulting. Political consultants also work on elections, referendums, recalls and other public policy issues.

CHECKING YOUR MEDIA LITERACY

- **Is it näive to think a candidate for federal or statewide office can succeed without political consultants?**

IMAGE CONSULTING

A growing specialized branch of public relations has been image consulting. In the first energy crisis of the 1970s, oil companies realized that their side of the story wasn't getting across. These companies turned to image consultants to groom corporate spokespersons, often chief executives, to meet reporters one on one and go on talk shows. The groomers did a brisk business, and it paid off in countering the stories and rumors that were blaming the oil companies for skyrocketing fuel prices.

CHECKING YOUR MEDIA LITERACY

- **What would Ivy Lee think of image consulting for top executives?**

FINANCIAL PUBLIC RELATIONS

In the 1920s and 1930s the U.S. Securities and Exchange Commission cracked down on abuses in the financial industry. Regulations on promoting sales of securities are complex. It is the job of people in financial public relations to know not only the principles of public relations but also the complex regulations governing the promotion of securities in corporate mergers, acquisitions, new issues and stock splits.

political communication
Advising candidates and groups on public policy issues, usually in elections

contingency planning
Developing programs in advance of an unscheduled but anticipated event

crisis management
Helping a client through an emergency

CONTINGENCY PLANNING

Many organizations rely on public relations people to design programs to address problems that can be expected to occur, known as **contingency planning.** Airlines, for example, need detailed plans for handling inevitable plane crashes—situations requiring quick, appropriate responses under tremendous pressure. When a crisis occurs, an organization can turn to public relations people for advice on dealing with it. Some agencies specialize in **crisis management,** which

MEDIA PEOPLE

Jack Abramoff

In college Jack Abramoff was smitten with politics. From his base at Brandeis University, Abramoff rallied Massachusetts college students statewide for Ronald Reagan's presidential bid in 1980. Reagan took the state in an upset. On to Washington, Abramoff rose quickly in the national College Republicans, moving the organization into right-wing activism.

Not all went well. The College Republicans vastly overspent their budget with a poorly conceived direct-mail campaign in 1982. The party elders threw out the free-spending Abramoff. Irrepressible, Abramoff found a spot running the privately funded Citizens for America, which campaigned for conservative causes. Under the group's banner Abramoff organized some audacious projects. His climactic accomplishment—a convention in a remote part of Angola for a motley bunch of anticommunist guerrillas from disparate Afghanistan, Laos and Nicaragua. The project was costly. The sugar daddy who financed Citizens for America fired Abramoff for taking too many liberties with the group's $3 million budget.

In all this, and in a checkered résumé of more Republican-related jobs, mostly in Washington, the young, energetic Abramoff made contacts. His reputation grew rapidly as one of the most influential lobbyists on Capitol Hill and in numerous executive branch agencies.

By 2000, with Republicans controlling the federal government, Abramoff had amassed the biggest lobbying portfolio in Washington. For the right ambiance to make pitches to members of Congress and top aides and also to acknowledge favors, Abramoff opened two posh restaurants down the street from the Capitol. He bought a fleet of casino boats. He leased four arena and stadium skyboxes. He sponsored golf outings to exclusive St. Andrews in Scotland and to the South Pacific.

The party began imploding in 2003 with revelations by Susan Schmidt of the Washington *Post.* Schmidt tracked $45 million in lobbying fees from Indian tribes that were desperate to protect their casino revenue from possible taxation. There were irregularities galore, including massive overbilling. Abramoff told one aide, for example, to find some way to bill a Choctaw band $150,000 one month: "Be sure we hit the $150k minimum. If you need to add time for me, let me know." The aide responded: "You only had two hours." Abramoff fired back: "Add 60 hours for me."

An avalanche of other revelations followed in what became one of the biggest congressional corruption scandals in history. The scandal was a centerpiece issue in the 2006 elections. Abramoff went to jail. It was not only a few members of Congress and their aides who worried about subpoenas for accepting Abramoff's largesse. For lobbyists who conduct themselves honorably, it all was an embarrassing sullying of their craft.

Jail-Bound. *Crooked Washington lobbyist Jack Abramoff is on his way to court, nattily attired. Soon thereafter, his garb was a prison jumpsuit.*

WHAT DO YOU THINK?

- If you were the judge, how would you have sentenced Jack Abramoff? Would you have set him free?
- Would you require public relations students to study Jack Abramoff's practices? Which lessons would you want them to learn?

involves picking up the pieces either when a contingency plan fails or when there was no plan to deal with a crisis.

CHECKING YOUR MEDIA LITERACY

If you were hired by an airline to design a contingency plan for an eventual inevitability of an accident, what would you lay out?

POLLING

Public opinion sampling is essential in many public relations projects. Full-service agencies can either conduct surveys themselves or contract with companies that specialize in surveying.

EVENTS COORDINATION

Many public relations people are involved in coordinating a broad range of events, including product announcements, news conferences and convention planning. Some in-house public relations departments and agencies have their own artistic and audiovisual production talent to produce brochures, tapes and other promotional materials. Other agencies contract for these services.

Public Relations and Advertising

STUDY ***PREVIEW***

Although public relations and advertising both involve crafting media messages for mass audiences, public relations is involved in creating policy. Advertising is not. Even so, there has been a recent blending of the functions, some under the umbrella concept of integrated marketing.

DIFFERENT FUNCTIONS

Both public relations and advertising involve persuasion through the mass media, but most of the similarities end there.

>> **Management Function.** Public relations people help to shape an organization's policy. This is a management activity, ideally with the organization's chief public relations person offering counsel to other key policymakers at the vice presidential level. **Advertising,** in contrast, is not a management function. The work of advertising is much narrower. It focuses on developing persuasive messages, mostly to sell products or services, after all the management decisions have been made.

>> **Measuring Success.** Public relations "sells" points of view and images. These are intangibles, and therefore success is hard to measure. In advertising, success is measurable with tangibles, such as sales, that can be calculated from the bottom line.

>> **Control of Messages.** When an organization decides that it needs a persuasive campaign, there is a choice between public relations and advertising. One advantage of advertising is that the organization controls the message. By buying space or time in the mass media, an organization has the final say on the content of its advertising messages. In public relations, by contrast, an organization tries to influence the media to tell its story a certain way, but the message that actually reaches a mass audience is up to the media. For example, a news reporter may lean heavily on a public relations person for information about an organization, but the reporter also may gather information from other sources. In the end, it is the reporter who writes the story. The upside of this is that the message, coming from a journalist, has a credibility with the mass audience that advertisements don't. Advertisements are patently self-serving. The downside of leaving it to the media to create the messages that reach the audience is surrendering control over the messages that go to the public.

CHECKING YOUR MEDIA LITERACY

◇ **What are the similarities of advertising and public relations? The differences?**

advertising
Unlike public relations, advertising seeks to sell a product or service

integrated marketing communication (IMC)
Comprehensive program that links public relations and advertising

INTEGRATED MARKETING

For many persuasive campaigns, organizations use both public relations and advertising. Increasingly, public relations and advertising people find themselves working together. This is especially true in corporations that have adopted **integrated marketing communication,** which attempts to coordinate advertising as a marketing tool with promotion and publicity of the sort that public relations experts can provide. Several

MEDIA PEOPLE

Leslie Unger

Leslie Unger was there at the beginning, when in 1992 the Academy of Motion Picture Arts & Sciences created an in-house communication unit. In her early 20s, after a couple of entry-level public relations jobs, Unger found herself helping run logistics for the Academy Awards.

Now, even after so many times through the annual Hollywood extravaganza, Unger at moments can't believe what she's in the middle of. She pinches herself in a reality check: "I'm at the Academy Awards!"

Working up to Oscar night occupies Unger full time-plus for five months beginning in November. Her usual seven-person staff is bulked up to 12 to handle news media requests for credentials. In recent years there have been 500 to 600 requests. Only about half are cleared.

For the audience, much of Unger's media-support work is invisible. She decides where individual reporters will be placed so they don't stumble over each other, at least not too much. Interview rooms need to look good on television. Even often-ratty pressrooms must be presentable. And are there enough jacks for bloggers and all the laptops?

There are countless meetings with fire and security experts and art directors. The network covering the event has its own marketing and publicity team with which Unger must coordinate. To do it all, Unger has to bring in outside public relations help, most recently from the Dobbin/Bolgla agency in New York.

Unger learned publicity and event management out of college in the public affairs department of the Los Angeles County Public Works Department. Then for a year she was a junior account executive at Ruder Finn, a public relations agency, in Los Angeles. Ruder Finn had handled the Academy Awards account until 1992 when the Academy created an internal communications unit—and Unger joined the Academy payroll.

The five-month buildup to the climactic Oscar night hardly ends Unger's work. Countless queries come in for days, like, she says, "What was the instrument Sting played?" After a while, though, she moves into less hectic months, an interlude of sorts. She works on Academy programs to promote film appreciation and literacy and the Academy's film archives, and to encourage student moviemaking. Those activities include Unger generating a couple of new releases a week—although nothing like the two-a-day rate in the pre-Oscar months.

WHAT DO YOU THINK?

- Would college alone have prepared Leslie Unger to be the event coordinator of the Academy Awards?
- What career-building advice do you infer from Leslie Unger's experience?

Academy Awards Preparation. *Making Oscar night work right, look good.*

major advertising agencies, aware of their clients' shift to integrated marketing, have acquired or established public relations subsidiaries to provide a wider range of services under their roof.

It is this overlap that has prompted some advertising agencies to move more into public relations. The WWP Group of London, a global advertising agency, has acquired both Hill & Knowlton, one of the public relations company in the United States, and the large Ogilvy PR Group. The Young & Rubicam advertising agency has three public relations subsidiaries: Burson-Marsteller, Cohn & Wolf, and Creswell, Munsell, Fultz & Zirbel. These are giant enterprises that reflect the conglomeration and globalization of both advertising and public relations.

To describe integrated marketing communication, media critic James Ledbetter suggests thinking of the old Charlie the Tuna ads, in which a cartoon fish made you chuckle and identify with the product—and established a brand name. That's not good enough for IMC. "By contrast," Ledbetter says, "IMC encourages tuna buyers to think about all aspects of the product. If polls find that consumers are worried about dolphins caught in tuna nets, then you might stick a big 'Dolphin Safe' label on the tins and set up a web site featuring interviews with tuna fishermen." The new wave of IMC, according to one of its primary texts, is "respectful, not patronizing; dialogue-seeking, not monologic; responsive, not formula-driven. It speaks to the highest point of common interest—not the lowest common denominator."

Public relations and advertising crossovers are hardly new. One area of traditional overlap is **institutional advertising,** which involves producing ads to promote an image rather than a product. The fuzzy, feel-good ads of agricultural conglomerate Archer Daniels Midland, which pepper Sunday morning network television, are typical.

institutional advertising
Paid space and time to promote an institution's image and position

CHECKING YOUR MEDIA LITERACY

- **Interagency competition among advertising agencies has blurred some distinctions between public relations and advertising. How so? And why?**

Media Relations

STUDY PREVIEW

Public relations people generally favor candor in working with the news media. Even so, some organizations opt to stonewall journalistic inquiries. An emerging school of thought in public relations is to challenge negative news coverage aggressively and publicly.

OPEN MEDIA RELATIONS

The common wisdom among public relations people today is to be open and candid with the mass media. It is a principle that dates to Ivy Lee, and case studies abound to confirm its effectiveness. A classic case study on this point is the Tylenol crisis.

Johnson & Johnson had spent many years and millions of dollars to inspire public confidence in its painkiller Tylenol. By 1982 the product was the leader in a crowded field of headache remedies with 36 percent of the market. Then disaster struck. Seven people in Chicago died after taking Tylenol capsules laced with cyanide. James Burke, president of Johnson & Johnson, and Lawrence Foster, vice president for public relations, moved quickly. Within hours, Johnson & Johnson:

- Halted the manufacture and distribution of Tylenol.
- Removed Tylenol products from retailers' shelves.
- Launched a massive advertising campaign requesting people to exchange Tylenol capsules for a safe replacement.
- Summoned 50 public relations employees from Johnson & Johnson and its subsidiary companies to staff a press center to answer media and consumer questions forthrightly.
- Ordered an internal company investigation of the Tylenol manufacturing and distribution process.
- Promised full cooperation with government investigators.
- Ordered the development of tamper-proof packaging for the reintroduction of Tylenol products after the contamination problem was resolved.

Investigators determined within days that an urban terrorist had poisoned the capsules. Although exonerated of negligence, Johnson & Johnson nonetheless had a tremendous problem: how to restore public confidence in Tylenol. Many former Tylenol users were reluctant to take a chance, and the Tylenol share of the analgesic market dropped to 6 percent.

To address the problem, Johnson & Johnson called in the Burson-Marsteller public relations agency. Burson-Marsteller recommended a media campaign to capitalize on the high marks the news media had given the company for openness during the crisis. Mailgrams went out inviting journalists to a 30-city video teleconference to

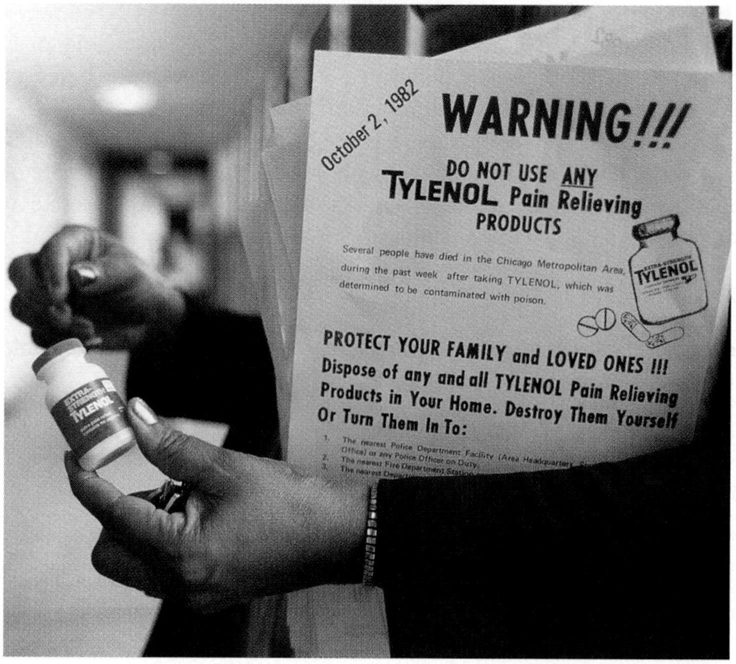

James Burke

Product-Tampering Crisis. *When cyanide-laced Tylenol capsules killed seven people in Chicago, the manufacturer Johnson & Johnson responded quickly. Company President James Burke immediately pulled the product off retailers' shelves and ordered company publicists to set up a press center to answer news media inquiries as fully as possible. Burke's action and candor helped to restore the public's shaken confidence in Tylenol, and the product resumed its significant market share after the crisis ended. It turned out that it probably was somebody outside Johnson & Johnson's production and distributing system who had contaminated the capsules rather than a manufacturing lapse.*

hear James Burke announce the reintroduction of the product. Six hundred reporters turned out, and Johnson & Johnson officials took their questions live.

To stir even wider attention, 7,500 **media kits** had been sent to newsrooms the day before the teleconference. The kits included a news release and a bevy of supporting materials: photographs, charts and background information.

The resulting news coverage was extensive. On average, newspapers carried 32 column-inches of copy on the announcement. Network television and radio as well as local stations also afforded heavy coverage. Meanwhile, Johnson & Johnson executives, who had attended a workshop on how to make favorable television appearances, made themselves available as guests on the network morning shows and talk shows. At the same time Johnson & Johnson distributed 80 million free coupons to encourage people to buy Tylenol again.

The massive media-based public relations campaign worked. Within a year, Tylenol had regained 80 percent of its former market share. Today, in an increasingly crowded analgesic field, Tylenol is again the market leader with annual sales of $670 million, compared with $520 million before the cyanide crisis.

CHECKING YOUR MEDIA LITERACY

- **Is there anything Ivy Lee would have done differently than Tylenol executives did after a terrorist replaced Tylenol with cyanide in Chicago drugstores?**

PROACTIVE MEDIA RELATIONS

Although public relations campaigns cannot control what the media say, public relations people can help to shape how news media report issues by taking the initiative. In the Tylenol crisis, for example, Johnson & Johnson reacted quickly and decisively and took control of disseminating information, which, coupled with full disclosure, headed off false rumors that could have caused further damage. This is a good example of **proactive media relations.**

media kit
A packet provided to news reporters to tell the story in an advantageous way

proactive media relations
Taking the initiative to release information

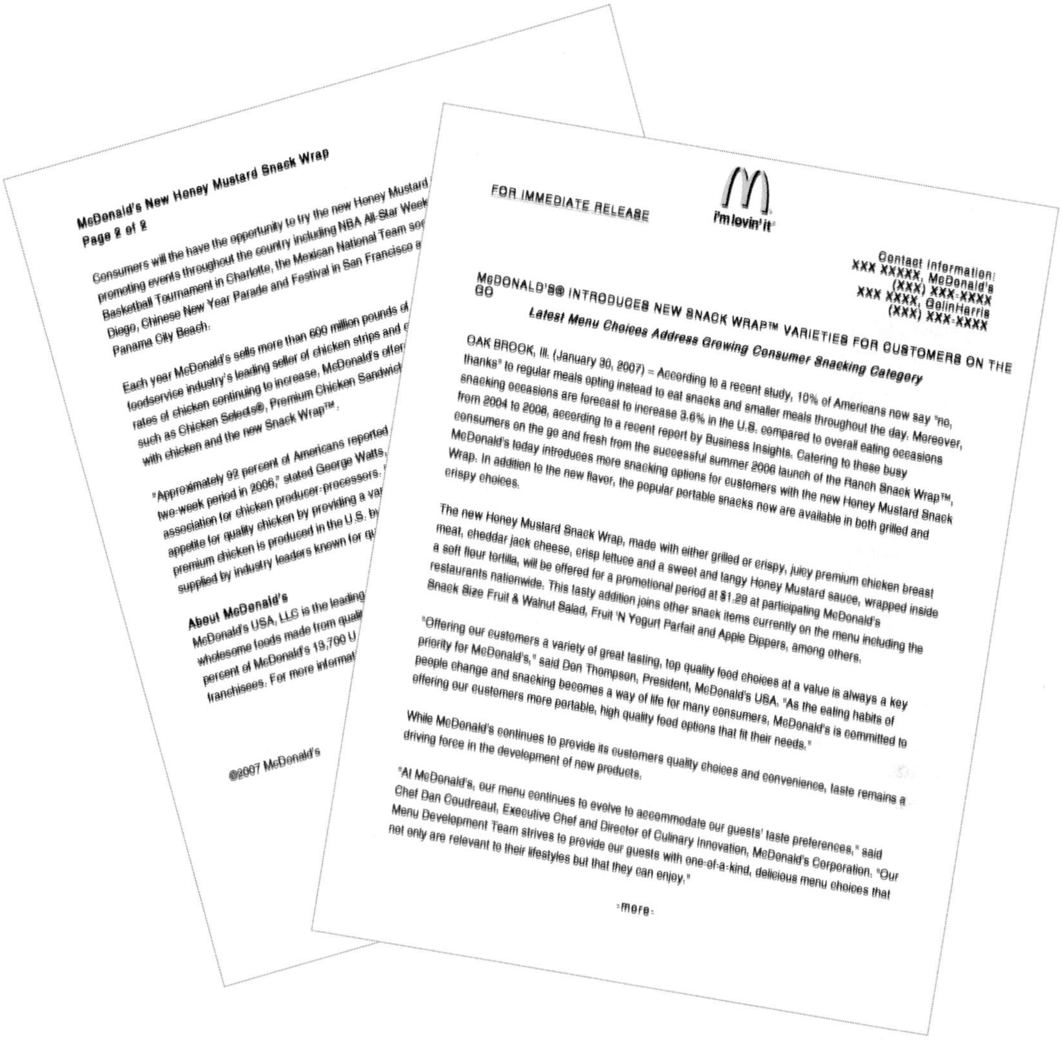

McDonald's New Honey Mustard Snack Wrap
Page 2 of 2

About McDonald's

©2007 McDonald's

FOR IMMEDIATE RELEASE

Contact Information:
XXX XXXXX, McDonald's
(XXX) XXX-XXXX
XXX XXXX, GolinHarris
(XXX) XXX-XXXX

MCDONALD'S® INTRODUCES NEW SNACK WRAP™ VARIETIES FOR CUSTOMERS ON THE GO

Latest Menu Choices Address Growing Consumer Snacking Category

OAK BROOK, Ill. (January 30, 2007) – According to a recent study, 10% of Americans now say "no, thanks" to regular meals opting instead to eat snacks and smaller meals throughout the day. Moreover, snacking occasions are forecast to increase 3.6% in the U.S. compared to overall eating occasions from 2004 to 2008, according to a recent report by Business Insights. Catering to these busy consumers on the go and fresh from the successful summer 2006 launch of the Ranch Snack Wrap™, McDonald's today introduces more snacking options for customers with the new Honey Mustard Snack Wrap. In addition to the new flavor, the popular portable snacks now are available in both grilled and crispy choices.

The new Honey Mustard Snack Wrap, made with either grilled or crispy, juicy premium chicken breast meat, cheddar jack cheese, crisp lettuce and a sweet and tangy Honey Mustard sauce, wrapped inside a soft flour tortilla, will be offered for a promotional period at $1.29 at participating McDonald's restaurants nationwide. This tasty addition joins other snack items currently on the menu including the Snack Size Fruit & Walnut Salad, Fruit 'N Yogurt Parfait and Apple Dippers, among others.

"Offering our customers a variety of great tasting, top quality food choices at a value is always a key priority for McDonald's," said Don Thompson, President, McDonald's USA. "As the eating habits of people change and snacking becomes a way of life for many consumers, McDonald's is committed to offering our customers more portable, high quality food options that fit their needs."

While McDonald's continues to provide its customers quality choices and convenience, taste remains a driving force in the development of new products.

"At McDonald's, our menu continues to evolve to accommodate our guests' taste preferences," said Chef Dan Coudreaut, Executive Chef and Director of Culinary Innovation, McDonald's Corporation. "Our Menu Development Team strives to provide our guests with one-of-a-kind, delicious menu choices that not only are relevant to their lifestyles but that they can enjoy."

-more-

News Release. *The workhorse of media relations is the news release, issued to newspapers, broadcast stations and other media to stir reporter interest in covering an event or developing a story or in hope of getting a point of view included in news stories. Studies have found that as many as 90 percent of news stories rely to some extent on information in news releases. Some releases even are reported verbatim, particularly in small-market, low-budget newsrooms.*

>> Crisis Response. For successful crisis management, public relations people need strong, ongoing relationships with their organization's top management. Otherwise, when crisis strikes, public relations people will face delays in rounding up the kind of breaking information they need to deal effectively with the news media. This was shown when President Bush, his popularity at an all-time low in 2006, brought in Tony Snow as White House news secretary to try to get media relations back on at least a less hostile track. Snow was a respected newsman and commentator in whom the White House reporting corps had confidence.

A principle in crisis management is to seize leadership on news reporting of the event. For public relations people, this means anticipating what news reporters will want to know and providing it even before reporters have time to formulate their questions. Ivy Lee invented this technique. Johnson & Johnson applied the technique with great success in 1982. At the White House in 2006, reporters saw spokesperson Tony Snow as someone they could trust, a straight-shooter who had the ear of the president.

media relations
Component of public relations that deals with press and other media

>> Ongoing Media Relationships. Good **media relations** cannot be forged in the fire of a crisis. Organizations that survive a crisis generally have a history of solid media relations. Their public relations staff people know reporters, editors and news directors

CASE STUDY

Crisis Management at *Time*

Dawn Bridges. *Public relations challenges include explaining decisions that may not be popular with everyone.*

When *Time's* cutting-edge journalism brings heat on the magazine, the Time Inc. senior vice president for corporate communications finds herself trying to set the facts straight from the company's perspective. In her job of handling media relations for the company, Dawn Bridges finds herself frequently put to the test.

In 2005, when *Time's* editor decided to comply with a federal prosecutor's demand for reporter Matt Cooper's notes in the Valerie Plame spy-outing scandal, everyone was clamoring for an explanation. In effect, Cooper's notes revealed his confidential source.

People wanted to know how *Time* could break the journalism standard of shielding confidential sources. Reporters were pounding at Bridges' door for answers. The crisis was a career challenge for Bridges. Many supporters of the Iraq War shuddered that Matt Cooper's notes would put the leak close to President Bush himself. The journalism community was outraged at the handover of the notes. At the same time, many people in the judicial system were pleased. There was court pressure for the notes.

Too, there was the drama of New York *Times* reporter Judith Miller gaining heroic martyrdom for refusing to give up notes for her Plame stories. Miller had gone to jail in the name of good journalism. How could *Time* have sold out?

To news reporters, Bridges made her points on behalf of *Time:*

- **Unfair Comparison.** Bridges explained to reporters that critics were taking shortcuts with the facts in equating the Judith Miller and Matt Cooper subpoenas. The New York *Times* was never asked for Judith Miller's notes. Miller's decision to go to jail was hers alone—not that of the newspaper as her employer. In the Cooper case, *Time* magazine was subpoenaed. Although the distinction was not at the heart of the criticism of *Time,* Bridges called the situations apples and oranges: To lionize the New York *Times* and to pillory *Time,* she said, was misleading.
- **Unique Situation.** The journalistic standard to shield whistleblowers, she argued, was less the issue than dirty politics. The allegation under federal investigation was that a political partisan had leaked Plame's name to discredit revelations from her husband. He had criticized the rationale for the U.S. war against Iraq and angered the White House. "This," said Bridges, "was allegedly a case of a political partisan breaking a law about national security in a time of war for political gain." Bridges said the case was far from a typical whistle-blowing confidential source issue.

DEEPENING YOUR MEDIA LITERACY

Crisis management is one of the greatest challenges for public relations. By definition, crises are unexpected. Each has twists that could not have been anticipated and require sharp analytical and communication skills.

EXPLORE THE ISSUE

Go to your library or online to brief yourself on the facts of the case.

DIG DEEPER

Next, tap into the wealth of commentary on both sides of the issue. Online search terms include *Valerie Plame, Judith Miller* and *Matt Cooper.*

WHAT DO YOU THINK?

If you were a journalist with grave doubts about *Time's* decision to surrender Matt Cooper's notes, what questions would you put to Dawn Bridges in an interview to expand on the points she made in her statement? If you were in Bridges' position, how would you respond to these questions? And what further questions would those answers beg be asked?

on a first-name basis. They avoid hyping news releases on routine matters, and they work hard at earning the trust of journalists.

Many public relations people, in fact, are seasoned journalists themselves, and they understand how journalists go about their work. It is their journalism background that made them attractive candidates for their public relations jobs.

>> **Sound Operating Principles.** An underlying strength that helped to see Johnson & Johnson through the Tylenol crisis was the company's credo. The credo was a written vow that Johnson & Johnson's first responsibility was to "those who use our products and services." Promoted in-house for years, the credo said, "Every time a business hires, builds, sells or buys, it is acting *for the people* as well as *for itself,* and it must be prepared to accept full responsibility." With such a sound operating principle, Johnson & Johnson's crisis response was, in some respects, almost reflexive. Going silent, for example, would have run counter to the principles that Johnson & Johnson people had accepted as part of their corporate culture for years.

CHECKING YOUR MEDIA LITERACY

- **Why are so many public relations jobs filled by people with journalism degrees and backgrounds?**

AMBIVALENCE IN MEDIA RELATIONS

Despite the advantage of open media relations, not all companies embrace the approach. Giant retailer Wal-Mart, as an example, long resisted putting resources into public relations. Founder Sam Walton saw public relations as a frill. It didn't fit his keep-costs-minimal concept. By 2005, even with Walton dead, his philosophy remained in place. The company had only a 17-member public relations staff—minuscule in business. How minuscule? Wal-Mart sales exceeded $285 billion, yet the company had but one public relations staffer per $16 billion in earnings. Put another way, the company had one public relations person per 76,000 employees.

With a new store opening every day in 2005, Wal-Mart's spectacular growth masked problems. The company was generating legions of critics, whose mantra was epitomized in Anthony Bianco's choice of a title for his Wal-Mart-bashing book in 2006—*The Bully of Bentonville.* In Irvine, California, voters killed a planned store. Public opposition undid plans in the Queens section of New York City for another store. Reflecting growing employee discontent, there were rumblings to unionize—anathema in the Wal-Mart culture. There was a scandal about illegal aliens doing overnight cleanup work. A class-action suit alleging gender discrimination was filed by some women employees.

Wal-Mart's attempts at damage control were clumsy. Occasional spectacular public relations successes flowed more from a corporate conscience in crisis than a methodical public relations strategy. In 2005, for example, Wal-Mart upstaged federal agencies in moving relief supplies to the Gulf Coast after Hurricane Katrina. More than 2,400 truckloads of merchandise were dispatched to stricken communities, the first 100 loads of donated merchandise arriving before the fumbling federal mobilization. Wal-Mart drivers also transported water and other essentials.

Wal-Mart to the Rescue. *While the federal emergency response agency was spinning bureaucratic wheels in hopeless confusion and disarray, Wal-Mart dispatched 2,400 truckloads of relief supplies to victims of Hurricane Katrina. Wal-Mart scored mightily with the public, although the rescue caravans were more a demonstration of the company's adroit delivery system than a sound public relations strategy. In public relations, Wal-Mart flies mostly blind.*

Occasional image successes, however, weren't doing the job. With a vague sense that something methodical in the public relations spirit was needed, Wal-Mart created an executive position in 2006 with the curious title "senior director stakeholder engagement." The job description had some earmarks of public relations, albeit not quite at the vice presidential level. Strangely, perhaps in homage to Sam Walton, the words *public relations* appeared nowhere in the job description's 3,000 words. You could, however, read a lot into wording like "an innovative out-of-the-box thinker" and "fundamental changes in how the company does business" and "social responsibility."

CHECKING YOUR MEDIA LITERACY

- **These companies have notorious histories for weak media relations, often snubbing reporter queries—Amerada Hess, IBM, Texas Instruments, Wal-Mart, Apple, Winn-Dixie. Would you defend the practice? Why or why not?**

Adversarial Public Relations

Public relations sometimes takes on aggressive, even feisty tactics. A pioneer in **adversarial public relations,** a vice president at Mobil Oil in the 1970s, **Herb Schmertz,** launched an assault on the ABC television network for a documentary critical of the U.S. oil industry. Schmertz bought full-page newspaper and magazine space for **advertorials,** a contrived word splicing *advertising* and *editorial,* for word-heavy, point-by-point rebuttals. Schmertz gave six Mobil executives a crash course on becoming spiffy interviewees and sent them on the talk-show circuit. They appeared on 365 television and 211 radio shows and talked with 85 newspaper reporters, not only tackling the ABC show but also spinning Mobil practices in an upbeat light.

Another adversarial approach is the corporate pout. Upset with the *Wall Street Journal,* carmaker General Motors once launched an **information boycott** of the newspaper. Contact with *Journal* reporters was cut off. So was GM advertising in the *Journal.* General Motors eventually came to its senses, after learning that information boycotts carry great risks:

- By going silent, an organization loses avenues for conveying messages to mass audiences.
- Yanking advertising is perceived by the public as coercive wielding of economic might.
- Because advertising is designed to boost sales, discontinuing ads is counterproductive.

Thirty years later, the jury is still out on Schmertz's adversarial public relations. Certainly, though, it has not been widely adopted, perhaps because more sophisticated tools have emerged for getting institutional messages across in society's ever-richer media mix. Glossy magazines are rife with paid content deliberately intended to blend with articles. Spokespersons are more practiced in avoiding a bite as they counter detractors in media forums.

adversarial public relations
Attacking critics openly

Herb Schmertz
Pioneered advertorials

advertorial
A public relations message, taking an editorial position, that appears in paid space or time; a term contrived from *advertisement* and *editorial*

information boycott
A policy to ignore news coverage and reporter queries

CHECKING YOUR MEDIA LITERACY

- **If you were president of a major corporation, would you hire Herb Schmertz as your public relations vice president? Why or why not?**

Directions for Public Relations

STUDY PREVIEW

New sensitivity about the ethical practice of public relations is being generated by theorists who favor open, honest dialogue with publics. Although not without risks, dialogic thinking has the potential to move public relations closer to ethical high ground. Ethics discussions and accreditation also aim to improve the practice of public relations.

A TARNISHED IMAGE

Unsavory elements in the heritage of public relations remain a heavy burden. P. T. Barnum, whose name became synonymous with hype, attracted crowds to his stunts and shows in the late 1800s with extravagant promises. Sad to say, some promoters still use Barnum's tactics. The claims for snake oil and elixirs from Barnum's era live on in commercials for pain relievers and cold remedies. The early response of tycoons to muckraking attacks, before Ivy Lee came along, was **whitewashing**—covering up the abuses but not correcting them. It is no wonder that the term *PR* is sometimes used derisively. To say something is "all PR" means that it lacks substance. Of people whose apparent positive qualities are a mere façade, it may be said that they have "good PR."

CHECKING YOUR MEDIA LITERACY

- **Will contemporary public relations people ever live down the legacy of P. T. Barnum? Of Jack Abramoff?**

STANDARDS AND CERTIFICATION

The Public Relations Society of America, which has grown to 28,000 members in 114 chapters, has a different approach: improving the quality of public relations work, whatever the label. In 1951 the association adopted a code of professional standards. In a further professionalization step, PRSA has established a credentialing process. Those who meet the criteria, including significant professional experience, and who then pass exams are allowed to place **APR,** which stands for "accredited in public relations," after their names. About 5,000 PRSA members hold APR status.

Since 1998 the APR program has been operated by the Universal Accreditation Board, which was created for that purpose by PRSA and a consortium of nine other public relations organizations. It is a rigorous process. Nationwide, only 80 to 90 practitioners a year earn the right to use APR with their signatures.

CHECKING YOUR MEDIA LITERACY

- **If you were in a capacity to hire someone for an entry-level public relations position in your organization, would you make a journalism degree a requirement? How about APR accreditation?**
- **How about for a senior public relations position?**

whitewashing
Covering up

APR
Indicates PRSA accreditation

dialogic theory
Dialogue-based approach to negotiating relationships

DIALOGIC PUBLIC RELATIONS

Among scholars an enthusiasm has developed for applying **dialogic theory** for a kinder, gentler practice of public relations. Advocates draw on the concept of genuine dialogue, which is deeply rooted in philosophy, psychology, rhetoric and relational communication. Rather than communication to publics, the traditional public relations model, dialogic theory insists on genuine listening in a true exchange. The theoretical shift is from managing communication to using communication as a tool for negotiating relationships without any manipulative or Machiavellian tricks.

Scholars Michael Kent and Maureen Taylor have summarized five major features of dialogic theory in operation:

>> **Mutuality.** A corporation or other institution engaged in public relations must recognize a responsibility to engage in communication on an even playing field. This means not taking advantage of financial might to talk down or push ideas without also listening.

>> **Propinquity.** For communication to be genuine, interaction with publics must be spontaneous.

>> **Empathy.** The institution must have a sincere sympathy in supporting and confirming public goals and interests.

>> **Risk.** Dialogic theory can work only if there is a willingness to interact with individuals and publics on their own terms.

>> **Commitment.** An institution must be willing to work at understanding its interactions with publics. This means that significant resources must be allocated not only to the dialogue but also to interpretation and understanding.

Dialogic theory offers a framework for a highly ethical form of public relations, but it is not without difficulties. As Kent and Taylor have noted, institutions have many publics, which makes dialogue a complex process. Participants in dialogic public relations put themselves in jeopardy. When publics engage in dialogue with organizations, they run the risk that their disclosures will be used to exploit or manipulate them.

Even so, discussion about dialogic theory is sensitizing many people in public relations to honesty and openness as ideals in the democratic tradition of giving voice to all. The theory is based on principles of honesty, trust and positive regard for the other rather than simply a conception of the public as a means to an end.

CHECKING YOUR MEDIA LITERACY

How could dialogic theory improve the practice of public relations?

TECHNOLOGY AND PUBLIC RELATIONS

The workhorse of public relations, the news media, made an easy transition to the Internet in the 1990s but pretty much only the medium changed—a mass-delivered e-mail of the standard release that once was snailed. In 2006 a Boston public relations agency, Shift Communications, reinvented the news release for the digital age. Shift's Todd Defren, who devised the new release, called it one-stop shopping for journalists to whom releases are targeted. The release includes tech-rich features, such as links to blogs that relate to the subject, links to related news releases and sites, downloadable company logos and videos.

Defren calls it the **social media news release** because it encourages interactive and ongoing communication. With a Shift release posted to the DIGG consumer-generated news site, journalists and bloggers and anyone else can click to sites that add to the dialogue. "This gives journalists everything they need in one place," Defren said.

The basis of Defren's invention is the Web 2.0 bevy of Internet services that facilitate the creation of content and exchange of information online. Within months of the Shift creation, which was downloadable free as a template, larger public relations agencies were on to the concept. PR giant Edelman unveiled its variation by the end of the year.

social media news release
Internet-based news releases with links to related material and interactive opportunities for news reporters

Edward Bernays

MEDIA PEOPLE

After graduation from college in 1912, Edward Bernays tried press agentry. He was good at it, landing free publicity for whoever would hire him. Soon his bosses included famous tenor Enrico Caruso and actor Otis Skinner. Bernays felt, however, that his success was tainted by the disdain in which press agents were held in general. He also saw far greater potential for affecting public opinion than his fellow press agents did. From Bernays' discomfort and vision was born the concept of modern public relations. His 1923 book *Crystallizing Public Opinion* outlined a new craft he was the first to call public relations.

Bernays saw good public relations as counsel to clients. He called the public relations practitioner a "special pleader."

The concept was modeled partly on the long-established lawyer–client relationship in which the lawyer, or counselor, suggests courses of action.

Because of his seminal role in defining what public relations is, Bernays sometimes is called the "Father of PR," although some people say the honor should be shared with Ivy Lee. No matter, there is no question of Bernays' ongoing contributions. He taught the first course in public relations in 1923 at New York University.

Bernays encouraged firm methodology in public relations, a notion that was captured in the title of a book he edited in 1955: *The Engineering of Consent.* He long advocated the professionalization of the field, which laid the groundwork for the accreditation of the sort the Public Relations Society of America has developed. Throughout his career Bernays stressed that public relations people need a strong sense of responsibility.

In one reflective essay, he wrote, "Public relations practiced as a profession is an art applied to a science in which the public interest and not pecuniary motivation is the primary consideration. The engineering of consent in this sense assumes a constructive social role. Regrettably, public relations, like other professions, can be abused and used for anti-social purposes. I have tried to make the profession socially responsible as well as economically viable."

Bernays became the Grand Old Man of public relations, still attending PRSA and other professional meetings past his 100th birthday. He died in 1993 at age 102.

WHAT DO YOU THINK?

- Edward Bernays liked to call himself the Father of Public Relations. Who deserves the accolade more—Bernays or Ivy Lee? Explain your choice.
- Bernays likened the relationship of public relations practitioners and their clients to lawyer–client relationships. Is it a fair comparison?

Edward Bernays. *Integrity was important to public relations pioneer Edward Bernays. When he was asked by agents of fascist dictators Francisco Franco and Adolf Hitler to improve their images in the United States, he said no. "I wouldn't do for money what I wouldn't do without money," Bernays said.*

CHAPTER WRAP-UP

Importance of Publics Relations (Pages 269–271)

- Public relations is a tool of leaders in business, government and other institutions to create beneficial relationships with other institutions and groups. Used well, public relations facilitates discussion that otherwise might not occur on issues of importance to constituent groups within society. This is discussion that affects the interests of the organization that has a stake in the issues—a kind of honest advocacy. This all puts public relations in an important role in the functioning of a democratic society. Key in public relations is the crafting of messages for mass audiences. The messages are delivered largely by mass media.

Origins of Public Relations (Pages 272–276)

- Modern public relations was the concept of Ivy Lee, who in 1906 began providing counsel to corporate clients that were under siege because of a wide range of abusive practices. These practices included exploitation of labor and unfair monopolistic policies against consumers and competitors. Lee urged corporations to soften their closed-door and arrogant practices. Lee also recommended an end to cover-ups when things go badly and facing issues publicly, honestly and openly. Lee had disdain for misleading, circus-like publicity excesses of the P. T. Barnum variety. These not only were less than honest but also were wearing thin with the public.

Structure of Public Relations (Pages 277–278)

- A revised model for corporate structures emerged in the late 1920s, putting an executive in charge of public relations. Typically a vice president, this executive provides input in corporate policies that would serve the interests not only of the organization but also of various constituencies. These constituencies are called publics, hence the term *public relations.* These executives head in-house public relations operations. Many organizations also draw on outside public relations agencies for special needs. Most public relations activities are either external communication, which is aimed at external publics, or internal communication, which is aimed at employees, shareholders and other groups within the organization.

Public Relations Services (Pages 278–281)

- Public relations covers a wide range of activities. These include lobbying on public policy and providing advocacy on organizational and public interests to legislators and other government officials. Lobbying done dishonestly can be against the public interest, as attested in occasional scandals about bribes and improper attempts to influence public policy. Done properly, however, lobbying is important in creating good public policy. Public relations also involves fund-raising, image management, crisis management and events coordination.

Public Relations and Advertising (Pages 281–283)

- Although public relations and advertising both involve crafting media messages for mass audiences, public relations is involved in creating policy. Advertising is not. Even so, there has been a recent blending of the functions, some under the umbrella concept of *integrated marketing.* This blending has blurred some traditional distinctions between public relations and advertising, especially as major advertising agencies have bought up public relations agencies to offer their clients a broader range of services.

Media Relations (Pages 283–288)

- The news media are especially important for public relations because they are the primary venue for distributing an organization's messages to groups in the public. The workhorse of media relations is the news release—a statement from an organization sent to newspapers, magazines and broadcasters. Newspeople decide what to pick up from these statements and how to integrate them into their news packages. Some studies have found that as much as 90 percent of news in U.S. media has roots in information from public relations sources. Media relations, however, is more than news releases. Most public relations involves making an organization accessible to the news media. Such open relations are valuable in emergencies because they help public relations people handle communication in crisis situations.

Directions for Public Relations (Pages 289–291)

- New sensitivity about the ethical practice of public relations is being generated by theorists who favor open, honest dialogue with publics. Although not without risks, dialogic thinking has the potential to move public relations closer to ethical high ground. Ethics discussions and accreditation also aim to improve the practice of public relations.

Review Questions

1. What is public relations? How is public relations connected to the mass media?
2. Why did big business become interested in the techniques and principles of public relations beginning in the late 1800s?

3. How is public relations a management tool?
4. What is the range of activities in which public relations people are involved?
5. What is the difference between public relations and advertising? What are the similarities?
6. What kind of relationship do most PR people strive to have with the mass media?
7. Why does public relations have a bad image? What are public relations professionals doing about it?

Concepts

Terms

People

Media Sources

- Joseph R. Hayden. *A Dubya in the Headlights: President George W. Bush and the Media.* Lexington, 2009. Hayden a journalism scholar, is harsh on the Bush White House's media relations.
- The industry's dominant trade journal is *PRWeek*.
- Kathryn Allamong Jacob. *King of the Lobby: The Life and Times of Sam Ward, Man-About-Washington in the Gilded Age.* Johns Hopkins, 2009. Jacob, a cultural historian on the post-Civil War era, profiles the public relations practitioner who perfected lobbying techniques to swoon Congress on behalf of banks, railroads and other clients.
- Michael L. Kent and Maureen Taylor. "Toward a Dialogic Theory of Public Relations," *Public Relations Review* (February 2002), pages 21–27. Kent and Taylor, both scholars, draw on a wide range of disciplines to argue for genuine dialogue as a basis for the moral practice of public relations.
- George S. McGovern and Leonard F. Guttridge. *The Great Coalfield War.* Houghton Mifflin, 1972. This account of the Ludlow Massacre includes the success of the Ivy Lee-inspired campaign to rescue the Rockefeller reputation but is less than enthusiastic about Lee's corporate-oriented perspective and sometimes shoddy fact gathering.
- Ray Eldon Hiebert. *Courtier to the Crowd: The Story of Ivy Lee and the Development of Public Relations.* Iowa State University Press, 1966. Professor Hiebert's flattering biography focuses on the enduring public relations principles articulated, if not always practiced, by Ivy Lee.

PUBLIC RELATIONS

In this chapter you have deepened your media literacy by revisiting several themes. Here are thematic highlights from the chapter:

MEDIA ECONOMICS

To the Rescue. Ivy Lee helped major corporations out of dilemmas resulting from their economic success.

The dark side of capitalism, unmitigated greed, marked the rise of corporations into unprecedented wealth and power in the latter 1800s. Abusive practices, often from monopolies, included the pursuit of profit over and above any sense of social responsibility. The Populist movement, led by underclass farmers and laborers, caught the ear of government. Public policy reforms followed, forcing industry to find new ways to conduct itself. Public relations, using a model devised by Ivy Lee in 1906, guided corporations toward behavior that served their own good and also took note of the needs and interests of society's other constituency groups. (Pages 271–275)

MEDIA AND DEMOCRACY

Sullied Reputation. Jack Abramoff's excesses hurt public relations.

Public relations ensures more diversity in public dialogue by giving an articulate voice to organizations. The best practice of public relations seeks win-win solutions on issues not only for the organization being represented but also for other constituencies with a stake in the issues. Public relations, practiced well, is honest advocacy in society's marketplace of ideas. One public relations activity, lobbying, goes to the heart of public policy by providing information and arguments to legislators in the creation of public policy. Lobbyists also work with government officials who put public policy into effect. Unethical and illegal lobbying activities, which sometimes make headlines, malign an otherwise honorable public relations activity that helps democracy work. (Pages 278–280)

ELITISM AND POPULISM

Enlightened Self-Interest. At General Motors in the 1930s, Paul Garrett pioneered the concept of sensitivity to public needs and interests as an element in high-level corporate decision making.

The Industrial Revolution that transformed U.S. society in the decades following the Civil War created a two-tiered society—the haves and the have-nots. Many in the upper class, panged to varying degrees with guilt about their unprecedented wealth, drew on the survival-of-the-fittest theory of Charles Darwin, the new rage of the time, to justify their privileged position. They called it social Darwinism, which meant they had acquired their advantage of superior status by being the most fit. The theory was cast in terms of a religious theme. It wasn't the fault of rich people that the Creator had imbued them with special gifts at amassing fortunes that enabled extravagant lifestyles. The notion was insulting to laborers, farmers and other ordinary blokes. A new political movement, Populism, arose to give voice to the underprivileged "inferiors" who, according to social Darwinism, had been left behind. The Populist movement inspired public policy changes that shook industry. Into this environment came public relations, as a way for industry to both listen to and communicate with the whole range of society's constituent groups. (Pages 271–272)

MEDIA FUTURE

News Releases. To encourage news coverage, public relations people prepare statements to the press.

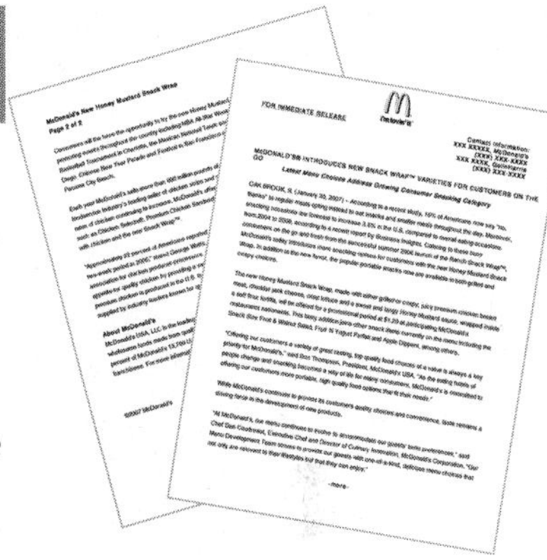

Public relations has a bum rap in many quarters. Take, for example, the derogatory phrase "It's only PR" to suggest something illusory and less than honest. The public relations profession has been working at the tarnished image, encouraging good practice through codes of ethics and accreditation. Scholars are working on new theories to guide public relations practitioners. These include dialogics, which emphasizes genuine listening before developing positions on issues. (Pages 289–290)

AUDIENCE FRAGMENTATION

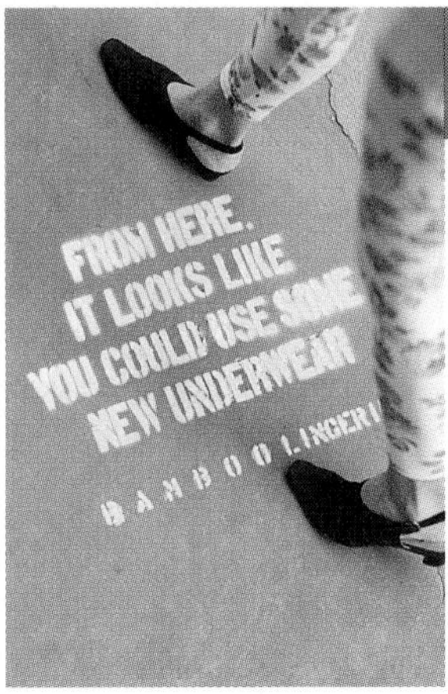

Two Tiers. The fragmentation of society into thousands of subgroups offers new challenges for public relations communication.

The concept of publics, groups within society that are identifiable and addressable, has grown more complex with the proliferation of special interest groups. People once identified themselves mostly as members of large groups, like political parties, religious denominations, ethnic communities and geographic areas. The old categories today have subcategories and subcategories within them, most with articulate leadership and their own channels of communication. This all adds layers of challenge for public relations practitioners in listening to the growing diversity of voices and designing campaigns to build support for mutually beneficial goals. (Page 290)

MEDIA TECHNOLOGY

Michael J. Fox. Special interest groups can personify their messages and broaden their appeals through celebrity support for the cause. Michael J. Fox not only drew support for stem-cell research funding, he also drew more people into the debate.

Not being a mass medium itself but relying on media to carry its messages, public relations has no technology unique to itself. But technology for other media, particularly the Internet, has opened fascinating new wrinkles for the conduct of public relations. One is online news releases with links to blogs and a wide range of related sites. Called the *social media news release,* the innovation encourages interactive and ongoing communication. It makes public relations more than ever a two-way street for communication. (Page 290)

chapter 11

ADVERTISING

Bob Greenberg *His crystal ball sees advertising not in packaging ads inside entertainment and news but in advertising so compelling that it's why people tune in.*

LEARNING AHEAD

- Advertising is key in consumer economies, democracy and the mass media.
- Most advertising messages are carried through the mass media.
- Advertising agencies create and place ads for advertisers.
- Advertisements are placed with care in media outlets.
- Advertisers are experimenting with new platforms.
- Brand names as an advertising strategy are in transition.
- Advertising tactics include lowest common denominators, positioning, redundancy and testimonials.
- New advertising tactics include encouraging word-of-mouth testimonials.
- Challenges ahead for advertisers include ad clutter and creative excesses.

ADVERTISING OUTSIDE THE BOX

If advertising had a guru, it would be Bob Greenberg. He was the first to talk about cell phones as a new advertising medium—the "third screen," he called it, coming after movies and television. In the fast-changing media environment, those insights were ages ago—at least a couple years. Now Greenberg is into massive outdoor signage becoming even more massive. Think Times Square.

Greenberg shares his observations freely, but, no mere armchair commentator, he practices post-mass media advertising at his R/GA agency in New York, part of the global Interpublic agency chain. R/GA designed the Nikeid web site, where footwear freaks can spend hours designing their own. That's customer interactivity that sells products, he says.

The era of entertainment that brought massive audiences to advertising messages is fast fading, Greenberg says. It's time to think outside the box.

Greenberg pities those ad agency execs who still pitch the 30-second television spot to clients because it's all they know. It's not that television, radio, magazines and newspapers are dead but that their heyday is past and their near-monopoly as carriers of advertising is fading fast. As Greenberg tells it, ad agencies that don't find new models to reach consumers are setting themselves up for extinction.

Greenberg's answer: Rather than ads being sandwiched into entertainment products, the ads themselves must be the entertainment. Greenberg has been called a media futurist, but there is evidence that the future is now. Samsung and Verizon have tripled their Internet ad budgets. American Express has shifted away from network television. At R/GA Greenberg has integrated information technologists, data analysts and what he calls "experience designers" into his staff. He must be doing something right. His staff has quintupled to 400.

Importance of Advertising

STUDY PREVIEW

Advertising is vital in a consumer economy. Without it people would have a hard time even knowing what products and services are available. Advertising, in fact, is essential to a prosperous society. Advertising also is the financial basis of important contemporary mass media.

CONSUMER ECONOMIES

Advertising is a major component of modern economies. In the United States the best estimates are that advertisers spend about 2 percent of the gross domestic product to promote their wares. When the nation's production of goods and services is up, so is advertising spending. When production falters, as it did in the early 2000s, many manufacturers, distributors and retailers pull back their advertising expenditures.

The essential role of advertising in a modern consumer economy is obvious if you think about how people decide what to buy. If a shoe manufacturer were unable to tout the virtues of its footwear by advertising in the mass media, people would have a hard time learning about the product, let alone knowing whether it is what they want.

CHECKING YOUR MEDIA LITERACY

- **Could a consumer economy work without advertising? Explain.**

ADVERTISING AND PROSPERITY

Advertising's phenomenal continuing growth has been a product of a plentiful society. In a poor society with a shortage of goods, people line up for necessities like food and clothing. Advertising has no role and serves no purpose when survival is the main concern. With prosperity, however, people have not only discretionary income but also a choice of ways to spend it. Advertising is the vehicle that provides information and rationales to help people decide how to enjoy their prosperity.

Besides being a product of economic prosperity, advertising contributes to prosperity. By dangling desirable commodities and services before mass audiences, advertising can inspire people to greater individual productivity so that they can have more income to buy the things that are advertised.

Advertising also can introduce efficiency into the economy by allowing comparison shopping without in-person inspections of all the alternatives. Efficiencies also can result when advertising alerts consumers to superior and less costly products and services that have displaced outdated, outmoded and inefficient offerings.

Said Howard Morgens when he was president of Procter & Gamble: "Advertising is the most effective and efficient way to sell to the consumer. If we should ever find better methods of selling our type of products to the consumer, we'll leave advertising and turn to these other methods." Veteran advertising executive David Ogilvy once made the point this way: "Advertising is still the cheapest form of selling. It would cost you $25,000 to have salesmen call on a thousand homes. A television commercial can do it for $4.69." McGraw-Hill, which publishes trade magazines, has offered research showing that a salesperson's typical call costs $178, a letter $6.63 and a phone call $6.35. For 17 cents, says McGraw-Hill, an advertiser can reach a prospect through advertising. Although advertising does not close a sale for all products, it introduces products and makes the salesperson's job easier and quicker.

Here are estimates of how much the leading advertisers spend in U.S. mass media:

Procter & Gamble	$5.2 billion
AT&T	3.2 billion
Verizon	3.0 billion
General Motors	3.0 billion
Time Warner	3.0 billion
Ford	2.5 billion
GlaxoSmithKline	2.5 billion
Johnson & Johnson	2.4 billion
Disney	2.3 billion
Unilever	2.2 billion

A Society of Choices. *By presenting choices to consumers, advertising mirrors the democratic ideal of individuals choosing intelligently among alternatives. The emphasis is on individuals making up their own minds: McCain or Obama? Nike or Reebok? Chevrolet or Ford?*

CHECKING YOUR MEDIA LITERACY

- **What is the link between advertising and prosperity?**

ADVERTISING AND DEMOCRACY

Advertising first took off as a modern phenomenon in the United States, which has given rise to the theory that advertising and democracy are connected. This theory notes that Americans, early in their history as a democracy, were required by their political system to hold individual opinions. They looked for information so that they could evaluate their leaders and vote on public policy. This emphasis on individuality and reason paved the way for advertising: Just as Americans looked to the mass media for information on political matters, they also came to look to the media for information on buying decisions.

In authoritarian countries, by contrast, people tend to look to strong personal leaders, not reason, for ideas to embrace. This, according to the theory, diminishes the demand for information in these non-democracies, including the kind of information provided by advertising.

Advertising has another important role in democratic societies in generating most of the operating revenue for newspapers, magazines, television and radio. Without advertising, many of the media on which people rely for information, for entertainment and for the exchange of ideas on public issues would not exist as we know them.

CHECKING YOUR MEDIA LITERACY

- **How does advertising dovetail with the democratic ideal of individual decision making?**

PERSUASION VERSUS COERCION

Advertising has critics who point out that almost all ads are one-sided. Ads don't lay out options, which violates the principle of honesty that is essential in persuasive communication. Persuasiveness requires a full presentation of available options and then argumentation based on all the evidence and premises. Ads don't do that. The argument in advertisements, sometimes screaming, often emotional, is direct: "Buy me." What an ad doesn't say speaks volumes. This makes advertising, say the critics, a type of coercive communication—far short of honest persuasion.

Whatever the criticism, advertising is a major element in mass communication. The financial base of newspapers, magazines, radio, television—and more and more the Internet—depends on advertising. The role of advertising both in the media as we know them today as well as in our consumer economy cannot be denied.

CHECKING YOUR MEDIA LITERACY

- **What is the difference between coercive and persuasive communication?**
- **Can you find any ads that meet the criteria of being persuasive rather than coercive?**

Origins of Advertising

STUDY PREVIEW

Advertising is the product of great forces that have shaped modern society, beginning with Gutenberg's movable type, which made mass-produced messages possible. Without the mass media there would be no vehicle to carry advertisements to mass audiences. Advertising also is a product of the democratic experience; of the Industrial Revolution and its spin-offs, including vast transportation networks and mass markets; and of continuing economic growth.

STEPCHILD OF TECHNOLOGY

Advertising is not a mass medium, but it relies on media to carry its messages. **Johannes Gutenberg**'s movable type, which permitted mass production of the printed word, made mass-produced advertising possible. First came flyers. Then advertisements, as newspapers and magazines were introduced. In the 1800s, when technology created high-speed presses that could produce enough copies for larger audiences, advertisers used these media to expand markets. With the introduction of radio, advertisers learned how to use electronic communication. Then came television.

Flyers were the first form of printed advertising. The British printer **William Caxton** issued the first printed advertisement in 1468 to promote one of his books. In America publisher **John Campbell** of the Boston *News-Letter* ran the first advertisement in 1704, a notice from somebody wanting to sell an estate on Long Island. Colonial newspapers listed cargo arriving from Europe and invited readers to come, look and buy.

Johannes Gutenberg
Progenitor of advertising media

William Caxton
Printed first advertisement

John Campbell
Published first ad in British colonies

CHECKING YOUR MEDIA LITERACY

- **How is advertising dependent on media technology?**
- **How is advertising efficient for selling products and services?**

INDUSTRIAL REVOLUTION

The genius of **Benjamin Day**'s New York *Sun*, in 1833 the first penny newspaper, was that it recognized and exploited so many changes spawned by the Industrial Revolution. Steam-powered presses made large pressruns possible. Factories drew great numbers of people to jobs in cities that were geographically small areas to which newspapers could be distributed quickly. The jobs also drew immigrants who were eager to learn—from newspapers as well as other sources—about their adopted country. Industrialization, coupled with the labor union movement, created unprecedented wealth, with laborers gaining a share of the new prosperity. A consumer economy was emerging, although it was primitive by today's standards.

A key to the success of Day's *Sun* was that, at a penny a copy, it was affordable for almost everyone. Of course, Day's production expenses exceeded a penny a copy. Just as the commercial media do today, Day looked to advertisers to pick up the slack. As Day wrote in his first issue, "The object of this paper is to lay before the public, at a price within the means of everyone, all the news of the day, and at the same time afford an advantageous medium for advertising." Day and imitator penny press publishers sought larger and larger circulations, knowing that merchants would see the value in buying space to reach so much purchasing power.

National advertising took root in the 1840s as railroads, another creation of the Industrial Revolution, spawned new networks for mass distribution of manufactured goods. National brands developed, and their producers looked to magazines, also delivered by rail, to promote sales. By 1869 the rail network linked the Atlantic and Pacific coasts.

Benjamin Day
His penny newspaper brought advertising to new level

CHECKING YOUR MEDIA LITERACY

- **What was the genius of Benjamin Day?**

Advertising Agencies

STUDY PREVIEW

Central in modern advertising are the agencies that create and place ads on behalf of their clients. These agencies are generally funded by the media in which they place ads. In effect, this makes agency services free to advertisers. Other compensation systems are also emerging.

PIONEER AGENCIES

By 1869 most merchants recognized the value of advertising, but they grumbled about the time it took away from their other work. In that grumbling, a young Philadelphia man sensed opportunity. **Wayland Ayer,** age 20, speculated that merchants, and even national manufacturers, would welcome a service company to help them create advertisements and place them in publications. Ayer feared, however, that his idea might not be taken seriously by potential clients because of his youth and inexperience. So when Wayland Ayer opened a shop, he borrowed his father's name for the shingle. The father was never part of the business, but the agency's name, N. W. Ayer & Son, gave young Ayer access to potential clients, and the first advertising agency was born. The Ayer agency not only created ads but also offered the array of services that agencies still offer clients today:

- Counsel on selling products and services.
- Design services, that is, actually creating advertisements and campaigns.
- Expertise on placing advertisements in advantageous media.

Full-service advertising agencies conduct market research for their clients, design and produce advertisements and choose the media in which the advertisement will run. The 500 leading U.S. agencies employ 120,000 people worldwide. In the United States they employ about 73,000.

Wayland Ayer
Founded first ad agency

MEDIA TIMELINE

	ADVERTISING MILESTONES	PIVOTAL EVENTS
1400s–1600s	**First Ad** In England William Caxton promoted a book with first printed advertisement (1468)	>> Gutenberg invented movable metal type (1440s) >> First colonial newspaper (1690)
1700s	**Colonial Ad** Joseph Campbell included advertisements in his Boston *News-Letter* (1704)	
1800s	**Penny Press** Benjamin Day created New York *Sun* as combination news, advertising vehicle (1833) **Ad Agency** Wayland Ayer opened first advertising agency, Philadelphia (1869)	>> Civil War (1861–1865) >> Penny press period (1833–) >> Mass production, railroads contribute to creation of national market economy (1870s–)
1900–1949	**Ethics** Edward Bok of *Ladies' Home Journal* established advertising code (1919) **Regulation** Congress created Federal Trade Commission to combat unfair advertising (1914) **Broadcast Code** NBC established code of acceptable advertising (1929) **Ad Council** Media industries created predecessor to Ad Council (1942)	>> Women's rights movement succeeds in suffrage (1920) >> Great Depression (1930s) >> World War II (1941–1945)
1950–1999	**Brands** David Ogilvy devised brand imaging (1950s) **TV Ads** Network television surpassed magazines as national advertising medium (1960s) **USP** Rosser Reeves devised unique selling proposition (1960s) **Regulation** Federal crackdown on misleading claims (1980s)	>> Korean War (1950–1953) >> Vietnam War (1964–1973) >> Humans reached moon (1969) >> Carter presidential administration (1981–1984)
2000s	**Store Brands** Store brands emerged as major challenge to brand names (2000s) **Viral** Ongoing story lines used to generate buzz (2000s) **Super Bowl** Thirty-second spot on televised game reached record $2.6 million (2006)	>> 9/11 terrorist attacks (2001) >> Iraq War (2003–) >> Hurricane Katrina (2005)

Ben Day's one-cent New York Sun *was dependent on advertising*

David Ogilvy championed a first-class image for branded products

Dave Balter has freelanced buzzing with agents to whom he issues sample products

Hybrid branding, like Paris Hilton fragrances, integrates implied testimonials and celebrity names

The world's largest advertising agencies, ranked by revenue from their core domestic clients:

Omnicon (New York)	$6.9 billion
WWP (London)	$4.6 billion
Interpublic (New York)	$3.8 billion
Publicis (Paris)	$2.9 billion
Dentsu (Tokyo)	$111 million

CHECKING YOUR MEDIA LITERACY

- What services of a modern advertising agency can be traced to Wayland Ayer?

AGENCY COMPENSATION

Advertising agencies once earned their money in a standard way—15 percent of the client advertiser's total outlay for space or time. On huge accounts, like Procter & Gamble, agencies made killings.

>> Commissions. The 15 percent **commission contract** system broke down in the 1990s when U.S. businesses scrambled to cut costs to become more competitive globally. Today, according to a guesstimate by the trade journal *Advertising Age,* only 10 to 12 percent of agency contracts use a standard percentage. Agency compensation generally is negotiated. Big advertisers, like P&G, are thought to be paying 13 percent on average, but different agencies handle the company's brands, each with a separate contract. For competitive reasons all parties tend to be secretive about actual terms.

In one sense, advertising under the commission system is free for advertisers. Most media companies offer a 15 percent discount to ad agencies for ads placed by agencies. In effect, media companies induce agencies to place their clients' messages with them. Media companies and agencies prefer, however, to explain the discount as compensation for bulk purchases of time and space.

>> Performance. Commission contracts have been replaced largely by **performance contracts.** With these contracts, pioneered by Procter & Gamble, an advertiser pays an agency's costs plus a negotiated profit. In addition, if a campaign works spectacularly, agencies land bonuses.

A variation that Coca-Cola forced on agencies for 2010 contracts was to cover agency costs for a campaign with nothing additional if a campaign flopped but as much as 30 percent extra if a campaign met all targets. Agencies weren't pleased. One concern was that Coke was transferring all the risk for daring creativity to agencies. But Coke, with ad spending of $3 billion a year worldwide, held the upper hand in negotiating new contracts. Said Coke executive Sarah Armstrong: "We want our agencies to earn their profitability."

>> Equity. In the 1990s dot-com boom, a performance contract variation was to pay agencies with shares in the company. **Equity contracts** are chancy for agencies because an advertiser's success hinges on many variables, not just the advertising, but the return for an agency with a soaring client can be stratospheric.

commission contract
An advertising agency earns an agreed-upon percentage of what the advertising client spends for time and space, traditionally 15 percent

performance contract
An advertising agency earns expenses and an agreed-upon markup for the advertising client, plus bonuses for exceeding minimal expectations

equity contract
An advertising agency is compensated with shares of stock in an advertising client

CHECKING YOUR MEDIA LITERACY

- How does the commission system in advertising work?
- What has forced changes in the commission system? What are the changes?

CASE STUDY

Kids in Army Marketing Cross-Hairs?

Alarms sounded at the Pentagon when the U.S. Army missed its recruiting goal of 80,000 new soldiers for the first time in years. Short 7,000, the Army launched multiple programs to restore its strength. New financial incentives were offered. The high-school diploma requirement was dropped. Applicants with criminal records were accepted. Waivers became more frequent for bad physical and medical deficiencies. It all worked. Recruiters met goals the next few years.

But what of the long term?

The Army reshaped its marketing to create a stronger and positive impression with the next generation from which soldiers would be recruited. Among tactics:

- At a Philadelphia mall, next door to an indoor skate park, the Army set up a 14,500-square-foot experimental exhibit. Displays included a Humvee and hands-on helicopter simulators.
- The online game *America's Army,* already with more than nine million registered users, was updated for a new release in 2009.
- Through an Army-approved licensing intermediary, Sears Roebuck & Co. issued a First Army Division apparel collection featuring the division's legendary Big Red One insignia. Prices of the apparel, starting in boys' sizes, began at $11.99.

The new marketing initiatives raised eyebrows. Was the Army softening a market of teen and even pre-pubescent kids? Was it right for the Army to glamorize itself to kids whose critical-assessment skills were still in formative stages? It was the same question that had been put to breakfast cereal makers for decades. Toy-makers had been similarly gigged for their ads. Were the promotions exploiting immature minds that could infer less than the whole truth of what products really delivered?

One critic of the new Army initiatives, Robert Weissman of Commercial Alert, talked about "the infusion of militaristic trappings into children's culture."

The Army was ready for critics. The game *America's Army* was rated T, meaning teens can buy it but not pre-teens. Army marketing spokesperson Paul Boyce told the trade journal *Advertising Age* that the helicopter simulators at the Philadelphia mall exhibit were for kids 13 and older only. Also, he said, the Big Red One apparel had no overt combat element—no fatigues, steel-toe boots or Kevlar helmets, just T-shirts, sweatshirts, jeans and jackets.

Big Red One. *Has the Army gone too far in recruiting when kids are part of the target that receives the pitches?*

DEEPENING YOUR MEDIA LITERACY

EXPLORE THE ISSUE

Look for online links to Army Experience Center at Franklin Mall in Philadelphia. Search the web also for Big Red One and other apparel with Army insignia. Search too for retailers selling the online game *America's Army.*

DIG DEEPER

Do you find any appeals to children, indirect or explicit, in these elements of the Army's marketing? If not, do you see how others might?

WHAT DO YOU THINK?

Robert Weissman of Commercial Alert has argued against Army marketing that reaches kids: "You see the glamorization and romanticism of the military in a context that is targeted at kids who don't probably have broader vantage to understand that complexity of military operations." How do you respond?

Placing Advertisements

STUDY PREVIEW

The placement of advertisements is a sophisticated business. Different media have inherent advantages and disadvantages in reaching potential customers. So do individual publications and broadcast outlets.

MEDIA PLANS

Agencies create **media plans** to ensure that advertisements reach the right target audience. Developing a media plan is no small task. Consider the number of media outlets available: 1,400 daily newspapers in the United States alone, 8,000 weeklies, 1,200 general-interest magazines, 13,000 radio stations and 1,200 television stations. Other possibilities include direct mail, banners on web sites, billboards, blimps, skywriting and even printing the company's name on pencils.

media plans
Lay out where ads are placed

cost per thousand
A tool to determine the cost-effectiveness of different media

Audit Bureau of Circulations
Verifies circulation claims

Media buyers use formulas, some very complex, to decide which media are best for reaching potential customers. Most of these formulas begin with a factor called **CPM,** short for cost per thousand. If airtime for a radio advertisement costs 7.2 cents per thousand listeners, it's probably a better deal than a magazine with a 7.3-cent CPM, assuming that both reach the same audience. CPM by itself is just a starting point in choosing media. Other variables that media buyers consider include whether a message will work in a particular medium. For example, radio wouldn't work for a product that lends itself to a visual pitch and sight gags.

Media buyers have numerous sources of data to help them decide where advertisements can be placed for the best results. The **Audit Bureau of Circulations,** created by the newspaper industry in 1914, provides reliable information based on independent audits of the circulation of most dailies. Survey organizations like Nielsen and Arbitron conduct surveys of television and radio audiences. Standard Rate and Data Service publishes volumes of information on media audiences, circulations and advertising rates.

Global Marketing. *Knowing the following that Houston Rockets star Yao Ming has in his China homeland, the distributor for the Chinese beer Yanjing paid $6 million for Chinese-language billboards at the Rockets' arena. When Rockets games were broadcast in China, millions of viewers saw Yanjing signs. Also, the imported Yanjing beer picked up customers in Houston.*

CHECKING YOUR MEDIA LITERACY

- **Why are media plans necessary in advertising?**
- **Why is CPM an essential advertising tool?**
- **How do advertisers know they are getting the audience to which they buy access?**

TRADITIONAL CHOICES

Here are pluses and minuses of major advertising vehicles:

>> **Newspapers.** The hot relationship that media theorist Marshall McLuhan described between newspapers and their readers attracts advertisers. Newspaper readers are predisposed to consider information in advertisements seriously because the act of reading requires them to be focused. Studies show that people, when ready to buy, look more to newspapers than to other media. Because newspapers are tangible, readers can refer back to advertisements just by picking up the paper a second time, which is not possible with ephemeral media like television and radio. Coupons are possible in newspapers. Newspaper readers tend to be older, better educated and higher earning than

television and radio audiences. Space for newspaper ads usually can be reserved as late as 48 hours ahead, and 11th-hour changes are possible.

However, newspapers are becoming less valuable for reaching young adults. To the consternation of newspaper publishers, there has been an alarming drop in readership among these people in recent years, and it appears that, unlike their parents, young adults are not picking up the newspaper habit as they mature.

Another drawback to newspapers is printing on newsprint, a relatively cheap paper that absorbs ink like a slow blotter. The result is that ads do not look as good as they do in slick magazines. Slick, stand-alone inserts offset the newsprint drawback somewhat, but many readers pull the inserts out and discard them as soon as they open the paper.

shelf life
How long a periodical remains in use

pass-along circulation
All the people who see a periodical

ad clutter
So many competing ads that all lose impact

>> **Magazines.** As another print medium, magazines have many of the advantages of newspapers plus longer **shelf life,** an advertising term for the amount of time that an advertisement remains available to readers. Magazines remain in the home for weeks, sometimes months, which offers greater exposure to advertisements. People share magazines, which gives them high **pass-along circulation.** With slick paper and splashier graphics, magazines provide a more prestigious context for advertisements than newspapers. With precise color separations and enameled papers, magazine advertisements can be beautiful in ways that newspaper advertisements cannot. Magazines, specializing as they do, offer more narrowly defined audiences than do newspapers.

On the downside, magazines require reservations for advertising space up to three months in advance. Opportunities for last-minute changes are limited, often impossible.

The Geico Spurt. *Discount insurer Geico credits its rapid growth to heavy advertising geared to different market segments. For young buyers, the Martin Agency of Richmond, Virginia, created the hilarious cavemen series with cavemen sighing and making their way through tony lifestyle situations—airports, psychotherapy, ritzy restaurants. For the older set, Geico has performers like Little Richard in campy self-mockery. Then there's the chatty gecko. Over five years Geico moved from 4.6 percent of the competitive U.S. insurance market to 6.3 percent. Industry insiders say Geico spent $499 million for advertising time and space in 2006.*

>> **Radio.** Radio stations with narrow formats offer easily identified target audiences. Time can be bought on short notice, with changes possible almost until airtime. Comparatively inexpensive, radio lends itself to repeated play of advertisements to drive home a message introduced in more expensive media like television. Radio also lends itself to jingles that can contribute to a lasting image.

However, radio offers no opportunity for a visual display, although the images that listeners create in their minds from audio suggestions can be more potent than those set out visually on television. Radio is a mobile medium that people carry with them. The extensive availability of radio is offset, however, by the fact that people tune in and out. Another negative is that many listeners are inattentive. Also, there is no shelf life.

>> **Television.** As a moving audio-visual medium, television offers special impact for advertising messages. Throughout its history, dating to the 1950s until recently, television has outpaced the growth of other media as an advertising vehicle. Today, the web is growing faster but remains a mere blip compared with network, cable and local television.

Drawbacks to placing ads on television include production costs. Because of cost, many advertisers have gone to shorter and shorter commercials. The resulting **ad clutter** overwhelms many viewers and diminishes the punch of the ads.

Limited inventory is also a problem for advertisers considering television. The networks, for example, have only so many ad slots available within and between programs. Historically, demand for slots has outstripped availability.

Slots for some hours are locked up months, even whole seasons, in advance. The networks historically have used the short supply of slots to push rates to what every year seems to be even more astronomical levels. The demand, however, appears to be softening with the fragmentation of television's audiences and the advent of new media.

Because of the television audience's diversity, especially at local stations and major networks, targeting potential customers with any precision is difficult. Narrowly focused cable services are an exception.

>> **Online.** Hesitation about using the Internet for advertising has yielded to the advantages. Literally thousands of sites serve niche audiences, enhancing the likelihood of reaching people with an inherent interest in specific products. For advertisers that choose the right sites, there is less waste than with traditional mass media, like the television networks that seek massive heterogeneous audiences.

For mail-order products, orders can be placed over the Internet right from the ad. With older media, ads only whet the consumer's appetite. A phone call or a visit to a showroom is necessary—and lots of otherwise likely customers frequently don't take that next step.

Another advantage of Internet advertising is cost. Except for high-demand sites, space is relatively inexpensive.

Some advertisers have experimented with consumer-created content on sponsored blog sites. An advantage of these post-your-own-clip sites is the consumer interest created by the bizarre stuff that people post. The sites have a high level of credibility because of their free-for-all nature. But there is also great risk. General Motors, for example, invited homemade clips about its Chevrolet Tahoe, a large sport-utility. The site ended up hosting TV spot-like messages about the Tahoe contributing to global warming. An advertiser that edits or shuts off negative input runs the risk of losing credibility.

Heavy consumer traffic on social networking sites like MySpace, YouTube and Facebook attracts advertising. But these sites also carry risk because people can post pretty much whatever they want on their pages, including negative stuff on a product that works against the effectiveness of the paid-for sponsored ads.

Among the five major media, here is how U.S. advertising dollars were spent, both nationally and locally, according to a 2005 projection:

Television	$62.1 billion
Newspapers	31.6 billion
Radio	16.5 billion
Magazines	12.1 billion
Online	11.9 billion

CHECKING YOUR MEDIA LITERACY

- **What are the advantages of each of the advertising-funded mass media? The disadvantages?**

New Advertising Platforms

STUDY PREVIEW

Internet search engines are a growing advertising vehicle, not only because of their high traffic but also because they organize the audience into subject categories. What better place to advertise skin-care products than on an index page for dermatology sites? Game sites attract advertisers because of their young, male audience, which has always been hard to reach.

SEARCH ENGINES

The Internet search engine Google, capitalizing on its super-fast hunt technology, has elbowed into the traditional placement service provided by advertising agencies. Google arranges for advertising space on thousands of web sites, many of them narrowly focused, like blogs, and places ads for its clients on the sites. Every blog visitor who clicks a **sponsored link** placed by Google will go to a fuller advertisement.

Google charges the advertiser a **click-through fee.** Google pays the site for every click-through. Google matches sites and advertisers—so a search for new Cadillacs doesn't display ads for muffler shops.

Google also places what it calls "advertiser links" on search screens. The New York *Times,* for example, has a license to use Google technology when readers enter search terms on the *Times* site. The license allows Google to display ads of likely interest whenever a *Times* site reader conducts an internal site search. A search for *Times* coverage of Jamaica news, for example, will produce links to *Times* stories on Jamaica, as well as to advertisements for Caribbean travel elsewhere on the Internet. If a *Times* reader clicks on an ad, Google pays the *Times* a click-through fee—from the revenue the advertiser paid to Google to place its ads.

Google has quickly become a major player in web advertising. Of the estimated advertisers' spending for online messages by 2010, Google had nearly $20 billion. That was more than 90 percent of the company's revenue.

CHECKING YOUR MEDIA LITERACY

- **Why are search engines a hot new medium for advertising?**

sponsored link
On-screen hot spot to move to an online advertisement

click-through fee
A charge to advertisers when an online link to their ads is activated; also, a fee paid to web sites that host the links

GAMING

To catch consumers who spend less time with television and more time with video games, advertisers have shifted chunks of their budgets to gaming. The potential is incredible. Half of Americans age 6 and older play games, and that elusive target for advertisers, men 18 and older, makes up 26 percent of the gamers.

For an on-screen plug, advertisers pay typically $20,000 to $100,000 for a message integrated into the game. In gaming's early days, game makers and product

Game Platform. *Jeep has found video games a new advertising platform. Background billboards on* Tony Hawk's Pro Skater 2 *can be updated with new products either as new DVD editions are issued or with downloads for Internet-connected games.*

markets worked directly with each other, but now many ad agencies have gaming divisions that act as brokers.

Game ads have advantages, particularly for online games. Messages can be changed instantly—a background billboard with a Pepsi ad can become a Chevy Cobalt ad or a movie trailer. One company, Massive, uses unseen interactive coding to identify gamers and adjust plugs that, for example, list stores near specific players and make geographic and other ad content adjustments. Nielsen, known mostly for television ratings, and game publisher Activision have an interactive system for tracking how many players see advertiser impressions—how many gamers see an ad and even how many recall an ad.

Although online gaming has advantages for advertisers, there are downsides. Online gaming ads, although generally cost-effective, are problematic. Games can take months to develop, requiring far more lead time than advertisers usually have for rolling out a comprehensive multimedia campaign. For simple billboard messages, however, games have the advantage of being instantly changeable.

Established brands have created their own games, which appear on their web sites. In an early **advergame,** as these ads are called, the shoe manufacturer Nike created a soccer game at Nikefootball.com. Kraft Foods had an advergaming race at Candyland.com. A downside: Because advergames are accessible only through a brand's site, they don't make sense for emerging brands.

CHECKING YOUR MEDIA LITERACY

- **What are the attractions of Internet-based games for advertisers?**

PRE-MOVIE ADVERTISING

Although it has been around a long time, advertising as a lead-in for movies is just now taking off. Why? Because it works. The research company Arbitron surveyed moviegoers as they left theaters and found that 80 percent remembered ads shown at the beginning of the movie. Other media aren't close, recently spurring a 37 percent increase in movie ad revenue to $356 million in one year. Also, according to Arbitron, the notion that most people resent ads is mythical. Of viewers between ages 12 and 24, 70 percent weren't bothered by the ads.

advergame
A sponsored online game, usually for an established brand at its own site

Brand Strategies

STUDY PREVIEW

Branding is a time-proven advertising strategy for establishing a distinctive name among consumers to set a product apart from competitors. The recent history of branding has moved beyond products into arrays of unrelated products. Special K is no longer just a breakfast cereal. Now it's an extensive line of diet products. Branding now includes building lines of products around celebrity images.

BRAND NAMES

A challenge for advertising people is the modern-day reality that mass-produced products intended for large markets are essentially alike: Toothpaste is toothpaste is toothpaste. When a product is virtually identical to the competition, how can one toothpaste maker move more tubes?

By trial and error, tactics were devised in the late 1800s to set similar products apart. One tactic, promoting a product as a **brand** name, aims to make a product a household word. When it is successful, a brand name becomes almost the generic identifier, like Coke for cola and Kleenex for facial tissue.

Techniques of successful brand-name advertising came together in the 1890s for an English product, Pears' soap. A key element in the campaign was multimedia

brand
A nongeneric product name designed to set the product apart from the competition

saturation. Advertisements for Pears' were everywhere—in newspapers and magazines and on posters, vacant walls, fences, buses and lampposts. Redundancy hammered home the brand name. "Good morning. Have you used Pears' today?" became a good-natured greeting among Britons that was still being repeated 50 years later. Each repetition reinforced the brand name.

CHECKING YOUR MEDIA LITERACY

- **What brand names would you list as household words?**
- **How effective are brand names with you personally?**
- **Do you resent the manipulation that is part of brand-name advertising?**

BRAND IMAGES

David Ogilvy, who headed the Ogilvy & Mather agency, developed the **brand image** in the 1950s. Ogilvy's advice: "Give your product a first-class ticket through life."

Ogilvy created shirt advertisements with the distinguished Baron Wrangell, who really was a European nobleman, wearing a black eye patch—and a Hathaway shirt. The classy image was reinforced with the accoutrements around Wrangell: exquisite models of sailing ships, antique weapons, silver dinnerware. To some seeing Wrangell's setting, the patch suggested all kinds of exotica. Perhaps he had lost an eye in a romantic duel or a sporting accident.

Explaining the importance of image, Ogilvy once said: "Take whisky. Why do some people choose Jack Daniels, while others choose Grand Dad or Taylor? Have they tried all three and compared the taste? Don't make me laugh. The reality is that these three brands have different images which appeal to different kinds of people. It isn't the whisky they choose, it's the image. The brand image is 90 percent of what the distiller has to sell. Give people a taste of Old Crow, and tell them it's Old Crow. Then give them another taste of Old Crow, but tell them it's Jack Daniels. Ask them which they prefer. They'll think the two drinks are quite different. They are tasting images."

David Ogilvy
Championed brand imaging

brand image
Spin put on a brand name

CHECKING YOUR MEDIA LITERACY

- **What twist did David Ogilvy put on brand names?**

First-Class Ticket. *In one of his most noted campaigns, advertising genius David Ogilvy featured the distinguished chair of the company that bottled Schweppes in classy locations. Said Ogilvy, "It pays to give products an image of quality—a first-class ticket." Ogilvy realized how advertising creates impressions: "Nobody wants to be seen using shoddy products."*

David Ogilvy

WHITHER BRAND NAMES?

Perhaps prematurely, perhaps not, obituaries are being written for brand names—and brand-name advertising.

>> Store Brands. Retailers are pushing **store brands,** on which they typically score 10 percent higher profits. Every time somebody buys Wal-Mart's Ol' Roy dog chow, Purina and other brand-name manufacturers lose a sale. Wal-Mart spends virtually nothing other than packaging costs for in-store displays to advertise Ol' Roy, which has knocked off Purina as top-seller. The store-brand assault has struck at a whole range of venerable brand names: Kellogg's, Kraft, Procter & Gamble and Unilever. Forrester Research, which tracks consumer trends, said in a 2002 report: "Wal-Mart will become the new P&G."

Some brands remain strong, like automobile lines, but many manufacturers of consumer goods, whose advertising has been a financial mainstay of network television and magazines as well as newspapers and radio, have had to cut back on ad spending. P&G spent $13.9 million advertising its Era detergent in 2001, only $5.4 million in 2002. Some manufacturers have dropped out of the brand-name business. Unilever has only 200 brands left, compared to 1,600 in the mid-1990s.

Retail chains, led by Wal-Mart, have the gigantic marketing channels to move great quantities of products without advertising expenses. Some retailers even own the factories. The Kroger chain owns 41 factories that produce 4,300 store-brand products for its grocery shelves.

store brands
Products sold with a store brand, often manufactured by the retailer. Also called *house brands* and *private labels.*

Before the mega-retailers, brand names gave products an edge—with network television and national magazines carrying the messages. In those days the major networks—ABC, CBS and NBC—delivered messages to millions of consumers with greater effect than could small retailers. Not only are small retailers disappearing, but the networks also can't deliver what they used to. Television systems with

Sam Walton

Store Brands. *Changes in retailing to one-stop superstores have diluted the value of traditional brand names. Chains, meanwhile, have introduced their own brands. Wal-Mart's Ol' Roy pet food and related pet products pick up on the name of company founder Sam Walton's favorite dog.*

Celebrity Branding. *Hybrid branding, like for Paris Hilton productions, integrates implied testimonials and celebrity names. For her namesake hair extensions, Hilton showed off the product at a hyped launch.*

500 channels and the highly diverse web have divided and subdivided the audience into fragments. In a 2003 newsletter to clients, the ad agency Doremus noted despairingly that "it's almost impossible to get your name in enough channels to build substantial awareness." Willard Bishop Consulting came to a similar conclusion from a study on network television, noting that three commercials could reach 80 percent of one target audience, 18-to 49-year-old women, in 1995. That penetration level required 97 ads in 2000.

In an analysis of the phenomenon, *Fortune* magazine writer Michael Boyle said the big superstores are displacing brand-name advertising as the new direct connection to consumers. The new mass channel, he said, is the superstore.

>> **Branding.** Brand names have taken on a new dimension. Today the concept includes lending a recognized name to an array of unrelated products: a Paris Hilton handbag, a Paris Hilton wristwatch, a Paris Hilton whatever. It's called **branding.** Originally, brand names were for products from a particular company, but the concept now includes unconnected products whose only connection is a name. Celebrities willing to objectify their image lend their names to arrays of products, giving the products a marketing cachet.

branding
Enhancing a product image with a celebrity or already established brand name, regardless of any intrinsic connection between the product and the image

CHECKING YOUR MEDIA LITERACY

- **Is there evidence that brand names are losing their luster? Explain.**
- **How has branding drifted from the original brand-name concept?**

Advertising Tactics

STUDY PREVIEW

When the age of mass production and mass markets arrived, common wisdom in advertising favored aiming at the largest possible audience of potential customers. These are called lowest common denominator approaches, and such advertisements tend to be heavy-handed so that no one can possibly miss the point. Narrower pitches, aimed at segments of the mass audience, permit more deftness, subtlety and imagination.

LOWEST COMMON DENOMINATOR

Early brand-name campaigns were geared to the largest possible audience, sometimes called an LCD, or **lowest common denominator,** approach. The term *LCD* is adapted from mathematics. To reach an audience that includes members with IQs of 100, the pitch cannot exceed their level of understanding, even if some people in the audience have IQs of 150. The opportunity for deft touches and even cleverness is limited by the fact they might be lost on some potential customers.

lowest common denominator
Messages for broadest audience possible

unique selling proposition
Emphasizes a single feature

>> **Unique Selling Proposition.** LCD advertising is best epitomized in contemporary advertising by USP, short for **unique selling proposition,** a term coined by

Rosser Reeves of the giant Ted Bates agency in the 1960s. Reeves' prescription was simple: Create a benefit of the product, even if from thin air, and then tout the benefit authoritatively and repeatedly as if the competition doesn't have it. One early USP campaign boasted that Schlitz beer bottles were "washed with live steam." The claim sounded good—who would want to drink from dirty bottles? However, the fact was that every brewery used steam to clean reusable bottles before filling them again. Furthermore, what is "live steam"? Although the implication of a competitive edge was hollow, it was done dramatically and pounded home with emphasis, and it sold beer. Just as hollow as a competitive advantage was the USP claim for Colgate toothpaste: "Cleans Your Breath While It Cleans Your Teeth."

A unique selling proposition need be neither hollow nor insulting, however. Leo Burnett, founder of the agency bearing his name, refined the USP concept by insisting that the unique point be real. For Maytag, Burnett took the company's slight advantage in reliability and dramatized it with the lonely Maytag repairman.

Rosser Reeves
Devised unique selling proposition

Jack Trout
Devised positioning

positioning
Targeting ads for specific consumer groups

flight (or wave)
Intense repetition of ads

>> **Positioning.** Rather than pitching to the lowest common denominator, advertising executive **Jack Trout** developed the idea of **positioning.** Trout worked to establish product identities that appealed not to the whole audience but to a specific audience. The cowboy image for Marlboro cigarettes, for example, established a macho attraction beginning in 1958. Later, something similar was done with Virginia Slims, aimed at women.

Positioning helps to distinguish products from all the LCD clamor and noise. Advocates of positioning note that there are more and more advertisements and that they are becoming noisier and noisier. Ad clutter, as it is called, drowns out individual advertisements. With positioning, the appeal is focused and caters to audience segments, and it need not be done in such broad strokes.

Campaigns based on positioning have included:

- Johnson & Johnson's baby oil and baby shampoo, which were positioned as adult products by advertisements featuring athletes.
- Alka-Seltzer, once a hangover and headache remedy, which was positioned as an upscale product for stress relief among health-conscious, success-driven people.

Over and Over. *The redundancy of ShamWow! ads, hammering away at its unique abilities to mop up spills, is enough to give you a headache. But the redundancy establishes a product in the minds of consumers. When a moisture-control emergency strikes, consumers reach for heavily promoted ShamWow! No matter how annoying, redundancy has proven to work to propel a product to success and maintain sales.*

CHECKING YOUR MEDIA LITERACY

- **What is lowest common denominator advertising?**
- **What is a unique selling proposition in advertising? Give examples from your own experience.**
- **How has the concept of positioning added dimension to advertising commodities?**

REDUNDANCY TECHNIQUES

Advertising people learned the importance of redundancy early on. To be effective, an advertising message must be repeated, perhaps thousands of times. Redundancy is expensive, however. To increase effectiveness at less cost, advertisers use several techniques:

- **Barrages.** Scheduling advertisements in intensive bursts called **flights** or **waves.**
- **Bunching.** Promoting a product in a limited period, such as running advertisements for school supplies in late August and September.

- **Trailing.** Running condensed versions of advertisements after the original has been introduced, as automakers do when they introduce new models with multipage magazine spreads and follow with single-page placements.
- **Multimedia trailing.** Using less expensive media to reinforce expensive advertisements. Relatively cheap drive-time radio in major markets is a favorite follow-through to expensive television advertisements created for major events like the Super Bowl.

Repetition can be annoying, especially with heavy-handed, simplistic messages. Hardly any American has escaped the repeated line for a roll-on headache remedy: "Head-On: Apply directly to the forehead." A follow-up ad series acknowledged the irritation with users proclaiming: "I hate your ads, but I love your product." And then repeating the annoying line. Annoying or not, redundancy can work. The chairman of Warner-Lambert, whose personal products include Rolaids gastric-relief tablets, once joked that the company owed the American people an apology for insulting their intelligence with the redundant line that "R-O-L-A-I-D-S spells relief." Warner-Lambert, however, has never been apologetic to shareholders about Rolaids maintaining its market dominance.

Marshall McLuhan, the media theorist prominent in the 1960s, is still quoted as saying that advertising is important after the sale to confirm for purchasers that they made a wise choice. McLuhan's observation has not been lost on advertisers that seek repeat customers.

Celebrity Ads. *When pop performer Michael Jackson pitched Pepsi in a 1984 advertisement, celebrities began to abandon their historic disdain for celebrity endorsements. Pepsi followed its $5 million deal with Jackson with Madonna, Michael J. Fox, Ray Charles, Cindy Crawford and Britney Spears. Soon, everybody was doing it: presidential candidate Bob Dole, the Kansas senator, extolled how Viagra worked for him.*

CHECKING YOUR MEDIA LITERACY

- **If repeating an advertisement annoys people, why do advertisers do it?**

TESTIMONIALS

Celebrity endorsements have long been a mainstay in advertising. Testimonials can be less than classy, though. Actress Rita Hayworth offered testimonials to a denture adhesive, quarterback Joe Montana to a jock-itch potion, former presidential candidate Bob Dole to an erectile-dysfunction prescription, former Surgeon General Everett Koop to an emergency-call device. Professional fund-raising, a growth industry, includes pleas from celebrity volunteers. For commercial products, however, testimonials are given only for compensation.

During Jimmy Carter's presidential administration in the 1980s, the Federal Trade Commission was among the federal agencies that cracked down on excessive business practices. The FTC saw testimonials getting out of hand and required that endorsers actually be users of the product. The commission also clamped down on implied expert endorsements, like actors wearing white coats to suggest they were physicians while they extolled the virtues of over-the-counter remedies. That led to one laughable FTC-ordered disclaimer that has endured as a comedy line: In the interest of full disclosure, one soap-opera star in a white frock opened an ad: "I'm not really a doctor but I play one on TV." Then he made the spiel.

CHECKING YOUR MEDIA LITERACY

- **How has the government policed testimonial advertising?**

New Advertising Techniques

STUDY PREVIEW

What goes around comes around. The original pre-media advertising, word of mouth, has new currency in techniques that go by the name "buzz communication." The goal is to create buzz about a product. Many buzz campaigns originate on the Internet with the hope of something virus-like. The term *viral advertising* has come into fashion.

WORD-OF-MOUTH ADVERTISING

A problem in advertising is credibility. Consumers are hardly blotters who absorb any line laid on them through the mass media. Far more credible are stories from friends and acquaintances who have had a favorable experience with a product.

>> Buzz Advertising. Word-of-mouth testimonials, friends talking to friends, is strong advertising. But how does word-of-mouth advertising get the buzz going? And how can the buzz be sustained? In the advertising industry's desperation in recent years to find new avenues for making pitches, buzzing has turned into an art. Several agencies specialize in identifying individuals with a large circle of contacts and introducing them to a product. These agents sample the product, generally being able to keep the samples for their help in talking them up with family, coworkers and anyone else in earshot. The agents file occasional reports, with the incentive of being eligible for prizes.

viral advertising
Media consumers pass on the message, like a contagious disease, usually on the Internet

How does buzz stack up against traditional advertising media? Nobody knows, but it's cheap enough that advertisers have seen it as worth trying.

Viral Advertising. *Automakers have experimented with what's called "viral advertising," producing compelling action stories on the web that viewers will want to pass on, virus-like, to friends. Embedded in story lines, like Ford's* Evil Twin *for its SportKa in Europe, are product messages.*

>> Viral Advertising. Another word-of-mouth tactic is **viral advertising,** so called because, when successful, it spreads contagion-like through the population. Advertisers create clever clips that they hope will prompt visitors to pass them on to friends. People open messages from friends, which tangentially increases an ad's reach at low cost. Viral advertising works particularly well on the web. Automakers were among the first to experiment with viral techniques. Ford promoted its SportKa in Europe with story lines designed to stir conversation and draw people in for other installments. BMW estimated that 55.1 million people saw its *For Hire* series. Honda could not have been happier with its *Cog* mini-story. Said a Honda executive: "I have never seen a commercial that bolted around the world like *Cog* in two weeks."

On the downside, however, advertisers can't cancel viral ads, which have a life of their own and can float around the Internet for months, even years. An advertisement for beach vacations in Beirut would have been fine in 2005 but grotesquely inappropriate a year later with Israeli air attacks on Hezbollah targets in the city, mass evacuations and hundreds of casualties.

CHECKING YOUR MEDIA LITERACY

- **Who in your group of friends would make a good buzz agent? Why? How about you?**
- **Where did the term *viral advertising* come from?**
- **What are examples of viral advertising?**

stealth ads
Advertisements, often subtle, in nontraditional, unexpected places

product placement
Writing a brand-name product into a television or movie script

TiVo
A television recording and playback device that allows viewers to edit out commercials. A competing device is ReplayTV.

UNDER-THE-RADAR ADVERTISING

Inundated with advertisements, 6,000 a week on network television, double since 1983, many people tune out. Some do it literally with their remotes. Ad people are concerned that traditional modes are losing effectiveness. People are overwhelmed. Consider, for example, that a major grocery store carries 30,000 items, each with packaging that screams "Buy me." More commercial messages are there than a human being can handle. The problem is ad clutter. Advertisers are trying to address the clutter in numerous ways, including stealth ads, new-site ads and alternative media. Although not hidden or subliminal, stealth ads are subtle—even covert. You might not know you're being pitched unless you're attentive—really attentive.

>> Stealth Ads. So neatly can **stealth ads** fit into the landscape that people may not recognize they're being pitched. Consider the Bamboo lingerie company, which stenciled messages on a Manhattan sidewalk: "From here it looks like you could use some new underwear."

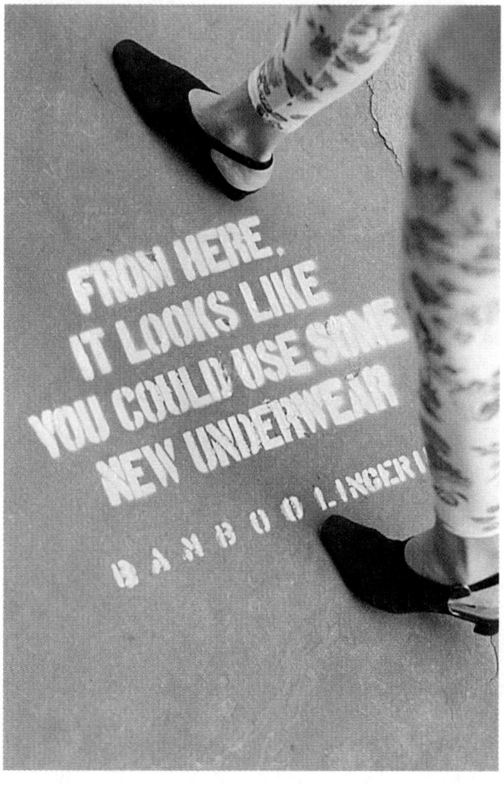

Omnipresent Ads. *Bamboo Lingerie's stenciled sidewalk messages may have been unsettling to some folks, but they sold underwear. Like many advertisers worried that their messages are lost in ad-crammed traditional media, Bamboo has struck out for nontraditional territory to be noticed. Regina Kelley, director of strategic planning for the Saatchi & Saatchi agency in New York, said: "Any space you can take in visually, anything you can hear, in the future will be branded."*

Sports stadiums like FedEx Field outside of Washington, D.C., work their way into everyday dialogue, subtly reinforcing product identity.

Not all stealth advertising is so harmless. In early 2007 some motorists in Boston began noticing suspicious-looking black boxes covered with lights and wires clamped to bridge supports near busy motorways. Roads were shut down and the bomb squad called in to remove what turned out to be battery-powered LED displays to advertise a TV show on the Cartoon Network. It was part of a campaign of "guerrilla marketing" carried out by Interference, Inc., a New York marketing firm. Two Boston artists, Peter Berdovsky and Sean Stevens, were arrested and charged with placing a hoax device in a way that causes panic, a crime carrying a maximum penalty of five years. The two were released after they performed community service, and the charges were dropped. But the public outrage over the hoax was so great that Cartoon Network General Manager Jim Samples was forced to resign. The network's parent company, Turner Broadcasting, paid more than $2 million restitution to the City of Boston.

>> Product Placement. In the 1980s advertisers began wiggling brand-name products into movie scripts, creating an additional although minor revenue stream for moviemakers. The practice, **product placement,** stirred criticism about artistic integrity, but it gained momentum. Fees zoomed upward. For the 2005 release of *The Green Hornet,* Miramax was seeking an automaker willing to pay at least $35 million for its products to be written into the script, topping the $15 million that Ford paid for its 2003 Thunderbird, Jaguar and Aston Martin lines to be in the James Bond movie *Die Another Day.*

Later, placing products into television scenes gained importance with the advent of **TiVo** and other devices that allow people to record shows and replay them commercial-free at their convenience. By 2004 about one million people owned these devices. Their growing popularity worried the television industry, whose business model was dependent on revenue from advertisers to which it guaranteed an audience for ads.

MEDIA PEOPLE

Dave Balter

Out of Skidmore College with a psych degree, Dave Balter set out to be a romance author. Sidetracked, he instead landed jobs on the periphery of advertising in direct marketing and promotion. In time, seeing the slipping effectiveness of traditional advertising, Balter toyed in his mind with word of mouth. Today at his marketing company in Boston, he's known around the office as buzzagent Dave.

The company, BzzAgent, is at the vanguard of the explosive word-of-mouth segment of the advertising industry—WOM, for short. BzzAgent handles about 300 campaigns simultaneously. Clients include Levi's Dockers, Anheuser-Busch and Cadbury-Schweppes.

By age 40 Balter, an absolute believer in buzz, had founded the Word-of-Mouth Marketing Association and chaired the association's ethics committee. Balter was in the process of securing a patent on the buzz schemes he had devised at BzzAgent. In 2005 he cemented his place in the evolution of advertising with a book fittingly titled *Grapevine.*

The premise of Balter's system is the universally acknowledged fact that people are more influenced by people around them, no matter how much they're also immersed in traditional advertising messages. BzzAgent signs up volunteers who meet a profile of "influentials," as they're called, and matches them up with a client's products—jeans, perfumes, cheese goodies, you name it—to sample and then chat up the products among family, friends, associates and anybody else. The buzzing is unscripted, mostly just everyday conversation, although some agents use the Internet to spread the word. The buzz agents file reports on their buzzing and earn buzz points that can be redeemed for rewards. iPods go over well. So do cameras and books. Balter's agents constitute an army, as many as 117,000 at any one point. Does buzz marketing work? Measures are elusive, but WOM is so cheap compared to buying space and time in traditional media that advertisers figure, what's to lose?

Anecdotal evidence of the effectiveness abounds. For example, the influential book-retailing trade journal *Publishers Weekly,* after receiving advance proofs of Balter's book *Grapevine,* issued a negative review that normally would be a death knell: "Balter's gee-whiz, narcissistic writing voice won't help win converts." But Balter also had put 2,000 copies into the hands of buzz agents. The book became a best-selling business title.

WHAT DO YOU THINK?

- Which products lend themselves to buzz promotion? Which do not?
- If you were an executive at an automobile manufacturer, how much of your advertising budget would you risk on buzz tactics? Explain your reasoning.
- What if the product were a new book? A new toothpaste? Or new athletic shoe aimed at pre-teens? An iPhone competitor?

Buzzmeister. *They call Dave Balter the master of buzz. His BzzAgent company stirs up word-of-mouth promotion for products through networks of people he calls "influentials." These people are given a product to try and to talk up to friends and associates.*

With TiVo, audiences no longer were trapped into watching commercials. Was the 30-second spot commercial doomed? The television and advertising industries struck product placement deals that went beyond anything seen before. For a fee, products are being built into scripts not only as props but also for both implicit and explicit endorsement.

infomercial
Program-length broadcast commercial

>> Infomercials. Less subtle is the **infomercial,** a program-length television commercial dolled up to look like a newscast, a live-audience participation show or a chatty talk show. With the proliferation of 24-hour television service and of cable channels, airtime is so cheap at certain hours that advertisers of even offbeat products can afford it. Hardly anybody is fooled into thinking that infomercials are

Product Placement. *For NBC and Ford, product placement was a win-win. NBC picked up a reported $25 to $50 million from Ford to make a throaty Shelby Mustang GT500KR the talking star of a revived* Knight Rider *series. That's far less than $8 million per episode that analysts say Ford would have paid for comparable screen time for conventional advertising. And, according to growing conventional wisdom in advertising, the impact of in-script product exposure exceeds overt advertising pitches. Ford's Hollywood branding chief, Al Uziella, called the Mustang placement a "golden egg" for the automaker. Ford threw in as many Mustangs as script-writers needed to wreck and otherwise blow to bits.*

anything but advertisements, but some full-length media advertisements, like Liz Taylor wandering through CBS sitcoms, are cleverly disguised.

A print media variation is the **'zine**—a magazine published by a manufacturer to plug a single line of products with varying degrees of subtlety. 'Zine publishers, including such stalwarts as IBM and Sony, have even been so brazen as to sell these wall-to-wall advertising vehicles at newsstands. One example was a splashy new magazine called *Colors,* for which you paid $4.50. Once inside, you probably realized it was a thinly veiled ad for Benetton casual clothes. *Guess Journal* may look like a magazine, but guess who puts it out as a 'zine: the makers of the Guess fashion brand.

Stealth advertisements try "to morph into the very entertainment it sponsors." wrote Mary Kuntz, Joseph Weber and Heidi Dawley in *Business Week*. The goal, they said, is "to create messages so entertaining, so compelling—and maybe so disguised—that rapt audiences will swallow them whole, oblivious to the sales component."

'zine
Magazine whose entire content, articles and ads, pitches a single product or product line

CHECKING YOUR MEDIA LITERACY

- **How do advertisers try to avoid being lost in ad clutter?**

Problems and Issues

STUDY PREVIEW

People are exposed to such a blur of ads that advertisers worry that their messages are being lost in the clutter. Some advertising people see more creativity as the answer so that people will want to see and read ads, but there is evidence that creativity can work against an ad's effectiveness.

ADVERTISING CLUTTER

Leo Bogart of the Newspaper Advertising Bureau noted that the number of advertising messages doubled through the 1960s and 1970s. Except during recessions, the trend continues. This proliferation of advertising creates a problem: too many ads. The problem has been exacerbated by the shortening of ads from 60 seconds in the early days of television to today's widely used 15-second format.

At one time the National Association of Broadcasters had a code limiting the quantity of commercials. The Federal Communications Commission let station owners know that it supported the NAB code, but in 1981, as part of the Reagan administration's deregulation, the FCC backed away from any limitation. In 1983 a federal court threw out the NAB limitation as a monopolistic practice.

Ad clutter is less of an issue in the print media. Many people buy magazines and newspapers to look at ads as part of the comparative shopping process. Even so, some advertisers, concerned that their ads are overlooked in massive editions, such as the old seven-pound metro Sunday newspapers or a 700-page bridal magazine, are looking to alternative means to reach potential customers in a less cluttered environment.

The clutter that marks much of commercial television and radio today may be alleviated as the media fragment further. Not only will demassification create more specialized outlets, such as narrowly focused cable television services, but there will be new media. The result will be advertising aimed at narrower audiences.

One measure of network television ad clutter is the average number of messages per commercial break, here including network program promotions:

ABC 7.1
CBS 6.3
NBC 6.2
Fox 6.0

CHECKING YOUR MEDIA LITERACY

- **Why is ad clutter more of a problem in broadcast than in print media?**
- **How might demassification ease the ad clutter problem?**

CREATIVE EXCESSES

Advertisers are reviewing whether creativity is as effective an approach as hard sell. **Harry McMahan** studied **Clio Awards** for creativity in advertising and discovered that the 36 agencies that produced 81 winners of the prestigious awards for advertisements had either lost the winning account or gone out of business.

Predicts advertising commentator E. B. Weiss: "Extravagant license for creative people will be curtailed." The future may hold more heavy-handed pitches, perhaps with over-the-counter regimens not only promising fast-fast-fast relief but also spelling it out in all caps and boldface with exclamation marks: **F-A-S-T! F-A-S-T!! F-A-S-T!!!**

A London agency, Naked Communications, set up a New York office in 2005 and became the talk of the industry for eschewing creativity. Rather than catchy slogans and clever jingles, Naked focuses first on strategy, identifying the audience for a product or service, then identifying how to reach that audience. Only then does Naked begin work on the message. As Naked executives put it, the rest of the advertising industry for too long has let the tail wag the dog by going for creative glitz before devising strategy. Naked worked wonders for early clients, including Heineken beer and Honda cars.

Harry McMahan
Dubious about ad creativity

Clio Award
Award for advertising creativity

CHECKING YOUR MEDIA LITERACY

- **Does creativity in advertising translate into sales successes? Explain.**

CHAPTER WRAP-UP

Importance of Advertising (Pages 297–299)

- Modern consumer economies are driven by the demand stirred by advertising for products. The demand contributes to economic growth and prosperity. Also, because advertising brings attention to consumer choices, it fits well with the democratic notion of people making decisions individually on what serves their interests. The question can be asked whether advertising is a negative in consumer decision making because it is aimed at selling products and not at promoting the common good. Conversely, it can be argued that prosperity is the common good. Also, advertising messages are one-sided and often filled with emotional appeals. The messages thus are more coercive communication than persuasive communication. Despite the critics, the role of advertising is undeniable. Some estimates put advertising spending at 2 percent of the U.S. gross domestic product.

Origins of Advertising (Pages 299–300)

- The printing technology that developed from Johannes Gutenberg's movable metal type made possible the mass production of advertising messages. Actual advertising evolved slowly, but some 400 years later, when the Industrial Revolution was in full swing, advertising became integral in the nascent U.S. national consumer economy. Mass-produced products for far-flung markets were promoted through national advertising with ads in national magazines and in hundreds of local newspapers. Later, radio and television became part of the media mix through which manufacturers, distributors and retailers promoted their wares nationally and locally—and increasingly globally.

Advertising Agencies (Pages 300–303)

- Retailers and other advertisers tried managing their own promotions in the growing U.S. consumer economy in the 1870s. Gradually they farmed out the advertising to new agencies that specialized in creating advertising. These agencies also chose media outlets for reaching the most potential customers efficiently. Agencies charged for the services, generally as a percentage of the cost of the time or space purchased from media companies to carry the ads. More variations on this so-called commission system have been introduced in recent years.

Placing Advertisements (Pages 304–306)

- Advertisements don't appear magically in the mass media. Media companies, dependent on advertising revenue, energetically court agencies and advertisers. Also, agencies and advertisers conduct extensive research before buying space and time to reach target consumers. Each type of media outlet has advantages.

New Advertising Platforms (Pages 306–308)

- Advertisers covet the millions of eyeballs that browse the Internet. But how to reach the right ones? The hottest Internet advertising vehicle has become search engines, which help people find sites they're interested in. The search engine Google lines up sites with advertisers seeking likely cohorts of consumers for their products. It's ads for high-end products on sites that attract upper-crust visitors. You won't find Mercedes ads on a skateboarding site, nor muffler shop ads on a site for luxury vacations. Another new advertising platform is video game sites that attract the young male audience that advertisers have always found elusive.

Brand Strategies (Pages 308–311)

- Brand names became a vehicle for distinguishing a product from competitors in the late 1800s. Brand names have endured as an advertising strategy. For commodities, with products largely the same, advertisers linked brands with extraneous qualities—like racing excitement with Dodges, daring and adventure with Hathaway shirts, class with Grand Dad whisky. Today, it seems, everything is branded. Does a Paris Hilton watch keep better time than a Timex? In the media, CNN is promoted as a brand. So is Fox News. Each has its own cachet. Less glamorous than branding in promoting products are hard-sell pitches, especially those that refrain from going over anyone's head by using lowest common denominator messages that hammer away. Redundancy works in selling, which makes those hard-sell messages annoying but no less effective.

Advertising Tactics (Pages 311–314)

- Like all mass messages, advertising has the potential to reach the largest possible audience when it appeals to a lowest common denominator. Tactics include often-grating, heavy-handed messages and repetition.

New Advertising Techniques (Pages 314–317)

- The original pre-media advertising, word-of-mouth, is back. This time it's called *buzz communication*. The goal is to get people talking about a product. Many buzz campaigns originate on the Internet with the hope of spreading virus-like. The term *viral advertising* has come into favor.

Problems and Issues (Pages 317–318)

- Modern life has become advertising saturated. On prime-time network television, dozens of 15-second spots drown each other out. Inundated, viewers zone out. The problem, called *ad clutter,* is a critical challenge for the advertisers that need somehow to get their messages across. Is creativity the answer, with ads that stand out for their cleverness? Evidence suggests, counterintuitive though it may seem, that the creativity may get attention but not move products. One answer seems to be more research to target audiences and to craft ads that rise above the clutter.

Review Questions

1. What is advertising's role in a capitalistic society? In a democracy? In the mass media?
2. Trace the development of advertising since Johannes Gutenberg.
3. What is the role of advertising agencies? How do agencies work?
4. Why do some ads appear in some media products and not in others?
5. What new platforms are advertisers trying? What are long-term prospects for each?
6. How is brand-name advertising morphing?
7. What are major tactics in advertising? Who devised each one?
8. What new advertising tactics are being devised? Why?
9. What unanswered issues face the advertising industry? What answers do you see?

Concepts

ad clutter (Page 305)
branding (Page 311)
lowest common denominator (Page 311)
pass-along circulation (Page 305)
shelf life (Page 305)

Terms

Audit Bureau of Circulations (Page 304)
commission contract (Page 302)
media plans (Page 304)
stealth ads (Page 315)

People

Benjamin Day (Page 300)
David Ogilvy (Page 309)
Jack Trout (Page 312)
Rosser Reeves (Page 312)
Wayland Ayer (Page 300)

Media Sources

- Brian Dolan. *The First Tycoon.* Viking, 2004. This is a biography of Josiah Wedgwood, the mid-1700s English potter whose china became the first consumer brand name.
- Tom Reichert and Jacqueline Lamblase, editors. *Sex in Consumer Culture: The Erotic Content of Media and Advertising.* Erlbaum, 2006. Reichert and Lamblase, both professors, have collected quantitative and qualitative articles on gender differences and representation in mass media.
- Helen Katz. *Media Handbook: A Complete Guide to Advertising, Media Selection, Planning, Research and Buying,* third edition. Erlbaum, 2006. Katz, a media buying executive, assesses categories of media for advertising choices.
- Dave Balter and John Butman. *Grapevine: The New Art of Word-of-Mouth Marketing.* Portfolio, 2005. With chatty enthusiasm, Balter and Butman extol the cost-efficiency and also fun of buzz marketing as the next wave in advertising.

ADVERTISING

In this chapter you have deepened your media literacy by revisiting several themes. Here are thematic highlights from the chapter:

MEDIA TECHNOLOGY

As a form of media message, advertising didn't take off quickly after Johannes Gutenberg's invention of movable metal type. But by the time the Industrial Revolution was transforming economies 400 years later, advertising became key to drawing customers to new mass-produced products. Printing technology was advanced to the point that thousands of copies of a message could be distributed. Broadcasting, particularly the networks, augmented the audience. (Pages 297–300)

MEDIA ECONOMICS

Create Demand. Advertising spurs economic growth by encouraging people to spend. When consumer purchases increase, so does prosperity. In a more abstract sense, advertising dazzles consumers with products beyond their means—like a teenage boy on a $10-a-week allowance coveting a 600- horsepower Corvette. To attain the dream promoted enticingly in advertising, the kid may do what's necessary, like go to college and study for a career. Advertising thus encourages financial achievement. Critics fault advertising for encouraging materialistic values.

Of all the messages that use mass media to reach huge audiences, advertising is the most obvious. It's in-your-face, sometimes shouting: "See me. Buy this." The core message of advertising smacks of a circus sideshow barker, but the media magnification adds potency of which a circus barker could only dream. In the United States it's estimated that 2 percent of the gross domestic product goes to advertising. When advertising succeeds in exciting consumer demand and spending, it contributes to prosperity. Not unimportantly, advertising is the economic engine for the newspaper, magazine, radio and television industries and increasingly the Internet. It is from these media outlets that advertisers buy time and space for their spiels. (Pages 297–299)

MEDIA AND DEMOCRACY

Choices. A premise for democracy is that citizens will make intelligent decisions about public policy if competing ideas are afloat in what's called the marketplace of ideas. Individual choice is a key element. Choice also is a premise in advertising. The goal of an advertisement is to convince consumers to choose a particular product over competitors or to give a new product a try.

When democracy works well, people choose their common course through informed decision making. This conceptually dovetails with the societal role of advertising, which provides people with information to make choices as consumers. The emphasis is on individuals reasoning their own way to conclusions about what's best. In some ways, however, advertising falls short. Ads seldom are aimed at even-handed and intelligent discourse but rather at a quick sell, often with emotional and one-sided appeals. (Pages 298–299)

AUDIENCE FRAGMENTATION

Advertisers see no point in buying time and space in media outlets that don't deliver the likeliest customers. The American Association of Retired Persons, for example, doesn't recruit members through the magazine *Seventeen.* To deliver the audiences that advertisers want, media companies have narrowed the focus of their products to coincide with what advertisers are seeking. The mutual interests of media companies and advertisers have led to fragmentation of the mass audience into countless subsets. Even the media products that continue in the tradition of seeking mega-audiences with something for everyone are dissected by advertisers and advertising agencies for modicums of difference. Demographically there are differences between CBS and Fox prime-time audiences. Advertisers know whether the New York *Times* or the New York *Daily News* is better for delivering the customers they seek. (Pages 304–306)

MEDIA FUTURE

Newspaper and magazine publishers delight when ads comprise 70 percent of the space in their publications. That's the max allowed by the U.S. Postal Service to qualify for discount mail rates. In television, networks can cram six to seven ads in sequence during single prime-time breaks. Consumers, overwhelmed by the quantity, tune out. This *ad clutter,* as it's called, is a major problem that the advertising industry needs to solve. A message lost in the clutter is wasted. One answer has been to find alternate media with better chances for ads to get attention. New tactics also include word-of-mouth campaigns. Another tactic, called *viral advertising,* offers compelling story lines continued through a series of ads. Stealth advertising is a tactic that puts messages where people least expect them, sometimes as time-proven as skywriting and chalked messages on sidewalks. (Pages 306–308, 310–311, 314–318)

ELITISM AND POPULISM

Over and Over. Redundancy establishes a product in the minds of consumers. No matter how annoying, redundancy can propel a product to success and maintain sales. Some ads air so often, and strike such a chord with the public, they become part of the popular culture. The incessant braying of the ShamWow! spokesman won the spot honors as #1 infomercial of all time, according to CNBC.

Advertising messages generally are brief. A rule of thumb for billboards is no more than seven words. Any more than that, motorists going 60 mph will miss the message. The requirement for ads to be compact can make for cleverness, but it also can lead to simplistic "Buy me" exhortations that not only lack cleverness but are downright annoying. Worse is "buy me" in all caps, bold type and italics and followed by multiple exclamation marks. These are appeals to the lowest common denominator among consumers. On a populist-elitist scale, these LCD appeals, repeated to the point of being annoying, are at the populist extreme. (Pages 311–313, 318)

chapter 12

MASS AUDIENCES

Susan Whiting

The president of Nielsen stands behind the company's television viewership tracking.

LEARNING AHEAD

- Sophisticated new methods measure and assess audiences.
- Statistics are a foundation for measuring mass audiences.
- Mass audience size is measured by pressruns, sales and surveys.
- Audience-measuring companies have gone electronic to track media habits.
- Reactions of mass audiences are part of media content decision-making.
- Audience analysis includes demographics, geodemographics and psychographics.

MAKING AND BREAKING TELEVISION PROGRAMS

Susan Whiting had critics waiting when, after 26 years at the Nielsen audience rating service, she was named president. Media mogul Rupert Murdoch was irate. He accused Nielsen of underrating the audience of his Fox television network. Nielsen data, he said, were costing him millions in advertising revenue. Reverend Al Sharpton was storming that urban blacks were underrepresented in Nielsen ratings. Then there were advertisers, which rely on Nielsen. They complained that the data were insufficient to help them make intelligent decisions in negotiating with networks on what to pay for 30-second spots.

Whiting, 47 at the time, had her hands full. The fact is that a lot is at stake in Nielsen television data. It is hardly an overstatement to say that Nielsen is called the most influential company in the television industry. Nielsens are used to determine the price of some $60 billion in television commercials a year. Network shows depend on the Nielsens for renewal. Ad agencies pay for access to Nielsen data. Time Warner itself pays more than $20 million a year. NBC, Viacom and Disney pay much more.

Whiting, from Quaker roots, joined Nielsen at 21 as a trainee. In 2004, when she was put in charge, Whiting immediately set out to double the number of Nielsen "families," the 5,000 households nationwide that Nielsen taps to measure network viewership. Because the television audience was fragmenting with the growth of cable and satellite television, a larger sample was needed for detailed information on proliferating niche networks.

A perennial complaint against Nielsen is that networks and advertisers have no alternative. There is no competitor. In the 1990s, upset at slipping viewership data from Nielsen, NBC threatened to form a separate service. Nothing came of the grumbling, but later Murdoch, displeased with the Nielsens for his Fox network, decried Nielsen as a monopoly. Murdoch's claim was that Nielsen undercounted urban blacks, which he said were a substantial 25 percent of Fox's audience. Murdoch went so far as to place an ad in the New York *Times:* "Don't Count Us Out," the ad shouted, claiming that "flawed" Nielsen numbers could have "a dramatic effect on the diversity of television programming."

Quietly but firmly, Whiting methodically defended Nielsen methodology. Black viewers, she demonstrated, were as accurately represented in new meters being introduced in major cities as they had been by earlier methods. Simultaneously, she stepped up plans to reduce statistical margins of error and to track where viewers were going in the fragmented universe of television choices.

Discovering Mass Audiences

STUDY PREVIEW

Mass media research has origins as folksy as eavesdropping on what people are talking about to decide what kind of stories to put in the newspaper. But today the research is sophisticated, with more at stake than ever—like which television programs survive and which get axed. Media research techniques overlap into many aspects of modern life, including marketing, politics and governance.

AUDIENCE RESEARCH EVOLUTION

Stories abound about Joseph Pulitzer wandering the streets of New York and looking over shoulders to see what people were reading. Too, Pulitzer listened to what people were taking about. It was research, 1880s style. Indeed, his research was a building block of Pulitzer's success at building his New York *World* into a circulation leader. What about today? New local television anchors hired from out of town have their own variation on Pulitzer's audience research. They hang out at barbershops and eavesdrop at mall eateries. Woe be to an anchor in Milwaukee who doesn't know what a bubbler is. Or in New Orleans who doesn't know a po'boy.

Today's media people also have vast additional resources to learn about their audiences, albeit less colorful. These are data from research that can be sliced and diced into useful truths about audience. Lots of the research is census like—income levels, educational attainment, religious and other affiliations. Other research focuses on attitudes and values or habits and motivations and reactions to new things.

The informal audience research of Joseph Pulitzer still has its place, but an entire industry today provides far more audience information than Pulitzer could gather in a lifetime of eavesdropping. Used well, the new data, gathered largely by surveys, can

MEDIA PEOPLE

George Gallup

George Gallup was excited. His mother-in-law, Ola Babcock Miller, had decided to run for secretary of state. If elected, she would become not only Iowa's first Democrat but also the first woman to hold the statewide office. Gallup's excitement, however, went beyond the novelty of his mother-in-law's candidacy. The campaign gave him an opportunity to pull together his three primary intellectual interests: survey research, public opinion and politics. In that 1932 campaign George Gallup conducted the first serious poll in history for a political candidate. Gallup's surveying provided important barometers of public sentiment that helped Miller to gear her campaign to the issues that were most on voters' minds. She won and was re-elected twice by large margins.

Four years after that first 1932 election campaign, Gallup tried his polling techniques in the presidential race and correctly predicted that Franklin Roosevelt would beat Alf Landon. Having called Roosevelt's victory accurately, Gallup had clients knocking at his door.

Gallup devoted himself to accuracy. Even though he had predicted Roosevelt's 1936 victory, Gallup was bothered that his reliability had not been better. His method, quota sampling, could not call a two-way race within 4 percentage points. With quota sampling, a representative percentage of women and men was surveyed, as was a representative percentage of Democrats and Republicans, Westerners and Easterners, Christians and Jews, and other constituencies.

In 1948 Gallup correctly concluded that Thomas Dewey was not a shoo-in for president. Nonetheless, his pre-election poll was 5.3 percentage points off. So he decided to switch to a tighter method, probability sampling, which theoretically gives everyone in the population being sampled an equal chance to be surveyed. With probability sampling, there is no need for quotas because, as Gallup explained in his folksy Midwestern way, it was like a cook making soup: "When a housewife wants to test the quality of the soup she is making, she tastes only a teaspoonful or two. She knows that if the soup is thoroughly stirred, one teaspoonful is enough to tell her whether she has the right mixture of ingredients." With the new method, Gallup's **statistical extrapolation** narrowed his error rate to less than 2 percentage points.

Even with improvements pioneered by Gallup, public opinion surveying has detractors. Some critics say that polls influence undecided voters toward the front-runner—a bandwagon effect. Other critics say that polls make elected officials too responsive to the momentary whims of the electorate, discouraging courageous leadership. George Gallup, who died in 1984, tirelessly defended polling, arguing that good surveys give voice to the "inarticulate minority" that legislators otherwise might not hear.

Gallup was convinced that public opinion surveys help to make democracy work.

WHAT DO YOU THINK?

- What variables determine how close is close enough in probability sampling?
- Explain George Gallup's metaphor of polling and making soup.
- Do you trust election polls? What do you need to know to have confidence in a poll?

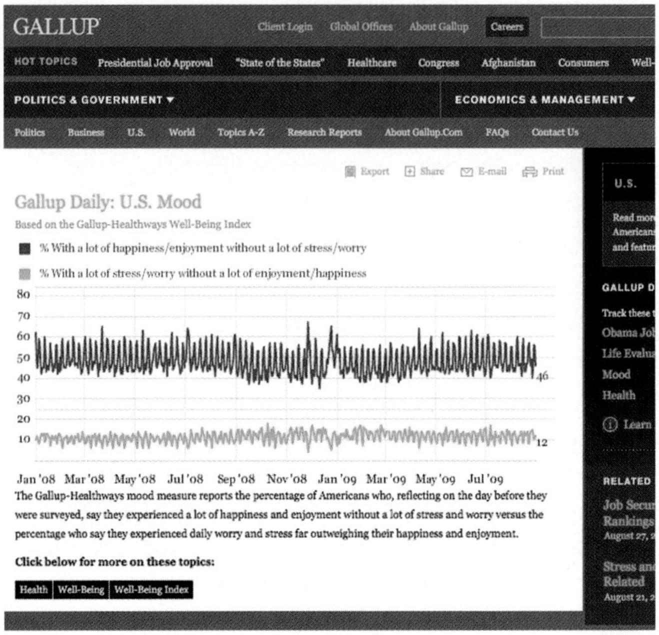

Probability Sampling. *Data collection has become more sophisticated since George Gallup began polling in the 1930s. Polls today track changes in public attitudes over the several decades that data have been accumulated.*

George Gallup

lead to successful decision-making in television programming, advertising campaigns and be a useful factor in choosing what makes news.

CHECKING YOUR MEDIA LITERACY

- How has audience research changed since the Pulitzer era?

SURVEY INDUSTRY

Public opinion surveying is a $5 billion-a-year business whose clients include major corporations, political candidates and the mass media. Today, just as in 1935 when **George Gallup** founded it, the **Institute of American Public Opinion** cranks out regular surveys for clients. Major news organizations hire survey companies to tap public sentiment regularly on specific issues.

About 300 companies are in the survey business in the United States, most performing advertising and product-related opinion research for private clients. During election campaigns, political candidates become major clients. There are dozens of other survey companies that do confidential research for and about the media. Their findings are important because they determine what kinds of advertising will run and where, what programs will be developed and broadcast, and which ones will be canceled. Some television stations even use such research to choose anchors for major newscasts.

The major companies:

>> **Nielsen.** The Nielsen Company is the leading global provider of information and analytics around what consumers watch and buy. While Nielsen is known widely for its television ratings, the company provides viewership data and analytics across television, online and mobile screens. It also measures retail transactions and consumer shopping behavior.

>> **Arbitron.** Arbitron measures mostly radio audiences in local markets.

>> **Gallup.** The Gallup Organization studies human nature and behavior and specializes in management, economics, psychology and sociology.

>> **Pew.** The Pew Research Center is an independent opinion research group that studies attitudes toward the press, politics and public policy issues.

>> **Harris.** Market research firm Harris Interactive Inc. is perhaps best known for the Harris Poll and for pioneering and engineering Internet-based research methods.

statistical extrapolation
Drawing conclusions from a segment of the whole

George Gallup
Introduced probability sampling

Institute of American Public Opinion
Gallup polling organization

CHECKING YOUR MEDIA LITERACY

- Name as many major public opinion sampling companies as you can.
- To whom do polling companies sell their information?

Number-Crunching Center. *Every night, ratings of every network television show in the country are tabulated at Nielsen's facility in Oldsmar, Florida.*

Audience Measurement Principles

STUDY PREVIEW

The effectiveness of mass media messages is measured through research techniques that are widely recognized in the social sciences and in business. These techniques include public opinion polling, which relies on statistical extrapolation that can be incredibly accurate. Sad to say, less reliable survey techniques also are used, sullying the reputation of serious sampling.

PROBABILITY SAMPLING

Although polling has become a high-profile business, many people do not understand how questions to a few hundred individuals can indicate the mood of 300 million Americans. In the **probability sampling** method pioneered by George Gallup in the 1940s, four factors figure into accurate surveying:

>> **Sample Size.** To learn how Layne College students feel about abortion on demand, you start by asking one student. Because you can hardly generalize from one student to the whole student body of 2,000, you ask a second student. If both agree, you start developing a tentative sense of how Layne students feel, but because you cannot have much confidence in such a tiny sample, you ask a third student and a fourth and a fifth. At some point between interviewing just one and all 2,000 Layne students, you can draw a reasonable conclusion.

How do you choose a **sample size**? Statisticians have found that **384** is a magic number for many surveys. Put simply, no matter how large the **population** being sampled, if every member has an equal opportunity to be polled, you need ask only 384 people to be 95 percent confident that you are within 5 percentage points of a precise reading. For a lot of surveys, that is close enough. Here is a breakdown, from Philip Meyer's *Precision Journalism,* a book for journalists on surveying, on necessary sample sizes for 95 percent confidence and being within 5 percentage points:

Population Size	Sample Size
500,000 or more	384
100,000	383
50,000	381
10,000	370
5,000	357
3,000	341
2,000	322
1,000	278

probability sampling
Everyone in the population being surveyed has an equal chance to be sampled

sample size
Number of people surveyed

384
Number of people in a properly selected sample for results to provide 95 percent confidence that results have less than a 5 percent margin of error

population
Group of people being studied

sample selection
Process for choosing individuals to be interviewed

At Layne, with a total enrollment of 2,000, the sample size would need to be 322 students.

>> **Sample Selection.** Essential in probability sampling is **sample selection,** the process of choosing whom to interview. A good sample gives every member of the population being sampled an equal chance to be interviewed. For example, if you want to know how Kansans intend to vote, you cannot merely go to a Wichita street corner and survey the first 384 people who pass by. You would need to

check a list of the state's 675,000 registered voters and then divide by the magic number, 384:

$$675{,}000/384 = 1{,}758$$

You would need to talk with every 1,758th person on the list. At Layne College, 2,000 divided by 322 would mean an interval of 6.2. Every sixth person in the student body would need to be polled.

Besides the right sample size and proper interval selection, two other significant variables affect survey accuracy: margin of error and confidence level.

>> Margin of Error. For absolute precision, every person in the population must be interviewed, but such precision is hardly ever needed, and the process would be prohibitively expensive and impracticable. Pollsters must therefore decide what is an acceptable **margin of error** for every survey they conduct. This is a complex matter, but in simple terms, you can have a fairly high level of confidence that a properly designed survey with 384 respondents can yield results within 5 percentage points, either way, of being correct. If the survey finds that two candidates for statewide office are running 51 to 49 percent, for example, the race is too close to call with a sample of 384. If the survey says that the candidates are running 56 to 44 percent, however, you can be reasonably confident who is ahead because, even if the survey is 5 points off on the high side for the leader, the candidate at the very least has 51 percent support (56 percent minus a maximum 5 percentage points for possible error). At best, the trailing candidate has 49 percent (44 percent plus a maximum 5 percentage points for possible error).

Increasing the sample size will reduce the margin of error. Meyer gives this breakdown:

Population Size	Sample Size	Margin of Error
Infinity	384	5 percentage points
Infinity	600	4 percentage points
Infinity	1,067	3 percentage points
Infinity	2,401	2 percentage points
Infinity	9,605	1 percentage point

Professional polling organizations that sample U.S. voters typically use sample sizes between 1,500 and 3,000 to increase accuracy. Also, measuring subgroups within the population being sampled requires that each subgroup, such as men and women, Catholics and non-Catholics or Northerners and Southerners, be represented by 384 properly selected people.

>> Confidence Level. With a sample of 384, pollsters can claim a relatively high 95 percent **confidence level,** that is, that they are within 5 percentage points of being on the mark. For many surveys, this is sufficient statistical validity. If the confidence level needs to be higher, or if the margin of error needs to be decreased, the number of people surveyed will need to be increased. In short, the level of confidence and margin of error are inversely related. A larger sample can improve confidence, just as it also can reduce the margin of error.

margin of error
Percentage that a survey may be off mark

confidence level
Degree of certainty that a survey is accurate

CHECKING YOUR MEDIA LITERACY

- **How does probability sampling work?**
- **Does probability sampling necessarily yield accurate results with samples of 384?**
- **What is margin of error?**
- **What could make an election race too close to call?**

QUOTA SAMPLING

Besides probability sampling, pollsters survey cross-sections of the whole population. This quota sampling technique gave Gallup his historic 1936 conclusions about the Roosevelt-Landon presidential race. With **quota sampling,** a pollster checking an election campaign interviews a sample that includes a quota of men and women that corresponds to the number of male and female registered voters. The sample might also include an appropriate quota of Democrats, Republicans and independents; of poor, middle-income and wealthy people; of Catholics, Jews and Protestants; of Southerners, Midwesterners and New Englanders; of the employed and unemployed; and other breakdowns significant to the pollster.

Both quota sampling and probability sampling are valid if done correctly, but Gallup abandoned quota sampling because he could not pinpoint public opinion more closely than within 4 percentage points on average. With probability sampling, he regularly came within 2 percentage points.

CHECKING YOUR MEDIA LITERACY

- **How does quota sampling differ from probability sampling?**
- **What attracted George Gallup to probability sampling?**

EVALUATING SURVEYS

Sidewalk interviews cannot be expected to reflect the views of the population. The people who respond to such polls are self-selected by virtue of being at a given place at a given time. Just as unreliable are call-in polls with 800 or **900 telephone numbers.** These polls test the views only of people who are aware of the poll and who have sufficiently strong opinions to go to the trouble of calling in.

Journalists run the risk of being duped when special interest groups suggest that news stories be written based on their privately conducted surveys. Some organizations selectively release self-serving conclusions.

To guard against being duped, the Associated Press insists on knowing methodology details before running poll stories. The AP tells reporters to ask:

- **How many people were interviewed and how were they selected?** Any survey of fewer than 384 people selected randomly from the population group has a greater margin for error than is usually tolerated.
- **When was the poll taken?** Opinions shift over time. During election campaigns, shifts can be quick, even overnight.
- **Who paid for the poll?** With privately commissioned polls, reporters should be skeptical, asking whether the results being released constitute everything learned in the survey. The timing of the release of political polls to be politically advantageous is not uncommon.
- **What was the sampling error?** Margins of error exist in all surveys unless everyone in the population is surveyed.
- **How was the poll conducted?** Whether a survey was conducted over the telephone or face-to-face in homes is important. Polls conducted on street corners or in shopping malls are not worth much statistically. Mail surveys are flawed unless surveyors follow up on people who do not answer the original questionnaires.
- **How were questions worded and in what order were they asked?** Drafting questions is an art. Sloppily worded questions yield sloppy conclusions. Leading questions and loaded questions can skew results. So can question sequencing.

Polling organizations get serious when someone misuses their findings. In 1998 the Gallup organization publicly told the tobacco industry to stop saying that a 1954 Gallup poll found that 90 percent of Americans were aware of a correlation between smoking and cancer. Not so, said Gallup. The question was "Have you heard or read

quota sampling
Demographics of the sample coincide with those of the whole population

900 telephone number
Used for call-in surveys; respondents select themselves to participate and pay for the call

MEDIA TIMELINE

MEDIA RESEARCH MILESTONES

1900–1949

Pressruns
Audit Bureau of Circulations created to verify circulation claims (1914)

Radio
Archibald Crossley conducted first listenership survey (1929)

Gallup Poll
George Gallup used quota sampling in Iowa election (1932)

Quota Sampling
Gallup used quota sampling in presidential election (1936)

Demographics
A. C. Nielsen conducted demographic listenership survey (1940s)

Probability Sampling
Gallup used probability sampling in presidential election (1948)

1950–1999

VALS
Psychographics introduced (1970s)

Geodemographics
Jonathan Robbin introduced PRIZM geodemographics (1979)

2000s

Bigger Samples
Nielsen committed to double the number of homes for television ratings (2004)

More Media
Nielsen added measures of Internet, iPod and cell phone devices (2006)

Billboards
Nielsen introduced cell phone-based Go Meters (2008)

George Gallup

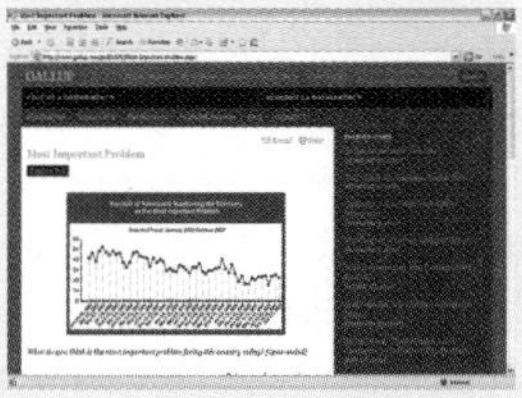

Polls trace changing attitudes

Visceral news judgment

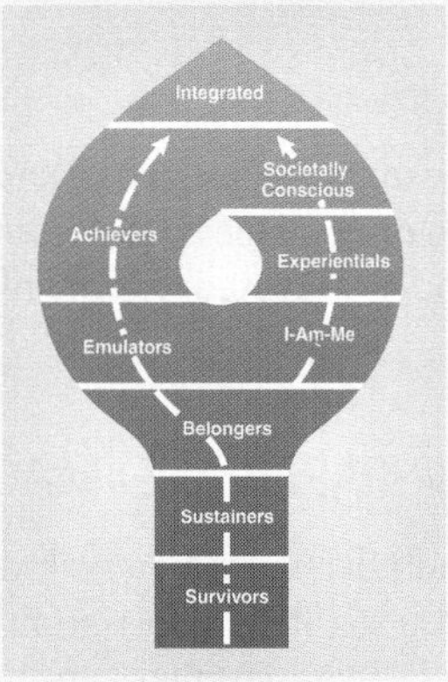

Psychographics

PIVOTAL EVENTS

1900–1949

- >> Radio emerged as commercial medium (late 1920s)
- >> Great Depression (1930s)
- >> World War II (1941–1945)
- >> Russian–Western Cold War (1945–1989)

1950–1999

- >> Television emerged as commercial medium (early 1950s)
- >> Vietnam war (1964–1973)
- >> Humans reached moon (1969)
- >> Internet emerged as commercial medium (late 1990s)

2000s

- >> 9/11 terrorist attacks (2001)
- >> Iraq war (2003–)
- >> Hurricane Katrina (2005)

anything recently that cigarette smoking may be a cause of cancer of the lung?" Ninety percent said that they were aware of a controversy, but, says Gallup, that doesn't necessarily mean those people believed there was a smoking-cancer correlation. Gallup threatened to go to court to refute the flawed conclusion if a tobacco company used it again in any wrongful-death lawsuit. Lydia Saad of Gallup told the *Wall Street Journal* that her organization gives people lots of latitude in interpreting its surveys. But this, Saad added, "really crosses the line."

It is with great risk that a polling company's client misrepresents survey results. Most polling companies, concerned about protecting their reputations, include a clause in their contracts with clients that gives the pollster the right to approve the release of findings. The clause usually reads: "When misinterpretation appears, we shall publicly disclose what is required to correct it, notwithstanding our obligation for client confidentiality in all other respects."

CHECKING YOUR MEDIA LITERACY

- **What information do you need to assess what a survey purports to have found?**
- **How can survey outcomes be manipulated?**

LATTER-DAY STRAW POLLS

The ABC and CNN television networks and other news organizations have dabbled, some say irresponsibly, with phone-in polling on public issues. These **straw polls** are conducted on the Internet too. While they can be fun, statistically they are meaningless.

Just as dubious are the candid-camera features, popular in weekly newspapers, in which a question is put to people on the street. The photos of half a dozen individuals and their comments are then published, often on the editorial page. These features are circulation builders for small publications whose financial success depends on how many local names and mug shots can be crammed into an issue, but it is only coincidental when the views expressed are representative of the population as a whole.

These **roving photographer** features are at their worst when people are not given time to formulate an intelligent response. The result too often is contributions to the public babble, not public understanding. The result is irresponsible pseudo-journalism.

straw polls
Respondents select themselves to be polled; unreliable indicator of public opinion

roving photographer
Statistically unsound way to tap public opinion

CHECKING YOUR MEDIA LITERACY

- **Why are listener call-in polls statistically suspect?**

Measuring Audience Size

STUDY PREVIEW

To attract advertisers, the mass media need to know the number and kinds of people they reach. This is done for the print media by audits and for the broadcast media by surveys. Although surveying is widely accepted for obtaining such data, some approaches are more reliable than others.

NEWSPAPER AND MAGAZINE AUDITS

The number of copies a newspaper or magazine puts out, called **circulation,** is fairly easy to calculate. It is simple arithmetic involving data like pressruns, subscription sales and unsold copies returned from newsracks. Many publishers follow strict procedures that are checked by independent audit organizations, like the **Audit Bureau of Circulations,** to assure advertisers that the system is honest and circulation claims comparable.

The Audit Bureau of Circulations was formed in 1914 to remove the temptation for publishers to inflate their claims to attract advertisers and hike ad rates. Inflated claims,

circulation
Number of readers of a publication

Audit Bureau of Circulations
Checks newspaper and magazine circulation claims

contagious in some cities, were working to the disadvantage of honest publishers. Today, most magazines and daily newspapers belong to ABC, which means that they follow the bureau's standards for reporting circulation and are subject to the bureau's audits.

CHECKING YOUR MEDIA LITERACY

- **How do advertisers know how much circulation they are buying in print media?**

BROADCAST RATINGS

Radio and television audiences are harder to measure, but advertisers have no less need for counts to help them decide where to place ads and to know what a fair price is. To keep track of broadcast audiences, a whole **ratings** industry, now with about 200 companies, has developed. **Nielsen Media Research** tracks network television viewership.

Radio ratings began in 1929 when advertisers asked pollster **Archibald Crossley** to determine how many people were listening to network programs. Crossley checked a small sample of households and then extrapolated the data into national ratings, the same process that radio and television audience-tracking companies still use, though there have been refinements.

In the 1940s **A. C. Nielsen** showed up in the broadcasting ratings business. Nielsen began telling advertisers which radio programs were especially popular among men, women and children. Nielsen also divided listenership into age brackets: 18 to 34, 35 to 49 and 50 plus. These were called **demographic** breakdowns. When Nielsen moved into television monitoring in 1950, it expanded audience data into more breakdowns. Today breakdowns include income, education, religion, occupation, neighborhood and even which products the viewers of certain programs use frequently.

While Archibald Crossley's early ratings were sponsored by advertisers, today networks and individual stations also commission ratings. The television networks pass ratings data on to advertisers immediately. Local stations usually recast the raw data for brochures that display the data in ways that put the stations in the most favorable light. These brochures are distributed by station sales representatives to advertisers. While advertisers receive ratings data from the stations and networks, major advertising agencies have contracts with Nielsen, Arbitron and other market research companies to gather audience data to meet their specifications.

ratings
Measurements of broadcast audience size

Nielsen Media Research
Surveys television viewership

Archibald Crossley
Conducted first polls on broadcast audience size

A. C. Nielsen
Founder of broadcast survey firm bearing his name

demographic
Characteristics of groups within a population being sampled, including age, gender and affiliations

Broadcast Ratings Council
Accredits ratings companies

CHECKING YOUR MEDIA LITERACY

- **How did Nielsen advance broadcast ratings from Crossley's early approach?**
- **Why are advertisers interested in broadcast audience ratings?**
- **How do television networks and stations use ratings?**
- **How have broadcast ratings improved since Archibald Crossley's telephone calls?**

CRITICISM OF RATINGS

However sophisticated the ratings services have become, they have critics. Many fans question the accuracy of ratings when their favorite television program is canceled because the network finds the ratings inadequate. Something is wrong, they say, when the viewing preferences of a few thousand households determine network programming for the entire nation. Though it seems incredible to someone who is not knowledgeable about statistical probability, the sample base of major ratings services like Nielsen generally is considered sufficient to extrapolate reliably on viewership in the 97 million television-equipped U.S. households.

It was not always so. Doubts peaked in the 1940s and 1950s when it was learned that some ratings services lied about sample size and were less than scientific in choosing samples. A congressional investigation in 1963 prompted the networks to create the **Broadcast Ratings Council** to accredit ratings companies and audit their reports.

Ratings have problems, some inherent in different methodologies and some attributable to human error and fudging.

NIELSEN MEDIA RESEARCH

10/29/07–11/04/07

MONDAY

	ABC	CBS	NBC	FOX	Univision	Telemundo	myTV	CW
8:00	**1 Dancing With the Stars 14.1/21**	53 How I Met/Mother 4.8/7	57 Chuck 4.3/6	67 House 3.9/6	103 Amar Sin Limites 1.6/2	128 Madre Luna 0.7/1	134 Celebrity Exposé 0.6/1	100 Evrybdy Hates Chris 1.7/3
8:30		45 Big Bang Theory 5.3/8						114 Aliens in America 1.4/2
9:00		16 Two and a Half Men 8.5/12	32 Heroes 6.1/9	86 K-Ville 2.7/4	82 Destilando Amor 3.0/4	134 La Esclava Isaura 0.6/1	134 Celebrity Exposé 0.6/1	103 Girlfriends 1.6/2
9:30	**19 Samantha Who? 9.8/14**	27 Rule/Engagement 6.7/10						100 The Game 1.7/2
10:00	25 The Bachelor 6.9/11	**20 CSI: Miami 9.8/16**	71 Journeyman 3.7/6		89 Cristina 2.5/4	174 Pecados Ajenos 0.3/1		
10:30								

TUESDAY

	ABC	CBS	NBC	FOX	Univision	Telemundo	myTV	CW
8:00	29 It's the Great Pumpkin, Charlie Brown 6.6/10	**7 NCIS 10.4/16**	71 Singing Bee 3.7/6	41 Bones 5.7/9	103 Amar Sin Limites 1.6/3	134 Madre Luna 0.6/1	103 Breaking the Magician's Code 1.6/2	103 Beauty and the Geek 1.6/2
8:30			61 The Biggest Loser 4.1/6					
9:00	**3 Dancing With the Stars Results 12.3/18**	26 The Unit 6.8/10		8 House 10.3/15	79 Destilando Amor 3.1/5	128 La Esclava Isaura 0.7/1	122 Iron Mask 0.8/1	100 Reaper 1.7/3
9:30								
10:00	**22 Boston Legal 7.7/13**	22 Cane 5.5/9	40 Law & Order: SVU 5.8/10		109 Como Ana Una Mujer 1.5/3	160 Pecados Ajenos 0.4/1		
10:30								

WEDNESDAY

	ABC	CBS	NBC	FOX	Univision	Telemundo	myTV	CW
8:00	**43 Pushing Daisies 5.6/10**	57 Kid Nation 4.3/8	67 Phenomenon 3.9/7	77 Back to You 3.4/6	114 Amar Sin Limites 1.4/2	134 Madre Luna 0.6/1	134 Decision House 0.6/1	93 America's Next Top Model 2.2/4
8:30				78 'Til Death 3.2/6				
9:00	20 Private Practice 7.8/13	13 Criminal Minds 9.5/15		89 Kitchen Nightmares 2.5/4	83 Destilando Amor 2.8/4	134 La Esclava Isaura 0.6/1	134 Decision House 0.6/1	121 Gossip Girl 1.1/2
9:30								
10:00	41 Dirty Sexy Money 5.7/10	**15 CSI: NY 8.7/15**	71 Life 3.7/6		93 Don Francisco Presents 2.0/4	174 Pecados Ajenos 0.3/1		
10:30								

THURSDAY

	ABC	CBS	NBC	FOX	Univision	Telemundo	myTV	CW
8:00	27 Ugly Betty 6.7/11	**16 Survivor: China 8.5/14**	54 My Name is Earl 4.6/7	47 Are You Smarter Than a 5th Grader? 5.2/8	98 Amar Sin Limites 1.8/3	128 Madre Luna 0.7/1	124 My Thursday Night Movie–Hot Shots! Part Deux 0.8/1	86 Smallville 2.7/4
8:30								
9:00	**2 Grey's Anatomy 12.6/19**	4 CSI 11.9/18	50 The Office 4.9/7	47 Are You Smarter Than a 5th Grader? 5.3/8	79 Destilando Amor 3.1/5	128 La Esclava Isaura 0.7/1		95 Supernatural 2.0/3
9:30			67 Scrubs 3.9/6					
10:00	48 Big Shots 5.1/9	**12 Without a Trace 9.7/15**	38 ER 5.9/10		97 Aquí y Ahora 1.9/3	160 Pecados Ajenos 0.4/1		
10:30								

FRIDAY

	ABC	CBS	NBC	FOX	Univision	Telemundo	myTV	CW
8:00	65 Men in Trees 4.0/7	**34 Ghost Whisperer 6.0/11**	**34 Deal or No Deal 6.0/1**	109 Next Great American Band 1.5/3	114 Amar Sin Limites 1.6/3	134 Madre Luna 0.7/1	124 My Friday Night Movie–Rocky 0.8/1	83 Friday Night Smackdown 2.8/5
8:30								
9:00	**30 Women's Murder Club 6.5/11**	50 Moonlight 4.9/9	74 Friday Night Lights 3.6/6		83 Destilando Amor 3.1/5	134 La Esclava Isaura 0.6/1		
9:30								
10:00	48 20/20 5.1/9	**32 Numb3rs 6.1/11**	50 Las Vegas 4.9/9		93 La Familia P Luche 2.2/4	174 Pecados Ajenos 0.4/1		
10:30					98 Retro P Luche 1.8/3			

SATURDAY

	ABC	CBS	NBC	FOX	Univision	Telemundo	myTV	CW
8:00	**61 Saturday Night Football 4.1/8**	**(nr) College Football–LSU vs. Alabama 4.0/8**	89 Bionic Woman 2.5/5	74 Cops 3.6/7	117 Sábado Gigante 1.3/2	174 Cine de Impacto–Enter the Dragon 0.3/1	174 NFL Network Total Access 0.3/1	
8:30				67 Cops 3.9/7				
9:00			92 Chuck 2.3/4	65 America's Most Wanted: Amer Fights Back 4.0/7			160 IFL Battleground 0.4/1	
9:30		**61 Crimetime Saturday 4.1/7**				134 Cinede Impacto–The Fast and the Furious 0.6/1		
10:00			76 Law & Order: SVU 3.5/6					
10:30		54 Crimetime Saturday 4.6/8						

SUNDAY

	ABC	CBS	NBC	FOX	Univision	Telemundo	myTV	CW
7:00	(nr) NASCAR Nextel Cup 3.7/7	**(nr) NFL Game 2 20.1/36**	Football Night Pt. 1 Sustaining	83 The Simpsons 2.8/4	117 Festival Mariachi Disney 1.3/2	174 Marav Mundo Disney–Spy Kids 3: Game Over 0.3/1		134 CW Now 0.6/1
7:30	57 Amer Fun Home Vid 4.3/7	**4 60 Minutes 11.9/19**	61 Football Night Pt. 2 4.1/7	56 The Simpsons 4.5/7				134 Aliens in America 0.6/1
8:00	20 Extreme Makeover: Home Edition 7.8/12		61 F'ball Night Pt. 3 5.9/10	31 The Simpsons 6.4/10				124 Life is Wild 0.8/1
8:30		18 The Amazing Race 8.3/12		34 Family Guy 6.0/9				
9:00	**6 Desperate Housewives 11.8/18**		**9 NFL Sunday Night Football–Dallas Cowboys vs. Philadelphia Eagles 10.2/16**	34 Family Guy 6.0/9	117 Cine Especial–Tonta, Tonta. Pero no Tonta 1.3/2	149 Cine Millonario–The Hulk 0.5/1		122 America's Next Top Model 0.9/1
9:30		14 Cold Case 9.0/14		60 American Dad 4.2/6				
10:00	19 Brothers & Sisters 8.1/14							
10:30		23 Shark 7.6/14						

Nielsen Ratings. *Every prime-time network show is ranked by audience in weekly Nielsens. ABC's* Dancing with the Stars *at 8 p.m. Monday led this week. Second, also on ABC, was* Grey's Anatomy, *Thursday night at 9 p.m.*

Ratings: *One measure of audience is the rating. This is the percentage of television-equipped households viewing a program. Because 97 million U.S. households have television sets, each percentage point represents 970,000 households.* Dancing's *rating was 14.1.*

Shares: *A second audience measure, share, is a show's percentage of all television sets that are turned on.* Dancing *had a 21 share, far outdistancing CBS's* How I Met Your Mother *with 7, NBC's* Chuck *and Fox's* House, *both with 6. Univision, Telemundo, MyTV and CW all picked up splinters.*

Source: Nielsen Media Research, adapted from Broadcasting & Cable, *November 12, 2007, 24.*

>> **Discrepancies.** When different ratings services come up with widely divergent findings in the same market, advertisers become suspicious. Minor discrepancies can be explained by different sampling methods, but significant discrepancies point to flawed methodology or execution. It was discrepancies of this sort that led to the creation of the Broadcast Ratings Council.

>> **Slanted Results.** Sales reps of some local stations, eager to demonstrate to advertisers that their stations have large audiences, extract only the favorable data from survey results. It takes a sophisticated local advertiser to reconcile slanted and fudged claims.

>> **Sample Selection.** Some ratings services select their samples meticulously, giving every household in a market a statistically equal opportunity to be sampled. Some sample selections are seriously flawed: How reliable, for example, are the listenership claims of a rock 'n' roll station that puts a disc jockey's face on billboards all over town and then sends the disc jockey to a teenage dance palace to ask about listening preferences?

>> **Hyping.** Ratings-hungry stations have learned how to build audiences during **sweeps** weeks in February, May and November when major local television ratings are compiled. Consider these examples of **hyping:**

- Radio giveaways often coincide with ratings periods.
- Many news departments promote sensationalistic series for the sweeps and then retreat to routine coverage when the ratings period is over.
- Besides sweeps weeks, there are **black weeks** when no ratings are conducted. In these periods some stations run all kinds of odd and dull serve-the-public programs that they would never consider running during a sweeps period.

>> **Respondent Accuracy.** With handwritten diaries, respondents don't always answer honestly. People have an opportunity to write that they watched *Masterpiece Theatre* on PBS instead of less classy fare. For the same reason, shock radio and trash television probably have more audience than the ratings show.

In a project to tighten measurement techniques, Nielsen gradually began eliminating diaries in local television markets in 2006. In the 10 largest markets, Nielsen redesigned its people meters, which measure both what network shows are being watched and who is in the room watching. The new meters also track local viewing choices. Gradually Nielsen sought to eliminate diary-based in smaller markets too.

>> **Zipping, Zapping and Flushing.** Ratings services measure audiences for programs and for different times of day, but they do not measure whether commercials are watched. Advertisers are interested, of course, in whether the programs between which their ads are sandwiched are popular, but more important to them is whether people are watching the ads.

This vacuum in audience measurements was documented in the 1960s when somebody with a sense of humor correlated a major drop in Chicago water pressure with the Super Bowl halftime. The drop became known as the **flush factor.** Football fans were getting off the couch by the thousands at halftime to go to the bathroom. Advertisers were missing many people because although viewers were tuned in, many were not watching the ads.

This problem has been exacerbated with the advent of handheld television remote controls and systems like TiVo. Viewers can **zip** from station to station to

sweeps
When broadcast ratings are conducted

hyping
Intensive promotion to attract an audience during ratings periods

black weeks
Periods when ratings are not conducted

flush factor
Viewers leave during commercials to go to refrigerator, bathroom, etc.

zipping
Viewers change television channels to avoid commercials

avoid commercials, and when they record programs for later viewing, they can **zap** out the commercials.

CHECKING YOUR MEDIA LITERACY

- How are broadcast ratings susceptible to manipulation?
- Besides deliberate manipulations, what vulnerabilities beset ratings?

ENGAGEMENT RATINGS

In the quest to spend their advertising dollars to the greatest effect, some advertisers have taken a liking to **engagement ratings.** These are attempts to gauge how attentive people are to certain programs and ads. To be sure, engagement ratings are imprecise—a combination of data and intuitiveness.

>> **Television Engagement.** Ford, for example, was won over to advertising its new F-series pickup trucks on Mike Rowes' *Dirty Jobs* on the Discovery Channel. It was not because *Dirty Jobs* was a ratings leader. In fact, the audience was not impressive in size. But the engagement metrics indicated that the viewers were deeply immersed in the show and were disproportionately 18- to 45-year-old men. That's an audience segment loaded with pickup buyers. By 2009 half of the 100 major advertisers on U.S. network television were pressing the networks for engagement ratings.

The research firm IAG pioneered engagement ratings in 2004 by asking viewers how well they recalled programs and ads. Within a year Toyota was using the data in negotiating rates with the networks. With the engagement ratings catching on, Nielsen put up $225 million in 2008 and bought IAG. The acquisition put Nielsen in a position to report not only how many households have their television sets tuned to certain programs but also how engaged they are—how much they're paying attention.

Engagement ratings can also be used to gauge the effectiveness of ads themselves. The ad agency Crispin Porter + Bogusky found that ads for the Volkswagen Jetta and Tiguan had 75 percent more viewers paying attention if an old VW Bug were a character in the ads.

>> **Internet Engagement.** Nielsen actually had earlier experimented with engagement ratings on the Internet. Until 2007 Nielsen had ranked web sites by page views. Because people race through views until they find what they want, the method missed engagement. To track what sites both attracted and kept web users, Nielsen switched in 2007 to checking how much time was spent at a site. Measuring web audiences, whatever the system, remains an inexact science, but advertisers now have a firmer feel for how many eyeballs their web advertising is reaching.

What difference did Nielsen's post-click counting method yield? Gaming company Electronic Arts suddenly was in the Top 10. Gamers stay at a game a while. Apple iTunes with its 90-second sampler of songs also moved up.

Advertisers quickly began pressing for engagement data for television, which commands five times more advertising revenue than the Internet. Hence came Nielsen's IAG acquisition and television engagement ratings.

zapping
Viewers record programs and eliminate commercial breaks

engagement
The time that audience people stay with media products and advertisements

CHECKING YOUR MEDIA LITERACY

- How do engagement ratings differ from traditional television ratings?
- What do engagement ratings measure? And how?

Audience Measurement Techniques

STUDY PREVIEW

Traditional polling techniques include interviews and diaries, both of which are being eclipsed by meters. Some devices even track which billboards a person passes and how often. These new devices track usage of new media forms, including the Internet, and the extension of television viewing beyond the living room and also playback viewing with TiVo and similar devices.

BASIC TOOLS

The primary techniques, sometimes used in combination, for measuring broadcast audiences are interviews, diaries and meters.

>> Interviews. In his pioneer 1929 listenership polling, Archibald Crossley placed telephone calls to randomly selected households. Although many polling companies use telephone **interviews** exclusively, they're not used much in broadcasting anymore. Also rare in broadcasting are face-to-face interviews. Although eyeball-to-eyeball interviewing can elicit fuller information, it is labor-intensive and relatively expensive.

>> Diaries. Nielsen began using **diaries** in the 1950s. Instead of interviews, Nielsen mailed forms to selected families in major markets for them to list program titles, times and channels and who was watching. This was done in major sweep periods: February, May, July and November. Although diaries were cost-efficient, many viewers would forget their duty and then try to remember days later what they had watched. The resulting data were better than no data but rather muddy.

>> Meters. Meters were introduced in the 1970s as a supplement to diaries to improve accuracy. Some Nielsen families had their television sets wired to track what channel was on. Some were issued meters that household members could click so that Nielsen could determine for whom programs have their appeal—men, women, children, oldsters. Some set-top meters even traced who was watching by sensing body mass.

>> People Meters. In 1987 Nielsen introduced **People Meters.** These were two-function units, one on the television set to scan the channels being watched every 2.7 seconds and a handheld remote that monitored who was watching. With data flowing in nightly to Nielsen's central computers, the company generates next-day reports, called **overnights,** for the networks and advertisers.

>> Portable Meters. In 2001 Nielsen and Arbitron, which focuses on radio audiences, jointly tested portable meters that people can carry around. The pager-size meters, weighing $2\frac{1}{2}$ ounces, are set to pick up inaudible signals transmitted with programs. The goal: to track away-from-home audiences at sports bars, offices and airports and, in the case of radio, cars. ESPN estimates that 4 million people watch its sports away from home in a typical week. The "walking meters," as they are called, also track commuter radio habits for the first time.

interviews
Face-to-face, mail, telephone survey technique

diaries
Sampling technique in which respondents keep their own records

People Meters
Devices that track individual viewers

overnights
Next-morning reports on network viewership

Media Metrix
A service measuring Internet audience size

CHECKING YOUR MEDIA LITERACY

<> What methods do ratings companies use to measure broadcast audiences?

INTERNET AUDIENCE MEASURES

The leading Internet audience measuring company, **Media Metrix,** uses a two-track system to determine how many people view web sites. Media Metrix gathers data from 40,000 individual computers whose owners have agreed to be monitored. Some of these computers are programmed to track Internet usage and report data back by e-mail. In addition, Media Metrix has lined up other computer users to mail in a tracking disc periodically. The Nielsen ratings company has set up a similar methodology. Other companies also are in the Internet ratings business.

How accurate are Internet ratings? Some major content providers, including CNN, ESPN and Time Warner, claim that the ratings undercount their users. Such claims go beyond self-serving comments because, in fact, different rating companies come up with widely divergent ratings. The question is: Why can't the ratings companies get it

Billboard Meter. *To measure the number of people who pass electronically tagged billboards, Nielsen Media Research issues palm-size devices that tell when participants pass an electronically coded billboard. Data are uploaded from the device to a satellite, then down to Nielsen data keepers who score billboards. Competitor Arbitron has a similar device.*

right? The answer, in part, is that divergent data flow from divergent methodologies. Data need to be viewed in terms of the methodology that was used. Also, the infant Internet ratings business undoubtedly is hobbled by methodology flaws that have yet to be identified and corrected.

CHECKING YOUR MEDIA LITERACY

- **How accurate are ratings of commercial Internet sites?**

MULTIMEDIA MEASURES

Recognizing that television viewers were increasingly mobile and less set-bound, Nielsen began remaking its ratings system in 2006 to measure the use of personal computers, video game players, iPods, cell phones and other mobile devices. Nielsen said the program, called **Anytime Anywhere Media Measurement,** or **A2/M2** for short, represented a commitment to "follow the video" with an "all-electronic measurement system that will deliver integrated ratings for television viewing regardless of the platform." Nielsen's chief researcher, Paul Donato, put it this way: "The plan is to try to capture it all."

An initial step was creating a panel of 400 video iPod users to track the programs they download and watch. Nielsen also began fusing data from its television-tracking unit and its Nielsen/Net Ratings unit to measure the relation between conventional television viewing and web surfing with meters on both televisions and personal computers.

CHECKING YOUR MEDIA LITERACY

- **What is A2/M2? Why is it important?**

MOBILE AUDIENCE MEASURES

Anytime Anywhere Media Measurement (A2/M2)
Nielsen plan to integrate audience measurements on a wide range of video platforms

Over-air networks tried addressing the audience leakage to DVD and TiVo-like devices when the Nielsen rating service introduced its Live Plus Seven measure in 2006. The new measure tracked live viewing plus any viewing within seven days. The networks built the extended period into their audience guarantees with advertisers. The network argument was that DVD and TiVo viewers are more affluent as a group and therefore worth more to advertisers. Advertisers balked. Advertisers argued that ads viewed after the fact have diminished value. Also, the new Nielsen gizmo for recording viewers didn't record ads that were skipped, which TiVo facilitates.

Advertisers were more comfortable with Nielsen's live-plus-same-day counts, which included DVD viewing before the next morning. Despite the issue over the counting period being spread out, Nielsen continued to install the new measuring devices. By 2007 about 18 percent of measured U.S. households were included.

Measuring Audience Reaction

STUDY PREVIEW

The television ratings business has moved beyond measuring audience size to measuring audience reaction. Researchers measure audience reaction with numerous methods, including focus groups, galvanic skin checks and prototypes.

focus groups
Small groups interviewed in loosely structured ways for opinion, reactions

FOCUS GROUPS

Television consulting companies measure audience reaction with **focus groups.** Typically, an interview crew goes to a shopping center, chooses a dozen individuals by gender and age, and offers them cookies, soft drinks and $25 each to sit

CASE STUDY

Tracking Technology

Research companies once collected data on television audiences by asking people to fill out a paper diary. Then Nielsen began using its electronic People Meter, which automatically recorded what channel a television set was tuned to.

Now Nielsen is planning to provide ratings for television regardless of the platform on which it is viewed. Its Anytime Anywhere Media Measurement A2/M2 will assess the new ways that people are watching television, including on the Internet, outside the home and via personal mobile devices.

Nielsen also is developing and testing new personal meters to measure television viewership away from home, including at work and in bars, restaurants, hotels and airports. The Go Meters are designed to collect audio signatures. One device places metering technology in cell phones, and the other is a customized meter that resembles an MP3 player.

The company also plans to expand the use of electronic metering to smaller television markets and by 2011 to have replaced paper diaries and logs with electronic meters in smaller cities. The Solo Meter that the company is developing can be used with any portable media system. For wireless connections, Nielsen is working on a tiny wireless meter that will passively listen to communication between mated devices. For wired systems, Nielsen is building a diminutive meter that will be physically inserted between the device and its earphones. These Solo Meters also will identify viewing by collecting audio signatures.

For advertisers, Nielsen plans to adopt a measure of engagement for television. Engagement assesses how deep an impression an ad or program has made on a viewer. As audiences for programming and advertising grow narrower, the need to make a deeper impression on a smaller group of people becomes more important than the conventional focus on reaching as many people as possible. Recent research points toward the possibility of a link between media engagement and advertising engagement.

As the technology of the mass media continues to progress, audience measurement companies must find ways to keep up. Sometimes that could mean dramatic changes in the way viewership figures are tallied. And that could result in major shifts in the way advertising dollars are spent and received. Stay tuned.

Jogging Viewers. *Television watching in a Minnesota State University, Mankato, workout gym misses the radar of Nielsen audience tracking. New audience tracking devices will cast their nets wider to recognize the reality that television is no longer only an at-home activity. Nielsen had been missing sports bars, airport waiting lounges, luxury SUVs and other non-living room audiences.*

DEEPENING YOUR MEDIA LITERACY

EXPLORE THE ISSUE

Find someone who has been asked to participate in a public opinion poll. Does that person know why he or she was chosen?

DIG DEEPER

Ask about the reliability of the information given to the polling company. Were answers based on recollection? Ask the person how completely he or she collected the information. Was it merely from memory or recollection?

WHAT DO YOU THINK?

Will consumers benefit as much as advertisers from the newest audience tracking technology?

down and watch a taped local newscast. A moderator then asks for reactions, sometimes with loaded and leading questions to open them up. It is a tricky research method that depends highly on the skill of the moderator. In one court case, an anchor who had lost her job as a result of responses to a focus group complained that the moderator had contaminated the process with prejudicial assertions and questions:

- "This is your chance to get rid of the things you don't like to see on the news."
- "Come on, unload on those sons of bitches who make $100,000 a year."
- "This is your chance to do more than just yell at the TV. You can speak up and say I really hate that guy or I really like that broad."
- "Let's spend 30 seconds destroying this anchor. Is she a mutt? Be honest about this."

Even when conducted skillfully, focus groups have the disadvantage of reflecting the opinion of the loudest respondent.

CHECKING YOUR MEDIA LITERACY

- **What is the role of analysis in focus group research?**
- **What is the role of a focus group moderator?**

SIT-DOWN INTERVIEWS

Surveying may need to shift to more personal methods. A growing number of people refuse to participate in telephone surveys. They covet their time. They resent the intrusion. There also is growing skepticism that surveys are not always seeking information or opinion but are sly marketing or opinion-manipulating tactics. This distrust extends beyond the telephone to Internet and mail polls.

What eases the resistance to participate? One research company, Jacobs Media, recommends an introduction that promises the survey will be simple and fast, serve a worthy cause, and offer compensation for the participant's time. Jacobs offered this introduction for a survey of young adults on media performance:

"By participating in this *brief* and *simple* survey, you will *be contributing to improving the media and technology that you use,* and you will be *paid* for your time."

The Bedroom Project
Fascinating new research that lets you hear the thoughts and opinions of 18- to 28-year-olds.
The Bedroom Project
ARBITRON
jacobs media

Natural Habitat Interviews. *To learn how young people used media and technology, Jacobs Media recognized shortcomings of traditional surveys. Focus groups also were ruled out. Instead, small teams of peer interviewers, all specially trained, went to visit young people where they do most of their media consultation, often in dorm rooms or bedrooms, and videotaped natural-habitat conversation that averaged two hours.*

GALVANIC SKIN CHECKS

Consulting companies hired by television stations run a great variety of studies to determine audience reaction. Local stations, which originate news programs and not much else, look to these consultants for advice on news sets, story selection and even which anchors and reporters are most popular. Besides surveys, these consultants sometimes use **galvanic skin checks.** Wires are attached to individuals in a sample group of viewers to measure pulse and skin reactions, such as perspiration. Advocates of these tests claim that they reveal how much interest a newscast evokes and whether the interest is positive or negative.

If It Bleeds, It Leads. *Audience researchers have found newscast ratings go up for stations that consistently deliver graphic video. This has prompted many stations to favor fire stories, for example, even if the fire wasn't consequential, if graphic video is available. The ratings quest also prompts these stations to favor crimes and accidents over more substantive stories, like government budgets, that don't lend themselves to gripping graphics.*

These tests were first used to check audience reaction to advertisements, but today some stations look to them in deciding whether to remodel a studio. A dubious use, from a journalistic perspective, is using galvanic skin checks to determine what kinds of stories to cover and whether to find new anchors and reporters. The skin checks reward short, photogenic stories like fires and accidents rather than significant stories, which tend to be longer and don't lend themselves to flashy video. The checks also favor good-looking, smooth anchors and reporters, regardless of their journalistic competence. One wag was literally correct when he called this "a heart-throb approach to journalism."

CHECKING YOUR MEDIA LITERACY

- **How would you as a television program executive use physiological indicators from galvanic skin checks?**

PROTOTYPE RESEARCH

Before making major investments, media executives seek as much information as they can obtain in order to determine how to enhance a project's chances for success or whether it has a chance at all. This is known as **prototype research.**

>> **Movie Screenings.** Movie studios have previewed movies since the days of silent film. Today the leading screening contractors are units of Nielsen and OTX. Typically about 300 people, selected carefully to fit a demographic, watch the movie and fill out comment cards. Were they confused at any point? Did they like the ending? What were their favorite scenes? Would they recommend the movie to a friend? The audience usually is filmed watching the movie, and producers and studio executives later look for reactions on a split screen with the movie running. Usually 20 or so testers are kept after a screening as a sit-down focus group with the studio people listening in.

Screenings make a difference. How a movie is promoted can be shaped by the test audience's reactions. Some endings have been changed. Astute moviegoers noticed that Vince Vaughn seemed thinner toward the end of *The Break Up.* The fact is that Universal executives had decided for a happier ending and ordered Vaughn and a crew back to Chicago to reshoot. He had lost weight in the meantime. More widely known is that Paramount took the advice of a Nielsen screener and had Glenn Close's character in *Fatal Attraction* be murdered rather than commit suicide.

Many directors don't like their creative control contravened by test screenings. Some directors, indeed, have the clout to refuse screenings. Steven Spielberg famously forsakes them. The usual objection from directors is that they don't want to surrender creative control. Put another way, some directors see screenings as a way for studio executives to cover their backsides by claiming to their supervisors, if a movie flops, that they did all they could to ensure its success.

In recent years, screenings have been squeezed out of tighter and tighter production schedules, especially when computer-generated imaging plays a big role in a movie. For *The Da Vinci Code, Superman Returns* and *Pirates of the Caribbean: Dead Man's Chest,* all big summer releases, there were no screen tests. There was no time to line up preview audiences, let alone make any changes that might have bubbled up through the process.

Some studio execs also have cooled to screenings because of negative leaks that can derail promotion plans. In 2006 a blogger had posted a review of Oliver Stone's *World*

galvanic skin checks
Monitor pulse, skin responses to stimuli

prototype research
Checks audience response to a product still in development

Trade Center within hours of a screening in Minneapolis. One site, Ain't It Cool News, works at infiltrating screenings. Drew McSweeney, a site editor, defends the crashing as a way to stunt executive interference in movies and return power to directors.

>> **Publication Protoypes.** When Gannett decided to establish a new newspaper, *USA Today*, it created prototypes, each designed differently, to test readers' reactions. Many new magazines are preceded by at least one trial issue to sample marketplace reaction and to show to potential advertisers.

Advertising agencies, too, often screen campaigns before launch to fine-tune them.

>> **Television Pilots.** In network television a prototype can even make it on the air in the form of a **pilot.** One or a few episodes are tested, usually in prime time with a lot of promotion, to see whether the audience goes for the program concept. Some made-for-television movies actually are test runs to determine whether a series might be spun off from the movie.

CHECKING YOUR MEDIA LITERACY

- **Why do strong-willed screenwriters and directors bristle at prototype research to adjust story lines?**
- **What role should an audience have in determining the mass media's literary content?**
- **What about a Hemingway novel? A James Cameron movie? A Ken Burns documentary? The *Sopranos* finale?**

pilot
A prototype television show that is given an on-air trial

Audience Analysis

STUDY PREVIEW

Traditional demographic polling methods divided people by gender, age and other easily identifiable population characteristics. Today, media people use sophisticated lifestyle breakdowns such as geodemographics and psychographics to match the content of their publications, broadcast programs and advertising to the audiences they seek.

DEMOGRAPHICS

Early in the development of public opinion surveying, pollsters learned that broad breakdowns had limited usefulness. Archibald Crossley's pioneering radio surveys, for example, told the number of people who were listening to network programs, which was valuable to the networks and their advertisers, but Crossley's figures did not tell how many listeners were men or women, urban or rural, old or young. Such breakdowns of overall survey data, called *demographics,* were developed in the 1930s as Crossley, Gallup and other early pollsters refined their work.

Today, if demographic data indicate that a presidential candidate is weak in the Midwest, campaign strategists can gear the candidate's message to Midwestern concerns. Through demographics, advertisers keen on reaching young women can identify magazines that will carry their ads to that audience. If advertisers seek an elderly audience, they can use demographic data to determine where to place their television ads.

While demographics remains valuable today, newer methods can break the population into categories that have even greater usefulness. These newer methods, which include cohort analysis, geodemography and psychographics, provide lifestyle breakdowns.

CHECKING YOUR MEDIA LITERACY

- **What are common demographic breakdowns in survey research?**

COHORT ANALYSIS

Marketing people have developed **cohort analysis,** a specialized form of demographics, to identify generations and then design and produce products with generational appeal. Advertising people then gear media messages to the images, music, humor and other generational variables that appeal to the target cohort. The major cohorts are dubbed:

- **Generation X,** who came of age in the 1980s.
- **Baby Boomers,** who came of age in the late 1960s and 1970s.
- **Postwar Generation,** who came of age in the 1950s.
- **World War II Veterans,** who came of age in the 1940s.
- **Depression Survivors,** who came of age during the economic depression of the 1930s.

Cohort analysis has jarred the traditional thinking that as people get older, they simply adopt their parents' values. The new 50-plus generation, for example, grew up on Coke and Pepsi drinks and, to the dismay of coffee growers, may prefer to start the day with cola—not the coffee their parents drank.

The Chrysler automobile company was early to recognize that Baby Boomers aren't interested in buying Cadillac-type luxury cars even when they have amassed the money to afford them. Chrysler determined that graying Baby Boomers preferred upscale Jeeps to the luxo-barge cars that appealed to the Postwar Generation.

Advertising people who use cohort analysis know that Baby Boomers, although now in their 50s, are still turned on by pizzas and the Rolling Stones. In short, many of the habits of their youth stick with a generation as it gets older. What appealed to the 30-something group a decade ago won't necessarily sail with today's 30-something set. David Bostwick, Chrysler's marketing research director, puts it this way: "Nobody wants to become their parents."

When the guerrilla war in Iraq began hurting U.S. military recruiting, the Pentagon desperately needed to fine-tune its message to reach the young men and women who were the most likely prospects to enlist. Applying analytical tools to its own existing data, the Pentagon identified ethnic, geographical and income cohorts that are more receptive to the military. The analysis also identified media for reaching these cohorts. Prospective Army recruits, for example, listen more to Spanish radio than the general population does. *Bassmaster* magazine is more the style of Air Force prospects. Marine prospects lean to *Car Craft, Guns & Ammo* and *Outdoor Life.*

Here are seven cohorts that the Pentagon identified to target their recruiting pitches:

Cohort	Urbanization	Ethnicity	Income
Beltway Boomers	Suburban	White/Asian	Upper-middle
Kids and Cul de Sacs	Suburban	White/Asian/Hispanic	Upper-middle
Big Sky Families	Town/rural	White	Midscale
Blue-Chip Blues	Suburban	White/black/Hispanic	Midscale
Shotguns and Pickups	Town/rural	White	Lower-middle
Suburban Pioneers	Suburban	White/black/Hispanic	Lower-middle
Bedrock America	Town/rural	White/black/Hispanic	Downscale

CHECKING YOUR MEDIA LITERACY

- **How can cohort analysis help mass communicators craft their messages?**
- **What kind of cohort would be useful for analysis by an advertiser for toothpaste? The Marine Corps? An automobile?**
- **Do you like being pigeonholed as a target for advertising and other media messages?**

cohort analysis

Demographic tool to identify marketing targets by common characteristics

GEODEMOGRAPHICS

While demographics, including cohort analysis, remain valuable today, new methods can break the population into categories that have even greater usefulness. These newer methods, which include geodemography, provide lifestyle breakdowns.

Computer whiz **Jonathan Robbin** provided the basis for more sophisticated breakdowns in 1974 when he began developing his **PRIZM** system for **geodemography.** From census data Robbin grouped every zip code by ethnicity, family life cycle, housing style, mobility and social rank. Then he identified 34 factors that statistically distinguished neighborhoods from each other. All this information was cranked through a computer programmed by Robbin to plug every zip code into 1 of 40 clusters. Here are the most frequent clusters created through PRIZM, which stands for Potential Rating Index for Zip Markets, with the labels Robbin put on them:

- **Blue-Chip Blues.** These are the wealthiest blue-collar suburbs. These make up about 6 percent of U.S. households. About 13 percent of these people are college graduates.
- **Young Suburbia.** Childrearing outlying suburbs, 5.3 percent of the U.S. population; college grads, 24 percent.
- **Golden Ponds.** Rustic mountain, seashore or lakeside cottage communities, 5.2 percent; college grads, 13 percent.
- **Blue-Blood Estates.** Wealthiest neighborhoods; college grads, 51 percent.
- **Money and Brains.** Posh big-city enclaves of townhouses, condos and apartments; college grads, 46 percent.

Geodemographic breakdowns are used not only by advertisers on ad placement decisions but also for editorial content. At Time Warner magazines, geodemographic analysis permits issues to be edited for special audiences. *Time,* for example, has a 600,000 circulation edition for company owners, directors, board chairs, presidents, other titled officers and department heads. Among others are editions for physicians and college students.

CHECKING YOUR MEDIA LITERACY

- **How is geodemographics different from demographics?**
- **Geodemographics cubbyholes people. In what cubbyholes do you fit more or less?**

Jonathan Robbin
Devised PRIZM geodemography system

PRIZM
Identifies population characteristics by zip code

geodemography
Demographic characteristics by geographic area

psychographics
Breaking down a population by lifestyle characteristics

VALS
Psychographic analysis by values, lifestyle and life stage

PSYCHOGRAPHICS

A refined lifestyle breakdown introduced in the late 1970s, **psychographics,** divides the population into lifestyle segments. One leading psychographics approach, the Values and Life-Styles program, known as **VALS** for short, uses an 85-page survey to identify broad categories of people:

>> **Belongers.** Comprising about 38 percent of the U.S. population, these people are conformists who are satisfied with mainstream values and are reluctant to change brands once they're satisfied. Belongers are not very venturesome and fit the stereotype of Middle America. They tend to be churchgoers and television watchers.

>> **Achievers.** Comprising about 20 percent of the population, these are prosperous people who fit into a broader category of inner-directed consumers. Achievers pride themselves on making their own decisions. They're an upscale audience to which a lot of advertising is directed. As a group, achievers aren't heavy television watchers.

>> **Societally Conscious.** Comprising 11 percent of the population, these people are aware of social issues and tend to be politically active. The societally conscious also are upscale and inner-directed, and they tend to prefer reading to watching television.

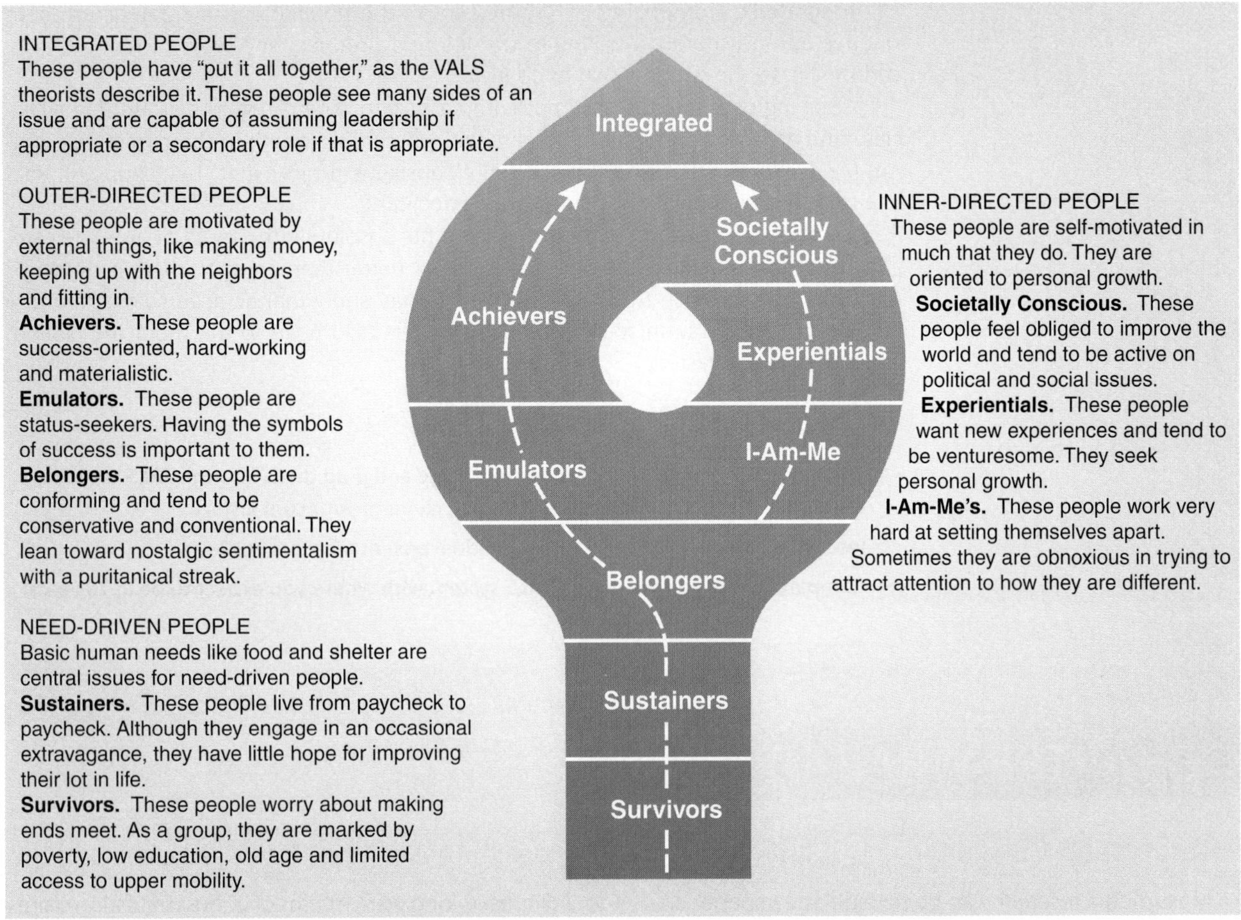

INTEGRATED PEOPLE
These people have "put it all together," as the VALS theorists describe it. These people see many sides of an issue and are capable of assuming leadership if appropriate or a secondary role if that is appropriate.
OUTER-DIRECTED PEOPLE
These people are motivated by external things, like making money, keeping up with the neighbors and fitting in.
Achievers. These people are success-oriented, hard-working and materialistic.
Emulators. These people are status-seekers. Having the symbols of success is important to them.
Belongers. These people are conforming and tend to be conservative and conventional. They lean toward nostalgic sentimentalism with a puritanical streak.
NEED-DRIVEN PEOPLE
Basic human needs like food and shelter are central issues for need-driven people.
Sustainers. These people live from paycheck to paycheck. Although they engage in an occasional extravagance, they have little hope for improving their lot in life.
Survivors. These people worry about making ends meet. As a group, they are marked by poverty, low education, old age and limited access to upper mobility.
Integrated
Societally Conscious
Achievers
Experientials
Emulators
I-Am-Me
Belongers
Sustainers
Survivors
INNER-DIRECTED PEOPLE
These people are self-motivated in much that they do. They are oriented to personal growth.
Societally Conscious. These people feel obliged to improve the world and tend to be active on political and social issues.
Experientials. These people want new experiences and tend to be venturesome. They seek personal growth.
I-Am-Me's. These people work very hard at setting themselves apart. Sometimes they are obnoxious in trying to attract attention to how they are different.

VALS Hierarchy. *Developmental psychologists have long told us that people change their values as they mature. Today, many advertisers rely on the Values and Life-Style model, VALS for short, which was derived from developmental psychology, to identify potential consumers and to design effective messages. Relatively few advertising messages are aimed at survivors and sustainers, who have little discretionary income. However, belongers and people on the divergent outer-directed or inner-directed paths are lucrative advertising targets for many products and services.*

>> **Emulators.** Comprising 10 percent of the population, these people aspire to a better life but, not quite understanding how to do it, go for the trappings of prosperity. Emulators are status seekers, prone to suggestions on what makes the good life.

>> **Experientials.** Comprising 5 percent of the population, these people are venturesome, willing to try new things in an attempt to experience life fully. They are a promising upscale audience for many advertisers.

>> **I-Am-Me's.** Comprising 3 percent of the population, these people work hard to set themselves apart and are susceptible to advertising pitches that offer ways to differentiate themselves, which gives them a kind of subculture conformity. SRI International, which developed the VALS technique, characterized a member of the I-Am-Me's as "a guitar-playing punk rocker who goes around in shades and sports an earring." Rebellious youth, angry and maladjusted, fit this category.

>> **Survivors.** This is a small downscale category that includes pensioners who worry about making ends meet.

>> **Sustainers.** These people live from paycheck to paycheck. Although they indulge in an occasional extravagance, they have slight hope for improving their lot in life. Sustainers are a downscale category and aren't frequent advertising targets.

>> **Integrateds.** Comprising only 2 percent of the population, integrateds are both creative and prosperous—willing to try different products and ways of doing things, and they have the wherewithal to do it.

Applying psychographics is not without hazard. The categories are in flux as society and lifestyles change. SRI researchers who chart growth in the percentage of I-Am-Me's, experientials and the societally conscious project that they soon will total one-third of the population. Belongers are declining.

Another complication is that no person fits absolutely the mold of any one category. Even for individuals who fit one category better than another, there is no single mass medium to reach them. VALS research may show that achievers constitute the biggest market for antihistamines, but belongers also head to the medicine cabinet when they're congested.

CHECKING YOUR MEDIA LITERACY

- **Think about a person your grandparents' age and plug them into the VALS category that today fits them best. Discuss how you came to your conclusion.**
- **Into what category did this same individual best fit 40 years ago?**
- **Compare where you are on the VALS system with where you expect to be in 20 years.**

CHAPTER WRAP-UP

Discovering Mass Audiences (Pages 325–327)

- Mass media research can be traced to newspaper entrepreneurs who eavesdropped on street corners to hear what was on people's minds—and then edited the next edition to pander to those interests. Today the research is sophisticated. For mass media companies, a lot is at stake in understanding the audience. Basic techniques include polling with many of the techniques used for surveying in marketing, politics and governance.

Audience Measurement Principles (Pages 328–332)

- Surveying for opinions plays a growing role in our society's public life, in public policy and in decisions about advertising and other media content. Survey techniques have become increasingly complex and statistically more reliable. Generally the best surveys use probability sampling, which statistically chooses respondents whose responses will coincide with the whole group. All surveys have caveats, however. Some surveys are hocus-pocus with no statistical reliability, including 800 and 900 number call-ins and man-on-the-street interviews.

Measuring Audience Size (Pages 332–336)

- Advertisers long were victims of bogus circulation claims by newspapers and magazines, whose advertising rates were based on unverified audience rates. The Audit Bureau of Circulations largely cleaned up false claims beginning in 1914. ABC checked pressruns. Radio, then television audiences were not so easily measured. In 1929 Archibald Crossley used extrapolations from small samples to see how many people were tuned to network radio programs. The networks, of course, wanted the information to guide programming decisions. Today Nielsen is the largest player in television ratings.

Audience Measurement Techniques (Pages 336–338)

- Traditional polling techniques include interviews and diaries. Meters have added new precision in recent years. Some new devices even track which billboards a person passes and how often.

Measuring Audience Reaction (Pages 338–342)

- Special techniques have been devised to measure how audiences react to media messages. This includes focus groups to generate feedback on media content, like a television program, a publication redesign, and advertisements. Visceral effects can be tracked by charting heartbeat, brain activity and other physiological reactions as a message is being presented. The fate of a pilot for a television program can hang on these measures. So can an advertising campaign. Some movies are adjusted by analyzing audience reactions to pre-final cuts. Advisers to large-budget political candidates also use these techniques to hone messages to various blocs of voters.

Audience Analysis (Pages 342–346)

- The imperative to match messages with audience has created a relatively new component of analysis. The historical breakdowns—demographics like age, gender and affiliations—have become much more sophisticated. Some analysis looks at media habits in highly defined neighborhoods in assessing how to craft media messages, particularly advertising and political spots. Called geodemographics, the method clusters people by income, education and geography. Psychographics looks at lifestyles and motivations. Some groupings include high achievers, followers, and convention-defiers.

▼ Review Questions

1. What variables determine whether surveys based on probability sampling can be trusted?
2. How is the size of newspaper audiences measured? Radio? Television?
3. What lifestyle and media changes have prompted media survey companies to update their techniques? What are these new techniques?
4. How are audience reactions to mass media content measured? What results from these measurements?
5. What are techniques of audience analysis? How are data from these analyses used?

Concepts

cohort analysis (Page 343)
geodemography (Page 344)
probability sampling (Page 328)
statistical extrapolation (Page 327)
VALS (Page 344)

Terms

Anytime Anywhere Media Measurement (A2/M2) (Page 338)
Audit Bureau of Circulations (Page 332)
margin of error (Page 329)
quota sampling (Page 330)
ratings (Page 333)

People

Archibald Crossley (Page 333)
A. C. Nielsen (Page 333)
George Gallup (Page 327)
Jonathan Robbin (Page 344)

Media Sources

- James Webster, Patricia Phalen and Lawrence W. Lichty. *Ratings Analysis: The Theory and Practice of Audience Research,* third edition. Erlbaum, 2006. The authors, all professors, discuss how to conduct audience research and how to make use of the findings.
- Kenneth F. Warren. *In Defense of Public Opinion Polling.* Westview, 2001. Warren, a pollster, acknowledges that bad polling exists but explains and defends good practices and notes their growing role in democracy.
- Dan Fleming, editor. *Formations: 21st Century Media Studies.* Manchester University Press, 2001. In this collection of essays, Fleming lays out the groundwork for students interested in advanced media studies.

A Thematic Chapter Summary

MASS AUDIENCES

In this chapter you have deepened your media literacy by revisiting several themes. Here are thematic highlights from the chapter:

MEDIA TECHNOLOGY

The Go Meter. Following the viewers.

Traditional techniques to measure media audiences focused on the advertising-supported mass media of newspapers, magazines, radio and television. For broadcast media these techniques have fallen short over time. The proliferation of television to follow people out of their homes—to dentists' waiting rooms and pizza joints, for example—left millions of viewing hours untracked. VCRs and DVDs complicated the tracking of audiences. And what of web browsing? Advertisers wanted wider and better measuring techniques to help them find the right media for their messages and to weigh competing advertising rates. Survey companies are introducing gizmos to provide more detailed media usage data. These include A2/M2 devices, short for Anytime Anywhere Media Measurement, to track television viewing regardless of platform—over-air stations, cable, satellite, even the web. Some devices even count how many billboards a person passes. (Pages 336–338)

MEDIA ECONOMICS

Nielsen Headquarters. Home of a leading company in a major industry. News reports based on these surveys also help citizens track shifting moods in the country. These reports are an important part of the nation's grassroots dialogue on the direction of public policy.

John Wanamaker, the department store magnate of 100 years ago, said he recognized that half of his advertising budget was wasted on reaching people who had no interest in shopping at his stores. Alas, he added, he didn't know which half. Today a major industry exists to help advertisers make informed decisions on where to place their advertising. For a fee, these survey companies provide data on audience size and breakdowns of demographics and lifestyle. Media companies use these data in choosing content that will attract the kinds of audiences that advertisers covet. (Pages 327, 336–338)

MEDIA AND DEMOCRACY

George Gallup. Pioneer pollster.

Techniques for measuring media audiences were pioneered and honed by George Gallup's political polling in the 1930s. His core contribution, probability sampling, is the backbone of surveying today. The data are important for political candidates in shaping campaign strategies and tactics. (Pages 326, 330–332)

AUDIENCE FRAGMENTATION

Psychographic Audience Analysis. The VALS model.

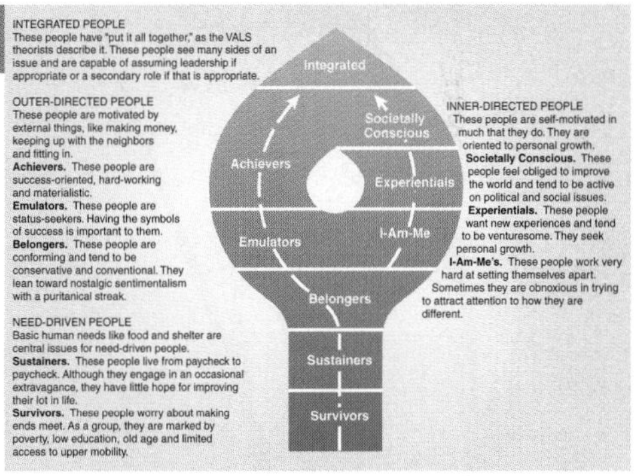

INTEGRATED PEOPLE
These people have "put it all together," as the VALS theorists describe it. These people see many sides of an issue and are capable of assuming leadership if appropriate or a secondary role if that is appropriate.
OUTER-DIRECTED PEOPLE
These people are motivated by external things, like making money, keeping up with the neighbors and fitting in.
Achievers. These people are success-oriented, hard-working and materialistic.
Emulators. These people are status-seekers. Having the symbols of success is important to them.
Belongers. These people are conforming and tend to be conservative and conventional. They lean toward nostalgic sentimentalism with a puritanical streak.
NEED-DRIVEN PEOPLE
Basic human needs like food and shelter are central issues for need-driven people.
Sustainers. These people live from paycheck to paycheck. Although they engage in an occasional extravagance, they have little hope for improving their lot in life.
Survivors. These people worry about making ends meet. As a group, they are marked by poverty, low education, old age and limited access to upper mobility.
Integrated
Societally Conscious
Achievers
Experientials
Emulators
I-Am-Me
Belongers
Sustainers
Survivors
INNER-DIRECTED PEOPLE
These people are self-motivated in much that they do. They are oriented to personal growth.
Societally Conscious. These people feel obliged to improve the world and tend to be active on political and social issues.
Experientials. These people want new experiences and tend to be venturesome. They seek personal growth.
I-Am-Me's. These people work very hard at setting themselves apart. Sometimes they are obnoxious in trying to attract attention to how they are different.

Recent refinements in surveying have yielded data that provide advertisers with incredible tools for designing messages and then buying media time and space to reach their most likely customers. The Army, for example, has breakdowns to match its media buys with specific targets for recruiting ads on scales of an urban-rural lifestyle, ethnicity and socioeconomics. This goes beyond the broad categories of traditional demographics like age and gender. The use of these data, from techniques like geodemographics and psychographics, has prompted media companies to shape their products more precisely to match slivers of the mass audience with advertisers. This has furthered media demassification—the Cartoon Network for kids' breakfast cereals and HGTV for Home Depot, for example. (Pages 342–346)

MEDIA EFFECTS

POLICE LINE DO NOT CROSS
POLICE

More Action, Less Substance. Visceral news judgment.

Media companies that seek the biggest possible audiences, including over-air television stations, use research to identify what goes over with the most people. The result, say critics, has been a coarsening of what's on the air and a trend away from news and information that contributes to public understanding and participation in significant issues. Research has found, for example, that a roaring house fire with its visceral visuals attracts more viewers than a report on a municipal budget crisis. Wags have said of TV news: "If it bleeds, it leads." The obsession of many media products on celebrities is a reflection of offering what draws the largest viewership. Celeb news displaces what's more important. A proliferation of violence in movies and television also reflects what survey data say about audience preferences. (Pages 340–342)

chapter 13

MASS MEDIA EFFECTS

War of the Worlds

Young Orson Welles scared the living daylights out of thousands of radio listeners with the 1938 radio drama War of the Worlds. *Most of the fright was short-lived, though. All but the most naïve listeners quickly realized that Martians really had not had the time within a one-hour real-time drama to devastate the New Jersey militia en route to wading the Hudson River to destroy Manhattan.*

LEARNING AHEAD

- Scholars today believe that the effects of mass communication generally are cumulative over time.
- Mass messages are significant in helping children learn society's expectations.
- Most of the effects of mass communication are difficult to measure and predict.
- Mass communication binds large audiences culturally but also can reinforce cultural fragmentation.
- Some notions about the effects of mass messages, including subliminal messages, have been overstated.
- Scholars differ on whether media-depicted violence triggers aggressive behavior.

ORSON WELLES

The boy genius Orson Welles was on a roll. By 1938, at age 23, Welles' dramatic flair had landed him a network radio show, *Mercury Theater on the Air*, at prime time on CBS on Sunday nights. The program featured adaptations of well-known literature. For their October 30 program, Welles and his colleagues decided on a scary 1898 British novel, H. G. Wells' ***War of the Worlds.***

Orson Welles opened with the voice of a wizened chronicler from some future time, intoning an unsettling monologue. That was followed by an innocuous weather forecast, then hotel dance music. Then the music was interrupted by a news bulletin. An astronomer reported several explosions on Mars, propelling something at enormous velocity toward Earth. The bulletin over, listeners were transported back to the hotel orchestra. After applause the orchestra started up again, only to be interrupted by a special announcement:

Seismologists had picked up an earthquake-like shock in New Jersey. Then it was one bulletin after another.

The story line accelerated. Giant Martians moved across the countryside spewing fatal gas. One at a time, reporters at remote sites vanished off the air. The Martians decimated the Army and were wading across the Hudson River. Amid sirens and other sounds of emergency, a reporter on a Manhattan rooftop described the monsters advancing through the streets. From his vantage point he described the Martians felling people by the thousands and moving in on him, the gas crossing Sixth Avenue, then Fifth Avenue, then 100 yards away, then 50 feet. Then silence.

To the surprise of Orson Welles and his crew, the drama triggered widespread mayhem. Neighbors gathered in streets all over the country, wet towels held to their faces to slow the gas. In Newark, New Jersey, people—many undressed—fled their apartments. Said a New York woman, "I never hugged my radio so closely. . . . I held a crucifix in my hand and prayed while looking out my open window to get a faint whiff of gas so that I would know when to close my window and hermetically seal my room with waterproof cement or anything else I could get a hold of. My plan was to stay in the room and hope that I would not suffocate before the gas blew away."

Researchers estimate that one out of six people who heard the program, more than 1 million in all, suspended disbelief and braced for the worst.

The effects were especially amazing considering that:

- An announcer identified the program as fiction at four points.
- Almost 10 times as many people were tuned to a popular comedy show on another network.
- The program ran only one hour, an impossibly short time for the sequence that began with the blastoffs on Mars, included a major military battle in New Jersey and ended with New York's destruction.

Unwittingly, Orson Welles and his *Mercury Theater* crew had created an evening of infamy and raised questions about media effects to new intensity. In this chapter you will learn what scholars believe to be true about the effects of the mass media on individuals and society.

Effects Theories

STUDY ***PREVIEW***

Early mass communication scholars assumed that the mass media were so powerful that ideas and even ballot-box instructions could be inserted as if by hypodermic needle into the body politic. It's called the *bullet theory.* Doubts arose in the 1940s about whether the media were really that powerful, and scholars began shaping their research questions on the assumption that media effects are more modest. Most scholars now look to long-term, cumulative media effects.

BULLET THEORY

The first generation of mass communication scholars thought the mass media had a profound, direct effect on people. Their idea, called **powerful effects theory,** drew heavily on social commentator **Walter Lippmann**'s influential 1922 book *Public Opinion.* Lippmann argued that we see the world not as it really is but as "pictures in our heads." The "pictures" of things we have not experienced personally, he said, are shaped by the mass media. The powerful impact that Lippmann ascribed to the media was a precursor to the powerful effects theory that evolved among scholars over the next few years.

War of the Worlds
Novel that inspired a radio drama that became the test bed of the media's ability to instill panic

Orson Welles
His radio drama cast doubt on powerful effects theory

powerful effects theory
Theory that media have immediate, direct influence

Walter Lippmann
His *Public Opinion* assumed powerful media effects in 1920s

Yale psychologist **Harold Lasswell,** who studied World War II propaganda, embodied the effects theory in his famous model of mass communication:

Who says what,
In which channel,
To whom,
With what effect.

At their extreme, powerful effects theory devotees assumed that the media could inject information, ideas and even propaganda into the public consciousness. The theory was explained in terms of a hypodermic needle model or **bullet model.** Early powerful effects scholars would agree that newspaper coverage and endorsements of political candidates decided elections.

The early scholars did not see that the hypodermic metaphor was hopelessly simplistic. They assumed, wrongly, that individuals are passive and absorb uncritically and unconditionally whatever the media spew forth. The fact is that individuals read, hear and see the same things differently. Even if they did not, people are exposed to many, many media—hardly a single, monolithic voice. Also, there is a skepticism among media consumers that is manifested at its extreme in the saying "You can't believe a thing you read in the paper." People are not mindless, uncritical blotters.

A remnant of now-discredited perceptions that the media have powerful and immediate influence is called **third-person effect.** In short, the theory holds that people overestimate the impact of media messages on other people. Scholar **W. P. Davison,** who came up with the concept, told a story about a community film board that censored some movies because they might harm people who watch them—even though the board members denied that they themselves were harmed by watching them. The theory can be reduced to this notion: "It's the other guy who can't handle it, not me."

Davison's pioneering scholarship spawned many studies. Most of the conclusions can be boiled down to these:

- Fears about negative impact are often unwarranted.
- Blocking negative messages is often unwarranted.

Harold Lasswell
His mass communication model assumed powerful effects

bullet model
Another name for the overrated powerful effects theory

third-person effect
One person overestimating the effect of media messages on other people

W. P. Davison
Scholar who devised third-person effect theory

CHECKING YOUR MEDIA LITERACY

- **Explain the ink-blotter metaphor for mass audiences in the early thinking about mass communication effects.**
- **What evidence supports the conclusion that the magic bullet theory simplistically overstates the effects of mass communication?**

MINIMALIST EFFECTS THEORY

Scholarly enthusiasm for the hypodermic needle model dwindled after two massive studies of voter behavior, one in Erie County, Ohio, in 1940 and the other in Elmira, New York, in 1948. The studies, led by sociologist **Paul Lazarsfeld** of Columbia University, were the first rigorous tests of media effects on elections. Lazarsfeld's researchers went back to 600 people several times to discover how they developed their candidate preferences. Rather than citing particular newspapers, magazines or radio stations, as had been expected, these people generally mentioned friends and acquaintances. The media had hardly any direct effect. Clearly, the hypodermic needle model was off base, and the powerful effects theory needed rethinking. From that rethinking emerged the **minimalist effects theory,** which includes:

Paul Lazarsfeld
Found voters are more influenced by other people than by mass media

minimalist effects theory
Theory that media effects are mostly indirect

two-step flow
Media affects individuals through opinion leaders

opinion leaders
Influence friends, acquaintances

>> Two-Step Flow Model. Minimalist scholars devised the **two-step flow** model to show that voters are motivated less by the mass media than by people they know personally and respect. These people, called **opinion leaders,** include many clergy, teachers and neighborhood merchants, although it is impossible to list categorically all those who are opinion leaders. Not all clergy, for example, are influential, and opinion leaders are not necessarily in authority roles. The minimalist scholars' point is that personal contact is more important than media contact. The two-step flow model, which replaced the hypodermic needle model, shows that whatever effect the media have on the majority of the population is through opinion leaders. Later, as mass communication research became more sophisticated, the two-step model was expanded into a **multistep flow** model to capture the complex web of social relationships that affects individuals.

multistep flow
Media affects individuals through complex interpersonal connections

status conferral
Media attention enhances attention given to people, subjects, issues

agenda-setting
Media tell people what to think about, not what to think

Maxwell McCombs and Don Shaw
Articulated agenda-setting theory

narcoticizing dysfunction
People deceive themselves into believing they're involved when actually they're only informed

Elisabeth Noelle-Neumann
Leading cumulative effects theorist

cumulative effects theory
Theory that media influence is gradual over time

>> **Status Conferral.** Minimalist scholars acknowledge that the media create prominence for issues and people by giving them coverage. Conversely, neglect relegates issues and personalities to obscurity. Related to this **status conferral** phenomenon is **agenda-setting.** Professors **Maxwell McCombs** and **Don Shaw,** describing the agenda-setting phenomenon in 1972, said the media do not tell people *what to think* but tell them *what to think about.* This is a profound distinction. In covering a political campaign, explain McCombs and Shaw, the media choose which issues or topics to emphasize, thereby helping set the campaign's agenda. "This ability to affect cognitive change among individuals," say McCombs and Shaw, "is one of the most important aspects of the power of mass communication."

>> **Narcoticizing Dysfunction.** Some minimalists claim that the media rarely energize people into action, such as getting them to go out to vote for a candidate. Rather, they say, the media lull people into passivity. This effect, called **narcoticizing dysfunction,** is supported by studies that find that many people are so overwhelmed by the volume of news and information available to them that they tend to withdraw from involvement in public issues. Narcoticizing dysfunction occurs also when people pick up a great deal of information from the media on a particular subject—poverty, for example—and believe that they are doing something about a problem when they are really only smugly well informed. Intellectual involvement becomes a substitute for active involvement.

CHECKING YOUR MEDIA LITERACY

◇ **What layers of complexity did Paul Lazarsfeld add to our understanding of the effects of mass communication?**

CUMULATIVE EFFECTS THEORY

In recent years some mass communication scholars have parted from the minimalists and resurrected the powerful effects theory, although with a twist that avoids the simplistic hypodermic needle model. German scholar **Elisabeth Noelle-Neumann,** a leader of this school, concedes that the media do not have powerful, immediate effects but argues that effects over time are profound. Her **cumulative effects theory** notes that nobody can escape either the media, which are ubiquitous, or the media's messages, which are driven home with redundancy. To support her point, Noelle-Neumann cites multimedia advertising campaigns that hammer away with the same message over and over. There's no missing the point. Even in news reports there is a redundancy, with the media all focusing on the same events.

Elisabeth Noelle-Neumann. *Her spiral of silence theory sees people with minority viewpoints being discouraged into silence by louder majority views. These majority views sometimes come into dominance through media amplification. The more the dominance, the less these views are subject to continuing review and evaluation.*

Noelle-Neumann's cumulative effects theory has troubling implications. She says that the media, despite surface appearances, work against diverse, robust public consideration of issues. Noelle-Neumann bases her observation on human psychology, which she says encourages people who feel they hold majority viewpoints to speak out confidently. Those views grow in credibility when they are carried by the media, whether they really are dominant or not. Meanwhile, says Noelle-Neumann, people who perceive that they are in a minority are inclined to speak out less, perhaps not at all. The result is that dominant views can snowball through the media and become consensus views without being sufficiently challenged.

To demonstrate her intriguing theory, Noelle-Neumann has devised the ominously labeled **spiral of silence** model, in which minority views are intimidated into silence and obscurity. Noelle-Neumann's model raises doubts about the libertarian concept of the media providing a marketplace in which conflicting ideas fight it out fairly, all receiving a full hearing.

CHECKING YOUR MEDIA LITERACY

spiral of silence
Vocal majority intimidates others into silence

- **Explain the way that Elisabeth Noelle-Neumann and most contemporary scholars see mass communication as having effects on people.**
- **Do you have an example of the spiral of silence model from your own experience? Explain.**

Lifestyle Effects

STUDY PREVIEW

Mass media have a large role in initiating children into society. The socialization process is essential in perpetuating cultural values. For better or worse, mass media have accelerated socialization by giving youngsters access to information that adults kept to themselves in earlier generations. While the mass media affect lifestyles, they also reflect lifestyle changes that come about for reasons altogether unrelated to the mass media.

SOCIALIZATION

Nobody is born knowing how to fit into society. This is learned through a process that begins at home. Children imitate their parents and brothers and sisters. From listening and observing, children learn values. Some behavior is applauded, some is scolded. Gradually this culturization and **socialization** process expands to include the influence of friends, neighbors, school and at some point the mass media.

In earlier times the role of the mass media came into effect in children's lives late because books, magazines and newspapers require reading skills that are learned in school. The media were only a modest part of early childhood socialization.

Today, however, television is omnipresent from the cradle. A young person turning 18 will have spent more time watching television than in any other activity except sleep. Television, which requires no special skills to use, has displaced much of the socializing influence that once came from parents. *Sesame Street* imparts more information on the value of nutrition than does Mom's admonition to eat spinach.

By definition, socialization is **prosocial.** American children learn that motherhood, baseball and apple pie are valued; that buddies frown on tattling; that honesty is virtuous; and that hard work is rewarded. The stability of a society is ensured through the transmission of such values to the next generation.

CHECKING YOUR MEDIA LITERACY

socialization
Learning to fit into society

- **Why is mass communication a growing issue in child development?**

prosocial
Socialization perpetuates positive values

LIVING PATTERNS

The mass media both reflect lifestyles and shape them. The advent of television in the mid-1950s, for example, kept people at home in their living rooms in the

MEDIA TIMELINE

MASS MEDIA EFFECTS MILESTONES

Pre-1950

Cathartic Theory
Aristotle dismissed notion that depictions of violence beget violence (350 B.C.)

Powerful Effects Theory
The media shape the pictures in our heads (1922)

Minimalist Effects Theory
Paul Lazarsfeld tested media effects on elections (1940s)

Aristotle saw the depictions of violence as cathartic

1950–1969

Bobo Doll Studies
Albert Bandura concluded media cause violence (1960)

Cognitive Dissonance
Media depictions cause overt racism to fade (1960s)

Cultural Imperialism
Herbert Schiller examined media's impact on indigenous cultures (1969)

Orson Welles' radio drama stirred panic—or did it?

1970–1979

Agenda Setting
Maxwell McCombs and Don Shaw showed that media set agendas, not opinions (1972)

Cumulative Effects Theory
Elisabeth Noelle-Neumann theorized media effects (1973)

Media-depicted violence: fun or dangerous?

1980–1989

Intergenerational Eavesdropping
Joshua Meyrowitz observed that television was eroding childhood innocence (1985)

What Causal Connection? Scholar William McQuire: Studies flawed on violence causality (1986)

1990–1999

2000–

Offensive Mascots Debated
Nebraska *Journal Star* banned offensive sports mascots (2005)

Elisabeth Noelle-Neumann says media effects are seldom sudden 180-degree reversals

PIVOTAL EVENTS

Pre-1950

- >> Greek Hellenistic period
- >> Right to vote for women (1920)
- >> Radio emerged as commercial medium (late 1920s)
- >> Great Depression (1930s)
- >> World War II (1941–1945)

1950–1969

- >> Television emerged as commercial medium (early 1950s)
- >> Vietnam war (1964–1973)
- >> Humans reached moon (1969)

1990–1999

- >> Internet emerged as commercial medium (late 1990s)

2000–

- >> 9/11 terrorist attacks (2001)
- >> Iraq war (2003–)
- >> Hurricane Katrina (2005)

evening. Lodge memberships tumbled. Wednesday-night vespers became an anachronism of earlier times. Television supplanted crossroads taverns in rural areas for socializing and keeping up to date.

Media and lifestyle are intertwined. To find and keep audiences, media companies adjust their products according to the changes caused by other changes. Department stores, a phenomenon in the 1880s, put shopping into the daily routine of housewives, giving rise to evening newspapers carrying store ads so that women could plan their next day's shopping expeditions. Newspapers previously were almost all in morning publication.

A century later, with the growing influx of women into full-time, out-of-the-house jobs, newspapers dropped their evening editions. Today almost all U.S. newspapers have only morning publication. Other societal changes also contributed to the demise of evening newspapers. In the old industrial economy, most jobs were 7 a.m. to 3 p.m., which allowed discretionary evening time to spend with a newspaper. With the emergence of a service economy, with 9 a.m. to 5 p.m. jobs coming into dominance, the market for evening newspapers withered. Television, as an alternative evening activity, also squeezed into the available time for people to read an evening paper.

CHECKING YOUR MEDIA LITERACY

- **Can you offer examples from your own experience of mass media reflecting**
- **lifestyles?**
- **How about examples of lifestyles reflecting mass media?**

INTERGENERATIONAL EAVESDROPPING

The mass media, especially television, have eroded the boundaries between the generations, genders and other social institutions that people once respected. Once, adults whispered when they wanted to discuss certain subjects, like sex, when children were around. Today, children "eavesdrop"on all kinds of adult topics by seeing them depicted on television. Though meant as a joke, these lines ring true today to many squirming parents:

> **Father to a friend:** My son and I had that father-and-son talk about the birds and the bees yesterday.
> **Friend:** Did you learn anything?

Joshua Meyrowitz, a communication scholar at the University of New Hampshire, brought the new socialization effects of intergenerational eavesdropping to wide attention with his 1985 book, *No Sense of Place.* In effect, the old socially recognized institution of childhood, which long had been protected from "grown-up issues" like money, divorce and sex, is disappearing. From television sitcoms, kids today learn that adults fight and goof up and sometimes are just plain silly. These are things kids may always have been aware of in a vague sense, but now they have front-row seats.

Television also cracked other protected societal institutions, such as the "man's world." Through television many women enter the man's world of the locker room, the fishing trip and the workplace beyond the home. Older mass media, including books, had dealt with a diversity of topics and allowed people in on the "secrets" of other groups, but the ubiquity of television and the ease of access to it accelerated the breakdown of traditional institutional barriers.

Joshua Meyrowitz
Noted that media have reduced generational and gender barriers

CHECKING YOUR MEDIA LITERACY

- **Has modern media content eroded the innocence of childhood? Explain.**

Attitude Effects

STUDY PREVIEW

When media messages rivet people's focus, public opinion can take new forms almost instantly. These quick cause-and-effect transformations are easily measured. More difficult to track are the effects of media messages on opinions and attitudes that shift over time—like customs and social conventions. Studies on role models and stereotype shifts seek to address these more elusive effects and how media messages can be manipulated to influence opinions and attitudes.

INFLUENCING OPINION

How malleable are opinions? People, in fact, change their minds. In politics, the dominance of political parties shifts. Going into the 2008 election, polls found a growing disaffection with the Democratic and Republican parties. More people were calling themselves independents. Enthusiasm for products can spiral to success overnight and collapse just as fast. We know that people adjust their opinions, sometimes gradually, sometimes suddenly. Also, we know that media messages are important in these processes.

Some cause and effect is tracked easily. A horrendous event, like the unexpected Japanese attack on U.S. Navy facilities at Pearl Harbor in 1941, instantly transformed American public opinion. Before the attack, sentiment had been against armed resistance to Japanese and German expansionism. In an instant, a massive majority decided to go to war. In 2005 public confidence in the federal government bottomed with the failure to deal with the hurricane devastation in New Orleans and the Gulf coast. Such sudden shifts result from information carried by mass media, including statements from opinion leaders.

Causal explanations for gradual opinion shifts are elusive, although mass messages are a factor. What puts a company atop lists of most-admired brands? What makes the rest of the country view California as it does? Or New York? Or New Jersey? Many institutions, including state tourism agencies, budget millions of dollars to promote an image that they hope will be absorbed over time. One concentration of corporate image messages airs weekly on Sunday-morning television talk shows.

Scholars have puzzled for decades over how to measure the effects of media content on opinion. Except for major events that trigger sudden turnarounds, media effects on opinion are gradual.

CHECKING YOUR MEDIA LITERACY

- **Give an example of sudden and drastic changes in public opinion based on media information and other content.**
- **How frequently do mass media trigger turnarounds in public opinion?**

ROLE MODELS

The extent of media influence on individuals may never be sorted out with any precision, in part because every individual is a distinct person and because media exposure varies from person to person. Even so, some media influence is undeniable. Consider the effect of entertainment idols as they come across through the media. Many individuals, especially young people casting about for an identity all their own, groom themselves in conformity with the latest heartthrob. Consider the Mickey Mantle butch haircuts in the 1950s and then Elvis Presley ducktails, Beatle mopheads in the 1960s and punk spikes in the 1980s. Then there were all the Spice Girls lookalikes in high school some years ago. This imitation, called **role modeling,** even

role modeling
Basis for imitative behavior

Asics Revival. *When Uma Thurman slashed her way through Quentin Tarantino's movie* Kill Bill, *the 1949-vintage Asics sneakers she wore, the Onitsuka Tiger model, were suddenly a hit again. In the first quarter after the movie, Asics net profits outperformed $1.8 billion in expectations to $2.6 billion.*

includes speech mannerisms from whoever is hip at the moment—"Show me the money," "Hasta la vista, baby" and "I'm the king of the world." Let's not forget "yadda-yadda-yadda" from *Seinfeld.*

No matter how quirky, fashion fads are not terribly consequential, but serious questions can be raised about whether role modeling extends to behavior. Many people who produce media messages recognize their responsibility for role modeling. Whenever Batman and Robin leaped into their Batmobile in the campy 1960s television series, the camera always managed to show them fastening their seat belts. Many newspapers have a policy of mentioning in accident stories whether seat belts were in use. In the 1980s, as concern about AIDS mounted, moviemakers went out of their way to show condoms as a precaution in social situations. For example, in the movie *Broadcast News*, the producer character slips a condom into her purse before leaving the house on the night of the awards dinner.

If role modeling can work for good purposes, such as promoting safety consciousness and disease prevention, it would seem that it could also have a negative effect. Some people linked the Columbine High School massacre in Littleton, Colorado, to a scene in the Leonardo DiCaprio movie *The Basketball Diaries.* In one scene, a student in a black trench coat executes fellow classmates. An outbreak of shootings followed other 1990s films that glorified thug life, including *New Jack City*, *Juice* and *Boyz N the Hood.*

CHECKING YOUR MEDIA LITERACY

- **From your experience, cite examples of role modeling on issues more consequential than fashion and fads.**

STEREOTYPES

Close your eyes. Think "professor." What image forms in your mind? Before 1973 most people would have envisioned a harmless, absent-minded eccentric. Today, *The*

Nutty Professor movie remake is a more likely image. Both the absent-minded and later nutty professor images are known as stereotypes. Both flow from the mass media. Although neither is an accurate generalization about professors, both have long-term impact.

Stereotyping is a kind of shorthand that can facilitate communication. Putting a cowboy in a black hat allows a movie director to sidestep complex character exploration and move quickly into a story line because moviegoers hold a generalization about cowboys in black hats: They are the bad guys—a stereotype.

Newspaper editors pack lots of information into headlines by drawing on stereotypes held by readers. Consider the extra meanings implicit in headlines that refer to the "Castro regime," a "Southern belle" or a "college jock." Stereotypes paint broad strokes that help create impact in media messages, but they are also a problem. A generalization, no matter how useful, is inaccurate. Not all Scots are tightfisted, nor are all Wall Street brokers crooked, nor are all college jocks dumb—not even a majority.

By using stereotypes, the mass media perpetuate them. With benign stereotypes there is no problem, but the media can perpetuate social injustice with stereotypes. In the late 1970s the U.S. Civil Rights Commission found that blacks on network television were portrayed disproportionately in immature, demeaning or comic roles. By using a stereotype, television was not only perpetuating false generalizations but also being racist. Worse, network thoughtlessness was robbing black people of strong role models.

Feminists have leveled objections that women are both underrepresented and misrepresented in the media. One study by sociologist Eve Simson found that most female television parts are decorative, played by pretty California women in their 20s. Worse are the occupations represented by women, said Simson. Most frequent are prostitutes, at 16 percent. Traditional female occupations—secretaries, nurses, flight attendants and receptionists—represent 17 percent. Career women tend to be man-haters or domestic failures. Said Simson: "With nearly every family, regardless of socioeconomic class, having at least one TV set and the average set being turned on seven hours per day, TV has emerged as an important source for promulgating attitudes, values and customs. For some viewers it is the only major contact with outside 'reality,' including how to relate to women. Thus, not only is TV's sexism insulting, but it is also detrimental to the status of women."

Media critics like Simson call for the media to become activists to revise demeaning stereotypes. Although often right-minded, such calls can interfere with accurate portrayals. Italian-Americans, for example, lobbied successfully against Mafia characters being identified as Italians. Exceptions like HBO's Soprano family remained irritants, however. In general, activists against stereotyping have succeeded. Simson would be pleased with the women and black and Latino characters in non-stereotypical roles in popular shows like NBC's *Law & Order* and CBS's *CSI*.

CHECKING YOUR MEDIA LITERACY

- **Why are stereotypes an essential element in mass communication?**
- **What media-perpetuated stereotypes do you see that are false, misleading and damaging?**

AGENDA-SETTING AND STATUS CONFERRAL

Media attention lends a legitimacy to events, individuals and issues that does not extend to things that go uncovered. This conferring of status occurs through the media's role as agenda-setters. It puts everybody on the same wavelength, or at least a similar one, which contributes to social cohesion by focusing our collective attention on issues we can address together. Otherwise, each of us could be going in separate directions, which would make collective action difficult if not impossible.

Examples of how media attention spotlights certain issues abound. An especially poignant case occurred in 1998 when a gay University of Wyoming student, Matthew Shepard, was savagely beaten, tied to a fence outside of town and left to die. It was

stereotyping
Using broad strokes to facilitate storytelling

MEDIA PEOPLE ▶ Kathleen Rutledge

To people who criticize the mass media for trafficking in misleading stereotypes, Kathleen Rutledge is a hero. Rutledge, editor of the Lincoln, Nebraska, *Journal Star*, has banned references to sports mascots and nicknames that many American Indians consider insulting. Readers of the *Journal Star*, circulation 74,000, no longer read about the Washington Redskins, just Washington. Instead of the Fighting Sioux, it's just North Dakota. The Cleveland Indians' mascot, Chief Wahoo, whose weird grin irked many Indians, doesn't appear in the newspaper either.

Rutledge acknowledges that the policy change rankled some readers when it was announced. In 500-some letters and e-mail messages, readers accused the newspaper of abandoning tradition and succumbing to the leftist politically correct agenda. Leftist? Hardly, responds Rutledge, noting that the *Journal Star* endorsed the self-proclaimed "compassionate conservative" George Bush for president in 2000.

Rather, she says, the newspaper is working hard to recognize diversity. Influxes of people from Latin America, Africa and Asia have changed the Lincoln area. "We've just become more aware of other cultures, other ethnicities," Rutledge said.

WHAT DO YOU THINK?

- Should sports teams be required to choose kinder, gentler mascots and nicknames so as not to offend?
- Can a media ban on references to a controversial mascot be effective in reducing stereotyping?

Banned in Lincoln. *Kathleen Rutledge, editor of the Lincoln* Journal Star *in Nebraska, doesn't allow nicknames and mascots that offend many American Indians to appear in the newspaper. Chief Wahoo, mascot of the Cleveland professional baseball team, doesn't appear in the newspaper. Nor does the tribal name Fighting Illini for the University of Illinois athletic teams. In 2005 the National Collegiate Athletic Association stepped up pressure on other college teams to drop Indian nicknames like the Fighting Sioux at North Dakota and the Savages at Southeastern Oklahoma State.*

Kathleen Rutledge

tragic gay-bashing, and coverage of the event moved gay rights higher on the national agenda. Coverage of the gruesome death was an example of the media agenda-setting and of status conferral.

CHECKING YOUR MEDIA LITERACY

- **How does mass communication wield power through status conferral on some issues and neglect others?**

Cultural Effects

STUDY PREVIEW

Mass media messages to large audiences can be culturally unifying, but media demassification, with messages aimed at narrower audiences, has had a role also in the fragmentation of society. On a global scale, media have imposed U.S. and Western values on the traditional values of other cultures. Even in countries with emerging media systems, the indigenous media continue to be influenced by media content from dominant cultures.

VALUES

>> **Historical Transmission.** Human beings have a compulsion to pass on the wisdom they have accumulated to future generations. There is a compulsion, too, to learn from the past. In olden times, people gathered around fires and in temples to hear storytellers. It was a ritual through which people learned the values that governed their community. This is a form of **historical transmission.**

Five-thousand years ago, the oral tradition was augmented when Middle Eastern traders devised an alphabet to keep track of inventories, transactions and rates of exchange. When paper was invented, clay tablets gave way to scrolls and eventually books, which became the primary vehicle for storytelling. Religious values were passed on in holy books. Military chronicles laid out the lessons of war. Literature provided lessons by exploring the nooks and crannies of the human condition.

Books remain a primary repository of our culture. For several centuries it has been between hard covers, in black ink on paper, that the experiences, lessons and wisdom of our forebears have been recorded for posterity. Other mass media today share in the preservation and transmission of our culture over time. Consider these archives:

- **Paley Center for Media** in New York, with 50,000 television and radio performances, productions, debuts and series.
- **Library for Communication and Graphic Arts** at Ohio State University, whose collection includes editorial cartoons.
- **Vanderbilt Television News Archive** in Nashville, Tennessee, with 900,000 items from network nightly news programs and also special coverage such as political conventions and space shots.

>> **Contemporary Transmission.** The mass media also transmit values among contemporary communities and societies, sometimes causing changes that otherwise would not occur. This is known as **contemporary transmission.** Anthropologists have documented that mass communication can change society. When Edmund Carpenter introduced movies to an isolated New Guinea village, the men adjusted their clothing toward the Western style and even remodeled their houses. This phenomenon, which scholars call **diffusion of innovations,** occurs when ideas move through the mass media. Consider the following:

- *American Revolution.* Colonists up and down the Atlantic seaboard took cues on what to think and how to act from newspaper reports on radical activities, mostly in Boston, in the decade before the Declaration of Independence. These included inflammatory articles against the 1765 Stamp Act and accounts of the Boston Tea Party in 1773.
- *Music, fashion and pop culture.* In modern-day pop culture, the cues come through the media, mostly from New York, Hollywood and Nashville.
- *Third World innovation.* The United Nations creates instructional films and radio programs to promote agricultural reform in less developed parts of the world. Overpopulated areas have been targets of birth control campaigns.
- *Democracy in China.* As China opened itself to Western tourists, commerce

historical transmission
Communication of cultural values to later generations

contemporary transmission
Communication of cultural values to different cultures

diffusion of innovations
Process through which news, ideas, values and information spread

and mass media in the 1980s, the people glimpsed Western democracy and prosperity, which precipitated pressure on the Communist government to westernize and resulted in the 1989 Tiananmen Square confrontation. A similar phenomenon was a factor in the glasnost relaxations in the Soviet Union in the late 1980s.

- *Demise of Main Street.* Small-town businesses are boarding up throughout the United States as rural people see advertisements from regional shopping malls, which are farther away but offer greater variety and lower prices than Main Street.

Scholars note that the mass media can be given too much credit for the diffusion of innovations. Diffusion almost always needs reinforcement through interpersonal communication. Also, the diffusion is hardly ever a one-shot hypodermic injection but a process that requires redundancy in messages over an extended period. The 1989 outburst for democracy in China did not happen because one Chinese person read Thomas Paine on a sunny afternoon, nor do rural people suddenly abandon their local Main Street for a Wal-mart 40 miles away. The diffusion of innovations typically involves three initial steps in which the mass media can be pivotal:

- *Awareness.* Individuals and groups learn about alternatives, new options and possibilities.
- *Interest.* Once aware, people need to have their interest further whetted.
- *Evaluation.* By considering the experience of other people, as relayed by the mass media, individuals evaluate whether they wish to adopt an innovation.

cultural imperialism
One culture's dominance over another

The adoption process has two additional steps in which the media play a small role: the trial stage, in which an innovation is given a try, and the final stage, in which the innovation is either adopted or rejected.

CHECKING YOUR MEDIA LITERACY

- **What is the role of mass communication in connecting us to the past?**
- **How does mass communication resolve diverse values in contemporary society?**

Herbert Schiller. *Schiller sounded the alarm that Western culture, epitomized by Hollywood, was flooding the planet. The result, he said, was that traditions and values in other cultures were being drowned out. The phenomenon, called cultural imperialism, has been offset somewhat by the growth in media content originating in other countries and targeted at U.S. and other Western audiences.*

CULTURAL IMPERIALISM

Nobody could provoke debate quite like Herbert Schiller, whether among his college students or in the whole society. He amassed evidence for a pivotal 1969 book, *Mass Communications and American Empire.* His argument: U.S. media companies were coming to dominate cultural life abroad. He called it **cultural imperialism.**

Schiller sensitized readers to the implications of exporting movies and other U.S. media products. He also put leading media companies on notice that Mickey Mouse in Borneo, no matter how endearing, had untoward implications for the indigenous culture. U.S. corporate greed, he said, was undermining native cultures in developing countries. He described the process as insidious. People in developing countries found U.S. media products so slickly produced and packaged that, candy-like, they were irresistible no matter the destruction they were causing to the local traditions and values that were fading fast into oblivion.

Plenty of evidence supported Schiller's theory. In South Africa, robbers have taken to shouting, "Freeze," a word that had no root in either Afrikaans or other indigenous languages. The robbers had been watching too much American television. A teen fashion statement in India became dressing like *Baywatch* characters, a fashion hardly in subcontinent tradition. In India, too, television talk shows began an American-like probing into private lives. Said media observer Shailja Bajpai: "American television has loosened tongues, to say nothing of our morals."

Schiller's observations were a global recasting of populist-elitist arguments. Populists, whose mantra is "Let the people choose," called Schiller hysterical. These populists noted that Hollywood and other Western media products weren't being forced on anyone. People wanted the products. Some elitists countered that

Devi. *In an attempt to stop Bala, a fallen god, the other gods each place a part of themselves into a warrior woman to create Devi. The manga comic book is part of an exploding mix of transcultural media content from East to West and every other direction on the globe.*

traditional values, many going back centuries, were like endangered species and needed protection against Western capitalistic instincts that were smothering them pell-mell. Elitists noted too that the Western media content that was most attractive abroad was hardly the best stuff. *Rambo* was a case in point at the time that Schiller was becoming a best-selling author with his ideas.

>> **Post-Schiller Revisionism.** Schiller's ideas took firmer hold in the 1990s as major U.S. and European media companies extended their reach. MTV and ESPN turned themselves into global brands. The Murdoch empire was flying high as his SkyTV satellite serviced virtually all of Asia plus similar ventures in Europe and Latin America. Hollywood was firmly in place as a reigning international icon. The largest U.S. newspaper, *USA Today*, launched editions in Europe and Asia.

At the same time, cracks were appearing in Schiller's model. Homegrown television production powerhouses in Latin America, like TV Globo in Brazil and Televisa in Mexico, were pumping programs into the United States. In Asia and the Middle East, Western programming ideas were being adapted to local cultures. Countless variations of *American Idol*, for example, from a growing number of independent companies in the Middle East, went on the air in Arabic countries. Pokémon wasn't invented in America, nor was Hello Kitty. Manga comics from Japan have mushroomed into $180 million in U.S. sales, roughly a third of comic sales.

Richard Branson. *The aviation entrepreneur and adventurer sees a future in exporting Indian legends, complete with underlying Hindu themes, to global audiences.*

Too, Western media products are adapted to local cultures. Profanities are edited from movies exported to Malaysia. For India, Spider-Man switched his crotch-hugging tights for the traditional billowing Hindu dhoti. He also wears pointy sandals.

By the first decade of the 21st century, the idea of a monolithic Western culture displacing everything else on the globe needed rethinking. Yes, Hollywood was still big globally, but other players were emerging.

>> **Transcultural Enrichment.** Turning the cultural imperialism model on its head has been the British-based Virgin Comics, a Johnny-come-lately to the comic book business. With London capital and Bangalore studios, comics with story lines from Indian religion and mythology were launched in U.S. and other markets in 2007. Other themes were drawn from the epic Sanskrit poem *Ramayana*. Could this be called cultural counter-imperialism?

Adventurer-entrepreneur Richard Branson, who is masterminding Virgin Comics, has set his sights far beyond just another product on magazine racks. Aware that the sources for franchise movie series like

CASE STUDY

Media Agenda-Setting

Immigration Demonstration. *An estimated 500,000 people took to the streets in Los Angeles to protest a proposal in Congress to criminalize millions of unauthorized workers in the United States from other countries. Critics faulted the news media for picking up the protesters' arguments in the coverage. What all sides agreed on was that news coverage kept the issue on the public agenda.*

A few years ago hardly anyone cared, but pick up any newspaper today and you'll find a story about immigration. It's a hot-button issue filled with emotion, conflict and drama. Many claim the immigration debate parallels the debate about black civil rights.

Just as 50 years ago, the news media kept the immigration story to the forefront of American consciousness, and today's media advocacy mirrors the role of the media in the older civil rights movement.

In California in 2006 a few advocacy groups wanted to organize a protest to a bill in Congress that would criminalize millions of unauthorized workers and punish those who helped them, including social and religious groups. It also called for the construction of a wall along the U.S.–Mexico border.

About 10 groups wanted to organize a protest in Los Angeles, said Noé Hernández, an immigrant rights activist. "Then they invited members of the Spanish press, and everything changed." Spanish-language DJs spread the word. So did television stations with information on how to participate.

The stunned mainstream news media stepped up coverage. An estimated 500,000 people took to the streets of Los Angeles. About 300,000 participated in Chicago. Similar protests were held in other cities across the country. In Atlanta 80,000 Latinos did not show up for work one day as part of a citywide boycott.

The media were criticized, mostly by those who leaned to the right politically. They charged that the news coverage was advocacy. Critics on the left criticized the words used in the media to frame the debate. Saurav Sarkar of Fairness & Accuracy in Reporting said: "The mainstream media helped to set the terms of the debate by endlessly repeating catchphrases and buzzwords like *porous borders* and *comprehensive immigration reform.*"

The words most often criticized were *illegal* and *alien*. The National Association of Hispanic Journalists said the words dehumanized people and stereotyped them as having committed a crime. An estimated 40 percent of the group referred to as illegal immigrants initially had valid visas but did not return to their native countries when their visas expired. Some former students fell into this category. However it was worded, the media set the country's agenda to debate the immigration question.

DEEPENING YOUR MEDIA LITERACY

EXPLORE THE ISSUE

Check a major news site like CNN or *USA Today* for a recent story on illegal immigration in which a special interest group is a source for information or opinion.

DIG DEEPER

What can you find out about this group and its leadership, financing, positions, activism and lobbying?

WHAT DO YOU THINK?

Does media coverage of the group help set the agenda for national debate on immigration policy? Should media coverage be setting the agenda? If not the media, who?

Superman, *Batman*, *Spider-Man* and *X-Men* are nearing exhaustion, Branson is looking to Indian mythology as a Next Big Thing. The comic *Sudhu*, about a Brit who discovers he was a Hindu holy man in a previous life, will become a Virgin movie. Self-help author Deepak Chopra has been contracted to write the screenplay, with actor Nicolas Cage to play the lead. John Woo, whose action films include *Mission: Impossible 2*, cocreated a China-themed story, *Seven Brothers*, for Virgin. For other story lines, Branson is leaning on movie director Guy Ritchie.

The Virgin Comics phenomenon is hardly isolated. Think Al-Jazeera, the Middle Eastern news channel that went global in 2006. Think the Chinese policy to become a global player in motion pictures. This can be seen as enriching. Scholar George Steiner has made the point that U.S. and European cultures are the richer for, not corrupted by, the continuing presence of Greek mythology from over 2,000 years ago. Sociologist Michael Tracey points to silent-movie comedian Charlie Chaplin, whose humor traveled well in other cultures: "Was it not Chaplin's real genius to strike some common chord, uniting the whole of humanity?"

CHECKING YOUR MEDIA LITERACY

- **Why was Herbert Schiller alarmed by what he called cultural imperialism?**
- **Was Schiller's concern about cultural imperialism warranted?**
- **Can transcultural communication be enriching even if also imperialist? Why or why not?**

Behavioral Effects

STUDY PREVIEW

The overstated magic bullet theory on how mass communication affects people has been perpetuated by advertising. The message is "buy me" or "test me" either immediately or soon. Manipulative advertising can have behavioral effects, although some techniques, like subliminal messages, are overrated and dubious.

MOTIVATIONAL MESSAGES

The 1940s marked the beginning of a confusing period about the effects of mass communication that remains with us. Early magic bullet theories, challenged by Lazarsfeld and others, were falling apart. Even so, as World War II progressed, people had a growing uneasiness about how media might be affecting them. Sinister possibilities were evident in the work of Joseph Goebbels, the minister of propaganda and public enlightenment in Nazi Germany. His mantra for using the media: Tell lies often enough and loudly enough, and they'll be believed. In the Pacific the Japanese beamed the infamous Tokyo Rose radio broadcasts to GIs to lower morale. Then during the Korean war in the early 1950s, a macabre fascination developed with so-called brainwashing techniques used on U.S. prisoners of war. In this same period, the work of Austrian psychiatrist **Sigmund Freud,** which emphasized hidden motivations and repressed sexual impulses, was being popularized in countless books and articles.

Sigmund Freud
Austrian neurologist who theorized that the human mind is unconsciously susceptible to suggestion

Ernest Dichter
Pioneered motivational research

motivational research
Seeks subconscious appeals that can be used in advertising

No wonder, considering this intellectual context, that advertising people in the 1950s looked to the social sciences to find new ways to woo customers. Among the advertising pioneers of this period was **Ernest Dichter,** who accepted Freud's claim that people act on motivations that they are not aware of. Depth interviewing, Dichter felt, could reveal these motivations, which could then be exploited in advertising messages.

Dichter used his interviewing, called **motivational research,** for automotive clients. Rightly or wrongly, Dichter determined that the American male is loyal to his wife but fantasizes about having a mistress. Men, he noted, usually are the decision makers in purchasing a car. Then, in what seemed a quantum leap, Dichter equated sedans, which were what most people drove, with wives. Sedans were familiar, reliable. Convertibles, impractical for many people and also beyond their reach financially, were equated with mistresses—romantic, daring, glamorous. With these conclusions in hand, Dichter devised advertisements for a new kind of sedan without a center door pillar. The hardtop, as it was called, gave a convertible effect when the windows were down. The advertisements, dripping with sexual innuendo, clearly reflected Dichter's thinking: "You'll find something new to love every time you drive it." Although they were not as solid as sedans and tended to leak air and water, hardtops were popular among automobile buyers for the next 25 years.

Dichter's motivational research led to numerous campaigns that exploited sexual images. For Ronson lighters, the flame, in phallic form, was reproduced in extraordinary proportions. A campaign for Ajax cleanser, hardly a glamorous product, had a white knight charging through the street, ignoring law and regulation with a great phallic lance. Whether consumers were motivated by sexual imagery is hard to establish. Even so, many campaigns based on motivational research worked.

To some extent, mass communication can move people to action—at least, to sample a product. This, of course, is far short of brainwashing. Also, the effect is uneven—not everybody buys. And the effect can be short-lived if an advertised product fails to live up to expectations. Seen many pillarless sedans lately?

CHECKING YOUR MEDIA LITERACY

- **What in the mid-century American experience contributed to the belief that mass messages can force people to change their behavior radically?**

SUBLIMINAL MESSAGES

Some concern, stirred by market researcher **Jim Vicary,** about mass communication as a hidden persuader was wacky. He claimed in 1957 that he had inserted messages like "Drink Coca-Cola" and "Eat Popcorn" into movies. The messages were flashed too fast to be recognized by the human eye, but, Vicary claimed, were nonetheless recognized by the brain. Prompted by the **subliminal message,** he claimed that people flocked mid-movie to the snack bar. Vicary had impressive numbers from his experiments, supposedly conducted at a New Jersey movie house. Coke sales increased 18 percent, popcorn almost 60 percent. Vicary's report stirred great interest, and also alarm, but researchers who tried to replicate his study found no evidence to support his claim.

Despite doubts about Vicary's claims, psychologists have identified a phenomenon they call **subception,** in which certain behavior sometimes seems to be triggered by messages perceived subliminally. Whether the effect works outside laboratory experiments and whether the effect is strong enough to prod a consumer to go out and buy are uncertain. Nevertheless, there remains a widespread belief among the general population that subliminal advertising works, and fortunes are being made by people who peddle various devices and systems with extravagant claims that they can control human behavior. Among these are the "hidden" messages in stores' sound systems that say shoplifting is not nice.

David Ogilvy, founder of the Ogilvy & Mather agency, once made fun of subliminal effects claims, pointing out the absurdity of "millions of suggestible consumers getting up from their armchairs and rushing like zombies through the traffic on their way to buy the product at the nearest store." The danger of "Go Taliban" being flashed during the *NBC Nightly News* is remote, and whether it would have any effect is dubious.

Jim Vicary
Made dubious subliminal advertising claims

subliminal message
Cannot be consciously perceived

subception
Receiving subconscious messages that trigger behavior

CHECKING YOUR MEDIA LITERACY

- **Why does the fraudulent research of Jim Vicary persist as urban legend?**
- **To what extent can subliminal messages be effective?**

Media-Depicted Violence

STUDY *PREVIEW*

Some individuals mimic the aggressive behavior they see in the media, but such incidents are exceptions. Some experts argue, in fact, that media-depicted violence actually reduces real-life aggressive behavior.

LEARNING ABOUT VIOLENCE

The mass media help to bring young people into society's mainstream by demonstrating dominant behaviors and norms. This prosocial process, called **observational learning,** turns dark, however, when children learn deviant behaviors from the media. In Manteca, California, two teenagers, one only 13, lay in wait for a friend's father in his own house and attacked him. They beat him with a fireplace poker, kicked him and stabbed him, and choked him to death with a dog chain. Then they poured salt in his wounds. Why the final act of violence—the salt in the wounds? The 13-year-old explained that he had seen it on television. While there is no question that people can learn about violent behavior from the media, a major issue of our time is whether the mass media are the cause of aberrant behavior.

Individuals on trial for criminal acts occasionally plead that "the media made me do it." That was the defense in a 1974 California case in which two young girls playing on a beach were raped with a beer bottle by four teenagers. The rapists told police they had picked up the idea from a television movie they had seen four days earlier. In the movie a young woman was raped with a broom handle, and in court the youths' attorneys blamed the movie. The judge, as is typical in such cases, threw out media-projected violence as an unacceptable scapegoating defense and held the young perpetrators responsible.

Although the courts have never accepted transfer of responsibility as legal defense, it is clear that violent behavior in the media can be imitated. Some experts, however, say that the negative effect of media-depicted violence is too often overstated and that media violence actually has a positive side.

CHECKING YOUR MEDIA LITERACY

- **Why do the courts refuse to excuse violent criminals who blame their behavior on media-depicted violence?**

MEDIA VIOLENCE AS POSITIVE

People who downplay the effect of media portrayals of blood, guts and violence often refer to a **cathartic effect.** This theory, which dates to ancient Greece and the philosopher **Aristotle,** suggests that watching violence allows individuals vicariously to release pent-up everyday frustration that might otherwise explode dangerously. By seeing violence, so goes the theory, people let off steam. Most advocates of the cathartic effect claim that individuals who see violent activity are stimulated to fantasy violence, which drains latent tendencies toward real-life violence.

In more recent times, scholar **Seymour Feshbach** has conducted studies that lend support to the cathartic effect theory. In one study, Feshbach lined up 625 junior-high school boys at seven California boarding schools and showed half of them a steady diet of violent television programs for six weeks. The other half were shown nonviolent fare. Every day during the study, teachers and supervisors reported on each boy's behavior in and out of class. Feshbach found no difference in aggressive behavior between the two groups. Further, there was a decline in aggression among boys who had been determined by personality tests to be more inclined toward aggressive behavior.

observational learning
Theory that people learn behavior by seeing it in real life, in depictions

cathartic effect
People release violent inclinations by seeing them portrayed

Aristotle
Defended portrayals of violence

Seymour Feshbach
Found evidence for media violence as a release

Opponents of the cathartic effect theory, who include both respected researchers and reflexive media bashers, were quick to point out flaws in Feshbach's research methods. Nonetheless, his conclusions carried a lot of influence because of the study's unprecedented massiveness—625 individuals. Also, the study was conducted in a real-life environment rather than in a laboratory, and there was a consistency in the findings.

CHECKING YOUR MEDIA LITERACY

- **How did Aristotle defend violence as a spectator activity?**
- **How is the cathartic effect theory controversial?**

PRODDING SOCIALLY POSITIVE ACTION

Besides the cathartic effect theory, an argument for showing violence is that it prompts people to engage in socially positive action. This happened after NBC aired *The Burning Bed*, a television movie about an abused woman who could not take any more and set fire to her sleeping husband. The night the movie was shown, battered-spouse centers nationwide were overwhelmed by calls from women who had been putting off doing something to extricate themselves from relationships with abusive mates.

On the negative side, one man set his estranged wife afire and explained that he was inspired by *The Burning Bed*. Another man who beat his wife senseless gave the same explanation.

CHECKING YOUR MEDIA LITERACY

- **Offer an example from your experience of media-depicted violence having a positive effect on an individual.**

MEDIA VIOLENCE AS NEGATIVE

The preponderance of evidence is that media-depicted violence has the potential to cue real-life violence. However, the **aggressive stimulation** theory is often overstated. The fact is that few people act out media violence in their lives. For example, do you know anybody who saw a murder in a movie and went out afterward and murdered somebody? Yet you know many people who see murders in movies and *don't* kill anyone.

We need to be careful when we talk about aggressive stimulation. Note how scholar Wayne Danielson, who participated in the 1995–1997 National Television Violence Study, carefully qualified one of the study's conclusions: "Viewing violence on TV *tends* to increase violent behavior in viewers, more *in some situations* and less in others. For whatever reason, *when the circumstances are right*, we *tend* to imitate what we see others doing. Our inner resistance to engage in violent behavior *weakens*."

The study concluded that children may be more susceptible than adults to copying media violence, but that too was far, far short of a universal causal statement.

Why, then, do many people believe that media violence begets real-life violence? Some early studies pointed to a causal link. These included the 1960 **Bobo doll studies** of **Albert Bandura,** who showed children a violent movie and then encouraged them to play with oversize, inflated dolls. Bandura concluded that kids who saw the film were more inclined to beat up the dolls than were other kids. Critics have challenged Bandura's methodology and said that he mistook childish playfulness for aggression. In short, Bandura and other aggressive stimulation scholars have failed to prove their theory to the full satisfaction of other scholars.

When pressed, people who hold the aggressive stimulation theory point to particular incidents they know about. A favorite is the claim by serial killer Ted Bundy that *Playboy* magazine had led him to stalk and kill women. Was Bundy telling the

aggressive stimulation
Theory that people are inspired to violence by media depictions

Bobo doll studies
Kids seemed more violent after seeing violence in movies

Albert Bandura
Found that media violence stimulated aggression in children

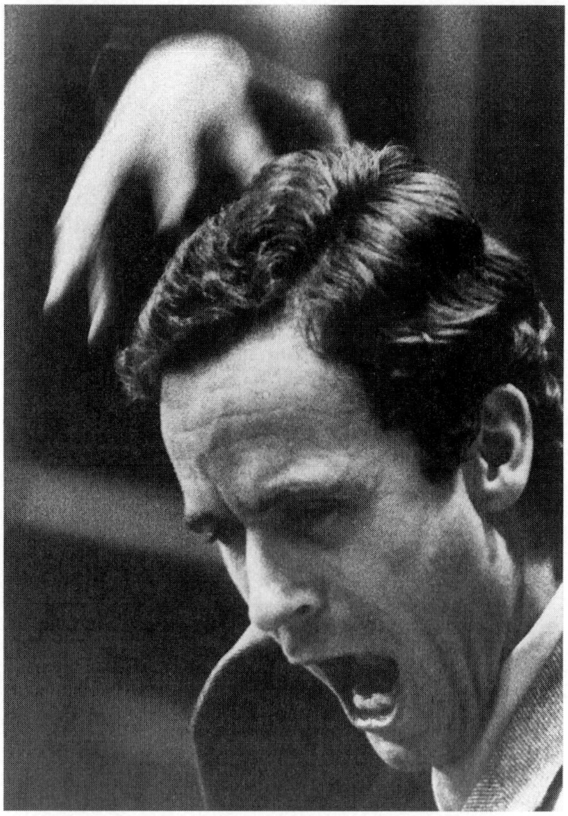

Scapegoating. *On the eve of his execution, serial killer Ted Bundy claimed that his violence had been sparked by girlie magazines. Whatever the truth of Bundy's claim, scholars are divided about whether media depictions precipitate violent behavior. At one extreme is the view that media violence is a safety valve for people inclined to violence. At the other extreme is the aggressive stimulation theory that media violence causes real-life violence. The most prevalent thinking, to paraphrase a pioneer 1961 study on television and children, is that certain depictions under certain conditions may prompt violence in certain people.*

truth? We will never know. He offered the scapegoat explanation on his way to the execution chamber, which suggests that there may have been other motives. The Bundy case is anecdotal, and anecdotes cannot be extrapolated into general validity.

An alternative to aggressive stimulation theory is a theory that people whose feelings and general view of the world tend toward aggressiveness and violence are attracted to violence in movies, television and other media depictions of violence. This alternative theory holds that people who are violent are predisposed to violence, which is far short of saying that the media made them do it. This leads us to the **catalytic theory,** which sees media-depicted violence as having a contributing role in violent behavior, not a triggering one.

CHECKING YOUR MEDIA LITERACY

- **What evidence supports the theory that media-depicted violence leads to real-life violence?**
- **How are catalytic effects of media-depicted violence different from causal effects?**

CATALYTIC THEORY

Simplistic readings of both cathartic and aggressive stimulation effects research can yield extreme conclusions. A careful reading, however, points more to the media having a role in real-life violence but not necessarily triggering it and doing so only infrequently—and only if several nonmedia factors are also present. For example, evidence suggests that television and movie violence, even in cartoons, is arousing and can excite some children to violence, especially hyperactive and easily excitable children. These children, like unstable adults, become wrapped up psychologically with the portrayals and are stirred to the point of acting out. However, this happens only when a combination of other influences is also present. Among these other influences are:

- **Whether violence portrayed in the media is rewarded.** In 1984 David Phillips of the University of California at San Diego found that the murder rate increases after publicized prizefights, in which the victor is rewarded, and decreases after publicized murder trials and executions, in which, of course, violence is punished.
- **Whether media exposure is heavy.** Researcher Monroe Lefkowitz studied upstate New York third-graders who watched a lot of media-depicted violence. Ten years later, Lefkowitz found that these individuals were rated by their peers as violent. This suggests cumulative, long-term media effects.
- **Whether a violent person fits other profiles.** Studies have found correlations between aggressive behavior and many variables besides violence viewing. These include income, education, intelligence and parental childrearing practices. This is not to say that any of these third variables cause violent behavior. The suggestion, rather, is that violence is far too complex to be explained by a single factor.

catalytic theory
Media violence is among factors that sometimes contribute to real-life violence

Most researchers note, too, that screen-triggered violence is increased if the aggression:

- *Is realistic and exciting,* like a chase or suspense sequence that sends adrenaline levels surging.

- *Succeeds in righting a wrong,* like helping an abused or ridiculed character get even.
- *Includes situations or characters* similar to those in the viewer's own experience.

All these things would prompt a scientist to call media violence a catalyst. Just as the presence of a certain element will allow other elements to react explosively but itself is not part of the explosion, the presence of media violence can be a factor in real-life violence but not be a cause by itself. This catalytic theory was articulated by scholars **Wilbur Schramm,** Jack Lyle and Edwin Parker, who investigated the effects of television on children and came up with this statement in their 1961 book *Television in the Lives of Our Children*, which has become a classic on the effects of media-depicted violence on individuals: "For *some* children under *some* conditions, *some* television is harmful. For *other* children under the same conditions, or for the same children under *other* conditions, it *may* be beneficial. For *most* children, under *most* conditions, *most* television is *probably* neither particularly harmful nor particularly beneficial."

CHECKING YOUR MEDIA LITERACY

- **Why is it difficult to demonstrate that media-depicted violence directly causes real-life violence?**
- **What variables may contribute to a person's proneness for violence after an experience with media-depicted violence?**

SOCIETALLY DEBILITATING EFFECTS

Media-depicted violence scares far more people than it inspires people to commit violence, and this, according to **George Gerbner,** a leading researcher on screen violence, leads some people to believe the world is more dangerous than it really is. Gerbner calculated that 1 in 10 television characters is involved in violence in any given week. In real life the chances are only about 1 in 100 per *year.* People who watch a lot of television, Gerbner found, see their own chances of being involved in violence nearer the distorted television level than their local crime statistics or even their own experience would suggest. It seems that television violence leads people to think they are in far greater real-life jeopardy than they really are.

The implications of Gerbner's findings go to the heart of a free and democratic society. With exaggerated fears about their safety, Gerbner said, people will demand greater police protection. They are also likelier, he said, to submit to established authority and even to accept police violence as a trade-off for their own security.

CHECKING YOUR MEDIA LITERACY

- **Does media-depicted violence misrepresent the extent of real-life violence in society?**
- **Does media-depicted violence lead people to unwarranted concern for their personal safety?**

MEDIA VIOLENCE AND YOUTH

Nobody would argue that Jerry Springer's television talk show is a model of good taste and restraint. In fact, the conventional wisdom is that such shows do harm. But do they? Two scholars at the University of Pennsylvania, Stacy Davis and Marie-Louise Mares, conducted a careful study of 292 high-school students in North Carolina, some from a city and some from a rural area, and concluded from their data: "Although talk shows may offend some people, these data do not suggest that the youth of the U.S. is corrupted by watching them."

One issue was whether talk-show viewing desensitizes teenagers to tawdry behavior. The conventional wisdom, articulated by many politicians calling for

Wilbur Schramm
Concluded that television has minimal effect on children

George Gerbner
Speculated that democracy is endangered by media violence

television reform, is that teenagers are numbed by all the antisocial, deviant and treacherous figures on talk shows. Not so, said Davis and Mares: "Heavy talk-show viewers were no less likely than light viewers to believe that the victims of antisocial behavior had been wronged, to perceive that the victim had suffered, or to rate the antisocial behavior as immoral."

Do talk shows undercut society's values? According to Davis and Mares, "In fact, the world of talk shows may be quite conservative. Studio audiences reinforce traditional moral codes by booing guests who flout social norms, and cheering those who speak in favor of the show's theme. So, actually, it looks almost as though talk shows serve as cautionary tales, heightening teens' perceptions of how often certain behaviors occur and how serious social issues are."

CHECKING YOUR MEDIA LITERACY

- **How can it be argued that media portrayals of deviant behavior discourage real-life deviance?**

TOLERANCE OF VIOLENCE

An especially serious concern about media-depicted violence is that it has a numbing, callousing effect on people. This **desensitizing theory,** which is widely held, says not only that individuals are becoming hardened by media violence but also that society's tolerance for such antisocial behavior is increasing.

Media critics say that the media are responsible for this desensitization, but many media people, particularly movie and television directors, respond that it is the desensitization that has forced them to make the violence in their shows even more graphic. They explain that they have run out of alternatives to get the point across when the story line requires that the audience be repulsed.

Some movie critics, of course, find this explanation a little too convenient for gore-inclined moviemakers and television directors, but even directors who are not inclined to gratuitous violence feel that their options for stirring the audience have become scarcer. The critics respond that this is a chicken-or-egg question and that the media are in no position to use the desensitization theory to excuse including more and more violence in their products if they themselves contributed to the desensitization. And so the argument goes on about who is to blame.

Desensitization is apparent in news also. In 2004 the New York *Times*, traditionally cautious about gore, showed a photo of victims' corpses hanging from a bridge in war-torn Iraq. Only a few years earlier there had been an almost universal ban on showing the bodies of crime, accident and war victims in newspapers and on television newscasts. Photos of U.S. troops torturing Iraqi prisoners, integral in telling a horrible but important story, pushed back the earlier limits. No mainstream media showed the videotaped beheading of U.S. businessman Nick Berg by terrorists in Iraq, but millions of people found the gruesome sequence online. This desensitizing did not come suddenly with the Iraq war and its aftermath, but the war has clearly established new ground rules.

It is undeniable that violence has had a growing presence in the mass media, which makes even more poignant the fact that we know far less about media violence than we need to. What do we know? Various theories explain some phenomena, but the theories themselves do not dovetail. The desensitizing theory, for example, explains audience acceptance of more violence, but it hardly explains research findings that people who watch a lot of television actually have heightened anxiety about their personal safety. People fretting about their own safety are hardly desensitized.

CHECKING YOUR MEDIA LITERACY

- **Does media-depicted violence desensitize us individually to be more tolerant of real-life violence?**
- **Is society more tolerant of real-life violence because of exposure to media depictions?**

desensitizing theory
Tolerance of real-life violence grows because of media-depicted violence

MEDIA PEOPLE

George Gerbner

George Gerbner worried a lot about media violence. And when he died in 2005, he had been doing this longer than just about anybody else. In 1967 Gerbner and colleagues at the University of Pennsylvania created a television violence index and began counting acts of violence. Today, more than three decades later, the numbers are startling. Gerbner calculated that the typical American 18-year-old has seen 32,000 murders and 40,000 attempted murders at home on television.

In a dubious sense, there may be good news for those who fear the effects of media violence. Gerbner's index found no significant change in the volume of violence since the mid-1970s. Maybe it maxed out.

Gerbner theorized that the media violence has negative effects on society. It's what he called "the meanworld syndrome." As he saw it, people exposed to so much violence come to perceive the world as a far more dangerous place than it really is. One of his concerns was that people become overly concerned for their own safety and, in time, may become willing to accept a police state to ensure their personal security. That, he said, has dire consequences for the free and open society that has been a valued hallmark of the American lifestyle.

Are there answers? Gerbner pointed out that the global conglomeration of mass media companies works against any kind of media self-policing. These companies are seeking worldwide outlets for their products, whether movies, television programs or music, and violence doesn't require any kind of costly translations. "Violence travels well," he said. Also, violence has low production costs.

Gerbner noted that violence is an easy fill for weak spots in a television story line. Also, in television, violence is an effective cliff-hanger before a commercial break.

While Gerbner's statistics are unsettling, there are critics who say his numbers make the situation seem worse than it really is. The Gerbner index scores acts of violence without considering their context. That means that when Bugs Bunny is bopped on the head, it counts the same as Rambo doing the same thing to a vile villain in a skull-crushing, bloodspurting scene. A poke in the eye on *The Three Stooges* also scores as a violent act.

Despite his critics, Gerbner provided a baseline for measuring changes in the quantity of television violence. Virtually every scholar cites him in the ongoing struggle to figure out whether media violence is something that should worry us all.

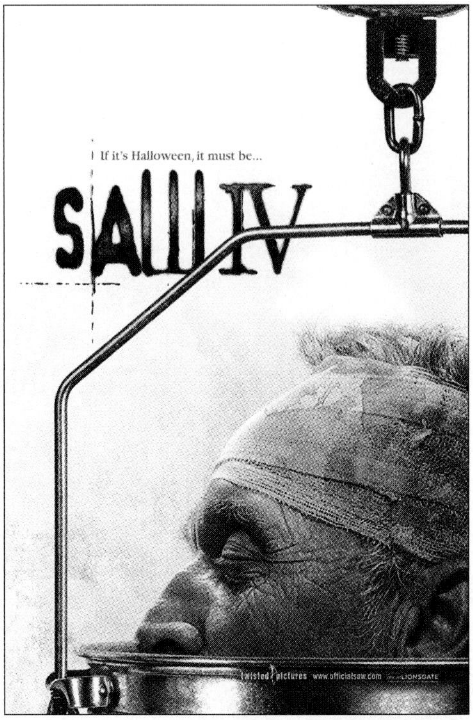

If it's Halloween, it must be...
SAW IV

WHAT DO YOU THINK?

- Why do scholars need to measure the incidence of media violence?
- Kung fu blood and guts or Bugs Bunny being bopped on the head—how do you classify the media depiction of violence?
- What do you make of Gerbner's observation that violence travels well?

George Gerbner

It's a Mean World. *Scholar George Gerbner, who began tracking television violence in 1967, found that the typical American child sees 32,000 on-screen murders before age 18. The result, he said, is that many people see the world as much meaner than it really is.*

VIOLENCE STUDIES

The mass media, especially television and movies that deal in fiction, depict a lot of violence. Studies have found as many as six violent acts per hour on prime-time network television. In and of itself, that may seem a lot, but a study at the University of California, Los Angeles, operating on the premise that the issue should not be how much violence is depicted but the context in which it occurs, came to a less startling conclusion: Slapstick comedic violence shouldn't be lumped with graphic homicide in counting depictions of violence. Nor should a violent storm.

The UCLA research, called the **Violence Assessment Monitoring Project,** concluded in its first year that distressing human violence was much less prevalent than earlier studies had counted. Of 121 prime-time episodes, only 10 had frequent violence and only eight had occasional violence. This was after comedic violence and nonhuman violence, such as hurricanes, were screened out. The next year, 1996, found violence in only five prime-time shows—half the number of the year before. Also, most of the shows didn't survive the season. In 1998, the number was down to two series.

The UCLA study added sophistication to Gerbner's counting acts of media-depicted violence but still didn't assess whether the violence affected people. In 1986 scholar **William McQuire** reviewed the literature on mediated violence and found that hardly any of the studies' evidence was statistically reliable. The exception was controlled laboratory studies, for which the statistics were more meaningful but did not indicate much causality.

Violence Assessment Monitoring Project
Conducted contextual nonviolence studies and found less serious media depictions than earlier thought

William McQuire
Found most media violence research flawed

CHECKING YOUR MEDIA LITERACY

- **What difficulty do researchers have in measuring violent media content?**

CHAPTER WRAP-UP

Effects Theories (Pages 351–354)

- Early mass communication scholars assumed that media messages had powerful and direct impacts on people. At an extreme, the bullet theory said the media could immediately affect behavior. Further scholarship found that the bullet theory was simplistic and vastly overstated the effects of mass communication. This does not mean that the media are without effect but that the dynamics of the effects generally are gradual over time.

Lifestyle Effects (Pages 354–356)

- In most of the world, mass media are integrated into people's lives from the cradle. In fact, media have a large role in initiating children into society by instilling cultural values. It is worth asking whether the media's role in childhood development is good, bad or neutral. The answer is not obvious. It can be said, however, that media reflect existing cultural values. This reflection, because values are in continuing flux, means that media content includes a rich mix of values. The mix includes traditional values as well as challenges to tradition.

Attitude Effects (Pages 357–360)

- Mass messages bring information and opinions to large numbers of people, in effect setting an agenda and conferring status on issues. What is missed by the media generally doesn't get on the public radar. But what are the effects of media content on attitudes and opinions? Scholars know a lot about the effect of stereotypes, which, when repeated, can have a compounding effect. Also, there is a copycat factor, at least for superficial issues like fashion and style. Which celebrity haircut will be the rage tomorrow? On more significant issues, shifts in attitudes and opinions generally are gradual.

Cultural Effects (Pages 361–365)

- Cultural values of dominant societies, as depicted in mass media content, have had unmistakable effects on developing societies. The extent of this so-called cultural imperialism can be debated, as can whether the effects are good, bad or nil. The export of dominant cultural values has been mitigated by the rise of indigenous media in developing countries, but there remains a lot of transcultural influence, some with content that imitates content from other countries and also the direct importation of content.

Behavioral Effects (Pages 365–366)

- Advertising research has found ways to tap into consumer psyches, sometimes with tactics so subtle as to be unrecognized for what they are. Precise control on hidden persuasion, however, is impossible. The larger the audience, the more exponentially the degree of influence decreases. Even so, a mythology exists about the effect of hidden persuasion. The power of subliminal communication has never been demonstrated conclusively to be a trigger of behavior. This is not to say, however, that media content has no effect on behavior. Media depictions of unacceptable behavior, especially when widely publicized, can have a dampening effect on such behavior. Also, media campaigns that explicitly encourage certain behaviors, as in Ad Council public-service announcements, can have an impact, albeit one that is difficult to measure.

Media-Depicted Violence (Pages 367–373)

- Media-depicted violence has been around forever. Read any Shakespeare lately? Despite anecdotal stories and testimony that "the media made me do it," scholars have come up empty in confirming the claim that media-depicted violence causes mentally healthy people to commit real-life violence. In fact, there is a line of reasoning dating to Aristotle that says witnessing violence sways people away from committing violence. There are, however, people, including the mentally deranged, who are susceptible to what's called aggressive stimulation. Research goes both ways on whether children are moved to violence by seeing it. The classic study on the issue says some children may be affected some of the time in some circumstances. That hardly is a firm conclusion of a predictable causal effect.

▼ Review Questions

1. Why has the bullet theory of mass communication effects lost support? What has replaced the bullet theory?
2. How is the role of mass messages in childhood development changing?
3. What are examples of the influence of mass communication on attitudes and opinions?
4. How has advertising perpetuated myths about the effects of mass communication?
5. What continues to fuel magic bullet theory beliefs about immediate, powerful effects of mass messages, including subliminal messages?
6. Identify and discuss different ideas about the effects of media-depicted violence.

Concepts

catalytic theory (Page 369)

cathartic effect (Page 367)

cultural imperialism (Page 362)

powerful effects theory (Page 351)

Terms

Bobo doll studies (Page 368)

bullet model (Page 352)

narcoticizing dysfunction (Page 353)

socialization (Page 354)

two-step flow (Page 352)

People

Elisabeth Noelle-Neumann (Page 353)

George Gerbner (Page 370)

Jim Vicary (Page 366)

Orson Welles (Page 351)

Wilbur Schramm (Page 370)

Media Sources

- Charles P. Pierce. *Idiot America: How Stupidity Became a Virtue of the Land of the Free.* Doubleday, 2009. Pierce, a journalist and humorist, blames the media for undoing the vision for the United States as an Enlightenment-based nation. He targets the political right for being satisfied with unscientifically verified and wild claims that, sadly, he says, find audiences.
- Christopher Pullen. *Gay Identity, New Storytelling, and the Media.* Palgrave Macmillan, 2009. Pullen, a British scholar, credits performers, artists and entertainers who publically acknowledged being homosexual as enabling gays to displace old myths with a new visibility and image. The shift, he notes, is largely in Western societies and that punishment, including death, is widespread in many parts of the world.
- Daniel Herwitz. *The Star as Icon: Celebrity in the Age of Mass Consumption.* Columbia, 2008. Herwitz, a philosopher of aesthetics, examines the phenomenon of audience senses of the charisma that makes stars and how it affects modern consumer culture, and individual lives.
- Elizabeth M. Peers. *Media Effects and Society.* Erlbaum, 2001. Peers, a communication scholar, offers an advanced overview of studies on media effects, including their effect on public opinion and voting.
- Lisa Blackman and Valerie Walkerdine. *Mass Hysteria: Critical Psychology and Media Studies.* Palgrave, 2001. Blackman and Walkerdine draw on numerous psychology theories to examine the relationship between psychology and the mass media.
- John Gosling. *Waging The War of the Worlds: A History of the 1938 Radio Broadcast and Resulting Panic.* McFarland, 2009. Includes original script. Gosling's almost life-long interest in the broadcast has led to a thorough review of the people behind the program and variations and translations in other countries.
- Michael Pickering. *Stereotyping: The Politics of Representation.* Palgrave, 2001. As a social science researcher, Pickering sees limitations to stereotyping as a construct.

A Thematic Chapter Summary

MASS MEDIA EFFECTS

In this chapter you have deepened your media literacy by revisiting several themes. Here are thematic highlights from the chapter:

MEDIA EFFECTS

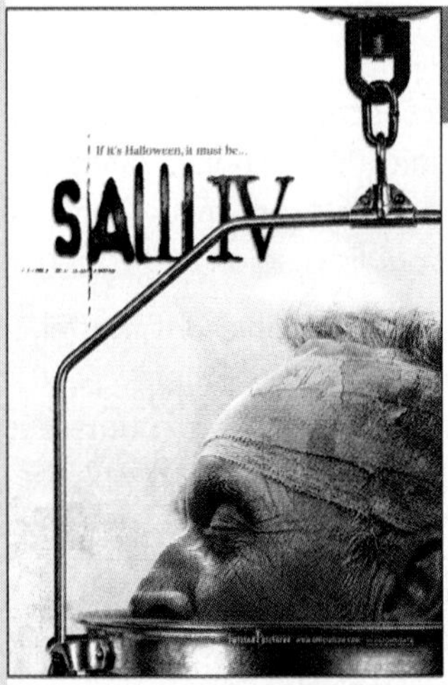

Seeing Is Doing? Personal experience tells us that media axe murders don't turn us into axe murderers, or at least not many of us.

Scholars know that mass messages don't have a sudden, bullet-like impact that affects behavior, but the idea of immediate, powerful media effects persists in our cultural mythology. A lot of the fears about the effects of media-depicted violence, for example, are drawn from the bullet theory. Scholars have come to the conclusion that the effects of mass messages are gradual, building up over time—a cumulative effect, not a bullet effect. (Pages 351–354)

MEDIA AND DEMOCRACY

On the Stump. No matter how good the campaign speech, most voters look to respected acquaintances for guidance in voting.

Pioneering studies by sociologist Paul Lazarsfeld in the 1940s discovered that most voters don't make their decisions based on campaign speeches, news accounts or advertisements. Lazarsfeld found that the greatest influence comes from opinion leaders with whom voters are in regular contact, like a respected neighbor, a teacher or a wizened uncle. He concluded that media messages are their most effective when they reach these opinion leaders, who then, often not recognizing their influence, shape how people around them vote. (Pages 352–353, 370)

MEDIA AND CULTURE

Stereotypes. Mass communication can strengthen stereotypes, as with loose characterizations of American Indians. Mass communication can also help dismantle stereotypes.

Media messages hardly are products of immaculate conception. They flow from their culture. Indeed, they are products of their culture. To find an audience, messages need to resonate fundamental values of the culture. Mass media products thus perpetuate existing values, although there can also be challenges to tradition in mass messages. But messages never can be so out of line that they won't find an audience. This process is called cultural transmission. (Pages 358–359)

MEDIA GLOBALIZATION

Cultural Imperialism. Herbert Schiller cautioned that media-exported Western culture could wipe out indigenous values elsewhere.

Media content can be pivotal when cultures collide. Scholar Herbert Schiller called it cultural imperialism when media content from economically, politically and militarily dominant parts of the world, such as the United States, finds audiences in less developed regions. Dominant values begin displacing native values, which can be lost forever. There is strong evidence of cultural imperialism at superficial levels—styles, fads, idioms. Contrarians note, however, that Schiller may have overstated his case. Not all displaced values are worth preserving, at least from a Western perspective. These include slavery, subjugation of women and suppression of free expression. (Pages 362–365)

ELITISM AND POPULISM

The elitism-populism prism that explains some mass communication effects has global applications. Scholar Herbert Schiller has seen people in developing cultures as unschooled in media literacy. These people, Schiller said, are especially vulnerable to alien values that media from developed societies export. He called the phenomenon *cultural imperialism.* Although criticized in recent years, Schiller's idea explains a lot of the gradual global homogenization in values. (Pages 362–365)

MEDIA ECONOMICS

Testimonials. Celebrities and other cultural icons help motivate people toward buying products.

Advertising has found success in associating products with celebrities and other people with bigger-than-life reputations and followings. Golfer Tiger Woods is worth millions for helping sell Buicks, geriatric actor James Garner for reverse mortgages, Paris Hilton for her product du jour. The role model phenomenon, although hardly recent, especially worries traditionalists when cultural icons engage in errant behavior. Like it or not, 50 Cent has a following that translates into retail sales of a clothing line. (Pages 357–358)

chapter 14

MEDIA AND DEMOCRACY

Arnold Schwarzenegger *Celebrity bids for public office can be disastrous—they can also be successes. Body-builder movie star Arnold Schwarzenegger, after a slow start, has won improving marks during his tenure as California's governor.*

LEARNING AHEAD

- The U.S. news media are a watchdog of government on the people's behalf.
- The mass media are major shapers of the public's agenda of issues.
- Government has many tools for manipulating media coverage.
- Watchdog performance is uneven, with voids in some government coverage.

POPULIST APPEALS

Arnold Schwarzenegger had made up his mind. In advance of an appearance on the *Tonight Show*, he had told host Jay Leno, his friend, that he wouldn't run for governor of California. On the edge of the set before going on, Schwarzenegger stood chatting with his adviser, George Gorton, who held a news release ready to be issued. It began: "I am not running for governor." Then and there, as Gorton tells it, Schwarzenegger changed his mind: "Let's go do it."

The rest, after that August 2003 announcement, became history that raised anew questions about populism and the role of the mass media in the process of representative government. Schwarzenegger was in the tradition of populist candidates, who, as newcomers to politics, rally sectors of the society against existing institutions. "Hasta la vista, baby," Schwarzenegger taunted incumbent Governor Gray Davis, using a famous line from one of his movies. He vowed to clean house at the Sacramento Capitol. To attract support, he drew on public dissatisfaction with record state government deficits, college tuition hikes and higher auto registration fees.

Was Schwarzenegger qualified? His popularity came not from political experience. He had none. When he was a young man, Schwarzenegger was a photogenic, world-class bodybuilder. He later made a fortune in movies, the most successful being high-energy action flicks that were short on dialogue except for pithy deadpan phrases like "Hasta la vista, baby." Critics said that the media made Schwarzenegger—or, perhaps more accurately, Schwarzenegger used the media to create a persona.

Is populism a good thing? Critics note that populist appeals often are simplistic and don't work. Despite downsides, populist candidates can draw new voters to the polls, increasing political participation in the spirit of fuller democracy. Schwarzenegger, for example, proclaimed himself the "people's candidate." The core question, however, is whether people are participating knowledgeably and intelligently or responding to simplistic and panacean policy proposals that aren't well thought out. Populism carries a risk of uninformed though popular-at-the-time policy changes that end up doing more harm than good.

The mass media, of course, are key in helping people sort through issues as they participate in the political process. How hard do news reporters push candidates to defend their proposals? How responsible, forthcoming and honest are candidates in their advertising, photo ops and other media manipulation? These are questions you will be exploring in this chapter on the mass media and governance.

Media Role in Governance

STUDY ***PREVIEW***

The news media are sometimes called *the fourth estate* or *the fourth branch of government*. These terms identify the independent role of the media in reporting on the government. The media are a kind of watchdog on behalf of the citizens.

FOURTH ESTATE

Medieval English and French societies were highly structured into classes of people called *estates*. The first estate was the clergy. The second was the nobility. The third was the common people. After Gutenberg, the mass-produced written word began emerging as a player in the power structure, but it couldn't be pigeonholed as part of one or another of the three estates. In time the press came to be called the **fourth estate.** Where the term came from isn't clear, but **Edmund Burke,** a member of the British Parliament, used it in the mid-1700s. Pointing to the reporters' gallery, Burke said, "There sat a Fourth Estate more important by far than them all." The term is applied to all journalistic activity today. The news media report on the other estates, ideally with roots in none and a commitment only to truth.

The fourth-estate concept underwent an adaptation when the United States was created. The Constitution of the new republic, drafted in 1787, set up a balanced form of government with three branches: the legislative, the executive and the judicial. The republic's founders implied a role for the press in the new governance structure when they declared in the Constitution's First Amendment that the government should not interfere with the press. The press, however, was not part of the formal structure. This led to the press informally being called the **fourth branch** of government. Its job is to monitor the other branches as an

fourth estate
The press as a player in medieval power structures, in addition to the clerical, noble and common estates

Edmund Burke
British member of Parliament who is sometimes credited with coining the term *fourth estate*

fourth branch
The press as an informally structured check on the legislative, executive and judicial branches of government

CASE STUDY

Governance Failure? Journalistic Failure?

Bridge Disaster. *Failed 1,900-foot Minneapolis span drops dozens of vehicles.*

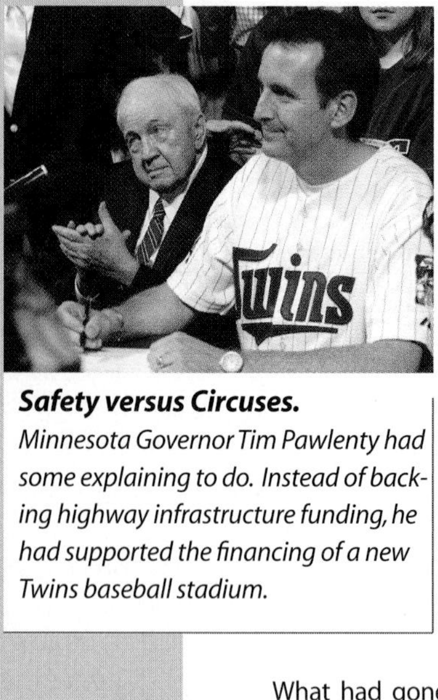

Safety versus Circuses. *Minnesota Governor Tim Pawlenty had some explaining to do. Instead of backing highway infrastructure funding, he had supported the financing of a new Twins baseball stadium.*

Bumper to bumper, commuters inched their way through a construction zone on a major federal highway across the Mississippi River in Minneapolis. Without warning, the central eight-lane span collapsed. The 60-foot free-fall was over in four seconds. Within another 10 seconds, other spans of the 1,900-foot bridge went down too. Miraculously, dozens of motorists survived, albeit many with injuries. Others were battered or crushed to death or drowned.

What had gone wrong? Within hours, journalists had access to reports that showed the bridge, part of the nation's government-built-and-maintained interstate highway system, had received bad inspection marks for years. But neither federal nor state authorities responded with any type of repairs. Clearly there had been a failure of government.

News reporters were quick to divulge that the Minnesota highways department had been starved of funds for years. Money instead had been committed recently to build a lavish stadium for professional baseball. The dichotomy was ghoulish: Romanesque priorities of circuses and games over public safety.

Negligence? Lawsuits followed the Minneapolis tragedy.

The public policy question, however, is broader than the individual tragedies. How could the government have so distorted its priorities for always-limited financial resources—and done so for years? Public policy is in fact the operational vehicle through which society decides which decisions to make. It's like your checking account. There is never enough money to buy everything you want. You have to make choices. Government at many levels had made many, many wrong decisions.

The news media, true to their watchdog function, identified the failures. But too late. Journalists reacted to government's negligence only after the tragedy. The watchdog was sleeping. It was a government failure but a journalistic failure as well.

DEEPENING YOUR MEDIA LITERACY

EXPLORE THE ISSUE

How complete is the coverage of state government in your news media? Check your daily newspaper for a day when your state legislature was last in session. Count the stories from the Capitol. Also count the words. This will be a rough indicator of the resources your newspaper puts into covering state public policy decisions.

DIG DEEPER

For the same day 10 years earlier, count the Capitol stories and do a word count.

WHAT DO YOU THINK?

From your two snapshots of state public policy coverage, what appears to have happened to public policy coverage in your state?

Edmund Burke. *The British political philosopher Edmund Burke concocted the term* fourth estate *for the press. Pointing to reporters in the gallery, he told fellow members of Parliament: "There sat a Fourth Estate more important by far than them all." Burke was adding to the three recognized estates—the nobility, the clergy and the common people.*

external check on behalf of the people. This is the **watchdog role** of the press. As one wag put it, the founders saw the role of the press as keeping tabs on the rascals in power to keep them honest.

CHECKING YOUR MEDIA LITERACY

- **What is meant when the news media are called watchdogs?**
- **What did Edmund Burke mean by his term the *fourth estate*?**

GOVERNMENT–MEDIA RELATIONS

Although the First Amendment says that the government shouldn't place restrictions on the press, the reality is that exceptions have evolved.

>> Broadcast Regulation. In the early days of commercial radio, stations drowned one another out. Unable to work out mutually agreeable transmission rules to help the new medium realize its potential, station owners went to the government for help. Congress obliged by creating the Federal Radio Commission in 1927. The commission's job was to limit the number of stations and their transmitting power to avoid signal overlaps. This the commission did by requiring stations to have a government-issued license that specified technical limitations. Because more stations were broadcasting than could be licensed, the commission issued and denied licenses on the basis of each applicant's potential to operate in the public interest. Over time, this criterion led to numerous requirements for broadcasters, in radio and, later, television, to include public issues in their programming.

Because of the limited number of available channels, Congress tried to ensure even-handedness in political content through the **equal time rule.** If a station allows one candidate to advertise, it must allow competing candidates to advertise under the same conditions, including time of day and rates. The equal-time requirement is in the law that established the Federal Radio Commission and also the 1934 law that established its successor, the Federal Communications Commission. The rule has since been expanded to require stations to carry a response from the opposition party immediately after broadcasts that can be construed as political, like the president's State of the Union address.

From 1949 to 1987 the Federal Communications Commission also required stations to air all sides of public issues. The requirement, called the **fairness doctrine,** was abandoned in the belief that a growing number of stations, made possible by improved technology, meant the public could find plenty of diverse views. Also, the FCC figured the public's disdain for unfairness would undermine the ability of lopsided stations to keep an audience. The commission, in effect, acknowledged that the marketplace could be an effective force for fairness—without further need for a government requirement.

Abandonment of the fairness doctrine was part of the general movement to ease government regulation on business. This shift has eased the First Amendment difficulties inherent in the federal regulation of broadcasting. Even so, the FCC remains firmly against imbalanced political broadcasting. In 1975, for example, the commission refused to renew the licenses of stations owned by **Don Burden** after learning that he was using them on behalf of political friends. At KISN in Vancouver, Washington, Burden had instructed the news staff to run only favorable stories on one U.S. Senate candidate and only negative stories on the other. At WIFE in Indianapolis he ordered "frequent, favorable mention" of one U.S. senator. The FCC declared it would not put up with "attempts to use broadcast facilities to subvert the political process." Although the Burden case is a quarter-century old, the FCC has sent no signals that it has modified its position on blatant slanting.

>> Print Regulation. The U.S. Supreme Court gave legitimacy to government regulation of broadcasting, despite the First Amendment issue, in its 1975 **Tornillo opinion.**

watchdog role
Concept of the press as a skeptical and critical monitor of government

equal time rule
Government requirement for stations to offer competing political candidates the same time period and the same rate for advertising

fairness doctrine
Former government requirement that stations air all sides of public issues

Don Burden
Radio station owner who lost licenses because he favored some political candidates over others

Tornillo opinion
The U.S. Supreme Court upheld First Amendment protection for the print media even if they are imbalanced and unfair

Pat Tornillo, a candidate for the Florida legislature, sued the Miami *Herald* for refusing to print his response to an editorial urging voters to vote for the other candidate. The issue was whether the FCC's fairness doctrine could apply to the print media—and the Supreme Court said no. As the Court sees it, the First Amendment applies more directly to print than to broadcast media.

This does not mean, however, that the First Amendment always protects print media from government interference. The Union Army shut down dissident newspapers in Chicago and Ohio during the Civil War. Those incidents were never challenged in the courts, but the U.S. Supreme Court has consistently said it could envision circumstances in which government censorship would be justified. Even so, the Court has laid so many prerequisites for government interference that censorship seems an extremely remote possibility.

>> **Internet Regulation.** The Internet and all its permutations, including chatrooms and web sites, are almost entirely unregulated in terms of political content. The massive quantities of material, its constant flux and the fact that the Internet is an international network make government regulation virtually impossible. Even Congress' attempts to ban Internet indecency in 1996 and again in 1999 fell apart under judicial review. The only inhibition on Internet political content is through civil suits between individuals on issues like libel and invasion of privacy, not through government restriction.

CHECKING YOUR MEDIA LITERACY

- **What controls does government exert over political news coverage in the United States?**
- **How do these controls comport with the First Amendment?**

Media Effects on Governance

STUDY PREVIEW

Media coverage shapes what we think about as well as how we think about it. This means the media are a powerful linkage between the government and how people view their government. A negative aspect is the trend of the media to pander to transitory public interest in less substantive subjects, like scandals, gaffes and negative events.

AGENDA-SETTING

A lot of people think the news media are powerful, affecting the course of events in godlike ways. It's true that the media are powerful, but scholars, going back to sociologist Paul Lazarsfeld in the 1940s and even Robert Park in the 1920s, have concluded that it's not in a direct tell-them-how-to-vote-and-they-will kind of way. Media scholars **Maxwell McCombs** and **Don Shaw** cast media effects succinctly when they said the media don't tell people *what to think* but rather *what to think about*. This has come to be called **agenda-setting.**

Maxwell McCombs, Don Shaw
Scholars whose agenda-setting ideas further displaced powerful effect theory

agenda-setting
The process through which issues bubble up into public attention through mass media selection of what to cover

>> **Civil Rights.** The civil rights of American blacks were horribly ignored for the century following the Civil War. Then came news coverage of a growing reform movement in the 1960s. That coverage, of marches and demonstrations by Martin Luther King Jr. and others, including film footage of the way police treated peaceful black demonstrators, got the larger public thinking about racial injustice. In 1964, Congress passed the Civil Rights Act, which explicitly forbade discrimination in hotels and eateries, government aid and employment practices. Without media coverage, the public agenda would not have included civil rights at a high enough level to have precipitated change as early as 1964.

>> **Watergate.** Had the Washington *Post* not doggedly followed up on a breakin at the Democratic Party's national headquarters in 1972, the public would never have learned that people around the Republican president, Richard Nixon, were behind it. The *Post* set the national agenda.

>> **White House Sex Scandals.** Nobody would have spent much time pondering whether President Bill Clinton engaged in sexual indiscretions if David Brock, writing in the *American Spectator* in 1993, had not reported allegations by Paula Jones. Nor would the issue have reached a feverish level of public attention without Matt Drudge's 1997 report about Monica Lewinsky in his online *Drudge Report.*

By and large, news coverage does not call for people to take positions, but on the basis of what they learn from coverage, people do take positions. It's a catalytic effect. The coverage doesn't cause change directly but serves rather as a catalyst.

CHECKING YOUR MEDIA LITERACY

- **How is news coverage catalytic in public decision making?**
- **What is media agenda-setting?**

CNN Effect
The ability of television, through emotion-raising video, to elevate distant issues on the domestic public agenda

framing
Selecting aspects of a perceived reality for emphasis in a mass media message, thereby shaping how the audience sees the reality

CNN EFFECT

Television is especially potent as an agenda-setter. For years, nobody outside Ethiopia cared much about the devastating famine. Not even after four articles in the New York *Times* was there much response. The Washington *Post* ran three articles, and the Associated Press distributed 228 stories—still hardly any response. The next year, however, disturbing videos aired by BBC captured public attention and triggered a massive relief effort. In recent years, many scholars looking at the agenda-setting effect of television vis-à-vis other media have focused on CNN, whose extensive coverage lends itself to study. As a result, the power of television to put faraway issues in the minds of domestic audiences has been labeled the **CNN Effect.**

A Failure of Government. *CNN deployed hundreds of staff to the Gulf Coast when Hurricane Katrina struck, documenting not only the disaster but the failure of the federal government to respond adequately. The coverage, including anchor Soledad O'Brien on the scene, kept the failure on the public agenda and forced President Bush to adjust his initially rosy claims about the federal response. The influence of the news media, particularly television, to propel issues powerfully into public consciousness has been dubbed the CNN Effect.*

CHECKING YOUR MEDIA LITERACY

- **What examples of the CNN Effect have you seen in your campus news media? In other local news media?**

FRAMING

Related to agenda-setting and the CNN Effect is a process called **framing,** in which media coverage shapes how people see issues. Because the Pentagon has allowed news reporters to accompany combat units in the Iraq and Afghan wars, there has been concern that the war coverage might be decontextualized. Critics foresaw coverage focusing on tactical encounters of the combat units, missing larger, strategic stories. In other words, highly dramatic and photogenic stories from combat units might frame the telling of the war story in terms of the minutiae of the conflict. Too, Pentagon war planners were aware that reporters living with combat units would, not unnaturally, see the story from the soldiers' perspective. The Pentagon, in fact, had carefully studied the 1982 war between Britain and Argentina, in which embedded British journalists were entirely reliant on the military not only for access to the battle zone but even for such basics as food. The resulting camaraderie gave a not unnatural favorable twist to coverage. As it turned out, scholars who analyzed the coverage concluded that the framing from combat zones is largely, though not wholly, as the Pentagon had intended. The tone is favorable to the military and individual combat units. However, the reports from embedded reporters are packaged in larger-perspective accounts that also include material from war protesters, mostly in Europe, and the fractured diplomatic front.

In the 2004 presidential campaign, advertising in support of President Bush hammered at inconsistencies in the Senate voting record of Democratic challenger John Kerry. The goal was to frame Kerry in the public mind as wavering and unreliable. The Bush campaign also emphasized Bush's consistency on national defense. Kerry, on the other hand, worked at framing Bush as single-minded, if not simple-minded, on military issues and easily misled, even duped, by ideologues among his advisers.

Partisan framing is the easiest to spot. But news, though usually cast in a dispassionate tone, is also subject to framing. Framing cannot be avoided. Not everything about an event or issue can be compacted into a 30-second television story item or even a 3,000-word magazine article. Reporters must choose what to include and what not to. Whatever a reporter's choices, the result is a framing of how the audience will see the reality.

CHECKING YOUR MEDIA LITERACY

Why is it impossible for the news media to be complete and comprehensive?

MEDIA OBSESSIONS

Although critics argue that the media are politically biased, studies don't support this. Reporters perceive themselves as middle-of-the-road politically, and by and large they work to suppress personal biases. Even so, reporters gravitate toward certain kinds of stories to the neglect of others, and this flavors coverage.

>> **Presidential Coverage.** News reporters and editors have long recognized that people like stories about people, so any time an issue can be personified, so much the better. In Washington coverage, this has meant focusing on the president as a vehicle for treating issues. A study of the *CBS Evening News* found that 60 percent of the opening stories featured the president. Even in non-election years, the media have a near-myopic fix on the White House. This displaces coverage of other important government institutions, like Congress, the courts, and state and local government.

>> **Conflict.** Journalists learn two things about conflict early in their careers. First, their audiences like conflict. Second, conflict often illustrates the great issues by which society is defining and redefining its values. Take, for example, capital punishment, abortion or the draft. People get excited about these issues because of the fundamental values involved.

Part of journalists' predilection for conflict is that conflict involves change—whether to do something differently. All news involves change, and conflict almost always is a signal to the kind of change that's most worth reporting. Conflict is generally a useful indicator of newsworthiness.

Presidents and Reporters. *In populous political entities, the best shot for the people to be heard by political leadership is through mass media. News reporters are surrogates for the public. Reporters seek information that citizens need to know and want to know.*

>> **Scandals.** Journalists know too that their audiences like scandal stories—a fact that trivializes political coverage. Talking about the coverage of Bill Clinton early in his presidency, political scientists Morris Fiorina and Paul Peterson said: "The public was bombarded with stories about Whitewater, Vince Foster's suicide, $200 haircuts, parties with

Sharon Stone, the White House travel office, Hillary Clinton's investments, and numerous other matters that readers will not remember. The reason you do not remember is that, however important these matters were to the individuals involved, they were not important for the overall operation of government. Hence, they have been forgotten."

No matter how transitory their news value, scandal and gaffe stories build audiences, which explains their increased coverage. Robert Lichter and Daniel Amundson, analysts who monitor Washington news coverage, found policy stories outnumbered scandal stories 13 to 1 in 1972 but only 3 to 1 in 1992. During that same period, news media have become more savvy at catering to audience interests and less interested in covering issues of significance. This also has led to more negative news being covered. Lichter and Amundson found that negative stories from Congress outnumbered positive stories 3 to 1 in 1972 but 9 to 1 in 1992.

>> **Horse Races.** In reporting political campaigns, the news media obsess over reporting the polls. Critics say this treating of campaigns as **horse races** results in substantive issues being underplayed. Even when issues are the focus, as when a candidate announces a major policy position, reporters connect the issue to its potential impact in the polls.

>> **Brevity.** People who design media packages, such as a newspaper or newscast, have devised presentation formats that favor shorter stories. This trend has been driven in part by broadcasting's severe time constraints. Network anchors have complained for years that they have to condense the world's news into 23 minutes on their evening newscasts. The result: short, often superficial treatments. The short-story format shifted to many newspapers and magazines, beginning with the launch of *USA Today* in 1982. *USA Today* obtained extremely high story counts, covering a great many events by running short stories—many only a half-dozen sentences. The effect on political coverage has been profound.

The **sound bites** in campaign stories, the actual voice of a candidate in a broadcast news story, dropped from 47 seconds in 1968 to 10 seconds in 1988 and have remained short. Issues that require lengthy explorations, say critics, get passed up. Candidates, eager for airtime, have learned to offer quippy, catchy, clever capsules that are likely to be picked up rather than articulate, thoughtful, persuasive statements. The same dynamic is apparent in *USA Today*-style brevity.

Some people defend brevity, saying it's the only way to reach people whose increasingly busy lives don't leave them much time to track politics and government. In one generalization, brevity's defenders note that the short attention span of the MTV generation can't handle much more than 10-second sound bites. Sanford Ungar, the communication dean at American University, applauds the news media for devising writing and reporting styles that boil down complex issues so that they can be readily understood by great masses of people. Says Ungar: "If *USA Today* encourages people not to think deeply, or not to go into more detail about what's happening, then it will be a disservice. But if *USA Today* teaches people how to be concise and get the main points across sometimes, they're doing nothing worse than what television is doing, and doing it at least as well."

While many news organizations have moved to briefer and trendier government and political coverage, it's unfair to paint too broad a stroke. The New York *Times*, the Washington *Post* and the Los Angeles *Times* have resisted the trend to scrimp on coverage, and even *USA Today* has begun to carry more lengthy articles on government and politics. The television networks, which have been rapped the most for sound-bite coverage, also offer in-depth treatments outside of newscasts—such as the Sunday-morning programs.

Candidates have also discovered alternatives to their words and views being condensed and packaged. Not uncommon are candidate appearances on the Oprah Winfrey, Jay Leno and David Letterman shows and even on *Saturday Night Live.*

horse race

An election campaign treated by reporters like a game—who's ahead, who's falling back, who's coming up the rail

sound bites

The actual voice of someone in the news, sandwiched into a correspondent's report

CHECKING YOUR MEDIA LITERACY

- **What is the problem with political news that fits predictable models?**
- **How are people short-changed by sound bites and other media tools that are used for brevity?**

MEDIA PEOPLE

Helen Thomas

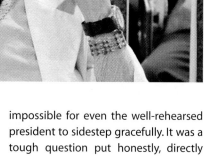

Helen Thomas grew up in Detroit, one of nine children of Syrian immigrants. Her father couldn't read or write English. Helen and her brothers and sisters read the newspapers to him. By high school she had decided to be a journalist. After graduating from her hometown Wayne State University, she headed to Washington. That was in 1942, and prospects for women in the male-dominated capital press corps were not as bleak as usual because World War II was sucking almost every able-bodied male, including journalists, into the military. Helen Thomas landed a job as a copy girl with the Washington *Daily News* for $17.50 a week. Somehow she survived the pink slips that most women journalists received when men began returning to their old jobs from the war.

In 1961 Helen Thomas switched to the White House. Within a few years she found herself the senior reporter, which meant, by tradition, that she and the Associated Press reporter alternated asking the first question of the president at news conferences. Also as senior reporter, it fell to her to close news conferences after an agreed-upon 30 minutes by saying, "Thank you, Mr. President."

During her tenure Helen Thomas consistently improved the status of women in journalism and the respect they deserve. She joined the Women's National Press Club, which had been formed in 1908 because the National Press Club refused to admit women even to cover newsworthy speeches. Thomas became president of the women's club in 1960 and kept pressure on its male counterpart to admit women. Finally, in 1971, the National Press Club admitted women.

Things have changed dramatically since then in Washington journalism. Thomas herself was elected president of the National Press Club in 1975, and she broke gender barriers at the Overseas Press Club, the White House Correspondents Association and the Gridiron Club.

It was the 2006 Gridiron Club dinner that gave Thomas a segue into her most memorable news conference question with President George W. Bush.

Dean of White House Correspondents. *At age 85, Helen Thomas is as quick as ever with questions that go to the core. She has covered news conferences of every president back to Franklin Roosevelt.*

THOMAS: After that brilliant performance at the Gridiron [dinner], I am ...(*fellow reporters and Bush break into laughter*). You're going to be sorry. (*more laughter*)

BUSH: Well, then, let me take it back. (*more laughter*)

THOMAS: I'd like to ask you, Mr. President, your decision to invade Iraq has caused the deaths of thousands of Americans and Iraqis, wounds of Americans and Iraqis for a lifetime. Every reason given, publicly at least, has turned out not to be true. My question is, why did you really want to go to war? From the moment you stepped into the White House, from your Cabinet—your Cabinet officers, intelligence people and so forth—what was your real reason? You have said it wasn't oil—quest for oil, it hasn't been Israel or anything else. What was it?

It was the first time, three years after the U.S.-led invasion of Iraq, that a reporter had capsulized growing frustration at the war in a direct question to President Bush. In a few words, without showing disrespect for the office of the presidency, Thomas had framed a truth-seeking question in a way that was impossible for even the well-rehearsed president to sidestep gracefully. It was a tough question put honestly, directly and poignantly.

It also was the kind of question that Thomas, in her 2006 book *Watchdogs of Democracy?*, argued is too seldom asked anymore. The Washington press corps has gone soft, she argues. She said media owners, beholden to government for broadcast licenses, had incubated a get-along mentality. Tightened news budgets meant short-staffing that precluded lots of labor-intensive journalistic digging. She also blamed government for a growing aggressive tendency to wield its bully pulpit to discredit news reports and reporters who venture from the party line.

WHAT DO YOU THINK?

- A seating chart that aides gave President Bush for a late 2007 news conference had Thomas marked as someone not to call on. Why would that be?
- Is Thomas correct in criticizing the White House news corps as having become wimpy?

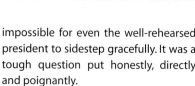

Government Manipulation of Media

STUDY PREVIEW

Many political leaders are preoccupied with media coverage because they know the power it can have. Over the years they have developed mechanisms to influence coverage to their advantage.

INFLUENCING COVERAGE

Many political leaders stay up nights figuring out ways to influence media coverage. James Fallows, in his book *Breaking the News,* quoted a Clinton White House official: "When I was there, absolutely nothing was more important than figuring out what the news was going to be. . . . There is no such thing as a substantive discussion that is not shaped or dominated by how it is going to play in the press."

The game of trying to outsmart the news media is nothing new. Theodore Roosevelt, at the turn of the 20th century, chose Sundays to issue many announcements. Roosevelt recognized that editors producing Monday newspapers usually had a dearth of news because weekends, with government and business shut down, didn't generate much worth telling. Roosevelt's Sunday announcements, therefore, received more prominent play in Monday editions. With typical bullishness, Roosevelt claimed that he had "discovered Mondays." Compared to how sophisticated government leaders have become at manipulating press coverage today, Roosevelt was a piker.

CHECKING YOUR MEDIA LITERACY

- **How do political leaders use the calendar and news flow to their advantage?**

TRIAL BALLOONS AND LEAKS

To check weather conditions, meteorologists send up balloons. To get an advance peek at public reaction, political leaders float **trial balloons.** When Richard Nixon was considering shutting down radio and television stations at night to conserve electricity during the 1973 energy crisis, the idea was floated to the press by a subordinate. The reaction was so swift and so negative that the idea was shelved. Had there not been a negative reaction or if reaction had been positive, the president himself would have unveiled the plan as his own.

Trial balloons are not the only way in which the media can be used. Partisans and dissidents use **leaks** to bring attention to their opponents and people they don't much like. In leaking, someone passes information to reporters on condition that he or she not be identified as the source. While reporters are leery of many leakers, some information is so significant and from such reliable sources that it's hard to pass up.

It's essential that reporters understand how their sources intend information to be used. It is also important for sources to have some control over what they tell reporters. Even so, reporter–source relationships lend themselves to abuse by manipulative government officials. Worse, the structures of these relationships allow officials to throttle what's told to the people. As political scientists Karen O'Connor and Larry Sabato said: "Every public official knows that journalists are pledged to protect the confidentiality of sources, and therefore the rules can be used to an official's own benefit—by say, giving reporters derogatory information to print about a source without having to be identified with the source." This manipulation is a regrettable, though unavoidable, part of the news-gathering process.

trial balloon
A deliberate leak of a potential policy, usually from a diversionary source, to test public response

leak
A deliberate disclosure of confidential or classified information by someone who wants to advance the public interest, embarrass a bureaucratic rival or supervisor, or disclose incompetence or skullduggery

CHECKING YOUR MEDIA LITERACY

- **How do reporter relationships with sources affect news positively? And negatively?**
- **Should reporter–source relationships be transparent to news audiences? How?**

MEDIA PEOPLE

Jon Favreau

Barack Obama has no discomfort invoking Christian scripture in his oratory. But the line in his inaugural address, about it being time to end partisanship and "put away childish things," from the Gospel of Paul, was crafted into the speech by Jon Favreau. Jon who? At age 27, after service as news aide to Massachusetts Senator John Kerry, Favreau had joined the Obama White House staff as chief speech-writer.

Favreau, "Favs" to his friends, got his start writing speeches at age 23. Just after college, he had volunteered for the 2004 John Kerry presidential campaign. For the Democratic National Convention, Favreau was assigned to check the keynote speech written by the little-known Illinois Senator Barack Obama to avoid redundancies with Kerry's acceptance. Favreau helped Obama rewrite an overlapping line.

When Obama began putting together his own presidential bid in 2007, he sat down with Favreau in the Senate cafeteria. Obama had no questions about Favs' resume, impressive though it was—college valedictorian, lots of civic and political activism, the Kerry campaign. Obama wanted to know Favreau's theory of speech-writing. As Favreau recalls his response: "A speech can broaden the circle of people who care about this stuff. How do you say to the average person that's been hurting, 'I hear you, I'm there'?"

As Favreau sees it, the key to good speeches that resonate powerfully through the mass media is not trickery with words but a quality message. Favreau applauded Obama as in tune with mass audiences in his 2004 Democratic keynote speech. "When I saw you at the convention, you basically told a story about your life from beginning to end, and it was a story that is the larger American narrative. People applauded you not because you had an applause line but because you touched something in the party and the country that people had not touched before."

No one challenges that Obama's strengths include his oratory, but even a consummate speech-giver needs help for dozens upon dozens of public statements a week. Not every script is spectacular oratory. But for the president of the United States, every utterance is crucial—even five-minute ceremonial appearances, condolences at a death, opening lines for news conferences, reactions to breaking news.

As Obama's speech-writer, Favreau isn't alone. He has two assistants. Their job, like that of any speech-writer, is not to put words into their boss's mouth but to know the boss so well they can help craft messages with which the president is comfortable and that will settle well with multiple audiences. When Favreau joined the Obama campaign, he wrote down everything the senator said and worked to absorb it—the words, the ideas, the rhythm. Favreau said he has found inspiration in works of Franklin Roosevelt, John and Bobby Kennedy, and Martin Luther King Jr. He consulted with legendary Ronald Reagan speech-writer Peggy Noonan.

Day to day Favreau and Obama have a close collaboration, which he has explained this way: "What I do is sit down with him for half an hour. He talks, and I type everything he says. I reshape it. I write. He writes. I reshape it. That's how we get a finished product."

Pressures can be heavy. Ahead of a major event, Favreau not uncommonly spends 16-hour days poring over Obama policy statements and speeches and news coverage and commentary, and history. It was that kind of backgrounding that inspired Favreau to take an old Obama campaign line, "Yes We Can," and turn it into a catchphrase for the 2008 bid for the presidency. It was how he crafted the Gospel of Paul and putting away childish things into the Obama inaugural.

To concentrate, Favreau sometimes bolts the intensity of the White House for the anonymity of a quiet corner in a nearby coffee house with his laptop. Caffeine is a core in his regimen: Red Bulls, double espressos, diet colas. He can't remember ever sleeping more than six hours at night. For crunch projects Favreau is up until 3, then again at 5.

WHAT DO YOU THINK?

- What is the role of a speech-writer for a political figure?
- Is it disingenuous for a public figure to have a ghost writer?
- What career path opportunities can you learn from Jon Favreau?

Jon Favreau. *At 27, as Barack Obama's speech-writer, Favreau became second only to James Fallows as the youngest presidential speech-writer in U.S. history. Fallows served two years for Jimmy Carter in the 1970s.*

Recollection Lapses. *The chief of the U.S. Justice Department later in the Bush administration, Attorney General Alberto Gonzales frustrated congressional critics with repeated claims that he couldn't remember details about controversial decisions that raised constitutional issues. Gonzales didn't grant news media interviews. Critics challenged his credibility. After months of stonewalling, he resigned.*

STONEWALLING

When Richard Nixon was under fire for ordering a cover-up of the Watergate break-in, he went months without a news conference. His aides plotted his movements to avoid even informal, shouted questions from reporters. He hunkered down in the White House in a classic example of **stonewalling.** Experts in the branch of public relations called political communications generally advise against stonewalling because people infer guilt or something to hide. Nonetheless, it is one way to deal with difficult media questions.

A variation on stonewalling is the **news blackout.** When U.S. troops invaded Grenada, the Pentagon barred the press. Reporters who hired runabout boats to get to the island were intercepted by a U.S. naval blockade. While heavy-handed, such limitations on media coverage do, for a limited time, give the government the opportunity to report what's happening from its self-serving perspective.

CHECKING YOUR MEDIA LITERACY

- **Do "no comment" answers from political leaders serve democracy well?**
- **How about ducking questions or giving evasive answers?**

OVERWHELMING INFORMATION

During the Persian Gulf buildup in 1990 and the war itself, the Pentagon tried a new approach in media relations. Pete Williams, the Pentagon's chief spokesperson, provided so much information, including video, sound bites and data, that reporters were overwhelmed. The result was that reporters spent so much time sorting through Pentagon-provided material, all of it newsworthy, that they didn't have time to compose difficult questions or pursue fresh story angles of their own. As a result, war coverage was almost entirely favorable to George H. W. Bush's administration.

stonewalling
To refuse to answer questions, sometimes refusing even to meet with reporters

news blackout
When a person or institution decides to issue no statements despite public interest and also declines news media questions

CHECKING YOUR MEDIA LITERACY

- **How can newspeople deal with information overloads that work against sorting out significant news from lesser stuff?**

Political Campaigns

STUDY PREVIEW

Elections are a key point in democratic governance, which explains the scrutiny that news media coverage receives. Also, the partisanship inherent in a campaign helps ensure that media missteps are identified quickly. Some criticism of media is of news, other of advertisements that media are paid to carry.

CAMPAIGN COVERAGE

Critics fault the news media for falling short in covering political campaigns. These are frequent criticisms:

>> **Issues.** Reporters don't push hard enough for details on positions or ask tough questions on major issues, and instead accept generalities. They need to bounce one candidate's position off other candidates, creating a forum of intelligent discussion from which voters can make informed choices.

>> **Agenda.** Reporters need to assume some role in setting a campaign agenda. When reporters allow candidates to control the agenda of coverage, reporters become mere conduits for self-serving news releases and images from candidates. **Pseudo-events** with candidates, like visits to photogenic flag factories, lack substance. So do staged **photo ops.** Reporters need to guard against letting such easy-to-cover events squeeze out substantive coverage.

>> **Interpretation.** Campaigns are drawn out and complicated, and reporters need to keep trying to pull together what's happened for the audience. Day-to-day spot news isn't enough. There also need to be explanation, interpretation and analysis to help voters see the big picture.

pseudo-event
A staged event to attract media attention, usually lacking substance

>> **Inside coverage.** Reporters need to cover the machinery of the campaigns—who's running things and how. This is especially important with the growing role of campaign consultants. Who are these people? What history do they bring to a campaign? What agenda?

photo op
Short for "photo opportunity." A staged event, usually photogenic, to attract media attention.

>> **Polling.** Poll results are easy to report but tricky and inconsistent because of variations in methodology and even questions. News operations should report on competing polls, not just their own. In tracking polls, asking the same questions over time for consistency is essential.

Not MyTube. *Presidential hopeful Mitt Romney initially declined to appear on the CNN–YouTube debate for Republican candidates in 2007. Romney said the format was insufficiently "respectful." In the initial CNN–YouTube debate for Democratic candidates, voters cast questions with creative videos, some putting candidates on the spot. Referring to a cartoon video about global warming, Romney said he didn't want to take questions from snowmen. In the end, Romney decided to participate. In general, the format was praised for bridging the gap between candidates and the people. YouTube questions came mostly from young people, who have absorbed the video-upload site into their lifestyles.*

>> **Depth.** With candidates going directly to voters in debates and talk show appearances and on blogs, reporters need to offer something more than what voters can see and hear for themselves. Analysis and depth add a fresh dimension that is not redundant to what the audience already knows.

>> **Instant feedback.** Television newsrooms have supplemented their coverage and commentary with instant e-mail feedback from viewers. Select messages are flashed on-screen within minutes. In some programs a reporter is assigned to analyze incoming messages and identify trends. While all this makes for "good television," the comments are statistically dubious as indicators of overall public opinion. Too much can be read into them.

CHECKING YOUR MEDIA LITERACY

◇ **Rank the list of common criticisms of campaign news coverage. How do you justify your ranking?**

ATTACK ADS

The 2004 presidential campaign spawned **negative ads** in unprecedented quantity. With little regard for facts or truth, Republicans loosely connected to the Bush campaign, under the banner of Swift Boat Veterans for Truth, ripped at the war-hero record of Democratic candidate John Kerry. Then there was the entry in a campaign advertising contest that likened George W. Bush to Hitler, which an anti-Bush group, moveon.org, let sit on its web site for days.

Negativism is not new in politics. An 1884 ditty that makes reference to Grover Cleveland's illegitimate child is still a favorite among folk singers. Negativism took center stage in 1952 when the Republican slogan "Communism, Corruption, Korea" slammed outgoing President Truman's Korea policy. Two hunkered-down soldiers, portrayed by actors, were lamenting a shortage of weapons. Then one soldier was killed, and the other charged courageously into enemy fire. The **attack ad** demonstrated the potency of political advertising in the new medium of television.

>> **527 Financing.** The 2004 wave of attack ads was mostly from shadowy groups not directly affiliated with candidates or parties. These groups operated under what was called **527 status** in the federal campaign law. Unlike the parties and candidates, the 527s were allowed to collect unlimited money independently. The 527s had raised an incredible $240 million within a month of Election Day. Although there was widespread disgust at the nastiest 527 ads, experts who tracked polls concluded they had significant influence. When Congress reconvened in 2005, there were cries for reforms to curb the influence of the 527 organizations. Nothing happened.

>> **Making Light.** Amid the 2004 campaign negativity, Senator Russ Feingold of Wisconsin took a different tack—humor. Just as commercial advertising relies largely on evoking chuckles, Feingold did the same and won re-election. Whether easygoing self-deprecation and deft fun-poking are antidotes that will displace attack ads, or at least reduce their role, may be determined by whether future candidates and their advisers have a good sense of humor and also decency and good taste.

CHECKING YOUR MEDIA LITERACY

◇ **Negative political advertising is easy to criticize, but what can be done about it?**

negative ads
Political campaign advertising, usually on television, in which candidates criticize the opponents rather than emphasizing their own platforms

attack ads
A subspecies of negative ads, especially savage in criticizing an opponent, many playing loosely with context and facts

527 status
Used by groups unaffiliated with candidates or parties to collect and spend unlimited funds

CHAPTER WRAP-UP

Media Role in Governance
(Pages 379–382)

- The U.S. democratic system relies on the mass media as an outside check to keep government accountable to the people. The concept has many labels, including the press as a fourth branch of government. The similar label *fourth estate* comes from feudal European times. A more modern variation characterizes the press as a watchdog on government. The concept has given rise to the informally put goal of "keeping them honest." The First Amendment gives an autonomous role to the press, although government regulation exists, particularly of broadcasting, as an anomaly.

Media Effects on Governance
(Pages 382–386)

- For lack of time and space to report all that might be reported, the media are selective in their coverage. What makes the news ends up on the public's agenda. The rest misses radar screens. This reality has been described in numerous variations, including agenda-setting, the CNN Effect and framing. What it all means is that we are dependent on the intelligence and goodwill of newspeople to use good judgment in their news choices. News people can be faulted for their focus on easily told aspects of stories, for superficiality, and for missing stories worth telling. Competition among news sources helps correct the worst shortcomings.

Government Manipulation of Media
(Pages 387–389)

- Political leaders quickly learn techniques to influence if not manipulate news coverage in their favor. Floating ideas, sometimes with plausible deniability as to their source, is one method for peeking at how the media and the public might respond on an issue. It's called the *trial balloon*. Leaks of explosive information to the press, sometimes intended to damage reputations, are another method of bending the news media for ulterior motives.

Political Campaigns (Pages 389–391)

- The same factors that lead to formulaic and superficial government news coverage extend also to political campaigns. Issues take a backseat to the latest poll numbers, reducing campaigns to a kind of horse-race caricature. Polls are important, but no less is citizens' thorough attention to candidates' character and positions. Besides news coverage, the mass media carry advertisements paid for by candidates and their supporters and, also, sometimes attack ads from opponents who can get really nasty and are not always accurate or honest. Dealing with the worst negative advertising is an unresolved issue. Everybody talks about it, but not much is being done.

Review Questions

1. By what authority are news media the people's watchdog for government accountability?
2. How do mass media influence public policy?
3. What are major government tools for manipulating news coverage?
4. Why is news coverage of political issues often formulaic and superficial?

Concepts

agenda-setting (Page 382)
CNN Effect (Page 383)
fairness doctrine (Page 381)
fourth estate (Page 379)
Tornillo opinion (Page 381)

Terms

attack ads (Page 391)
equal time rule (Page 381)
527 status (Page 391)
stonewalling (Page 389)
watchdog role (Page 381)

People

Edmund Burke (Page 379)
Maxwell McCombs, Don Shaw (Page 382)

Media Sources

- Kate Kenski, Bruce W. Hardy and Kathleen Hall Jamieson. *The Obama Victory: How Media, Money and Messages Shaped the 2008 Election*. Oxford, 2010. The authors, all scholars, offer a comprehensive empirical-based analysis that is informed also by interviews with insiders with the Obama and McCain campaigns.
- Kate Kaye. *Campaign '08: A Turning Point for Digital Media.* Kate Kaye, 2009. Kaye, a journalist on marketing news, offers a breezy account of the McCain and Obama media strategies.
- Costas Panagopolous, editor. *Politicking Online: The Transformation of Election Campaign Communications.* Rutgers University Press, 2009. Panagopolous has collected observations from fellow political scientists on new media applications in election campaigns and the effect on democracy.
- Helen Thomas. *Watchdogs of Democracy? The Waning Washington Press Corps and How It Has Failed the Public.* Scribner/Lisa Dew, 2006. Thomas, a veteran White House reporter, blames adversarial news media on an unholy alliance of big government and big business to control the news, sometimes subtly, sometimes not.
- David D. Perlmutter. "Political Blogs: The New Iowa?" *Chronicle of Higher Education* (May 26, 2006), Pages B6–B8. Perlmutter, a political scientist, examines the potential of blogs in presidential campaigns. He has as many questions as answers about this new medium in candidates' quivers.
- Craig Crawford. *Attack the Messenger: How Politicians Turn You Against the Messenger.* Littlefield, 2005. Crawford, a *Congressional Quarterly* columnist, examines White House policies in the Bush administrations to undermine the mainstream news media.

MEDIA AND DEMOCRACY

In this chapter you have deepened your media literacy by revisiting several themes. Here are thematic highlights from the chapter:

MEDIA TECHNOLOGY

Photogenic Candidates. The role of television and other visual media in politics is undeniable. Could the portly William Howard Taft, who won the presidency in pretelevision 1912, be elected president today? Taft carried 321 pounds. In 1960, John Kennedy's calm command of issues won over voters in a televised debate as his opponent, Richard Nixon, sweated in obvious discomfort in the studio lights. Kennedy won.

Since the earliest days of the republic, political candidates and leaders have used leading media technology to seek public support. Newspapers were the medium of choice back then. Newspapers were joined by radio in the 1930s, when President Franklin Roosevelt combined the novelty of the emerging medium and a public yearning for leadership to solve the Great Depression. As a political tool, radio came of age during Roosevelt's four terms. In 1960, Senator John Kennedy exuded confidence, some said charisma, on television. He won the presidency. A former Vermont governor, Howard Dean, relied on the Internet to raise funds for his 2004 presidential bid and to spread his message. Dean washed out in later primaries. Nonetheless, he wrote the how-to book for other candidates on the potential of the latest mass medium and of blogging. (Page 387)

ELITISM AND POPULISM

Edmund Burke. His contributions to modern political thought came in essays and speeches, mostly in the 1770s and later. Burke, who served in Parliament, saw the role of political parties as an important link between competing branches of government and as vehicles for continuity. He saw the press as a powerful vehicle in the political process. He called the press a *fourth estate* and declared it as powerful as the traditional institutions of society—the nobility, the clergy and commoners.

British political philosopher Edmund Burke put a name to the role of the news media in the political life of a democratic society. Burke called the press a *fourth estate*, every much as powerful as the nobility, the clergy and the common people as institutions that influence the course of events. The founders of the United States saw the press as a conduit for information and ideas, back and forth between the people and the elected leadership. In the United States the press came to be called a *fourth branch* of government, in addition to the executive, legislative and judicial branches, but functioning outside the structure of the constituted branches. (Pages 379–382)

MEDIA AND DEMOCRACY

Mass media have essential roles in democracy, including that of watchdog. Theoretically immune to government control under the U.S. Constitution, the media are like an outside auditor to assure the people of government accountability. The media accountability system, however, lacks the precision of audits in the sense of bookkeeping and works unevenly. Working against the accountability system is that political leaders have mastered tools for influencing news coverage to their advantage. Also, the media sometimes falter in their watchdog function. (Pages 379–382)

MEDIA FUTURE

Fourth Estate. The rationale for news being independent of government control worked, albeit too late, when a commuter-clogged bridge collapsed in Minneapolis because of unmended structural shortcomings. To the chagrin of Minnesota Governor Tim Pawlenty, news reports divulged the governor's support of state spending to build a new Twins baseball stadium even as the state's highway infrastructure was falling apart. The dichotomy was driven home by photos of Pawlenty grinning at Twins fans three months earlier while signing the stadium legislation. Within a week of the bridge collapse, however, Pawlenty announced that he had changed his position against a gasoline tax increase to generate new revenue for highway repairs.

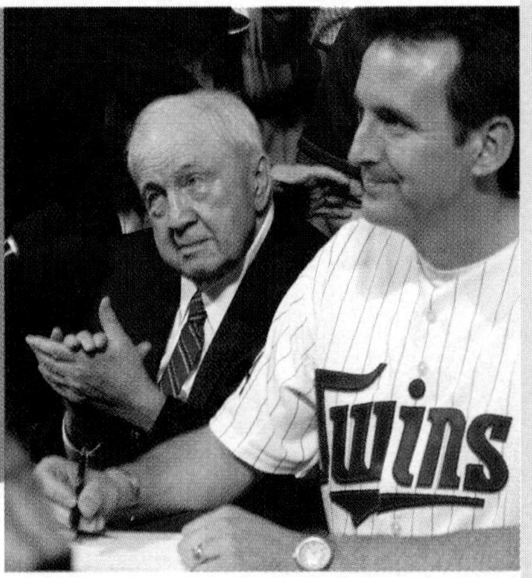

With the first $1 billion presidential campaign in 2008, most of it for television advertising, campaign spending reform is a bigger issue than ever. The costs have forced candidates into a financial dependency on big donors, many with self-serving public policy agendas. Existing limits on campaign spending donations are so big that deep-pocket donors could drive truckloads of cash through. Major advertising, for example, is funded by shadowy partisan organizations that support some candidates but have no direct ties to the candidates. Proposals also grew to give candidates free time for advertising on television, the most-used medium. (Pages 389–391)

MEDIA AND CULTURE

Not MyTube. Presidential hopeful Mitt Romney turned down an initial invitation to the CNN–YouTube debates. He didn't want to encourage "disrespectful" questions. Whether Romney's refusal hurt his standing with young voters, many for whom YouTube is a favorite site, wasn't clear. One wag encouraged Romney to loosen up: "Maybe Mrs. Romney should put less starch in his boxers." In the end, Romney relented and participated in the debate.

Lifestyle changes wrought by mass media technology don't settle easily with everyone. In political life, candidates and leaders with squeaky voices and shrill pitches don't come across effectively. The CNN-YouTube presidential debates in 2007 attempted to employ the immense new popularity of video sharing on the Internet, a sudden staple in the U.S. youth culture, in the public policy dialogue in the presidential campaigns. One candidate, Mitt Romney, at first declined to participate in the debates. He said he preferred questions from professional journalists and characterized YouTube questions as "disrespectful." (Pages 389–391)

chapter 15

MASS MEDIA GLOBALIZATION

Hellfire Evidence *Missile fragments photographed by Hayatullah Khan suggest that the U.S. Central Intelligence Agency was responsible for a remote-control bombing in a remote Pakistani region that killed an Al-Qaeda leader. It was contrary to official policy for the U.S. military to be venturing into Pakistan.*

LEARNING AHEAD

- Mass media reflect a nation's political system.
- War can force compromises in media freedom.
- Market forces are transforming some Arab media.
- Terrorists have adapted digital media as a propaganda tool.
- Media are central in a Cold War-style battle for reforms in Iran.
- China has the broadest censorship apparatus in history.
- Variations exist among national media systems, even in democracies.

THE HELLFIRE PICTURES

When journalist Hayatullah Khan heard that an important Al-Qaeda commander had been killed in the tribal-controlled Waziristan region of Pakistan, he rushed to the scene. Khan took photos of the shambles of the house where, the government said, the Al-Qaeda leader had been making a bomb when it blew up. Khan's photos showed something else—fragments of a U.S.

Hellfire missile. Khan's story, with photos, reported that the missile had been fired from a U.S. spy drone—a sensational report that contradicted both U.S. and Pakistani official insistence that the U.S. anti-terrorism resources were honoring Pakistan's sovereignty and staying within the borders of neighboring Afghanistan.

Officials at the U.S. Central Intelligence Agency, which operates drones, were displeased with Khan's reporting. So was the Pakistani government. Within days of Khan's revelations, Khan vanished. Six months later, his body was found dumped in northern Waziristan, handcuffed and shot in the back.

Khan's family blamed the Pakistani government. The government blamed intrigue—somebody out to malign the government. Whatever the truth, Khan's death is testimony to the danger facing war correspondents, especially in tribal no-man's territories. Over two years, five reporters who ventured into Waziristan were killed. Now almost all reporting from the area is secondhand, with reporters using telephones to call into the region from the relative safety of Peshawar and faraway cities.

In this chapter you will discover how the mass media fit into the global geopolitical environment. The media are players not only in crisis moments, like war, but also in evolving globalization.

Mass Media and Nation-States

STUDY ***PREVIEW***

The world's nations and media systems fall into competing, philosophically irreconcilable systems. Authoritarianism places confidence in political and sometimes theocratic leadership for governance. In contrast, libertarianism emphasizes the ability of human beings to reason their own way to right conclusions and therefore believes humans are capable of their own governance. Democracy and a free mass media are in the libertarian tradition.

AUTHORITARIANISM

Throughout mass media history, **authoritarian** political systems have been the most common. The powerful monarchies were authoritarian. In 1529, King Henry VIII of England outlawed imported publications because many presses were producing materials that bordered on sedition and treason. Also authoritarian were Nazi Germany and Franco's Spain in the 1900s. The Soviets had their own twist on authoritarianism. Today, dictatorships and theocracies continue the tradition. A premise of authoritarian systems is that the government is infallible, which places its policies beyond questioning. The media's role in an authoritarian society is subservience to government.

>> **Censorship.** Authoritarian regimes have found numerous ways, both blatant and subtle, to control mass media. Censorship is one. The most thorough censoring requires that manuscripts be read by government agents before being printed or aired. To work, **pre-publication censorship** requires a government agent in every newsroom and everywhere else that mass media messages are produced. Such thorough censorship is hardly practicable, although governments sometimes establish censorship bureaucracies during wartime to protect sensitive military information and to ban information that runs counter to their propaganda. Most authoritarian regimes have opted instead for post-publication action against dissidents. The effect of the execution of a media person who strayed beyond what's acceptable can be chilling to like-minded people.

authoritarianism
Top-down governance such as a monarchy or dictatorship

pre-publication censorship
Authorities preview material before dissemination

>> **Authoritarian Effectiveness.** Authoritarian controls can have short-term effectiveness, but truth is hard to suppress for very long. In Franco's Spain, which was allied with Germany in World War II, the news media were mum for years

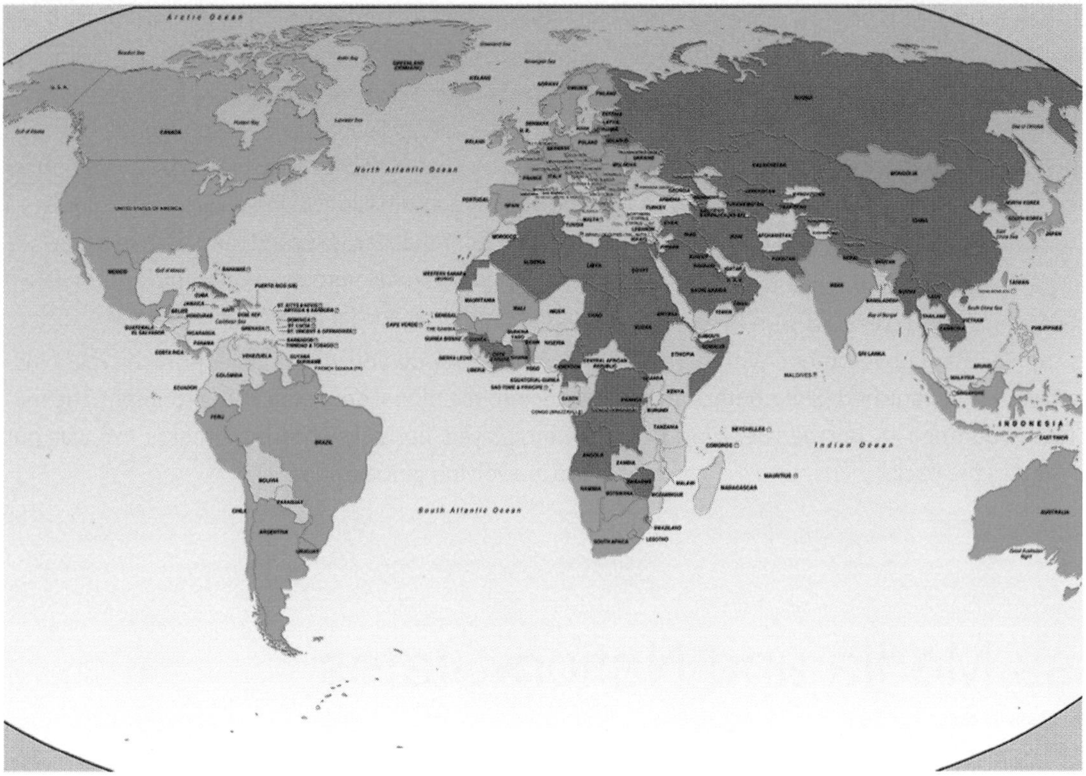

Color-Coding Freedom. *Freedom House, which tracks the freedom of the news media worldwide, reports relatively few countries where news and information flow freely within and across their borders. Green shows countries that Freedom House regards as free, yellow as partly free, and purple as not free. The number of free countries has grown over 20 years from 31 percent to 40 percent.*

about Nazi atrocities against Jews. Despite the media blackout, the Spanish people were aware of the Holocaust. People do not receive all their information through the mass media. Especially if people have come to distrust the accuracy or thoroughness of an authoritarian medium, they pay special attention to alternative sources. They talk to travelers. They read contraband publications. They listen secretly to transborder newscasts. They tap into the Internet. In recent years, China has created the largest censorship apparatus in history to maintain ideological control, complete with electronic and Internet monitoring and intercepts, but the system leaks. It's an open question whether the Chinese will come to recognize the futility of pre-publication censorship, as have earlier authoritarian-minded regimes.

Authoritarian Execution. *Authoritarian governments prevent mass media criticism of their policies with numerous methods, including execution. In authoritarian England, the Crown made spectacles of executions. Here, a crowd gathered in 1619 to witness the execution of John de Barneveld, which had a chilling effect on other people who might have challenged the Crown.*

Divine Right. *King James I, who fancied himself a scholar, wrote a treatise in 1598 that claimed monarchies were legitimate because of a pipeline to God. His theory, called the divine right of kings, is a classic defense for authoritarian political and media systems.*

>> Global Authoritarianism. Authoritarianism dies hard. The organization Freedom House, which monitors press freedom worldwide, lists 45 nations that deny a broad range of freedoms. The eight worst-rated countries include Cuba and North Korea, both Marxist-Leninist regimes. Turkmenistan and Uzbekistan in central Asia are ruled by dictators with roots in the Soviet period. Arab countries Libya and Syria are under secular dictatorships. Sudan is under leadership that has elements of both radical Islamism and military juntas. Burma has a tightly controlled military dictatorship. Tibet, although not a country but under Chinese jurisdiction, rates among the bottom-most territories. So does the former Soviet republic of Chechnya, where an indigenous Islamic population is engaged in a brutal guerrilla war for independence from Russia.

>> Authoritarian Premises. Authoritarian media systems make sense to anyone who accepts the premise that the government, whether embodied by a monarch or a dictator, is right in all that it says and does. Such a premise is anathema to most people in democracies today, but merely 400 years ago it was mainstream Western thought. **King James VI** of Scotland, who later became James I of England, made an eloquent argument for the **divine right of kings** in 1598. He claimed that legitimate monarchs were anointed by an Almighty and thereby were better able to express righteousness and truth than anyone else. By definition, therefore, anybody who differed with the monarch was embracing falsity and probably heresy.

The authoritarian line of reasoning justifies suppression of ideas and information on numerous grounds:

- Truth is a monopoly of the regime. Commoners can come to know truth only through the ruler, who in King James' thinking had an exclusive pipeline to an Almighty. Advocates of authoritarianism hold little confidence in individuals.
- Challenges to government are based on falsity. It could not be otherwise, considering the premise that rulers are infallible.
- Without strong government, the stability necessary for society to function may be disrupted. Because challenges to government tend to undermine stability and because challenges are presumed to be false to begin with, they must be suppressed.

To the authoritarian mind, media people who support the government are purveying truth and should be rewarded. The unfaithful, those who criticize, are spreading falsity and should be banished. It all makes sense if King James was right about his divine right theory. It's no wonder that John Twyn was sentenced to die so gruesomely.

CHECKING YOUR MEDIA LITERACY

- **Give examples of authoritarian censorship and bribery.**
- **Why do authoritarian governments generally favor post-publication review to prepublication censorship?**
- **What is the notion of truth that is at the heart of authoritarianism?**

King James I
Articulated the divine right of kings theory

divine right of kings
Proper decisions follow the monarch's will, which is linked to an Almighty

John Milton
Early libertarian thinker

marketplace of ideas
An unbridled forum for free inquiry and free expression

LIBERTARIANISM

Libertarian thinkers, in contrast to authoritarians, have faith in the ability of individual human beings to come to know great truths by applying reason. This distinction is the fundamental difference between libertarian and authoritarian perspectives.

>> Marketplace of Ideas. An English writer, **John Milton,** was the pioneer libertarian. In his 1644 pamphlet *Areopagitica,* Milton made a case for free expression based on the idea that individual human beings are capable of discovering truth if given the opportunity. Milton argued for a free and open exchange of information and ideas—a **marketplace of ideas.** Just as people at a farmers' market can pinch and inspect a lot of vegetables until they find the best, so can people

MEDIA TIMELINE

GLOBAL MASS MEDIA MILESTONES

1500s

Censorship
Henry VIII placed limits on imported publications (1529)

Licensing
British set up Stationers Company to license printers (1557)

Authoritarianism Justified
James I claimed kings held a divine right to rule (1598)

King James saw divine anointment.

1600s

Areopagitica
John Milton argued for robust discourse in seeking truth (1644)

Milton would let Truth and Falsehood grapple

1700s

First Amendment
U.S. Constitution bars government control of press (1791)

1800s

Civil War
U.S. government limited war reporting (1862)

1900s

Global Shortwave
British Broadcasting Corporation created (1927)

Uniformed Journalists
U.S. government credentialed reporters (1942)

Airwave Propaganda
U.S. created Voice of America (1942)

Voice of America as a Cold War tool

Satellite Broadcasting
CNN launched a 24/7 news channel, later went global (1976)

Reporter Pools
Government allowed coverage of Panama invasion through reporter pools (1989)

Embeds
Reporters embedded with combat units (1993)

Al-Jazeera
Qatar sheik created Al-Jazeera news channel (1996)

Al-Jazeera sought pan-Arab, global news audience

2000s

Chinese Censorship
China installed filters on incoming Internet communication (2001)

Pan-Arab Media
Dubai launched media enterprise for multinational audiences (2003)

Iraq Infowar
Digital media used by Iraqi insurgents for propaganda (2003–)

Liu Di under lifetime of Chinese government "permanent surveillance"

PIVOTAL EVENTS

1500s
- Printing presses throughout Europe (1500–)

1600s
- Age of Science, Age of Reason, Enlightenment

1700s
- Revolutionary War (1776–1781)

1800s
- Morse invented telegraph (1844)
- U.S. Civil War (1861–1865)

1900s
- World War II (1941–1945)
- Russian–Western rivalry triggered Cold War (1945)
- Vietnam war (1964–1973)
- Soviet empire imploded (1989)
- Persian Gulf war (1991)

2000s
- 9/11 terrorist attacks (2001)
- Iraq war (2003–)

Marketplace of Ideas. *A marital spat and a confrontation with the king led John Milton to write* Areopagitica *in 1644. The tract challenged royal authority on intellectual and moral grounds and paved the way for libertarianism. Milton made a case that everyone should be free to express ideas for the consideration of other people, no matter how traitorous, blasphemous, deleterious or just plain silly. It was a strong argument against restrictions on free speech.*

find the best ideas if they have a vast array from which to choose. Milton's marketplace is not a place but a concept. It exists whenever people exchange ideas, whether in conversation or letters or the printed word.

Milton was eloquent in his call for free expression. He saw no reason to fear any idea, no matter how subversive, because human beings inevitably will choose the best ideas and values. He put it this way: "Let Truth and Falsehood grapple: whoever knew Truth put to the worse in a free and open encounter." Milton's line is perhaps the greatest insight in the period in intellectual history called the **Enlightenment.** Milton reasoned that people would gain confidence in their ideas and values if they tested them continually against alternative views. It was an argument against censorship. People need to have the fullest-possible choices in the marketplace if they are going to go home with the best product, whether vegetables or ideas. Also, bad ideas should be present in the marketplace because, no matter how objectionable, they might contain a grain of truth.

Milton and his libertarian successors acknowledged that people sometimes err in sorting out alternatives, but these mistakes are corrected as people continually reassess their values against competing values in the marketplace. Libertarians see this truth-seeking as a never-ending, life-long human pursuit. Over time, people will shed flawed ideas for better ones. This is called the **self-righting process.**

>> First Amendment. Libertarianism took strong root in Britain's North American colonies in the 1700s. Thomas Paine stirred people against British authoritarianism and incited them to revolution. The rhetoric of the Enlightenment was clear in the Declaration of Independence, which was drafted by libertarian philosopher Thomas Jefferson. His document declares that people have **natural rights** and are capable of deciding their own destiny. No king is needed. There is an emphasis on liberty and individual rights. Libertarianism spread rapidly as colonists rallied against Britain in the Revolutionary War.

Not everyone who favored independence was a firm libertarian. When it came time to write a constitution for the new republic, there was a struggle between libertarian and authoritarian principles. The libertarians had the greater influence, but sitting there prominently were Alexander Hamilton and a coterie of individuals who would have severely restricted the liberties of the common people. The constitution that resulted was a compromise. Throughout the Constitution, an implicit trust of the people vies with an implicit distrust. Even so, the government that emerged was the first to be influenced by libertarian principles, and so began "the great experiment in democracy," as it's been called.

By the time the Constitution was ratified, it had been expanded to include the **First Amendment,** which bars government from interfering in the exchange of ideas. The First Amendment declares that "Congress shall make no law . . . abridging the freedom of speech, or of the press. . . ."

In practice there have been limits on both free speech and free expression since the beginning of the republic. Legal scholars debate where to draw the line when the First Amendment comes into conflict with other civil rights, such as the right to a fair trial. Even so, for 200 years the First Amendment has embodied the ideals of the Enlightenment. The United States clearly is in the libertarian tradition, as are the other Western-style democracies that followed.

>> Global Libertarianism. On its scale of *Free* and *Not Free,* the Freedom House organization, which tracks freedom globally, says that democracy and freedom are the dominant trends in Western and East-central Europe, in the Americas, and increasingly in the Asia-Pacific region. In the former Soviet Union, Freedom House says the

Enlightenment
A movement emphasizing reason and individualism

self-righting process
Although people make occasional errors in truth-seeking, they eventually discover and correct them

natural rights
Inherent human rights, including self-determination

First Amendment
The free expression section of the U.S. Constitution

picture remains mixed. In Africa, free societies and electoral democracies are a minority despite recent progress. The Middle East has experienced gains for freedom, although the region as a whole overwhelmingly consists of countries that Freedom House rates as *Partly Free* or *Not Free.*

CHECKING YOUR MEDIA LITERACY

- **Explain how libertarianism is optimistic about human reason and how authoritarianism is pessimistic.**
- **How does the Enlightenment relate to libertarianism?**
- **How does the First Amendment embody the ideals of the Enlightenment?**

War as a Libertarian Test

STUDY PREVIEW

From the fog of war can come defining clarity on the irreconcilable clash between authoritarianism and libertarianism. The trials of combat, with national survival at issue, can put even the greatest democracies to a test of their libertarian ideals. Expedience can lead to contradictory policies—such as censorship and suppression of dissent.

COMBAT REPORTING

The ordeal of combat is perhaps the greatest test not only of personal courage but also of democratic nations' commitment to their ideals. In crisis situations, with national survival at issue, can a government allow unfettered news coverage? The struggle for an answer is rooted deeply in the American experience.

>> **Civil War.** The war between the states was the first war to have a large contingent of reporters accompanying the armies, about 500. After some fumbling with how to deal with the reporters, the secretary of war, **Edwin Stanton,** ordered that stories go to censors to delete sensitive military matters. In general, the system worked from Stanton's perspective. Toward the end of the war General William Sherman marched all the way from Chattanooga, Tennessee, through hostile Georgia to the sea at Savannah, a nine-month campaign, without a hint in the press to tip off the Confederacy.

>> **World War II.** In World War II correspondents wore uniforms with the rank of captain and usually had a driver and a Jeep. The reporters generated lots of field coverage, but the reporting, reflecting the highly patriotic spirit of the times, as evident in the reporters wearing military uniforms, was hardly dispassionate and sometimes propagandist.

>> **Vietnam.** Reporters had great freedom in reporting the Vietnam war in the 1960s and 1970s. Almost at will, reporters could link up with South Vietnamese or U.S. units and go on patrols. The result, dubbed **rice-roots reporting,** included lots of negative stories on what was, in fact, an unsuccessful military campaign unpopular among many soldiers and a growing majority at home. For the first time the reporting was filmed for television, with networks pumping gruesome footage

Edwin Stanton
U.S. secretary of state who organized Civil War censorship of sensitive military news

rice-roots reporting
Uncensored field reporting from the Vietnam war

into living rooms across the nation on the evening news, deepening opposition to the war.

Commanders didn't like negative reports, which some blamed for losing the public's support for the war. In the end, demoralized, the United States withdrew in defeat—the first war in its history the nation had lost.

>> Grenada. For the next wars, relatively quick incursions, the Pentagon had new rules. In 1983, when the United States took over the Caribbean nation of Grenada, a naval blockade kept reporters out. Secretly planned, the war surprised the news media. Scrambling to get on top of the story but barred from the action, enterprising reporters hired small boats to run the blockade but were intercepted.

Major newspapers, the networks and news agencies protested loudly at being excluded from covering the Grenada invasion. Acknowledging that the policy had ridden roughshod over the democratic principles on which the United States was founded, with an informed electorate essential for the system to work, the Pentagon agreed to sit down with news media leaders to devise new ground rules. The result was a **pool system,** in which a corps of reporters would be on call on a rotating basis to be shuttled to combat areas on short notice for the next quick war.

CHECKING YOUR MEDIA LITERACY

- **Would news audiences have problems today with a policy to put journalists in military uniforms?**
- **What are the advantages and disadvantages of reporter pools?**

EMBEDDED REPORTERS

The Iraq war, beginning in 2003, was covered by journalists like no other. The U.S. government, after flip-flopping on rules for war correspondents for 50 years, seemed to recognize the futility of trying to manipulate information in the digital age. Months before the invasion, the Pentagon chief for media relations, Victoria Clarke, invited news organizations to send reporters to special combat mini-courses to get up to speed—and also into physical shape—to go to war with combat units. Commanders were told to let the cameras roll whenever the journalists wanted.

The embed system has been fine-tuned as the war has ground on. Even so, the system has problems. A military unit with an embedded reporter needs to assign additional soldiers to address security. If a reporter is wounded, resources have to be diverted from the mission to evacuate the reporter. This became a growing issue in the Iraq war. More than 100 reporters have been mortally wounded. Bureau chiefs for U.S. news organizations in Baghdad left it to individual reporters to decide whether to embed with a combat unit.

CHECKING YOUR MEDIA LITERACY

- **Have embedded reporters given you a clearer feel for what's happening in the Iraq war?**
- **Does embedding as a policy resolve the vexing issue of how an independent news media can cover combat without jeopardizing military tactics?**
- **As a reporter in a Baghdad news bureau, would you volunteer for embed missions? Explain.**

pool system
Reporters chosen on a rotating basis to cover an event to which access is limited

MEDIA PEOPLE

Hazardous Duty

For a story on U.S. soldiers on patrol in a ravaged Baghdad neighborhood, a three-person CBS television crew joined an infantry unit for the day. **Embeds,** the reporters were called. For most practical purposes, they were part of the unit, embedded. As their Hummer negotiated the streets, a yellow taxi alongside, packed with 300 to 500 pounds of explosives, was detonated remotely. Cameraman Paul Douglas and soundman James Brolan were wounded mortally. So were an Army captain and his Iraqi translator.

The wounded also included CBS correspondent Kimberly Dozier. Near death with shredded upper legs, severe burns and shrapnel in her head, Dozier was rushed to a combat hospital. Unconscious, having lost tremendous amounts of blood, Dozier's heart stopped twice. Technically, she was dead. Both times surgeons brought her back and kept her alive.

Two dozen surgeries later back in the United States, Dozier was considering how to resume her work as a foreign correspondent. She had been in Baghdad three years, knowing every day the dangers. The work, she said, was essential: "The world is watching. The story needs to be told." At the same time, Dozier was hesitant to put her family through the trauma of her again being anyplace as dangerous as Iraq had become. By mid-2007 104 journalists had died covering the war.

She noted an irony about the embed duty for which she, Paul Douglas and James Brolan had volunteered the day they were attacked. They had chosen to go with soldiers assigned to a neighborhood thought to be relatively safe although a bomb had exploded there just the day before.

Another irony: The bomb that day was relatively small for the improvised devices that insurgents had been perfecting since early in the Iraq war.

Although a veteran war reporter, Dozier said the experience that fateful day was a revelation: "You think how many lives, day after day after day, are being torn apart, how many sacrifices are being made. I thought I understood that, but I didn't really understand it until I lived through it."

WHAT DO YOU THINK?

- What if all reporters were afraid to volunteer for Iraq assignments?

Kim Dozier

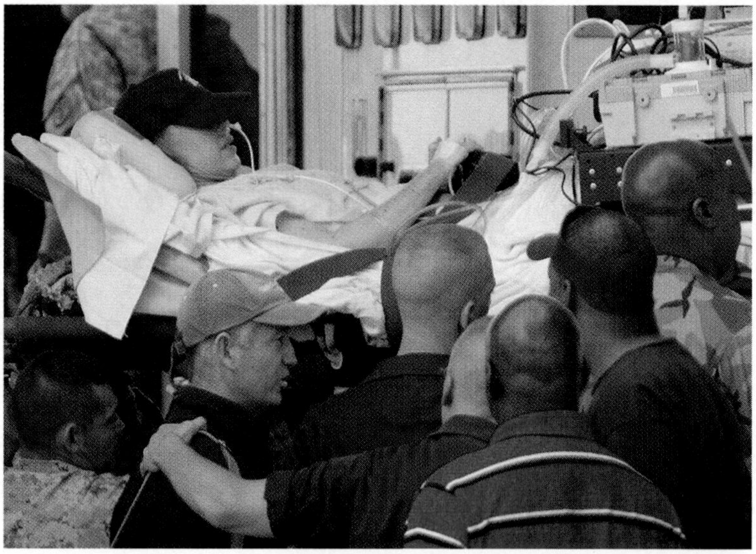

Medical Evacuation. *CBS reporter Kimberly Dozier survived a car bombing in which two crew members were killed, among 104 reporters who had died in the Iraq war by mid-2007. Also killed in the explosion were an Army captain and a translator.*

+ Pay-to-Publish

When the U.S. Defense Department realized it couldn't control news and information getting to Iraqis during the war in Iraq, it turned to private companies, including the Lincoln Group, a Washington-based public relations firm.

To Willem Marx, it looked like his dream of being a foreign correspondent was coming true. After his final semester at Oxford, he was offered an internship with Lincoln. Marx was ready for some real-world experience before starting journalism school in the fall.

In a tell-all piece in *Harper's* magazine, Marx described his job as choosing which stories submitted by U.S. military writers would be translated and published in Iraqi newspapers. He knew the stories were "far from exemplars of objective journalism." But, he said, he was told to think of them "not so much as news but as messages Iraqis needed to hear." Propaganda? That's the issue. Certainly, the stories being planted in Iraqi newspapers were not from the detached, neutral journalistic perspective that is the American democratic ideal.

During one two-month period, the Lincoln Group proposed a $19 million multimedia blitz. Marx found an Iraqi company that would produce a half-minute television spot for $10,000. Iraq's national station said it could air the spot during its most expensive time for $2,000. The Lincoln Group was charging the military $1 million for the spot. Marx found himself driving through Baghdad with $3 million in cash in the trunk of the car. For his summer internship, Marx was paid $1,000 a month.

The Los Angeles *Times* broke the story about Lincoln's contract with the Pentagon to pay Iraqi news media to anonymously publish stories written by U.S. military personnel. Soon after, the Pentagon launched an investigation, which ultimately concluded that legally the government could spread propaganda in foreign nations.

The Lincoln Group defended its work as an attempt to level the playing field in Iraqi media. Said one Lincoln adviser: "The opposition is very clever and basically gets a free run in the media over there." Other Pentagon defenders argued that different ethical standards are needed in a combat zone.

There is no evidence that the stories planted in Iraqi media were untrue. The controversy is whether the stories, for the sake of honesty and transparency, should have been attributed to the U.S. military.

Government manipulation of media content bothers John Schulz, dean of communication at

Old Tech Message. *Despite a costly U.S. information campaign that vilified Iraq leader Saddam Hussein, the people of Fallujah renamed one of their streets the Street of the Martyr Saddam Hussein. Slickly produced media messages for television, no matter the budget or talent that goes into them, failed to offset insurgents' YouTube-type calls for resistance. George Bush was there, old-media style, and not getting through. Everybody, it seems, has a video cell phone.*

Boston University. Schulz sees the issue going to the core of an American ideal. "In the very process of attempting to either lead by example or actually instill a democracy, which is the main mission in Iraq as we understand it now, we're subverting democracy at the very core by subverting the legitimate process of journalism," Schulz said. "There needs to be an agonizing reappraisal of what they mean about trusting the news media and whether soldiers and plants and public relations firms can function in the place of effective news media. I don't think so."

DEEPENING YOUR MEDIA LITERACY

EXPLORE THE ISSUE

List the reasons the U.S. military would pay to have its own stories published in the Iraqi press. Then list ways that democracy and an effective media interact.

DIG DEEPER

Do you see any intersections between your two lists? Where do ethics fit into them?

WHAT DO YOU THINK?

Is a trust in the media necessary for a successful democracy? Is it OK to follow different media ethics in a new, unstable democracy? Was it worth the price the United States paid to get its stories in the Iraqi press?

Arab Media Systems

STUDY PREVIEW

Media in Islamic regions do not fit a single mold. These media operate in diverse political systems, some driven by theologies that themselves are inconsistent. Others are pragmatically oriented to create pan-Arabic mass audiences. Among the most successful is Al-Jazeera.

DIVERSE MEDIA STRUCTURES

Media systems of the nations comprising Islam-dominated regions are as diverse as the nations themselves. These nations span from northern Africa to southeast Asia. Many resemble classic authoritarian systems, some being among the planet's last theocracies with clerics dominating public policy. Variations, however, are significant. Islamic dogma ranges widely among sects vying for dominance. The civil war into which Iraq fell during the U.S. occupation, for example, was a clash of different traditions and strains of Islam going back centuries. In contrast, in the sheikdom of Dubai, whose governance resembles a monarchy, economic growth has trumped divisive issues with overt pan-Arabic attempts to accommodate diverse traditions.

Media systems in some Arabic areas reflect values from periods of overbearing European dominance, mixed with resurgent indigenous traditions and values. Some of this Western influence continued long after this dominance had ended. In the 1990s, for example, the British Broadcasting Corporation, with a history of international broadcasting in the region, spent two years setting up an Arab-language service. Obstacles led BBC to abandon the project in 1996. But, seeing a vacuum, the government of the tiny Gulf state of Qatar, already committed to creating itself as a regional media center, created a 24/7 television news service, modeled on U.S.-based CNN. Sheikh **Hammad bin Khalifa** put up the money. Thus **Al-Jazeera** was born, which today has been ranked the world's fifth best-known brand.

CHECKING YOUR MEDIA LITERACY

- **Describe the diversity in political systems and their media components in Arabic and Islamic regions.**

AL-JAZEERA

Al-Jazeera picked up its journalistic tradition largely through Brits who had been with the abandoned BBC project. For the Middle East, the approach was fresh—live coverage of breaking news told dispassionately and as thoroughly as possible, no holds barred. Viewers glommed to the channel. Call-in shows were uncensored. Arabs suddenly had an avenue to unload on their governments, many of them despotic and unevenly responsive to public needs.

Al-Jazeera was applauded in the West as a voice for democracy and reform. But things changed after Arab terrorists killed thousands of people in New York City and Washington in 2001. As the Bush administration responded by moving toward war in Iraq, the Arab perspective inherent in Al-Jazeera included independent reporting that sometimes was at odds with U.S. portrayals. Commentary was from all sides, including insurgents whom the U.S. government wanted to deny a voice. According to news reports, in a 2004 meeting with the British prime minister, President Bush stepped out of the U.S. libertarian tradition in an unguarded moment and suggested bombing Al-Jazeera's headquarters in Qatar.

Meanwhile, Al-Jazeera's reporting continued in the BBC tradition, seeking multiple perspectives to get at the facts and truth. The reporting carried a high price to intolerant factions that claimed their own monopolies on truth. Twice Al-Jazeera bureaus were bombed, including a 2001 U.S. aerial attack on the Al-Jazeera bureau in

embeds
News reporters who are with military units on missions

Hammad bin Khalifa
Founder of Al-Jazeera television news network

Al-Jazeera
Qatar-based satellite news channel for Arab audiences; now global

Control Room. *The Al-Jazeera control room in Qatar is staffed by a mix of former British Broadcasting Corporation employees and Arabian journalists. Al-Jazeera's reporting during the U.S.-led war on Iraq displeased President Bush, who, according to British press reports, suggested to British Prime Minister Tony Blair in 2004 that the network's headquarters be bombed.*

Baghdad. Several Arab governments banned Al-Jazeera, although with little effect. The audience, already 50 million in 2000, has continued to grow.

So has Al-Jazeera's influence. In 2003 the network entered a news-sharing agreement with BBC. CNN added Al-Jazeera to its sources of video feeds. Al-Jazeera launched an English-language network in 2006 to extend its global reach. The English language anchors have familiar faces, some formerly with CNN, Sky News and BBC.

CHECKING YOUR MEDIA LITERACY

- **What are challenges facing Al-Jazeera and its competitors in reaching Arab audiences?**
- **When agents of master terrorist Osama Bin Laden supplied video of his anti-Western political messages to Al-Jazeera, the network aired them as news. Was this the right thing to do?**
- **The White House said the Bin Laden tapes might carry embedded instructions to terror cells and asked U.S. television networks not to air the tapes. How would you as a network executive respond to the White House request?**

DUBAI MEDIA INCORPORATED

As a nation, Dubai might seem a mere speck of sand on the Persian Gulf—674,000 people, only 265,700 in its main city. From under the sand, though, has come oil that has brought spectacular wealth to the tiny emirate. But what will happen when the wells run dry? Resources extractable from the earth inevitably run out.

The government has set a deliberate course to create a post-oil financial infrastructure. The plan includes lavish hotels to transform Dubai into a tourism magnet. Beaches line the Gulf for miles, easily only a day's flight from major population centers in Europe, south Asia and, of course, the rest of the Arab world.

And so much sunshine. Could Dubai also become the Arabian Hollywood? It was California sunshine, after all, that drew the infant U.S. filmmaking industry from the East Coast to Hollywood early in the 1900s. The more sunshine, the more days for outdoor shooting. With moviemaking could come a host of related media industries—particularly television.

Dubai Media Incorporated
Quasi-government agency building Dubai to be a Mideast entertainment production center

The brainstorming that began with a tourist-oriented Dubailand complex mushroomed. In 2003 the government converted its Ministry of Information into **Dubai Media Incorporated** to run the nation's television system. DMI is a quasi-government agency but is set up to operate like a private company. Ninety-seven billion dollars, much of it borrowed, which created a fiscal crisis in 2009, has gone into construction. More than 1,000 television and film companies have taken up residence, availing themselves of the sunshine and also the government's tax-free incentives.

Dubai Media Incorporated, with audience goals far beyond the emirate's borders, operates four television channels. These include an Arab-language general entertainment channel. The channel became the most-watched pan-Arabian satellite station, second only to the older Saudi-owned, London-based MBC. The Dubai Sports Channel, the only 24-hour Arab sports channel, has exclusive rights to the World Cup of horse racing. Arab soccer also is exclusive. An English-language service carries mostly movies and imported programs. In addition, a local channel aims at audiences within the United Arab Emirates, of which Dubai is part.

In the culturally and religiously fractured Arab region, Dubai TV and its competitors are on a tightrope in choosing content. Hussein Ali Lootah, chief executive, sees Dubai TV's greatest achievement in introducing Gulf-oriented programming that has not alienated Arabs on the Mediterranean. Creativity is within the bounds of local sensitivities, he says. For news, Dubai TV avoids the hard-hitting journalism of Al-Jazeera by having a deliberately friendly, informal approach. On magazine and talk shows there is more analysis, less polemics.

On the English-language One TV, programs and movies are chosen because they are "relevant and sensitive to our culture," says manager Naila Al-awadhi. Shows are subtitled and promoted in Arabic.

Dubai TV claims 50 percent market penetration, which means a reach of 100 million Arabs across the region. Dubai's pre-2004 predecessor earned less than $4 million. The 2006 gross reached $40 million. DMI claims English-language One TV can reach 70 million Arab households.

CHECKING YOUR MEDIA LITERACY

- **How is the emirate of Dubai seeking to become a global entertainment industry player?**
- **What obstacles does the Dubai enterprise face?**

Media and Terrorism

STUDY PREVIEW

Mass media are a new battleground in civilization's great struggles. Saudi Arabians have tackled terrorism with pan-Arab television drama. But old-style media may have maxed out their effectiveness. In Iraq, despite the high production quality and big spending, U.S. messages have failed to offset the insurgents' YouTube-style video calls for violent resistance.

SAUDI ANTI-TERRORISM

What a difference a major terrorism attack can make. Until November 2003, some members of the royal family that controls Saudi Arabia were channeling their oil wealth into Al-Qaeda terrorism and to militant Islam imams who saw their holy book, the Koran, as justifying terrorism. Then came a 2003 terrorist bombing in Saudi Arabia itself. Eighteen people, all Arabs, were killed. It was a pivotal moment. Soon came a wave of mini-series and dramas, some produced in Saudi Arabia, challenging the notion that Islam somehow justifies terrorism. These programs play on Arab channels throughout the Middle East. Some, like *The Beautiful Virgins,* led the ratings with an anti-terrorism theme woven into a trans-Arab story line with characters of Egyptian, Jordanian, Lebanese, Moroccan, Palestinian and Syrian descent.

Written by a former Al-Qaeda member, *The Beautiful Virgins* is narrated by a Syrian girl who was burned in the 2003 attack. Amid all kinds of problems, including marital infidelity, drug addiction and wife beating, the core issue is the loving versus the dark side of Islam as told through the conflict within a young Saudi man torn between militant and moderate readings of the Koran. Which way does he go to find the virgins whom the Koran, at least metaphorically, says await good Islamic men in paradise?

Militant imams deride *Beautiful Virgins* as sacrilege, which points out that Islamic Arabs are hardly of one mind. The show was panned on militant web sites. Station executives have received death threats. Even so, the show has led viewership not only in Saudi Arabia but also in other Islamic countries. At the Saudi-owned Middle East Broadcasting Corporation, based in Dubai, production manager Abe al Masry has described *Beautiful Virgins* as an integral part of the new Arab battle against terrorism.

It wasn't always so. The producer of a 2001 show, *The Road to Kabul,* which portrayed the Afghan Taliban negatively, caved to death threats after eight installments. But that was before the 2003 attack in Saudi Arabia. Today, the story line continues in *The Rocky Road* with hints at hypocrisy and Afghan corruption. Another show, *What Will Be, Will Be,* portrays conservative village sheiks as bumbling bumpkins, not unlike the sheriff in *The Dukes of Hazzard,* albeit with political edginess.

CHECKING YOUR MEDIA LITERACY

- **Why has anti-terrorism become fashionable in Saudi Arabian media?**

MEDIA AS TERRORISM TOOL

Islamic radicals including Al-Qaeda have adapted low-cost digital media to their needs. During the U.S. presence in Iraq, insurgents have learned to plan multicamera, high-resolution video shots of large-scale attacks on U.S. forces. The videos are quickly edited into hyped narratives and spliced with stock clips of snipers felling U.S. soldiers, all with backgrounds of religious music or martial chants. The videos are meant to inspire triumphal passions. The videos sell in Baghdad markets, fundraisers for the cause. More potently, they make the rounds on video cell phone incredibly quickly. Within minutes after an attack, video is in virtually unlimited circulation on handheld devices.

The adroit use of technology—all it takes is a laptop—figures into internecine tensions. A ghoulish sectarian video of a Sunni militiaman sawing off the head of a Shiite prisoner with a five-inch knife stirred Sunni emotion. The Shiites, of course, have no monopoly on the new tools of the information and propaganda war. When secretly shot video of the hanging of Iraqi leader Saddam Hussein leaked onto the Internet, his neck cracked in the noose, close up, incensed Shiites rioted in Anbar province.

New media can give underdogs an identity against forces that are superior by traditional measures. In Fallujah, an insurgent stronghold northwest of Baghdad, the United States created a multimillion-dollar campaign with traditional public relations and propaganda tools to win over the people. The other side, however, carried the day. The people renamed a major thoroughfare the Street of the Martyr Saddam Hussein.

CHECKING YOUR MEDIA LITERACY

- **How have underground forces glommed onto inexpensive new media forms to mobilize many Iraqis to their cause?**
- **How can the United States deal with grassroots media tactics that use new digital media?**

Battle for Iran

STUDY PREVIEW

Geopolitically strategic Iran has emerged in the crosshairs of the East-West confrontation that has been shaped by global terrorism. In Los Angeles, where many Iranian expatriates live, satellite television stations aim at homeland reforms. The U.S. State Department, meanwhile, has implemented soft diplomacy with its own media messages. In reaction, the Iran government is trying to block transborder communication.

TEHRANGELES

Outside of Iran itself, no city is home to more Iranians than Los Angeles. The nickname **Tehrangeles,** however, didn't catch on much until Zia Atabay realized he could lease time on an orbiting satellite to send television programs from Los Angeles to anybody with a dish receiver in Iran. Atabay's goal: to encourage political reform and democracy in an Islamic society that's divided between old ways and new. Thus in 2000 was born, in Los Angeles, the National Iranian Television network.

Atabay poured $6 million into NITV, hoping it would become financially self-sustaining through advertising. It didn't. In 2006 the operation went dark. By then, however, 20 other satellite stations, funded by Iranians in the United States, were beaming signals to Iran. Although most are talk shows, programming at surviving Tehrangeles operations is all over the map. Think Iranian MTV. Or Iranian ESPN.

Tehrangeles
Nickname for Los Angeles as home to more Iranians than any city other than Tehran

Radio Farda
U.S. government-funded Farsi-language service aimed at Iran

Voice of America
U.S. government-funded broadcast service sent into nations with state-controlled media to articulate U.S. policies directly to the people

How effective has Tehrangeles television been as an alternative to state-controlled television and radio in Iran, all heavily censored? Measures are hard to come by. No doubt, though, the Los Angeles stations have audiences, judging by talk-show call-ins from Iran. Too, although satellite television is illegal in Iran, about half the population, roughly 20 million people, have dishes. But is it effective? The 2005 election of conservative Islamic Mahmoud Ahmadinejad as president has been called a backlash against the often-virulent anti-regime polemics from Los Angeles. Some observers say, however, that the music clips and sports on other satellite stations may be doing more to encourage social and other fundamental reforms by broadening the cultural exposure of Iranian young people.

Ahmadinejad's controversial re-election in 2009 spurred riots and bloodshed. Despite media coverage, the dissent was suppressed brutally.

Tehrangeles. *Half a world away in Los Angeles, Alireza Nourizadeh offers commentary aimed at Iranian viewers of Channel One's* Window on the Fatherland. *Nourizadeh, who favors regime change, takes calls from Iranians in and out of the country.*

CHECKING YOUR MEDIA LITERACY

- **Is it wrong for Iranian ex-patriates to try to influence public policy in Iran with appeals directly to the Iranian people?**
- **Can such projects succeed?**

U.S.-SPONSORED MEDIA

For years the U.S. government has funded **Radio Farda,** a 24-hour service in the Farsi language. Farda transmits from facilities in the Czech Republic. There also is a **Voice of America** satellite television service that the State Department beams into Iran. Unlike the fiery commercial stations broadcast from Los Angeles, the State Department hopes to sway Iranians with "soft diplomacy." This includes news programs that, although from a U.S. perspective, are not propagandistic.

The U.S. State Department has decades-long experience in broadcasting directly to people in repressed areas. Radio Free Europe and Voice of

Voice of America. *From studios in Washington, D.C., Luna Shadzi anchors a Persian-language news program beamed into Iran. Voice of America broadcasters believe Iranians deserve an alternative to the propaganda from their government.*

America were created after World War II, first under the guise of being citizen-generated projects. The goal ostensibly was to present information on U.S. positions on issues that were being distorted or unreported in Eastern Europe and the Soviet Union. It was soft-sell propaganda, but also was exposing people behind the so-called Iron Curtain to insights into Western pop culture and music, as well as dangling lures of advanced Western countries before repressed, impoverished people.

Old-style Voice of America and similar U.S. projects, including Radio Martí and television aimed at Cuba, also carry an antagonistic message to regimes in target countries. The projects have since added digital components. Attempts by the government to connect directly with Iranians, for example, include a Farda web site. The main Iranian target is young adults, who tend to be well educated, technically savvy and more inclined as a group to political reform.

CHECKING YOUR MEDIA LITERACY

- **What do you know about the role of Voice of America in facilitating the collapse of the Soviet Union and ending the Cold War?**
- **What are the prospects for the U.S. State Department's Radio Farda?**

IRAN BLOCKAGES

Typical of authoritarian regimes, the Iranian government tries to block signals from sources it considers unfavorable. The militia-like Revolutionary Guard jams signals. The British Broadcasting Corporation's Farsi service is a frequent target. The state Administration for Culture and Islamic Guidance assumed control of blogs in 2006 with robot and human censors and blocking. In addition, the agency hired hundreds of agents to create blogs carrying the government's message.

Blogging has worked against the government in specific cases. In 2006, word came from a prison that dissident journalist Akbar Ganji, who had been locked up five years earlier, was engaging in a hunger strike and could die. After bloggers spread the word about Ganji's prison treatment, re-igniting public interest in his case, the government freed him.

Citizen blogging was less successful in the massive 2009 protests about election irregularities. Government agents and goons succeeded in putting down the protests.

CHECKING YOUR MEDIA LITERACY

- **Eastern European regimes jammed Voice of America and similar programs during the Cold War but with limited success. VOA changed frequencies often. Would you expect Iran to be more successful in its blockage attempts?**

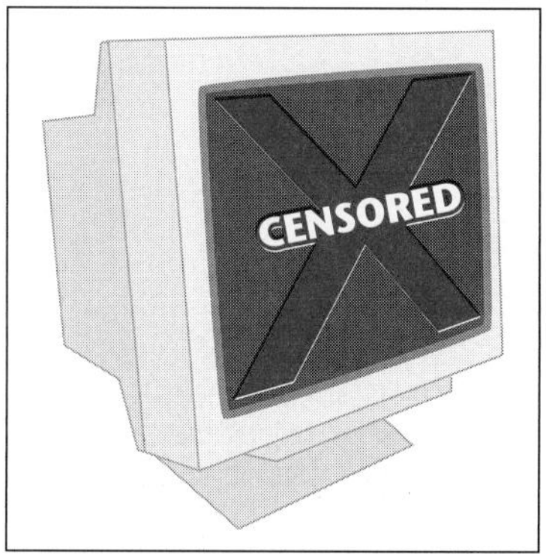

"Watch Your Step." *China and Iran are the most aggressive nations in blocking political content from other countries but they are not alone. The Open Net Initiative—a consortium of Harvard, Cambridge, Oxford and Toronto universities—says at least 25 nations restrict citizen access to certain web sites, some for political reasons, some for cultural reasons, some for both. The consortium noted that the study was limited to 40 countries and the Palestinian territories, so this may be only a partial picture of the state of the web internationally. Besides China and Iran, the study reported that Myanmar, Syria, Tunisia and Vietnam focus on political content. Oman, Saudi Arabia, Sudan, Tunisia, United Arab Emirates and Yemen try mostly to filter socially unacceptable sites featuring pornography, gambling and homosexual material.*

China Media

STUDY PREVIEW

The struggle between freedom and tyranny plays and replays itself out with the mass media offering case studies on broader issues. Among major nations, China has suppressed challenges to government authority with the most labor-intensive censorship initiative in history.

Liu Di. *Government agents arrested college student Liu Di for her Internet essays, some of which mocked the government. Agents jailed her in a cell with a convicted murderer. After a year she was released subject to "permanent surveillance." She was told never to speak to foreign journalists.*

CHINESE POLICY

Chinese authorities were less than amused at the free-wheeling satire of someone on the Internet going by the name Stainless Steel Mouse. The Mouse was tapping out stinging quips about ideological hypocrisy among the country's communist leaders. When government agents tracked the commentaries to **Liu Di,** a psychology major at a Beijing university, they jailed her for a year without charges. Finally, figuring the publicity about the arrest would be enough to chill other freethinkers into silence, the authorities let Liu Di go—on the condition that she not return to her old ways.

The government's rationale has been articulated at the highest levels. In a speech, President Jiang Zemin put the necessity of absolute government control this way: "We must be vigilant against infiltration, subversive activities, and separatist activities of international and domestic hostile forces. Only by sticking to and perfecting China's socialist political system can we achieve the country's unification, national unity, social stability, and economic development. The Western mode of political systems must never be copied."

CHECKING YOUR MEDIA LITERACY

- **How does China justify its tight controls on media content?**

CHINESE NEWS CONTROL

The rise of a market economy in China has loosened the financial dependence of newspapers on the ruling Communist Party. Competing for readers in this emerging marketplace, the predictable and dull propagandist thrust of many newspapers has begun to dim. More reporting is appearing, for example, on disasters and other previously off-limits spot news.

In 2005, after 121 Guangdong miners died in a mine flood, *China Business Times* launched a journalistic examination that concluded that mine authorities had known of safety violations and had taken bribes to look the other way. With the revelation, there was no choice but for the government to prosecute. Eighteen men, including a high-ranking government official, were hauled into court. In the past, misdeeds within the power structure had been ignored or dealt with quietly. That is no longer so easily done, now that a journalistic dragon is stirring.

Most accidents, even disasters, still go unreported. Of the 3,300 mine accidents in China in 2005, few garnered much coverage. But some newspapers have started going after these kinds of stories. When a Jilin factory explosion dumped 100 tons of toxic chemicals into the Songhua River, the government naïvely assumed it could keep a lid on the situation. Wrong. Chinese newspapers told the story, albeit in bits and pieces. The government was embarrassed when downstream Russians learned the river was dangerous. It was an international incident that the government then blamed on the newspapers.

> **Liu Di**
> Under the pseudonym Stainless Steel Mouse, she satirized the Chinese government until arrested and silenced

The extent to which the Chinese go to keep negative information out of circulation was demonstrated in 2007 when a contaminated ingredient imported from China began killing pets in the United States. When international inspectors arrived at the facilities of origin, the equipment was nowhere to be found. It was as if the

Never Happened. *A major industrial fire in China wasn't what authorities regarded as something that should be reported. A careful reading of Jilin newspapers, however, revealed bits and pieces that something catastrophic had occurred. When pollution from tons of toxic chemicals released in the explosions and fires reached the Russian border downstream, the fire became an international issue.*

place had never existed. The Chinese explained that they had completed their own inspection and corrected any problems. No plant, no story.

To rein in journalism, the influential State Council has proposed an **Emergency Response Law** to "manage news" about emergencies. Censorship? The proposal's language is iffy. Permission would be required for reporting that "causes serious consequences." What does that mean? The State Council says "normal" reporting would be OK under its law, whatever that means.

The government's justification for the restrictions on coverage is to encourage stability. News about government corruption, as in the Guangdong mine flood, or government incompetence, as in disaster relief, does not inspire public confidence in the government. The nation's leadership is aware of an estimated 87,000 demonstrations in 2005 alone, many directed against public policies and government action—and inaction.

The Emergency Response Law would cover 812,500 news outlets. Some newspapers, feeling a new sense of journalistic self-empowerment, have taken strident positions against the proposed law. Editors have scoffed in print at the law's provision for local governments to be the sole source of disaster and accident information and to report such information in "a timely manner." The problem, the editors argue, is government cover-ups. And who defines "timely"? Who decides how much information is released? And which is, and which isn't?

CHECKING YOUR MEDIA LITERACY

- **How would China's proposed Emergency Response Law affect reporting about disasters?**
- **If the United States had such a law, how would government sluggishness have been reported in the 2005 Hurricane Katrina disaster on the U.S. Gulf coast?**
- **Do you accept the Chinese government's argument that restrictions on journalists are needed to prevent inaccuracies in reporting that could work against social and political stability?**

CHINESE FIREWALL

Emergency Response Law
Chinese limits on news reporting of disasters, ostensibly to ensure social stability

firewall
A block on unauthorized access to a computer system while permitting outward communication

The Chinese government has expended major resources to limit Internet communication, particularly from abroad. To exclude unwanted messages, the Chinese government has undertaken numerous initiatives. One of them has been likened to a 21st century version of the Great Wall of China, a 1,500-mile fortress barrier built in ancient times along the Mongolian frontier to keep invaders out.

The Chinese didn't invent their **firewall.** It came from the U.S. network design company Cisco, which devised filters in the early 1990s for corporate clients to filter employee access to the Internet. The goal of these firewalls was productivity, to keep employees who are equipped with desktop computers from whiling away company minutes, hours even, on sites featuring entertainment and diversions. When Cisco went courting the Chinese as customers, the filters seemed perfect for China to block unwanted material from outside the country. Cisco filters soon were installed at the gateways for Internet messages into China. Here's how it works: The filters subtly "lose" messages from banned sites abroad. If a Chinese user seeks access to a verboten foreign site, an error message or a message saying "site not found" appears on the screen. Whether it's censorship or a technical glitch, the user never knows.

There is dark humor among critics of the Chinese firewall. Noting the role of Cisco, they say: "The modern Great Wall of China was built with American bricks."

CHECKING YOUR MEDIA LITERACY

- **How does the Chinese firewall work?**

INTERNAL CHINESE CONTROLS

To control communication within the country, the Chinese Ministry of Public Security bans Internet service providers from carrying anything that might jeopardize national security, social stability—or even spread false news, superstition or obscenity. As a condition of doing business in China, the U.S. company Yahoo agreed to the terms in 2002. So have Microsoft and other service providers. The system is called the **Golden Shield.** The shield complements the work of the firewall against unwanted foreign messages by controlling communication inside the country.

Even tighter control is expected through a huge intranet that the Chinese government is building within the country—the **Next Carrying Network.** CN2, as it's called for short, was designed from scratch—unencumbered by the older technical standards cobbled together for the system that serves the rest of the planet. CN2's technical advantages include exceptional capacity and speed. Also, because CN2 uses its own technical standards that are not easily compatible with the global Internet, the system fits neatly with the government's policy to limit contact with the outside. Communications from abroad can be received on CN2 only after code translations that stall delivery and, not unimportantly, make them subject to more scrutiny.

CHECKING YOUR MEDIA LITERACY

- **How will China's CN2 strengthen the Golden Shield?**
- **How could CN2 work against Chinese integration into the global community?**
- **Could this work against China's commercial goals?**

CHINESE CENSORSHIP APPARATUS

Because **prior censorship,** reviewing messages before they reach an audience, is hugely labor-intensive, seldom in human history has it been practiced on a large scale. Past authoritarian regimes have relied almost wholly on post-publication sanctions with severe penalties against wayward printers and broadcasters to keep others in line. The Chinese, however, are engaging in pre-publication censorship on an unprecedented scale.

Chinese censorship is partly automated. Internet postings are machine-scanned for words and terms like *human rights*, *Taiwan independence* and *Falun Gong* (a forbidden religious movement) and dropped from further routing. The system also catches other terms that signal forbidden subjects, like *oral sex* and *pornography.*

No one outside the government has numbers on the extent of human involvement in censorship, but there appears to be significant human monitoring at work. Western organizations, including Reporters Without Borders, occasionally test the Chinese system by posting controversial messages, some with terms that machines can easily spot, some with trickier language. Postings with easy-to-catch terms like *Falun Gong* never make it.

Golden Shield
Chinese system to control internal Internet communication within the country

Next Carrying Network (CN2)
Fast Chinese Internet protocols built on new technical standards; incompatible with other protocols

prior censorship
Government review of content before dissemination

Postings with harder-to-spot language but nonetheless objectionable content last a bit longer, although seldom more than an hour, which suggests a review by human eyes.

Who are these censors? How many are there? The consensus among experts outside the country is that China, whose Internet users number 100 million-plus, must be a massive censorship bureaucracy. A rare peek into the system appeared in a 2005 interview in *Nanfang Weekend* with a censor in Siquan, Ma Zhichun, whose background is in journalism. Ma discusses his job as an *Internet coordinator* in the municipal External Propaganda Office, where, without identifying himself online as a government agent, he guides discussions in the government's favor. Ma is part of elaborate mechanisms to keep online dialogue on the right track, particularly in chatrooms, but like thousands of other propaganda officers throughout the country, Ma is in a position to spot banned postings and report them.

CHECKING YOUR MEDIA LITERACY

- **If you were a Chinese censor, what terms would you use to intercept Internet content that should be checked?**

OVERT CHINESE CONTROLS

Although a lot of Chinese government control of Internet postings is invisible, some is overt. Because users are required to use a government-issued personal identification number to log on, citizens know they're subject to being monitored. Operators of blog sites, which number 4 million, need to register with the government. Cybercafés, which have been woven into the lifestyles of many Chinese, must be licensed. At cybercafés, cameras look over users' shoulders for what's on-screen. Police spend a lot of time in cafés looking over shoulders too.

The government's seriousness about regulating the Internet was unmistakable when thousands of illegal cafés were shut down in a series of sweeps in the early 2000s.

Arrests are publicized, which has a chilling effect. One especially notable case involved Wang Youcai, who, during President Clinton's historic 1998 visit to China, proposed an opposition political party in the U.S. tradition. Wang filed papers to register the China Democratic Party. Within a day, government officials knocked on his door, interrogated him for three hours, and hauled him away. He was sent to prison for 11 years and ordered into political abstinence for an additional three years for "fomenting opposition against the government."

The later case of the imprisonment of Liu Di, the Stainless Steel Mouse, for satirizing the government was a similarly chilling warning to those who want to engage in full and open dialogue.

CHECKING YOUR MEDIA LITERACY

- **Chinese punishment for bloggers who engage in frowned-upon content has a chilling effect. What is that chilling effect?**
- **As a traveler in China, would you be comfortable in a cybercafé engaging in the kinds of everyday Internet communication that you do at home?**

CHINESE BROADCASTING

Although political issues are the major focus of Chinese censorship, the government discourages what it sees as a creeping intrusion of Western values and sexuality. In a clampdown on racy radio gab and, lo and behold, orange-tinted hair on television, the State Administration for Radio, Film and Television issued an edict: Enough. To television hosts, the order was no vulgarity. That includes "overall appearance." Specifically forbidden: "multicolor dyed hair" and "overly revealing clothing." There also are new bans on things sexual. Violence, murder and horrors are out until 11 p.m. So too are "fights, spitting, littering and base language."

The restrictions, which are periodically issued as media stray, are consistent with the communist notion that government and media are inseparably linked in moving the society and culture to a better future. As the Chinese put it, the media are the *houshe*, the throat and tongue, of the ruling Communist Party.

Chinese nationalism takes unexpected turns. Broadcasters, for example, periodically are instructed to use only Mandarin. Foreign words, including Westernisms like *OK* and *yadda-yadda*, are not allowed. Not allowed either are dialects from separatist Taiwan. Also, a strict cap was put on imported soap operas and martial arts programs for television. Imports can't constitute more than 25 percent of the total of such programs.

Even in Hong Kong, the British colony that was returned to China in 1997 and that was to be governed by different rules that honored its tradition of free expression, Beijing-approved governors were appointed to comport with official policies. Political cartoonists also have been reined in.

Is government pressure effective? In Fujian province, the hosts of the program *Entertainment Overturning the Skies* gave up their blond dye jobs after one crackdown.

Some television programs imported from Taiwan, the United States and elsewhere suddenly and quietly disappear. Hong Kong radio is tamer. But clampdowns come and go. Kenny Bloom of the Beijing-based AsiaVision production house told a *Wall Street Journal* interviewer: "Commentators will follow the rules for a couple months, and then their clothes will get tighter and their hair will get wilder."

Even so, legal scholars Jack Goldsmith of Harvard and Tim Wu of Columbia, who have studied government controls on media content globally, say controls do not have to be absolute to be effective. Goldsmith and Wu offer copyright law as an example. Infringements of copyright in, say, illegal music downloads, are inevitable, but the threat of civil or criminal sanctions keeps violations at a rate that copyright owners are willing to live with. Such, they note, is the same with the censorious Chinese government. Nobody is so unrealistic to claim that all dissidence can be suppressed. The goal, rather, is to keep dissidence from breaking beyond an easily manageable level.

CHECKING YOUR MEDIA LITERACY

- **Why are Chinese media discouraged from using Westernisms in scripts, like *yadda-yadda* and *OK*?**

EFFECTIVENESS OF CHINESE CONTROLS

An *Idol*-like mania swept China when an upstart television station in remote Hunan province put its show *Supergirl* on satellite. Despite admonitions against lyrics in English and gyrating hips, contestants pushed the envelope of

Yogurt Girl. *A touch of democracy swept China when people were asked to vote for their favorite talent in an* Idol*-style television show sponsored by the Mongolian Cow Sour Yogurt brand. Authorities didn't much like the idea. Whether societal reforms will be inspired by the show seems dubious, although Mongolian Cow Sour Yogurt Supergirl winners have catapulted their acts into entertainment careers.*

government acceptability in front of huge audiences. That viewers could vote their preferences by mobile phones raised a specter of nascent democracy in a country where people can't vote for their leadership. Most analysts, however, have concluded that the phenomenon was an anomaly in the tightly controlled society. Even so, winners, who are called Mongolian Cow Sour Yogurt Supergirls, because of the dairy that sponsored the show, have gone on to singing and modeling careers.

CHECKING YOUR MEDIA LITERACY

- **Could *American Idol*-like television shows that encourage viewers to vote be a preamble to democracy in China?**

Distinctive Media Systems

STUDY PREVIEW

Nations organize their media systems differently. Even largely similar systems like those in Britain and the United States have distinctive methods for funding. Some countries like India have unique features. Some countries have unique developmental needs.

BRITAIN

Almost everybody has heard of the BBC, Britain's venerable radio and television system. Parliament created the British Broadcasting Corporation in 1927 as a government-funded entity that, despite government support, would have as much programming autonomy as possible. The idea was to avoid private ownership and to give the enterprise the prestige of being associated with the Crown. The government appoints a 12-member board of governors to run the BBC. Although the government has the authority to remove members of the board, it never has. The BBC has developed largely independently of the politics of the moment, which has given it a credibility and stature recognized worldwide.

The Beeb, as the BBC is affectionately known, is financed through an annual licensing fee, about $230, on television receivers.

The BBC is known for its global news coverage. It has 250 full-time correspondents, compared to CNN's 113. The Beeb's reputation for first-rate dramatic and entertainment programs is known among English-speaking people everywhere. The 1960s brought such enduring comedies as David Frost's *That Was the Week That Was* and later *Monty Python's Flying Circus.* Sir Kenneth Clark's *Civilisation* debuted in 1969. Then came dramatic classics like *The Six Wives of Henry VIII, War and Peace* and *I, Claudius.*

The great issue today is whether the BBC should leave the government fold. Advocates of privatization argue that the BBC could exploit its powerful brand name better if it were privatized. The privatization advocates also say that the BBC's government ties are keeping it from aggressively pursuing partnerships that could make it a global competitor with companies like Time Warner and Rupert Murdoch's News Corporation. But continuing to do business as usual, they say, will leave the Beeb in everybody else's dust.

CHECKING YOUR MEDIA LITERACY

- **What sets the BBC apart from other international broadcast organizations?**
- **Is the BBC a government mouthpiece? Explain.**

INDIA

The world's largest democracy, India, has a highly developed movie industry that took root by providing affordable entertainment to mass audiences when the country was largely impoverished. The industry, called **Bollywood,** a contrivance of its historic roots in Bombay and the U.S. movie capital Hollywood, is adapting as India moves rapidly out of its Third World past. Today India is becoming a model for new media applications, like wi-fi, as the country brings itself into modern times.

>> **Bollywood.** At 85 cents a seat, people jam Indian movie houses in such numbers that some exhibitors schedule five showings a day starting at 9 a.m. Better seats sell out days in advance in some cities. There is no question that movies are the country's strongest mass medium. Even though per capita income is only $1,360 a year, Indians find enough rupees to support an industry that cranks out as many as 1,200 movies a year, twice as many as U.S. moviemakers. Most are B-grade formula melodramas and action stories. Screen credits often include a director of fights. Despite their flaws, Indian movies are so popular that it is not unusual for a movie house in a Hindi-speaking area to be packed for a film in another Indian language that nobody in the audience understands. Movies are produced in 16 Indian languages.

The movie mania centers on stars. Incredible as it may seem, M. G. Ramachandran, who played folk warriors, and M. R. Radha, who played villains, got into a real-life gun duel one day. Both survived their wounds, but Ramachandran exploited the incident to bid for public office. He campaigned with posters that showed him bound in head bandages and was elected chief minister of his state. While in office, Ramachandran continued to make B-grade movies, always as the hero.

Billboards, fan clubs and scurrilous magazines fuel the obsession with stars. Scholars Erik Barnouw and Subrahmanyam Krishna, in their book *Indian Film*, characterize the portrayals of stars as "mythological demigods who live on a highly physical and erotic plane, indulging in amours." In some magazines, compromising photos are a specialty.

Bollywood
Nickname for India's movie industry

wi-fi
Wireless fidelity technology, which offers limited-range downloading

>> **Wi-Fi.** India has taken a lead in linking remote villages with the rest of the world through wireless technology. Villagers and farmers who once had to walk several miles to pay their power bills now go to a "knowledge center," as it's called—several rooms equipped with desktop computers, connected by **wi-fi** to the Internet—and pay online. Such "knowledge centers" are being installed in 600,000 villages in a government-enterpreneurial program launched in 2005. Eventually, all 237,000 villages in India large enough to have a governing unit will be equipped.

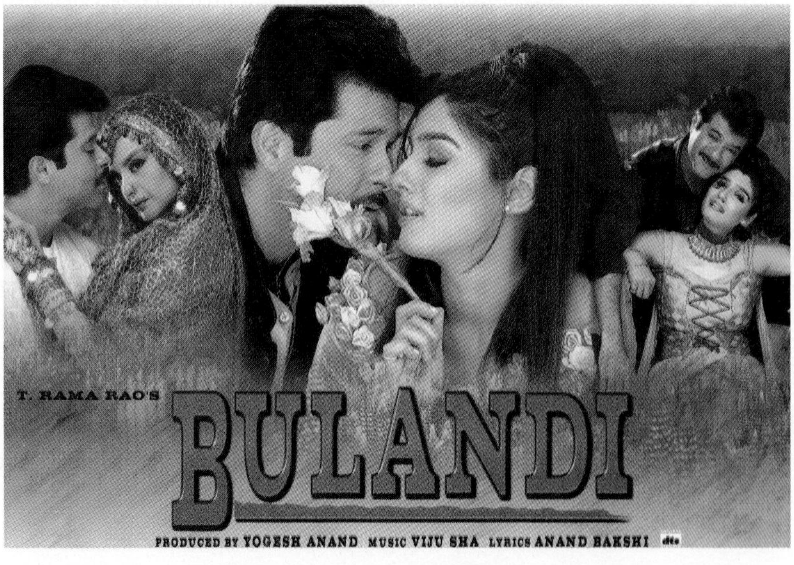

Bollywood. *The Indian movie industry, centered in Bombay and sometimes called Bollywood, pumps out an incredible 1,200 movies a year. Although India has some internationally recognized moviemakers, most Bollywood productions are formulaic action movies that critics derisively label "curry westerns."*

India Censorship. *After 207 people were killed by terrorist bombs on Mumbai commuter trains, India's Department of Telecommunications ordered Google and other web portal companies to block access to specified web sites. The action was inconsistent with India's democratic tradition, but the government decreed that continuing access to the sites was a threat to security. The bombings were blamed on militant Islamists from neighboring Pakistan.*

The Indian experience is a model for extending mass media links into isolated, poverty-ridden areas in Africa and eastern Europe. Farmers can learn market corn prices to decide when it's best to sell. Faraway doctors can diagnose illnesses through digital electrocardiography. In India a company named n-Logue has designed wi-fi kiosks for rural villages at $1,200 a unit, complete with a computer, software, a digital camera, paper and a backup power supply. Kiosks can have ATM banking too.

A remaining obstacle is the diversity in languages in many underdeveloped parts of the world. Google doesn't translate universally.

CHECKING YOUR MEDIA LITERACY

- **How do you explain the powerful influence of the Indian movie industry?**
- **Is wi-fi the way to bring remote parts of India into the country's mainstream economic expansion? How so?**

COLOMBIA

High drama is popular on Colombian radio stations, but it is hardly theatrical. In Colombia thousands of people, both wealthy and ordinary, are kidnapped captives. Families go on the air to express their love and support in the hope that their kidnapped kin are listening. It makes for powerful radio. Tragically, it's real.

Drug lords and petty criminals alike have found kidnapping to be lucrative in a country where anarchy is practically an everyday reality. The mass media are hardly immune. In the 1990s, according to the U.S.-based Committee to Protect Journalists, 31 journalists were killed because of their work. Sixteen others have died in incidents that may or may not have been related to their work. In a typical year, six to 10 journalists are kidnapped in a country whose population is less than that of the U.S. Pacific Coast states.

A political satirist, Jamie Garzón, was shot to death in 1999 after a television show. *El Espectador*, a leading newspaper, has armed guards at every entrance and around the perimeter, as do most media operations. Many reporters are assigned bodyguards, usually two, both armed. Two *El Espectador* reporters have fled the country under threat. The editor of another daily, *El Tiempo*, fled in 2000 after supporting a peace movement.

Beset with corruption fueled by the powerful cocaine industry, the government has no handle on assaults against the media. Although hypersensitive to negative coverage, the drug industry is not the only threat to the Colombian media. The Committee to Protect Journalists, Human Rights Watch, Amnesty International and other watchdogs blame renegade paramilitary units and guerrillas, some of whom are ideologically inspired. Also, the Colombian military itself and some government agencies have been implicated.

CHECKING YOUR MEDIA LITERACY

- **What steps can be taken in a country like Colombia to create an environment in which newspeople can perform their highest service?**

CHAPTER WRAP-UP

Mass Media and Nation-States
(Pages 397–402)

- The world's nations and media systems can be measured on a scale of media freedom. At one extreme are nations in a libertarian tradition, which accords high levels of autonomy and independence to the mass media. Libertarianism emphasizes the ability of human beings to reason their own way to right conclusions and therefore believes humans are capable of their own governance. Democracy and a free mass media are in the libertarian tradition. At the other extreme are authoritarian nations with top-down leadership in control, sometimes overtly and onerously, sometimes less so. Libertarianism and authoritarianism are philosophically irreconcilable systems, a fact that explains many divisions in the world.

Arab Media Systems
(Pages 406–408)

- Although most nations in Islam-dominated regions are authoritarian, they also are diverse. Some are theocracies for all practical purposes, even when internal Islamic sects are hardly of one mind. Some of these countries, however, have moved beyond religion and pragmatically sought to be part of the modern world. Examples include the Qatar-based Al-Jazeera news network that seeks pan-Arabic, even global mass audiences. Media production centers, notably in Lebanon and Dubai but also elsewhere, are cultivating transborder and transcultural Arab and Islamic audiences.

War as a Libertarian Test (Pages 402–405)

- For all of its attractions for Americans, whose traditions are libertarian, the concept has had a rough history. U.S. leadership hasn't always been responsive to the idea of grassroots governance nor to the ideal of a free press as embodied in the nation's Constitution. In times of war, even little wars like Grenada, leadership consistently has declared that national survival trumps free expression and a free press. The trials of combat put even the greatest democracies to the test of libertarian ideals. Contradictory policies result, including censorship and suppression of dissent.

Media and Terrorism (Pages 408–409)

- Terrorism has emerged as a major weapon in the global culture wars, aimed both at Western institutions from Islamic-dominated regions and at battling Islamic factions. The techniques of terrorism, low-cost and mostly with easily mastered technology, have become a major propaganda tool in stirring odd mixes of religious pride and intolerance and also mindless hatred. Partisans find video cell phones a powerful tool for recruiting support. Insurgents in Iraq use YouTube-style videos to easily outflank sophisticated U.S. appeals for popular support.

Battle for Iran (Pages 410–411)

- Strategically located Iran, bristly in international relations, has become the target of outside media bombardment for reform. The U.S. State Department has fine-tuned its lessons from the Cold War and regeared its Voice of America to influence internal affairs in Iran. Meanwhile, in Los Angeles, home to thousands of Iranian expatriates, entrepreneurs have financed satellite television stations to encourage change. The satcast services are a transforming entry in global communication. In response, the government of Iran is employing traditional methods from the Cold War to block out transborder communication.

China Media (Pages 412–417)

- China's emergence as a global economic power hinges in part on its tightly controlling mass media. Government policy is to let nothing interfere with the stability necessary for the nation's economic engine to remain in high gear. The government has created the largest pre-publication censorship apparatus in human history, called the Chinese Firewall, to monitor and censor incoming communication. Within the country, both entertainment and news media are kept in check—although signs of loosening appear from time to time.

Distinctive Media Systems (Pages 417–420)

- Nations organize their media systems differently. Even largely similar systems like those in Britain and the United States have distinctive methods for funding. Some countries like India have unique features. Some countries have unique developmental needs. In a nation like Colombia, where drug lords and gangs exercise heavy influence on media content through threats of violence, including kidnapping and murders, media have a unique set of obstacles.

▼ Review Questions

1. List countries that fit the definition of *libertarian*. List also those that fit the definition of *authoritarian*. Justify your choices.
2. How well have various wartime efforts to accommodate free news reporting worked throughout U.S. history?
3. What generalizations can be made about government and media systems in Islam-dominated regions? How do these generalizations miss many realities?
4. Are insurgents destined to forever have an advantage through low-cost new technology in information and propaganda wars?
5. What are the echoes of the Cold War in the battle over information and ideas in Iran? What are the differences?
6. How effective have China's efforts at controlling mass media been? What do you see as the future of these efforts?

Concepts

authoritarianism (Page 397)
divine right of kings (Page 399)
marketplace of ideas (Page 399)
self-righting process (Page 401)

Terms

Al-Jazeera (Page 406)
embeds (Page 406)
Emergency Response Law (Page 413)
Enlightenment (Page 401)
pool system (Page 403)

People

Hammad bin Khalifa (Page 406)
Henry VIII (Page 397)
John Milton (Page 399)
Liu Di (Page 412)

Media Sources

Scholarly journals that carry articles on foreign media systems and issues include the *International Communication Bulletin*.

- Charles Hirschkind. *The Ethical Soundscape: Cassette Sermons and Islamic Counterpublics.* Columbia University Press, 2006. Hirschkind, an anthropologist whose interests bridge media and religion, examines the role of cassette sermons in the daily lives of Muslims in the Middle East.
- Thomas L. Friedman. *The World Is Flat: A Brief History of the 21st Century.* Farrar, Straus and Giroux, 2005. Friedman, a journalist, provides an overview of how media resulting from new technology are transforming global economics.
- Michael S. Sweeney. *Secrets of Victory: The Office of Censorship and the American Press and Radio in World War II.* University of North Carolina Press, 2001. Sweeney, a scholar, examines the U.S. government's World War II censorship program and attempts to explain its success. Sweeney, once a reporter himself, draws on archival sources.
- Daya Kishan Thussu, editor. *Electronic Empires: Global Media and Local Resistance.* Arnold, 1999. Sixteen essays evaluate media globalization, especially television, from a diverse range of perspectives, including cultural imperialism and audience liberation.

MASS MEDIA GLOBALIZATION

In this chapter you have deepened your media literacy by revisiting several themes. Here are thematic highlights from the chapter:

MEDIA TECHNOLOGY

Who's Watching? *The U.S. message to Iraqis, omniscient in a big budget media campaign, hasn't carried the day. Meanwhile, insurgents are splicing motivational music with anti-American combat scenes and getting their message out on ubiquitous video cell phones.*

Media technology that's accessible on a small budget is changing global mass communication. With $6 million, a fraction of what it would cost to build a traditional television station, Iranian expatriate Zia Atabay built a satellite station in Los Angeles to encourage political reform in his homeland. Now 20 such stations in the United States are beaming messages to Iran. Low-cost media technology is leapfrogging traditional media thinking. The government of Iran, for example, is trying old-style broadcast blocking and Internet intercepts with limited success. Elsewhere, financially accessible technology, especially cell phone videos, have given terrorists an advantage in propaganda wars against major powers like the United States. (Pages 410–411)

MEDIA ECONOMICS

Al-Jazeera. *The pan-Arab news channel has become the world's fifth most-recognized brand.*

Advertising revenue goes to the media that amass audiences that advertisers covet. This financial incentive has become a factor in burgeoning broadcast services in Islamic-dominated regions. The 24-hour Arab television news service Al-Jazeera, for example, was designed to attract a pan-Arab audience that never existed before. Other Middle East enterprises have the same goal, some aiming for global audiences. (Pages 406–407)

MEDIA AND DEMOCRACY

Chinese Democracy. *Cell phone voting for the Mongolian Cow Sour Yogurt Supergirl may be as close as China has come to democracy. Could a taste of majority rule be a prelude?*

The democratic ideal of government enacting the will of the people requires an informed populace. The ideal is from the philosophical school of libertarianism, which holds that people can reach good conclusions through the open exchange of ideas. This principle was articulated by the English poet and novelist John Milton in 1644. Libertarianism became the philosophical basis for the form of democracy pioneered by the United States when it was a new country in the late 1700s. (Pages 399–402, 402–410, 412)

MEDIA EFFECTS

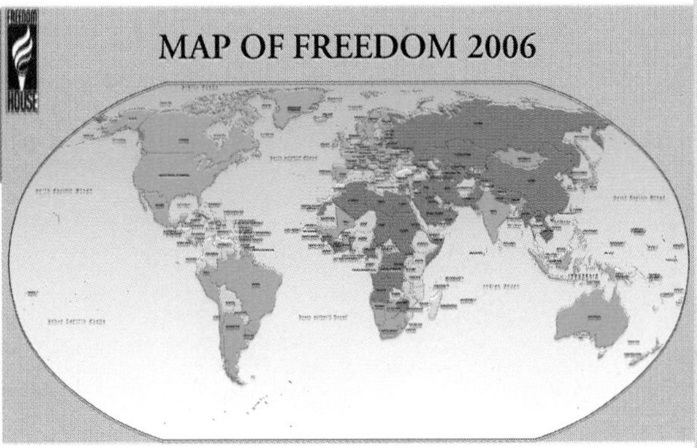

Measuring Freedom. *The greening of the planet by Freedom House, which tracks global press freedom, has been gradual but steady for 20 years. Russia wobbles. Most of Asia and Africa have consistently been in the authoritarian tradition.*

Although media effects are difficult to measure, governments, including that of the United States, have invested heavily in directly reaching people in other countries to encourage political reforms if not outright revolt. The United States became heavily involved in transborder broadcasting during World War II with Voice of America. VOA and similar services continued into the Cold War with programming aimed at Russia and Eastern Europe. Today variants are targeting people in Cuba, Arab nations and wherever it suits U.S. national policy. Governments of target nations hardly see these projects as benign. Attempts are made to block incoming programs. (Page 410–412)

ELITISM AND POPULISM

Rival Theorists. *What a conversation King James and John Milton would have had. The scholarly British king defended monarchical systems as divine and thus beyond criticism. Two generations later, Milton made the case for libertarianism in* Areopagitica.

Authoritarian government systems are elitist. A monarch or a coterie of governing elite are presumed to hold answers that common folks can't recognize without guidance. This monopoly on knowing what's best includes social policies, cultural affairs and other matters, including media content. In contrast, libertarianism has confidence in individual human beings. Given enough time to sort through even the most complex issues, according to libertarians, people individually and collectively will reach correct conclusions. To work well, libertarianism requires that mass media be an uncensored forum for people to gather information and exchange ideas. (Pages 397–402)

chapter 16

MEDIA LAW

Waiting for the Judge *Jon Lech Johansen waits for his case to begin in a Norway court. The U.S. movie industry had gone after DVD-Jon, as he came to be called, for publishing code that enabled others to copy disks. He was acquitted.*

LEARNING AHEAD

- Copyright law protects intellectual property, with a lot of twists wrought by emerging technology.
- The heart of U.S. mass media law is the First Amendment's guarantee of free expression.
- The First Amendment has come to be applied more broadly over the years.
- Anyone falsely slandered by the mass media may sue for libel.
- Mass media generally may not intrude on someone's solitude.

SHAKING UP HOLLYWOOD

By age 12, Jon Lech Johansen had written his first computer program. That made him a wunderkid of sorts. But nobody foresaw that he would, while still a teenager, devise programs that would shake the billion-dollar Hollywood movie industry to its core. His genius also would make him a folk hero to millions of movie-lovers worldwide.

Jon-Lech, as he came to be lionized in his native Norway, began his trek to notoriety unwittingly. He loved movies. By 15 he owned 360 DVDs. Some he bought at jacked-up Norwegian prices because Hollywood's geographical coding prevented European computers from playing U.S.-issued versions. Other DVDs he bought from U.S. sources, and with coding he invented, he played them on his computer in Oslo. It all was perfectly legal in Norway. He recalls reveling at his accomplishment when he first ripped copies of *The Matrix* and *The Fifth Element.*

"Why shouldn't others share my enjoyment?" he asked himself. A week later, he posted his coding on the Internet.

Hollywood went ballistic, recognizing that Jon-Lech's coding could be used to bypass the encrypting that prevented their DVD movies from being easily swapped through file-sharing. The revenue loss could be devastating. The Motion Picture Association of America pushed Norwegian authorities to act. Police raided the Johansen home, confiscated Jon-Lech's computer, and put him through seven hours of interrogation. Confident he had done nothing wrong, Jon-Lech even gave police the password to his computer.

Johansen thus found himself at the vortex of a continuing struggle between the rights of megamedia conglomerates that own creative material and the rights of individuals to do what they want with products they buy—in this case copying DVDs, and also music, to play on any number of their own devices.

For the trial, Hollywood executives flew to Oslo to argue that Johansen had unleashed software that facilitated movie piracy and could put the movie industry in ruins. Johansen responded that he had committed no wrongdoing, let alone piracy, and that he had a fundamental human right of free expression to share his coding however he wanted. In effect, he said: "Go after the pirates, not me." Jon-Lech fancied himself a consumer advocate, allowing people to use their DVD purchases as they wanted—on computers at home, on laptops on the road, on handheld devices anywhere else. The court agreed. In fact, when the prosecution appealed, the court again agreed.

In the run-up to the trial, Jon-Lech supporters worldwide distributed T-shirts and neckties printed with his software. In the May Day parade in Oslo, backers carried a banner "Free DVD-Jon." The issue inspired a haiku. Meanwhile, more than 1 million copies of his anti-DVD encryption software had been downloaded from Johansen's site.

For better or worse, depending on your perspective, Norway later revised its laws to forbid software that could be used to undermine copyright protections, as the United States had done earlier at the behest of giant media companies. But the issue lives on, as you will discover in this chapter on mass media law. The chapter includes the most pressing media law dilemma in the early 21st century—the protection of intellectual property.

Intellectual Property

STUDY ***PREVIEW***

Products produced by mass media companies go by the legal name of *intellectual property*. Copyright law protects ownership rights to intellectual property. Other rights, including consumer rights and free expression rights, have arisen to challenge the long-held supremacy of copyright. Mass media companies are worried.

COPYRIGHT

copyright
Protects the ownership rights of creative works, including books, articles and lyrics

intellectual property
Creative works

Copyright has been around since the beginning of the Republic. The founders wrote copyright law into the Constitution. When Congress first convened in 1790, the second law to be passed was for copyright. The whole idea was to encourage creativity. With creative work classified as property, creative people have a legal right to derive income from their works by charging for their use. An author, for example, can charge a book publisher a fee for publishing the book. Actually, it's a little more complicated, but that's the idea. The goal was to guarantee a financial incentive for creative people to keep creating. Why? The rationale was that a society is richer for literature and music and other creative works. Inventions, which are covered by patents, are a separate area of **intellectual property** law.

CASE STUDY

The Price of Free Music

IF 1
YOU 2
CAN'T 3
SEE THAT 4
ILLEGAL DOWNLOADING 5
IS STEALING 6
THEN KEEP READING 7
If you download music illegally, you are stealing music.
Every month, thousands of students face university disciplinary action or lawsuits and fines that cost thousands of dollars.
Legal downloading doesn't cost much. The choice is yours. Pay a little now or a lot more later.
RIAA
Developed by university students for the RIAA.

Piracy Not Nice. *The recording industry, crippled by revenue losses from music file-swapping, has gone after downloaders, mostly college students, for copyright infringement. Legal settlements can run into thousands of dollars.*

Imagine opening an urgent e-mail from the Recording Industry Association of America accusing you of illegally downloading hundreds of songs onto your computer. Indeed, you have used a file-sharing program you found on the Internet to build your music collection. By doing this, the e-mail charges, you have violated federal copyright law. The law, you're reminded, grants rights to an artist, publisher or distributor for exclusive publication, production, sale or distribution of artistic work. The message from the RIAA is threatening: Settle now for several thousand dollars or we'll see you in federal court.

A hoax? Not for several hundred college students who have received these "prelitigation" e-mails. Most students settle, despite feeling that they were unfairly singled out. After all, it's estimated that more than half of all college students illegally download copyrighted music and movies. As one 20-year-old student who recently received the RIAA e-mail explained: "I knew it was illegal, but no one got in trouble for it."

Copyright violations continue to cost the artistic community billions of dollars. And with less money to reward artistic endeavors, some are concerned that artists will not be able to support themselves and that the companies that distribute the art will be less willing to invest because of diminishing returns. There are also those who argue that copyright violators hurt honest people because the artistic community has to increase prices to offset losses to copyright infringers.

DEEPENING YOUR MEDIA LITERACY

EXPLORE THE ISSUE

Think of web sites that allow people to download music or movies legally.

DIG DEEPER

Do you think the lawsuits brought by the recording industry will solve the problem of illegal downloading? Are there alternatives? Would legislation help? How about education programs starting in grade school?

WHAT DO YOU THINK?

Individuals who download music may not be the only ones being sued. Media giant Viacom has sued YouTube because its users can illegally upload Viacom movies. Is it just a matter of time before individual YouTube users are also sued for sharing copyrighted media without permission?

>> **Permissions.** Copyright law allows creators to control their creation. They can sell it, lease it, give it away or just sit on it. The law is the vehicle through which creative people earn a livelihood, just as someone in the trades, like a carpenter earning money from carpentry or a landlord earning money by renting out real estate. Creators of intellectual property grant **permissions** for the use of their work, usually for a fee. Freelance photographers charge magazines that want to use their photographs. Composers charge music publishers that want to issue their music.

>> **Assignments.** As a practical matter, most photographers, composers, authors and other creators of intellectual property don't have the expertise or means to exploit the commercial potential of their work. Simon & Schuster, for example, can better market a hot murder mystery than can its best whodunit author. Imagine Jay-Z without Def Jam. Or a Mark Burnett eco-adventure show without CBS. Although there are notable Lone Rangers, the resources of major media companies make it attractive for the creators of intellectual property to sell or assign their rights to a media company. In exchange for the **assignment** of their rights, the originating creator usually receives a flat fee or a percentage of the eventual revenue.

Also, media companies hire creative people whose work, as part of their employment, belongs automatically to the company.

For media companies, these rights are a treasure trove. It's their product. It's what they have to sell. No surprise, media companies vigilantly guard their intellectual property against theft, or **piracy,** as they call it. Hollywood studios have dozens of attorneys who monitor for **infringements** of their copyrights. So do music companies. Magazines and newspapers are increasingly active in identifying infringements. Not uncommonly, media companies go to court against anyone who expropriates their property without permission and without paying a fee.

CHECKING YOUR MEDIA LITERACY

- **Who are the various parties that can own a copyright?**
- **What recourse do copyright owners have against infringements?**

CONSUMER RIGHTS

Predictably, mass media companies overreact when a threat to their tried-and-true business models presents itself. This has been no more true than in frenzied, almost Luddite attempts by media companies to apply copyright law to shield their old and comfortable ways of doing business. Time and again, media companies, wedded to the past, have failed to think outside the box and exploit new technologies. In fact, not since the glory days of RCA, which prided itself on research and development under David Sarnoff, have established companies been on the technological cutting edge.

Recent history has shown media companies merely making tepid applications of technology for modest advantages in efficiency. Then, wham, they find their existence on the verge of being upended by innovators who are seeing new basic infrastructures and saying to hell with old business models. Consider the recorded music industry in the Napster and Grokster cases, and the book industry in the Google case.

>> **Grokster.** In the 1990s, the music recording industry, entrenched in its traditional ways of doing business, was in a frenzy with music-swapping software sales eroding profits dramatically. First with Napster, then other peer-to-peer music-sharing services, people were bypassing the retail CD bins. Napster was the first to hit the dust, in a 2001 federal court case. Then came the case against **Grokster,** another peer-to-peer service. Grokster argued that its software was neutral as to the rights and wrongs of copyright law. Yes, said Grokster, there could be misuses but the recording industry's legal target should be the misusers—not Grokster.

permissions
Grant of rights for a second party to use copyright-protected work

assignment
Transfer of ownership interest in a piece of intellectual property

piracy
Theft of copyright-protected material

infringement
A violation of copyright

Grokster
Involved in U.S. Supreme Court case that said promoting the illegal copying of intellectual property is an infringement on copyright

Download Protest. *Among young people, emotions run high about music. A widely held view is that access to music should be free. When the U.S. Supreme Court was hearing the Grokster case over software intended to facilitate music downloads without the permission of copyright holders, protesters displayed their disdain for the record industry's initiative to shut down file-sharing.*

In deciding the case in 2005, the Supreme Court noted that Grokster had explicitly promoted the copyright-infringement potential of its software. It was right there in the company's own advertising. The ads were self-incriminating ads, the Court said. Grokster was out of business. The lesson is that infringement-enabling devices are all right as long as infringement isn't encouraged.

In any event, the music recording industry was shaken by Napster and look-alike systems like Grokster. The end result, after the legal battles, was that the industry came out of its decades-old buffered ways, which had been shielded by copyright law, and embraced the new technology. Even by the time of the Grokster decision, the German-owned global media giant Bertelsmann had bought the remnants of Napster to find ways to market its music online. Also, Apple's online music store, iTunes, introduced in 2002, was an instant success. Other online music sales outlets cropped up, sponsored by record makers, to capitalize on new technology—not to fight it or go into denial.

>> **Google.** The book industry, also entrenched in old ways, missed the potential of digital technology. Except for back-shop production efficiencies, which were invisible to readers, and marketing web sites and minor forays with e-books, publishers had to be dragged kicking and screaming into the 21st century, like the movie and recording industries before them. Google was the reason.

Fueled with untold revenues from its massively successful search engine in the early 2000s, Google expanded rapidly into new ventures. In 2005, Google executives talked five major libraries into allowing it to digitize their entire collections, 15 million books in the English language. The goal, then, was to create a single online index system, the **Google Print Library Project,** with worldwide free access.

Publishers first bristled, then sued. The claim was that their intellectual property interests would be jeopardized through free online access to copyright-protected works not yet in the public domain.

Google and the Association of American Publishers reached a settlement in 2009. Almost immediately other groups including the Authors Guild as well as industry groups in other countries questioned the settlement and raised objections of their own. These issues may create new parameters on the protections afforded by copyright law. Whatever the outcome, the case further illustrates that mass media companies are less in control of the technology that is reshaping the world than are companies and individuals who specialize in the research and creative thinking that brings about technical revolution.

Google Print Library Project
Digitizes 15 million English-language books for online index access by Google

CHECKING YOUR MEDIA LITERACY

- How have the consumer rights movement and the copyright community collided?
- What lessons about copyright can be derived from the Grokster decision?
- What are the copyright issues in the Google library project?

Free Expression

STUDY PREVIEW

A core American value is that the government cannot impede free expression, which, of course, extends to the mass media. Although the U.S. Constitution bars government censorship, the courts have allowed exceptions. These exceptions include utterances that could undermine national security in wartime. In general the Supreme Court has expanded the prohibition on censorship over the years.

DISTRUST OF GOVERNMENT

In colonial times, before the formation of the United States, a critical mass of libertarians ascended into leadership roles as ill feeling grew against British authority. These people were still in critical leadership roles when the Revolutionary War ended. These included many luminaries of the time—Thomas Jefferson, Benjamin Franklin, James Madison and John Adams. Their rhetoric excoriated the top-down authoritarian British governance system.

In drafting the Constitution for the new republic, the founders, mindful of their experience as part of the British empire, were firm in their distrust of governmental authority. Also, they exalted the ability of people individually and collectively to figure out their way to the best courses of action through free inquiry and free expression in an unregulated marketplace of ideas. No surprise, the Constitution they put together prohibited government from interfering in free expression. The prohibition is in the Constitution's **First Amendment:** "Congress shall make no law... abridging the freedom of speech or of the press." The amendment, a mere 45 words, also prohibits government from interfering in religion. Also, it guarantees people the right to complain about the government and demand that wrongs be righted. Most relevant for media people are the free speech and free press clauses, which can be summed up as the **free expression provision.**

Implicit in the First Amendment is a role for the mass media as a watchdog guarding against government misdeeds and policies. In this respect, the media, in news as well as in other content areas, are an informal **fourth branch of government**—in addition to the executive, judicial and legislative branches. The media have a role in governance to, in effect, ensure that the government is accountable to the people.

First Amendment
Prohibits government interference in free expression, religion and individual and public protests against government policies

CHECKING YOUR MEDIA LITERACY

- Describe the roots of the First Amendment in libertarian principles.

free expression provision
First Amendment ban against government abridgment of freedom of speech and freedom of the press

fourth branch of government
The mass media

Alien and Sedition acts
1798 laws with penalties for free expression

FIRST AMENDMENT REDISCOVERED

As ironic as it seems, merely six years after the Constitution and the First Amendment were ratified, Congress passed laws to limit free expression. People were jailed and fined for criticizing government leaders and policies. These laws, the **Alien and Sedition acts** of 1798, ostensibly were for national security at a time of paranoia about a French invasion. One of the great mysteries in U.S. history is how Congress, which included many of the same people who had created the Constitution, could so contradict the anti-censorship provision of the First Amendment.

The fact, however, is that nobody paid much attention to the First Amendment for more than 100 years of the nation's history. It was a nice idea but complicated.

Nobody wanted to tackle tough questions, such as in the case of the 1798 laws, whether exceptions to free expression were needed in times of war or a threat.

Many states, meanwhile, had laws that explicitly limited freedom of expression. The constitutionality of these laws too went unchallenged.

Not until 1919 did the U.S. Supreme Court decide a case on First Amendment grounds. Two Socialists, husband and wife **Charles Schenck** and **Elizabeth Baer,** had been arrested by federal agents for distributing an antiwar pamphlet. They sued, contending that the government had violated their free-expression rights as guaranteed by the First Amendment. The Supreme Court turned down their appeal, saying that censorship is reasonable in war, but the justices acknowledged in the case, usually called *Schenck* v. *U.S.,* that freedom from government restraint is a civil right of every citizen.

Numerous other censorship cases also flowed from World War I. In 1925 the Court overruled a New York state law under which antiwar agitator **Benjamin Gitlow** had been arrested. Gitlow lost his case, but importantly, the Court said that state censorship laws in general were unconstitutional.

CHECKING YOUR MEDIA LITERACY

- **Explain the anomalies of the 1798 Alien and Sedition acts.**
- **Explain the Supreme Court's 130 years of First Amendment silence.**

Charles Schenck, Elizabeth Baer
Principal plaintiffs in 1919 U.S. Supreme Court opinion decided on First Amendment grounds

Benjamin Gitlow
Principal in 1924 U.S. Supreme Court decision that barred state censorship laws

Near* v. *Minnesota
U.S. Supreme Court case that barred government interference with free expression in advance

prior restraint
Prohibiting expression in advance

Clarence Brandenburg
Ku Klux Klan leader whose conviction was overturned because his speech was farfetched

PRIOR RESTRAINT

On a roll with the First Amendment, the Supreme Court in 1931 barred the government in most situations from silencing someone before an utterance. The ruling, in ***Near* v. *Minnesota,*** banned **prior restraint.** A Minneapolis scandal sheet had been padlocked by the sheriff under a state law that forbade "malicious, scandalous and defamatory" publications. The great libertarian John Milton, who had articulated the marketplace of ideas concept in 1644, would have shuddered at the law. So did the U.S. Supreme Court. In a landmark decision against government acts to preempt free expression before it occurs, the Court ruled that any government unit at any level is in violation of the First Amendment if it suppresses a publication because of what might be said in the next issue.

Nobody would much defend Near's paper, the *Saturday Press,* just his right to write whatever he wanted. Stories were peppered with bigoted references to "niggers," "yids," "bohunks" and "spades." The court did say, however, that prior restraint might be justified in extreme situations. But exceptions must be extraordinary, such as life-and-death situations in wartime.

Since *Near* the Supreme Court has moved to make it even more difficult for the government to interfere with freedom of expression. In an important case, from the perspective of free-expression advocates, the Court overturned the conviction of a white racist, **Clarence Brandenburg,** who had been jailed after a Ku Klux Klan rally in the woods outside Cincinnati. Brandenburg had said hateful and threatening things, but the Court, in a landmark decision in 1969, significantly expanded First Amendment protection for free expression. Even the advocacy of lawless actions is protected,

Clarence Brandenburg

Jay Near

Free Expression Landmarks. *Obscure, despised and discredited, John Near and Clarence Brandenburg were little noted in obituaries when they died. Decent photos weren't even available. Even so, Near and Brandenburg were key in important court cases that bar government interference with free expression. Near's Minnesota scandal sheet had been shut down by a sheriff in the 1920s. He argued that the sheriff had violated the U.S. First Amendment, which forbids government interference with free expression. The U.S. Supreme Court agreed, in effect noting that Near's outrageous hatemongering must be tolerated. In the case of Brandenburg, a white supremacist in the 1950s, the court built on its Near reasoning with explicit requirements that the government must prove to justify limiting free expression. The requirements have virtually precluded government censorship.*

according to the Brandenburg decision, as long as it's unlikely that lawlessness is imminent and probable. This is called the **Incitement Standard.** The distinction is that advocacy is protected up to the moment that lawlessness is incited. According to the Incitement Standard, authorities can justify silencing someone only if:

- The statement advocates a lawless action.
- The statement aims at producing lawless action.
- Such lawless action is imminent.
- Such lawless action is likely to occur.

Unless an utterance meets all four tests, it cannot be suppressed by the government.

CHECKING YOUR MEDIA LITERACY

- **How can restrictions on free expression be justified in view of the absolutist language of the First Amendment?**
- **What was the significance of *Near* v. *Minnesota*?**
- **What is the Incitement Standard?**

ALLOWABLE ABRIDGMENTS

In its wisdom the U.S. Supreme Court has avoided creating a rigid list of permissible abridgments to freedom of expression. No matter how thoughtfully drafted, a rigid list could never anticipate every situation. Nonetheless, the Supreme Court has discussed circumstances in which censorship is sometimes warranted.

>> **National Security.** The federal government jailed dozens of antiwar activists during World War I. Many appealed, prompting the U.S. Supreme Court to consider whether the First Amendment's prohibition against government limitations should be waived in wartime. A federal prosecutor had gone after Charles Schenck of Philadelphia, general secretary of the Socialist Party, and his wife, Elizabeth Baer, for handing out leaflets aimed at recently drafted men. The pamphlets made several points:

- The draft violated the 13th Amendment, which prohibits slavery.
- The draft was unfair because clergy and conscientious objectors, like Quakers, were exempted.
- The war was being fought for the profit of cold-blooded capitalists, who, the leaflets claimed, controlled the country.
- Draftees should join the Socialists and work to repeal the draft law.

Incitement Standard
A four-part test to determine whether an advocacy speech is constitutionally protected

Martyred Political Prisoner. *Eugene Debs, a Socialist Party leader, had run four times for the presidency, in 1900, 1904, 1908 and 1912. He ran a fifth time, in 1920—this time from prison. Here, party officials pose with Debs at the prison after notifying him that he had been nominated. He had been sent to jail for making an antiwar speech, a conviction that was upheld by the U.S. Supreme Court because of special national security considerations in time of war. Debs' 1920 campaign photograph showed him in prison garb with bars in the background—the martyred political prisoner. He won almost 1 million votes. A year later, President Warren Harding pardoned Debs, who by then was aged and ailing.*

As the government prosecutor saw it, the leaflets encouraged insubordination and disloyalty in the military, even mutiny. The Supreme Court agreed that the government can take exceptional prerogatives when the nation is at war. Schenck and Baer lost.

Since *Schenck* in 1919 the Court has repeated its point that national security is a special circumstance in which government restrictions can be justified. Even so, the Court's thinking has evolved in specifics, and many scholars believe that Schenck and Baer today would have prevailed. Support for this assessment of the Court's revised thinking came in an important 1972 case, during the Vietnam war, when the Court overruled the government for threatening the New York *Times* for a series of articles drawn from classified defense documents. In the so-called **Pentagon Papers** case, the Court said that the people's right to know about government defense policy was more important than the government's claim that the *Times* was jeopardizing national security.

>> Public Endangerment. In the Schenck case, the eloquent Justice **Oliver Wendell Holmes** wrote these words: "The most stringent protection of free speech would not protect a man in falsely shouting 'Fire' in a crowded theater and causing panic." His point was that the First Amendment's ban on government abridgment of freedom of expression cannot be applied literally. Holmes was saying that reasonable people agree that there must be exceptions. Since then, lesser courts have carved out allowable abridgments. Some have been endorsed by the Supreme Court. On other cases the Court has been silent, letting lower-level court decisions stand.

In a 1942 New Hampshire case, the police were upheld in jailing **Walter Chaplinsky,** who had taken to the streets to deride religions other than his own as "rackets." Somebody called the police. Chaplinsky then turned his venom on the marshal who showed up, calling him, in a lapse of piety, "a God-damned racketeer" and "a damned fascist." From these circumstances emerged the **Fighting Words Doctrine.** The Court said someone might be justified taking a poke at you for using "fighting words," with perhaps a riot resulting. Preventing a riot was a justification for halting someone's freedom of expression. Again, whether courts today would uphold Chaplinsky being silenced is debated among legal scholars. Nonetheless, the Fighting Words Doctrine from *Chaplinsky* remains as testimony to the Court's willingness to consider public safety as a value that sometimes should outweigh freedom of expression as a value.

The courts also accept time, place and manner limits by the government on expression, using the **TPM Standard.** Cities can, for example, ban newsracks from busy sidewalks where they impede pedestrian traffic and impair safety, as long as the restriction is content-neutral—an important caveat. A newspaper that editorializes against the mayor cannot be restricted while one that supports the mayor is not.

Pentagon Papers
Case in which the government attempted prior restraint against the New York *Times*

Oliver Wendell Holmes
Justice who wrote that shouting "Fire!" in a crowded theater would be justification for abridgment of freedom of speech rights

Walter Chaplinsky
Namesake for the case in which the Fighting Words Doctrine was defined

Fighting Words Doctrine
The idea that censorship can be justified against inciting provocation to violence

TPM Standard
Government may control the time, place and manner of expression as long as limits are content-neutral

CHECKING YOUR MEDIA LITERACY

- **What are the allowable exceptions to the First Amendment prohibition on government interference with free expression? What is the basis for these exceptions?**
- **What is the Fighting Words Doctrine?**
- **Can you give an example of the TPM standard allowing government to ban a publication's distribution?**

Broadening Protection

STUDY PREVIEW

The U.S. Supreme Court's initial First Amendment decisions involved political speech. The justices had no problem applying protections against government interference to political discourse, which is essential in democracy. It became apparent, however, that a fence cannot easily be erected between political and nonpolitical discourse. Gradually, First Amendment protections have been broadened.

POLITICAL EXPRESSION

The strides of the U.S. Supreme Court in the 20th century for free expression first were limited to political expression. The justices saw free exchanges of political ideas as necessary for a functioning democracy. Entertainment and advertising initially were afforded no First Amendment protection. They were considered less important to democracy than political expression. New cases, however, made it difficult to draw the line between political and nonpolitical expression.

>> Literature. A 1930 tariff law was used as an import restriction to intercept James Joyce's *Ulysses* at the docks because of four-letter words and explicit sexual references. The importer, **Random House,** went to court, and the judge ruled that the government was out of line. The judge, **John Woolsey,** acknowledged "unusual frankness" in *Ulysses* but said he could not "detect anywhere the leer of the sensualist." The judge, who was not without humor, made a strong case for freedom in literary expression: "The words which are criticized as dirty are old Saxon words known to almost all men, and, I venture, to many women, and are such words as would be naturally and habitually used, I believe, by the types of folks whose life, physical and mental, Joyce is seeking to describe. In respect to the recurrent emergence of the theme of sex in the minds of the characters, it must always be remembered that his locale was Celtic and his season Spring."

Woolsey was upheld on appeal, and *Ulysses*, still critically acclaimed as a pioneer in stream-of-consciousness writing, remains in print today.

Postal restrictions were used against a 1928 English novel, *Lady Chatterley's Lover*, by D. H. Lawrence. The book was sold in the United States in expurgated editions for years, but in 1959 **Grove Press** issued the complete version. Postal officials denied mailing privileges. Grove sued and won.

In some respects the Grove case was *Ulysses* all over again. Grove argued that Lawrence, a major author, had produced a work of literary merit. Grove said the explicit, rugged love scenes between Lady Chatterley and Mellors the gamekeeper were essential in establishing their violent yet loving relationship, the heart of the story. The distinction between the *Ulysses* and *Lady Chatterley* cases was that one ruling was against the customs service and the other against the postmaster general.

>> Entertainment. Courts had once claimed movie censorship as involving something unworthy of constitutional protection. But movies can be political. Witness the movies of Michael Moore. The Supreme Court in 1952 widened First Amendment protection to movies in striking down a local ban on a controversial movie, *The Miracle,* in which a simple woman explained that her pregnancy was by St. Joseph. Some Christians saw the movie as blasphemy. The Court found, however, that government could not impede the exploration of ideas under the Constitution's guarantee that expression should be free of government control.

>> Advertising. Advertising, called **commercial speech** in legal circles, also was not easily separated from political speech, as the Supreme Court discovered in a libel case out of Alabama. The case originated in an advertisement carried by the New York *Times* to raise money for the civil rights cause. The ad's sponsors included negative statements about Montgomery, Alabama, police. Was this commercial speech, being an ad? Or was it political speech, being on a public policy issue? In the 1964 landmark case *New York Times* v. *Sullivan*, the Court found the ad to be political speech and began opening the door for First Amendment protection of advertising—although the process of full protection for advertising remains a work in progress.

>> Emotive Speech. Polite society has never been particularly tolerant of vulgarities, but what if the vulgarity is clearly political? The issue was framed in the Vietnam war-protest era when a young man showed up at the Los Angeles courthouse wearing a jacket whose back carried a message: "Fuck the Draft." Paul Robert Cohen was sent to jail for 30 days. The Supreme Court overturned the conviction. Justice John Harlan wrote

Random House
Fought against censorship of James Joyce's *Ulysses*

John Woolsey
Judge who barred import law censorship of *Ulysses*

Grove Press
Fought against censorship of D. H. Lawrence's *Lady Chatterley's Lover*

commercial speech
Legalese for advertising

Joey Johnson. *Flag-burning protester whose conviction was overturned on First Amendment grounds.*

that linguistic expression needs to allow for "inexpressible emotions," sometimes called **emotive speech.** As one wag put it: Cohen wouldn't have been arrested if his jacket had said, "The Heck with Conscription" or "I Really Don't Like the Draft Very Much." Instead Cohen chose more charged language, the F-word. His jacket conveyed the depths of his feelings about the draft. Justice Harlan said: "One man's vulgarity is another's lyric. Words are often chosen as much for their emotive as their cognitive force."

>> Hate Speech. Emotions run high on First Amendment issues when national security is at stake or when expression is obnoxious or even vile. The Supreme Court, however, takes the position that a society that is free and democratic cannot have a government that silences somebody just because that person's views don't comport with mainstream values. In effect, the Court says that people need to tolerate a level of discomfort in a society whose core principles value freedom of expression.

This point, made in the Brandenburg case, has come up in Court decisions against **hate speech** laws that grew out of the political correctness movement of the 1990s. Especially notable was *R.A.V.* v. *St. Paul.* Several punks had burned a cross, KKK style, on the lawn of a black family in St. Paul, Minnesota. They were caught and convicted under a municipal ordinance against "hate speech." One of them, identified only as R.A.V. in court documents, appealed to the U.S. Supreme Court on First Amendment grounds. The Court found that the ordinance was aimed at the content of the expression, going far beyond allowable time, place or manner restrictions. The decision was a slap at the political correctness movement's attempts to discourage language that can be taken offensively.

emotive speech
Expressions whose excesses underscore the intensity of an emotion

hate speech
Offensive expressions, especially those aimed at racial, ethnic and sexual-orientation minorities

John Brinkley
Radio quack who challenged government regulation of radio

CHECKING YOUR MEDIA LITERACY

- **What kinds of expressions beyond political speech have been gaining First Amendment protection?**
- **Does the U.S. Supreme Court see four-letter vulgarities as protected by the First Amendment? How about flag burning? How about hate speech?**

John Brinkley

John Brinkley and his bride arrived in Milford, Kansas, population 200, in 1917 and rented the old drug store for $8 a month. Mrs. Brinkley sold patent medicines out front, while Brinkley talked to patients in a back room. One day an elderly gentleman called on "Dr. Brinkley" to do something about his failing manhood. As the story goes, the conversation turned to Brinkley's experience with goats in the medical office of the Swift meat-packing company, a job he had held for barely three weeks. Said Brinkley, "You wouldn't have any trouble if you had a pair of those buck glands in you." The operation was performed in the back room, and word spread. Soon the goat gland surgeon was charging $750 for the service, then $1,000, then $1,500. In 1918 Brinkley, whose only credentials were two mail-order medical degrees, opened the Brinkley Hospital. Five years later he set up a radio station, KFKB, to spread the word about his cures.

Six nights a week, Brinkley extolled the virtues of his hospital over the air. "Don't let your doctor two-dollar you to death," he said. "Come to Dr. Brinkley." If a trip to Milford was not possible, listeners were encouraged to send for Brinkley compounds. Soon the mail-order demand was so great that Brinkley reported he was buying goats from Arkansas by the boxcar. "Dr. Brinkley" became a household word. *Radio Digest* awarded Brinkley's KFKB its Golden Microphone Award as the most popular radio station in the country. The station had received 356,827 votes in the magazine's write-in poll. Brinkley was a 1930 write-in candidate for governor. Harry Woodring won with 217,171 votes to Brinkley's 183,278, but Brinkley would have won had it not been for misspellings that disqualified thousands of write-in ballots.

Also in 1930 the KFKB broadcast license came up for renewal by the Federal Radio Commission, which had been set up to regulate broadcasting. The American Medical Association wanted the license revoked. The medical profession had been outraged by Brinkley but had not found a way to derail his thriving quackery. In fact, Brinkley played to the hearts of thousands of Middle America listeners when he attacked the AMA as "the meat-cutter's union." At the license hearing, Brinkley argued that the First Amendment guaranteed him freedom to speak his views on medicine, goat glands and anything else he wanted. He noted that Congress had specifically forbidden the FRC to censor. It would be a censorious affront to the First Amendment, he said, to take away KFKB's license for what the station put on the air. Despite Brinkley's arguments, the FRC denied renewal.

Brinkley challenged the denial in federal court, and the case became a landmark on the relationship between the First Amendment and U.S. broadcasting. The appeals court sided with the FRC, declaring that broadcast licenses should be awarded for serving "the public interest, convenience and necessity." It was appropriate, said the court, for the commission to review a station's programming to decide on renewal. Brinkley appealed to the U.S. Supreme Court, which declined to hear the case. The goat gland surgeon was off the air, but not for long. In 1932 Dr. Brinkley, proving himself unsinkable, bought a powerful station in Villa Acuna, Mexico, just across the Rio Grande from Del Rio, Texas, to continue peddling his potions. By telephone linkup from his home in Milford, Brinkley continued to reach much of the United States until 1942, when the Mexican government nationalized foreign-owned property.

WHAT DO YOU THINK?

- How do you explain the skirting of First Amendment issues in early court decisions about federal regulation of broadcasting?
- Do you see a problem in a government agency establishing the requirements for a license to broadcast?
- Can you defend the broadcast licensing standard of "public interest, convenience and necessity"?

Goat Gland Surgeon. *Eager for publicity, John Brinkley obliges a photographer by placing a healing hand on a supposedly insane patient he is about to cure. Broadcasting such claims from his Kansas radio station, Brinkley developed a wide market for his potions. Because of his quackery, he lost the station in a significant First Amendment case.*

BROADCAST REGULATION

Early commercial radio was a horrendous free-for-all. Government licensing was a joke. Stations went on the air at any frequency with as much wattage as they wanted. As the number of stations grew, they drowned each other out. To end the cacophony and create a national radio system, Congress established the Federal Radio Commission in 1927 to facilitate the orderly development of the new radio industry. A no-nonsense licensing system was put in place with licenses going to stations that could best demonstrate they would operate in "the public interest, convenience and necessity."

Wait a minute? Government licensing based on performance sure smacks of government regulation. What about the First Amendment?

To sidestep the First Amendment issue, Congress embraced the concept that the airwaves, which carried radio signals, were a public asset and therefore, somewhat like a public park, were subject to government regulation for the public good. The **public airwaves** concept was useful for justifying regulation of the 1927 chaos on the airwaves, but it also was problematic. Some stations that lost licenses made First Amendment objections, but the courts declined to address the inherent constitutional contradictions. The radio industry overall was pleased with the new federal regulatory structure. The system, today under the Federal Communications Commission, later was expanded to television.

Over time many early restrictions have been relaxed. No longer, for example, are stations expected to air public affairs programs as a condition for license renewal. Although the FCC talks tough about on-air indecency, old bans have become loosened with the times.

public airwaves
Concept that broadcast should be subject to government regulation because the electromagnetic spectrum is a public asset

CHECKING YOUR MEDIA LITERACY

- **How has government regulation of broadcasting been justified when regulation of print media is clearly unconstitutional?**

Defamation

STUDY PREVIEW

When the mass media carry disparaging descriptions and comments, they risk being sued for libel. The media have a strong defense if the libel was accurate. If not, there can be big trouble. Libel is a serious matter. Not only are reputations at stake when defamation occurs, but also losing a suit can be so costly that it can put a publication or broadcast organization out of business.

LIBEL AS A CONCEPT

If someone punched you in the face for no good reason, knocking out several teeth, breaking your nose and causing permanent disfigurement, most courts would rule that your attacker should pay your medical bills. If your disfigurement or psychological upset causes you to lose your job, to be ridiculed or shunned by friends and family or perhaps to retreat from social interaction, the court would probably order your attacker to pay additional amounts. Like fists, words can cause damage. If someone writes false, damaging things about you, you can sue for **libel.** Freedom of speech and the press is not a license to say absolutely anything about anybody.

If a libeling statement is false, the utterer may be liable for millions of dollars in damages. The largest jury award to date, in 1997 against the *Wall Street Journal*, was almost twice the earnings that year of the *Journal*'s parent company, Dow Jones Inc. The award was reduced substantially on appeal, but the fact

libel
A written defamation

MEDIA TIMELINE

MASS MEDIA LAW MILESTONES

1700s

Intellectual Property
Congress passed first copyright law (1790)

Free Expression
States ratified First Amendment to U.S. Constitution (1791)

1800s

Censorship
Wartime newspapers closed (1864–1865)

Opposition newspapers padlocked on Lincoln's watch

1900s

Cherry Sisters
Iowa Supreme Court ruled that performers must accept criticism of performances (1901)

Prior Restraint
Justice Oliver Wendell Holmes coined "Fire!" in a crowded theater example for prior restraint (1919)

Book Ban
Court overruled import restriction against *Ulysses* (1930)

Landmark Case
U.S. Supreme Court banned prior restraint in *Near* v. *Minnesota* (1931)

Sullivan Case
U.S. Supreme Court ruled that public figures can sue for libel only if media were reckless (1964)

Obscenity
U.S. Supreme Court ruled that local community standards determine obscenity (1968)

National Security
U.S. Supreme Court banned prior restraint in Pentagon Papers case (1971)

Celebrated and ridiculed vaudeville troupe

Jay Near won against prior restraint

2000s

Download Piracy
Recording industry won case against Grokster and other Internet file-swap enablers (2005)

Napster-like file-swaps outlawed

PIVOTAL EVENTS

1700s

- Revolutionary War (1776–1781)
- Alien and Sedition acts (1798)

1800s

- Civil War (1861–1865)

1900s

- World War I (1914–1918)
- Right to vote extended to women (1920)
- Great Depression (1930s)
- World War II (1941–1945)
- Civil rights movement (1960)
- Humans reached moon (1969)
- Vietnam war (1964–1973)
- Nixon resigns presidency (1974)

2000s

- 9/11 terrorist attacks (2001)
- Iraq war (2003–)
- Hurricane Katrina (2005)

remains that awards have grown dramatically in recent years and can hurt a media company seriously.

CHECKING YOUR MEDIA LITERACY

- **What is the rationale for libel law?**

RECKLESS DISREGARD

Elected officials have a hard time winning libel suits today. Noting that democracy is best served by robust, unbridled discussion of public issues and that public officials are inseparable from public policy, the U.S. Supreme Court has ruled that public figures can win libel suits only in extreme circumstances. The Court has also said that people who thrust themselves into the limelight forfeit some of the protection available to other citizens.

The key Court decision in developing current U.S. libel standards originated in an advertisement carried by the New York *Times* in 1960. A civil rights coalition, the Committee to Defend Martin Luther King and the Struggle for Freedom in the South, escalated its antisegregationist cause by placing a full-page advertisement in the *Times.* The advertisement accused public officials in the South of violence and illegal tactics against the civil rights struggle. Although the advertisement was by and large truthful, it was marred by minor factual errors. Police Commissioner L. B. Sullivan of Montgomery, Alabama, filed a libel action saying that the errors damaged him, and he won $500,000 in an Alabama trial. On appeal to the U.S. Supreme Court, the case, ***New York Times* v. *Sullivan,*** became a landmark in libel law. The Supreme Court said that the importance of "free debate" in a democratic society generally was more important than factual errors that might upset and damage public officials. To win a libel suit, the Court said, public officials needed to prove that damaging statements were uttered or printed with the knowledge that they were false. The question in the *Sullivan* case became whether the *Times* was guilty of "**reckless disregard** of the truth." The Supreme Court said it was not, and the newspaper won.

Questions lingered after the *Sullivan* decision about exactly who was and who was not a public official. Lower courts struggled for a definition, and the Supreme Court eventually changed the term to *public figure.* In later years, as the Court refined its view on issues raised in the *Sullivan* case through several decisions, it remained consistent in giving the mass media a lot of room for error, even damaging error, in discussing government officials, political candidates and publicity hounds.

- **Government officials.** All elected government officials and appointed officials with high-level policy responsibilities are public figures as far as their performance in office is concerned. A member of a state governor's cabinet fits this category. A cafeteria worker in the state capitol does not.
- **Political candidates.** Anyone seeking public office is subject to intense public review, during which the courts are willing to excuse false statements as part of robust, wide-open discussion.
- **Publicity hounds.** Court decisions have gone both ways, but generally people who seek publicity or intentionally draw attention to themselves must prove "reckless disregard of the truth" if they sue for libel.

How far can the media go in making disparaging comments? It was all right, said a Vermont court, when the Barre *Times Argus* ran an editorial that said a political candidate was "a horse's ass, a jerk, an idiot and a paranoid." The court said open discussion on public issues excused even such insulting, abusive and unpleasant verbiage. Courts have generally been more tolerant of excessive language in opinion pieces, such as the Barre editorial, than in fact-based articles.

New York Times v. Sullivan
Libel case that largely barred public figures from the right to sue for libel

reckless disregard
Supreme Court language for a situation in which public figures may sue for libel

CHECKING YOUR MEDIA LITERACY

- **How did *New York Times* v. *Sullivan* significantly change libel law?**
- **How many people can you name who fall into a gray area between public figure and private figure? Discuss their ambiguous status.**

COMMENT AND CRITICISM

People flocked to see the **Cherry Sisters'** act. Effie, Addie, Jessie, Lizzie and Ella toured the country with a song-and-dance act that drew big crowds. They were just awful. They could neither sing nor dance, but people turned out because the sisters were so funny. Sad to say, the Cherry Sisters took themselves seriously. In 1901, desperate for respect, the sisters decided to sue the next newspaper reviewer who gave them a bad notice. That reviewer, it turned out, was Billy Hamilton, who included a lot of equine metaphors in his piece for the Des Moines *Leader*: "Effie is an old jade of 50 summers, Jessie a frisky filly of 40, and Addie, the flower of the family, a capering monstrosity of 35. Their long skinny arms, equipped with talons at the extremities, swung mechanically, and anon waved frantically at the suffering audience. The mouths of their rancid features opened like caverns, and sounds like the wailings of damned souls issued therefrom. They pranced around the stage with a motion that suggested a cross between the *danse du ventre* and the fox trot—strange creatures with painted faces and hideous mien. Effie is spavined, Addie is stringhalt, and Jessie, the only one who showed her stockings, has legs with calves as classic in their outlines as the curves of a broom handle."

Cherry Sisters
Complainants in a case that barred performers from suing critics

fair comment and criticism
Doctrine that permits criticism of performers, performances

The outcome of the suit was another setback for the Cherrys. They lost in a case that established that actors or others who perform for the public must be willing to accept both positive and negative comments about their performance. This right of **fair comment and criticism,** however, does not make it open season on performers in aspects of their lives that do not relate to public performance. The *National Enquirer,* for example, could not defend itself when entertainer Carol Burnett sued for a story that described her as obnoxiously drunk at a restaurant. Not only was the description false (Carol Burnett abstains from alcohol), but Burnett was in no public or performing role at the restaurant. This distinction

Fair Comment and Criticism. *Upset with what an Iowa reviewer had written about their show, the Cherry Sisters sued. The important 1901 court decision that resulted said that journalists, critics and anybody else can say whatever they want about a public performance. The rationale was that someone who puts on a performance for public acceptance has to take a risk also of public rejection.*

between an individual's public and private lives also has been recognized in cases involving public officials and candidates.

CHECKING YOUR MEDIA LITERACY

- **How did *New York Times* v. *Sullivan* enable news reporters to do their work better?**
- **Disparaging comments about an individual in the mass media are acceptable for some situations but not others. Consider a major celebrity. What's off-limits? What's not?**

TRESPASS, FRAUD AND LIBEL

An emerging legal tactic against the news media for disparaging coverage is not libel but trespass and other laws. In 1998 the Utah Restaurant Association sued television station KTVX for a report on roaches in restaurant kitchens and unsanitary food handling and storage. Wesley Sine, attorney for the restaurants, did not sue for libel. Sine argued instead that it was illegal for news reporters to go into a private area, like a kitchen, without permission.

Such end runs around libel law worry media people. The defenses that usually work in libel cases are hard to apply if the media are sued over disparaging reports on grounds other than libel. This was a factor in a case involving the Food Lion supermarket chain that resulted in a $5.5 million jury verdict against ABC television. Food Lion was riled over a report on rats and spoilage in store backrooms as well as unfair labor practices. In its suit, Food Lion never challenged ABC's accuracy. Rather, Food Lion said, among other things, that ABC had committed fraud by sending undercover reporters to get on the Food Lion payroll to investigate the backrooms. On appeal, the damages against ABC were reduced almost to zero—a moral victory for ABC, but it took seven years and lots of expensive lawyers.

CHECKING YOUR MEDIA LITERACY

- **What alternatives to libel law are litigants using against defamatory reporting that is accurate and true?**

Indecency

STUDY PREVIEW

Despite the First Amendment's guarantee of freedom of expression, the U.S. government has tried numerous ways during the past 100 years to regulate obscenity and pornography.

PORNOGRAPHY VERSUS OBSCENITY

Through U.S. history, governments have attempted censorship of various sorts at various levels of jurisdiction. But since the courts over-ruled a government effort to ban James Joyce's classic novel *Ulysses* in the 1930s, much has occurred to discourage censorship.

The U.S. Supreme Court has ruled that **pornography,** material aimed at sexual arousal, cannot be stopped. Import and postal restrictions, however, still can be employed against obscene materials, which the Court has defined as going beyond pornography. Obscenity restrictions apply, said the Court, if the answer is yes to *all* of the following questions:

- Would a typical person applying local standards see the material as appealing mainly for its sexually arousing effect?
- Is the material devoid of serious literary, artistic, political or scientific value?
- Is sexual activity depicted offensively, in a way that violates state law that explicitly defines offensiveness?

pornography
Sexually explicit depictions that are protected from government bans

CHECKING YOUR MEDIA LITERACY

- **How are pornography and obscenity different?**

PROTECTING CHILDREN

Although the Supreme Court has found that the First Amendment protects access to pornography, the Court has stated on numerous occasions that children must be protected from sexually explicit material. It's a difficult double standard, as demonstrated by 1996 and 1999 federal forays into systematically regulating media content with ill-conceived communications decency laws. Without hearings or formal debate, Congress created the laws to keep smut away from children who use the Internet. Although hardly anyone defends giving kids access to indecent material, the laws had two flaws: the difficulty of defining **indecency** and the impossibility of denying questionable material to children without restricting freedom of access for adults.

Before a Philadelphia federal appeals court that reviewed the 1996 Communications Decency Act, witnesses from the Justice Department testified that the law went ridiculously far. The law, they said, required them to prosecute for certain AIDS information, museum exhibits, prize-winning plays and even the *Vanity Fair* magazine cover of actress Demi Moore nude and pregnant.

>> **Access.** When it reviewed the 1996 Communications Decency Act in 1999, the U.S. Supreme Court noted that the Internet is the most democratic of the media, enabling almost anyone to become a town crier or pamphleteer. Enforcing the law would necessarily inhibit freedom of expression of the sort that has roots in the Revolution that resulted in the creation of the Republic and the First Amendment, the court said. The 7-2 decision purged the law from the books.

How, then, are government bans of indecency on radio and television justified but not on the Internet? Justice John Stevens, who wrote the majority Supreme Court opinion, said the Internet is hardly an "invasive broadcasting." The odds of people encountering pornography on the Internet are slim unless they're seeking it, he said. Underpinning the Court's rejection of the **Communications Decency Act** was the fact that the Internet lends itself to free-for-all discussions and exchanges with everybody participating who wants to, whereas other media are dominated by carefully crafted messages aimed at people whose opportunity to participate in dialogue with the message producers is so indirect as to be virtually nil.

Even while politicians and moralists rant at indecency, people seem largely unperturbed by the issue. The V-chip, required by a 1996 law to be built into every television set, allows parents to block violence, sexual explicitness and vulgarity automatically. Although the V-chip was widely praised when it became a requirement, hardly anybody uses it.

In 2006, when Congress was in a new dither over objectionable content, movie industry lobbyist Jack Valenti came out of retirement to lead a $300 million campaign to promote the V-chip. Valenti made the point that stiff fines being levied against broadcasters for indecency are unnecessary because people already have the tool they need to block it, if they want.

indecency
Term used by the Federal Communications Commission to encompass a range of words and depictions improper on public airwaves

Communications Decency Act
Failed 1996 and 1999 laws to keep indecent content off the Internet

Patriot Act
2001 law that gave federal agents new authority to pre-empt terrorism

CHECKING YOUR MEDIA LITERACY

What is the difficulty of enforcing indecency restrictions for children but not adults?

PATRIOT ACT

Immediately after the 9/11 terrorist attacks on New York and Washington in 2001, the Bush administration quickly drafted multiprong legislation to give authorities more power to track terrorists. Despite criticism among civil libertarians that some provisions would allow federal agents to ignore constitutionally guaranteed citizen rights, Congress reasoned that it was better to be safe than sorry and went along, passing the **Patriot Act** by an overwhelming majority.

The book industry mobilized against a provision that allowed federal agents to go into bookstores, unannounced and without close judicial oversight, and confiscate customer records to see who had bought books that might be used to aid or promote terrorism. The provision also allowed agents to go into libraries to see who had been reading what. To book publishers, authors, librarians and indeed all civil liberty advocates, the implications were alarming. They launched a massive lobbying effort to rescind parts of the law that could chill citizen inquiry and expression. Their point was that the law's effect would be to discourage people from reading works on a secret or even nongovernment list of seditious literature.

Four years later, as fear about massive, imminent terrorism eased, Congress pushed to delete Section 215 from the Patriot Act. Earlier attempts in U.S. history to place federal limits on what citizens read had failed too—though through the courts, not the executive or legislative branch of government.

The Patriot Act was rigorously defended in its entirety by President Bush, including Section 215, which especially concerned the book industry, librarians and civil libertarians. Bush argued that the provision had not been used much. But, he said, it needed to be in the government's anti-terrorism arsenal. The law remained in force.

CHECKING YOUR MEDIA LITERACY

- **What is Section 215 of the Patriot Act?**
- **Why do the book industry, librarians and civil libertarians object to Section 215?**

CHAPTER WRAP-UP

Intellectual Property (Pages 425–429)

- Copyright law protects mass communicators and other creative people from having their creative work used without their permission. It's an issue of property rights. Also, copyright law encourages creativity in society with a profit incentive for creative people. They can charge for the use of their work. The financial structure of mass media industries has been built around the copyright concept. Time and again technology has challenged media control over copyrighted content, most recently with downloaded music and video.

Free Expression (Pages 429–432)

- The First Amendment to the U.S. Constitution guarantees freedom to citizens and the mass media from government limitations on what they say. The guarantee has solid roots in democratic theory. Even so, the U.S. Supreme Court has allowed exceptions. These mostly commonsense exceptions include utterances that could undermine national security in wartime. In general, however, the Supreme Court has expanded the prohibition on censorship over the years, all in the libertarian spirit articulated by John Milton in the 1600s.

Broadening Protection (Pages 432–436)

- The U.S. Supreme Court addressed First Amendment issues for the first time after World War I and had little problem in declaring that government limitations were unacceptable for political discourse, albeit with specific exceptions. It turned out, however, that political speech has lots of crossover with literature, entertainment and advertising. Over time, the Supreme Court has broadened First Amendment protection into these additional areas of expression—although less exuberantly than for political issues. An odd exception has been broadcasting, for which the Court has never squarely addressed the contradictions between federal regulation and the First Amendment.

Defamation (Pages 436–440)

- Someone who is defamed can sue for libel. This generally is not a constitutional free expression issue but a civil issue. If the defamation was false and caused someone to suffer public hatred, contempt or ridicule, civil damages can be awarded by the courts. Judgment can be severe, sometimes approaching $100 million. The courts have found some defamations excusable. The landmark *New York Times* v. *Sullivan* decision of 1964 makes it difficult for public figures to recover damages unless there has been reckless disregard for truth. Also, performers cannot sue for criticism of their performances, no matter how harsh.

Indecency (Pages 440–442)

- Indecency revolts many people, but the U.S. Supreme Court in struggling with the issue has said, in effect, that indecency like beauty is in the eye of the beholder. The Court says the media are guaranteed freedom to create pornography and citizens are guaranteed freedom of access. However, sexually explicit material that goes too far—obscenity, the Court has called it—cannot be tolerated. But the Court has never devised a clear distinction between pornography, which is protected, and obscenity, which it says is not. In both categories, however, the Court has endorsed laws to punish purveyors of sexually explicit material to children.

▼ Review Questions

1. What is the rationale underlying copyright law?
2. Why is the First Amendment important to mass media in the United States?
3. What was the direction of court interpretation of the First Amendment in the 1900s?
4. Who can sue for libel?
5. How are obscenity and pornography different?

Concepts

copyright (Page 425)
indecency (Page 441)
libel (Page 436)

Terms

fair comment and criticism (Page 439)
First Amendment (Page 429)
Incitement Standard (Page 431)
pornography (Page 440)
prior restraint (Page 430)

People

Charles Schenck, Elizabeth Baer (Page 430)
Cherry Sisters (Page 439)
Clarence Brandenburg (Page 430)

Media Sources

- James Sullivan. *Seven Dirty Words: The Life and Crimes of George Carlin.* De Capo, 2010. Sullivan, a music journalist and culture critic, tracks Carlin from his radio disc-jockey days through his meteoric ascent from night club gigs into national prominence and controversy.
- Gabriel Schoenfeld. *Necessary Secrets: National Security, the Media and the Rule of Law.* Norton, 2010. Schoenfeld builds a thesis on an interpretation that the founders at the First and Second Continental congresses believed that national defense is less important than transparency in government. His focal point is the 2005 decision of *The New York Times* to reveal massive and secret government wire-tapping that included taps on U.S. citizens.
- Robert J. Wagman. *The First Amendment Book.* Paros, 1991. This lively history of the First Amendment is a solid primer on the subject.
- Clark R. Mollenhoff. "25 Years of *Times* v. *Sullivan,*" *Quill* (March 1989), pages 27–31. A veteran investigative reporter argues that journalists have abused the landmark *Sullivan* decision and have been irresponsibly hard on public figures.
- Fred W. Friendly. *Minnesota Rag: The Dramatic Story of the Landmark Supreme Court Case That Gave New Meaning to the First Amendment.* Random House, 1981. A colorful account of the *Near* v. *Minnesota* prior restraint case.
- Lawrence Lessig. *Remix: Making Art and Commerce Thrive in a Hybrid Economy.* Penguin, 2008. Lessig, a leading theorist on intellectual property, calls for loosening copyright restrictions that he sees as inhibiting creativity.

A Thematic Chapter Summary

MEDIA LAW

In this chapter you have deepened your media literacy by revisiting several themes. Here are thematic highlights from the chapter:

MEDIA TECHNOLOGY

Free Stuff. Feelings run strong on the recording and movie industries' call for court protection against downloading and file-swapping that threatens their franchises.

New technologies keep creating new mass media legal issues. The first home video recording equipment in the 1970s, Betamax, raised questions of whether people have a legal right to duplicate copyright-protected movies. Despite Hollywood's objections, the answer of the U.S. Supreme Court was yes. For more than a century, photography has created poignant privacy questions that nobody ever thought about before. The problem with copyright law is that lawmakers are no better than the rest of us at seeing what future technology will bring. Copyright law has been revisited over and over in the history of the Republic, most recently because of Internet-related issues like unauthorized downloading that have shaken media industries. (Pages 424–429)

MEDIA ECONOMICS

John Lech Johansen. He became Hollywood's Norwegian nightmare with software that cracked regional coding for movies.

At the core of mass media infrastructure is copyright law, which gives exclusive rights to creative people to profit from their creations. The Internet has broken the control of media companies on distribution of their creations. Anybody with a few pieces of low-cost, easy-to-use computer equipment can distribute media content for free downloading by anyone on the planet. Most threatened have been the recording and movie industries, which have scrambled in the courts for protection of assets under copyright law. Both industries have cast the issue as economic survival. (Pages 424–429)

MEDIA AND DEMOCRACY

IF
YOU
CAN'T
SEE THAT
ILLEGAL DOWNLOADING
IS STEALING

Prior Restraint. The sheriff was wrong to padlock the Minnesota paper.

The democratic ideal of self-governance through grassroots political participation requires that people have full access to information. The ideal also requires that people have the freedom to sort through and hash out the facts to arrive at the best possible public policy. The First Amendment to the U.S. Constitution guarantees these freedoms of inquiry and expression to all citizens and to the mass media. The guarantee, however, is limited only to a ban on government interference in inquiry and expression. Citizens who feel wronged can seek compensation from other citizens and corporate entities, including media companies. Also, the courts have carved out some areas, including national security, in which the government can restrict access to and sharing of information. (Pages 429–436)

MEDIA AND CULTURE

The polarizing Culture Wars that have divided American society in recent years are not new except in their shrill intensity. Sexual explicitness is a hot-button cultural issue that goes way back. The U.S. Supreme Court has barred government interference with adult access to sexually explicit material. The Court has said that the access is a right under the free expression guarantee of the First Amendment, but the Court also has created limits. Some of these limits are clear, like protecting children. Some are vague, like the distinction between pornography, which is acceptable, and obscenity, which is not. In short, though, the mass media have had growing latitude in dealing with sexuality through the First Amendment. (Pages 440–442)

ELITISM AND POPULISM

Public Figures. They must take criticism as well as praise.

Elected and appointed governing elites have been largely stripped of the ability to sue their critics. In a landmark 1964 decision, *New York Times* v. *Sullivan,* the U.S. Supreme Court ruled that a democracy requires full and robust citizen discourse on public policy issues. The Court said that defamations that occur in this discourse are excusable, except for egregious and intentional untruths. The *Sullivan* decision gave new leeway for criticism of political leadership to the people and also to the media. The decision also opened up the range of negative comments on a broad range of other public figures. (Pages 439–440)

MEDIA FUTURE

Lingering Issue. Can government restrict on-air quacks?

Our understanding of the First Amendment is evolving. It's been clear since the U.S. Supreme Court began examining the First Amendment after World War I that discussion of political issues must be protected for democracy to function. But numerous practices, also endorsed by the courts, leave many contradictions unresolved. For example, the government in 1927 gave itself the authority to decide who could broadcast and who couldn't. Criteria for a broadcast license still include on-air performance expectations, a kind of government content control that the Court would never countenance for print media. Also not addressed squarely by the courts so far are a wide range of government restrictions on advertising. (Pages 432–434)

chapter 17

ETHICS

Jim DeFede *Reflexively, Miami* Herald *columnist Jim DeFede did what seemed right when a suicidal friend called: He taped the call. But in Florida taping a call without permission is against the law. But does being illegal make an act necessarily wrong? Such are the issues that make ethics essential to understand.*

LEARNING AHEAD

- Mass media ethics codes cannot anticipate all moral questions.
- Mass media people draw on numerous moral principles, some inconsistent with each other.
- Some mass media people prefer process-based ethics systems, while some prefer outcome-based systems.
- Potter's Box is a useful tool to sort through ethics issues.
- Some mass media people confuse ethics, law, prudence and accepted practices.
- Dubious mass media practices confound efforts to establish universal standards.

DOES ILLEGAL EQUAL IMMORAL?

Jim DeFede, a hard-hitting Miami *Herald* investigative reporter, was home late in the afternoon when his phone rang. It was an old friend, former city and county commissioner Arthur Teele Jr. Teele was distraught that another newspaper had outed him for trysts with a transvestite prostitute. "What did I do to piss off this town?" Teele asked. The transvestite allegation had followed 26 charges of fraud and money laundering. Teele said he was being smeared by prosecutors. He was afraid the transvestite story would hurt him with "the ministers and the church."

Worried about his friend's anguish, DeFede turned on his telephone recorder to record Teele's pain. He also asked if Teele wanted to go public about the prosecutors using the media to smear him. Teele said no, but the discussion meandered back and forth to a potentially explosive story for which Teele said he had documents. A couple hours later, Teele called and said he was leaving the documents for DeFede. Then he hung up, put a pistol to his head, and shot himself dead.

DeFede briefed his editor, Judy Miller, who told him to write a front-page story. In the meantime, higher executives at the *Herald* realized that DeFede had violated a state law that forbade taping a telephone conversation without permission. Over Miller's objections, publisher Jesus Diaz Jr. and corporate attorney Robert Beatty and two other corporate executives decided to fire DeFede—even though the *Herald* had once fought the Florida law, even though anyone who calls a reporter implicitly is consenting to being quoted, even though tape recording is just a more detailed form of note taking—and even though, in this case, *Herald* executives decided to draw on DeFede's notes from the taped conversation to be used in a story on the suicide.

If indeed DeFede had acted unethically, then how about the fact that the *Herald* drew on his information from the phone call? And how's this for a twist to make the issue murkier? The state's attorney cleared DeFede of violating the anti-recording statute. Also, only 12 states, including Florida, have such a law. If what DeFede did was unethical in Florida, is it less so in the 38 states that don't have such restrictions?

Clearly, the law and ethics don't coincide lockstep, which is a major issue in media ethics. In this chapter you will learn tools that have been developed through the centuries to sort through complexities posed by dilemmas of right and wrong, when choosing a course has downsides as well as upsides.

The Difficulty of Ethics

STUDY **PREVIEW**

Mass media organizations have put together codes of ethics that prescribe how practitioners should go about their work. Although useful in many ways, these codes neither sort through the bedeviling problems that result from conflicting prescriptions nor help much when the only open options are negative.

PRESCRIPTIVE ETHICS CODES

The mass media abound with **codes of ethics.** The earliest was adopted in 1923, the **Canons of Journalism** of the American Society of Newspaper Editors. Advertising, broadcast and public relations practitioners also have codes. Many newcomers to the mass media make an erroneous assumption that the answers to all the moral choices in their work exist in the prescriptions of these codes, a stance known as **prescriptive ethics.** While the codes can be helpful, ethics is not so easy.

The difficulty of ethics becomes clear when a mass communicator is confronted with a conflict between moral responsibilities to different concepts. Consider:

code of ethics
Statement that defines acceptable, unacceptable behavior

Canons of Journalism
First media code, 1923

prescriptive ethics
Follow the rules and your decision will be the correct one

>> **Respect for Privacy.** The code of the Society of Professional Journalists prescribes that reporters will show respect for the dignity, privacy, rights and well-being of people "at all times." The SPJ prescription sounds excellent, but moral priorities such as dignity and privacy sometimes seem less important than other priorities. The public interest, for example, overrode privacy in 1988 when the Miami *Herald* staked out presidential candidate Gary Hart overnight when he had a woman friend in his Washington townhouse.

>> **Commitment to Timeliness.** The code of the Radio-Television News Directors Association prescribes that reporters be "timely and accurate." In practice, however, the virtue of accuracy is jeopardized when reporters rush to the air with stories. It takes time to confirm details and be accurate—and that delays stories and works against timeliness.

>> Being Fair. The code of the Public Relations Society of America prescribes dealing fairly with both clients and the general public. However, a persuasive message prepared on behalf of a client is not always the same message that would be prepared on behalf of the general public. Persuasive communication is not necessarily dishonest, but how information is marshaled to create the message depends on whom the Public Relations person is serving.

CHECKING YOUR MEDIA LITERACY

- **How can codes of ethics help media people make the right decisions? Do codes always work? Why or why not?**
- **Is it always a virtue to respect privacy? Why or why not?**

CONFLICT OF DUTIES

Media ethics codes are well-intended, often helpful guides, but they are simplistic when it comes to knotty moral questions. These inherent problems become obvious if you consider how the various duties of mass communicators can conflict. Media ethicist Clifford Christians and others have examined, for example, conflicts in duties to audience, to employer, to society, to the profession and to self.

>> Duty to Self. Self-preservation is a basic human instinct, but is a photojournalist shirking a duty to subscribers by avoiding a dangerous combat zone?

Self-aggrandizement can be an issue too. Many college newspaper editors are invited, all expenses paid, to Hollywood movie premieres. The duty-to-self principle favors going: The trip would be fun. In addition, it is a good story opportunity, and as a free favor, it would not cost the newspaper anything. However, what of an editor's responsibility to readers? Readers have a right to expect writers to provide honest accounts that are not colored by favoritism. Can a reporter write fairly after being wined and dined and flown across the continent by movie producers who want a gung-ho story?

Even if reporters rise above being affected and are true to conscience, there are the duty-to-employer and the duty-to-profession principles to consider. The newspaper and the profession itself can be tarnished by audience suspicions, whether or not they are unfounded, that a reporter has been bought off.

>> Duty to Audience. Television programs that reenact violence are popular with audiences, but do they do a disservice because they frighten many viewers into inferring that the streets are more dangerous than they really are?

Tom Wicker of the New York *Times* tells a story about his early days as a reporter in North Carolina. He was covering a divorce case involving one spouse chasing the other with an ax. Nobody was hurt physically, and everyone who heard the story in the courtroom, except the divorcing couple, had a good laugh. "It was human comedy at its most ribald, and the courtroom rocked with laughter," Wicker recalled years later. In writing his story, Wicker captured the darkly comedic details so skillfully that his editor put the story on the front page. Wicker was proud of the piece until the next day when the woman in the case visited him. Worn-out, haggard, hurt and angry, she asked, "Mr. Wicker, why did you think you had a right to make fun of me in your paper?"

The lesson stayed with Wicker for the rest of his career. He had unthinkingly hurt a fellow human being for no better reason than to evoke a chuckle, or perhaps a belly laugh, from his readers. For Wicker, the duty-to-audience principle would never again transcend his moral duty to the dignity of the subjects of his stories. Similar ethics questions involve whether to cite AIDS as a contributor to death in an obituary, to identify victims in rape stories, or to name juveniles charged with crimes.

>> Duty to Employer. Does loyalty to an employer transcend the ideal of pursuing and telling the truth when a news reporter discovers dubious business deals involving

Charlie Gay

MEDIA PEOPLE

Unusual among U.S. newspapers, the Shelton, Washington, *Journal* prints the names of rape victims and even gets into X-rated details in covering trials. The publisher, Charlie Gay, knows the policy runs against the grain of contemporary news practices. It's also, he says, "good basic journalism."

Most newsrooms shield the names of rape victims, recognizing a notion, flawed though it is, that victims invite the crime. This stigma sets rape apart from other crimes, or at least so goes one line of thinking. Thus, naming should be at the victim's discretion, not a journalist's. To that, Charlie Gay says balderdash. Silence and secrecy only perpetuate stigmas, he says. As he sees it, only with the bright light of exposure can wrong-headed stigmas be cleansed away.

Gay says the journalist's duty is to tell news fully and fairly. "If we did follow a policy of no victims' names, we'd be horribly unfair to the other party, the person who's picked up for the crime and who is innocent until proved guilty," he says. It's unfair reporting to be "stacking everything against the accused."

In a speech to the Shelton Rotary Club, Gay said: "The *Journal* is reporting a crime and a trial. We're not trying to protect one party or make judgments about one party." The ideal to Gay is full, fair, detailed stories that inform without prejudicing.

The *Journal's* victim-naming policy has rankled many readers. Letters flood the opinion page with every rape case. The newspaper has been picketed. Critics have tried organizing an advertiser boycott and called on readers to cancel subscriptions.

At one point the state legislature responded. After lengthy debate about whether naming names should be outlawed, the legislature decided to bar reporters from naming child victims. The law was later ruled unconstitutional. It violated the First Amendment because government was abridging freedom of the press. The flap, however, demonstrated the intensity of feelings on the subject.

Police, prosecutors and social workers generally want names withheld, saying that some victims won't come forward for fear of publicity. Gay is blunt about that argument: The job of the press is to report the news, not to make the job of government easier. He says it is the job of government agents, including police and social workers, to persuade victims to press charges.

Although decidedly with a minority view, Gay has some support for including names and gripping detail in reporting sex crimes. Psychologist Robert Seidenberg, for example, believes that rape victims may be encouraged to report the crime by reading the accounts of victims with whom they can relate because details make compelling reading that helps them sort through their own situation more clearly.

WHAT DO YOU THINK?

- What do you think of the rationale for publishing the names of accusers in criminal cases, including rape?
- Will the policy of the Shelton *Journal* contribute to eliminating an undeserved stereotypical stigma that some rape victims feel?
- Should the First Amendment protect news organizations that choose to publish the names of crime victims?

Rape Names. *Editor Charlie Gay sees a journalistic duty to include victim names in rape stories.*

the parent corporation? This is a growing issue as the mass media become consolidated into fewer gigantic companies owned by conglomerates.

In a classic case, the executive producer of the NBC *Today* show, Marty Ryan, ordered a reference to General Electric deleted from an affiliate-provided news story on untested and sometimes defective bolts in jet engines manufactured by GE. The owner of NBC at the time was GE.

>> **Duty to the Profession.** At what point does an ethically motivated advertising agency person blow the whistle on misleading claims by other advertising people?

>> **Duty to Society.** Does duty to society ever transcend duty to self? To the audience? To the employer? To colleagues? Does ideology affect a media worker's sense of duty to society? Consider how Joseph Stalin, Adolf Hitler and Franklin Roosevelt would be covered by highly motivated communist, fascist and libertarian journalists.

Are there occasions when the duty-to-society and duty-to-audience principles are incompatible? Nobody enjoys seeing the horrors of war, for example, but journalists may feel that their duty to society demands that they go after the most grisly photographs of combat to show how horrible war is and, thereby, in a small way, contribute to public pressure toward a cessation of hostilities and eventual peace.

CHECKING YOUR MEDIA LITERACY

- **If you were a college newspaper editor and were offered an all-expenses-paid trip to a Hollywood movie premiere, would you accept? In explaining your decision, keep in mind that avoiding controversy may be an attractive response but would be a weak ethical choice.**

Media Ethics

STUDY PREVIEW

Media ethics is complicated by the different performance standards that mass media operations establish for themselves. This is further complicated by the range of expectations in the mass audience. One size does not fit all.

MEDIA COMMITMENT

A single ethics standard is impossible to apply to the mass media. Nobody held the supermarket tabloid *News of the World*, which specialized in celebrities being visited by aliens, to the same standard as the New York *Times*. Why the difference? Media ethics, in part, is a function of what a media operation promises to deliver to its audience and what the audience expects. The *News of the World* commitment was fun and games in a tongue-in-cheek news context. The New York *Times* considers itself a "newspaper of record." There is a big difference.

CNN touts accuracy in its promotional tagline: "News You Can Trust." Explicitly, the network promises to deliver truthful accounts of the day's events. CNN establishes its own standards. A lapse, like a misleading story—especially if intentional or the result of sloppiness—represents a broken promise and an ethics problem.

A media organization's commitments may be implicit. Disney, for example, has cultivated an image of wholesome products with which the whole family can be comfortable. It's a commitment: nothing bordering on smut here.

AUDIENCE EXPECTATION

The audience brings a range of ethics expectations to media relations, which further thwarts any attempt at one-size-fits-all media ethics. From a book publisher's fantasy science-fiction imprint, readers have far different expectations than they do from the *NBC Nightly News*, which, except for plainly labeled opinion, is expected to deliver unmitigated nonfiction.

A range in the type of messages purveyed by the mass media also bespeaks a variety of ethics expectations. Rarely is falsity excusable, but even the courts allow puffery in advertising. The news releases that public relations people produce are expected, by their nature, to be from a client's perspective, which doesn't always coincide with the perspective that people expect of a news reporter.

Media messages in the fiction story tradition don't unsettle anyone if they sensationalize to emphasize a point. Sensationalistic exaggeration in a serious biography, however, is unforgivable.

ETHICS AS AN INTELLECTUAL PROCESS

A set of rules, easily memorized and mindlessly employed, would be too easy. It doesn't work that way. Ethics, rather, needs to be an intellectual process of sorting through media commitments, audience expectations and broad principles. But even on broad principles there is more.

CHECKING YOUR MEDIA LITERACY

- **Why do ethics expectations differ among media organizations?**

Moral Principles

STUDY PREVIEW

Concern about doing the right thing is part of human nature, and leading thinkers have developed a great number of enduring moral principles over the centuries. The mass media, like other institutions and also like individuals, draw on these principles, but this does not always make moral decisions easy. The principles are not entirely consistent, especially in sorting through dilemmas.

Aristotle
Advocate of the Golden Mean

Golden Mean
Moderation is the best course

"Do unto others"
Judeo-Christian principle for ethical behavior

Aristotle. *The Greek thinker Aristotle told his students 2,400 years ago that right courses of action avoid extremes. His recommendation: moderation.*

THE GOLDEN MEAN

The Greek philosopher **Aristotle,** writing almost 2,400 years ago, devised the **Golden Mean** as a basis for moral decision making. The Golden Mean sounds simple and straightforward: Avoid extremes and seek moderation. Modern journalistic balance and fairness are founded on this principle.

The Golden Mean's dictate, however, is not as simple as it sounds. As with all moral principles, application of the Golden Mean can present difficulties. Consider the federal law that requires over-the-air broadcasters to give equal opportunity to candidates for public office. If one candidate buys 30 seconds at 7 p.m. for $120, a station is obligated to allow other candidates for the same office to buy 30 seconds at the same time for the same rate. On the surface this application of the Golden Mean, embodied in federal law, might seem to be reasonable, fair and morally right, but the issue is far more complex. The equality requirement, for example, gives an advantage to candidates who hold simplistic positions that can be expressed compactly. Good and able candidates whose positions require more time to explain are disadvantaged, and society is damaged when inferior candidates win public office.

"DO UNTO OTHERS"

The Judeo-Christian principle of "**Do unto others** as you would have them do unto you" appeals to most people. Not even the do-unto-others prescription is without problems, however. Consider the photojournalist who sees virtue in serving a mass audience with a truthful account of the human condition. This might manifest itself in portrayals of great emotions, like grief. But would the photojournalist appreciate being photographed herself in a grieving moment after learning that her own infant son had died in an accident? If not, her pursuit of truth through photography for a mass audience would be contrary to the "do-unto-others" dictum.

Immanuel Kant
Advocated the categorical imperative

categorical imperative
A principle that can be applied in any and all circumstances with moral certitude

John Stuart Mill
Advocated utilitarianism

principle of utility
Best course bestows the most good for the most people

John Dewey
Advocate of pragmatism

pragmatic ethics
Judge acts by their results

John Rawls
Advocated egalitarianism

veil of ignorance
Making decisions with a blind eye to extraneous factors that could affect the decision

egalitarianism
Treat everyone the same

CATEGORICAL IMPERATIVES

About 200 years ago, German philosopher **Immanuel Kant** wrote that moral decisions should flow from thoroughly considered principles. As he put it, "Act on the maxim that you would want to become universal law." He called his maxim the categorical imperative. A **categorical imperative,** well thought out, is a principle that the individual who devised it would be willing to apply in all moral questions of a similar sort. In a way, Kant recast the Judeo-Christian "do unto others" admonition but more intellectually and less intuitively.

Kant's categorical imperative does not dictate specifically what actions are morally right or wrong. Moral choices, says Kant, go deeper than the context of the immediate issue. He encourages a philosophical approach to moral questions, with people using their intellect to identify principles that they, as individuals, would find acceptable if applied universally.

Kant does not encourage the kind of standardized approach to ethics represented by professional codes. His emphasis, rather, is on hard thinking. The point has been put this way by scholar Patricia Smith, writing in the *Journal of Mass Media Ethics*: "A philosophical approach to ethics embodies a commitment to consistency, clarity, the principled evaluation of arguments and unrelenting persistence to get to the bottom of things."

UTILITARIAN ETHICS

In the mid-1800s British thinker **John Stuart Mill** declared that morally right decisions are those that result in "happiness for the greatest number." Mill called his idea the **principle of utility.** It sounds good to many of us because it parallels the democratic principle of majority rule, with its emphasis on the greatest good for the greatest number of people.

By and large, journalists embrace Mill's utilitarianism today, as evinced in notions like the *people's right to know*, a concept originally meant to support journalistic pursuit of information about government, putting the public's interests ahead of government's interests, but which has come to be almost reflexively invoked to defend pursuing very personal information about individuals, no matter what the human toll.

PRAGMATIC ETHICS

John Dewey, an American thinker who wrote in the late 1800s and early 1900s, argued that the virtue of moral decisions had to be judged by their results. Dewey's **pragmatic ethics,** like other ethics systems, has problems. One is that people do not have crystal balls to tell them for sure whether their moral actions will have good consequences.

Robert Hutchins. *His commission elevated social responsibility as a factor in ethics decisions in mass communication.*

EGALITARIAN ETHICS

In the 20th century, philosopher **John Rawls** introduced the **veil of ignorance** as an element in ethics decisions. Choosing a right course of action, said Rawls, requires blindness to social position or other discriminating factors. This is known as **egalitarianism.** An ethical decision requires that all people be given an equal hearing and the same fair consideration.

To Rawls, a brutal slaying in an upscale suburb deserves the same journalistic attention as a similarly brutal slaying in a poor urban neighborhood. All other things being equal, a $20,000 bank burglary is no more newsworthy than a $20,000 embezzlement.

MEDIA TIMELINE

ETHICS MILESTONES

Early Eras

Aristotle
The Golden Mean (400 B.C.)

Jesus Christ
"Do unto others as you would have them do unto you" (20)

Kant, less intuitive on ethics, more intellectual

1700s

Immanuel Kant
Categorical imperatives (1785)

Hutchins, a paradigm shift to social responsibility

1800s

John Stuart Mill
Utilitarianism (1865)

Wayland Ayer
First advertising agency (1869)

Yellow Press
Sensationalism grew as factor in news (1890s)

1900s

John Dewey
Pragmatism (1903)

World War I
U.S. government stirred war enthusiasm with comprehensive promotion (1917)

News Ethics
Upton Sinclair exposed newsroom abuses in *The Brass Check* (1919)

Ethics Code
American Society of Newspaper Editors adopted first media ethics code (1923)

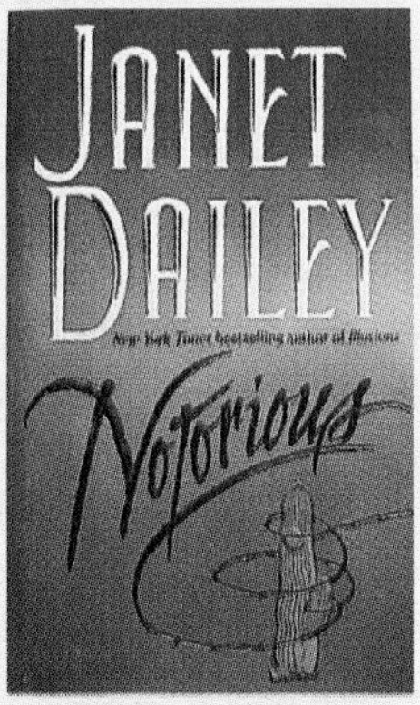

Copycat romance novel a plagiarist embarrassment

Social Responsibility
Hutchins Commission urged media to be socially responsible (1947)

Ethics as Process
Ralph Potter devised quadrants as a model to deal with dilemmas (1965)

John Rawls
The veil of ignorance (1971)

Quadrants for grasping the dynamics of dilemmas

2000s

Internet
Plagiarism swelled with growing access to digitized media (2000s)

PIVOTAL EVENTS

Early Eras

- Greek defeat of Persians at Marathon (490 B.C.)
- Athenian democracy (430 B.C.–)
- Roman domination of Mediterranean (250–300 B.C.)

1700s

- Johannes Gutenberg's movable metal type (1440s)
- Martin Luther launched Reformation (1517)
- Age of Science, Age of Reason began (1600s–)
- Isaac Newton's natural laws (1687)
- Industrial Revolution (1760s–)
- Revolutionary War (1776–1781)

1800s

- Morse invented telegraph (1844)
- Darwin's seminal work on human evolution (1859)
- U.S. Civil War (1861–1865)
- Railroad link of Atlantic and Pacific coasts (1869)

1900s

- Right to vote extended to women (1920)
- Radio emerged as mass medium (1920s)
- Great Depression (1930s)
- World War II (1941–1945)
- Television emerged as mass medium (1950s)
- Humans reached moon (1969)
- Netscape browser ignited the Internet as a mass medium (1997)

2000s

- 9/11 terrorist attacks (2001)
- Iraq war (2003–)
- Hurricane Katrina (2005)

SOCIAL RESPONSIBILITY ETHICS

Hutchins Commission
Advocated social responsibility as goal and result of media activities

Robert Hutchins
Called for the new media to emphasize its social responsibility, not only its freedom

social responsibility
Making decisions that serve society responsibly

The **Hutchins Commission**, a learned group led by intellectual **Robert Hutchins** that studied the U.S. mass media in the 1940s, recommended that journalists and other media people make decisions that serve society responsibly. For all its virtues the **social responsibility** system, like all ethics systems, has difficulties. For one thing, decision-makers can only imperfectly foresee the effects of their decisions. It is not possible to predict with 100 percent confidence whether every decision will turn out to be socially responsible. Also, well-meaning people may differ honestly about how society is most responsibly served.

CHECKING YOUR MEDIA LITERACY

- **Can you identify the ethics principle or system most associated with Aristotle? Immanuel Kant? John Stuart Mill? John Dewey? Robert Hutchins? John Rawls?**

Process versus Outcome

STUDY PREVIEW

The various approaches to ethics fall into two broad categories: deontological ethics and teleological ethics. Deontologists say people need to follow good rules. Teleologists judge morality not by the rules but by the consequences of decisions.

DEONTOLOGICAL ETHICS

The Greek word *deon*, which means "duty," is at the heart of **deontological ethics**, which holds that people act morally when they follow good rules. Deontologists feel that people are duty bound to identify these rules.

Deontologists include people who believe that Scripture holds all the answers for right living. Their equivalent among media practitioners are those who rely entirely on codes of ethics drafted by organizations they trust. Following rules is a prescriptive form of ethics. At first consideration, ethics might seem as easy as following the rules, but not all questions are clear-cut. In complicated situations, the rules sometimes contradict each other. Some cases are dilemmas with no right option—only a choice among less-than-desirable options.

deontological ethics
Good actions flow from good processes

theory of divine command
Proper decisions follow God's will

theory of divine right of kings
Monarchs derive authority from God, not from their subjects

theory of secular command
Holds that authorities legitimately hold supreme authority although not necessarily with a divine authority

libertarian theory
Given good information and time, people ultimately make right decisions

Deontological ethics becomes complicated, and also more intellectually interesting, when individuals, unsatisfied with other people's rules, try to work out their own universally applicable moral principles.

Here are some major deontological approaches:

- **Theory of divine command.** This theory holds that proper moral decisions come from obeying the commands of God, with blind trust that the consequences will be good.
- **Theory of divine right of kings.** This theory sees virtue in allegiance to a divinely anointed monarch.
- **Theory of secular command.** This theory is a nonreligious variation that stresses allegiance to a dictator or other political leader from whom the people take cues when making moral decisions.
- **Libertarian theory.** This theory stresses a laissez-faire approach to ethics: Give free rein to the human ability to think through problems, and people almost always will make morally right decisions.
- **Categorical imperative theory.** This theory holds that virtue results when people identify and apply universal principles.

TELEOLOGICAL ETHICS

Unlike deontological ethics, which is concerned with the right actions, teleological ethics is concerned with the consequences of actions. The word ***teleology*** comes from the Greek word *teleos*, which means "result" or "consequence."

Teleologists see flaws in the formal, legalistic duty to rules of deontologists, noting that great harm sometimes flows from blind allegiance to rules.

Here are some major teleological approaches:

- **Pragmatic theory.** This theory encourages people to look at human experience to determine the probable consequences of an action and then decide its desirability.
- **Utilitarian theory.** This theory favors ethics actions that benefit more people than they damage—the greatest good for the greatest number.
- **Social responsibility theory.** This theory judges actions by the good effect they have on society.

SITUATIONAL ETHICS

Firm deontologists see two primary flaws in teleological ethics:

- Imperfect foresight.
- Lack of guiding principles.

Despite these flaws, many media practitioners apply teleological approaches, sometimes labeled **situational ethics,** to work through moral issues. They gather as much information as they can about a situation and then decide, not on the basis of principle but on the facts of the situation. Critics of situational ethics worry about decisions governed by situations. Much better, they argue, would be decisions flowing from principles of enduring value. With situational ethics the same person might do one thing one day and on another day go another direction in a similar situation.

Consider a case at the *Rocky Mountain News* in Denver. Editors learned that the president of a major suburban newspaper chain had killed his parents and sister in another state when he was 18. After seven years in a mental hospital the man completed college, moved to Colorado, lived a model life and became a successful newspaper executive. The *Rocky Mountain News* decided not to make a story of it. Said a *News* official, "The only reason for dredging up [his] past would be to titillate morbid curiosity or to shoot down, maliciously, a successful citizen."

However, when another newspaper revealed the man's past, the *Rocky Mountain News* reversed itself and published a lengthy piece of its own. Why? The newspaper that broke the story had suggested that *News* editors knew about the man's past and had decided to protect him as a fellow member of the journalistic fraternity. *News* editors denied that their motivation was to protect the man. To prove it, they reconsidered their decision and published a story on him. The *News* explained its change of mind by saying that the situation had changed. *News* editors, concerned that their newspaper's credibility had been challenged, thought that printing a story would set that straight. Of less concern, suddenly, was that the story would titillate morbid curiosity or contribute to the destruction of a successful citizen. It was a classic case of situational ethics.

Flip-flops on moral issues, such as what happened at the *Rocky Mountain News*, bother critics of situational ethics. The critics say that decisions should be based on deeply rooted moral principles—not immediate, transient facts or changing peripheral contexts.

teleology
Good decisions are those with good consequences

situational ethics
Make ethics decisions on the basis of situation at hand

CHECKING YOUR MEDIA LITERACY

- **As someone who reads newspapers and watches newscasts, do you favor deontological or teleological ethics? Which system do you think most journalists favor? Why?**
- **What is the attraction of situational ethics for sorting out dilemmas? And what is the problem?**

Potter's Box

STUDY ***PREVIEW***

Moral problems in the mass media can be so complex that it may seem there is no solution. While ideal answers without any negative results may be impossible, a process exists for identifying a course of action that integrates an individual's personal values with moral principles and then tests conclusions against loyalties.

Ralph Potter
Ethicist who devised Potter's Box

Potter's Box
Tool for sorting through the pros and cons of ethics questions

FOUR QUADRANTS

A Harvard Divinity School professor, **Ralph Potter,** devised a four-quadrant model for sorting through ethics problems. Each quadrant of the square-like model, called **Potter's Box,** poses a category of questions. Working through these categories helps to clarify the issues and leads to a morally justifiable position. These are the quadrants of Potter's Box:

>> Situation. In Quadrant 1 the facts of the issue are decided. Consider a newsroom in which a series of articles on rape is being developed and the question arises of whether to identify rape victims by name. Here is how the situation could be defined: The newspaper has access to a young mother who has been abducted and raped and who is willing to describe the assault in graphic detail and to discuss her experience as a witness at the assailant's trial. Also, the woman is willing to be identified in the story.

>> Values. Moving to Quadrant 2 of Potter's Box, editors and reporters identify the values that underlie all the available choices. This process involves listing the positive and negative values that flow from conscience. One editor might argue that full, frank discussion on social issues is necessary to deal with them. Another might say that identifying the rape victim by name might discourage others from even reporting such a crime. Other positions:

- Publishing the name is in poor taste.
- The newspaper has an obligation to protect the victim from her own possibly bad decision to allow her name to be used.
- The purpose of the rape series can be accomplished without using the name.

Readers have a right to all the relevant information that the newspaper can gather. An editor who is torn between such contrary thoughts is making progress toward a decision by at least identifying all the values that can be posited.

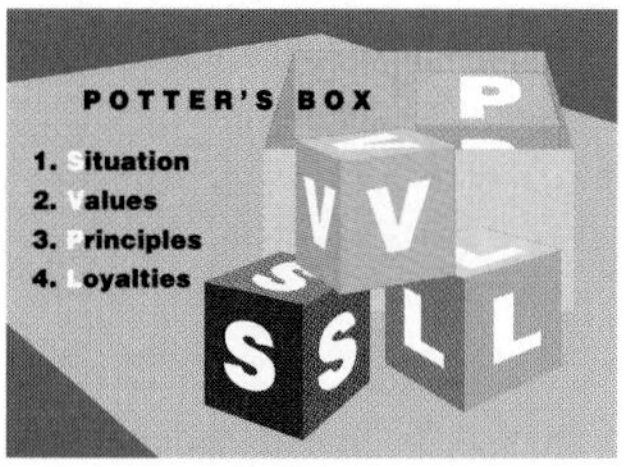

Potter's Box offers four categories of questions to help develop morally justifiable positions. Ralph Potter, the divinity professor who devised the categories, said to start by establishing the facts of the situation. Next, identify the values that underpin the options, recognizing that some values may be incompatible with others. Then, consider the moral principles that support each of the values. Finally, sort through loyalties to all the affected interests. Potter's Box is not a panacea, but it provides a framework for working through ethics issues in a thorough way.

>> Principles. In Potter's Quadrant 3, decision-makers search for moral principles that uphold the values they identified in Quadrant 2. John Stuart Mill's principle of utility, which favors the majority over individuals, would support using the victim's name because it could add poignancy to the story, enhancing the chances of improved public sensitivity, and perhaps even lead to improved public policy, all of which, Mill would say, outweigh the harm that might come to an individual. On the other hand, people who have used Immanuel Kant's ideas to develop inviolable operating principles—categorical imperatives—look to their rule book: We never publish information that might offend readers. One value of Potter's Quadrant 3 is that it gives people confidence in the values that emerged in their debates over Quadrant 2.

>> Loyalties. In Quadrant 4 the decision-maker folds in an additional layer of complexity that must be sorted through: loyalties. The challenge is to establish a hierarchy of loyalties. Is the first loyalty to a code of ethics, and if so, which code? To readers, and if so, which ones? To society? To the employer? To self? Out of duty to self, some reporters and editors might want to make the rape

Ralph Potter

series as potent as possible, with as much detail as possible, to win awards and bring honor to themselves and perhaps a raise or promotion or bigger job in another newsroom. Others might be motivated by their duty to their employer: The more detail in the story, the more newspapers it will sell. For others their duty to society may be paramount: The newspaper has a social obligation to present issues in as powerful a way as possible to spur reforms in general attitudes and perhaps public policy.

Potter's Box does not provide answers. Rather, it offers a process through which the key elements in ethics questions can be sorted out.

Also, Potter's Box focuses on moral aspects of a problem, leaving it to the decision-maker to examine practical considerations separately, such as whether prudence supports making the morally best decision. Moral decisions should not be made in a vacuum. For example, would it be wise to go ahead with the rape victim's name if 90 percent of the newspaper's subscribers would become so offended that they would quit buying the paper and, as a result, the paper would go out of business?

Other practical questions can involve the law. If the morally best decision is to publish the name but the law forbids it, should the newspaper proceed anyway? Does journalistic virtue transcend the law? Is it worth it to publish the name to create a First Amendment issue? Are there legal implications, like going to jail or piling up legal defense costs?

Is it worth it to go against generally accepted practices and publish the victim's name? Deciding on a course of action that runs contrary to tradition, perhaps even contrary to some ethics codes, could mean being ostracized by other media people, whose decisions might have gone another way. Doing right can be lonely.

CHECKING YOUR MEDIA LITERACY

- **You are a news reporter. A candidate for mayor tells you that the incumbent mayor is in cahoots with organized crime. It's a bombshell story! Use Potter's Box to decide whether to rush to your microphone with the story.**

Ethics and Related Issues

STUDY PREVIEW

Right and wrong are issues in both ethics and law, but ethics and law are different. Obedience to law, or even to professional codes of ethics, will not always lead to moral action. There are also times when practical issues can enter moral decisions.

DIFFERENTIATING ETHICS AND LAW

Ethics is an individual matter that relates closely to conscience. Because conscience is unique to each individual, no two people have exactly the same moral framework. There are, however, issues about which there is consensus. No right-minded person condones murder, for example. When there is a universal feeling, ethics becomes codified in law, but laws do not address all moral questions. It is the issues of right and wrong that do not have a consensus that make ethics difficult. Was it morally right for *USA Today* to initiate coverage of tennis superstar Arthur Ashe's AIDS?

Ethics and law are related but separate. The law will allow a mass media practitioner to do many things that the practitioner would refuse to do. Since the 1964 *New York Times* v. *Sullivan* case, the U.S. Supreme Court has allowed mass media to cause tremendous damage to public officials, even with false information. However, rare is the journalist who would intentionally push the *Sullivan* latitudes to their limits to pillory a public official.

The ethics decisions of an individual mass media practitioner usually are more limiting than the law. There are times, though, when a journalist may choose to break the law on the grounds of ethics. Applying John Stuart Mill's principle of "the greatest good," a radio reporter might choose to break the speed limit to reach a chemical plant where an accident is threatening to send a deadly cloud toward where her listeners live. Breaking a speed limit might seem petty as an example, but it demonstrates that obeying the law and obeying one's conscience do not always coincide.

CHECKING YOUR MEDIA LITERACY

- **Can breaking the law ever be justified?**

ACCEPTED PRACTICES

Just as there is no reliable correlation between law and ethics, neither is there one between accepted media practices and ethics. What is acceptable at one advertising agency to make a product look good in photographs might be unacceptable at another. Even universally **accepted practices** should not go unexamined, for unless accepted practices are examined and reconsidered on a continuing basis, media practitioners can come to rely more on habit than on principles in their work.

PRUDENCE AND ETHICS

Prudence is the application of wisdom in a practical situation. It can be a leveling factor in moral questions. Consider the case of Irvin Lieberman, who had built his *Main Line Chronicle* and several other weeklies in the Philadelphia suburbs into aggressive, journalistically excellent newspapers. After being hit with nine libel suits, all costly to defend, Lieberman softened the thrust of his newspapers. "I decided not to do any investigative work," he said. "It was a matter of either feeding my family or spending my whole life in court." Out of prudence, Lieberman decided to abandon his commitment to hard-hitting, effective journalism.

Courageous pursuit of morally lofty ends can, as a practical matter, be foolish. Whether Irvin Lieberman was exhibiting a moral weakness by bending to the chilling factor of libel suits, which are costly to fight, or being prudent is an issue that could be debated forever. The point, however, is that prudence cannot be ignored as a factor in moral decisions.

accepted practices
What media do as a matter of routine, sometimes without considering ethics implications

prudence
Applying wisdom, not principles, to an ethics situation

Unsettled, Unsettling Questions

STUDY PREVIEW

When mass media people discuss ethics, they talk about right and wrong behavior, but creating policies on ethics issues is not easy. Many standard media practices press the line between right and wrong, which muddies clear-cut standards that are universally applicable and recognized. There is further muddiness because many ethics codes confuse unethical behavior with behavior that may appear unethical but is not necessarily so.

PLAGIARISM

Perhaps the most fiercely loyal media fans are those who read romance novels and swear by a favorite author. In an Internet chatroom in 1997, romance writer Janet Dailey found herself boxed into an admission that she had plagiarized from rival writer Nora Roberts. There is no scorn like that of creative people for those who steal their work, and Roberts was "very, very upset." HarperCollins recalled *Notorious*,

Janet Dailey

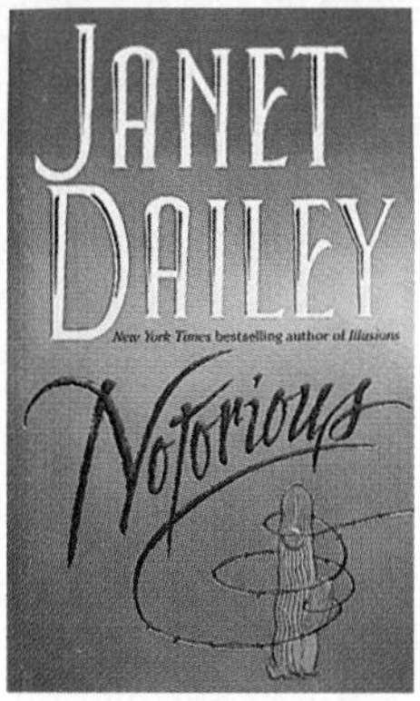

Copycat Romance. *Widespread Internet access is facilitating plagiarism, much of it among people who don't know better. But it remains a taboo in media work. Janet Dailey's* Notorious *was withdrawn and shredded by publisher HarperCollins after rival romance writer Nora Roberts spotted passages that Dailey had lifted.*

Dailey's book that contained the plagiarism, and Roberts' fans, many of them long-time Dailey detractors, began a hunt for other purloined passages.

What is **plagiarism**? Generally, it's considered passing off someone else's creative work as your own, without permission. It's still plagiarism even if the original is changed a tad, as was Dailey's loose paraphrasing.

The fact that Dailey's 93 books over 20 years had sold an average of more than 2 million each made the scandal all the juicier. In the end Roberts proposed a financial settlement, and the proceeds went to promote literacy.

Everyone agrees that plagiarism, a form of thievery, is unethical, but the issue is not simple. The fact is that many media people draw heavily on other people's ideas and work. Think about sitcom story lines that mimic each other or the bandwagon of movies that follow an unexpected hit with an oddball theme that suddenly becomes mainstream. Journalists, most of whom consider themselves especially pristine compared to their media brethren, have standard practices that encourage a lot of "borrowing."

Among factors that make journalists uncomfortable when pressed hard on plagiary questions are:

- Institutionalized exchanging of stories
- The role of public relations in generating news stories
- Monitoring the competition
- Subliminal memory and innocent recall

This all is further complicated by a cut-and-paste mentality that has been facilitated by digitized messages on the Internet. A whole new generation is missing a level of sensitivity to traditionally recognized rights of people who create or own intellectual property to control its reuse.

>> Swapping Stories. Some creative work, like scholarship, requires that information and ideas be attributed to their sources. Journalists are not so strict, as shown by story swapping through the Associated Press. The AP picks up stories from its members and distributes them to other members, generally without any reference to the source. Some publications and broadcasters do not even acknowledge AP as the intermediary.

Conditioned by 150 years of the AP's being a journalistic model and under pressure to gather information quickly, many journalists have a high tolerance for "borrowing." When the Chicago *Tribune* was apologizing for a story cribbed from the Jerusalem *Post*, for example, one of the writer's colleagues defended the story: "Everybody rewrites the Jerusalem *Post*. That's how foreign correspondents work."

Incredible as it seems, journalistic tolerance for plagiarism once even allowed radio stations to pilfer the local newspaper for newscasts. Sometimes you could hear the announcer turning the pages. A sad joke that acknowledged this practice was that some stations bought their news at 50 cents a copy, which was cheaper than hiring reporters to cover the community. So pervasive was the journalistic tolerance for "borrowing" that few newspapers protested even mildly when their stories were pirated.

plagiarism
Using someone else's work without permission or credit

Janet Cooke
Classic case of representing fiction as truth

MISREPRESENTATION

Janet Cooke's meteoric rise at the Washington *Post* unraveled quickly the day after she received a Pulitzer Prize. Her editors had been so impressed with her story "Jimmy's World," about a child who was addicted to heroin, that they had nominated it for a Pulitzer Prize. The gripping tale began: "Jimmy is 8 years old and a third-generation

CASE STUDY

Penguin Spoof Video

Gore Lampoon. *Anonymous postings of partisan videos give corporations and special interests an avenue to disguise their role in public dialogue. The viciously funny video on Al Gore's* Penguin Army *has been linked to ExxonMobil, although the company denied it. ExxonMobil had been roasted earlier by Gore for its record on pollution-causing global warming.*

After Al Gore's documentary *An Inconvenient Truth* began firing-up public awareness of the dangers of global warming, somebody put together a spoof for the post-your-own video site YouTube. Thousands of YouTube habitués chuckled, albeit at Gore's expense. There the former vice president was in the two-minute clip, blaming everything on global warming—even Lindsay Lohan's shrinking waist. Gore was portrayed as hopelessly out of touch, boring movie audiences but hypnotizing penguins.

The clip had all the earmarks of an amateur taking sophomoric delight in undermining someone else's dignity. The art was jerky, the production quality second-rate. But even Al Gore probably couldn't resist chuckling.

Who did it? Videos can be posted anonymously on YouTube, but this one was signed Toutsmith and carried a link to a personal profile. The profile claimed that Toutsmith was 29, from Hollywood, but not much more. Two *Wall Street Journal* reporters, however, tracked numerical data in an e-mail from Toutsmith and found the message originated on a computer registered to DCI Group, a public relations firm in Washington, D.C., whose clients, they reported, included ExxonMobil.

In *An Inconvenient Truth,* Gore excoriates ExxonMobil, among other giant energy companies, for a long-term campaign to discredit evidence about contributing to global warming: "These companies want to prevent any new policies that would interfere with their current business plans that rely on the massive unrestrained dumping of global warming pollution of the Earth's atmosphere every hour of every day."

Had ExxonMobil attempted, under the cloak of YouTube anonymity, to discredit Gore?

No matter how suspicious the Exxon–DCI connection, ExxonMobil responded with plausible deniability. Dave Gardner, a spokesperson confronted by *Journal* reporters, said: "We, like everyone else on the planet, have seen it, but did not fund it, did not approve it, and did not know what its source was." At DCI, spokesperson Matt Triaca declined to confirm or deny anything. And how was it that Toutsmith was sending messages from a DCI computer? Said Triaca: "DCI Group does not disclose the names of its clients, nor do we discuss the work that we do on our clients' behalf."

Probably there was no legal issue. As a former vice president and as an author and movie producer, Gore's work is subject to public comment and criticism. Also, the courts give broad protection for satire.

Even so, who to sue? The truth of the penguin video may never be known, but it points up the potential of special interests to create covert presences on the Internet to promote their interests.

DEEPENING YOUR MEDIA LITERACY

EXPLORE THE ISSUE

Toutsmith's Penguin Army remains accessible on YouTube. Is it a funny spoof? Or pure nastiness?

DIG DEEPER

Gore's criticism of ExxonMobil is explicit in his book *An Inconvenient Truth.* Check what Gore wrote.

WHAT DO YOU THINK?

How far should an individual or organization go in responding to critics? Can anonymity be justified?

heroin addict, a precocious little boy with sandy hair, velvety brown eyes and needle marks freckling the baby-smooth skin of his thin brown arms." Janet Cooke claimed that she had won the confidence of Jimmy's mother and her live-in male friend, a drug dealer, to do the story. Cooke said she had promised not to reveal their identities as a condition for her access to Jimmy.

The story, which played on the front page, so shocked Washington that people demanded that Jimmy be taken away from his mother and placed in a foster home. The *Post* declined to help authorities, citing Cooke's promise of confidentiality to her sources. The mayor ordered the police to find Jimmy with or without the newspaper's help. Millions of dollars in police resources went into a door-to-door search. After 17 days the police gave up knocking on doors for tips on Jimmy. Some doubts emerged at the *Post* about the story, but the newspaper stood behind its reporter.

Janet Cooke, 25 when she was hired by the *Post*, had extraordinary credentials. Her résumé showed a baccalaureate degree, *magna cum laude*, from Vassar; study at the Sorbonne in Paris; a master's degree from the University of Toledo; abilities in several languages; and two years of journalistic experience with the Toledo *Blade*. Said Ben Bradlee, editor of the *Post*: "She had it all. She was bright. She was well spoken. She was pretty. She wrote well." She was also black, which made her especially attractive to the *Post*, which was working to bring the percentage of black staff reporters nearer to the percentage of blacks in the newspaper's circulation area.

Six months after "Jimmy's World" was published, the Pulitzer committee announced its decision and issued a biographical sheet on Janet Cooke. The Associated Press, trying to flesh out the biographical information, spotted discrepancies right away. Janet Cooke, it turned out, had attended Vassar for one year but had not graduated with the honors she claimed. The University of Toledo had no record of awarding her a master's. Suddenly, doubts that had surfaced in the days immediately after "Jimmy's World" was published took on a new intensity. The editors sat Cooke down and grilled her on the claims on which she was hired. No, she admitted, she was not multilingual. The Sorbonne claim was fuzzy. More important, they pressed her on whether there was really a Jimmy. The interrogation continued into the night, and finally Janet Cooke confessed all: There were no confidential sources, and there was no Jimmy. She had fabricated the story. She resigned, and the *Post*, terribly embarrassed, returned the Pulitzer.

In cases of outright fabrication, as in "Jimmy's World," it is easy to identify the lapses in ethics. When Janet Cooke emerged briefly from seclusion to explain herself, she said that she had been responding to pressures in the *Post* newsroom to produce flashy, sensational copy. Most people found the explanation unsatisfying, considering the pattern of deception that went back to her falsified résumé.

There are **misrepresentations,** however, that are not as clearly unacceptable. Much debated are the following:

>> Staging News. To attract favorable attention to their clients, public relations people organize media events, a practice known as **staging news.** These are designed to be irresistible to journalists. Rallies and demonstrations on topical issues, for example, find their way onto front pages, magazine covers and evening newscasts because their photogenic qualities give them an edge over less visual although sometimes more significant events. The ethics question is less important for publicists, who generally are up front about what they are doing. The ethics question is more serious for journalists, who claim that their job is to present an accurate, balanced account of a day's events but who regularly overplay staged events that are designed by publicists to be photogenic and easy to cover.

>> Re-Creations. Some television **reality programs** feature **reenactments** that are not always labeled as such. Philip Weiss, writing in *Columbia Journalism Review*, offered this litany: shadows on the wall of a woman taking a hammer to her husband, a faceless actor grabbing a tin of kerosene to blow up his son, a corpse in a wheelbarrow with a hand dangling, a detective opening the trunk of a car and reeling from the

misrepresentations
Deception in gathering or telling information

staging news
Creating an event to attract news media attention and coverage

reality programs
Broadcast shows with a nonfiction basis

reenactments
Re-creating real events

stench of a decomposing body. Although mixing re-creations with strictly news footage rankles many critics, others argue that it helps people understand the situation. The same question arises with docudramas, which mix actual events and dramatic re-creations.

>> **Selective Editing.** The editing process, by its nature, requires journalists to make decisions on what is most worth emphasizing and what is least worth even including. In this sense, all editing is selective, but the term **selective editing** refers to making decisions with the goal of distorting. Selective editing can occur in drama too, when writers, editors and other media people take literary license too far and intentionally misrepresent.

>> **Fictional Methods.** In the late 1960s many experiments in media portrayals of people and issues came to be called the **new journalism.** The term was hard to define because it included so many approaches. Among the most controversial were applications of fiction-writing methods to topical issues, an approach widely accepted in book publishing but suddenly controversial when it appeared in the news media. Character development became more important than before, including presumed insights into the thinking of people being covered. The view of the writer became an essential element in much of this reporting. The defense for these approaches was that traditional, facts-only reporting could not approach complex truths that merited journalistic explorations. The profound ethics questions that these approaches posed were usually mitigated by clear statements about what the writer was attempting. Nonetheless, it was a controversial approach to the issues of the day. There was no defense when the fictional approach was complete fabrication passing itself off as reality, as in "Jimmy's World."

CHECKING YOUR MEDIA LITERACY

- **How have mass media practices muddied plagiarism as an issue?**
- **If plagiarism is so bad, why do more and more people do it? Are there any ethics principles or systems that would condone plagiarism?**

GIFTS, JUNKETS AND MEALS

In his 1919 book ***The Brass Check,*** a pioneer examination of newsroom ethics, **Upton Sinclair** told how newspeople took bribes to put stories in the paper. Today all media ethics codes condemn gifts and certainly bribes. Even so, there are still people who curry favor with the mass media through gifts, such as a college sports publicist who gives a fifth of whisky at Christmas to a sportswriter as a gesture of goodwill. Favors can take many forms: media-appreciation lunches; free trips abroad, known as **junkets,** especially for travel writers; season passes to cover the opera; discounts at certain stores.

Despite the consistent exhortation of the ethics codes against gifts, favors, free travel and special treatment and privileges, there is nothing inherently wrong in taking them if they do not influence coverage and if the journalist's benefactor understands that. The problem with favors is more a practical one than one of ethics. Taking a favor may or may not be bad, but it *looks* bad. Many ethics codes do not make this important distinction. One that does is the code of the Associated Press Managing Editors, which states: "Journalists must avoid impropriety and *the appearance of impropriety* as well as any conflict of interest or *the appearance of conflict.* They should neither accept anything nor pursue any activity that might compromise or *seem to compromise* their integrity". The APME admonitions at least recognize the distinction between the inherent wrongness of impropriety, which is an ethics question, and the perception that something may be wrong, which is a perception that is unwise to encourage but is not necessarily unethical.

selective editing
Misrepresentation through omission and juxtaposition

new journalism
Mixing fiction techniques with nonfiction

The Brass Check
1919 book that exposed newsroom corruption

Upton Sinclair
Author of *The Brass Check*

junket
Trip with expenses paid by someone who may expect favors in return

While ethics codes are uniform in prohibiting **freebies,** as gifts and favors are called, many news organizations accept free movie, drama, concert and other tickets, as well as recordings, books and other materials for review. The justifications are usually that their budgets allow them to review only materials that arrive free and that their audiences would be denied reviews if the materials had to be purchased. A counterargument is that a news organization that cannot afford to do business right should not be in business. Many news organizations insist on buying tickets for their reporters to beauty pageants, sports events and other things to which there is an admission fee. A frequent exception occurs when a press box or special media facility is available. With recordings, books and free samples, some media organizations return them or pass them on to charity to avoid any appearance that they have been bought off.

When junkets are proposed, some organizations send reporters only if they can pay the fare and other expenses. The Louisville *Courier-Journal* is firm: "Even on chartered trips, such as accompanying a sports team, or hitchhiking on a State Police plane, we insist on being billed for our pro-rata share of the expense." An exception is made by some news organizations for trips that they could not possibly arrange on their own, such as covering a two-week naval exercise aboard a ship.

Some media organizations address the issue of impropriety by acknowledging favors. Many quiz shows say that "promotional consideration" has been provided to companies that give them travel, lodging and prizes. Just as forthright are publications that state that reviews are made possible through season passes or free samples. Acknowledging favors does not remove the questions, but at least it is up front.

CHECKING YOUR MEDIA LITERACY

As a news editor, how would you handle a proposal from the National Guard to ferry a reporter in a Guard aircraft to hometown unit training exercises? "Just have the reporter bring a pad, pencil and camera," says the Guard public relations officer. "We'll provide lodging, field meals, flak jackets and everything else—even a souvenir T-shirt and Guard baseball cap."

freebies
Gifts for which the giver may expect favors in return

CHAPTER WRAP-UP

The Difficulty of Ethics (Pages 447–450)

- Media people have no shortage of ethics codes. Every professional organization has one. This multitude of ethics codes makes it easy for people to infer that ethical behavior is a simple matter of learning and obeying the rules. But they are missing the complexity of moral issues. No matter how well intentioned the ethics codes, they have limited usefulness. Merely to follow prescribed rules with unique, sometimes nuanced subtleties makes for a particular dilemma. No prescriptive code, cast in broad terms as they must be, can replace a good mind and the application of broad, universal principles.

Media Ethics (Pages 450–451)

- Mass communicators try to do good in an often-confusing combination of obligations. One fundamental obligation, for example, is to serve the audience. But who decides what serves the audience best? The editors of the New York *Times* and the *National Enquirer* could debate endlessly on that. Imagine the conflict of advertising-supported media when the interests of advertisers and listeners don't coincide. That's been the crux of ethics debates on sugary, fat-laden snacks marketed to kids.

Moral Principles (Pages 451–454)

- Philosophers have struggled over the centuries to devise overarching principles to sort through moral dilemmas. In the 1700s Immanuel Kant proposed *categorical imperatives*—broad principles that everyone would see as acceptable for dealing with any and all situations. The Kant idea is not prescriptive as much as it is a call for thorough consideration, clarity of thinking, and consistency.

Potter's Box (Pages 456–457)

- By definition, a moral dilemma has no perfect solution. That's what makes a dilemma a dilemma. A useful process for working through problems, called Potter's Box, is to start with the facts and apply values and principles—and then to sort through loyalties that affect everyone involved. Potter's Box emphasizes not rules but an intellectual process in finding answers.

Process versus Outcome (Pages 454–455)

- Nothing better demonstrates the complexity of ethics than the conflict between deontologists and teleologists. Deontologists emphasize creating good rules. As deontologists see it, applying good rules results in good behavior. Whoa, say the teleologists. They can cite all kinds of well-intentioned rules that backfired in particular situations. Teleologists argue that behavior can be judged better by the results. A third school of ethicists approach each moral dilemma from scratch. The idea is to consider the facts of a situation without any larger or philosophical framework. Critics of situational ethics note, however, that no two human minds work alike. Without agreed-upon principles, people end up with very different ideas of how to handle a dilemma. Not everyone can be right.

Ethics and Related Issues (Pages 457–458)

- Ethics and law often are confused. The confusion is no better illustrated than by someone claiming to have been ethical for following a law. Ethics is not so simple. Think about the long history of whistleblowers who have violated national security laws and been lauded as heroes for exposing wrongheaded government practices. Sometimes ethics is confused with standard and accepted practices in a profession. The fact, however, is that accepted practices need continuing reconsideration as to their efficacy. Mimicking old ways of doing things may or may not be practicing good behavior.

Unsettled, Unsettling Questions (Pages 458–463)

- Many standard media practices border on the shady. None is more problematic than plagiarism. Everybody condemns plagiarism as thievery and dishonesty, but a tremendous amount of "borrowing" occurs in creating media content. The rash of movies picking up on a blockbuster theme is one example. It's similar with misrepresentation, which is easy to condemn. But what about John Howard Griffin, a white man who dyed his skin black and traversed the South in the 1950s to see racial injustices, which helped trigger the civil rights movement? Griffin misrepresented himself. Was it the right thing to do? Or was it wrong?

▼ Review Questions

1. Why can't ethics codes anticipate all moral questions? And does this limit the value of codes for mass media people?
2. List and explain moral principles that mass media people can use to sort through ethics questions.
3. How can mass media people come to different conclusions depending on whether they use process-based or outcome-based ethics?
4. Is ethics the same as law? As prudence? As accepted practice?
5. Discuss dubious mass media practices that are inconsistent with many moral principles.

Concepts

deontological ethics (Page 454)

libertarian theory (Page 454)

teleology (Page 455)

theory of divine command (Page 454)

veil of ignorance (Page 452)

Terms

categorical imperative (Page 452)

freebies (Page 463)

junket (Page 462)

pragmatic ethics (Page 452)

situational ethics (Page 455)

People

Aristotle (Page 451)

Immanuel Kant (Page 452)

John Stuart Mill (Page 452)

Ralph Potter (Page 456)

Robert Hutchins (Page 454)

Media Sources

- Thomas Bivins. *Mixed Media: Moral Distinctions in Advertising, Public Relations and Journalism.* Erlbaum, 2004. Professor Bivins stresses identifying the impact of ethics decisions in choosing courses of action.
- Clifford G. Christians, Kim B. Rotzoll and Mark Fackler. *Media Ethics,* sixth edition. Longman, 2002. These scholars are especially good at describing Kant's categorical imperative and other philosophical systems on which media ethics can be based.
- Ralph B. Potter. "The Structure of American Christian Responses to the Nuclear Dilemma, 1958–1963." Potter describes what came to be known as Potter's Box, in his Harvard University doctoral dissertation in 1965.

ETHICS

In this chapter you have deepened your media literacy by revisiting several themes. Here are thematic highlights from the chapter:

MEDIA TECHNOLOGY

Changing technology through the history of the mass media has posed ethics challenges that never could have been anticipated earlier. A growing contemporary issue is a lack of sensitivity among a new generation whose practices include wholesale cutting of Internet material and pasting it into their own work without credit. Plagiarism has always been a difficult issue for the mass media, especially with the vagaries imposed by deadlines and the continuing repackaging of material. For better or worse, media people have agreed upon all kinds of conditions and rules for swapping information. Even these accepted practices cause purists in some academic fields to shudder—"Egads! No footnotes?" The issue is becoming more critical with broadening acceptance of the rampant copying that's facilitated by digitization. Old ways of doing things need to be reconsidered. (Page 458–459)

MEDIA ECONOMICS

Advertising-dependent media have an obligation to advertisers as their financial supporters. But media also have obligations to other interests and values, including to their readers, to their owners and, let's not forget, to the truth. Weighing these obligations can expose all kinds of moral dilemmas. Consider a magazine that is financially dependent on ads for dubious Viagra substitutes. To turn away the ads could mean the magazine goes belly-up. What kind of service is that to readers who would benefit from the magazine's articles? (Pages 448–450, 458)

MEDIA AND DEMOCRACY

Social Responsibility. In 1947 a blue-ribbon task force of intellectuals headed by Robert Hutchins placed a premium on the media acting in socially responsible ways. The Hutchins ideas came to be embraced by the media, albeit with notable exceptions. But the media are no longer the easily identified companies that had the equipment and means to reach huge audiences. New technology has enabled just about anyone to enter the media marketplace, many who never heard of the Hutchins Commission and are completely oblivious to the Hutchins legacy.

For democracy to work as it should, people need accurate, timely and useful information. Ethical media conduct includes providing full reports, but are there no limits? During the 2000 presidential campaign, when an intrepid reporter in Maine unearthed a nearly 30-year-old drunken driving conviction against George Bush, the Bush campaign people were irate and used words like *irrelevant, unfair* and *smear.* Others saw evidence of Bush not owning up to his past. They argued that he had wanted to conceal his record, which they saw as a character flaw that voters should know about. (Page 454)

ELITISM AND POPULISM

Digitization has given almost everyone a mass media megaphone. Look around you. Who doesn't have the capability to set up a MySpace or Facebook page or become a blogger? This democratization of the mass media has triggered a need to reassess the rules by which traditional media have operated. Ethical conduct, for example, had been conditioned over the centuries and decades by conventions of copyright and widely accepted bounds on defamation, privacy and decency adopted by media organizations and the trained professionals who crafted media messages. These conventions were fortified by a broad range of institutions, including journalism schools and other career-oriented educational programs. Today, nobody needs a degree to blog or go on Facebook. (Pages 458–462)

MEDIA TOMORROW

Professional media associations will continue to tweak their ethics codes, especially to address issues that could never have been anticipated because of changes wrought by technology and evolving values in society. These codes will place pressure on media people who operate at the fringes of appropriate behavior, but, lacking the force of law, will wield influence mostly through moral persuasion. On complex issues with conflicting duties, the codes will continue to have limited roles in finding answers. Only through hard thinking can moral dilemmas be addressed and even then not to universal satisfaction. (Pages 447–450, 452)

INDEX

PHOTO CREDITS

The main photo usage appears first; additional uses follow in parentheses.

2 (20T) (295B): © TIM SLOAN/AFP/Getty Images; 5: Alex Brandon/AP Wide World Photos; 6: Courtesy of the Library of Congress; 7L: © Richard A. Bloom/CORBIS All Rights Reserved; 7R: Gerald Herbert/AP Wide World Photos; 8TL: IZEA; 8TR: IZEA; 8B (20C): Steve Wilkie/Everett Collection; 10 (145T): UPI/CORBIS-NY; 11 (20B): As seen on Shalom TV, America's National Jewish Cable Television Network; 14 (21): Kirk Schroeder/Courtesy Randy Baker and Beth Sanders; 16: Daniel Acker/Bloomberg Markets Magazine; 17: Fred Prouser/Landov Media; 22: *Harper's Weekly* drawing by Thomas Nast, "Compromise with the South" (1864). Public Domain; 26T (50T): Hilde Vanstraelen/iStockphoto; 26B (30T): North Wind Picture Archives; 28L: Public

Domain; 28R: Courtesy of the Library of Congress; 29L: © Justin Lane/CORBIS All Rights Reserved; 29R: The Image Works; 30TC: UPI/CORBIS-NY; 30C: Courtesy of the Library of Congress; 30BC: CORBIS-NY; 31L (51): Matthew B. Brady/AP Wide World Photos; 31R: The Granger Collection, New York; 34T: Courtesy of the Library of Congress; 34B: Hulton Archive/Getty Images; 36 (151TC): Bettmann/CORBIS; 37L (50C) (151C) (182T): Copyright Broadcasting & Cable Magazine, Photo Illustration by Forest Evashevski; 37R: The Image Works; 39L (30B): CORBIS-NY; 39R: Yale Joel/Getty Images/Time Life Pictures; 41: AP Photo/Lefebvre Communications, HO/AP Wide World Photos; 42T: Soren McCarty/Getty Images; 42B: Louis Lanzano/AP Wide World Photos; 45: Sean Hemmerle/Contact Press Images Inc.; 50B: Photo by Sara Chapman, originally in NDSU Newspaper, *The Spectrum*; 52: Peter Klaunzer/AP Wide World Photos; 59L: Courtesy of the Library of Congress; 59R (80T): © 2009 *The Christian Science Monitor* (www.CSMonitor.com). All Rights Reserved.; 62 (81C): Alex Wong/Getty Images; 66T (80B): CORBIS-NY; 66TC: The Granger Collection, New York; 66B: UPI/CORBIS-NY; 69 (66BC) (126T) (132L): Bettmann/CORBIS; 74 (81T): Robert Galbraith/Landov Media; 75 (80C): Public Domain; 76: © Brooks Kraft/Sygma/CORBIS All Rights Reserved; 77 (81B): Lawrence Jackson/AP Wide World Photos; 82 (192BC): © Rick Friedman/CORBIS All Rights Reserved; 86: Copyright 2009 The New York Times. All rights reserved. Used by permission and protected by the Copyright Laws of the United States.; 87TL: Public Domain; 87TR (89TC): The Image Works; 87B (114T): John Moore/Getty Images; 88L: Reprinted with permission of *The Wall Street Journal*, Copyright © 2009 Dow Jones & Company, Inc. All Rights Reserved Worldwide.; 88R (89BC): Copyright 2009, *USA TODAY*. Reprinted with permission.; 89T (238T) (301T): CORBIS-NY; 89B: © 2007 *The Christian Science Monitor* (www.CSMonitor.com). All Rights Reserved.; 91: Copyright TIME Inc.; 94T: Minnesota Historical Society; 94B: Reprinted with permission from *Reader's Digest*. Copyright © 2009 by The Reader's Digest Association, Inc.; 96T (92B): Alfred Eisenstaedt/Getty Images/Time Life Pictures; 96B: Joe Kohen/Getty Images; 97 (92T): Popperfoto/Getty Images; 98 (92TC): Cover/hologram photo illustration by Tom Schaefges. © National Geographic Society. Used with permission.; 99T: Photo by Oscar Graubner. Courtesy Margaret Bourke-White Estate, Life Magazine. © TimePix.; 99BL: Margaret Bourke-White/Life Magazine. © TimePix.; 99BR: George Strock/Time & Life Pictures; 100: Copyright © 1992 Watterson. Reprinted with permission of Universal Press Syndicate. All rights reserved.; 106L: The Image Works; 106R: Courtesy of the Library of Congress; 107: Paul Souders/Getty Images, Inc. Liaison; 108L: Basso Cannarsa/Opale/Retna Ltd.; 108R: Copyright Little, Brown and Company, a division of Hachette Book Group, Inc.; 110L (115C): Mike Segar/Landov Media; 110R: Krause Taylor Associates/© Plastic Logic; 114B (92BC): CORBIS; 115T: Chester Higgins Jr./Redux Pictures; 115B (219TC) (239C): North Wind Picture Archives; 116: Thor Swift/Thor Swift Photography; 118: Frank Trapper/CORBIS-NY; 120 (126TC): George DeSota/Getty Images; 121T (126C): Paul Sakuma/AP Wide World Photos; 121B: Lionel Vadam/Landov Media; 122 (126B): © Kim Kulish/CORBIS All Rights Reserved; 125 (145B): CORBIS-NY; 129: Bruce L. Flashnick/AP Wide World Photos; 131: AP Wide World Photos; 132R: CORBIS-NY; 137 (144B): Courtesy "Fresh Air with Terry Gross," produced in Philadelphia by WHYY. Photo by Miles Kennedy.; 139 (126BC) (144T): XM Satellite Radio; 146: Getty Images; 148: Picture Desk, Inc./Kobal Collection; 150: Buena Vista Pictures/Everett Collection; 151BC: © WARNER BROS/DC COMICS/THE KOBAL COLLECTION; 153: Picture Desk, Inc./Kobal Collection; 154 (238B): Jeff Reidel/Getty Images; 156: Lions Gate/Everett Collection; 157L: Everett Collection; 157R (151T): Photofest; 160: AP Wide World Photos; 161: Dreamworks/Everett Collection; 162: Epoch/The Kobal Collection; 163: Picture Desk, Inc./Kobal Collection; 165: The Granger Collection, New York; 166: K. C. Alfred/ZUMA Press; 170: Diane Bondareff/AP Wide World Photos; 171: Photofest; 172: Everett Collection; 175 (183C): © Tribune Media Services, Inc. All rights reserved. Reprinted with permission.; 177 (183T): Jim Cole/AP Wide World Photos; 182C: Jonathan Nourok/PhotoEdit Inc.; 182B: John Filo/CBS Photo Archive/CBS Broadcasting Inc.; 183B (151B): Justin Sullivan/Getty Images; 184: Landov Media; 185L (209T): CORBIS-NY: 185R: Landov Media; 187 (192TC): Robert Burroughs/Getty Images, Inc.-Liaison; 188 (208B): Gautam Singh/AP Wide World Photos; 189: Dennis Cook/AP Wide World Photos; 194: John MacDougal/Getty Images, Inc. AFP; 195: © David Brabyn/CORBIS All Rights Reserved; 196: The Doubleday Broadway Publishing Group/Copyright Doubleday and TurnHere, Inc.; 201 (192T): Marcio Jose Sanchez/AP Wide World Photos; 202L: Alessandro Della Valle/AP Wide World Photos; 202R: Linden Research, Inc./Second Life is a trademark of Linden Research, Inc. Certain materials have been reproduced with the permission of Linden Research, Inc.; 203L (192B) (208T): © 2004–2005 Geoffrey R. Hutchison, licensed under a Creative Commons license; 203R: Paul Sakuma/AP Wide World Photos; 205: Chester Higgins, Jr./Redux Pictures; 210: © M. Kaia Sand, Courtesy Jules and Maxwell Boykoff; 212 (219T): North Wind Picture Archives; 214: Getty Images Inc.-Hulton Archive Photos; 215L (219BC): Culver Pictures, Inc.; 215R: CORBIS-NY; 216TL: Culver Pictures, Inc.; 216BL: Culver Pictures, Inc.; 216R: CORBIS-NY; 222: © Matt Dellinger/The New Yorker; 223 (219B) (239T): SuperStock, Inc.; 228L: Public Domain; 228R: The Granger Collection, New York; 229: © Paul Chinn/CORBIS All Rights Reserved; 233: Landov Media; 239B: Reprinted with permission of *The Wall Street Journal*, Copyright © 2007 Dow Jones & Company, Inc. All Rights Reserved Worldwide.; 240: Shaun Curry/Getty Images, Inc. AFP; 242 (266B): Robert Voets/CBS/Everett Collection; 243: Damian Dovarganes/AP Wide World Photos; 245: © Kevin Mazure/WireImage/Getty Images; 247: Ben Kaller © TNT/Courtesy Everett Collection; 249: © Michael Ochs Archives/Getty Images; 250 (267B): Dima Gavrysh/AP Wide World Photos; 251: Ethan Miller/Getty Images; 255: CORBIS-NY; 256 (266T): Courtesy Electronic Arts; 260: Johan Spanner; 262 (267T): © Ezio Petersen/UPI/Landov; 268: Matthew Staver/Redux Pictures; 269: The North Face; 271 (294B): Copyright General Motors Corp. Used with permission of GM Media Archives.; 275L: Courtesy Colorado Historical Society; 275R (273TC) (294T): AP Wide World Photos; 276L (273T): The Granger Collection, New York; 276R: AP Wide World Photos; 280 (273B) (294C) Gerald Herbert/AP Wide World Photos; 282: Reed Saxon/AP Wide World Photos; 284L (273BC): © Kevin Horan/Chicago; 284R: CORBIS-NY; 285 (295T): Used with permission from McDonald's Corporation.; 286: Courtesy Dawn Bridges; 287: Nicholas Kamm/Getty Images, Inc. AFP; 291: UPI/CORBIS-NY; 296: Fred R. Conrad/*The New York Times*/Redux Pictures; 298 (322B): Gary Hershorn/Getty Images, Inc. AFP; 303: Mike Segar/Landov Media; 304: Pat Sullivan/AP Wide World Photos; 305: Gail Adler/Photofest; 307: DaimlerChrysler/Screenshot from Tony Hawk's Pro Skater 2, Courtesy Activision Publishing, Inc. © 2000 Activision Publishing, Inc. All Rights Reserved.; 309L: SCHWEPPES is a registered trademark of Dr Pepper/Seven Up, Inc. © 2007 Dr Pepper/Seven Up, Inc.; 309R (301TC): Courtesy Ogilvy & Mather; 310L: © RoadsideAmerica.com; 310R: Luke Frazza/Getty Images, Inc. AFP; 311 (238C) (301B): Brian Kersey/AP Wide World Photos; 312 (323): Square One Entertainment; 313: Richard E. Aaron/Getty Images; 314: Courtesy Ogilvy & Mather, London and Ford of Europe; 315 (295C): Courtesy Bamboo, Inc.; 316 (301BC): Richard Pasley/Richard Pasley Photography; 317 (322T): Virginia Sherwood/NBCU Photo Bank; 324: © Brendan McDermid/Reuters/Landov; 326T (331C): Copyright 2011 © The Gallup Organization; 326B (331T) (349T): AP Wide World Photos; 327 (348B): Courtesy Nielsen Media Research; 338 (348TR): Courtesy Nielsen Media Research; 339 (348TL): John Cross/The Free Press, Mankato/AP Wide World Photos; 340: Arbitron, Inc./Jacobs Media; 341 (331B) (349B): Dennis Kitchen/Getty Images Inc.-Stone Allstock; 350 (355TC): Bettmann/CORBIS; 353 (355B): © Patrick Seeger/DPA/Landov; 355T: Getty Images/Time Life Pictures; 358 (377B): A Band Apart/Miramax/Picture Desk, Inc./Kobal Collection; 360T (376B): AP Wide World Photos; 360B: © Lincoln Journal Star Library; 362 (377T): L. D. Ford/Scripps Institution of Oceanography Photographic Archives/SIO/UCSD; 363T (355BC): Provided by Virgin Comics, LLC. © 2006 DEVI, All rights reserved.; 363B: © Tim Ockenden/PA Photos/Landov; 364: J. Emilio Flores/Getty Images; 369: CORBIS-NY: 372T (376T): © Lions Gate/Courtesy Everett Collection; 372B: © Kyle Cassidy; 376C: Charles Dharapak/AP Wide World Photos; 378: Robert Galbraith/Landov Media; 380T: Richard Tsong-Taatarii/Landov Media; 380B (395T): Ann Heisenfelt/AP Wide World Photos; 381 (394B): Hulton Archive/Getty Images; 383: CNN Image Source/© CNN. All rights reserved.; 384: Kevin Lamarque/Landov Media; 386: Eduardo Sverdlin/UPI/Landov Media; 388: Jacob Silberberg/Redux Pictures; 389: Dennis Cook/AP Wide World Photos; 390L (395B): Brian Snyder/Landov Media; 390R: Christopher Morin/Landov Media; 394T: CORBIS-NY; 396: © Hayat Kahn/CORBIS All Rights Reserved; 398T (423T): Courtesy Freedom House; 398B: North Wind Picture Archives; 399 (400T) (423BL): Lebrecht Music & Arts Photo Library; 400C: Courtesy Voice of America; 401 (400TC) (423BR): Courtesy of the Library of Congress; 404T: Paul J. Richards/Getty Images, Inc. AFP; 404B: Win McNamee/Getty Images; 405 (422TL): Kamran Jebrelli/AP Wide World Photos; 407 (400BC) (422C): © RABIH MOGHRABI/AFP/Getty Images; 410: Courtesy Channel 1 and Alireza Nourizadeh; 411: Courtesy Voice of America; 412 (400B): © AFP/Getty Images; 413: Xinhua, Chi Haifeng/AP Wide World Photos; 416 (422B): China Photos/Getty Images; 418: Courtesy Video Sound, Inc., NJ; 419: Anupam Nath/AP Wide World Photos; 422TR: Justin Sullivan/Getty Images; 424 (444C): © Len Irish; 426 (444B): This advertisement, created by students enrolled in RIAA-EdVenture Partners classes, was provided courtesy of the Recording Industry Association of America (RIAA).; 428 (444T): Dennis Brack/Landov Media; 430L: Copyright © The New York Times Company. Reprinted with permission.; 430R (437BC): © Star Tribune. All rights reserved.; 431: CORBIS-NY; 434: David Leeson/Getty Images/Time Life Pictures; 435 (445B): UPI/CORBIS-NY; 437T: Courtesy of the Library of Congress; 437B: Napster logo and marks reprinted with the permission of Napster, LLC.; 439 (437TC) (445T): © State Historical Society of Iowa, Iowa City; 446: Wilfredo Lee/AP Wide World Photos; 449: Courtesy Charles Gay; 451: Getty Images/Time Life Pictures; 452 (453C) (466): Fritz Goro/Getty Images/Time Life Pictures; 453T: North Wind Picture Archives; 457: Courtesy Office of Communications at Harvard Divinity School; 459T: Ed Lallo/Getty Images/Time Life Pictures; 459B (453B): © David M. Grossman; 460: YouTube, LLC

STUDY GUIDE

CHAPTER 1

MEDIA LITERACY ACTIVITIES
CAN CHILDREN LEARN MEDIA LITERACY?

We are bombarded by media messages. Even children are targeted and, with today's spotlight on childhood obesity, those media messages are a target for action.

According to the Centers for Disease Control and Prevention, the percentage of young people who are overweight has more than tripled since 1980, with more than 9 million school-age children over the age of 5 in the U.S. considered overweight in 2010. In addition to the psychological and social issues of stigmatization, overweight children are at far greater risk of growing into adults who have cardiovascular disease, Type 2 diabetes, and other chronic diseases that may reduce the length and quality of their lives.

Most experts agree that there are lots of reasons the youth of America are increasingly overweight. But since, according to the American Academy of Pediatrics, the average child sees 40,000 TV commercials a year, it is almost certain that one of those reasons is advertising. Alluring ads for junk food and sugary treats are aimed at children, who for the most part don't understand that commercials are for selling products. The AAP says that kids 6 years and under are unable to distinguish content from commercials, especially if their favorite character is promoting the product. Even older kids may need to be reminded of the purpose of advertising.

First Lady Michelle Obama's national campaign to fight childhood obesity, called Let's Move, features public service announcements created by Scholastic Media and Warner Bros. The ads leverage the fun aspects and family appeal of the companies' characters to reach children "with important messages about being healthy." One series of ads features the Looney Tunes characters as they are paired with professional athletes to deliver an active lifestyle message that tells kids to "Be A Player." Another series features Maya & Miguel of PBS KIDS GO! and encourages children to "Take the Maya & Miguel Challenge" as a way to get more physically active and eat healthy. The ads were created in both English and Spanish.

At the same time the Let's Move campaign got underway, the advocacy group Corporate Accountability International called for the retirement of the venerable spokesclown for McDonald's, Ronald McDonald. Research has shown that a child already knows the McDonald's logo by the time he is two or three years old. Children who participated in a study done by Stanford doctors believed that a number of foods, including milk and carrots, tasted better when served in McDonald's packaging.

McDonald's declined to retire Ronald, saying he is the "heart and soul of Ronald McDonald Charities, which lends a helping hand to families in their time of need." The company pointed out that Ronald also delivers messages to families on issues such as safety, literacy, and the importance of physical activity and making balanced food choices.

- Think about a television ad that appeals to you and makes you want to buy the product. How does it do that?
- Is it possible to teach very young children how to be media literate?
- Is there anything McDonald's can do to help children learn media literacy? Is that their responsibility?
- Do you think the PSAs created by Let's Move can effectively mitigate the effect of advertising on childhood obesity?

PRACTICE QUIZ

1.1 True/False Questions

___ **1.** An example of media multitasking is washing the dishes and listening to the radio.
___ **2.** *USA Today* is an example of demassification.

1.2 Completion Questions

1. One-on-one communication is called ___________ communication.
2. When audiences across the country listened to the same radio programs, the effect was strong ___________ cohesion.

1.3 Multiple Choice Questions

1. According to the Veronis project, how much time did the average person spend watching television in 2004?
a. 78 hours
b. 219 hours
c. 1,057 hours
d. 3,584 hours

2. All but which of the following are reasons for the symbiosis of mass media and our lives?
a. persuasion
b. entertainment
c. acclimatization
d. information

3. An example of narrowcasting is
a. *Popular Mechanics.*
b. *PC World.*
c. *O* magazine.
d. all of the above.

4. Media create revenue streams by
a. selling advertising.
b. selling stock.
c. creating celebrities.
d. covering national issues.

1.4 Short Answer

1. List three "invisible" media messages you encountered today.
2. Give an example of a messenger who has been blamed for the message.

PRACTICE TEST

1.1 True/False Questions

___ 1. We spend about one-third of our waking hours involved with media.
___ 2. The book industry relies almost exclusively on direct sales for revenue.
___ 3. Editorial independence means that since advertisers help pay a media company's bills they are entitled to independent control of the media product.
___ 4. Fragmented audiences can be culturally polarized.
___ 5. The Internet is an example of broadcasting.
___ 6. Television has not helped in the processes of moral consensus and unification.
___ 7. As a member of a mass media audience, your feedback to a message can often be immediate.

1.2 Completion Questions

1. People expose themselves to competing ideas in the ____________ of ideas.
2. Media companies seeking smaller, niche audiences are creating ____________ audiences.
3. Shared knowledge leads to cultural ____________.
4. Mass communication is the technology-assisted transmission of ____________ to mass audiences.
5. Understanding how the media work is called media ____________.

1.3 Multiple Choice Questions

1. The interdependence of the audience and the media is called
   a. a marketplace of ideas.
   b. symbiosis.
   c. interpersonal communication.
   d. cultural identity.
2. Group communication is
   a. face to face.
   b. an email blast.
   c. television advertising.
   d. mass communication.
3. An essential part of mass communication is
   a. technology.
   b. an audience of any size.
   c. immediate feedback.
   d. a computer.
4. Editorial content of a media product includes
   a. all the content.
   b. editorials and opinion.
   c. all the nonadvertising content.
   d. everything written by the editor.
5. Revenue streams for media companies include
   a. subscriptions.
   b. direct sales.
   c. government funding.
   d. all of the above.
6. What is the biggest factor in explaining media behavior?
   a. editorial content
   b. mass communication
   c. making a profit
   d. use of technology

1.4 Essay Questions

1. Give an example of why knowing the motivation behind a media message is important.
2. How does the media help forge moral consensus with what seems like divisive coverage on controversial issues?
3. How did radio and magazines survive the advent of television?
4. Explain what the mass media and John Milton have in common.

CHAPTER 2

MEDIA LITERACY ACTIVITIES

LIBRARY OF CONGRESS AND GOOGLE APPLY NEW TECHNOLOGY TO NEW MEDIA

Twitter debuted on March 21, 2006. Four years later, the microblog service boasted 105.7 million users and 50 billion tweets a day. It has been one of the true success stories for social media.

On April 14, 2010, the Library of Congress announced its plans to digitally archive every public tweet since the launch of Twitter. The library made its announcement in a Twitter post. "It boggles my mind to think what we might be able to learn about ourselves and the world around us from this wealth of data," wrote Matt Raymond, the library's director of communications, in a blog post. "And I'm certain we'll learn things that none of us now can even possibly conceive."

As the largest library in the world, the Library of Congress is a research library. It receives copies of every book, pamphlet, map, print, and piece of music registered in the United States. The LOC began collecting materials from the Web with the congressional and presidential campaign Web sites in 2000. In 10 years it had amassed more than 167 terabytes of Web-based information.

That's a lot of information to search through if you just want to look at one topic or one event. Google, of course, had an answer to that problem. As the Library of Congress announced its plan to archive Twitter posts, Google announced a new feature that lets users search and explore the public archive of tweets. Google's real-time search already had content from MySpace, Facebook and Buzz. With tweets, the Google search function allows the user to zoom to any point in time and "replay" what people were saying publicly about a topic on Twitter.

"Want to know how the news broke about health care legislation in Congress ... or what people were tweeting during your own marathon run? These are the kinds of things you can explore with the new updates mode," said Dylan Casey, product manager for Google's Real-Time Search, in a blog post. "All of us are just beginning to understand the many ways real-time information and short-form Web content will be useful in the future, and we think being able to make use of historical information is an important part of that." Google named the new feature Google Replay because "it lets you relive a real-time search from specific moments in time."

- Do tweets fit in the concentric model of mass communication or in the web-like model of Web communication?
- How will researchers be able to use tweets?
- Is the Library of Congress archive of tweets another step in the democratization of the mass media? Why, or why not?

PRACTICE QUIZ

2.1 True/False Questions

___ **1.** Pulp paper and high-speed presses were some of the first chemical technology inventions of the Industrial Revolution that fueled the evolution of wood block printing.

___ **2.** Richard Hoe invented the Linotype machine.

___ **3.** Much of the control of the mass media communication process shifted to the sender.

2.2 Completion Questions

1. Flipping quickly through a series of still photos creates the ____________ of motion.

2. The precursor to today's television was Philo Farnsworth's ____________ ____________.

2.3 Multiple Choice Questions

1. How does mass communication differ from interpersonal communication?
- a. Mass communication uses written messages; interpersonal communication does not.
- b. Interpersonal communication uses technology; mass communication does not.
- c. Mass communication uses technology; interpersonal communication does not.
- d. Since both use technology, there is no difference.

2. The Chinese were printing
- a. 800 years before Europe
- b. 1,200 years before Europe
- c. 600 years after Europe
- d. 100 years before America

3. Who was not involved with the evolution of motion pictures?
- a. John Jacob Bausch
- b. Lumiére, Auguste and Louis
- c. George Eastman
- d. William Dickson

4. Arthur C. Clark
- a. wrote science fiction books.
- b. came up with the concept of geosynchronous orbit.
- c. envisioned a satellite in 1945.
- d. did all of the above.

5. The concentric circle model erects barriers to mass communication that include
- a. the medium.
- b. gatekeepers.
- c. a and b.
- d. none of the above.

2.4 Short Answer Questions

1. How did electricity change the way Americans consumed mass media?

2. How is media becoming democratized?

PRACTICE TEST

2.1 True/False Questions

___ **1.** Today, interpersonal communication depends on technology.
___ **2.** A halftone divides a photograph into a microscopic grid.
___ **3.** Telephone and television signals were uplinked to Telstar.
___ **4.** Fiber-optic cables carry light at 20,000 miles per second.
___ **5.** The first Internet was the military's ARPAnet.
___ **6.** The Laswell narrative model of mass communication asks which channel a message uses.

2.2 Completion Questions

1. Cable television distributes signals on ____________.
2. The first recording machine was invented by Thomas Edison in 1877 and was called the ____________.
3. The four primary technologies on which mass media are built are digital, printing, chemical, and ____________.

2.3 Multiple Choice Questions

1. What discovery in 1727 was a breakthrough in mass communication?
a. movable type
b. sending messages on radio waves
c. motion picture camera
d. the way light causes silver nitrate to darken

2. Johannes Gutenberg invented
a. bound books.
b. movable metal type.
c. chemical technology.
d. vellum.

3. Entrepreneur Mathew Brady's successful mass communication business venture sold
a. ads on fledgling radio stations.
b. printed Bibles.
c. books of Civil War photographs.
d. the first newspaper.

4. Before electricity, the only mass media was
a. radio.
b. print.
c. telegraph.
d. Morse code.

5. Movies and television were based on the concept of
a. persistence of vision.
b. an antenna.
c. electromagnetic waves.
d. all of the above.

6. Bardeen, Brittain and Shockley won the 1956 Novel prize for the
a. semiconductor.
b. fiber-optic cables.
c. Hertzian waves.
d. wireless radio.

7. Media convergence is affecting
a. media production.
b. media devices.
c. media distribution.
d. all of the above.

8. Tim Berners-Lee invented
a. hypertext markup language.
b. the World Wide Web.
c. universal resource locators.
d. all of the above.

9. Understanding a media message can be inhibited by
a. sequential presentation of messages.
b. psychological filters.
c. interrelations of message models.
d. all of the above.

2.4 Essay Questions

1. How did Gutenberg's invention spur the Age of Science and the Age of Reason?
2. What were three of the effects of the Industrial Revolution on printing?
3. How does a television signal use a geosynchronous orbiting satellite?

CHAPTER 3

MEDIA LITERACY ACTIVITIES
BUILDING BRIDGES TO ECONOMIC SUCCESS IN NEW MEDIA

The rise of online media and participatory media has challenged traditional media's business models. No one has found the definitive business model for new media yet, but some have made impressive forays into the battlefield.

Tina Brown, former editor of *Vanity Fair* and *The New Yorker,* is a journalist, magazine editor, columnist, talk-show host and author of *The Diana Chronicles,* a biography of Diana, Princess of Wales. She is now editor-in-chief of The Daily Beast. Brown created The Daily Beast, a mix of original journalism with celebrity gossip and high-class photography, for her friend, Internet mogul Barry Diller. Brown says that although she had to be dragged to do a Web site, she wouldn't ever want to go back to print. "After just a few months of working with this world, I realized how vibrant, exciting, and creative it is. I wouldn't want to go back to print now. Having an audience that you can immediately access and ask to collaborate in your work is absolutely thrilling. You can have an idea and try it so quickly. If it doesn't work, you can try something else. With print, it's rigid."

What does this mean for the way new media should do business? For The Daily Beast it means going for upper-echelon advertisers by maintaining a site that is "integrated and innovative and great to look at." Brown says after the site's first nine months, "we were up to millions of unique visits and we could ask advertisers what they want to do with us." The Daily Beast also built three or four revenue streams with television, conferences, and other Web sites as a "stopgap to get us through to the time when everything is really online."

The new media business models that so far have been successful are about being a bridge, not a gatekeeper, says Elisa Camahort. In 2006, Camahort and friends Jory Des Jardins and Lisa Stone, who respectively have backgrounds in technology product management, business development, and journalism, began a series of annual conferences and launched a Web site, BlogHer.com, to showcase some of the best blogs by women and to offer their readers and writers a place to meet. BlogHer "works with bloggers to provide quality sponsors and advertisers to support communities of women online, pay women bloggers and promote their excellent writing."

Just four years later, that community was reaching more than 20 million people each month via conferences and events, the BlogHer.com news service and the BlogHer Publishing Network of more than 2,500 blogs, 76,000 registered bloggers and 80 paid contributing editors. BlogHer content is syndicated to sites as diverse as iVillage and Yahoo!. Advertisers on the site reach the 2,500 affiliated bloggers with revenue-sharing agreements. The BlogHer ad network meets editorial guidelines that Camahort says are stricter than new Federal Trade Commission rules requiring bloggers to disclose paid posts. BlogHer raised $15 million in venture capital, and Camahort expected the company to become profitable in 2010, with about 80 percent of its revenue coming from its online operations.

- List the different revenue streams being used by The Daily Beast and BlogHer.
- List the different revenue streams being used by a large daily newspaper. How many are the same for BlogHer and The Daily Beast? Different?
- Do you think new media like The Daily Beast and BlogHer will survive and prosper? Will they replace traditional news media like large daily newspapers?
- How would you make a new media enterprise profitable?

PRACTICE QUIZ

3.1 True/False Questions

___ **1.** In Japan and Britain, the government collects money to finance television networks.

___ **2.** *The Christian Science Monitor* was founded by Mary Baker Eddy as a counterbalance to sensationalistic reporting.

___ **3.** The Corporation for Public Broadcasting is the Australian equivalent of the BBC Trust.

___ **4.** Many inventors never understand the commercial potential of their inventions.

3.2 Completion Questions

1. The death tax is levied on an ____________.

2. The U.S. Constitution acknowledges the role of the press as an independent check of government in the ____________ Amendment.

3. Graphical user interface was first used successfully by ____________ computers.

3.3 Multiple Choice Questions

1. Who is responsible for making decisions in a media conglomerate?
a. the editor
b. the company's board of directors
c. the station manager
d. the media mogul

2. Mass media's role as a monitor of government performance on behalf of citizens is called
a. watchdog.
b. bulldog.
c. glass ceiling.
d. coattails.

3. The Postal Acts of 1789, 1845 and 1879
   a. established postal rates west of the Mississippi.
   b. subsidized postage for newspapers.
   c. changed the way postage for magazines and newspapers was collected.
   d. did all of the above.
4. The Big Four in the recording industry and the Big Four in network television are examples of
   a. monopoly.
   b. conglomerates.
   c. oligopoly.
   d. personality-driven media.

3.4 Short Answer Questions

1. Why are so many news organizations dropping investigative journalism?
2. What is the purpose of trade groups for mass media?

PRACTICE TEST

3.1 True/False Questions

___ 1. In a dictatorship, media is financed by direct sales to minimize dissent.
___ 2. A media conglomerate condenses all its companies into one big company.
___ 3. An example of sponsored media is WCFL in Chicago.
___ 4. Any newspaper run by a community foundation would have hard-hitting reporting because foundations are nonprofit.
___ 5. The Medill Innocence Project is an example of a cooperative news agency.
___ 6. The U.S. record on government keeping its hands off content in subsidized noncommercial broadcasting is better than Great Britain's.
___ 7. JOAs were set up to preserve independent radio stations.

3.2 Completion Questions

1. A company that owns a number of newspapers, radio or TV stations is called a media ____________.
2. Reuters is an example of a ____________ nonprofit news organization.
3. Free newspaper exchanges authorized by the 1789 Postal Act was a government ____________ for producing content by reprinting news from afar.

3.3 Multiple Choice Questions

1. Why are revenue streams important to a media company?
   a. They help with distribution.
   b. They help generate a profit.
   c. They replace advertising.
   d. They replace direct sales.
2. A media conglomerate can own
   a. newspapers.
   b. gold mines.
   c. casinos.
   d. all of the above.
3. Media can be sponsored by
   a. religious groups.
   b. colleges.
   c. companies.
   d. all of the above.
4. Why were fireside chats significant?
   a. They became the model for podcasting.
   b. They preceded television by 200 years.
   c. They emphasized the importance of the consumer protection agency.
   d. The president could talk directly to the people.
5. Having second-class postal rates for print media
   a. institutionalizes postal subsidies.
   b. means that newspapers and magazines must cap their advertising at 70 percent.
   c. gives newspapers and magazines an economic advantage.
   d. does all of the above.
6. The U.S. government began regulating the broadcast industry because
   a. there was a scarcity of demand for frequencies.
   b. there was more demand than frequencies available.
   c. it wanted competition to flourish.
   d. satellite-delivery systems wanted to carry local TV stations.
7. What do Thomas Edison and George Eastman have in common?
   a. They worked on the invention of radiotelegraphy.
   b. They redefined radio.
   c. They saw the commercial potential of their inventions.
   d. Their commercial companies failed.
8. Which is not one of the five new possible funding mechanisms to replace advertising and subscriptions for mass media?
   a. auxiliary enterprises
   b. trade groups
   c. philanthropy
   d. micropayments

9. What are Andy Grove's final stages of an aging industry?
   a. set up studies, use dated technology, go bankrupt
   b. ignore new challenges, resist change, try radical reforms
   c. resist change, use dated technology
   d. ignore new challenges, blame someone else, go bankrupt

3.4 Essay Questions

1. What are the similarities and differences between a cooperative and a new nonprofit media organization?
2. Why do some people believe family-owned newspapers should be encouraged?

CHAPTER 4

MEDIA LITERACY ACTIVITIES
PAYING LESS FOR TEXTBOOKS

Open textbooks, an idea inspired by open-source software, are popping up everywhere. They are available on the Web and provide students with a free, digital version of the textbook. They can save students hundreds of dollars every semester.

Many open textbooks can be modified to suit course requirements by adding, removing or altering the content, and they can be used indefinitely, so instructors may opt to use the same book for a number of years.

Behind the open textbook is the open license, which allows users to read the textbook online, download it, or print it, all for free. This is a radical change to the traditional copyright model of author compensation. To make this new system work, an author must agree not to charge for access to his or her work. That means that users can use the textbook, copy it, distribute it noncommercially and shift the content into other formats—all without paying or even sometimes crediting the author.

So who will pay an author to spend years writing a textbook that will be given away free? Startup open textbook publisher Flat World Knowledge pays its authors on the sale of print copies and study aids. Other proposed models include grants, institutional support, and advertising. Some authors are hired by a school or foundation to write open textbooks for a particular reason or for a particular group of students. University of Colorado professor Ken Krauter, co-author of an open textbook for his principles in genetics course, said although the open textbook may provide a smaller profit up front for the author, he is looking to constant online updates and various digital formats that will give him a more consistent and longer-term revenue stream than traditional publishing.

A project funded by the William and Flora Hewlett Foundation, The Community College Open Textbook Collaborative, is working on the development of open textbooks. The collaborative is a collection of colleges, governmental agencies, educational nonprofits, and other education-related organizations. It has been working to create open textbook standards and guide their development. The collaborative has been providing training for instructors adopting open resources, peer reviews of open textbooks, an online professional network, support for authors opening their resources, and other services.

The textbook, like all books, is finding new methods of delivery in the digital age. Whether open textbooks are the future or just a step into the future remains to be seen, but whatever the form of textbooks in the future, students across the country are looking forward to paying less for the knowledge contained within their pages.

- Take a look at the graphic on page 104 that illustrates how the textbook dollar is divided. Draw a dollar showing the costs for an open textbook.
- In the future, do you think your textbook will have advertising? How will that affect your perception of the validity of the textbook?
- How will open textbooks affect traditional textbook publishers?

PRACTICE QUIZ

4.1 True/False Questions

___ **1.** When a newspaper's circulation increases, its market penetration falls.
___ **2.** The in-depth personality profile was refined by *Playboy's* long Q&As.
___ **3.** Trade books are limited to general-interest fiction.
___ **4.** An audio book is read on an e-reader.

4.2 Completion Questions

1. *The New York Times* prints important documents in their entirety, making it a newspaper ____________ ____________.

2. DeWitt and Lila Wallace founded The ____________ ____________.

4.3 Multiple Choice Questions

1. Who owned the first newspaper chain?
a. William Randolph Hearst
b. Benjamin Franklin
c. Ida Tarbell
d. Benjamin Day

2. A contributing editor at a magazine is
a. an unsalaried editor.
b. like an independent writer and reporter.
c. an editor paid by the piece.
d. all of the above.

3. What tradition did Daniel Defoe's *Weekly Review* establish?
a. highbrow slicks
b. aggregators
c. outsourcing
d. photojournalism

4.4 Short Answer Questions

1. What are the consequences of newspapers vanishing?

2. How did *National Geographic* and *Life* magazine change the magazine industry?

PRACTICE TEST

4.1 True/False Questions

___ **1.** Software that allows several people to write and edit the same article is called Nupedia.
___ **2.** Benjamin Day introduced advertising as a way to meet expenses not covered by selling copies of his newspaper for a penny.
___ **3.** Essays and commentaries are examples of long-form journalism that set many magazines apart from most Web-only content.
___ **4.** Demassification by the magazine industry often made CPM sense for advertisers.
___ **5.** CPM is advertising lingo for the cost per million.
___ **6.** Magazines have survived by catering to submass audiences.
___ **7.** E-books can be read on a dedicated reader, cell phones, or computers.

4.2 Completion Questions

1. Gannet was the largest newspaper ___________ in the 1900s.
2. The Supreme Court decided in the ___________ libel case that news media could have generous leeway in reporting public issues.
3. Investigative reporting is also called ___________.
4. A person who can read but doesn't is ___________.

4.3 Multiple Choice Questions

1. What did Ben Franklin and Ben Day have in common?
a. They owned chain newspapers.
b. They got rich from their newspapers.
c. Their newspapers catered to a mass audience.
d. All of the above.

2. The Tweed Scandal and the Pentagon Papers are examples of
a. courageous reporting.
b. government scandals.
c. reporting by *The New York Times.*
d. all of the above.

3. When did circulation peak for U.S. newspapers?
a. 2008
b. 1958
c. 1908
d. 1988

4. What do magazines outsource?
a. printing
b. writers
c. circulation
d. all the above

5. What magazine was the precursor to today's aggregator Web sites?
a. *Good Housekeeping*
b. *Harper's*
c. *Reader's Digest*
d. *TV Guide*

6. What do Upton Sinclair, Ida Tarbell and *McClure's Magazine* have in common?
a. exposing filth in meat-packing plants
b. exposing the Standard Oil monopoly
c. writing about international government scandals
d. doing some of the first investigative reporting

7. Women's magazines are now characterized as
a. shelter magazines.
b. food magazines.
c. lifestyle magazines.
d. all the above.

8. When an author's copyright has expired, his work becomes part of
a. Citizendium.
b. reference book footnotes.
c. the public domain.
d. online libraries.

9. What may breathe new life into backlist books?
a. Google Print Library
b. print on demand
c. space on bestseller lists
d. Project Gutenberg

4.4 Short Essay Questions

1. How did Benjamin Day's penny newspaper create a mass audience, and how did that change the newspaper industry?
2. Why did many newspapers go out of business in the early 2000s?
3. What advantages does the book industry have over magazines and newspapers in the shift to digital formats?

CHAPTER 5

MEDIA LITERACY ACTIVITIES
MAKING MUSIC A MULTIMEDIA EXPERIENCE

In 1998 Britpop artist Dam Albarn created Gorillaz, a virtual band, with Jamie Hewlett, co-creator of the comic book *Tank Girl.* The band's four animated members, 2D (lead vocals, keyboard), Murdoc Niccals (bass guitar), Noodle (guitar and occasional vocals) and Russel Hobbs (drums and percussion), play a fusion of various musical genres. The band's debut album in 2001 sold over 7 million copies.

The newest album by Gorillaz, *Plastic Beach,* debuted at number 2 on the U.S. and U.K. charts and sold over 200,000 copies in its first week in 2010. This was at a time when the Gorillaz label, EMI, was floundering in debt, and the whole music business was trying to find ways to recapture business lost in a 20 percent plummet in CD sales in 2009. Globally, recorded music sales fell from $26.5 billion in 2000 to just $17 billion in 2009.

One of the biggest problems for the music industry is the mass exodus of artists. Many artists have left the big labels and found other ways to produce and distribute their music, including signing with smaller labels and self-recording and self-distributing. These days an artist who wants control over his work is more likely to be looking for a financial investor than a label.

Artists have long complained that the music industry is slow to adopt new technologies, but several of the majors are working to change that. The release of *Plastic Beach* by EMI was a multimedia experience. Buyers were given a special code to access computer games, manga-style videos and live audio streamed on the Gorillaz Web site. And, EMI allowed fans to listen to the album for free on the *Guardian* newspaper's Web site. Instead of going after radio play to promote the album, the band and EMI partnered with YouTube to "premiere" the album's first single. The video featured Bruce Willis and the band in a car chase and generated a YouTube record of 900,000 views in its first 24 hours. That caused a spike in sales that lasted for weeks, according to Dan Sabbagh of *Time* magazine.

Universal Music also is dipping a toe into the digital swimming pool. The company is working on a new service that will allow consumers in England to listen to and download as much music as they want for a fixed fee per month. Spotify, a Swedish company, has proved that the model can work. The company has a catalog of 7.8 million songs licensed from the music majors, available for free to subscribers who just have to listen to a few advertisements between songs. By early 2010, Spotify had 7 million registered users. If Universal starts a service like that, the other majors—EMI, Warner Music, and Sony Music—will have to follow, says Sabbagh, although industry insiders are betting there will be a cap on the number of songs that can be downloaded in a month.

iTunes slowed the decline of the music industry by selling individual songs, but are the majors ready for the next jump in technology to online, subscription-based services and using new media for promotion and more?

- Visit the Web sites of three or four of your favorite bands or artists. Find a mix of artists on major labels and indie labels.
- List all the different ways the bands are promoting themselves. Are the indie labels or the major labels finding more creative methods of promotion?
- Do you think the majors will survive the next five years? Why or why not?

PRACTICE QUIZ

5.1 True/False Questions

___ **1.** Pandora uses the same model of communication with its listeners as traditional radio.
___ **2.** Gerald Levin came to Ice T's defense, saying that his song "Cop Killer" should be protected as artistic freedom, an essential value in free society.
___ **3.** Radio in the U.S. is regulated by the government.
___ **4.** When networks started providing programming to local affiliates, music for a national audience displaced local programming

5.2 Completion Questions

1. "A&R" stands for ___________ and repertoire.
2. Adam Curry invented ___________.
3. The 20 largest ___________ radio stations own 2,700 stations.
4. In 1971, the FCC said that radio stations have a responsibility to know "the content of ___________."

5.3 Multiple Choice Questions

1. What were the annual sales of the global recording industry in 2004?
a. $1.4 trillion
b. $2.4 million
c. $18.4 billion
d. $8.4 million

2. What innovation caused the demise of bricks and mortar music stores?
a. CDs
d. garage bands
c. downloading
d. chain stores

3. How has radio reinvented itself?
a. switched to all-news format
b. switched to recorded music
c. switched to listener call-in shows
d. all of the above

4. The Corporation for Public Broadcasting is a(n) ___________ agency that decides on federal funding for noncommercial radio and television.
   a. educational
   b. commercial
   c. quasi-government
   d. chain
5. A predominant characteristic of corporate radio is
   a. centralized playlists.
   b. voice tracking.
   c. high amounts of advertising.
   d. all of the above.

PRACTICE TEST

5.1 True/False Questions

___ 1. Music file swapping was upheld by the U.S. Supreme Court.
___ 2. During the Vietnam war, the government banned war protest songs.
___ 3. With the advent of iPods, the music recording industry no longer needs radio.
___ 4. Talk radio has put more news and public affairs on the radio than ever before.
___ 5. The 1967 Public Broadcasting Act established the deregulation of the broadcasting industry.

5.2 Completion Questions

1. The two kinds of recording companies are the majors and the ___________.
2. Sirius and XM are examples of ___________ radio.

5.3 Multiple Choice Questions

1. What usually happens to successful independent recording companies?
   a. They move into commercial radio.
   b. They are bought by one of the majors.
   c. They burn out.
   d. They move to Canada.
2. What innovation gave recording artists control over their art?
   a. low-cost recording equipment
   b. greater diversity at recording companies
   c. more chances to tour
   d. all of the above
3. What do Shawn Fanning and Steve Jobs have in common?
   a. They introduced new ways to access music.
   b. They made music file swapping lucrative.
   c. They used illicit copying of music files.
   d. They helped the music industry recover from losses to Napster.
4. The Parents Music Resource Center formed to
   a. provide resources to school music programs.
   b. protest offensive song lyrics.
   c. guarantee artistic freedom for songwriters.
   d. create archives of current music.
5. What helped new recordings in the 1950s be successful?
   a. the invention of hi-fi
   b. Victrolas
   c. radio airplay
   d. Ed Sullivan appearances
6. According to Arbitron, how many hours a week does the average teen or adult listen to radio?
   a. 22
   b. 2
   c. 12
   d. 52
7. What concept was necessary for the federal government to issue broadcast licenses?
   a. public service
   b. radio news
   c. public air waves
   d. all of the above
8. Congress decided that the Federal Radio Commission should award broadcast licenses based on
   a. public interest, convenience and necessity.
   b. advertising revenues.
   c. ownership caps.
   d. network availability.
9. The FRC's decision to limit the number of radio stations that could be owned by a single entity was made to promote
   a. capitalism.
   b. diversity.
   c. regulation.
   d. the marketplace.
10. The deregulation of the broadcasting industry replaced the trusteeship concept with the
    a. scarcity concept.
    b. marketplace concept.
    c. localism concept.
    d. network concept.
11. The FCC can't control the content of
    a. American Public Media.
    b. Jack radio.
    c. public broadcasting.
    d. satellite radio.
12. What do many people think was the biggest mistake made by radio stations in the 1990s?
    a. creating too many chains
    b. not converting to subscription radio
    c. not converting to digital transmission
    d. all of the above

5.4 Short Answer Questions

1. What effect did A&R units have on U.S. culture?
2. What did Steve Jobs do that may have saved the recording industry?
3. How does headline news differ from news packages?

CHAPTER 6

MEDIA LITERACY ACTIVITIES
WHEN A NATIONAL DEBATE BECOMES A PUBLIC SERVICE

When Congress established the concepts of public airwaves and public interest to decide who should be awarded licenses for local radio and television stations, those stations began broadcasting stories that served the public's interest. In the 1950s, Edward R. Murrow reported on the tactics being used by Senator Joseph McCarthy to label people as communists even if they weren't. Murrow's courageous reporting was one of the first examples of public affairs reporting on television, and public service became firmly entrenched in broadcasting. But starting in the 1980s, there was a trend toward deregulation that culminated in the 1996 Telecommunications Act. That meant that fewer and fewer broadcast stations aired pieces that could be considered a public service.

Univision, the dominant Spanish-language television network in the U.S., is challenging the current model of less public service. In 2010, as the national debate about immigration policy heated up, Univision was continuing the tradition begun by Murrow and CBS. Univision held a televised, prime-time, commercial-free forum in Phoenix and Miami, "Inmigración: Un Debate Nacional," to discuss the new law passed by Arizona that cracked down on illegal immigration. The Arizona law required police to ask a person about his or her immigration status if there was "reasonable suspicion" that the person was in the country illegally. Experts on immigration law and public policy, representatives of national Hispanic organizations and advocates for tougher enforcement against illegal immigrants attended the forum, as did members of Congress and Arizona state officials. The White House even sent a representative.

When pro-immigration rallies were held across the country, Univision carried hours of live coverage. Meanwhile, English-language cable news channels like CNN and Fox News featured the rallies in their newscasts but did not provide wall-to-wall coverage.

Univision also sponsored a poll done with the Associated Press that became big news when it showed that the country is divided over the immigration issue. "The debate on immigration reform continues to be one of the most important issues for our community," said Alina Falcón, president of news for Univision, in a statement. "We are happy to partner with the Associated Press on this poll to be able to present the current viewpoints of Hispanics around the country."

Univision seems to embrace its role of providing a public service to its viewers. Falcón says, "...we wish to provide a forum to debate these issues which are of vital importance to the daily lives of our viewers."

- Other than presidential candidate debates, can you remember one of the Big Four networks turning over an hour of prime time for a public affairs debate?
- What other national issues might benefit from public service reporting on radio or television?
- Pick one of those issues and make a plan of how you would cover it if you were in charge at a television network.
- What might change in the national debate about your issue if it got the same kind of coverage as Univision is providing the immigration issue?

PRACTICE QUIZ

6.1 True/False Questions

___ **1.** Audiences felt cheated when they saw the first narrative films that used close-up shots.
___ **2.** Michael Moore uses his films to persuade people to his point of view.
___ **3.** Control of the U.S. movie industry was spread among many companies in the 1920s.
___ **4.** The term "theme park" was coined to describe Walt Disney's amusement park, which opened in 1955.

6.2 Completion Questions

1. Natural skepticism is lost in the suspension of ___________.
2. Illusions in movies were replaced by ___________.
3. The technological breakthrough of *Gone with the Wind* was ___________.
4. Formulaic, low-budget movies that are almost sure to make money are called ___________ movies.

6.3 Multiple Choice Questions

1. The first talkie was
a. *The Black Pirate.*
b. *Gone with the Wind.*
c. *The Jazz Singer.*
d. *Life of a Fireman.*

2. Who pioneered animated movies in the 1920s?
a. Walt Disney
b. Al Gore
c. Thomas Edison
d. James Cameron

3. How did movie theater chains adapt to decreasing ticket sales in the 1970s?
a. They built multiplex theaters in the suburbs.
b. They added art-house movie theaters.
c. They started merchandise tie-ins.
d. all of the above

4. CBS Television established itself with soap operas and radio reporting by
a. Roone Arledge.
b. Edward R. Murrow.
c. David Sarnoff.
d. Barry Diller.

PRACTICE TEST

6.1 True/False Questions

___ **1.** More movies are imported than exported.
___ **2.** A docuganda presents a subject in a totally nonpartisan way.
___ **3.** Michael Eisner moved Disney away from collaborating with television.
___ **4.** The director of early blockbuster *Birth of a Nation* was Harvey Weinstein.
___ **5.** Movie studios charge companies for placing their products in a film.
___ **6.** Art houses mostly show films about art.
___ **7.** The release window for movies is shrinking.
___ **8.** Sales of DVD movies have been steadily increasing.
___ **9.** The Federal Communications Act of 1934 set up laws to regulate radio and television.
___**10.** David Sarnoff built the NBC radio network for RCA before he moved into television.
___**11.** HBO, ESPN and WTBS are broadcast stations.
___**12.** It's legal for one company to own both over-air networks and cable networks.

6.2 Multiple Choice Questions

1. What innovation did *I Love Lucy* borrow from the movies?
a. showing movies in prime time
b. three-camera production
c. live comedy
d. all of the above

2. Frank Capra's *Why We Fight* series is an example of
a. propagandist films.
b. animated films.
c. docugandas.
d. in-your-face documentaries.

3. What was the effect of the Paramount decision by the U.S. Supreme Court?
a. Movie studios could no longer own movie theaters.
b. Move studios could no longer use block booking.
c. Studios began hiring directors and actors by the project.
d. all of the above

4. Most independent movie studios
a. disappear.
b. make multiple breakthrough films.
c. find their own financing.
d. acquire other studios

5. At its peak, movie house attendance reached
a. 1 billion tickets a week in 2006.
b. 90 million tickets a week in 1946.
c. 2 million tickets a week in 1926.
d. 900,000 tickets a week in 1916.

6. What digital processes can be used by movies?
a. film and editing
b. distribution
c. exhibition
d. all of the above

7. Perry Mason and Mary Tyler Moore are examples of television's
a. common themes.
b. educational potential.
c. cultural role.
d. all the above

8. What is the drawback to time-shifting, TiVo and video on demand for advertisers?
a. Timeliness of ads is lost.
b. People don't have to own a television to watch shows.
c. On-demand movies have drained audiences.
d. all of the above

9. Newton Mills' accusation that television was a "vast wasteland" spurred Congress to create
a. educational television (ETV).
b. mobile television.
c. the Federal Communications Act.
d. the Corporation for Public Broadcasting.

Short Essay Question

1. What innovations did Adolph Zukor make in the movie business?

CHAPTER 7

MEDIA LITERACY ACTIVITIES
SOMEBODY IS ALWAYS WATCHING

Behavioral marketing—it's nothing new, but now it's everywhere on the Web. Every search on Google is tracked, and ads are displayed on your screen accordingly. Internet service providers often release information about what Web pages you visit, and marketers use that information to further target their ads. Cookies follow you as you click through a Web site; the information they gather is used to pick the ads and even the pages you are presented. Companies do this to enhance your experience on their site, and advertisers do it to market their products more effectively.

Some people see this trend in Web advertising as advantageous; they will see ads that they might actually want to see. Others, however—like people who spend hours researching topics for a job—say that the system would not be showing them ads they want to see.

For many, the problem with behavioral targeting is that it's an invasion of their privacy. Sir Tim Berners-Lee, credited with inventing the Web, agrees. He spoke to Britain's Parliament in 2009 "to raise awareness of the technical, legal and ethical implications of interception and profiling by ISPs in collaboration with behavioral targeting companies."

Marketers say that as more people become aware of this target marketing, they are starting to be more accepting of the practice. But David Hallerman, eMarketer senior analyst, says that the surveys that have been done don't agree. "A number of surveys reveal significantly divergent perspectives among consumers about the intersection of privacy, data collected about them and their relationship with targeted online advertising."

A survey done by TRUSTe, an online privacy watchdog group, backs up marketers who believe the practice is becoming more acceptable, and the survey suggests that "the more consumers understand these practices, the higher their comfort levels." Colin O'Malley, vice president of strategic business at TRUSTe, invited the advertising industry "to give its customers a newfound transparency into its tracking and profiling practices so that they may gain consumer trust and earn the right to continue to engage in behavioral advertising activities.... Behavioral tracking techniques represent the future in digital advertising, but as companies adapt to take advantage of these technologies, we are seeing some stumble as they struggle to provide transparency around privacy."

- One study suggests that women want more, not less, targeted offers from trusted brands. Does this seem to be true among your friends?
- When downloaded, Google's toolbar provides a measure of control over privacy. Is this enough control to satisfy people like Sir Tim Berners-Lee?
- Can you think of a way that Internet service providers—who can see where each of their users goes online—can provide privacy and transparency for their customers?

PRACTICE QUIZ

7.1 True/False Questions

___ **1.** Before browsers, subscription-based services like AOL provided walled-garden access to the Internet.
___ **2.** Both texting and tweeting can be done on a computer.
___ **3.** eBay is an example of an auction site.
___ **4.** Multiuser dungeons were the first online games with a mass media message.

7.2 Completion Questions

1. Video games sponsored by an advertiser are called ____________.

2. ____________ is the digital equivalent of Britannica.

7.3 Multiple Choice Questions

1. Blogging has created a platform for
a. AOL-type companies.
b. ARPAnet.
c. video gaming.
d. user-generated content.

2. What kind of site can carry commercial messages and advertising?
a. .com
b. .edu
c. .biz
d. all of the above

3. Pierre Omidyar created
a. Twitter.
b. YouTube.
c. eBay.
d. MySpace.

4. You create your own avatar when you play
a. Metabrain.
b. Second Life.
c. advergames.
d. Sim City.

PRACTICE TEST

7.1 True/False Questions

___ **1.** Search engines take snapshots of Web pages.
___ **2.** The U.S. military created the first e-mail network.
___ **3.** Twitter discussions cannot include links to other material.
___ **4.** Video sharing is a form of social networking.
___ **5.** Authoritarian governments welcome the opportunity for their citizens to use YouTube.
___ **6.** Both Amazon.com and iTunes caused physical stores to lose business.

___ **7.** Google's search algorithms allow advertisers to target their marketing.

___ **8.** Simulation games use artificial life to put players into make-believe situations.

7.2 Completion Questions

1. Marc Andreessen designed the first ____________ software and called it Netscape.

2. Jeff Bezos founded ____________.

7.3 Multiple Choice Questions

1. What two tools are essential to using the Internet?
  a. Netscape and Explorer
  b. walled gardens and AOL
  c. browsers and search engines
  d. advertising and e-mail

2. How do search engines make money?
  a. They carry advertising.
  b. They do targeted searches.
  c. They have expanded overseas.
  d. They offer e-mail services.

3. What do texting and e-mail have in common?
  a. They can take the place of letters.
  b. They can replace phone calls.
  c. They are generally not mass communications.
  d. all of the above

4. Facebook and YouTube are examples of
  a. social networking sites.
  b. user-generated content.
  c. a contrast to the walled garden.
  d. all of the above.

5. The creators of the Internet wanted to keep it
  a. video-free.
  b. commercial-free.
  c. politics-free.
  d. all of the above.

6. What concept did Amazon.com copy from iTunes?
  a. targeting e-mail promotions
  b. downloading an intangible product
  c. online auctioning
  d. commercial-free communication

7. Using personal information to match ads with potential customers is
  a. behavioral targeting.
  b. video sharing.
  c. social networking.
  d. all of the above.

8. What is the fundamental question that bothers critics of the Google Print Library?
  a. Where will Google store all that information?
  b. Will Wikipedia and other archive services survive?
  c. Should publishers and authors get paid for their work?
  d. all of the above

7.4 Short Essay Questions

1. How has blogging changed mass media?

2. What is the difference in how Google and Facebook target potential customers for advertisers?

CHAPTER 8

MEDIA LITERACY ACTIVITIES
OBJECTIVITY VS. EMPIRICISM

Former journalist and academic John H. McManus has proposed that journalism should adopt the goal of empiricism rather than objectivity when reporting the news.

McManus says we should get rid of the objectivity standard because not only is it unachievable but it also rejects biases that "are necessary if news is to be useful in a democracy—biases for the common good, for brevity, for making what's important interesting."

McManus' definition of empiricism is the "scientific method of inquiry based on careful observation from multiple perspectives and logic." It wouldn't even pretend to reflect reality because it recognizes that news represents a small part of reality with carefully selected words, sounds and images. Empiricism would take the social "fault lines" that Robert C. Maynard identified—race, class, gender, geography and generation—seriously. Empiricism, says McManus, would disclose how its version of what happened was gathered, and it would invite other credible versions. "Objectivity is a lecture. Empiricism is a conversation."

McManus uses what NBC reporter Ashleigh Banfield observed during the 2003 invasion of Iraq as an example of what's wrong with the current state of journalism. Banfield said that reporters embedded with U.S. soldiers "certainly did show the American side of things because that's where we were shooting [video] from. You didn't see what happened when the mortar landed. There are horrors that were completely left out of this war."

Objectivity has encouraged passivity and invited official manipulation, says McManus. Falling back on a "he said, she said" approach to reporting is safe and can help a media organization stay on the good side of politicians and advertisers, but "demagogues like Senator Joseph McCarthy and powerful industries like tobacco have taken advantage of such objectivity norms at great expense to society."

McManus suggests that journalism should become more independent and skeptical of powerful sources, even risking their wrath and denial of access. "Accuracy would become more necessary, but less sufficient, particularly when journalists asserted facts from their own investigations rather than relying on officials." He says providers of news should acknowledge their limitations of staff, space or time and invite the public as a partner "in what would be a more empowering and democratic form of journalism."

McManus argues that now is the time for a new standard. He sees the move of news to the web as an opportunity for media to more easily accommodate give and take with the community it serves. "There's room for diverse perspectives. Updates and revisions are easy to accomplish. And news is easier than ever to share."

- Take a second look at this article. Would it have been better if it had been objective and quoted another source that argued in favor of keeping the standard of objectivity for journalists?
- Write a checklist for figuring out if a journalist is using the standard of objectivity. Write a similar list for empiricism. Read an online news report and also watch one of the cable news shows. Does the journalist adhere to the standard of empiricism or objectivity? Is that a factor in how much you trust what he or she has to say?

PRACTICE QUIZ

8.1 True/False Questions

___ **1.** Benjamin Harris published the first U.S. newspaper in 1690.
___ **2.** Lightning news traveled via telegraph during the Civil War.
___ **3.** The media want to have unbiased reporting because it makes economic sense.
___ **4.** Rachel Maddow is a leading political commentator on Fox News.
___ **5.** Journalists are often blamed for the news they report.

8.2 Completion Questions

1. News is a report on ____________.
2. Bob Woodward and Carl Bernstein reported about the ____________ scandal.

8.3 Multiple Choice Questions

1. Who was the first editor to believe that his newspaper should be used for social good?
a. David Bowen
b. Horace Greeley
c. Benjamin Harris
d. Samuel Morse

2. William Randolph Hearst and Joseph Pulitzer were part of which period of journalism?
a. yellow
b. partisan
c. penny
d. colonial

3. What is the disadvantage of nonstop news coverage?
a. Quality of reporting decreases.
b. There is no time for in-depth reporting.
c. The number of live stand-ups increases.
d. All of the above

4. What do John McQuaid, Carl Bernstein and Ida Tarbell have in common?
a. investigative reporting
b. Watergate
c. blogging
d. live news reporting

PRACTICE TEST

8.1 True/False Questions

___ **1.** John Peter Zenger was convicted of writing stories critical of the crown.

___ **2.** James Gordon Bennett was the first newspaper publisher to organize the newsroom around beats so he could be the first with the news.

___ **3.** Complete objectivity in news reporting is impossible.

___ **4.** Publishers tell journalists which stories to report.

___ **5.** Journalists write from their own political bias when they write about changes proposed by candidates or governments.

___ **6.** All blogging news sites adhere to professional journalists' codes of ethics.

___ **7.** All new media [CE1]are trained to observe the journalistic ideal of accuracy in reporting the news.

___ **8.** Live coverage of the news is routinely and carefully edited by gatekeepers.

___ **9.** Soft news includes muckraking stories.

8.2 Completion Questions

1. The space left in a newspaper after all the ads have been placed on pages is called the ____________ ____________.

2. Many Web news sites, called ____________ sites, get their news from elsewhere.

8.3 Multiple Choice Questions

1. The Alien and Sedition acts prohibited
a. illegal immigration to the colonies.
b. criticism of the royal governor.
c. scandalous statements about the government.
d. opposition to the stamp tax.

2. What concept was adopted by the Associated Press to make its news stories usable by all its members?
a. Advertising content should be universal.
b. News reporting should be objective.
c. Partisan stories appeal to more people.
d. Papers should cost only a penny.

3. What happens on heavy news days?
a. Not all news stories are published or broadcast.
b. The news hole shrinks.
c. The news hole expands.
d. All news stories are published or broadcast.

4. The consensible nature of news is also called
a. quick updates.
b. aggregating journalism.
c. pack journalism.
d. none of the above.

5. Information that has not been verified but is included in online news is called
a. original reporting.
b. distributive journalism.
c. comprehensive coverage.
d. competitive journalism.

6. Who decides whether or not to use a story and if it has to be changed?
a. writer
b. editor
c. blogger
d. gatekeeper

7. The predominant characteristic of the yellow period of journalism is
a. accuracy.
b. lightning news.
c. sensationalism.
d. all of the above.

8. What news reporting convention came to be during the Civil War?
a. penny press
b. stunt reporting
c. yellow journalism
d. inverted pyramid

8.4 Short Essay Questions

1. How does ethnocentrism affect American journalists?

2. What have shrinking budgets meant for newsrooms?

CHAPTER 9

MEDIA LITERACY ACTIVITIES
LOST IN THE EXPERIENCE

Lost was not just a sci-fi mystery television show that followed a group of people whose airplane crashed on an enchanted island full of supernatural mysteries and threats—it was a multimedia experience. There was the show itself, but it was so much more—a cornucopia of *Lost* entertainment.

You could watch the long-running show on television when it aired, watch it again online, play online *Lost* games, watch webisodes, or listen to a podcast dedicated to the show. It spawned fan forums, blogs and its own reference sites like Lostpedia.org.

The Atlantic magazine offered a challenge to readers to sum up *Lost* in a single tweet. One of the entries from Vicky Page said, "Disproportionate number of good looking people on same plane. Crash. More good looking people show up. Things go badly. Wonder why." But there was more to *Lost* than good-looking people. Page referenced it with "wonder why." The twisted plot lines and references made for endless chatter about what it all meant. As producer and writer Damon Lindelof explained, the writers hoped that angst over the show's story line would be "replaced by a question along the lines of, What did they mean by that? And the question that we would throw back at the audience is, Well, what did it mean to you? Your own personal relationship with *Lost* actually trumps any intention that we had as storytellers. And we wanted that to be the legacy of the show."

"The next time someone tells you TV makes people stupid, think of the *Lost* fans chatting about Gnosticism, Einstein and the British East India Company," observed James Poniewozik, *Time* magazine's television critic.

The show ran on ABC for six seasons, and the last episode was aired on May 23, 2010. But it wasn't the end for fans. The *Lost Experience* online, interactive, multiplatform game carried on the *Lost,* well, experience. The alternate-reality game was described by reporter Lia Miller as a "multimedia treasure hunt that makes use of e-mail messages, phone calls, commercials, billboards and fake Web sites that are made to seem real." The game featured new characters, and it was devised by the show's writers, not marketers, according to Michael Benson, a senior vice president at ABC.

Writer and producer Carlton Cuse said, "We created it for purposes of understanding the world of the show but it was something that was always going to be sort of below the water, sort of the iceberg metaphor, and the Internet *Experience* sort of gave us a chance to reveal it."

Says Poniewozik, "The phenomenon that is *Lost*—a story authored by everyone who watches—will continue. And the way we watch TV will have changed into an experience that's more communal, demanding and rewarding."

- How did the producers of *Lost* use cross-media adaptations to promote their show?
- Would you describe the show as elitist or populist? Highbrow or lowbrow?
- What do you think is the future of entertainment as perceived by the producers and writers of *Lost*?

PRACTICE QUIZ

9.1 True/False Questions

___ **1.** An on-site audience is needed for an authentic performance.
___ **2.** Elvis Presley put a white face on the previously all-black rock 'n' roll.
___ **3.** Elitists favor lowbrow art.
___ **4.** Susan Sontag posited that popular entertainment and art could raise serious issues.

9.2 Completion Questions

1. Literature is adapted to new media with movies, radio and ____________.
2. Storytelling, sports and music are entertainment ____________.

9.3 Multiple Choice Questions

1. What kind of performance can be mediated?
a. football game
b. documentary movie
c. hip-hop concert
d. all of the above

2. Who do we have to thank to be able to read sports stories in a newspaper?
a. KDKA
d. Cecile Frot-Coutaz
c. Roone Arledge
d. James Gordon Bennett

3. Harlequin books are an example of
a. middlebrow art.
b. highbrow art.
c. nonfiction.
d. pulp fiction.

4. When Dwight Macdonald called pop art kitsch it was a
a. compliment.
b. put-down.
c. tribute.
d. misconception.

PRACTICE TEST

9.1 True/False Questions

___ **1.** Entertainment includes literature, sports, sex and music.
___ **2.** The medium does not transform a performance.

___ **3.** Poetry and fascism are both genres of literature.

___ **4.** Politicians often use music to inspire voters.

___ **5.** Movies based on games don't make much money.

___ **6.** It's been proven that games like *Grand Theft Auto* make teenagers violent.

___ **7.** People who are interested in art that supports their lifestyle and values are lowbrow.

___ **8.** A criticism of pop art is that it's market-driven.

9.2 Completion Questions

1. Pittsburgh's KDKA was the first ____________ station to carry a play-by-play sports event.

2. The ____________ Standard defines when sexual content is protected from government bans.

3. Movie versions of books are ____________ adaptations.

9.3 Multiple Choice Questions

1. When you attend a concert you are attending
a. a crossover performance.
b. a mediated performance.
c. an authentic performance.
d. all of the above.

2. Rhythm and blues emerged from
a. black music.
b. hillbilly music.
c. rock 'n' roll.
d. folk music.

3. The First Amendment protects
a. pornography and obscenity.
b. pornography.
c. obscenity.
d. none of the above.

4. The U.S. Supreme Court ruled that during the times when children are likely to be watching, over-air broadcast stations cannot air
a. adult education programming.
b. indecent programming.
c. live comedy programs.
d. foreign films.

5. What did French film critic André Bazin call cutting-edge, original filmmakers?
a. auteur
b. amateur
c. derivative
d. faux

6. Harlequin and the studio system are modeled after
a. factories.
b. kitsch.
c. tabloids.
d. Bollywood.

7. Sociologist Herbert Gans tied people's tastes in art to their
a. education.
b. intellect.
c. income.
d. all of the above.

8. Elitists who were influenced by Susan Sontag used what word to describe a sophisticated appeal in pop art?
a. avant-garde
b. highbrow
c. camp
d. visionary

9.4 Short Answer Question

1. Discuss why broadcast companies are willing to lose money on sports programs.

CHAPTER 10

MEDIA LITERACY ACTIVITIES

A BATTLE FOR THE HEART AND SOUL OF BRITISH PETROLEUM

British Petroleum had just been named a finalist for a federal award honoring offshore oil companies that displayed outstanding safety and pollution prevention, and the company had a successful marketing campaign, "Beyond Petroleum," that painted it as environmentally friendly.

BP seemed to be on a public relations roll—until its Deepwater Horizon oil rig exploded and caught fire in April 2010 in an accident that killed 11 of the rig's workers. The crisis kept growing as the days passed and oil spewed into the Gulf of Mexico in what many were calling the worst environmental disaster in decades. BP faced unprecedented technological and engineering challenges in trying to plug the oil well.

At first, BP played down the size of the spill, the company's own role in the explosion and the environmental damage that had occurred. At the same time, company spokespeople kept promising that BP would get the well plugged. BP's chief executive and public face, Tony Hayward, was prone to uttering provocative statements. He said the spill would not cause big problems because the gulf "is a very big ocean" and "the environmental impact of this disaster is likely to have been very, very modest." His most infuriating comment was, "I would like to have my life back."

BP enlisted the help of the Brunswick Group, a public relations and crisis management firm, to deal with the accident. It dedicated the home page of its Web site to the crisis and hired a new head of media relations in the U.S.

Another problem for BP was its low profile in Washington, D.C. The company's lobbying work and political contributions were behind other oil and gas giants like Exxon, Mobil and Chevron. BP didn't have as many friends in Washington as it might have, and this was a time when friends in Washington would have been important.

At the start of the crisis, BP promised to be transparent. At times BP kept its promise; but at other times it didn't. The company set up a Web site for the press where one could join a mailing list or submit an inquiry via e-mail. The site also provided links to social media sites, including Facebook, Twitter, and YouTube. But BP resisted putting up a live video feed of the underwater spill for weeks, agreeing to do it only after feeling intense pressure from Congress. The company also resisted using common scientific techniques to measure the spill, saying it was focused on shutting down the well. BP was accused of hiding the true dimensions of the leak for financial reasons. The company knew it would eventually pay a fine that would be based on the amount of oil that escaped its well. "They have tried to control the message, including controlling facts, because they have a direct financial interest in this," said David Pettit, a senior attorney with Natural Resources Defense Council.

According to Chris LeHane, a crisis communication expert, BP made several mistakes and was not open, transparent, or accessible. "You see this all the time. Typically publicly traded companies find themselves in a situation, and their immediate concern is to limit their legal exposure, as opposed to recognizing that this is really a fight for the heart and soul of the company."

LeHane thinks BP should not have promised that its proposed solutions would work. He also thinks the company should have brought in an outside expert or asked the federal government to be a partner in finding a solution to the spewing oil. Harlan Loeb, U.S. director of crisis and issues management at Edelman, the largest public relations agency in the world, finds the reports of BP's early offer to residents of a $5,000 settlement if they waived their rights to sue for any damages troubling. "The challenge in the face of crisis is to rise above the narrative of the crisis," Loeb said.

- Research what else BP did to handle this public relations crisis.
- Write out a crisis management plan for the BP crisis. Compare that to what BP actually did.
- Do you think BP rose to Loeb's challenge?

PRACTICE QUIZ

10.1 True/False Questions

___ **1.** When a company practices enlightened self-interest, the public perceives it as an unfriendly, industrial giant.

___ **2.** The democratic ideal of public relations creates a dialogue on issues.

___ **3.** A public relations service is to groom industry executives to go on talk shows.

___ **4.** Wal-Mart has good media relations and a good crisis management plan.

___ **5.** When a company has a public relations person, it negates the need to hire a PR agency.

10.2 Completion Questions

1. A news release and supporting materials is called a media ____________.

2. A public relations message that combines using paid space in a publication with editorial content is a(n) ____________.

10.3 Multiple Choice Questions

1. Who laid out the fundamentals of public relations?
a. Charles Darwin
b. John D. Rockefeller Jr.
c. Ivy Lee
d. William Henry Vanderbilt

2. Public relations based on dialogue with a company's public is
   a. reactive.
   b. whitewashing.
   c. dialogic
   d. prologic.
3. What is the role of public relations?
   a. contingency planning
   b. image consulting
   c. crisis management
   d. all of the above

PRACTICE TEST

10.1 True/False Questions

___ **1.** Institutions may interact with many different publics.
___ **2.** Ivy Lee proved to the railroads that secrecy about policies and business practices was best.
___ **3.** Giving decision-making responsibility to the public relations job at a company is wise.
___ **4.** Public relations companies that conduct their own polls are considered disreputable.
___ **5.** The Tylenol crisis is an example of bad open media relations.
___ **6.** A principle of crisis management is providing information for reporters before they know they want it.
___ **7.** The Public Relations Society of America has established a process to give members credentials.
___ **8.** A social media news release is interactive.

10.2 Completion Questions

1. Public relations is a management tool that establishes beneficial ___________.
2. When a company takes the initiative to disseminate information in a crisis, it is practicing ___________ media relations.
3. Mutuality, commitment, empathy, propinquity and risk are characteristics of the ___________ theory in practice.

10.3 Multiple Choice Questions

1. Who used the theory of social Darwinism to justify their practices?
   a. populists
   b. industry leaders
   c. muckrakers
   d. labor unions
2. Puffery is equivalent to
   a. exaggerated claims.
   b. fine pastries.
   c. whipping up opposition.
   d. muckraking.
3. What do George Creel and Elmer Davis have in common?
   a. They headed government public relations agencies.
   b. They used public relations on a giant scale.
   c. They were both journalists.
   d. all of the above
4. A company newsletter is an example of
   a. external public relations.
   b. media relations.
   c. internal public relations.
   d. all of the above.
5. A person who works to influence public policy on behalf of a client is a(n)
   a. advertiser.
   b. journalist.
   c. CEO.
   d. lobbyist.
6. Integrated marketing communication
   a. can make a campaign even more persuasive.
   b. has prompted some advertising agencies to move into PR.
   c. coordinates PR and advertising as a marketing tool.
   d. all of the above.
7. What mistakes did General Motors make when its leadership got angry with coverage in *The Wall Street Journal*?
   a. It bought more advertising to promote its point of view.
   b. It initiated an informational boycott.
   c. It created advertorials critical of *The Wall Street Journal.*
   d. all of the above
8. The early response of companies to muckraking was
   a. whitewashing.
   b. advertorials.
   c. proactive media relations.
   d. integrated marketing communication.
9. Who could be considered the father of public relations?
   a. Edward Bernays
   b. Ivy Lee
   c. neither
   d. both

Short Answer Questions

1. Discuss the differences between advertising and public relations.
2. Explain the differences in how Johnson & Johnson, Wal-Mart and Mobil Oil (in the 1970s) handle public relations.

CHAPTER 11

MEDIA LITERACY ACTIVITIES
ARVERTISING: A FAD OR A NEW DIRECTION?

ARvertising was the newest promotion concept in 2009. Augmented reality (AR) is the technology that augments a live direct or indirect view of a real-world environment with computer-generated imagery. Advanced AR technology could use the information about the real world of the user to make it interactive and digitally usable. Information on the objects and environment of the real world can be stored and retrieved as an information layer that can be imposed on the real worldview. An example of AR is the yellow "first down" lines seen in broadcasts of football games or the line ahead of a speed skater showing where his opponent was at the same moment. AR also can be used to enhance museum exhibitions by inserting objects into the real environment with projectors and screens. AR also is used in games to display various images that give information or clues.

In the summer of 2009, Best Buy started using augmented reality to make its weekly print ads that it inserts in newspapers interactive and three-dimensional. The ads invited readers to go to a dedicated Web site where they could hold the ad in front of their webcam. That triggered a 3D-style augmented reality animation of a Toshiba laptop computer that jumped out of the page, along with 3D speech bubbles that promoted a tech advice service from Best Buy employees delivered by Twitter. The ad could be viewed from different angles by moving the print ad around in front of the webcam.

Best Buy's director of brand identity, Spencer Knisely, said the company was trying to think of the advertising circular as not the end of all promotional activity but as the beginning. However, he admitted, "It's a great organizing tool for promotional activity, but it doesn't offer all the different connections we want." Based on Best Buy's estimates of how many people owned webcams, they were pleasantly surprised by how many used the AR experience. "We projected maybe 2,500 people would give it a shot. We were surprised to learn many more connected with and used the experience—6,500 for just one day."

Following the success of the trial experience with a Toshiba laptop ad, Best Buy was considering going to its manufacturer partners to ask if they had an interest in a similar promotion.

- Who was Best Buy's targeted audience with its ARvertising newspaper insert? Was this the best way to advertise a laptop computer? Do you think it was an effective use of Best Buy's advertising money?
- Is Best Buy still using augmented reality in its advertising?
- Was ARvertising just a fad, or will it have an enduring place in the changing technology of advertising?

PRACTICE QUIZ

11.1 True/False Questions

___ **1.** Advertising has a role in both rich and poor societies.
___ **2.** Advertising is one-sided communication.
___ **3.** Jeep is a brand name for four-wheel-drive vehicles.
___ **4.** Ads that are creative outsell hard-sell ads.

11.2 Completion Questions

1. Francis Wayland Ayer founded the first ad ___________.
2. Kraft Foods' online game is an example of a(n) ___________.
3. ___________ is used to distinguish products from the LCD clamor.
4. Viral advertising spreads like a ___________.

11.3 Multiple Choice Questions

1. When was the first advertisement printed by William Caxton?
a. 468
b. 1168
c. 1468
d. 1868

2. What did the penny press newspapers seek that helped them sell advertising?
a. larger circulation
b. ad agencies
c. more circulation
d. all of the above

3. What is the advantage of game ads?
a. Messages can change instantly.
b. Women 18 and older play games.
c. Games take months to develop.
d. all of the above

4. A factor used by advertisers to evaluate the effectiveness of an ad is
a. ABC.
b. CPM.
c. PAC.
d. all of the above.

5. An Internet ad intended for the widest possible audience will aim at
a. store brands.
b. the lowest common denominator.
c. celebrity branding.
d. under-the-radar advertising.

6. What can connect otherwise unrelated products?
a. gaming
b. shelf life
c. infomercials
d. branding

7. The Pepsi Center in Denver is an example of
   a. stealth ads.
   b. product placement.
   c. viral advertising.
   d. word of mouth.

PRACTICE TEST

11.1 True/False Questions

___ **1.** One theory holds that democracy's need to evaluate leaders led to advertising.
___ **2.** Advertising does not need mass media technology.
___ **3.** Full-service ad agencies not only design ads; they also give advice on selling products and services.
___ **4.** The advantage of a store brand is higher profits for the store.
___ **5.** Ocean Spray's claim that it's "Straight from the bog" is an example of a unique selling proposition.
___ **6.** With product placement, a company pays to have its product written into the script of a television show.
___ **7.** Ad clutter may be alleviated by demassification.

11.2 Completion Questions

1. In a(n) ____________ contract, an agency earns expenses, a negotiated markup, and something extra if the ad campaign succeeds.
2. CPM is short for cost per ____________.
3. Google pays a Web site a(n) ____________ fee every time someone opens an ad on the site.

11.3 Multiple Choice Questions

1. How does advertising contribute to prosperity?
   a. It uses word-of-mouth testimonials.
   b. It inspires greater individual productivity.
   c. It is in the forefront of technological innovations.
   d. all of the above
2. Which is the most effective way to reach consumers?
   a. salesmen
   b. advertising
   c. letters
   d. phone calls
3. How can an ad agency earn money?
   a. shares in the company
   b. commissions
   c. bonuses
   d. all of the above
4. An advantage of advertising in a magazine is
   a. longer shelf life.
   b. high pass-along circulation.
   c. slick paper.
   d. all of the above.
5. The high cost of television ads can be attributed to
   a. limited availability of slots.
   b. its niche audience.
   c. the opportunity for moving visual display.
   d. all of the above.
6. When David Ogilvy said, "Give your product a first-class ticket through life," he was developing a
   a. store brand.
   b. brand image.
   c. lowest common denominator.
   d. unique selling proposition.
7. Barrages, bunching and trailing are examples of
   a. redundancy.
   b. testimonials.
   c. LCD.
   d. branding.
8. Buzz advertising is
   a. anti big company.
   b. peer-initiated.
   c. word of mouth.
   d. product placement.
9. What do infomercials and 'zines have in common?
   a. They are produced by companies to sell products.
   b. They can be cleverly disguised.
   c. They are stealth advertising.
   d. all of the above

11.4 Short Answer Questions

1. What are the advantages of online advertising?
2. Why are traditional media, like newspapers, radio and television, losing advertisers?

CHAPTER 12

MEDIA LITERACY ACTIVITIES
TIVO AND GOOGLE TIE THE KNOT

For years, the major broadcast companies have threatened to start their own rating company to compete with Nielsen. In 2009 several of the biggest companies in television and advertising held discussions about forming a consortium to back a new ratings company. The group included the four major broadcast networks, cable channel operators, three of the country's biggest-spending advertisers, and two of the biggest advertising agency holding companies.

The group said a more precise and accurate measurement of viewership, particularly of TV on the Internet and mobile devices, was needed. Especially during the current economic recession, companies need to get better information to increase their efficiency and effectiveness. The group said that when its plan is completed it will take bids from outside firms to provide the service, which would be "years down the road"—and expensive. The service would measure programming and advertising across television, Web sites and mobile devices.

Earlier in 2009, Nielsen went three days without providing any prime-time rating information to its clients, blaming a computer flaw. In June, the company reported that ABC's newscast had scored by far the lowest rating in its history, a number it had to correct after ABC protested. And, in 1997 and 2003, Nielsen reported sudden drops in viewing by young men. Nielsen never admitted an error, and months later the young men simply reappeared.

This is just the latest threat from Nielsen's clients. Friction between Nielsen and its clients has been common for decades, fueled by Nielsen's monopoly over audience information and what its customers perceive as arrogance in dealing with their complaints. Now other players, like Google TV Ads, are finding ways to measure audience reaction.

What Google TV Ads offers its customers may be in the future for Nielsen or a possible competitor. Google TV Ads sells television ads on a CPM basis, charging advertisers only for the ad impressions viewed. Google TV Ads works with cable channels, including CNBC, MSNBC, Hallmark Channel, CBS College Sports and Syfy. The system allows advertisers to reach up to 96 million households. Launched in 2007, Google TV Ads had served 100 billion TV ad impressions by 2009.

In late 2009, Google and TiVo made a deal that enabled Google to integrate TiVo viewing data into its audience research for advertisements sold through Google TV Ads. Through a deal with Dish Network, Google TV Ads advertisers already had access to second-by-second data collected by set-top boxes. The new deal with TiVo gave advertisers a more detailed picture. TiVo now provides Google TV Ads with second-by-second viewing patterns of time-shifted programs in order to "enhance the measurement and accountability of ad impressions." TiVo collects a log of what commercials you watched and what commercials you skipped. TiVo promises that none of the data is tied to an individual, and its users can change their privacy settings on TiVo's Web site.

"Working with Google is an important milestone for our audience research business and represents a shared approach to developing innovative products and services to help the media industry better understand the effectiveness of ad campaigns in an evolving TV landscape," said Todd Juenger, vice president and general manager, TiVo Audience Research and Measurement. "Among the many innovative aspects of Google TV Ads, a critical role is in its ability to measure specific commercial ratings, not simply averages, which is a key attribute of the TiVo data. By using TiVo's massive samples and second-by-second granularity in its currency measurement, Google TV Ads can now provide an order of magnitude of improved accountability for advertisers."

- What is the "evolving TV landscape" that Juenger refers to?
- What parts of that landscape do Nielsen, Google and TiVo measure for advertisers?
- How would you measure the parts not currently being surveyed?

PRACTICE QUIZ

12.1 True/False Questions

___ **1.** Harris and Pew focus on researching television audiences.

___ **2.** A poll that shows two candidates running 62 to 38 percent with a 5 percent margin of error has a high probability of being inaccurate.

___ **3.** Diaries and People Meters are used to track television viewership.

___ **4.** Nielsen only measures broadcast audiences.

12.2 Completion Questions

1. The Audit Bureau of Circulation checks the number of ____________ of a magazine.

2. A(n) ____________ breakdown adds groups like age and gender.

12.3 Multiple Choice Questions

1. A survey where the respondents are self-selected and the results are unreliable is a
   a. straw poll.
   b. quota sampling.
   c. probability sampling.
   d. zipped poll.

2. In what way do television networks try to influence their ratings?
   a. hyping during sweeps week
   b. hyping during black weeks
   c. changing sample demographics
   d. all of the above

3. Galvanic skin checks measure
   a. perspiration.
   b. pulse.
   c. audience reaction.
   d. all of the above.
4. The system that divides people into categories based on their lifestyles is called
   a. PRIZM.
   b. cohort analysis.
   c. psychographics.
   d. focus groups.

PRACTICE TEST

12.1 True/False Questions

___ 1. Eavesdropping on the bus is one way to do audience research.
___ 2. For any location, a good sample will interview every 1,758th person.
___ 3. The extrapolation of data by the ratings industry is important to advertisers.
___ 4. The Broadcast Ratings Council accredits ratings companies but cannot audit their reports.
___ 5. The flush factor and zipping describe an audience's commercial avoidance.
___ 6. Nielsen can measure live television viewing habits and viewing within 30 days.
___ 7. Geodemography and psychographics measure acceptance of television programs.

12.2 Completion Questions

1. Everyone in a population has a(n) ___________ chance of being surveyed in a probability survey.
2. A ___________ group measures audience reaction.
3. VALS identifies people's ___________.

12.3 Multiple Choice Questions

1. After the 1948 presidential election, George Gallup switched his polling technique to
   a. quota sampling.
   b. probability sampling.
   c. public opinion sampling.
   d. a target sample size.
2. What is the magic sample size for many surveys to have a 95 percent chance of having less than a 5 percent margin of error?
   a. 1,384
   b. 2,100
   c. 384
   d. 7 percent of the population
3. The percentage representing the chance that a survey may be wrong is the
   a. sample error.
   b. margin of error.
   c. population factor.
   d. probability factor.
4. How did A.C. Nielsen expand on Archibald Crossley's ratings system?
   a. He added advertisers.
   b. He added demographic breakdowns.
   c. He added radio listeners.
   d. all of the above
5. Engagement ratings measure
   a. how well people recall an ad or a TV program.
   b. how long people stay on a Web page.
   c. how much attention viewers give to a TV program.
   d. all of the above.
6. Movie previews and pilot television shows are examples of
   a. galvanic skin checks.
   b. prototype research.
   c. sit-down interviews.
   d. focus groups.
7. When the Pentagon put people in a group called Kids and Cul de Sacs, it was using
   a. psychographics.
   b. emulators.
   c. geodemographics.
   d. cohort analysis.
8. Jonathan Robbins invented the PRIZM system to rank neighborhoods by
   a. geodemographics.
   b. housing style.
   c. social rank.
   d. all of the above.

12.4 Short Answer Questions

1. What are the differences between probability sampling and quota sampling?
2. What factors should you consider to evaluate a survey?
3. What are some dubious uses of galvanic skin checks? Why?

CHAPTER 13

MEDIA LITERACY ACTIVITIES
MTV GOES GLOBAL, TURNS LOCAL

MTV launched on August 1, 1981, as the first nonstop pop music video channel. Its launch marked a new era in promotion, consumption and power of pop music among the record-buying young. The new channel coined the expression the "MTV generation." Twenty years later, in 2001, MTV was beamed into 342 million homes and was a multimillion-dollar enterprise owned by Viacom.

When MTV first expanded outside the U.S. in 1987, it aired American programs with English-speaking VJs throughout Europe. But the company soon found that most people preferred local music, with the exception of a few global superstars like Michael Jackson and Madonna. Soon many local stations were copying the MTV format. Tom Freston, the former chairman of MTV Networks, said, "We were going for the most shallow layer of what united viewers and brought them together. It didn't go over too well."

To fight the leakage of viewers to the local copycats, MTV changed tactics in 1995 and adopted a strategy of localizing content according to the country where it was broadcasting. The strategy worked. By 2004, MTV had 72 channels and viewers in 140 countries. Today, all the MTV channels have the familiar frenetic look and feel of MTV, but much of the programming is localized. According to Charles Hill and Gareth Jones, authors of *Strategic Management Theory: An Integrated Approach,* "no matter what language they are using, MTV gets the local channels started by using expatriates from elsewhere in the world who can do a 'gene transfer' of the company's culture and operating principles." MTV "gets inside the heads" of the local population and produces programming that matches the locals' tastes and preferences. Once established, the expatriates move on, and the network switches to local employees.

Hill and Jones say that although many of MTV's programming ideas still originate in the U.S., with staples such as *The Real World* having equivalents in different countries, an increasing share of programming is local in conception. In Italy, *MTV Kitchen* combines cooking with a music countdown. In Brazil, *Erotica* features a panel of youngsters discussing sex. The Indian channel produces 21 homegrown shows hosted by local VJs who speak "Hinglish," a version of Hindi and English.

"Since 1987, MTV has become the most ubiquitous cable programmer in the world," say Hill and Jones. By 2009, the network reached 450 million households worldwide, and 300 million of them were in countries outside the U.S.

- Does what MTV is doing match the definition of cultural imperialism? Why or why not?
- Do you think MTV is exporting American culture even if it carries local programming?
- Do you think MTV will still be broadcasting in 10 years?

PRACTICE QUIZ

13.1 True/False Questions

___ **1.** The powerful effects theory and the third-person effect theory have been proven to be true in American society.
___ **2.** When media change their products, lifestyle changes follow.
___ **3.** Television eased the breakdown of traditional social institutional barriers.
___ **4.** Television has replaced much of the socializing influence that used to come from parents.
___ **5.** Most violent people are acting out media violence.
___ **6.** It's been proven that talk shows desensitize people to anti-social behavior.
___ **7.** According to minimalist scholars, the media does not give issues and people prominence by covering them.

13.2 Completion Questions

1. A generalization that college jocks are dumb is called ____________.
2. A message that cannot be consciously perceived is ____________.
3. Photos of U.S. troops torturing Iraqi prisoners have had the effect of ____________ viewers to violence.

13.3 Multiple Choice Questions

1. The linking of the Columbine High School massacre to a movie is called
  a. stereotyping.
  b. role modeling.
  c. socialization.
  d. cognitive dissonance.
2. Ernest Dichter created ads for cars based on
  a. Sigmund Freud's research.
  b. his own motivational research.
  c. subconscious appeals.
  d. all of the above.
3. The 1960 Bobo doll studies done by Albert Bandura seemed to substantiate the
  a. cathartic effect theory.
  b. subliminal message theory.
  c. aggressive stimulation theory.
  d. all of the above.

PRACTICE TEST

13.1 True/False Questions

___ **1.** The two-step flow model says that people are influenced more by people they know and respect than by the media.
___ **2.** The cumulative effects theory says that redundancy in the media makes a message powerful.

___ **3.** Researchers have proven that subliminal advertising works.

___ **4.** Media can affect public opinion only during major events.

___ **5.** Mass media perpetuate stereotypes by using them.

___ **6.** The way mass communication changes society is called diffusion of innovations.

___ **7.** Other countries have not yet begun to produce their own media products, and products from the U.S. still dominate the global market.

___ **8.** The statement "For most children, under most conditions, most television is probably neither particularly harmful nor particularly beneficial" exemplifies the catalytic theory.

___ **9.** The Violence Assessment Monitoring Project found that distressing human violence was less prevalent than previous studies had shown.

13.2 Completion Questions

1. The hypodermic needles model is also called the ___________ model.

2. Elisabeth Noelle-Neumann's theory that minority viewpoints are discouraged is called the ___________ of silence theory.

3. Herbert Schiller called the domination of cultural life around the world by the U.S. media cultural ___________.

13.3 Multiple Choice Questions

1. His radio show, based on H.G. Wells' *The War of the Worlds,* triggered widespread panic.
a. Walter Lippmann
b. Albert Bandura
c. Paul Lazarsfeld
d. Orson Welles

2. Paul Lazarsfeld's research of voters led to the
a. powerful effects theory.
b. minimalist effects theory.
c. third-person effect.
d. bullet model.

3. The theory that media do not tell people what to think but what to think about is called
a. agenda-setting.
b. third-person effect.
c. two-step flow.
d. powerful effects.

4. When the media cover an event or an issue, they make the event or issue
a. stereotypical.
b. legitimate.
c. innovative.
d. historical.

5. What do music archives and medieval storytellers have in common?
a. They are part of the historical transmission of culture.
b. They promote contemporary transmission of culture.
c. They both use status conferral.
d. all of the above

6. What step in the diffusion of innovations involves the mass media?
a. interest
b. awareness
c. evaluation
d. all of the above

7. The theory that media-depicted violence contributes to but doesn't trigger real-life violence is the
a. catalytic theory.
b. Bobo doll theory.
c. aggressive stimulation theory.
d. motivational message theory.

13.4 Short Answer Questions

1. Explain how media violence can be seen as positive or negative.

2. How can media-depicted violence affect a democratic society?

CHAPTER 14

MEDIA LITERACY ACTIVITIES
SOME NETWORKS LET POLITICIANS HAVE THEIR CAKE AND EAT IT TOO

The new trend of politicians as news analysts and of media stars running for office is troubling to critics. In early 2010, Sarah Palin, Mike Huckabee and Newt Gingrich were working as paid political analysts for Fox News. All three were potential candidates for the Republican presidential ticket in 2012.

Other analysts are considering runs for political office. They include Lou Dobbs, who left CNN in 2009. Lesser-known Angela McGlowan, a former Fox analyst, entered a House of Representatives race in Mississippi. Harold E. Ford Jr. worked at MSNBC before he contemplated a run for the Senate in New York.

Taking a part-time and highly paid job as an analyst increases the potential candidate's visibility, but to viewers "it seems to be an endless televised political campaign, with former, and possibly future, politicians biding their time giving sound-bite versions of stump speeches," observes Brian Stelter of *The New York Times.*

Some experts worry that the practice can cloud the objectivity of the news organizations. "As long as they are still newsmakers, there is a strong potential for conflict," said Andy Schotz, the chairman of the ethics committee for the Society of Professional Journalists.

Analysts working for CNN and the broadcast networks are not likely to run for office in 2010 or 2012, "but . . . Fox News has a veritable bullpen of potential conservative candidates," says Stelter. Television executives say they sign the politicians as analysts to make them easier to book and to keep them off rivals' programs.

In the case of Ford, as soon as he indicated that he was considering a run for office, MSNBC "froze him as an analyst." At Fox News, McGlowan was preparing for a Republican run for the House of Representatives for six months before she ended her Fox contract. McGlowan was a political analyst for Fox for 11 years. When Stelter asked her if her candidacy would benefit from her tie to Fox, McGlowan said, "I think it helps with getting ready to run, and it helps with name ID. But me having been on Fox News is not going to win this candidacy for me."

When Larry Kudlow was considering a run for Senate in Connecticut, the liberal media watchdog group Media Matters sent CNBC a letter demanding clarity about his on- and off-air roles. "As a private citizen, Mr. Kudlow has a right to explore a run for public office, but using his platform as a CNBC host to further his political ambitions jeopardizes the integrity of your network," the letter said. Chris Matthews chose to stay at MSNBC rather than run for the Senate in Pennsylvania after that network received similar complaints.

- Define conflict of interest.
- Do you think Andy Schotz has a point about the potential for conflict for news organizations that hire politicians as analysts?
- Can a media organization stay objective and continue to be a watchdog if it has politicians or potential politicians on the payroll?

PRACTICE QUIZ

14.1 True/False Questions

___ **1.** The First Amendment led to the press being called the third branch of government.

___ **2.** The FCC no longer requires that stations adhere to the fairness doctrine.

___ **3.** Congress passed a law that regulates Internet indecency.

___ **4.** The ability of the press to tell people what to think is called agenda-setting.

___ **5.** Watergate coverage is an example of agenda-setting.

___ **6.** The media's obsession with polls during political campaigns means more coverage of substantive issues.

14.2 Completion Questions

1. The function the press serves when monitoring the other branches of government is called the ____________ role.

2. A political leader who refuses to answer questions and avoids the press is ____________.

14.3 Multiple Choice Questions

1. When a reporter chooses what to include in a news story, he is
a. embedding the story.
b. framing the story.
c. creating sound bites.
d. using the CNN Effect.

2. The sound bite in campaign stories is now averaging
a. more than ever.
b. 0–3 seconds.
c. 10 seconds.
d. 1 minute.

PRACTICE TEST

14.1 True/False Questions

___ **1.** The FCC requires radio and television stations to carry a response from the opposition party immediately after political broadcasts.

___ **2.** Studies support the argument that the media are politically biased.

___ **3.** Helen Thomas has criticized the Washington press corps for being too tough on the president.

___ **4.** Providing too much information during the Persian Gulf buildup proved that the government didn't want to control media coverage.

___ **5.** Pseudo-events and photo ops can replace substantive coverage in political campaigns.

___ **6.** It's not necessary to ask the same questions over time for consistent poll results.

___ **7.** A frequent criticism of campaign coverage is that reporters don't help set the campaign agenda.

___ **8.** Critics say that reporters should stay away from stories about who is running a campaign and how.

___ **9.** Negative campaign ads are as old as 1884.

___ **10.** The federal campaign law that allows groups not affiliated with candidates or parties to raise money that can be used for advertising is called 527 status.

14.2 Completion Questions

1. Moving a foreign issue onto the national agenda by covering it on television is called the ___________ Effect.

2. A ___________ is a disclosure of confidential or classified information by a person who doesn't want to be identified as the source.

14.3 Multiple Choice Questions

1. The fourth estate in medieval power structure was the
a. noble.
b. clerical.
c. press.
d. common.

2. In the Tornillo opinion, the Supreme Court
a. gave legitimacy to government regulation of broadcasting.
b. said the FCC's fairness doctrine didn't apply to print media.
c. said the First Amendment applies more directly to print than broadcast media.
d. all of the above

3. The short-story format was first used by
a. *USA Today.*
b. *The New York Times.*
c. *The Los Angeles Times.*
d. *The Washington Post.*

4. Political leaders test how well the public will accept a potential policy by
a. asking their advisors.
b. floating a trial balloon.
c. driving around.
d. all of the above.

5. Barring the press from an event is
a. stonewalling.
b. a news blackout.
c. often wise.
d. a media tool.

6. An ad that criticizes an opponent with unsubstantiated facts is
a. an interpretive ad.
b. an attack ad.
c. inexpensive.
d. inconclusive.

14.4 Short Answer Questions

1. Why do reporters spend so much time covering the president and what does that mean for the American public?

2. Describe the methods used to influence the media.

CHAPTER 15

MEDIA LITERACY ACTIVITIES

THE ONGOING CENSORSHIP BATTLE IN CHINA

No longer willing to censor results from searches of Internet users in China, Google announced in early 2010 that it would redirect online traffic off the mainland. Google established Google.cn in 2006 and agreed at the time to control the results Chinese users could see. "We went into this with our eyes open," said a Google spokesperson. But after the Chinese government attempted to monitor the e-mails of human rights activists, Google said it was "no longer willing to continue censoring its results" in China, the world's biggest online community.

Fortunately, Google is a large enough company to be able to turn its back on the revenue it might get from operating in China. Microsoft, on the other hand, is a much larger company and its search engine, Bing, is available in China because the country is "the most important strategic market."

But for now, Google is standing fast on its principles. "Google is in the rare position of having an enormous amount of brand and financial brand capital, and the Chinese market is not fundamental to its midterm success. If there is regime change in 10 to 20 years, Google will be remembered for taking a principled stand," said Whit Andrews, lead Google analyst with research firm Gartner. Andrews says that Google "does not like to buckle to anyone else's idea of what is relevant and therefore censorship is anathema."

Following Google's announcement, China released a 31-page white paper on government policy defending its censorship. The paper said there were 384 million Chinese online, which is nearly a third of the population. The country routinely blocks Facebook, YouTube and Twitter, and the paper implied that there would be no easing of the "Great Firewall." The white paper makes it clear that it is up to companies to block content deemed sensitive. Lists of subjects upon which major media cannot report are regularly produced by the Chinese government and even leaked online. But the topics are always changing, making working with the government difficult.

China requires Internet service providers to set up "Internet security management systems and utilize technical measures to prevent the transmission of all types of illegal information." Anyone using the Internet in China has to respect its laws, the paper said. "Within Chinese territory the Internet is under the jurisdiction of Chinese sovereignty. The Internet sovereignty of China should be respected and protected."

- Find out how many other countries block or censor their citizens' use of Google.
- Do most of them use a firewall approach like China?
- How effective do you think it is for the governments of those countries to block or censor Google? Why?

PRACTICE QUIZ

15.1 True/False Questions

___ **1.** The media's role in an authoritarian society is subservience to government.

___ **2.** Libertarians believe that if people continually reassess their values in the marketplace of ideas, they can then choose the best ones.

___ **3.** Iran blocks signals from media sources and hires bloggers to spread the government's message.

___ **4.** Restrictions on Chinese media include censoring political opinions, but hair dye, American words, and gyrating hips are okay.

15.2 Completion Questions

1. The ____________ Amendment bars government from interfering with the exchange of ideas.

2. In the Iraq war, reporters have been ____________ with combat units.

3. The Chinese government practices prior ____________, reviewing messages before they reach an audience.

4. The nickname for India's movie industry is ____________.

15.3 Multiple Choice Questions

1. Reporters who have been chosen on a rotating basis to cover an event where access is limited are part of a
   a. rainbow.
   b. stable.
   c. pool.
   d. garden.

2. Reporting on Al Jazeera follows
   a. the Bush tradition.
   b. the BBC tradition.
   c. the Arabic tradition.
   d. the Islamic tradition.

3. The Emergency Response law would regulate the media in
   a. China.
   b. Iran.
   c. Poland.
   d. Burma.

PRACTICE TEST

15.1 True/False Questions

___ **1.** Prepublication censorship is more practical than postpublication censorship.

___ **2.** Sheikh Hamad bin Khalifa put up the money to found Al-Jazeera.

___ **3.** The news on Al-Jazeera follows a totalitarian tradition.

___ **4.** Dubai is transforming itself into a tourist magnet and a movie and television production hot spot.

___ **5.** *The Beautiful Virgins* is derided by militant imams as sacrilege.

___ **6.** Al-Qaida has yet to discover how to use digital media to its advantage.

___ **7.** The BBC is government funded.

___ **8.** The Indian government is connecting 237,000 villages to Wi-Fi to make them "knowledge centers."

___ **9.** Colombia is a relatively safe country for journalists.

15.2 Multiple Choice Questions

1. How do people get unbiased information in an authoritarian society?
a. They talk to travelers.
b. They read contraband.
c. They visit the Internet.
d. all of the above

2. In 1598 King James VII of Scotland argued for
a. executions of press people.
b. the use of propaganda.
c. the divine right of kings.
d. all of the above.

3. John Milton argued for free expression of ideas, called
a. the marketplace of ideas.
b. authoritarianism.
c. natural rights.
d. none of the above.

4. The Chinese government censors Internet use with
a. a law.
b. a firewall.
c. a proclamation.
d. all of the above.

5. The Declaration of Independence says that people have
a. enlightenment.
b. natural rights
c. libertarianism.
d. all of the above.

6. During the Civil War, Secretary of War Edwin Stanton
a. censored war stories.
b. embedded reporters
c. organized a firewall.
d. sent out press releases.

7. Liu Di, who was arrested and jailed for her Internet chatter that satirized the Chinese government, was also called the
a. Mouse that Roared.
b. Unification Child.
c. Student of Subversion.
d. Stainless Steel Mouse.

8. Expatriates in Tehrangeles are producing television shows beamed via satellite to
a. Iraq.
b. Iran.
c. Saudi Arabia
d. Dubai.

9. Radio Farda and Voice of America are examples of
a. Tehrangeles.
b. embeds.
c. soft diplomacy.
d. censorship.

10. The Open Net Initiative found that 25 nations restrict citizen access to some Web sites for
a. cultural reasons.
b. political reasons.
c. both cultural and political reasons.
d. none of the above.

11. Where do cameras look over the shoulders at the screens of computer users in cybercafes?
a. Russia
b. Slovakia
c. China
d. Dubai

15.4 Essay Question

1. Discuss the effects of the differences in how the government handled the media during the Civil War, WWII, Vietnam and Grenada.

CHAPTER 16

MEDIA LITERACY ACTIVITIES
IS GOVERNMENT READING OVER YOUR SHOULDER?

The USA Patriot Act was hurriedly passed by Congress in 2001 following the tragedy of 9/11. Many Congressmen didn't have time to read, much less thoroughly study, the 342-page law that was submitted to Congress by the Bush administration just 13 days after the 9/11 attack.

The act gave the government wider surveillance powers in an effort to fight terrorism. But many contend it also put civil liberties at risk. Among the act's more controversial provisions is Section 215, which allows investigators broad access to library, bookstore, rental car and many other records. The act prevents the recipient of such an order from disclosing the request for records.

But for many, concerns remain about the law's potential chilling effect on First Amendment rights and reader privacy because, even with the change, the government retains the right to secretly search the records of anyone who it believes is relevant to a terrorist investigation.

Before the Patriot Act, the government needed at least a warrant and probable cause to access private records. Now, whoever holds your financial, library, travel, video rental, phone, medical, church, synagogue or mosque records can be searched without your knowledge or consent, providing the government says it's trying to protect against terrorism.

The American Civil Liberties Union points out the irony in Section 215. "The FBI can investigate United States persons based in part on their exercise of First Amendment rights.... For example, the FBI could spy on a person because they don't like the books she reads, or because they don't like the Web sites she visits. They could spy on her because she wrote a letter to the editor that criticized government policy." Those served with Section 215 orders are prohibited from disclosing the fact to anyone else. So, if the government had been keeping track of what books a person had been reading, or what Web sites she had been visiting, the person would never know.

Changes to Section 215 were proposed in Congress in 2009. That year, the Senate and Judiciary Committees passed reauthorization bills that provided additional protections for bookstore and library records. The House bill prohibited the use of Section 215 to search the records of a library patron or bookstore customer unless there are "specific and articulable facts" to show that the person is "a suspected agent of a foreign power" or someone who is in contact or known to the suspected agent. The Senate bill provided enhanced protections for library patrons. But Congress was unable to consider the legislation before the Dec. 31 expiration date and voted a one-year temporary extension for Section 215 to Feb. 28, 2011.

An advocate for changes to Section 215, the Campaign for Reader Privacy, was organized in 2004 by the American Booksellers Association, the American Library Association, the Association of American Publishers, and PEN American Center. Its goal is "to ensure that Americans can purchase and borrow books without fear that the government is reading over their shoulder." It has been working to get Congress to modify Section 215 and believes that the proposed protections for bookstore and library records do not pose an impediment to anti-terrorism or law enforcement. The group is optimistic that Congress will finally pass the modifications to Section 215 sometime in 2011.

- What are the reasons the Supreme Court has said it's okay to abridge a person's First Amendment rights?
- Does Section 215 fit into any of these categories?
- Do you think Section 215 should be reauthorized, modified or thrown out?
- Do you see any similarities between the Patriot Act and the Alien and Sedition Acts?

PRACTICE QUIZ

16.1 True/False Questions

___ **1.** A songwriter can sell, lease or give away his intellectual property.
___ **2.** Eugene Debs was jailed for making an antiwar speech during WWI.
___ **3.** The Brandenburg decision expanded First Amendment protection of free expression by defining the Incitement Standard.
___ **4.** The right of fair comment and criticism does not include a performer's private life.

16.2 Completion Questions

1. The theft of intellectual property is called ___________.
2. Writing false, damaging words about someone is called ___________.
3. Words and depictions deemed improper for the public airwaves are considered ___________.

16.3 Multiple Choice Questions

1. Which amendment to the Constitution has the free expression provision?
a. First
b. Second
c. Fifth
d. Seventh

2. The Supreme Court has extended protection for freedom of expression to
a. entertainment.
b. emotive speech.
c. commercial speech.
d. all of the above.

3. What U.S. Supreme Court case said that promoting illegal copying of intellectual property was indeed a copyright infringement?
   a. Napster
   b. Grokster
   c. Google
   d. Bertelsmann

PRACTICE TEST

16.1 True/False Questions

___ 1. A writer can never assign his intellectual property to someone else.
___ 2. In both the Schenck and Pentagon Papers cases, the Supreme Court ruled that national security was more important than the people's right to know.
___ 3. The Fighting Words Doctrine says that preventing a riot is justification for halting someone's freedom of speech.
___ 4. Judge John Woolsey argued that James Joyce's *Ulysses* should be banned for "unusual frankness."
___ 5. The Supreme Court has found that we don't have to tolerate hate speech.
___ 6. The government sidestepped the First Amendment when it licensed radio stations.
___ 7. The Supreme Court decided that *The New York Times* was guilty of "reckless disregard of the truth" in *New York Times* v. *Sullivan.*
___ 8. The Cherry Sisters won their lawsuit against the newspaper reviewer who used equine metaphors to describe them.
___ 9. The Court has ruled that pornography cannot be censored.
___ 10. The Supreme Court threw out the Communications Decency Act saying that the Internet is not "invasive broadcasting."
___ 11. Section 215 of the Patriot Act enables federal agents to go to bookstores or libraries and find out what people have been reading.
___ 12. A presidential candidate who sues a columnist for libel will probably win his case.

16.2 Completion Questions

1. A person's creative work is considered his ____________ property.
2. In the *Near* v. *Minnesota* case, the U.S. Supreme Court ruled against ____________ restraint.

16.3 Multiple Choice Questions

1. What law encourages creativity?
   a. free expression
   b. piracy
   c. copyright
   d. all of the above
2. The mass media serves what purpose as the fourth branch of government?
   a. free expression
   b. consumer rights
   c. watchdog
   d. right to bear arms
3. The 1798 law that limited free expression was the
   a. National Security Act.
   b. Alien and Sedition acts.
   c. Fighting Words law.
   d. Hate Speech Act.
4. When did the Supreme Court first decide a case on First Amendment grounds?
   a. Civil War
   b. WWI
   c. WWII
   d. Indian wars
5. For what reason has the Supreme Court said it's acceptable to limit freedom of expression?
   a. when the nation is at war
   b. to prevent inciting violence
   c. if the TML standard is met
   d. all of the above
6. Who must prove "reckless disregard of the truth" to win a libel case?
   a. newspapers
   b. public figures
   c. criminals
   d. advertisers

16.4 Short Answer Question

1. Why are publishers and authors around the world concerned about the Google Print Library?

CHAPTER 17

MEDIA LITERACY ACTIVITIES
SELF-COVERAGE: A GAME CHANGER?

The New York Times broke the story in April 2010. Gannett's New Jersey newspapers had begun publishing sports stories under a new byline: Eric Marin.

Marin is employed by the New Jersey Devils, not Gannett.

Newspapers across the country have been struggling to find ways to survive within diminished budgets and smaller staffs, and many of them have been turning to outside organizations to supply articles. "At the same time," the *Times* article notes, "professional sports teams, trying to make up for declining news coverage, have been hiring journalists for their Web sites."

In this case, the Devils approached Gannett, offering coverage of the team by Marin, who was already writing stories for the Devils' Web site. Hollis Towns, executive editor of *The Asbury Park Press,* the largest of the state's six Gannett papers, said that Gannett does not pay for the articles, and there are no restrictions on who may edit them. He said that if the Devils were involved in a serious controversy, the papers would not publish an article sent by the team. He assured readers that the papers would not start carrying articles about school districts or hospitals written by their employees, that the current arrangement is limited to sports.

It's a sweet deal for the Devils, and "As long as it served our readers and we told them where that content was coming from, the readers were fine with it," Towns told the *Times.* The Ethics Committee of the Society of Professional Journalists disagrees. "The public expects journalists to be ethical—including fair and impartial—and holds us accountable when we fail," Ethics Committee Chairman Andy Schotz said. "We hear constantly from people upset about eroding standards by news organizations." He said ceding journalistic duties to newsmakers and giving space to what could be seen as glorified press releases cheapens journalism.

An Internet search done by SPJ showed that *The Asbury Park Press* ran Devils stories by Devils employee Marin with the label "Special to the Asbury Park Press" or "Special to the Press" or "correspondent." Other Gannett newspapers used the same "Special" designation, which is commonly used for work by freelancers or stringers.

When the *Times'* story exposed the newspaper's hidden relationship with the team, the papers added a tagline: "Eric Marin works for the New Jersey Devils and writes for newjerseydevils.com."

Disclosure is important but doesn't solve the powerful conflict of interest—actual and perceived—of having figures or organizations in the news cover themselves, Schotz said. "As the Fourth Estate, the press shouldn't abdicate its responsibilities to those with a vested interest in the news."

Towns' reply? "I think journalists get hung up on certain lines of what's ethical more than readers."

- As a reader, do you agree with Towns or with Schotz?
- If you were in editor Towns' position, would you run the stories by Marin?
- When you see that a story is written by the newsmakers themselves, does that change how much you trust the news and the media organization presenting the news?

PRACTICE QUIZ

17.1 True/False Questions

___ **1.** Different media operations that make different promises to readers or viewers are held to the same ethical standards.
___ **2.** The Golden Mean advocates moderation.
___ **3.** Media deontologists rely on ethics codes written by organizations they trust.
___ **4.** Newspapers have traditionally come down hard on reporters who "borrow" from other sources.
___ **5.** Egalitarianism gives everyone an equal hearing and fair consideration.

17.2 Completion Questions

1. The principle of ____________ declares that morally right decisions result in "happiness for the greatest numbers."
2. The four-quadrant model used for making ethics decisions is called ____________ box.
3. A public relations company that organizes an event for the media is ____________ news.

17.3 Multiple Choice Questions

1. The pragmatic and social responsibility theories are two approaches of
a. deontological ethics.
b. teleological ethics.
c. libertarianism.
d. categorical imperativeness.

2. A definition of acceptable and unacceptable behavior is a(n)
a. code of ethics.
b. prescription.
c. ethical charter.
d. categorical imperative.

3. Deontological ethics includes the theories of
a. divine command, libertarianism and situational ethics.
b. categorical imperative, situational ethics and divine right of kings.
c. egalitarianism, secular command and categorical imperative.
d. libertarianism, divine right of kings and categorical imperative.

PRACTICE TEST

17.1 True/False Questions

___ **1.** The American Society of Newspaper Editors adopted the Canons of Journalism in 1990.
___ **2.** The audience brings different ethics expectations to different media messages.
___ **3.** Aristotle was an advocate of the "Do unto others" principle.
___ **4.** Immanuel Kant believed in a standardized approach to ethics as represented by a code of ethics.
___ **5.** The "people's right to know" concept is based on John Stewart Mills' principle of utility.
___ **6.** John Dewey's idea that the virtue of moral decisions should be decided by their result is called pragmatic ethics.
___ **7.** Teleological ethics is concerned with right actions.
___ **8.** The law and ethics always agree.
___ **9.** It is illegal, but ethical, for a media organization to accept junkets.

17.2 Completion Questions

1. The Hutchins Commission advocated for ____________ responsibility.
2. Passing off someone else's creative work as your own is ____________.
3. Experiments in media portrayals of people and issues that used approaches like fiction-writing techniques is called ____________ journalism.

17.3 Multiple Choice Questions

1. The ethical choice made by people who believe all the answers are in the rules is
a. canonical.
b. utilitarian.
c. prescriptive.
d. pragmatic.

2. Modern journalistic principles of fairness and balance are based on
a. accepted practices.
b. the Golden Mean.
c. situational ethics.
d. deontological ethics.

3. A principle that can be applied in any and all circumstances is a
a. categorical imperative.
b. pragmatic principle.
c. social responsibility.
d. all of the above.

4. The veil of ignorance principle led to
a. Potter's box.
b. egalitarianism.
c. the principle of utility.
d. teleology.

5. Potter's Box asks questions in which categories?
a. prudence, law, ethics
b. situation, values, principles, loyalties
c. rights, loyalties, principles
d. all of the above

17.4 Short Answer Questions

1. Give an example of how a duty to audience and a duty to employer could conflict.
2. What are possible problems seen by critics of situational ethics?
3. What are some ethically questionable news practices?